W9-BTG-977

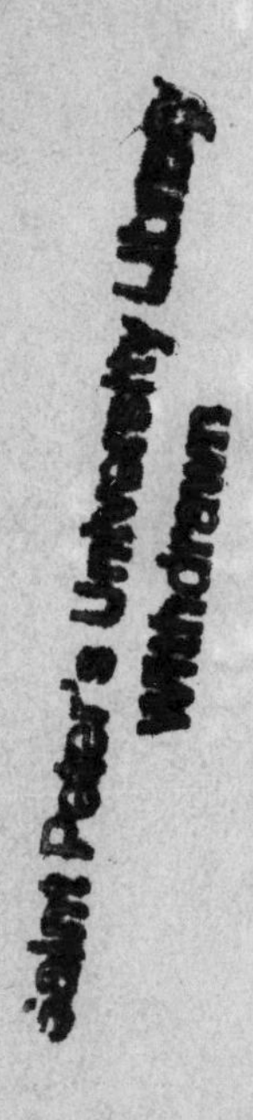
Saint Peter's University Library
Withdrawn

[illegible]

[illegible]

THE LOEB CLASSICAL LIBRARY

FOUNDED BY JAMES LOEB, LL.D.

PROCOPIUS

VII

GLORIAE
PERENNI
DOSI

FIFTEENTH-CENTURY DRAWING OF THE STATUE OF JUSTINIAN IN THE AUGUSTAEUM AT CONSTANTINOPLE

(See the Appendix)

PROCOPIUS

WITH AN ENGLISH TRANSLATION BY

H. B. DEWING, Ph.D., L.H.D.
FORMER PRESIDENT ATHENS COLLEGE, GREECE

WITH THE COLLABORATION OF

GLANVILLE DOWNEY, Ph.D.
THE INSTITUTE FOR ADVANCED STUDY

IN SEVEN VOLUMES

VII

BUILDINGS
GENERAL INDEX TO PROCOPIUS

VE
RI
TAS

CAMBRIDGE, MASSACHUSETTS
HARVARD UNIVERSITY PRESS
LONDON
WILLIAM HEINEMANN LTD
MCMXL

Printed in Great Britain

CONTENTS

	PAGE
PREFATORY NOTE	vii
INTRODUCTION	ix
BUILDINGS	1
APPENDIX: The Equestrian Statue of Justinian in the Augustaeum	395
LIST OF LATIN WORDS	399
GENERAL INDEX TO PROCOPIUS	401

PLANS—

ST. SOPHIA AT CONSTANTINOPLE	14, 15
SS. SERGIUS AND BACCHUS AT CONSTANTINOPLE	46
ST. JOHN AT EPHESUS	47
FORTIFICATIONS AT RUSAFA	104, 105

MAPS—

CONSTANTINOPLE	*At end*
EUPHRATES FRONTIER	*At end*
ROMAN EMPIRE	*At end*

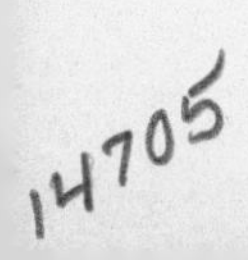
14705

PREFATORY NOTE

In the preparation of this translation for the press, Dr. Dewing has received the collaboration of Dr. Downey, of the Institute for Advanced Study, and of Professor E. Baldwin Smith, of Princeton University. Dr. Downey read the manuscript and made suggestions concerning the translation; he also contributed parts of the commentary and prepared the Introduction. Professor Smith revised those portions of the translation which are concerned with architectural matters, selected the architectural drawings, and also generously read the whole of the translation and offered valuable criticism of it.

The Editors

INTRODUCTION

THE praise which Procopius bestows on Justinian in the *Buildings* would, as Bury remarked, astonish us as coming from the author of the *Wars* even if the *Secret History* had been lost or never written.[1] The criticism of the Emperor which appears in veiled passages in the *Wars* had been elaborated with minute care in the *Secret History*, written in 550; but this libel of course was designed to remain unpublished during Justinian's lifetime, and the treatise on the *Buildings*, published in 560 or soon after,[2] would have presented, in appearance at least, a wonderful change in the writer's feelings. The introduction to the work declares that the Emperor saved and transformed the State, drove back the barbarians, rescued religion from error and reformed the laws; and when the writer goes on, in the remainder of the book, to tell how Justinian fortified the frontiers, restored and founded cities, and everywhere made provision for the safety and comfort of his subjects, no opportunity is lost to point out the Emperor's wisdom, generosity and ingenuity.

To account for this apparent change on the part of

[1] J. B. Bury, *History of the Later Roman Empire*, London, 1923, II, p. 428.

[2] The date is given by the statement (V. iii. 10) that the construction of a bridge over the Sangarius was in progress when Procopius wrote; Theophanes (A.M. 6052, I, p. 234, 15–18 ed. De Boor) states that this work was carried out in the year A.D. 559–60.

Procopius is not entirely possible, for the scanty evidence is capable of interpretation in different ways.[1] Though the wish to flatter the Emperor is obvious, it is difficult to determine whether the circumstances which furnished the immediate occasion for writing the book differed from the original motives which Procopius may have had for planning it. A number of reasons why Procopius should have written the treatise can be suggested. He may have wished to defend himself from the charges of disloyalty which could have been brought against him as a result of the criticisms of the administration which he allowed to appear in the *Wars*. On the other hand, he may have acted either in gratitude for official preferment or in the hope of it; but these motives must remain conjectural, for though we know that he had the title of *illustris*,[2] there is nothing to shew that this was given to him before or after the publication of the *Buildings*. Again, a Procopius was city-prefect of Constantinople in 562,[3] shortly after the publication of the *Buildings*; but the name was not uncommon, and it remains only a possibility that it was the author of the *Buildings* to whom this office was given as a reward for this work. Or it is possible

[1] *Cf.* F. Dahn, *Prokopius von Cäsarea*, Berlin, 1865, pp. 352–67; J. Haury, *Procopiana*, I, Augsburg, 1891, pp. 28–31, 34; K. Krumbacher, *Geschichte der byzantinischen Litteratur*, ed. 2, Munich, 1897, pp. 232 f.; Ch. Diehl, *Justinien et la civilisation byzantine au VIe siècle*, Paris, 1901, pp. xiii. xviii f.; P. Friedländer, *Johannes von Gaza und Paulus Silentiarius*, Leipzig, 1912, pp. 44, 54; Bury, *loc. cit.* On Procopius's relations with Justinian, see also Haury, "Prokop und der Kaiser Justinian," *Byzantinische Zeitschrift*, xxxvii, 1937, pp. 1–9.

[2] Suidas, *s.n.* Προκόπιος.

[3] Theophanes, A.M. 6055, I, pp. 238, 10; 239, 7 ed. De Boor; *cf.* Haury, *Procopiana*, I, pp. 34 f.

that the work was undertaken by imperial command or desire, directly or indirectly conveyed.[1] Finally, it is possible to detect a hint of personal gratitude in the introduction of the work,[2] and an effort has been made, though without complete success, to shew that there were circumstances in Procopius's life which caused him to feel such gratitude to the Emperor.[3] Depending upon one's belief or disbelief in these grounds, the work can be read either as a panegyric, containing a greater or less amount of irony, or as a recantation, spontaneous or constrained, of the writer's earlier criticism of the Emperor.[4]

[1] Procopius writes, in I. iii. 1: "We must begin with the churches of Mary Mother of God. For we know that this is the wish of the Emperor himself, and true reason manifestly demands that from God one must proceed to the Mother of God." This allusion does not, however, seem sufficient to prove that the Emperor ordered the work: he could, for example, have expressed his wish after he learned that the book was planned or was being written.

[2] I. i. 4: "Apart from all this, history shews that subjects who have received benefits have proved themselves grateful toward their benefactors, and that they have repaid them with thank-offerings in generous measure, seeing that while they have profited, it may be, for the moment only by the beneficence of their rulers, they nevertheless preserve their sovereigns' virtue imperishable in the memory of those who are to come after them."

[3] Haury believed (*Zur Beurteilung des Geschichtschreibers Procopius*, Munich, 1896, pp. 19, 44 f.) that Procopius was grateful to Justinian for avenging the murder of his father Stephanus, an official in Palestine, and saving the family property. Haury is, however, unable to find enough evidence to make the theory convincing; *cf.* Bury, *op. cit.*, II, p. 420, n. 1.

[4] Either interpretation is possible in several instances in which Procopius gives, in the *Buildings*, descriptions and

In the circumstances it is not possible to prove any one of these explanations satisfactorily. They need not, however, be mutually exclusive, and it is conceivable that all these motives may have been present in the author's mind, in various degrees and combinations, when he wrote the work. A passage in the *Wars* suggests, indeed, that Procopius contemplated writing such a book as early as 545;[1] but it is possible, if not likely, that when he actually wrote it he was impelled by motives quite different from those which he may originally have had.

The subject was inherently dull and monotonous, and much of Procopius's treatment of it is perfunctory, being controlled in large measure by his rhetorical tendency; he was also limited not only by the nature of his material but by the necessity of keeping the Emperor constantly in the foreground. Yet the flattery of the Emperor was not necessarily, to Procopius and his contemporaries, as exaggerated and pointless as it now seems. By long tradition each Roman and each Byzantine Emperor was regarded as the direct source and origin of all the

---

interpretations of events which are quite different from those which he gives elsewhere (*cf.* Haury, *Procopiana*, I, pp. 31–33). Compare, for example, *Buildings* I. i. 9 with *Secret History* xiii. 7; *Buildings* I. i. 25, 26 with *Secret History* xxi. 7, 9, 22–25; *Buildings* IV. ii. 15 with *Secret History* xxvi. 31–33.

[1] *Wars* II. xii. 29; *cf.* Haury, *Procopiana*, I, pp. 18, 28, and in *Byzantinische Zeitschrift*, xxxiv, 1934, p. 10. But there are many instances in which Procopius announced (as he does in the present passage) that he would describe a certain subject or incident in another place, and then failed to do so. There is also a passage in the *Secret History*, written in 550, in which Procopius seems to allude to his intention of writing the *Buildings*; see below, note on II. vii. 4.

public building operations executed during his reign.[1] In pagan thought the ruler was a god among men, and in the Christian Empire he became the Vice-regent of God on earth (the Empire being a *mimesis* of Heaven). The Hellenistic ruler and the Roman and the Christian Byzantine Emperor thus represented the source and " creator " of all things on earth. So if Justinian is portrayed as personally responsible for the design and construction of public buildings of all kinds and in every part of the Empire, his rôle was only one phase of his constant and pervading care for his subjects. The Emperor's importance in this respect is only heightened when on occasion he receives guidance and inspiration from God;[2] and the assistance which he receives from his master-builders is but another manifestation of God's watchfulness in providing the Emperor with the best means for the execution of his mission, which was, as Procopius says, " to watch over the whole Roman Empire and, so far as was possible, to remake it."[3]

Naturally, Procopius's adulation of the Emperor was not motivated entirely by this conception; but it certainly was made possible by it; and if Procopius felt any hesitation in heaping up the flattery

[1] On this conception *cf.* Downey, " Imperial Building Records in Malalas," *Byzantinische Zeitschrift*, xxxviii, 1938, pp. 1–15. In addition to the studies cited there, reference may be made to W. Schubart, " Das Gesetz und der Kaiser in griechischen Urkunden," *Klio*, xxx, 1937, pp. 54–69, and L. Berlinger, *Beiträge zur inoffiziellen Titulatur der römischen Kaiser : Eine Untersuchung ihres ideengeschichtlichen Gehaltes und ihrer Entwicklung*, Breslau, 1935.

[2] I. i. 71; II. iii. 8, 13; V. vi. 19, 20; *cf.* I. i. 61.

[3] II. vi. 6; *cf.* I. i. 25, 26, II. ix. 11.

of Justinian (though it is debatable whether such a scruple occurred to him) his doubts would have been removed by the thought that his account in this respect could be considered normal and in no way grotesque. And of course the official correctness of his presentation would provide an admirable screen for the irony which some scholars find in the work.

It is partly because of this conception that the titles which Procopius gives to Anthemius, Isidorus and Chryses have been translated here as "master-builder." Procopius generally uses *mechanikos* or *mechanopoios* in speaking of these men,[1] and Isidorus is called *mechanikos* in an inscription of Chalcis in Syria which records work executed there in A.D. 550–1 —evidently the repair of the circuit-wall which Procopius describes.[2] These craftsmen are always spoken of as "serving" or "assisting" the Emperor in his undertakings;[3] they apply to him for help when their skill is unable to cope with a difficult situation, and the devices with which he overcomes these problems are beyond their powers of imagination.[4] The implication conveyed in the modern term "master-builder" thus seems to express most closely the relationship which Procopius sought to depict. It is necessary to use it also because the modern terms "architect" and "engineer" impute to ancient workers methods and resources which, however great their skill, they did not possess.

[1] I. i. 24, 71, 76; II. iii. 2, 11, 14. Their craft is called μηχανική (I. i. 24; *Wars* II. xiii. 26) and τὰ μηχανικά (II. iii. 7).

[2] See the notes on II. xi. 1 and viii. 25.

[3] Their work is spoken of as ὑπουργία, *e.g.* II. viii. 25; *cf.* I. i. 24.

[4] I. i. 68–78; II. iii. 7–13.

There is a notable exception to Procopius's usage: in his reference to Trajan's bridge across the Danube he says that Apollodorus of Damascus was "*architektôn* of the whole work."[1] This is the only passage in the *Buildings* in which Procopius uses the word *architektôn*, and its appearance here suggests that he made a distinction between the relationship of the "master-builders" to Justinian and the relationship of similar craftsmen to other emperors: apparently Procopius wished to imply that Justinian had a greater share of originality and responsibility in such work than his predecessors had had, a thought which of course would not necessarily, in the case of Trajan, run counter to the conception of the ruler as the originator of public building operations.

For sources, it is plain from the amount of information which Procopius gives that he had access to official records of some sort: the use of such material is indicated particularly by his three long lists[2] of fortresses and other buildings. In addition, he must have used the knowledge acquired during his own travels,[3] and he probably drew also upon the experiences of others.[4] It is of course not to be expected that all his information, especially that concerning work done in remote districts, is completely accurate. Many of the place-names are corrupted, for in addition to the dangers of corruption in manuscript tradition to which unusual names are peculiarly exposed, the names may have been garbled in the records which Procopius used, and he may himself have transcribed them inaccurately. In the present edition it is impossible to deal with the problems

[1] IV. vi. 13.
[2] IV. iv. and xi.; V. ix.
[3] *Cf.* II. iv. 3; VI. vii. 18.
[4] *Cf.* VI. vii. 18.

thus created. The more important of the places mentioned have, however, been identified so far as it is possible, and their modern names given; and a few studies of individual sites have been mentioned in the notes.[1]

To facilitate the use of the translation by students of the history of architecture, the Greek architectural terms have sometimes been transliterated in the English version, and a selection of these words has been gathered in the Index under the heading Architectural Terms. When the same term occurs several times in a single passage, it has usually been transliterated only at its first occurrence, and when the English term which is used in that place recurs, the reader can assume that it represents the same Greek term. In certain passages, however, it has seemed desirable to repeat the transliteration of the same word several times in order to make clearer the way in which different terms are used by Procopius. When "stoa" has been used in the translation to represent Greek στοά, no transliteration has been added; but when it is necessary to translate Greek στοά by different words ("colonnaded stoa," "portico," etc.) the transliteration has been supplied.[2] Certain

[1] For a recent example of a study of the geographical material in the *Buildings*, see P. Skok, "De l'importance des listes toponomastiques de Procope pour la connaissance de la latinité balkanique," *Revue internationale des études balkaniques*, iii. 1937, pp. 47–58.

[2] Procopius nearly always employs *stoa* to describe any structure which consists basically of a covered colonnade (see the entry for *stoa* in the heading Architectural Terms in the Index); once he uses *embolos* for a covered portico in a wall (*Buildings*, III. v. 11) and twice he speaks of *peristyloi aulai* (*Buildings*, I. i. 58, II. x. 20). In this translation, "stoa" alone is employed when the nature of the structure is

terms with well-established and unmistakeable meanings (*e.g. peribolos*, " circuit-wall "; *proteichisma*, " outworks "; *pyrgos*, " tower ") occur so frequently in this work that it has seemed unnecessary to transliterate them except in passages in which it is desirable to distinguish them from other terms. In some instances, of course, Procopius employs literary locutions in place of technical terms, and it has usually seemed unnecessary to attempt to reproduce his phraseology in transliteration; in such cases the translation has generally been made as literal as possible.

The material gathered in the Index does not comprise all the occurrences of all the technical terms which Procopius uses. This collection is intended rather to represent unusual words, words which Procopius employs with different shades of meaning or in quite different senses, and in general terms such as *apsis*, *tholos* and *stoa* which are often used so loosely by ancient writers that it is always desirable to collect examples of them. In some instances words have been included because they happen to occur in contexts which make their meanings unusually clear. When the meaning of a word is well established, and when its use by Procopius has no significance either for his technique of description

---

clear from the context; " porch " and " portico " are sometimes employed in special cases, and sometimes " colonnaded stoa " and " stoa-like colonnade " are used when it is necessary to indicate that Procopius is using στοά to describe both the columns and the whole of the structure of which they form a part. *Cf.* Downey, " The Architectural Significance of the Use of the Words *Stoa* and *Basilikê* in Classical Literature," *American Journal of Archaeology*, xli, 1937, pp. 194–211.

or for the history of architecture, it has seemed unnecessary to list it.

The *Buildings* was first published, incompletely, by Beatus Rhenanus at Basel in 1531; his edition was reprinted at Paris in 1543. A more complete text was edited by David Hoeschel at Augsburg in 1607. The next edition was that of Claudius Maltretus (Paris, 1663), which was reprinted at Venice in 1729. The text was again edited by G. Dindorf at Bonn in 1838, largely on the basis of Maltretus's edition. The present edition is based upon that of J. Haury in the Teubner series (Leipzig, 1913), though his text occasionally has been modified. There is an English translation by Aubrey Stewart, with notes by C. W. Wilson and Hayter Lewis, in the series of the Palestine Pilgrims' Text Society (London, 1896).

The plans and elevations used in this book, while redrawn, have been taken from the following publications, to which due acknowledgement is hereby given:

W. R. Lethaby and W. Swainson, *The Church of Sancta Sophia*, London, Macmillan, 1894, Figs. 3 and 4.

A. Van Millingen, R. Traquair, and others, *Byzantine Churches in Constantinople*, London, Macmillan, 1912, Plan of SS. Sergius and Bacchus, p. 80.

K. Wulzinger, "*Die Apostelkirche und die Mehmedije zu Konstantinopel*," *Byzantion*, vii, 1932, Plan of St. John's at Ephesus, p. 26.

H. Spanner and S. Guyer, *Rusafa* (*Forschungen zur Islamischen Kunst*, hrsg. F. Sarre), Berlin, D. Reimer (E. Vohsen), 1926, Plans of fortifications, Plates 2, 4 and 5.

The maps have been taken, with the omission of certain details, from the following publications, to which acknowledgement is made:

Van Millingen, *op. cit.*, Map of Constantinople, facing p. 15.

Cambridge Ancient History (Cambridge University Press), Map of the Euphrates Frontier, vol. I, map no. 7; Map of the Roman Empire, vol. II, map no. 15.

At the last moment before this volume goes to press it is possible to add:

Kenneth J. Conant, "*The First Dome of St. Sophia and its Rebuilding*," *American Journal of Archaeology*, xliii (1940), 589–591, which has an important bearing upon the narrative of Procopius in I. 66 ff., pages 29–33 *infra*. Professor Conant's study of the architectural history of this church was to have appeared in the first issue for 1940 of the *Bulletin of the Byzantine Institute*, whose publication has been delayed by the war in Europe. In advance of that publication Professor Conant reproduces architectural drawings of the cross-section of the building which show (1) the original plan of the dome, (2) the deformation which occurred before the building settled, and (3) the reconstruction which took place in 558–563.

PROCOPIUS OF CAESAREA

BUILDINGS

ΠΡΟΚΟΠΙΟΥ ΚΑΙΣΑΡΕΩΣ

ΠΕΡΙ ΚΤΙΣΜΑΤΩΝ

ΛΟΓΟΣ Α΄

α΄. Οὐκ ἀρετῆς ἐπίδειξιν ποιεῖσθαι ἐθέλων, P 2 οὐδὲ λόγου δυνάμει θαρσῶν, οὐδὲ χωρίων ἐπὶ τῇ ἐμπειρίᾳ φιλοτιμούμενος, ἐς τῆσδε τῆς ἱστορίας τὴν γραφὴν ὥρμηκα· ἐπεὶ οὐκ εἶχον οὐδὲν ὑφ' 2 οὗ ἂν παρρησίας ἐς τόδε ἀγόμενος, ἀλλά μοι πολλάκις ἔννοια γέγονεν ὁπόσων τε καὶ πηλίκων ἀγαθῶν αἴτιον ἱστορία ταῖς πόλεσι γίνεσθαι εἴωθε, παραπέμπουσά τε εἰς τοὺς ἐπιγόνους τῶν προγεγενημένων τὴν μνήμην, καὶ ἀνταγωνιζομένη τῷ χρόνῳ κρυφαῖα ποιεῖσθαι διατεινομένῳ τὰ πράγματα, καὶ τὴν μὲν ἀρετὴν εὐφημίαις ἀεὶ τῶν ἀναλεγομένων αὐτὴν ἐπαίρουσα, τῆς δὲ κακίας ἐπιλαμβανομένη διηνεκές, ταύτῃ τε ἀπο3 κρουομένη τὴν αὐτῆς δύναμιν. τούτου οὖν δὴ μόνου ἐπιμελητέον ἡμῖν, ὅπως δὴ ἔνδηλα τὰ πεπραγμένα διαφανῶς ἔσται καὶ ὑφ' ὅτου ἐργασθείη τῶν πάντων ἀνθρώπων. ταῦτα δέ, οἶμαι, οὐδὲ γλώσσῃ τραυλιζούσῃ τε καὶ ἰσχνοφώνῳ οὔσῃ ἀμήχανά 4 ἐστι. χωρὶς δὲ τούτων εὐγνώμονας μὲν ἱστορία ἐς τοὺς εὐεργέτας ἐνδείκνυται γεγονέναι τῶν ἀρχομένων τοὺς εὖ πεπονθότας, ἐν μείζοσι δὲ

PROCOPIUS OF CAESAREA

BUILDINGS

BOOK I

i. It is not because I wish to make a display of skill, nor through any confidence in my eloquence, nor because I pride myself on my personal knowledge of many lands, that I have set about writing this record; for indeed I had no grounds for venturing so bold an intention. Yet the thought has many times occurred to me, how many and how great are the benefits which are wont to accrue to states through History, which transmits to future generations the memory of those who have gone before, and resists the steady effort of time to bury events in oblivion; and while it incites to virtue those who from time to time may read it by the praise it bestows, it constantly assails vice by repelling its influence. Wherefore our concern must be solely this—that all the deeds of the past shall be clearly set forth, and by what man, whosoever he might be, they were wrought. And this, I believe, is not an impossible task, even for a lisping and thin-voiced tongue. Apart from all this, history shews that subjects who have received benefits have proved themselves grateful toward their benefactors, and that they have repaid them with

αὐτοῖς ἐκτετικέναι τὰ χαριστήρια, οἵ γε, ἂν οὕτω τύχοι, ἐπὶ καιροῦ μὲν τῆς ἀγαθοεργίας τῶν ἐν σφίσιν ἡγησαμένων ἀπώναντο, ἀθάνατον δὲ αὐτοῖς τῶν εἰς τὸ ἔπειτα ἐσομένων τῇ μνήμῃ τὴν ἀρετὴν 5 διασώζουσι. διὰ ταῦτα γὰρ καὶ τῶν ἐπιγινομένων πολλοὶ ἀρετῶσι μὲν τὰς τῶν προγεγενημένων ζηλοῦντες τιμάς, ἐς δὲ τὰς βλασφημίας B 171 χαλεπῶς ἔχοντες τῶν ἐπιτηδευμάτων τὰ πονηρότατα, ὡς τὸ εἰκός, ἀναδύονται. ὅτου δὲ δὴ ἕνεκα ταῦτα ὑπεῖπον αὐτίκα δηλώσω.

6 Ἐν χρόνῳ τῷ καθ' ἡμᾶς Ἰουστινιανὸς ὁ[1] βασιλεὺς γέγονεν, ὃς[2] τὴν πολιτείαν πλημμελῶς κινουμένην παραλαβὼν μεγέθει μὲν αὐτὴν μείζω τε καὶ πολλῷ ἐπιφανεστέραν εἰργάσατο, ἐξελάσας ἐνθένδε τοὺς ἐκ παλαιοῦ βιασαμένους αὐτὴν βαρβάρους, ὥσπερ μοι λεπτολογουμένῳ ἐν τοῖς ὑπὲρ τῶν P 3 7 πολέμων δεδήλωται λόγοις. καίτοι λέγουσί ποτε Θεμιστοκλέα τὸν Νεοκλέους[3] ἀποσεμνύνεσθαι ὅτι δὴ οὐκ ἀνεπιστημόνως ἔχοι πόλιν μικρὰν[4] ποιῆσαι 8 μεγάλην. ὁ δὲ δὴ οὐκ ἀμελέτητός ἐστιν ἐμπορίζεσθαι πολιτείας ἑτέρας· πολλὰς ἀμέλει προσεποίησεν ἤδη τῇ Ῥωμαίων ἀρχῇ ἀλλοτρίας καθ' αὑτὸν οὔσας, πόλεις δὲ ἀναρίθμους δεδημιούργη9 κεν οὐ πρότερον οὔσας. πλανωμένην δὲ εὑρὼν τὴν ἀμφὶ τῷ θεῷ δόξαν τὰ πρότερα ἐς πολλά τε ἀναγκαζομένην ἰέναι, συντρίψας ἁπάσας τὰς ἐπὶ τὰς πλάνας φερούσας ὁδούς, διεπράξατο ἐν τῷ βεβαίῳ τῆς πίστεως ἐπὶ μιᾶς ἑστάναι κρηπῖδος.

[1] ὁ V : om A.
[2] γέγονεν, ὃς om. A.
[3] Νεοκλέους Hoeschel : νικοκλέους.
[4] μικρὰν Hoeschel : μὴ V.

thank-offerings in generous measure, seeing that, while they have profited, it may be, for the moment only by the beneficence of their rulers, they nevertheless preserve their sovereigns' virtue imperishable in the memory of those who are to come after them.[1] Indeed it is through this very service that many men of later times strive after virtue, by emulating the honours of those who have preceded them, and, because they cannot endure censure, are quite likely to shun the basest practices. And the reason why I have made this preface I shall forthwith disclose.

In our own age there has been born the Emperor Justinian, who, taking over the State when it was harrassed by disorder, has not only made it greater in extent, but also much more illustrious, by expelling from it those barbarians who had from of old pressed hard upon it, as I have made clear in detail in the Books on the Wars. Indeed they say that Themistocles, the son of Neocles, once boastfully said that he did not lack the ability to make a small state large. But this Sovereign does not lack the skill to produce completely transformed states—witness the way he has already added to the Roman domain many states which in his own times had belonged to others, and has created countless cities which did not exist before. And finding that the belief in God was, before his time, straying into errors and being forced to go in many directions, he completely destroyed all the paths leading to such errors, and brought it about that it stood on the firm foundation

[1] It has been thought that Procopius here alludes to personal gratitude to the Emperor on his own part; see the *Introduction*, p. x.

10 πρὸς δὲ καὶ τοὺς νόμους λαβὼν τῷ τε παμπληθεῖς οὐ δέον γεγονέναι σκοτεινοὺς ὄντας καὶ ξυγχεομένους διαφανῶς τῷ ἀπ' ἐναντίας ἀλλήλοις ἰέναι, καὶ τοῦ μὲν ὄχλου αὐτοὺς τῆς τερθρείας ἀποκαθάρας, τὸ δὲ ἐς[1] ἀλλήλους διχοστατεῖν βεβαιότατα κρατυνόμενος διεσώσατο. καὶ τοῖς μὲν ἐπιβουλεύουσιν αὐτεπάγγελτος τὰς αἰτίας ἀφείς, τοὺς δὲ βίου δεομένους πλούτῳ πεποιημένος κατακορεῖς καὶ τύχην αὐτοῖς τὴν ἐπηρεάζουσαν βιασάμενος, εὐδαίμονι βίῳ τὴν πολιτείαν 11 ξυνῴκισεν. ἀλλὰ καὶ βαρβάροις πανταχόθεν ὑποκειμένην (B 172) τὴν Ῥωμαίων ἀρχὴν στρατιωτῶν τε πλήθει ἐπέρρωσε καὶ ὀχυρωμάτων οἰκοδομίαις ἁπάσας αὐτῆς τὰς ἐσχατιὰς ἐτειχίσατο.

12 Ἀλλὰ τῶν μὲν ἄλλων τὰ πλεῖστα ἐν ἑτέροις μοι συγγέγραπται λόγοις, ὅσα δὲ αὐτῷ ἀγαθὰ οἰκοδομουμένῳ δεδημιούργηται, ἐν τῷ παρόντι γεγράψεται.[2] ἄριστον μὲν δὴ βασιλέα γεγονέναι Κῦρον τὸν Πέρσην φασίν, ὧν ἀκοῇ ἴσμεν, τοῖς τε ὁμογενέσιν 13 αἰτιώτατον τῆς βασιλείας. εἰ δὲ τοιοῦτός τις (P 4) ἦν ὁ Κῦρος ἐκεῖνος οἷος δὴ ὑπὸ Ξενοφῶντι τῷ 14 Ἀθηναίῳ παιδεύεται, οὐκ ἔχω εἰδέναι. τάχα γάρ που καὶ ἡ τοῦ γεγραφότος αὐτὰ δεξιότης κεκομψευμένῃ δυνάμει τοῦ λόγου ἐγκαλλώπισμα 15 τῶν ἔργων γενέσθαι[3] διαρκῶς ἴσχυσε. τοῦ δὲ

[1] τῷ before ἐς deleted by Maltretus.
[2] γεγράψεται Maltretus: γέγραπται.
[3] For γενέσθαι Capps conjectures γεννᾶσθαι ("create").

---

[1] Quite a different interpretation of Justinian's actions in this respect is given in the *Secret History*, xiii. 7.

[2] This is thought to be a disguised reference to the *Secret History*, which was written before the present work, but designed to remain unpublished during Justinian's lifetime:

of a single faith.[1] Moreover, finding the laws obscure because they had become far more numerous than they should be, and in obvious confusion because they disagreed with each other, he preserved them by cleansing them of the mass of their verbal trickery, and by controlling their discrepancies with the greatest firmness; as for those who plotted against him, he of his own volition dismissed the charges against them, and causing those who were in want to have a surfeit of wealth, and crushing the spiteful fortune that oppressed them, he wedded the whole State to a life of prosperity. Furthermore, he strengthened the Roman domain, which everywhere lay exposed to the barbarians, by a multitude of soldiers, and by constructing strongholds he built a wall along all its remote frontiers.

However, most of the Emperor's other achievements have been described by me in my other writings,[2] so that the subject of the present work will be the benefits which he wrought as a builder. They do indeed say that the best king of whom we know by tradition was the Persian Cyrus, and that he was chiefly responsible for the founding of the kingdom of Persia for the people of his race. But whether that Cyrus was in fact such a man as he whose education from childhood up is described by Xenophon the Athenian, I have no means of knowing. For it may well be that the skill of the writer of that description was quite capable, such was his exquisite eloquence, of coming to be a mere embellishment of the facts.

Procopius seems to have designed the present passage so that it could be taken by contemporaries to refer to the *Wars*, the eight books of which had already been published, while posterity would know that it referred to the *Secret History* (*cf.* Haury in *Byzantinische Zeitschrift*, xxxvii, 1937, p. 5).

καθ' ἡμᾶς βασιλέως Ἰουστινιανοῦ (ὃν δὴ καὶ φύσει βασιλέα καλῶν τις, οἶμαι, ὀρθῶς ἂν εἴποι, ἐπεὶ καὶ πατὴρ ὣς ἤπιός ἐστι, καθ' Ὅμηρον),[1] εἴ τις ἐς τὸ ἀκριβὲς τὴν βασιλείαν διασκοποῖτο,
16 παιδιάν τινα τὴν Κύρου ἀρχὴν οἰήσεται εἶναι. τεκμηριώσει δὲ τὸ τοιοῦτο ἡ μὲν πολιτεία πρὸς αὐτοῦ, ἧπέρ μοι ἔναγχος εἴρηται, τῇ τε χώρᳳ καὶ τῇ ἄλλῃ δυνάμει πλεῖν ἢ διπλασία γεγενημένη, οἱ δὲ τὴν ἐπιβουλὴν αὐτῷ σκαιωρησάμενοι μέχρι ἐς φόνον μὴ ὅτι βιοτεύοντες ἐς τόδε τοῦ χρόνου καὶ τὰ σφέτερα αὐτῶν ἔχοντες, καίπερ ἐξεληλεγμένοι διαφανῶς, ἀλλὰ καὶ στρατηγοῦντες Ῥωμαίων ἔτι καὶ ἐς τὸ τῶν ὑπάτων ἀναγεγραμμένοι τελοῦσιν [1] ἀξίωμα.

17 Τανῦν δέ, ὅπερ εἶπον, ἐπὶ τὰς οἰκοδομίας τούτου δὴ τοῦ βασιλέως ἡμῖν ἰτέον, ὡς μὴ ἀπιστεῖν τῷ τε πλήθει καὶ τῷ μεγέθει ἐς τὸν ὄπισθεν χρόνον τοῖς αὐτὰς [2] θεωμένοις ξυμβαίη ὅτι δὴ ἀνδρὸς ἑνὸς
B 173 18 ἔργα τυγχάνει ὄντα. πολλὰ γὰρ ἤδη τῶν προγεγενημένων οὐκ ἐμπεδωθέντα τῷ λόγῳ τῷ ὑπερβάλλοντι τῆς ἀρετῆς ἄπιστα γέγονεν. εἴη δ' ἂν εἰκότως τὰ ἐν Βυζαντίῳ παρὰ πάντα τῷ
19 λόγῳ κρηπίς. ἀρχομένου [3] γὰρ ἔργου, κατὰ δὴ τὸν παλαιὸν λόγον, πρόσωπον χρὴ θέμεναι τηλαυγές.

P 5 20 Ἄνδρες ἀγελαῖοί ποτε καὶ ὁ συρφετὸς ὅλος [4]

[1] τελοῦσιν A : om. V.
[2] αὐτὰς Hoeschel : αὐτὰ V.
[3] ἀρχομένου Dindorf : ἀρχομένῳ V.
[4] ὅλος suggested by Haury (appendix, p. 395) : ὄχλος.

---

[1] *Odyssey*, II. 47, XV. 152.
[2] In the original there is a play upon the words παιδεία

But in the case of the king of our times, Justinian (whom one would rightly, I think, call a king by nature as well as by inheritance, since he is, as Homer says,[1] " as gentle as a father "), if one should examine his reign with care, he will regard the rule of Cyrus as a sort of child's play.[2] The proof of this will be that the Roman Empire, as I have just said, has become more than doubled both in area and in power generally, while, on the other hand, those who treacherously formed the plot[3] against him, going so far even as to plan his assassination, are not only living up to the present moment, and in possession of their own property, even though their guilt was proved with absolute certainty, but are actually still serving as generals of the Romans, and are holding the consular rank to which they had been appointed.

But now we must proceed, as I have said, to the subject of the buildings of this Emperor, so that it may not come to pass in the future that those who see them refuse, by reason of their great number and magnitude, to believe that they are in truth the works of one man. For already many works of men of former times which are not vouched for by a written record have aroused incredulity because of their surpassing merit. And with good reason the buildings in Byzantium, beyond all the rest, will serve as a foundation for my narrative. For " o'er a work's beginnings," as the old saying has it,[4] " we needs must set a front that shines afar."

Some men of the common herd, all the rubbish of

(" education," the title of Xenophon's book mentioned above) and *παιδιά* (" child's play ").

[3] *Wars*, VII. xxxii.

[4] Pindar, *Ol.*, VI. 4, translated by Sandys (L.C.L.).

Ἰουστινιανῷ βασιλεῖ ἐν Βυζαντίῳ ἐπαναστάντες τὴν Νίκα καλουμένην στάσιν εἰργάσαντο, ἧπέρ μοι ἀπαρακαλύπτως ἀκριβολογουμένῳ ἐν τοῖς
21 ὑπὲρ τῶν πολέμων δεδιήγηται λόγοις. ἐνδεικνύμενοι δὲ ὡς οὐκ ἐπὶ τὸν βασιλέα μόνον, ἀλλ' οὐδέν τι ἧσσον ἐπὶ τὸν θεὸν ἅτε ἀποφράδες τὰ ὅπλα ἀντῆραν, ἐμπρῆσαι τῶν Χριστιανῶν τὴν ἐκκλησίαν ἐτόλμησαν (Σοφίαν καλοῦσιν οἱ Βυζάντιοι τὸν νεὼν ἐπικαιριώτατα τῷ θεῷ τὴν ἐπωνυμίαν ἀπεργασάμενοι), ἐπεχώρει δὲ αὐτοῖς ὁ θεὸς διαπράξασθαι τὸ ἀσέβημα, προειδὼς εἰς ὅσον τι [1] κάλλος τοῦτο τὸ ἱερὸν μεταστήσεσθαι ἔμελλεν.
22 ἡ μὲν οὖν ἐκκλησία ἐξηνθρακωμένη τότε ξύμπασα ἔκειτο. βασιλεὺς δὲ Ἰουστινιανὸς τοιαύτην ἀποτετόρνευται οὐ πολλῷ ὕστερον ὥστε, εἰ τῶν Χριστιανῶν τις ἐπύθετο πρότερον εἰ βουλομένοις αὐτοῖς διολωλέναι τὴν ἐκκλησίαν εἴη καὶ τοιάνδε γενέσθαι, δείξας τι αὐτοῖς τῶν νῦν φαινομένων ἐκτύπωμα, δοκοῦσιν ἄν μοι ὡς συντομώτατα εὔξασθαι πεπονθυῖαν σφίσι τὴν ἐκκλησίαν θεάσασθαι, ὅπως δὴ
23 αὐτοῖς ἐς τὸ παρὸν μεταβάλοιτο σχῆμα. ὁ μὲν οὖν βασιλεὺς ἀφροντιστήσας χρημάτων ἁπάντων
B 174 ἐς τὴν οἰκοδομὴν σπουδῇ ἵετο, καὶ τοὺς τεχνίτας
24 ἐκ πάσης γῆς ἤγειρεν ἅπαντας. Ἀνθέμιος δὲ Τραλλιανός, ἐπὶ σοφίᾳ τῇ καλουμένῃ μηχανικῇ λογιώτατος, οὐ τῶν κατ' αὐτὸν μόνον ἁπάντων,

[1] τι Haury : ἐς τὸ V, om. A.

---

[1] I. xxiv.
[2] "Wisdom"; *cf. Wars*, III. vi. 26.
[3] See the plan and section of St. Sophia on pp. 14 and 15.

the city, once rose up against the Emperor Justinian in Byzantium, when they brought about the rising called the Nika Insurrection, which has been described by me in detail and without any concealment in the Books on the Wars.[1] And by way of shewing that it was not against the Emperor alone that they had taken up arms, but no less against God himself, unholy wretches that they were, they had the hardihood to fire the Church of the Christians, which the people of Byzantium call " Sophia," [2] an epithet which they have most appropriately invented for God, by which they call His temple; and God permitted them to accomplish this impiety, forseeing into what an object of beauty this shrine was destined to be transformed. So the whole church at that time lay a charred mass of ruins. But the Emperor Justinian built not long afterwards a church [3] so finely shaped,[4] that if anyone had enquired of the Christians before the burning if it would be their wish that the church should be destroyed and one like this should take its place, shewing them some sort of model of the building we now see, it seems to me that they would have prayed that they might see their church destroyed forthwith, in order that the building might be converted into its present form. At any rate the Emperor, disregarding all questions of expense, eagerly pressed on to begin the work of construction, and began to gather all the artisans from the whole world. And Anthemius of Tralles, the most learned man in the skilled craft which is known as the art of building,[5] not only of all his contemporaries,

[4] Literally, "roundly turned," as by a lathe, *cf.* Plato, *Phaedrus*, 234e.

[5] On the use in this translation of the terms " building " and " master-builder," see the *Introduction*, p. x.

ἀλλὰ καὶ τῶν αὐτοῦ προγεγενημένων πολλῷ, τῇ βασιλέως ὑπούργει σπουδῇ, τοῖς τεκταινομένοις τὰ ἔργα ῥυθμίζων, τῶν τε γενησομένων προδιασκευάζων ἰνδάλματα, καὶ μηχανοποιὸς σὺν αὐτῷ ἕτερος, Ἰσίδωρος ὄνομα, Μιλήσιος γένος, ἔμφρων τε ἄλλως καὶ πρέπων Ἰουστινιανῷ
25 ὑπουργεῖν βασιλεῖ. ἦν δὲ ἄρα καὶ τοῦτο τῆς τοῦ θεοῦ περὶ τὸν βασιλέα τιμῆς, προκαταστησαμένου τοὺς ἐς τὰ πραχθησόμενα χρησιμωτά-
26 τους αὐτῷ ἐσομένους. καὶ αὐτοῦ δὲ τοῦ βασιλέως τὸν νοῦν εἰκότως ἄν τις ἀγασθείη τούτου δὴ ἕνεκα, ὅτι δὴ ἐκ πάντων ἀνθρώπων ἐς τῶν πραγμάτων τὰ σπουδαιότατα τοὺς καιριωτάτους ἀπολέξασθαι ἔσχε.

27 Θέαμα τοίνυν ἡ ἐκκλησία κεκαλλιστευμένον γεγένηται, τοῖς μὲν ὁρῶσιν ὑπερφυές, τοῖς δὲ ἀκούουσι παντελῶς ἄπιστον· ἐπῆρται μὲν γὰρ ἐς ὕψος οὐράνιον ὅσον, καὶ ὥσπερ τῶν ἄλλων οἰκοδομημάτων ἀποσαλεύουσα ἐπινένευκεν ὑπερκειμένη
P 6 τῇ ἄλλῃ πόλει, κοσμοῦσα μὲν αὐτήν, ὅτι αὐτῆς ἐστιν, ὡραϊζομένη δέ, ὅτι αὐτῆς οὖσα καὶ ἐπεμβαίνουσα τοσοῦτον ἀνέχει ὥστε δὴ ἐνθένδε ἡ
28 πόλις ἐκ περιωπῆς ἀποσκοπεῖται. εὖρος δὲ αὐτῆς καὶ μῆκος οὕτως ἐν ἐπιτηδείῳ ἀποτετόρνευται, ὥστε καὶ περιμήκης καὶ ὅλως εὐρεῖα οὐκ ἀπὸ τρόπου εἰρήσεται. κάλλει δὲ ἀμυθήτῳ

---

[1] In the *Secret History* (xxi. 7–25) Procopius gives a different account of the way in which Justinian chose his subordinates.

[2] On Procopius's description see O. Wulff, "Das Raumerlebnis des Naos im Spiegel der Ekphrasis," *Byzantinische Zeitschrift*, xxx, 1929–30, pp. 531–539. *Cf.* also K. Kumaniecki,

but also when compared with those who had lived long before him, ministered to the Emperor's enthusiasm, duly regulating the tasks of the various artisans, and preparing in advance designs of the future construction; and associated with him was another master-builder, Isidorus by name, a Milesian by birth, a man who was intelligent and worthy to assist the Emperor Justinian. Indeed this also was an indication of the honour in which God held the Emperor, that He had already provided the men who would be most serviceable to him in the tasks which were waiting to be carried out. And one might with good reason marvel at the discernment of the Emperor himself, in that out of the whole world he was able to select the men who were most suitable for the most important of his enterprises.[1]

So the church has become a spectacle of marvellous beauty, overwhelming to those who see it, but to those who know it by hearsay altogether incredible.[2] For it soars to a height to match the sky, and as if surging up from amongst the other buildings it stands on high and looks down upon the remainder of the city, adorning it, because it is a part of it, but glorying in its own beauty, because, though a part of the city and dominating it, it at the same time towers above it to such a height that the whole city is viewed from there as from a watch-tower. Both its breadth and its length have been so carefully proportioned, that it may not improperly be said to be exceedingly long and at the same time unusually broad. And it exults in an indescribable beauty.

"Eine unbekannte Monodie auf den Einsturz der Hagia Sophia im Jahre 558," *ibid.*, pp. 35–43 (especially the note on p. 41).

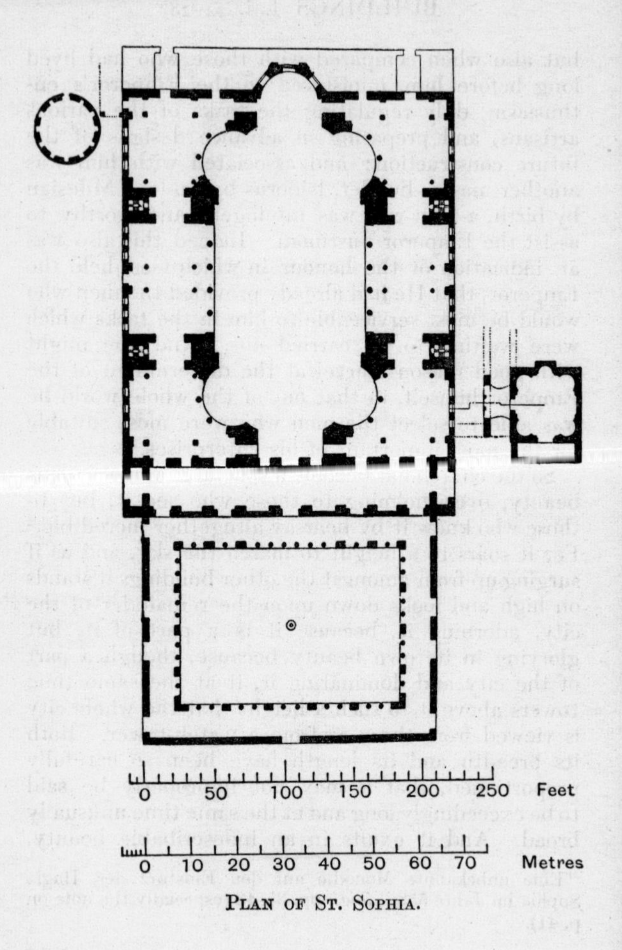
0 50 100 150 200 250 Feet
0 10 20 30 40 50 60 70 Metres

PLAN OF ST. SOPHIA.

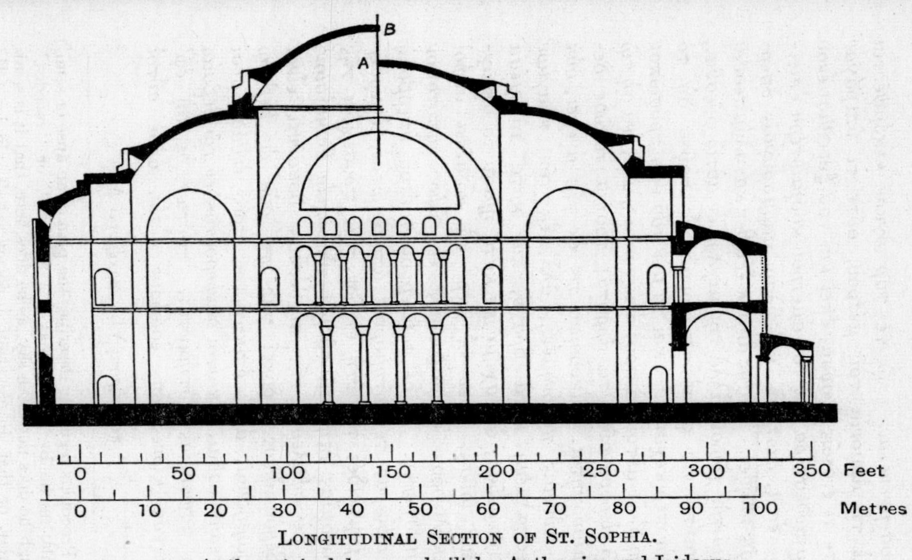
B
A
0
50
100
150
200
250
300
350 Feet
0
10
20
30
40
50
60
70
80
90
100
Metres

LONGITUDINAL SECTION OF ST. SOPHIA.

A, the original dome as built by Anthemius and Isidorus.
B, reconstruction of the dome in A.D. 558 by Isidorus the Younger.

29 ἀποσεμνύνεται. τῷ τε γὰρ ὄγκῳ κεκόμψευται καὶ τῇ ἁρμονίᾳ τοῦ μέτρου, οὔτε τι ὑπεράγαν
B 175 οὔτε τι ἐνδεῶς ἔχουσα, ἐπεὶ καὶ τοῦ ξυνειθισμένου κομπωδεστέρα καὶ τοῦ ἀμέτρου κοσμιωτέρα ἐπιεικῶς ἐστι, φωτὶ δὲ καὶ ἡλίου μαρμαρυγαῖς ὑπερ-
30 φυῶς πλήθει. φαίης ἂν οὐκ ἔξωθεν καταλάμπεσθαι ἡλίῳ τὸν χῶρον, ἀλλὰ τὴν αἴγλην ἐν αὐτῷ φύεσθαι, τοσαύτη τις φωτὸς περιουσία ἐς τοῦτο δὴ τὸ
31 ἱερὸν περικέχυται.[1] καὶ τὸ μὲν τοῦ νεὼ πρόσωπον (εἴη δ' ἂν αὐτοῦ τὰ πρὸς ἀνίσχοντα ἥλιον, ἵνα δὴ τῷ θεῷ ἱερουργοῦσι τὰ ἄρρητα) τρόπῳ τοιῷδε δε-
32 δημιούργηται. οἰκοδομία τις ἐκ γῆς ἀνέχει, οὐκ ἐπ' εὐθείας πεποιημένη, ἀλλ' ἐκ τῶν πλαγίων ὑπεσταλμένη κατὰ βραχύ, καὶ κατὰ τὰ μέσα ὑποχωροῦσα, ἐπὶ σχῆμά τε κατὰ ἥμισυ τὸ στρογγύλον ἰοῦσα, ὅπερ οἱ περὶ τὰ τοιαῦτα σοφοὶ ἡμικύλινδρον ὀνομάζουσιν, ἐς ὕψος ἀπότομον
33 ἐπανέστηκεν. ἡ δὲ τοῦ ἔργου τούτου ὑπερβολὴ ἐς σφαίρας τεταρτημόριον ἀποκέκριται, ὕπερθέν τε μηνοειδές τι αὐτῇ ἕτερον τοῖς προσεχέσι τῆς οἰκοδομίας ἐπῆρται, τῇ μὲν εὐπρεπείᾳ θαυμάσιον, τῷ δὲ σφαλερῷ τῆς συνθέσεως δοκοῦντι εἶναι
34 φοβερὸν ὅλως. δοκεῖ γάρ πη οὐκ ἐν βεβαίῳ ἐπῃωρῆσθαι, ἀλλ' ἐπικινδύνως τοῖς ἐνθάδε οὖσι μετεωρίζεσθαι. καίτοι διαφερόντως ἐν τῷ βεβαίῳ
35 τῆς ἀσφαλείας ἐστήρικται. τούτων δὲ δὴ ἐφ' ἑκάτερα κίονες ἐπ' ἐδάφους εἰσίν, οὐδὲ αὐτοὶ

[1] περικέχυται VL : διακέχυται A.

---

[1] Procopius regularly describes the plan of an apse or semicircular niche by saying that it "retreats" or "recedes," though he does not often say, as he does here, that it is semicircular, or that, in elevation, it forms a half-cylinder. He

For it proudly reveals its mass and the harmony of its proportions, having neither any excess nor deficiency, since it is both more pretentious than the buildings to which we are accustomed, and considerably more noble than those which are merely huge, and it abounds exceedingly in sunlight and in the reflection of the sun's rays from the marble. Indeed one might say that its interior is not illuminated from without by the sun, but that the radiance comes into being within it, such an abundance of light bathes this shrine. And the face itself of the church (which would be the part which faces the rising sun, that portion of the building in which they perform the mysteries in worship of God) was constructed in the following manner. A structure of masonry (*oikodomia*) is built up from the ground, not made in a straight line, but gradually curving inward on its flanks and receding at the middle, so that it forms the shape of half a circle, which those who are skilled in such matters call a half-cylinder (*hêmikylindron*); and so it rises precipitously to a height.[1] The upper part of this structure ends in the fourth part of a sphere (*sphaira*), and above it another crescent-shaped (*mênoeides*) structure rises, fitted to the adjoining parts of the building, marvellous in its grace, but by reason of the seeming insecurity of its composition altogether terrifying. For it seems somehow to float in the air on no firm basis, but to be poised aloft to the peril of those inside it. Yet actually it is braced with exceptional firmness and security. On either side of this are columns arranged on the pavement; these likewise do not

sometimes uses the same locutions to describe the arrangement of columns.

κατ' εὐθὺ ἑστῶτες, ἀλλ' εἴσω κατὰ σχῆμα τὸ ἡμίκυκλον ὥσπερ ἐν χορῷ ἀλλήλοις ὑπεξιστάμενοι, καὶ αὐτῶν ὑπεράνωθεν οἰκοδόμημα μηνοειδὲς ἀποκρέμαται. 36 τοῦ δὲ δὴ ἑῴου κατ' ἀντικρὺ[1] τὰς εἰσόδους ἔχων ἐγήγερται τοῖχος, καὶ αὐτοῦ ἑκατέρωθεν οἵ τε κίονες καὶ τὰ αὐτῶν ὕπερθεν ὁμοιότατα τοῖς δεδηλωμένοις ἐν ἡμικύκλῳ ἑστήκασι. 37 κατὰ δὲ τὰ τοῦ νεὼ μέσα λόφοι χειροποίητοι ἐπανεστήκασι τέσσαρες, οὓς καλοῦσι (B 176) πεσσούς, δύο μὲν πρὸς βορρᾶν, δύο δὲ πρὸς ἄνεμον νότον, ἀντίοι τε καὶ ἴσοι ἀλλήλοις, κίονας ἐν μέσῳ ἑκάτεροι κατὰ τέσσαρας μάλιστα ἔχοντες. 38 πεποίηνται δὲ οἱ λόφοι λίθοις εὐμεγέθεσι σύνθετοι, λογάδην μὲν συνειλεγμένοις, ἐς ἀλλήλους[2] δὲ πρὸς τῶν λιθολόγων ἐπισταμένως ἐναρμοσθεῖσιν,[3] ἐς ὕψος μέγα. εἰκάσαις ἂν αὐτοὺς εἶναι σκοπέλους ὀρῶν ἀποτόμους. 39 ἐπὶ τούτοις δὲ ἀψῖδες τέσσαρες ἐν τετραπλεύρῳ ἀνέχουσι· καὶ αὐτῶν τὰ μὲν ἄκρα ξύνδυο ξυνιόντα εἰς ἄλληλα ἐν τῇ ὑπερβολῇ ἠρήρεισται τῶν λόφων τούτων, τὰ δὲ δὴ ἄλλα ἐπηρμένα εἰς ἀπέραντον ὕψος ᾐώρηται. 40 τῶν δὲ ἀψίδων αἱ μὲν δύο κατὰ κενοῦ τοῦ ἀέρος ἐπανεστήκασι πρὸς ἀνίσχοντά τε καὶ δύοντά που τὸν ἥλιον, (P 7) αἱ δὲ λειπόμεναι οἰκοδομίαν τέ τινα καὶ κίονας

[1] So Hoeschel: τοῦ δὲ δὴ ἔω οὐ καταντικρὺ V, τοῦ δὲ δὴ νεὼ οὐκ ἀντικρὺ L.

[2] ἐς ἀλλήλους A: ἐπ' ἀλλήλοις VL, ἐς ἀλλήλους corrector of V in margin.

[3] ἐναρμοσθεῖσιν VL: ἐναρμοσθέντες A.

---

[1] It seems clear from the context that Procopius here uses *μάλιστα* in the sense of "just," either in order to indicate

stand in a straight line, but they retreat inward in the pattern of the semicircle (*hêmikyklon*) as if they were yielding to one another in a choral dance, and above them hangs a structure of crescent shape (*mênoeides*). And on the side opposite the east is reared a wall containing the entrances (*eisodoi*), and on either side of this there stand in a semicircle (*hêmikyklon*) not only the columns themselves but also the structure above them, all this being very similar to the columns and structure I have just described. And in the centre of the church stand four man-made eminences (*lophoi*), which they call piers (*pessoi*), two on the north side and two on the south, opposite and equal to each other, each pair having between them just four columns.[1] The piers (*lophoi*) are composed of huge stones joined together, carefully selected and skilfully fitted to one another by the masons, and rising to a great height. One might suppose that they were sheer mountain-peaks. From these spring four arches (*apsides*) which rise over the four sides of a square, and their ends come together in pairs and are made fast to each other on top of these piers (*lophoi*), while the other portions rise and soar to an infinite height. And while two of the arches rise over empty air, those namely on the east and the west sides, the other two have under them certain structural elements (*oikodomia*), including

that he is giving the number exactly, or in order to give it as his impression that the number four is a rather small one in relation to the large size of the building. He uses μάλιστα in this sense elsewhere in the *Buildings*: it certainly means "just" in I. vi. 9 and II. ii. 3, and may have this meaning also in I. vii. 1, II. viii. 14 and IV. x.

41 μικροὺς [1] κομιδῇ ἔνερθεν ἔχουσιν. ὕπερθεν δὲ αὐτῶν κυκλοτερὴς οἰκοδομία ἐν στρογγύλῳ ἐπῆρται· ὅθεν ἀεὶ διαγελᾷ πρῶτον ἡ ἡμέρα.
42 ὑπεραίρει γάρ, οἶμαι, τὴν γῆν ξύμπασαν, καὶ διαλείπει τὸ οἰκοδόμημα κατὰ βραχύ, ἐξεπίτηδες παρειμένον τοσοῦτον, ὅσον τοὺς χώρους, οὗ δὴ τὸ διῃρημένον τῆς οἰκοδομίας συμβαίνει εἶναι,
43 φέγγους διαρκῶς ἀγωγοὺς εἶναι. τῶν δὲ ἀψίδων τῆς συμπλοκῆς ἐν τετραγώνῳ ἐξειργασμένης, ἐς τρίγωνα τέσσαρα μεταξὺ τὸ ἔργον ἀποτετέλεσται.
44 καὶ ἡ μὲν τριγώνου ἑκάστη [2] κρηπὶς πεπιεσμένη τῇ ἐς ἀλλήλας τῶν ἀψίδων ἐνέρσει ὀξεῖαν ποιεῖται τὴν κάτω γωνίαν, συναναβαίνουσα δὲ τὸ λοιπὸν εὐρυνομένη τῇ μεταξὺ χώρᾳ ἐς τὸ κυκλοτερὲς τελευτᾷ, ὃ ταύτῃ ἀνέχει, γωνίας τε τὰς λειπομένας
45 ἐνταῦθα ποιεῖται. τούτου δὲ τοῦ κυκλοτεροῦς παμ-
B 177 μεγέθης ἐπανεστηκυῖά τις σφαιροειδὴς θόλος
46 ποιεῖται αὐτὸ διαφερόντως εὐπρόσωπον. δοκεῖ δὲ οὐκ ἐπὶ στερρᾶς τῆς οἰκοδομίας ἑστάναι, ἀλλὰ τῇ σφαίρᾳ [3] τῇ χρυσῇ ἀπὸ τοῦ οὐρανοῦ ἐξημμένη
47 καλύπτειν τὸν χῶρον. ταῦτα δὲ πάντα ἐς ἄλληλά τε παρὰ δόξαν ἐν μεταρσίῳ ἐναρμοσθέντα, ἔκ τε ἀλλήλων ᾐωρημένα καὶ μόνοις ἐναπερειδόμενα τοῖς ἄγχιστα οὖσι, μίαν μὲν ἁρμονίαν ἐκπρεπεστάτην τοῦ ἔργου ποιοῦνται, οὐ παρέχονται δὲ τοῖς θεωμένοις αὐτῶν τινι ἐμφιλοχωρεῖν ἐπὶ πολὺ τὴν ὄψιν, ἀλλὰ μεθέλκει τὸν ὀφθαλμὸν ἕκαστον, καὶ
48 μεταβιβάζει ῥᾷστα ἐφ' ἑαυτό. ἀγχίστροφός τε

[1] μικροὺς LA : μακροὺς V.
[2] ἑκάστη VL : ἑκάστου Hoeschel.
[3] σφαίρᾳ Haury : σειρᾷ.

a number of rather small columns. Upon the crowns of the arches rests a circular structure (*kykloterês oikodomia*), cylindrical (*strongylon*) in shape; it is through this that the light of day always first smiles. For it towers above the whole earth, as I believe, and the structure is interrupted at short intervals, openings having been left intentionally, in the spaces where the perforation of the stone-work takes place, to be channels for the admission of light in sufficient measure. And since the arches where they are joined together are so constructed as to form a four-cornered plan, the stonework between the arches produces four triangles (*trigôna*).[1] And while each supporting end (*krêpis*) of a triangle, having been contracted to a point by the coming together of each pair of arches, makes the lower point an acute angle, yet as the triangle rises and its width is extended by the intermediate surface, it ends in the segment of a circle (*kykloterês*) which it supports, and forms the remaining angles[2] at that level. And upon this circle rests the huge spherical dome (*sphairoeidês tholos*) which makes the structure exceptionally beautiful. Yet it seems not to rest upon solid masonry, but to cover the space with its golden dome (*sphaira*) suspended from Heaven. All these details, fitted together with incredible skill in mid-air and floating off from each other and resting only on the parts next to them, produce a single and most extraordinary harmony in the work, and yet do not permit the spectator to linger much over the study of any one of them, but each detail attracts the eye and draws it on irresistibly to itself. So the vision

[1] Pendentives.

[2] The two upper angles of each spherical triangle.

ἡ τῆς θέας μεταβολὴ ἐς ἀεὶ γίγνεται, ἀπολέξασθαι τοῦ ἐσορῶντος οὐδαμῆ ἔχοντος ὅ τι ἂν ποτε ἀγασθείη μᾶλλον τῶν ἄλλων ἁπάντων. 49 ἀλλὰ καὶ ὡς ἀποσκοποῦντες[1] πανταχόσε τὸν νοῦν, τάς τε ὀφρῦς ἐπὶ πᾶσι συννενευκότες, οὐχ οἷοί τέ εἰσι ξυνεῖναι τῆς τέχνης, ἀλλ' ἀπαλλάσσονται ἀεὶ ἐνθένδε καταπεπληγμένοι τῇ ἐς τὴν ὄψιν ἀμηχανίᾳ. ταῦτα μὲν οὖν τῇδέ πῃ ἔχει.

50 Μηχαναῖς δὲ πολλαῖς βασιλεύς τε Ἰουστινιανὸς καὶ Ἀνθέμιος ὁ μηχανοποιὸς σὺν τῷ Ἰσιδώρῳ οὕτω δὴ μετεωριζομένην τὴν ἐκκλησίαν ἐν τῷ ἀσφαλεῖ διεπράξαντο εἶναι· ὧνπερ τὰς μὲν ἄλλας ἁπάσας ἐμοὶ εἰδέναι τε ἄπορον καὶ λόγῳ φράσαι ἀμήχανον, μία δέ μοι μόνον ἔν γε τῷ παρόντι γεγράψεται ᾗ δύναιτ'[2] ἂν τις ξύμπασαν τοῦ 51 ἔργου τεκμηριῶσαι τὴν δύναμιν. ἔχει γὰρ ὧδε· οἱ λόφοι, ὧνπερ ἐπεμνήσθην ἀρτίως, οὐ κατὰ ταὐτὰ ταῖς ἄλλαις οἰκοδομίαις πεποίηνται, ἀλλὰ τρόπῳ τοιῷδε. λίθων ἐπιβολὴ ἐν τετραγώνῳ B 178 52 διαπεπόνηται, σκληρῶν μὲν φύσιν, ἐργασίαν δὲ λείων, ἐντομὴν[3] δέ, εἰ μὲν τὰ προὔχοντα ποιεῖσθαι τῶν τοῦ λόφου πλευρῶν μέλλοιεν, ἐγγωνίων, εἰ δὲ τὴν μεταξὺ κεκλήρωνται χώραν, ἐν τετρα53 πλεύρῳ γεγενημένων. συνήρμοσε δὲ αὐτοὺς οὐ τίτανος, ἥνπερ ἄσβεστον ὀνομάζουσιν, οὐκ ἄσφαλτος, ἡ Σεμιράμιδος ἐν Βαβυλῶνι φιλοτιμία, οὐκ

[1] ἀποσκοποῦντες: Haury proposes ἀποστρέφοντες.
[2] δύναιτ' Dindorf: δύναται VL. [3] ἐντομὴν V: ἐκτομὴν L.

---

[1] In describing the great piers, which are actually quite irregular in plan, Procopius uses the word "four-cornered" to convey a general impression of their somewhat rectangular appearance as they rise above the spectator.

constantly shifts suddenly, for the beholder is utterly unable to select which particular detail he should admire more than all the others. But even so, though they turn their attention to every side and look with contracted brows upon every detail, observers are still unable to understand the skilful craftsmanship, but they always depart from there overwhelmed by the bewildering sight. So much, then, for this.

It was by many skilful devices that the Emperor Justinian and the master-builder Anthemius and Isidorus secured the stability of the church, hanging, as it does, in mid-air. Some of these it is both hopeless for me to understand in their entirety, and impossible to explain in words; I shall record only one of them for the present, from which it should be possible to gain an impression of the strength of the whole work. It is as follows: The piers (*lophoi*) which I have just mentioned are not constructed in the same way as other structures, but in the following manner. The courses of stone were laid down so as to form a four-cornered shape, the stones being rough by nature but worked smooth; and they were cut to the angles when they were destined to form the projecting corners of the sides of the pier, but when they chanced to be assigned to a position between the angles, they were cut in rectangles (*tetrapleuron*).[1] These were held together neither by lime (*titanos*), which they call "asbestus",[2] nor by asphalt, the material which was the pride of Semiramis in Babylon,[3] nor by any other such thing,

[2] Because lime "cannot be quenched" by water; *cf.* *Wars*, VI. xxvii. 21.

[3] *Cf.* Diodorus, II. 12. Babylon was famous for its asphalt (Strabo, XVI. 743; Pliny, *Nat. Hist.*, XXXV. 178).

ἄλλο τοιοῦτον οὐδέν, ἀλλὰ μόλιβδος ἐς τέλμα
P 8 χυθείς, καὶ μεταξὺ πανταχόσε χωρήσας, τῶν τε
λίθων τῇ ἁρμονίᾳ ἐντετηκὼς καὶ συνδέων ἀλλήλοις
54 αὐτούς. τοῦτο μὲν οὖν ταύτῃ ἐξείργασται. ἐπὶ
τὰ λειπόμενα δὲ τοῦ νεὼ ἴωμεν.

Χρυσῷ μὲν ἀκιβδήλῳ καταλήλειπται ἡ ὀροφὴ
πᾶσα, κεραννῦσα τὸν κόμπον[1] τῷ κάλλει, νικᾷ
μέντοι ἡ ἐκ τῶν λίθων αὐγὴ ἀνταστράπτουσα
55 τῷ χρυσῷ. στοαί τέ εἰσιν ἑκατέρωθι δύο,
οἰκοδομίᾳ μὲν τοῦ νεὼ οὐδεμιᾷ διειργόμεναι,
ἀλλὰ καὶ μεῖζον αὐτοῦ ποιοῦσαι τοῦ εὔρους τὸ
μέτρον, καὶ τῷ μήκει μέχρι ἐς τὸ πέρας συνεξ-
56 ικνούμεναι, τὸ δέ γε ὕψος καταδεέστεραι. καὶ
αὐταῖς δὲ ἥ τε ὀροφὴ θόλος καὶ ὁ χρυσὸς ἐγκαλλώπισμα. ταύταιν δὲ[2] ταῖν στοαῖν ἁτέρα μὲν
τοὺς ἄνδρας εὐχομένους διακεκλήρωται, γυναιξὶ
57 δὲ ταὐτὸ ποιουμέναις ἡ ἄλλη ἀνεῖται. παραλ-
λὰξ δὲ οὐδὲν ἔχουσιν, οὐδὲ διαφέρουσι δήπου
ἀλλήλαιν, ἀλλὰ καὶ τὸ ἴσον αὐταῖν τῷ ἱερῷ ἐς

[1] κόμπον LA: κόσμον V.
[2] αὐταῖς δὲ VL: ταύταις A.

---

[1] Procopius evidently misunderstood what he had been told about the way in which the lead was employed, for it can scarcely have been poured into the joints in the manner which he describes. Paul the Silentiary, in his *Description of Saint Sophia*, says that sheets of lead were used in the piers (P. Friedländer, *Johannes von Gaza und Paulus Silentiarius*, Leipzig, 1912, p. 240, lines 476–480):

ἁρμονίαις δ' ἐνέηκε πλάκας μαλακοῖο μολύβδου,
ὄφρα κε μὴ λάιγγες ἐπ' ἀλλήλῃσι δεθεῖσαι
καὶ στυφελὰ στυφελοῖσιν ἐπ' ἄχθεσιν ἄχθεα θεῖσαι
νῶτα διαθρύψωσι· μεσοδμήτῳ δὲ μολύβδῳ
ἠρέμα πιληθεῖσα βάσις μαλθάσσετο πέτρου.

but by lead (*molibdos*) poured into the interstices (*telma*), which flowed about everywhere in the spaces between the stones and hardened in the joints (*harmonia*), binding them to each other.[1] Thus were these parts constructed; but let us proceed to the remaining portions of the church.

The whole ceiling is overlaid with pure gold, which adds glory to the beauty, yet the light reflected from the stones prevails, shining out in rivalry with the gold. And there are two stoa-like colonnades (*stoai*),[2] one on each side, not separated in any way from the structure of the church itself, but actually making the effect of its width greater,[3] and reaching along its whole length, to the very end, while in height they are less than the interior of the building. And they too have vaulted ceilings (*orophê tholos*) and decorations of gold. One of these two colonnaded stoas has been assigned to men worshippers, while the other is reserved for women engaged in the same exercise. But they have nothing to distinguish them, nor do they differ from one another in any way, but their very equality serves to beautify the church, and

"In the joints they have put sheets of soft lead, lest the stones, as they lie on one another, and heavy weight bears upon heavy weight, should have their backs broken; with the lead between, the stone foundation is pressed softly and is gently burdened." *Cf.* Lethaby and Swainson, *Sancta Sophia*, p. 259.

[2] The procedure followed in rendering Greek *stoa* in this translation is explained in the Introduction, p. x.

[3] Literally, Procopius says "the *measure* of its width." He seems to have been aware that the colonnades of the aisles and galleries, which he describes as stoas, increased the scale of the interior by making the great width of the nave seem more measurable and impressive in relation to the apparent size of the side aisles.

58 κάλλος διήκει καὶ ὡραΐζει τὸ ἐμφερές. τίς δ' ἂν τῶν ὑπερῴων τῆς γυναικωνίτιδος ἑρμηνεὺς γένοιτο, ἢ τάς τε παμπληθεῖς διηγοῖτο στοὰς καὶ τὰς περιστύλους αὐλάς, αἷς ὁ νεὼς περιβέβλη-
59 ται; τίς δὲ τῶν τε κιόνων καὶ λίθων διαριθμήσαιτο τὴν εὐπρέπειαν, οἷς τὸ ἱερὸν κεκαλλώ-
B 179 πισται; λειμῶνί τις ἂν ἐντετυχηκέναι δόξειεν
60 ὡραίῳ τὸ ἄνθος. θαυμάσειε γὰρ ἂν εἰκότως τῶν μὲν τὸ ἁλουργόν, τῶν δὲ τὸ χλοάζον, καὶ οἷς τὸ φοινικοῦν ἐπανθεῖ καὶ ὧν τὸ λευκὸν ἀπαστράπτει, ἔτι μέντοι καὶ οὓς ταῖς ἐναντιωτάταις ποικίλλει χροιαῖς ὥσπερ τις ζωγράφος ἡ φύσις.
61 ὁπηνίκα δέ τις εὐξόμενος ἐς αὐτὸ ἴοι, ξυνίησι μὲν εὐθὺς ὡς οὐκ ἀνθρωπείᾳ δυνάμει ἢ τέχνῃ, ἀλλὰ θεοῦ ῥοπῇ τὸ ἔργον τοῦτο ἀποτετόρνευται· ὁ νοῦς δέ οἱ πρὸς τὸν θεὸν ἐπαιρόμενος ἀεροβατεῖ, οὐ μακράν που ἡγούμενος αὐτὸν εἶναι, ἀλλ'
62 ἐμφιλοχωρεῖν μάλιστα οἷς αὐτὸς εἵλετο. καὶ τοῦτο οὐ τὴν πρώτην μόνον ἰδόντι ξυμβαίνει, ἀλλὰ διηνεκὲς ἑκάστῳ ταὐτὸ τοῦτο δοκεῖ, ὥσπερ
63 ἐνταῦθα τῆς ὄψεως ἀεὶ ἀρχομένης. τούτου κόρον οὐδεὶς τοῦ θεάματος ἔλαβε πώποτε, ἀλλὰ παρόντες μὲν [1] τῷ ἱερῷ ἄνθρωποι τοῖς ὁρωμένοις γεγήθασιν, ἀπιόντες δὲ τοῖς ὑπὲρ αὐτοῦ διαλόγοις
64 ἀποσεμνύνονται. ἔτι μέντοι [2] τῶν κειμηλίων τοῦ νεὼ τοῦδε τά τε χρυσώματα καὶ τὰ ἐν ἀργύρῳ καὶ λίθοις ἐντίμοις ξύμπαντα μὲν φράσαι ἀκριβολογουμένῳ ἀμήχανον ἅπερ Ἰουστινιανὸς βασιλεὺς τῇδε ἀνέθηκεν· ἑνὶ δὲ μόνῳ τεκμηριοῦσθαι
65 τοῖς τάδε ἀναλεγομένοις ἐφίημι· ὁ γὰρ τοῦ

[1] μὲν: μὲν ἐν Wahler.
[2] μέντοι VL: μὴν A.

their similarity to adorn it. But who could fittingly describe the galleries (*hyperôa*) of the women's side (*gynaikonitis*), or enumerate the many colonnades and the colonnaded aisles (*peristyloi aulai*) by means of which the church is surrounded? Or who could recount the beauty of the columns (*kiones*) and the stones with which the church is adorned? One might imagine that he had come upon a meadow with its flowers in full bloom. For he would surely marvel at the purple of some, the green tint of others, and at those on which the crimson glows and those from which the white flashes, and again at those which Nature, like some painter, varies with the most contrasting colours. And whenever anyone enters this church to pray, he understands at once that it is not by any human power or skill, but by the influence of God, that this work has been so finely turned. And so his mind is lifted up toward God and exalted, feeling that He cannot be far away, but must especially love to dwell in this place which He has chosen. And this does not happen only to one who sees the church for the first time, but the same experience comes to him on each successive occasion, as though the sight were new each time. Of this spectacle no one has ever had a surfeit, but when present in the church men rejoice in what they see, and when they leave it they take proud delight in conversing about it. Furthermore, concerning the treasures of this church—the vessels of gold and silver and the works in precious stones, which the Emperor Justinian has dedicated here—it is impossible to give a precise account of them all. But I shall allow my readers to form a judgment by a single example. That part of the shrine which is

ἱεροῦ τὰ μάλιστα χῶρος ἀβέβηλος καὶ μόνοις ἱερεῦσι βατός, ὅνπερ καλοῦσι θυσιαστήριον, λιτρῶν ἀργύρου μυριάδας ἐπιφέρεται τέτταρας.

66 Τὰ μὲν οὖν τῆς Κωνσταντινουπόλεως ἐκκλησίας, ἥνπερ μεγάλην καλεῖν νενομίκασι, συνελόντι τε καὶ ἄκρῳ δακτύλῳ διαριθμησαμένῳ εἰπεῖν, λόγῳ τε βραχυτάτῳ τὰ τῶν πραγμάτων ἀξιολογώτατα φράσαι, τῇδε Ἰουστινιανῷ δεδημι-

P 9 67 ούργηται βασιλεῖ. οὐ χρήμασι δὲ αὐτὴν ὁ βασι-

B 180 λεὺς ἐδείματο μόνον, ἀλλὰ καὶ πονουμένῃ τῇ διανοίᾳ καὶ τῇ ἄλλῃ τῆς ψυχῆς ἀρετῇ, ὥσπερ

68 ἐγὼ αὐτίκα δηλώσω. τῶν ἀψίδων, ὧνπερ ἐπεμνήσθην ἀρτίως (λώρους δὲ αὐτὰς οἱ μηχανοποιοὶ ἐπικαλοῦσι) μία τις, ἣ πρὸς ἀνίσχοντα ἥλιόν ἐστιν, ἐπανειστήκει μὲν ἑκατέρωθεν ἤδη, οὔπω δὲ ὅλη κατὰ τὸ μέσον συνετετέλεστο,

69 ἀλλ' ἔμενεν ἔτι. οἱ δὲ πεσσοὶ ὧν δὴ ὕπερθεν ἡ οἰκοδομία ἐγίνετο, τῶν ἐγκειμένων σφίσιν οὐκ ἐνεγκόντες τὸ μέγεθος, ἀμηγέπη ἐξαπιναίως ἀπορρηγνύμενοι, οὐκ ἐς μακρὰν διαλυθησομένοις

70 ἐῴκεσαν. οἱ μὲν οὖν ἀμφί τε Ἀνθέμιον καὶ Ἰσίδωρον τοῖς συμπεπτωκόσι περίφοβοι ὄντες ἐπὶ τὸν βασιλέα τὸ πρᾶγμα ἦγον, δυσέλπιδες ἐπὶ

71 τῇ τέχνῃ γεγενημένοι. αὐτίκα δὲ ὁ βασιλεύς, ὅτῳ [1] μέν ποτε ἠγμένος οὐκ οἶδα, θεῷ δέ, οἶμαι, οὐ γάρ ἐστι μηχανικός, ἐς τὸ πέρας αὐτοῖς περιελίξαι τὴν ἀψῖδα ταύτην ἐπήγγελλεν. αὐτὴ γάρ, ἔφη, ἐφ' ἑαυτῆς ἀνεχομένη τῶν ἔνερθεν

especially sacred, where only priests may enter, which they call the Inner Sanctuary (*thysiastêrion*), is embellished with forty thousand pounds' weight of silver.

So the church of Constantinople (which men are accustomed to call the Great Church), speaking concisely and merely running over the details with the finger-tips, as it were, and mentioning with a fleeting word only the most notable features, was constructed in such a manner by the Emperor Justinian. But it was not with money alone that the Emperor built it, but also with labour of the mind and with the other powers of the soul, as I shall straightway shew. One of the arches which I just now mentioned (*lôri*[1] the master-builders call them), the one which stands toward the east, had already been built up from either side, but it had not yet been wholly completed in the middle, and was still waiting. And the piers (*pessoi*), above which the structure was being built, unable to carry the mass which bore down upon them, somehow or other suddenly began to crack, and they seemed on the point of collapsing. So Anthemius and Isidorus, terrified at what had happened, carried the matter to the Emperor, having come to have no hope in their technical skill. And straightway the Emperor, impelled by I know not what, but I suppose by God (for he is not himself a master-builder), commanded them to carry the curve of this arch to its final completion. "For when it rests upon itself," he said, "it will no longer need

[1] Greek *λῶρος*, from Latin *lorus*, meaning a "thong" or "leash," and, in the plural, "reins."

---

[1] *ὅτῳ . . . μηχανικός* VL: *θέοθεν ἡγμένος* A.

72 πεσσῶν οὐκέτι δεήσει. καὶ εἰ μὲν ὁ λόγος ἀμάρτυρος ἦν, εὖ οἶδα ὅτι κόλαξ τε ἂν ἔδοξεν εἶναι καὶ ἄπιστος ὅλως, ἀλλ' ἐπεὶ μάρτυρες πάρεισι τῶν τηνικάδε πεπραγμένων πολλοί, οὐκ ὀκνητέα ἡμῖν ἐπὶ τὰ τοῦ λόγου λειπόμενά ἐστιν.
73 οἱ μὲν οὖν τεχνῖται τὰ ἐπιτεταγμένα ἐποίουν, ἡ δὲ ἀψὶς ἐπ' ἀσφαλοῦς ἠώρητο πᾶσα, ἐπισφραγί-
74 ζουσα τῇ πείρᾳ τὴν τῆς ἐννοίας ἀλήθειαν. τοῦτο μὲν οὖν ταύτῃ ἐξείργασται, κατὰ δὲ τὰς ἄλλας ἀψῖδας αἵ τε πρὸς μεσημβρίαν τετραμμέναι εἰσὶ καὶ βορρᾶν ἄνεμον, τοιόνδε ξυνηνέχθη γενέσθαι.
75 οἱ μὲν λῶροι καλούμενοι τοῦ νεὼ τῇ οἰκοδομίᾳ ἐξωγκωμένοι ἠώρηντο, βαρυνόμενοι δὲ αὐτοῖς ἐπεπονήκει τὰ ἔνερθεν πάντα, κίονές τε οἱ τῇδε ὄντες χάλικας σμικρὰς ὥσπερ ἀποξυσθέντες
76 ἀφίεσαν. καὶ αὖθις μὲν ἄθυμοι τοῖς συμπεπτωκόσιν οἱ μηχανικοὶ γεγενημένοι τῷ βασιλεῖ
B 181 77 τὰ σφίσι παρόντα ἐσήγγελλον. αὖθις δὲ ὁ βασιλεὺς ἀντεπετεχνήσατο[1] τάδε. τούτων δὴ τῶν πεπονηκότων τὰ ἄκρα, ὅσα τῶν ἀψίδων ἐπέψαυε, διελεῖν μὲν ἐν τῷ παραυτίκα ἐκέλευσεν, ἐντιθέναι δὲ πολλῷ ὕστερον, ἐπειδὰν τὸ τῆς οἰκοδομίας
78 ὑγρὸν ἀπολωφήσειεν αὐτοῖς μάλιστα.[2] καὶ οἱ μὲν κατὰ ταῦτα ἐποίουν· ἡ δὲ κτίσις διαγέγονε τὸ

[1] ἀντεπετεχνήσατο A: ἀντετεχνήσατο VL.
[2] μάλιστα VL: om. A.

the props (*pessoi*) beneath it."[1] And if this story were without witness, I am well aware that it would have seemed a piece of flattery and altogether incredible; but since there are available many witnesses of what then took place, we need not hesitate to proceed to the remainder of the story. So the artisans carried out his instructions, and the whole arch then hung secure, sealing by experiment the truth of his idea. Thus, then, was this arch completed; but in the process of building the other arches, indeed, those namely which are turned toward the south and the north, the following chanced to take place. The so-called *lôri* had been raised up, carrying the masonry of the church, but everything underneath was labouring under their load, making the columns (*kiones*) which stood there throw off tiny flakes, as if they had been planed. So once more the master-builders were dismayed at what had happened and reported their problem to the Emperor. And again the Emperor met the situation with a remedy, as follows. He ordered them immediately to remove the upper parts (*akra*) of the masonry which were strained, that is, the portions which came into contact with the arches, and to put them back much later, as soon as the dampness of the masonry should abate enough to bear them. These instructions they carried out, and thereafter the structure stood

[1] This passage is at first sight ambiguous because Procopius is using *pessoi* in two quite different senses. Obviously the statement that once the arch was completed it would no longer need the *pessoi* beneath it cannot refer to the main masonry piers (which Procopius has just called *pessoi*), but must refer to the scaffolding or centering (*pessoi*) which was holding up the great arch before its completion.

λοιπὸν ἐν ἀσφαλεῖ οὖσα. φέρεται[1] δέ τι καὶ μαρτύριον ὁ βασιλεὺς τοῦ ἔργου τοιόνδε.

β΄. Ἀγορά τις πρὸ τοῦ βουλευτηρίου ἐτύγχανεν οὖσα· καλοῦσι δὲ Αὐγουσταῖον τὴν ἀγορὰν οἱ Βυζάντιοι. ἐνταῦθα ξυνθῆκαι λίθων οὐχ ἧσσον ἢ ἑπτὰ ἐν τετραγώνῳ πεποίηνται, κατὰ μὲν ἀπόβασιν ξυγκείμεναι πᾶσαι, τοσοῦτον δὲ ἑκάστη (P 10) τῆς ἔνερθεν οὔσης ἐλασσουμένη καὶ ἀποδέουσα, ὥστε δὴ τῶν λίθων ἕκαστον τῇ ἐμβολῇ προὔχοντα βαθμὸν γεγονέναι τῶν τε ἀνθρώπων τοὺς ἐκείνῃ ἀγειρομένους ἐπ᾿ αὐτῶν ὥσπερ ἐπὶ βάθρων 2 καθῆσθαι. ἐν δὲ τῇ τῶν λίθων ὑπερβολῇ κίων ἐπανέστηκεν ἐξαίσιον ὅσον, οὐ μονοειδὴς μέντοι, ἀλλὰ λίθοις ἐν περιδρόμῳ εὐμεγέθεσι σύνθετος, ἐγγωνίοις μὲν τῇ ἐντομῇ οὖσιν, ἐς δὲ ἀλλήλους 3 ἐμπειρίᾳ τῶν λιθοδόμων ἐναρμοσθεῖσι. χαλκὸς δὲ ἄριστος ἔν τε πίναξι καὶ στεφάνοις διαχυθεὶς περιβάλλει πανταχόθι τοὺς λίθους, ἐν μὲν τῷ βεβαίῳ συνδέων, ἐν κόσμῳ δὲ αὐτοὺς συγκαλύπτων, καὶ τά τε ἄλλα σχεδόν τι πάντα καὶ διαφερόντως τά τε ἄνω καὶ τὰ κάτω ἐς τοῦ κίονος τὸν 4 τύπον ἀπομιμούμενος. ὁ δὲ χαλκὸς οὗτος τὸ μὲν χρῶμά ἐστι χρυσοῦ ἀκιβδήλου πρᾳότερος, τὴν δὲ ἀξίαν οὐ παρὰ πολὺ ἀποδέων ἰσοστάσιος (B 182) 5 ἀργύρῳ εἶναι. ἐν δὲ τοῦ κίονος τῇ κορυφῇ

[1] φέρεται . . . ὑπερβολῇ: ἐν δὲ τῷ καλουμένῳ αὐγουσταίῳ A.

---

[1] Procopius's account is not entirely clear, either because he did not understand what had happened, or because he was unable to describe the processes in technical language, or possibly because he wished to avoid a complicated technical description. His account suggests that the builders constructing the north and south arches used the walls and galleries

secure.[1] And the Emperor, in this way, enjoys a kind of testimonial from the work.

ii. Before the Senate House there happened to be a sort of market-place, which the people of Byzantium call the Augustaeum. In that place there is a structure of stones, which is made up of not less than seven courses, laid in a rectangle, all fitted to each other at their ends, but each course being narrower than that beneath, and set back, with the result that each of the stones becomes, from the way it is set, a projecting step, so that people assembled there sit upon them as upon seats. And at the top of the stones there rises a column of extraordinary size, not a monolith, however, but composed of large stones in circular courses, cut so as to form angles on their inner faces, and fitted to one another by the skill of the masons. And finest brass, cast in panels and garlands, covers the stones on every side, both serving to bind them securely, and covering them with adornment, and giving the shaft throughout, but particularly at the base and the capital, the appearance of a column. This brass, in its colour, is softer than pure gold, and its value is not much less than that of an equal weight of silver. And on the

at the sides as permanent centering for the great arches, with the result that the weight of these arches, before their keystones were in place, was too much for the thin clerestory walls and columns beneath, which were not designed to carry so much weight and would not have to do so after the arches were completed. It is even possible, from Procopius's description, that the builders were building up the spandrels of masonry above the haunches of the arches before they had completed their curve. Therefore, when Justinian ordered them to take out the strained portions and replace them later, he made it necessary for the builders to complete the arches before filling in the clerestory wall.

χαλκοῦς ἕστηκεν ὑπερμεγέθης ἵππος, τετραμμένος πρὸς ἕω, θέαμα λόγου πολλοῦ ἄξιον. ἔοικε δὲ βαδιουμένῳ καὶ τοῦ πρόσω λαμπρῶς ἐχομένῳ. 6 ποδῶν τῶν προσθίων ἀμέλει τὸν μὲν ἀριστερὸν μετεωρίζει, ὡς ἐπιβησόμενον τῆς ἐπίπροσθεν γῆς, ὁ δὲ δὴ ἕτερος ἐπὶ τοῦ λίθου ἠρήρεισται οὗ ὕπερθέν ἐστιν, ὡς τὴν βάσιν ἐκδεξόμενος· τοὺς δὲ ὀπισθίους οὕτω ξυνάγει ὡς, ἐπειδὰν τὸ μὴ ἑστήξειν αὐτοῖς[1] ἐπιβάλλοι, ἐν ἑτοίμῳ εἶεν. 7 τούτῳ δὴ τῷ ἵππῳ χαλκῆ ἐπιβέβηκε τοῦ βασιλέως εἰκὼν κολοσσῷ ἐμφερής. ἔσταλται δὲ Ἀχιλ-8 λεὺς ἡ εἰκών· οὕτω γὰρ τὸ σχῆμα καλοῦσιν ὅπερ ἀμπέχεται. τάς τε γὰρ ἀρβύλας ὑποδέδε-9 ται καὶ τὰ σφυρά ἐστι κνημίδων χωρίς. εἶτα ἡρωϊκῶς τεθωράκισται καὶ κράνος αὐτῷ τὴν κεφαλὴν σκέπει δόξαν ὡς κατασείοιτο παρεχόμενον, αἴγλη τέ τις ἐνθένδε αὐτοῦ ἀπαστράπτει. 10 φαίη τις ἂν ποιητικῶς εἶναι τὸν ὀπωρινὸν ἐκεῖνον ἀστέρα. βλέπει δὲ πρὸς ἀνίσχοντά που τὸν ἥλιον, τὴν ἡνιόχησιν ἐπὶ Πέρσας, οἶμαι, ποιού-11 μενος. καὶ φέρει μὲν χειρὶ τῇ λαιᾷ πόλον, παραδηλῶν ὁ πλάστης ὅτι γῆ τε αὐτῷ καὶ θάλασσα δεδούλωται πᾶσα, ἔχει δὲ οὔτε ξίφος οὔτε δοράτιον οὔτε ἄλλο τῶν ὅπλων οὐδέν, ἀλλὰ σταυρὸς αὐτῷ ἐπὶ τοῦ πόλου ἐπίκειται, δι' οὗ δὴ μόνου τήν τε βασιλείαν καὶ τὸ τοῦ πολέμου πεπόρισται 12 κράτος. προτεινόμενος δὲ[2] χεῖρα τὴν δεξιὰν ἐς τὰ πρὸς ἀνίσχοντα ἥλιον καὶ τοὺς δακτύλους

[1] αὐτοῖς VL: om. A. [2] δὲ A: δὲ τὴν VL.

---

[1] This statue is illustrated in the Frontispiece; see Appendix (pp. 295 ff.), where its significance is discussed. See also the

summit of the column stands a gigantic bronze horse, facing toward the east, a very noteworthy sight.[1] He seems about to advance, and to be splendidly pressing forward. Indeed he holds his left fore foot in the air, as though it were about to take a forward step on the ground before him, while the other is pressed down upon the stone on which he stands, as if ready to take the next step; his hind feet he holds close together, so that they may be ready whenever he decides to move. Upon this horse is mounted a colossal bronze figure of the Emperor. And the figure is habited like Achilles, that is, the costume he wears is known by that name. He wears half-boots and his legs are not covered by greaves. Also he wears a breastplate in the heroic fashion, and a helmet covers his head and gives the impression that it moves up and down,[2] and a dazzling light flashes forth from it. One might say, in poetic speech, that here is that star of Autumn.[3] And he looks toward the rising sun, directing his course, I suppose, against the Persians. And in his left hand he holds a globe, by which the sculptor signifies that the whole earth and sea are subject to him, yet he has neither sword nor spear nor any other weapon, but a cross stands upon the globe which he carries, the emblem by which alone he has obtained both his Empire and his victory in war.[4] And stretching forth his right hand toward the rising sun and spreading out his fingers, he

analysis of Procopius's description by P. Friedländer, *Johannes von Gaza und Paulus Silentiarius*, Leipzig, 1912, pp. 64–65.

[2] As if the horse were in motion.

[3] Sirius.

[4] The emblem of the Christian warrior: ἐν τούτῳ νίκα.

διαπετάσας ἐγκελεύεται τοῖς ἐκείνῃ βαρβάροις καθῆσθαι οἴκοι καὶ μὴ πρόσω ἰέναι. ταῦτα μὲν οὖν ὧδέ πη ἔχει.

13 Ἐκκλησίᾳ δὲ τῇ μεγάλῃ ὅμορον οὖσαν καὶ συγκαταφλεχθεῖσαν αὐτῇ πρότερον τὴν τῆς Εἰρή- B 183 νης ἐπώνυμον Ἰουστινιανὸς βασιλεὺς ὑπερμεγέθη ἐδείματο, ἱερῶν τῶν ἐν Βυζαντίῳ σχεδόν τι ἁπάντων, μετά γε τῆς Σοφίας τὸν νεών, οὐδενὸς[1] 14 δεύτερον. ἦν δέ τις μεταξὺ ταύταιν δὴ ταῖν ἐκκλησίαιν ξενών, ἀνθρώποις ἀνειμένος ἀπορουμένοις τε καὶ νοσοῦσι τὰ ἔσχατα, εἴ πρὸς τῇ 15 οὐσίᾳ καὶ τὸ σῶμα νοσοῖεν. τοῦτον ἀνήρ τις θεοσεβὴς ἐν τοῖς ἄνω χρόνοις ἐδείματο, Σαμψὼν P 11 ὄνομα. ἔμεινε δὲ οὐδὲ αὐτὸς[2] τοῖς στασιώταις ἀνέπαφος, ἀλλ' ἐκκλησίᾳ ἑκατέρᾳ συγκαταφλεχθεὶς 16 ἀπολώλει. Ἰουστινιανὸς[3] δὲ αὐτὸν ἀνῳκοδομήσατο βασιλεύς, κάλλει μὲν κατασκευῆς ἀξιώτερον, πλήθει δὲ οἰκιδίων παρὰ πολὺ μείζω· προσόδῳ τε αὐτὸν ἐπετείων δεδώρηται χρημάτων μεγάλων, ὅπως δὴ πλείοσιν ἐς ἀεὶ ταλαιπωρου- 17 μένοις ἀνθρώποις ἰῷτο τὰ πάθη. κόρον δὲ τῆς εἰς τὸν θεὸν τιμῆς ἢ πλησμονήν τινα ὡς ἥκιστα ἔχων, δύο ξενῶνας ἑτέρους ἀπ' ἐναντίας αὐτῷ ἔθετο ἐν ταῖς Ἰσιδώρου τε καὶ Ἀρκαδίου καλουμέναις οἰκίαις, τῆς βασιλίδος Θεοδώρας αὐτῷ τοῦτο δὴ τῶν ἔργων ξυνεπιλαμβανομένης τὸ 18 ἱερώτατον. τὰ δὲ δὴ ἄλλα ἱερὰ ξύμπαντα, ὅσα τῷ Χριστῷ ὁ βασιλεὺς οὗτος ἀνέθηκε, τοσαῦτα τὸ πλῆθος καὶ τοιαῦτα τὸ μέγεθός ἐστιν, ὥστε λεπτολογεῖσθαι μὲν ἀμφ' αὐτοῖς ἀμήχανα εἶναι. 19 οὐ γὰρ ἂν οὐδὲ ὁ λόγος οὐδὲ ὁ πᾶς ἡμῖν αἰὼν

[1] οὐδενὸς A: om. V. [2] αὐτὸς A : οὗτος V.

commands the barbarians in that quarter to remain at home and to advance no further. So much, then, for this statue.

The church called after Eirenê, which was next to the Great Church and had been burned down together with it, the Emperor Justinian rebuilt on a large scale, so that it was scarcely second to any of the churches in Byzantium, save that of Sophia. And between these two churches there was a certain hospice, devoted to those who were at once destitute and suffering from serious illness, those who were, namely, suffering in loss of both property and health. This was erected in early times by a certain pious man, Samson by name. And neither did this remain untouched by the rioters, but it caught fire together with the churches on either side of it and was destroyed. The Emperor Justinian rebuilt it, making it a nobler building in the beauty of its structure, and much larger in the number of its rooms. He has also endowed it with a generous annual income of money, to the end that through all time the ills of more sufferers may be cured. But by no means feeling either a surfeit or any sort of weariness in shewing honour to God, he established two other hospices opposite to this one in the buildings called respectively the House of Isidorus and the House of Arcadius, the Empress Theodora labouring with him in this most holy undertaking. All the other shrines which this Emperor dedicated to Christ are so numerous and so great in size, that it is impossible to write about them in detail. For neither the power of language, nor the whole span of eternity, would suffice

---

[3] *ἰουστινιανὸς . . . βασιλεύς* V: *ἀνῳκοδομήσατο δὲ τοῦτον ἰουλιανός* A.

ἐπαρκέσοι κατάλογον πεποιημένοις ἀποστοματίσαι πρὸς ὄνομα τούτων δὴ ἕκαστον. ἄχρι τοῦδε εἰπεῖν [1] ἡμῖν ἀποχρήσει.

γʹ. Ἀρκτέον δὲ ἀπὸ τῶν τῆς θεοτόκου Μαρίας νεών. τοῦτο γὰρ καὶ αὐτῷ βασιλεῖ ἐξεπιστάμεθα βουλομένῳ εἶναι, καὶ διαφανῶς εἰσηγεῖται ὁ ἀληθὴς λόγος ὅτι δὴ ἐκ τοῦ θεοῦ ἐπὶ τὴν B 184 2 αὐτοῦ μητέρα ἰτέον. πολλὰς τοίνυν ἐκκλησίας Ἰουστινιανὸς βασιλεὺς τῇ θεοτόκῳ ἐδείματο πανταχόθι τῆς Ῥωμαίων ἀρχῆς οὕτω δὴ μεγαλοπρεπεῖς τε καὶ παμμεγέθεις καὶ χρημάτων ὄγκῳ ἐξεργασθείσας ὑπερφυεῖ, ὥστε ἤν τις αὐτῶν μίαν κατὰ μόνας θεῷτο, εἰκάσειεν ἂν τοῦτο αὐτῷ μόνον εἰργάσθαι τὸ ἔργον καὶ περὶ τοῦτο ἠσχολημένον ἅπαντα τῆς βασιλείας κατα- 3 τρῖψαι τὸν χρόνον. ἀλλὰ νῦν, ὅπερ εἶπον, τὰ ἐπὶ Βυζαντίου ἱερά μοι γεγράψεται. τὸν μὲν οὖν ἕνα τῆς θεοτόκου νεὼν ᾠκοδομήσατο πρὸ τοῦ περιβόλου ἐν χώρῳ καλουμένῳ Βλαχέρναις· αὐτῷ γὰρ λογιστέον καὶ τὰ Ἰουστίνῳ εἰργασμένα τῷ θείῳ, ἐπεὶ καὶ αὐτοῦ τὴν βασιλείαν κατ᾽ ἐξουσίαν αὐτὸς διῳκεῖτο· ἐπιθαλάσσιος δὲ ὁ νεώς ἐστιν, ἱερώτατός τε καὶ σεμνὸς ἄγαν, ἐπιμήκης μέν, κατὰ λόγον δὲ περιβεβλημένος τῷ μήκει τὸ εὖρος, τά τε ἄνω καὶ τὰ κάτω ἄλλῳ οὐδενὶ ἀνεχόμενος ὅτι μὴ τμήμασι λίθου Παρίου ἐν κιόνων λόγῳ 4 ἐνταῦθα ἑστῶσι. καὶ τὰ μὲν ἄλλα τοῦ νεὼ μέρη κατ᾽ εὐθὺ ἑστᾶσιν οἱ κίονες, κατὰ δὲ τὰ μέσα 5 ὑποστέλλονται εἴσω. μάλιστα δὲ ἄν τις ἀγασθείη τοῦ ἱεροῦ τοῦδε εἴσω γενόμενος τὸ μὲν

[1] εἰπεῖν added by Haury, cf. *Buildings* I. iv. 31, IV. i. 26.

us to make a catalogue and by name descant upon each one of these. It will suffice us to have said thus much.

iii. We must begin with the churches of Mary the Mother of God. For we know that this is the wish of the Emperor himself, and true reason manifestly demands that from God one must proceed to the Mother of God. The Emperor Justinian built many churches to the Mother of God in all parts of the Roman Empire, churches so magnificent and so huge and erected with such a lavish outlay of money, that if one should see one of them by itself, he would suppose that the Emperor had built this work only and had spent the whole time of his reign occupied with this alone. But now, as I said, I must describe the sanctuaries of Byzantium. One of the churches of the Mother of God he built outside the fortifications in a place called Blachernae[1] (for to the Emperor's credit there must also be reckoned the buildings erected by his uncle Justinus, since Justinian administered the government also during his uncle's reign on his own authority). This church is on the sea, a most holy and very stately church, of unusual length and yet of a breadth well proportioned to its length, both its upper and its lower parts being supported by nothing but sections of Parian stone which stand there to serve as columns. And in all the other parts of the church these columns are set in straight lines, except at the centre, where they recede.[2] Anyone upon entering this church would marvel particularly at the greatness of the mass

[1] This was the outer edge of the city—toward the west—at the point where the land-walls meet the Golden Horn.

[2] See above, p. 16, note 1.

P 12 ὑπέρογκον τοῦ σφαλεροῦ χωρὶς τεταγμένον ὁρῶν, τὸ δὲ μεγαλοπρεπὲς τοῦ ἀπειροκάλου ἐλεύθερον.

6 Ἕτερον δὲ ἱερὸν αὐτῇ ἐν χώρῳ καλουμένῳ Πηγῇ ἀνέθηκεν.[1] ἐνταῦθά ἐστι δάσος κυπαρίσσων ἀμφιλαφές, λειμὼν ἐν ἁπαλαῖς ταῖς ἀρούραις τεθηλὼς ἄνθεσι, παράδεισος εὐφορῶν τὰ ὡραῖα, B 185 πηγὴ ἀψοφητὶ βλύζουσα γαληνὸν τὸ ὕδωρ καὶ 7 πότιμον, ἱεροπρεπῆ ἐπιεικῶς πάντα. ταῦτα μὲν ὁ ἀμφὶ τὸ τέμενος χῶρος· αὐτὸν δὲ τὸν νεὼν οὐδὲ ὀνόμασιν ἐπαξίοις συλλαβεῖν ῥᾴδιον, οὐδὲ διανοίᾳ σκιαγραφῆσαι, οὐδὲ διαψιθυρίσαι τῷ 8 λόγῳ. τοσοῦτον δὲ μόνον εἰπεῖν ἀποχρήσει, ὡς τῶν ἱερῶν κάλλει τε καὶ μεγέθει ὑπεραίρει 9 τὰ πλεῖστα. ταῦτα δὲ ἄμφω τὰ ἱερὰ πρὸ τοῦ τῆς πόλεως πεποίηται τείχους, τὸ μὲν ἀρχομένου παρὰ τὴν τῆς θαλάσσης ἠϊόνα, τὸ δὲ ἄγχιστά πη τῶν Χρυσῶν καλουμένων Πυλῶν, ἃς δὴ ἀμφὶ τὸ τοῦ ἐρύματος πέρας συμβαίνει εἶναι, ὅπως δὴ ἄμφω ἀκαταγώνιστα φυλακτήρια 10 τῷ περιβόλῳ τῆς πόλεως εἶεν. ἔτι μέντοι κἀν τῷ Ἡραίῳ, ὅπερ Ἱερὸν[2] καλοῦσι τανῦν, τῇ θεοτόκῳ νεὼν οὐκ εὐδιήγητον κατεστήσατο.

11 Ἐν χωρίῳ δὲ τῆς πόλεως ὃ Δεύτερον ἐπικαλεῖται, ἱεροπρεπές τε καὶ ἀγαστὸν ὅλως ἀνέθηκεν ἕδος Ἄννῃ ἁγίᾳ, ἣν τῆς μὲν θεοτόκου γεγονέναι μητέρα τινὲς οἴονται, τοῦ δὲ Χριστοῦ τιτθήν.

[1] ἀνέθηκεν V : ἀνέκαθεν A. [2] Ἱερὸν Haury : Ἱερεῖον.

---

[1] "Spring"; modern Balukli, to the west of the land-walls.

[2] *i.e.* the land-wall as distinguished from the harbour-wall.

which is held in place without instability, and at the magnificence which is free from bad taste.

He dedicated to the Virgin another shrine in the place called Pegê.[1] In that place is a dense grove of cypresses and a meadow abounding in flowers in the midst of soft glebe, a park abounding in beautiful shrubs, and a spring bubbling silently forth with a gentle stream of sweet water—all especially suitable to a sanctuary. Such are the surroundings of the sanctuary. But the church itself is not easy to describe in such terms as it deserves, nor can one readily form a mental vision of it, nor do it justice in whispering speech. It must suffice to say only this, that it surpasses most shrines both in beauty and in size. Both these churches were erected outside the city-wall,[2] the one where it starts beside the shore of the sea, the other close to the Golden Gate, as it is called, which chances to be near the end of the line of fortifications, in order that both of them may serve as invincible defences to the circuit-wall of the city.[3] Also in the Heraeum, which they now call the Hieron, he built a church to the Mother of God which it is not easy to describe.

In that section of the city which is called Deuteron[4] he erected a most holy and revered church to St. Anna, whom some consider to have been the mother of the Virgin and the grandmother

[3] The Church of the Spring was far removed from the Golden Gate and from the sea. Procopius forgets or wilfully distorts the facts of topography in depicting a purely fanciful arrangement of these two churches as guardians of the city-wall.

[4] "Second," as being marked by the second milestone from the original centre of the city, which was near the point of the peninsula.

12 ἄνθρωπος γὰρ ᾗπερ ἐβούλετο γεγονὼς ὁ θεὸς καὶ τριγονίας ἀνέχεται καὶ γενεαλογεῖται τὰ 13 ἐκ μητρὸς ἀνθρώπῳ ἴσα. τούτου δὲ δὴ τοῦ νεὼ οὐ πολλῷ ἄποθεν ἀμφὶ τῆς πόλεως ἀγυιὰν ἐσχάτην Ζωῇ μάρτυρι σεμνὸν ἐπιεικῶς ἕδος πεποίηται.

14 Τοῦ δὲ ἀρχαγγέλου Μιχαὴλ ἱερὸν εὗρεν ἐν Βυζαντίῳ βραχύ τε καὶ ἀφεγγὲς ἄγαν καὶ ὡς ἥκιστα τῷ ἀρχαγγέλῳ ἀνεῖσθαι πρέπον πρὸς σενάτορός τινος τῶν πατρικίων ἐν χρόνῳ γεγενημένον τῷ ἔμπροσθεν, κοιτωνίσκῳ οἰκίας ἀτεχνῶς 15 ἐμφερὲς οὐδὲ λίαν εὐδαίμονος. διὸ δὴ καθεῖλε B 186 μὲν αὐτὸ ἐς τὸ ἔδαφος ἐκ τῶν θεμελίων, ὡς μή τι αὐτῷ τῆς προτέρας ἀκοσμίας ἀπολειφθείη. 16 εὐμέγεθες δὲ τεκτηνάμενος κατὰ[1] τὸν νῦν φαινόμενον τρόπον, ἐς κάλλος μεταβιβάζει θαυμάσιον 17 οἷον. ἐν τετραπλεύρῳ μὲν γὰρ τὸ τέμενός ἐστιν, οὐ κατὰ πολὺ δὲ φαίνεται προέχον τοῦ εὔρους τὸ μῆκος. τῆς δὲ πλευρᾶς ἣ πρὸς ἀνίσχοντα ἥλιον τέτραπται κατὰ μὲν τὰ ἄκρα παχὺς ἑκατέρωθεν τοῖχος λίθοις ἐν πλήθει ξυγκειμένοις ἀποτετόρνευται, κατὰ δὲ τὰ μέσα ἐξ 18 ὑπαγωγῆς ἀποχωρῶν ὑποστέλλεται. καὶ αὐτῆς ἐφ' ἑκάτερα μὲν ἀνέχουσι τὸν νεὼν κίονες χροιαῖς τισι ποικιλλόμενοι φύσει. ὁ δὲ καταντικρὺ πρὸς δύοντά που τὸν ἥλιον τοῖχος ταῖς εἰς τὸν νεὼν εἰσαγούσαις διήρηται θύραις.

P 13 δ'. Ἐς δὲ τοῦ Χριστοῦ ἀποστόλους τὸ πιστὸν ἐπιδέδεικται τρόπῳ τοιῷδε. πρῶτα μὲν Πέτρῳ καὶ Παύλῳ νεὼν οὐ πρότερον ὄντα ἐν Βυζαντίῳ

[1] κατὰ V: ἐς A.

of Christ. For God, being born a man as was His wish, is subjected to even a third generation, and His ancestry is traced back from His mother even as is that of a man. Not far from this same church, near the last street within the city, he built a very imposing shrine to the martyr Zoê.

He found a shrine of the Archangel Michael in Byzantium which was small and very badly lighted, utterly unworthy to be dedicated to the Archangel; it was built in earlier times by a certain patrician senator, quite like a tiny bedroom of a dwelling-house, and that, too, of the house of one who is not very prosperous. So he tore this down, even to the lowest foundations, so that no trace of its earlier unseemliness might remain. And increasing its size to the proportions which it now displays, he transformed it into a marvellously beautiful building. For the church[1] is in the form of a rectangle (*tetrapleuron*), and the length appears not much greater than the width. And at either end of the side which faces the east a thick wall was perfectly constructed of many fitted stones, but in the middle it is drawn back so as to form a recess. On either side of this rise columns of naturally variegated hues which support the church. The opposite wall, which faces approximately the west, is pierced by the doors which lead into the church.

iv. His faith in the Apostles of Christ he displayed in the following manner. First he built a Church of Peter and Paul, which had not previously existed in

[1] Procopius often uses τέμενος (*temenos*), as here, to mean the church building itself, not the enclosure about it; sometimes he employs the word to mean both the building and the enclosure.

ἐδείματο παρὰ τὴν βασιλέως αὐλήν, ἣ Ὁρμίσδου
2 τὸ παλαιὸν ἐπώνυμος ἦν· ταύτην[1] γὰρ οἰκίαν
αὐτοῦ ἰδίαν Παλάτιον εἶναι δοκεῖν τε καὶ πρέπειν
τῷ μεγαλοπρεπεῖ τῆς οἰκοδομίας διαπραξάμενος,
ἐπειδὴ αὐτοκράτωρ κατέστη Ῥωμαίοις, τοῖς
3 ἄλλοις βασιλείοις ἐνῆψεν. οὗ δὴ καὶ τέμενος
ἄλλο ἁγίοις ἐπιφανέσι Σεργίῳ τε καὶ Βάκχῳ
ἐδείματο, καὶ ἔπειτα καὶ τέμενος ἄλλο ἐκ πλαγίου
4 τούτῳ παρακείμενον. ἄμφω δὲ τούτω τὼ νεὼ
οὐκ ἀντιπροσώπω, ἀλλ' ἐκ πλαγίας ἀλλήλοιν
ἑστᾶσι, συνημμένοι τε καὶ ἀλλήλοις ἐνάμιλλοι
ὄντες, καὶ τὰς εἰσόδους ἐπικοινούμενοι, καὶ ἴσα
ἀλλήλοις τά τε ἄλλα πάντα καὶ τὰ κράσπεδα
περιβεβλημένοι, καὶ ἅτερος θατέρου[2] οὔτε κάλ-
B 187 λους πέρι οὔτε μεγέθους οὔτε ἄλλου οὐδενὸς
5 πλεονεκτῶν ἢ ἐλασσούμενος δείκνυται. ὁμοίως
μὲν γὰρ ἑκάτερος τῇ αἴγλῃ τῶν λίθων ὑπεραστράπ-
τει τὸν ἥλιον, ὁμοίως δὲ χρυσοῦ περιουσίᾳ πανταχ-
χόθι κατακορής ἐστι καὶ κατακομᾷ τοῖς ἀναθή-
6 μασιν. ἑνὶ μέντοι διαλλάσσουσι μόνῳ. τὸ μὲν
γὰρ μῆκος αὐτοῖν τῷ μὲν κατ' εὐθὺ διαπεπόνηται,
τῷ δὲ οἱ κίονες ἐν ἡμικύκλῳ ἐκ τοῦ ἐπὶ πλεῖστον
7 ἑστᾶσιν. ἔστι δὲ αὐτοῖς μία μὲν ἡ ἐπὶ τῶν
προθύρων στοὰ ἐπὶ τοῦ νάρθηκος τῷ περιμήκης
εἶναι ὠνομασμένη· ἐπὶ κοινῆς δὲ προπύλαια

[1] ταύτην γὰρ οἰκίαν αὐτοῦ . . . ἐδείματο, καὶ V, ἔνθα τὴν οἰκίαν εἶχεν αὐτὸς πρὸ τοῦ βασιλεῦσαι A.
[2] ἅτερος θατέρου A: om. V, οὐδέτερος Maltretus.

---

[1] Hormisdas was a fugitive Persian prince, high in the counsels of the Emperor Constantius, A.D. 353–361.
[2] Justinian.

Byzantium, alongside the imperial residence which in former times was called by the name of Hormisdas.[1] For he[2] had contrived that this building, which was his private residence, should both seem to be a palace, and by the magnificence of its structure be as handsome as one; and when he became Emperor of the Romans he joined it to the Palace proper. There too he built another shrine to the famous Saints Sergius and Bacchus, and then also another shrine which stood at an angle to this one.[3] These two churches do not face each other, but stand at an angle to one another, being at the same time joined to each other and rivalling each other; and they share the same entrances (*eisodoi*) and are like each other in all respects, even to the open spaces (*kraspeda*) by which they are surrounded; and each of them is found to be neither superior nor inferior to the other either in beauty or in size or in any other respect. Indeed each equally outshines the sun by the gleam of its stones, and each is equally adorned throughout with an abundance of gold and teems with offerings. In just one respect, however, they do differ. For the long axis (*mêkos*) of one of them is built straight, while in the other church the columns stand for the most part in a semi-circle (*hêmikyklos*).[4] But whereas they possess a single colonnaded stoa,[5] called a narthex because of its great length, for each one of their porches (*prothyra*), they have their propylaea (*propylaia*) entirely in common, and

[3] See the plan of the Church of Saints Sergius and Bacchus on p. 46; the other church has been destroyed.

[4] This is a way of saying that one church was a basilica, in which the walls and aisles ran in a straight line, while the other (that of SS. Sergius and Bacchus) was built on a central plan with exedras.

[5] Cf. *infra* V. vi. 23.

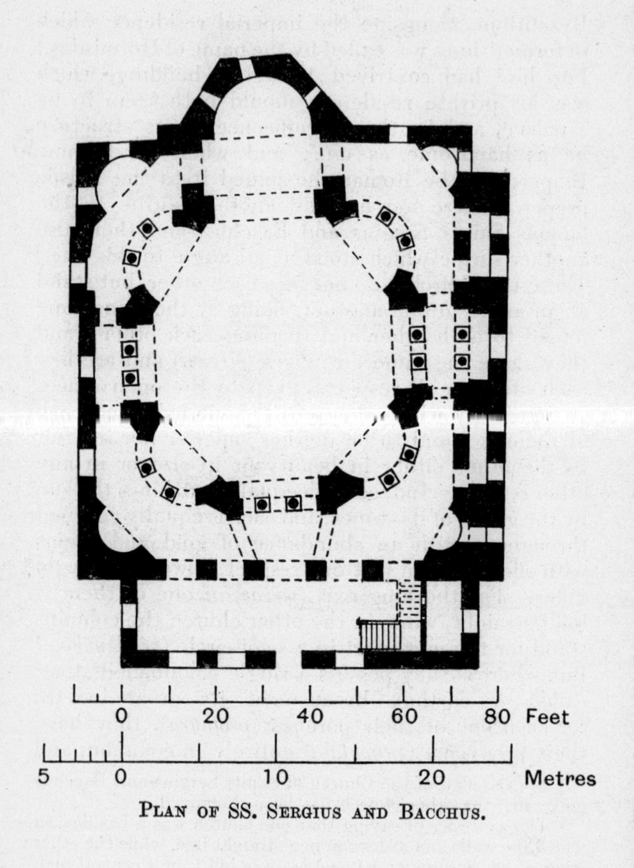
0
20
40
60
80
Feet
5
0
10
20
Metres
PLAN OF SS. SERGIUS AND BACCHUS.

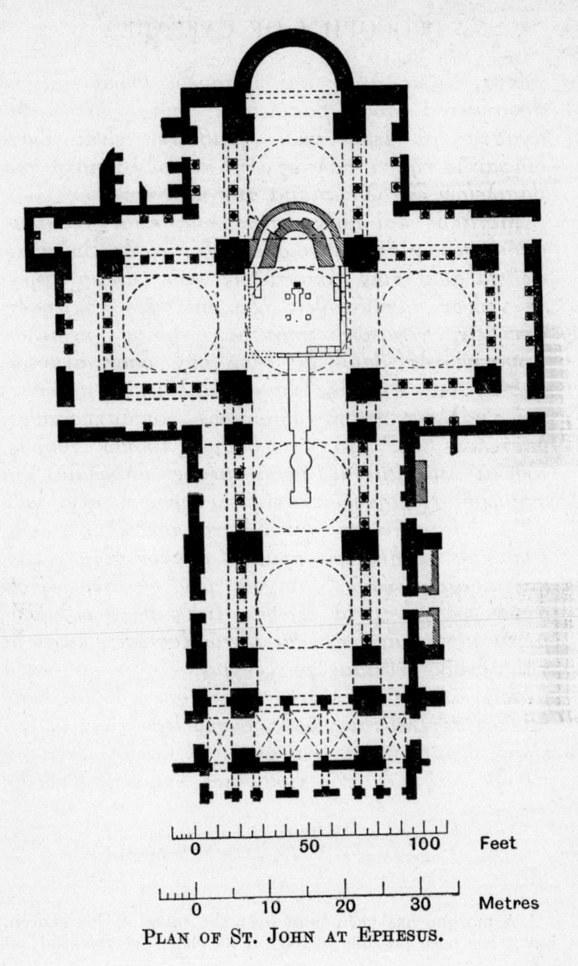
0
50
100
Feet
0
10
20
30
Metres

Plan of St. John at Ephesus.

πάντα, ἥ τε αὐλὴ καὶ μέταυλοι θύραι καὶ τὸ
8 προσήκειν[1] τοῖς βασιλείοις. οὕτω δὲ ἄμφω
ἀγαστὰ τὰ ἱερὰ τάδε ξυμβαίνει εἶναι ὥστε
διαφανῶς τῆς τε πόλεως ὅλης καὶ οὐχ ἥκιστα τῶν
βασιλείων ἐγκαλλώπισμα τυγχάνει ὄντα.

9 Μετὰ δὲ καὶ τοὺς ἀποστόλους ἅπαντας ὑπερφυῶς σέβων ἐποίει τοιάδε. ἦν τις ἐν Βυζαντίῳ
ἐκ παλαιοῦ τοῖς ἀποστόλοις νεὼς ἅπασι μήκει
τε χρόνου κατασεισθεὶς ἤδη καὶ πρὸς τὸ μηκέτι
10 ἑστήξειν γεγονὼς ὕποπτος. τοῦτον περιελὼν
Ἰουστινιανὸς βασιλεὺς ὅλον οὐχ ὅσον ἀνανεώ-
σασθαι διὰ σπουδῆς ἔσχεν, ἀλλὰ καὶ μεγέθους
καὶ κάλλους πέρι ἀξιώτερον καταστήσασθαι.
11 ὑπετέλεσε δὲ[2] τὸ σπούδασμα τρόπῳ τοιῷδε.
εὐθεῖαι συνημμέναι κατὰ μέσον ἀλλήλαις ἐπὶ
σταυροῦ σχήματος πεποίηνται δύο, ἡ μὲν ὀρθὴ
πρὸς ἀνίσχοντά τε καὶ δύοντα τὸν ἥλιον οὖσα,
ἐγκαρσία δὲ ἡ ἑτέρα πρός τε ἄρκτον τετραμμένη
P 14 12 καὶ ἄνεμον νότον. τοίχοις μὲν ἐκ περιφεροῦς
ἀποπεφραγμέναι τὰ ἔξωθεν, ἐντὸς δὲ περιβαλλό-
μεναι κίοσιν ἄνω τε καὶ κάτω ἑστῶσι· κατὰ δὲ
B 188 ταῖν δυοῖν εὐθείαιν τὸ ζεῦγμα, εἴη δ' ἂν κατὰ
μέσον αὐταῖν μάλιστα, τοῖς οὐκ ὀργιάζουσιν
ἄβατος τετέλεσται χῶρος, ὅνπερ ἱερατεῖον, ὡς τὸ
13 εἰκός, ὀνομάζουσι. καὶ αὐτοῦ αἱ μὲν ἐφ' ἑκάτερα
πλευραὶ τῆς ἐν τῷ ἐγκαρσίῳ κειμένης εὐθείας

[1] προσήκειν Maltretus for προσοικεῖν V.
[2] ὑπετέλεσέ τε V, ἐπετέλεσε δὲ Maltretus.

---

[1] A mosque has been built over the ruins of this church, but it has been possible to recover its plan; see the study of

they share a single court (*aulê*), and the same doors leading in from the court (*metauloi thyrai*), and they are alike in that they belong to the Palace. These two churches are so admirable that they manifestly form an adornment of the whole city, and not merely of the Palace.

Afterwards, as shewing very special honour to all the Apostles together, he did as follows. There was in Byzantium from ancient times a church dedicated to all the Apostles; but having by now been shaken by the passage of time, it had fallen under the suspicion that it would not continue to stand. This the Emperor Justinian pulled down entirely, and he was at pains not simply to restore it, but to make it more worthy both in size and in beauty. He carried out his effort as follows.[1] Two straight lines were drawn, intersecting each other at the middle in the form of a cross, one extending east and west, and the other which crossed this running north and south. On the outside these lines were defined by walls on all of the sides, while on the inside they were traced by rows of columns standing above one another. At the crossing of the two straight lines, that is to say at about the middle,[2] there was set aside a place which may not be entered by those who may not celebrate the mysteries; this with good reason they call the "sanctuary" (*hierateion*). The two arms (*pleurai*) of this enclosure which lie along the transverse line are equal

K. Wulzinger, "Die Apostelkirche und die Mehmedije zu Konstantinopel," *Byzantion*, vii., 1932, pp. 7–39. The plan is illustrated by that of the Church of St. John at Ephesus (above, p. 47), which Procopius says (below, V. i. 6) closely resembled the Church of the Apostles.

[2] *i.e.*, of the church.

ἴσαι ἀλλήλαις τυγχάνουσιν οὖσαι, τῆς μέντοι ὀρθῆς ἡ πρὸς δύοντα ἥλιον ἐς τόσον τῆς ἑτέρας πεποίηται μείζων ὅσον ἀπεργάσασθαι τὸ τοῦ
14 σταυροῦ σχῆμα. τῆς δὲ ὀροφῆς τὰ μὲν τοῦ ἱερατείου καλουμένου καθύπερθεν τῷ τῆς Σοφίας ἱερῷ κατά γε τὰ μέσα ἐμφερῆ εἴργασται, πλήν γε δὴ ὅτι ταῦτα ἐκείνων ἐλασσοῦσθαι μεγέθει
15 συμβαίνει. αἵ τε γὰρ ἀψῖδες τέσσαρες οὖσαι κατὰ τὸν αὐτὸν ᾐώρηνταί τε καὶ συνδέονται ἀλλήλαις τρόπον καὶ τὸ κυκλοτερὲς ὑπερανεστηκὸς κατὰ τὰς θυρίδας διῄρηται, τό τε σφαιροειδὲς ἐπικυρτούμενον ὕπερθεν μετεωρίζεσθαί που δοκεῖ καὶ οὐκ ἐπὶ στερρᾶς τῆς οἰκοδομίας ἑστάναι, καίπερ
16 ἀσφαλείας εὖ ἔχον. τὸ μὲν οὖν τῆς ὀροφῆς μέσον τῇδε πεποίηται· κατὰ δὲ τὰς πλευρὰς τέσσαρας οὔσας, ᾗπέρ μοι εἴρηται, κατὰ ταὐτὰ τῷ μέσῳ τὸ μέγεθος εἴργασται, τούτου δὴ μόνου ἐνδέοντος, ὅτι δὴ τοῦ σφαιρικοῦ ἔνερθεν οὐ διῄρη-
17 ται ἡ οἰκοδομία θυρίσιν. ἐπειδὴ δὲ αὐτῷ τὸ ἁγίστευμα τοῦτο ἐξείργαστο, καταφανεῖς[1] οἱ ἀπόστολοι πεποίηνται πᾶσιν ὡς γεγήθασί τε τῇ τοῦ βασιλέως τιμῇ καὶ κατακόρως ἐν-
18 αβρύνονται. σώματα γοῦν τῶν[2] ἀποστόλων Ἀνδρέου τε καὶ Λουκᾶ καὶ Τιμοθέου ἄδηλά τε καὶ ὅλως κρυφαῖα τὰ πρότερα ὄντα τηνικάδε πᾶσιν ἔνδηλα γέγονεν, οὐκ ἀπαξιούντων, οἶμαι, τὴν βασιλέως πίστιν, ἀλλ᾽ ἐπιχωρούντων αὐτῷ
B 189 διαρρήδην ὁρῶντί τε αὐτοὺς καὶ προσιόντι καὶ ἁπτομένῳ τῆς ἐνθένδε ὠφελείας τε καὶ περὶ τὸν βίον ἀσφαλείας ἀπόνασθαι. ἐγνώσθη δὲ ὧδε.

[1] καταφανεῖς Hoeschel : καταφανές.

to each other, but the arm which extends toward the west, along the upright line, is enough longer than the other to make the form of the cross. That portion of the roof which is above the sanctuary, as it is called, is built, in the centre at least, on a plan resembling that of the Church of Sophia, except that it is inferior to it in size. The arches, four in number, rise aloft and are bound together in the same manner, and the circular drum (*kykloteres*) which stands upon them is pierced by the windows, and the dome (*sphairoeides*) which arches above this seems to float in the air and not to rest upon solid masonry, though actually it is well supported. Thus, then, was the central portion of the roof constructed. And the arms of the building, which are four, as I have said, were roofed on the same plan as the central portion, but this one feature is lacking: underneath the domes (*sphairikon*) the masonry is not pierced by windows. And at the time when this shrine was completed by him, the Apostles made it manifest to all men how they delight in the honour shewn them by the Emperor and glory in it exceedingly. At any rate the bodies of the Apostles Andrew and Luke and Timothy, which previously had been invisible and altogether concealed, became at that time visible to all men, signifying, I believe, that they did not reject the faith of the Emperor, but expressly permitted him to see them and approach them and touch them, that he might thereby enjoy their assistance and the safety of his life. This was made known in the following way.

---

[2] τῶν added by Maltretus.

19 Κωνστάντιος[1] μὲν βασιλεὺς τοῦτον δὴ τὸν νεὼν ἔς τε τὴν τιμὴν καὶ τὸ ὄνομα τῶν ἀποστόλων ἐδείματο, τὰς θήκας γενέσθαι αὐτῷ τε καὶ τοῖς ἐς τὸ ἔπειτα βασιλεύσουσιν ἐνταῦθα τάξας, οὐκ ἀνδράσι μόνον, ἀλλὰ καὶ γυναιξὶν οὐδέν τι ἧσσον· ὅπερ καὶ διασώζεται ἐς τόνδε τὸν χρόνον· οὗ δὴ καὶ Κωνσταντίνου τοῦ πατρὸς τὸν νεκρὸν 20 ἔθετο. ἀποστόλων δὲ σώματα ἐνταῦθα εἶναι ὡς ἥκιστά πη ἐπεσημήνατο, οὐδέ τις ἐνταῦθα ἐφαίνετο χῶρος σώμασιν ἁγίοις ἀνεῖσθαι δοκῶν. 21 ἀλλὰ νῦν Ἰουστινιανοῦ βασιλέως ἀνοικοδομουμένου τὸ ἱερὸν τοῦτο, οἱ μὲν λιθουργοὶ τὸ ἔδαφος διώρυσσον ὅλον, τοῦ μή τι ἄκοσμον τῇδε λελεῖφθαι· θήκας δὲ ξυλίνας ἐνταῦθά πη ἀπημελημένας τεθέανται τρεῖς, γράμμασιν ἐγκειμένοις σφίσι δηλούσας, ὡς Ἀνδρέου τε καὶ Λουκᾶ καὶ Τιμοθέου 22 τῶν ἀποστόλων σώματα εἶεν· ἅπερ ἀσμενέστατα P 15 βασιλεύς τε αὐτὸς καὶ Χριστιανοὶ ξύμπαντες εἶδον, πομπήν τε αὐτοῖς καὶ πανήγυριν ἐπιτετελεκότες, τῇ τε περὶ αὐτοὺς τιμῇ ἐξοσιωσάμενοι τὰ εἰωθότα καὶ περιστείλαντες τὰς θήκας αὖθις τῇ γῇ ἔκρυψαν, οὐκ ἄσημον οὐδὲ ἀγείτονα λιπόντες τὸν χῶρον, ἀλλὰ σώμασιν ἀποστόλων 23 ἀνειμένον καταστησάμενοι ξὺν εὐσεβείᾳ. εὔδηλον δὲ ὡς ἀμειβόμενοι, ὅπερ μοι εἴρηται, οἱ ἀπόστολοι οἵδε τὴν ἐς αὐτοὺς βασιλέως τιμὴν πεφήνασι 24 τοῖς ἀνθρώποις τανῦν. βασιλέως γὰρ εὐσεβοῦντος οὐδὲ ἀποφοιτᾷ τῶν ἀνθρωπείων τὰ θεῖα πραγμάτων

[1] Κωνστάντιος Haury : κωνστα$\overset{\tau'}{\nu}$: Κωνσταντῖνος editors.

The Emperor Constantius [1] had built this church in honour of thc Apostles and in their name, decreeing that tombs for himself and for all future Emperors should be placed there, and not for the rulers alone, but for their consorts as well; and this custom is preserved to the present day. Here also he laid the body of his father Constantine. But neither did he give any intimation whatever that the bodies of Apostles were there, nor did any place appear there which seemed to be given over to the bodies of holy men. But when the Emperor Justinian was rebuilding this shrine, the workmen dug up the whole soil so that nothing unseemly should be left there; and they saw three wooden coffins lying there neglected, which revealed by inscriptions upon them that they contained the bodies of the Apostles Andrew and Luke and Timothy. And the Emperor himself and all the Christians saw these with the greatest joy, and having arranged a procession in their honour and a festival, and having performed the customary holy rites over them and having put the coffins in order, they laid them once more in the ground, not leaving the place unmarked or solitary, but piously ordaining that it be dedicated to the bodies of Apostles. And it is plain, as I have said, that it was in requital for this honour which the Emperor shewed them, that these Apostles appeared to men on this occasion. For when the Emperor is pious, divinity walks not

[1] Eusebius and others state that the church was founded by Constantine the Great, while Procopius and some writers attribute it to Constantius; evidently it was begun by Constantine and completed after his death by his son (*cf.* A. Heisenberg, *Grabeskirche und Apostelkirche*, Leipzig, 1908, II, p. 110).

B 190 ἀλλ᾽ ἐπιμίγνυσθαί τε καὶ ἐμφιλοχωρεῖν τῇ ἐς τοὺς ἀνθρώπους ὁμιλίᾳ φιλεῖ.

25 Τίς δ᾽ ἂν τὸν Ἀκακίου σιωπῴη νεών; ὅνπερ καταπεπονηκότα περιελὼν ἐξ αὐτῶν θεμελίων ἀνέστησε, μέγεθος περιβεβλημένον θαυμάσιον ἡλίκον· ὃς κίοσι μὲν ἐπῆρται πανταχόθι λευκοῖς ὑπεράγαν, λίθῳ δὲ τὰ ἐδάφη παραπλησίῳ ἠμφίεσται, ὧνπερ ἀπαστράπτει τοσοῦτον ἡ αἴγλη ὥστε καὶ δόξαν παρέχεσθαι ὅτι δὴ χιόσιν ὁ νεὼς 26 ἅπας κατάρρυτός ἐστι. στοαὶ δὲ αὐτοῦ προβέβληνται δύο, περίστυλος μὲν ἁτέρα οὖσα, ἡ δὲ πρὸς 27 ἀγορὰν νενευκυῖα. μικροῦ με τὸ μαρτύριον ἐκεῖνο παρῆλθεν εἰπεῖν, ὃ Πλάτωνι ἀνεῖται ἁγίῳ, ἱεροπρεπές τε ὡς ἀληθῶς ὂν καὶ σεμνὸν ἄγαν, οὐ πολλῷ τῆς ἀγορᾶς ἄποθεν ᾗ βασιλέως Κωνσταντίνου ἐπώνυμός ἐστιν· ἔτι μέντοι καὶ τὸν Μωκίῳ μάρτυρι ἀνειμένον νεών, οὗπερ τὰ 28 ἱερὰ πάντα μεγέθει ἐλάσσω. πρὸς δὲ καὶ τὸ Θύρσου μάρτυρος ἕδος καὶ μὴν τὸ Θεοδώρου ἁγίου τέμενος πρὸ τῆς πόλεως κείμενον ἐν χώρῳ καλουμένῳ Ῥησίῳ, καὶ τό τε Θέκλης μάρτυρος ἱερόν, ὃ παρὰ τὸν τῆς πόλεως λιμένα ἐστὶν ὅνπερ ἐπώνυμον Ἰουλιανοῦ ξυμβαίνει εἶναι, καὶ τὸ Θεοδότης ἁγίας ἐν προαστείῳ καλουμένῳ 29 Ἑβδόμῳ. ταῦτα γὰρ ἅπαντα ὁ βασιλεὺς οὗτος ἐπὶ τοῦ θείου Ἰουστίνου βασιλεύοντος ἐκ θεμελίων ἐδείματο, ἀπαγγέλλεσθαι μὲν οὐ ῥᾴδια λόγῳ,

---

[1] Acacius, said to have been a centurion from Cappadocia, was martyred at Byzantium under Maximianus. The Church of Acacius which was restored by Justinian had been built by Constantine the Great, and stood at the Heptascalum, on

afar from human affairs, but is wont to mingle with men and to take delight in associating with them.

Who could pass over in silence the Church of Acacius?[1] This had fallen into ruin, and he took it down and rebuilt it from the foundations, so as to make it a building of marvellous size. It is carried on all sides on columns of astonishing whiteness, and the floor is covered with similar stone, from which such a brilliant light is reflected that it gives the impression that the whole church is coated with snow. And two stoas are thrown out in front of it, one of them making a court (*peristylos*), the other facing[2] the market-place. I have almost omitted to mention that martyr's shrine which is dedicated to St. Plato, a truly holy and much revered building, not far from the market-place which bears the name of the Emperor Constantine; also the church dedicated to the marytr Mocius, to which all other shrines yield in size. There is also the resting-place of the martyr Thyrsus, and likewise the precinct of St. Theodore, situated outside the city at a place called Rhesium, as well as the sanctuary of the martyr Thecla, which is hard by the harbour of the city which chances to bear the name of Julian, and that of St. Theodota in the suburb called Hebdomum.[3] All these our present Emperor built from the foundations during the reign of his uncle Justinus, and they are not easy to describe in words, and

the Sea of Marmara. There was also an oratory at the place where Acacius was executed.

[2] Possibly "open towards" or "leading to."

[3] Modern Macrikeuy, called Hebdomum because it stood at the "seventh" milestone from the original centre of the city.

θαυμάζεσθαι[1] δὲ ὄψει κατὰ τὴν ἀξίαν ἀμήχανα.
30 ἕλκει τὸν λόγον ἐς αὑτὸν ὁ Ἀγαθονίκου τοῦ ἁγίου νεὼς καὶ βιάζεται οὐδὲ φωνὴν ἔτι ἔχοντα οὐδὲ ὀνόματα ἐφαρμόσαι τοῖς πράγμασι. διόπερ ἡμῖν μὲν ἄχρι τοῦδε εἰπεῖν ἀποχρήσει· φράσαι δὲ αὐτοῦ τό τε κάλλος καὶ τὸ ἐς ἅπαντα μεγαλοπρεπὲς ἑτέροις ἀφίεμεν, οἷς ἂν ὁ λόγος ἀκμάζων τε καὶ οὔπω πεπονηκὼς παντάπασιν εἴη.

P 16 ε΄. Καὶ ἄλλα δὲ τεμένη ἐν τῷ καλουμένῳ Ἀνάπλῳ καὶ κατὰ τὴν ἀντιπέρας ἤπειρον εὗρεν οὐ πρέποντα τῶν τινι ἀνεῖσθαι ἁγίων, ἔτι μέντοι καὶ ἀμφὶ τὸν κόλπον, ὅνπερ Κέρας οἱ ἐπιχώριοι Κεροέσσῃ[2] τῇ Βύζαντος μητρὶ τοῦ τῆς πόλεως οἰκιστοῦ ἐπωνύμως καλοῦσιν, ἐν τοῖς ἅπασιν ἐπιδέδεικται πολυτέλειαν ἐπιτηδείως βασιλεῖ ἔχουσαν, ἅπερ ἐγὼ αὐτίκα δηλώσω, ὑπειπὼν πρότερον ὅντινα διακοσμεῖ τρόπον ἡ θάλασσα τὸ Βυζάντιον.

2 Πρὸς τῇ ἄλλῃ εὐδαιμονίᾳ καὶ ἡ θάλασσα ἐν καλῷ τίθεται ἀμφ' αὐτὸ[3] μάλιστα, ἐγκολπουμένη τε καὶ εἰς πορθμοὺς ξυναγομένη καὶ χεομένη ἐς πέλαγος μέγα, ταύτῃ τε τὴν πόλιν εὐπρόσωπόν τε διαφερόντως ἐργαζομένη καὶ σκέπας λιμένων ἡσύχιον τοῖς ναυτιλλομένοις παρεχομένη, τά τε εἰς τὴν δίαιταν εὔπορον καὶ τὰ ἐς τὴν χρείαν
3 εὐδαίμονα. πελάγη γὰρ δύο ἀμφ' αὐτὴν ὄντα, ὅ τε δὴ Αἰγαῖος καὶ ὁ Εὔξεινος καλούμενος Πόντος, ξυνίασιν ἀλλήλοις ἐς τὰ πρὸς ἕω τῆς πόλεως καὶ ξυγκρουόμενα τῇ τοῦ ῥοθίου ἐπιμιξίᾳ, ταύτῃ τε τὴν ἤπειρον τῇ ἐσβολῇ βιαζόμενα,

[1] θαυμάζεσθαι V : φράζεσθαι A.
[2] Κεροέσσῃ Maltretus : κορέσσῃ V.
[3] αὐτὸ Hoeschel : αὐτὸ V, αὐτῷ A.

one cannot admire them sufficiently when they are seen. But the Church of St. Agathonicus now draws my narrative and constrains me, though I no longer have the voice or the words to do justice to it. So I must content myself with mention of this church, and leave it to others to describe its beauty and its magnificence in every detail—others whose power of utterance is fresh and not yet wholly spent.

v. There are other shrines also, both in the place called Anaplus [1] and on the shore of the opposite continent, which he found in a condition unworthy to be dedicated to any of the saints, as well as along the inlet which the inhabitants call Ceras,[2] after Ceroessa, the mother of Byzas, the founder of the city; and in all these he displayed a munificence altogether befitting an Emperor, as I shall presently shew, after first explaining how the sea adorns Byzantium.

Besides the city's other blessings the sea is set most beautifully all about it, forming curving bays, contracting into narrow straits, and spreading into a great open sea; and thus it makes the city exceptionally beautiful, and offers the quiet shelter of harbours to navigators, thereby abundantly providing the city with the necessities of life and making it rich in all useful things. For in reality there are two seas embracing it, the Aegean on the one side and the sea called the Euxine on the other; these unite with each other to the east of the city, and rushing together as they mingle their waves, and pushing back the solid land by this invasion, they beautify the

[1] Modern Arnautkeuy, on the European bank of the Bosporus.

[2] "Horn," now known as the "Golden Horn."

4 καλλωπίζουσι κύκλῳ τὴν πόλιν. πορθμοὶ τοίνυν αὐτὴν περιβάλλουσι τρεῖς, ἀλλήλοις μὲν ἀπερηρεισμένοι, ἐς κάλλος δὲ αὐτῇ διατεταγμένοι καὶ χρείαν, περιπλεῖσθαι μὲν ἥδιστοι ἅπαντες, ἀποσκοπήσασθαι δὲ ποθεινοί, ἐνορμίσασθαι δὲ λίαν
5 εὐλιμένες. καὶ ὁ μὲν αὐτῶν μέσος ἐκ Πόντου προϊὼν τοῦ Εὐξείνου εὐθὺ τῆς πόλεως ὡς διακοσμήσων αὐτὴν ἵεται, ἐφ' ἑκάτερα δὲ ἄμφω τὰ
B 192 6 ἠπείρω διακεκλήρωται. ὧν δὴ ταῖς ὄχθαις πεπίεσται, ἐπιφρίττων τε καὶ γαυρουμένῳ ἐοικὼς ὅτι δὴ ἐποχούμενος τῇ τε Ἀσίᾳ καὶ τῇ Εὐρώπῃ
7 προσβαίνει τῇ πόλει. δόξαις ἂν ποταμὸν τεθεᾶσθαι ἐπίπροσθεν προσηνεῖ τῷ ῥείθρῳ ἰόντα. ὁ δὲ δὴ αὐτοῦ ἐν ἀριστερᾷ θλίβεται μὲν ἑκατέρωθεν ἐπὶ μακρότατον ταῖς ἀκταῖς, τά τε ἄλση καὶ λειμώνων κάλλη καὶ τὰ ἄλλα τῆς ἀντιπέρας ἠπείρου ἐνδεικνύμενος ὑποκείμενα τῇ τῆς πόλεως ὄψει.
8 εὐρύνεται δὲ τὸ ἐντεῦθεν ἐξωθούμενος αὐτῆς πρὸς ἄνεμον νότον καὶ τὴν Ἀσίαν αὐτῆς ὡς πορρωτάτω
9 ἀποκομίζων. ἀλλὰ καὶ ὡς περιβάλλον διαμένει τὴν πόλιν τὸ ῥόθιον ἄχρι ἐς δύοντά που τὸν ἥλιον. ὁ δὲ δὴ τρίτος πορθμὸς τοῦ μὲν πρώτου ἐχόμενος ἐπὶ δεξιᾷ, ἐκ δὲ Συκῶν τῶν καλουμένων ἀρχόμενος, ἐπὶ πλεῖστον διήκει τῆς πόλεως πρὸς βορρᾶν ἄνεμον, οὗ δὴ ἐς κόλπον τελευτῶν παύεται.
10 οὕτω μὲν οὖν στεφανοῖ τὴν πόλιν ἡ θάλασσα, ἐκδέχεται δὲ ἀνὰ τὸ λειπόμενον ἡ γῆ, μεταξὺ
P 17 τοσαύτη οὖσα, ὅσον τὴν ἀπὸ τῆς θαλάττης

[1] The Bosporus.
[2] The northern extremity of the Sea of Marmara which lies along the east side of the city.

city as they surround it. So it is encircled by three straits which open into one another, so disposed that they both adorn and serve the city, all of them most delightful for sailing, each a pleasurable sight for the eyes, and very commodious for anchorage. And the middle one of them,[1] coming down from the Euxine Sea, flows straight toward the city, as though to beautify it, and on either side of it the two continents are placed. And it is pressed in by their banks, so that it ripples and seems to plume itself because it approaches the city mounted upon both Asia and Europe. One would imagine that he was looking upon a river moving toward him with gentle current. And the strait which lies on the left of this[2] is confined by its shores on either side for a very great distance, displaying the woods and the lovely meadows and all the other details of the opposite shore which lie open to view from the city. Then from that point it broadens as it is thrust away from the city toward the south, and carries the coast of Asia very far from the city. Yet the wash of the sea continues to envelop the city up to its western boundary. The third strait,[3] which branches off from the first toward the right, commencing at Sycae,[4] as it is called, extends for a very great distance along the side of the city which faces the north, and terminates in the bay which forms its end. Thus the sea forms a garland about the city; the remainder of the city's boundary is formed by the land which lies between the two arms of the sea, and is of sufficient size to bind together there the crown

[3] The Golden Horn.
[4] Literally, "Fig-trees"; modern Galata.

11 στεφάνην ἐνταῦθα ξυνδεῖσθαι. πραΰνεται δὲ διηνεκὲς ὁ κόλπος οὗτος καὶ ἀναθολοῦσθαι οὐδαμῆ πέφυκεν, ὥσπερ ὁρίων τῷ κλύδωνι κειμένων ἐνταῦθα καὶ σάλου τὸ ἐνθένδε παντὸς τῇ τῆς
12 πόλεως εἰργομένου τιμῇ. χειμῶνος δέ, ἂν οὕτω τύχῃ, καὶ ἀνέμων σκληρῶν τοῖς τε πελάγεσι καὶ τῷ πορθμῷ ἐπιπεσόντων, ἐπειδὰν ἐς τὴν εἴσοδον ἵκωνται τοῦ κόλπου αἱ νέες, ἀκυβέρνητοί τε τὸ
13 λοιπὸν ἴασι καὶ ἀπροβουλεύτως ὁρμίζονται. ἐς σταδίους μὲν γὰρ πλεῖν ἢ τεσσαράκοντα τὸ περίμετρον τοῦ κόλπου διήκει, λιμὴν δὲ ὅλος πανταχῇ ἐστιν· ὥστε ἀμέλει ὁρμιζομένης ἐνταῦθα νηὸς ἡ μὲν πρύμνα τῇ θαλάσσῃ ἐπῆρται, ἡ δὲ
B 193 πρῷρα ἐν τῇ γῇ κάθηται, ὥσπερ ἀλλήλοις τῶν στοιχείων ἁμιλλωμένων, ὁπότερον ἂν αὐτοῖν δύναιτο [1] μᾶλλον τὴν ἐς τὴν πόλιν ἐνεργολαβεῖν ὑπουργίαν.

ϛʹ. Τὰ μὲν οὖν τοῦ κόλπου τοῦδε τοιαῦτά ἐστι. βασιλεὺς δὲ Ἰουστινιανὸς κάλλος ἀμφ᾽ αὐτὸν ἐξ οἰκοδομίας πεποιημένος ἐπιφανέστερον ἐξειργά-
2 σατο. τό τε γὰρ ἐν ἀριστερᾷ τοῦ κόλπου Λαυρεντίου ἁγίου μαρτύριον ἀφεγγές τε τὰ πρότερα ὂν καὶ σκότους ἀτεχνῶς ἔμπλεων μεθαρμοσάμενος, ὡς διὰ βραχέων εἰπεῖν, ἐς τὸν νῦν
3 φαινόμενον ἀνέθηκε τρόπον. καὶ αὐτοῦ ἐπίπροσθεν τὸν τῆς θεοτόκου νεὼν ἐν χώρῳ καλουμένῳ Βλαχέρναις τοιοῦτον δεδημιούργηκεν οἷός
4 μοι ἔναγχος δεδιήγηται. ἐπέκεινά τε Πρίσκῳ τε καὶ Νικολάῳ ἁγίοις ἱερὸν ᾠκοδομήσατο, καινουργήσας αὐτός, οὗ δὴ οἱ Βυζάντιοι ἐμφιλοχωροῦντες ἐνδιατρίβουσιν ἐκ τοῦ ἐπὶ πλεῖστον, πὴ μὲν σέβοντές τε καὶ τεθηπότες τοὺς ἁγίους

of waters. This bay is always calm, being so fashioned by nature that it is never roiled, just as if limits were set there for the turbulent waters and all billows were excluded from that area so as to do honour to the city. And in winter, even should violent winds chance to fall upon the open spaces of the sea and upon the strait, as soon as ships reach the entrance to the bay, they proceed for the rest of the way without a pilot and are anchored without precautions. For the circuit of the bay extends to a distance of more than forty stades, and furnishes anchorage throughout its whole extent; so that when a ship anchors there the stern rides upon the sea while the prow rests upon the land, as if the two elements contended with each other to see which of them would be able to render the greater service to the city.

vi. Such is the nature of this bay. And the Emperor Justinian adorned it with buildings on all sides and thus made it still more notable. On the left of the bay he found the martyr's shrine of St. Lawrence, which previously had been without a ray of light and practically filled with darkness, and he remodelled it, to speak briefly, and consecrated it in the form in which it is now seen. Over against this, in the quarter called Blachernae, he built the Church of the Virgin which I just described.[1] Further on he established a shrine to St. Priscus and St. Nicholas, an entirely new creation of his own, at a spot where the Byzantines love especially to tarry, some worshipping and doing honour to these saints who

[1] Chap. iii. 3.

---

[1] δύναιτο Hoeschel: δύναιντο V.

ἐνδήμους σφίσι[1] γινομένους, πῇ δὲ τῆς τοῦ τεμένους ἀπολαύοντες εὐπρεπείας, ἐπεὶ τῆς θαλάσσης τὸ ῥόθιον βιασάμενος βασιλεὺς ὕπερθέν τε τοῦ κλυδωνίου ἐπὶ μακρότατον ἐνθέμενος τὰ θεμέλια τὸ ἱερὸν κατεστήσατο.

5 Κατὰ δὲ τοῦ κόλπου τὸ πέρας[2] ἔν τε τῷ ἀνάντει καὶ ἰσχυρῶς ὀρθίῳ τέμενος ἐκ παλαιοῦ Κοσμᾷ τε καὶ Δαμιανῷ ἁγίοις ἀνεῖται· οὗ δὴ αὐτόν ποτε νενοσηκότα πικρότατα[3] καὶ δόκησιν παρεχόμενον ὅτι δὴ ἀποθάνοι, πρός τε τῶν ἰατρῶν ἀπολελειμμένον ἅτε δὴ ἐν νεκροῖς κείμενον, ἐς ὄψιν ἐλθόντες ἐσώσαντο οἱ ἅγιοι οὗτοι ἐκ τοῦ παραδόξου καὶ τοῦ παραλόγου καὶ ὀρθὸν ἔστησαν. 6 οὓς δὴ εὐγνωμοσύνῃ ἀμειβόμενος ὅσα γε τὰ ἀνθρώπεια, ὅλην ἐναλλάξας τε καὶ μετασκευασάμενος τὴν προτέραν οἰκοδομίαν ἄκοσμόν τε καὶ ἄδοξον οὖσαν οὐδὲ ἀξιόχρεων τηλίκοις ἁγίοις (B 194, P 18) ἀνεῖσθαι, κάλλει τε καὶ μεγέθει τὸν νεὼν κατελάμπρυνε καὶ φωτὸς αἴγλῃ, ἄλλα τε πολλὰ οὐ πρότερον ὄντα ἀνέθηκεν. 7 ἐπειδάν τέ τινες ἀρρωστήμασιν ὁμιλήσαιεν ἰατρῶν κρείττοσιν, οἵδε τὴν ἀνθρωπείαν ἀπογνόντες ἐπικουρίαν ἐπὶ τὴν μόνην αὐτοῖς ὑπολελειμμένην ἐλπίδα χωροῦσι, καὶ γενόμενοι ἐν ταῖς βάρεσι πλέουσι διὰ τοῦ κόλπου ἐπὶ τοῦτον δὴ τὸν νεών. 8 ἀρχόμενοί τε τοῦ εἴσπλου εὐθὺς ὁρῶσιν ὥσπερ ἐν ἀκροπόλει τὸ τέμενος τοῦτο ἀποσεμνυνόμενόν τε τῇ τοῦ βασιλέως εὐγνωμοσύνῃ καὶ παρεχόμενον τῆς ἐντεῦθεν ἐλπίδος αὐτοῖς ἀπολαύειν.

[1] σφίσι l: σφ/// V, om. A.
[2] πέρας A: κέρας V.
[3] πικρότατα V: πικρῶ. A.

have come to dwell among them, and others simply enjoying the charm of the precinct, since the Emperor forced back the wash of the sea and set the foundations far out into the water when he established this sanctuary.[1]

At the far end of the bay, on the ground which rises steeply in a sharp slope,[2] stands a sanctuary dedicated from ancient times to Saints Cosmas and Damian. When the Emperor himself once lay seriously ill, giving the appearance of being actually dead (in fact he had been given up by the physicians as being already numbered among the dead), these Saints came to him here in a vision, and saved him unexpectedly and contrary to all human reason and raised him up. In gratitude he gave them such requital as a mortal may, by changing entirely and remodelling the earlier building, which was unsightly and ignoble and not worthy to be dedicated to such powerful Saints, and he beautified and enlarged the church and flooded it with brilliant light and added many other things which it had not before. So when any persons find themselves assailed by illnesses which are beyond the control of physicians, in despair of human assistance they take refuge in the one hope left to them, and getting on flat-boats they are carried up the bay to this very church. And as they enter its mouth they straightway see the shrine as on an acropolis, priding itself in the gratitude of the Emperor and permitting them to enjoy the hope which the shrine affords.

[1] The Emperor's passion for erecting buildings at the edge of the water is frequently criticised in the *Secret History* (viii. 7, xix. 6, xxvi. 23).

[2] Modern Eyoub.

9 Τοῦ δὲ κόλπου ἐπὶ θάτερα μαρτύριον οἰκοδομησάμενος βασιλεὺς οὗ πρότερον ὃν ἀνέθηκεν Ἀνθίμῳ μάρτυρι παρ' αὐτὴν μάλιστα τὴν τοῦ
10 κόλπου ἠϊόνα. καὶ τὰ μὲν κράσπεδα τοῦ ἱεροῦ πραϋνομένῃ ἐπικλυζόμενα τῇ τῆς θαλάσσης ἐπιρ-
11 ροῇ τὸ εὔχαρι ἐπιεικῶς ἔχει. οὐ γὰρ ξὺν θορύβῳ τὸ κλυδώνιον ἐπανεστηκὸς εἶτα [1] εἰς τοὺς ἐκείνῃ λίθους ἀράσσεται, οὐδὲ μεγάλα τὸ κῦμα ἠχῆσαν, οἷά γε τὰ θαλάττια, καὶ σχιζόμενον ἀποκρίνεται εἰς εἶδος ἀφρῶδες, ἀλλὰ πρόεισι μὲν προσηνές, σιωπηλὸν δὲ ὂν ἐπιψαύει τῆς γῆς, ἀναστρέφει δὲ
12 μόνον. ἐκδέχεται δὲ τὸ ἐνθένδε αὐλὴ ὁμαλή τε καὶ λίαν ὑπτία, μαρμάροις μὲν πανταχόθι κεκομψευμένη καὶ κίοσιν, ὄψει δὲ ὡραϊζομένη τῇ ἐς τὴν
13 θάλασσαν. στοὰ μετὰ ταύτην καὶ ὁ νεὼς ἐντὸς ἐν τετραγώνῳ ἐς ὕψος ἐπῆρται λίθων εὐπρεπείᾳ καὶ χρυσῷ κατακεχυμένῳ καλλωπιζόμενος.
14 τοσοῦτον δὲ προέχει μόνον τοῦ εὔρους τὸ μῆκος ἐς ὅσον δὴ [2] χῶρον τὸν ἀβέβηλον, ἐν ᾧ ὄργια τὰ ἄρρητα τελεῖσθαι θέμις, κατὰ τὴν πλευρὰν
B 195 ἣ πρὸς ἀνίσχοντα ἥλιον τέτραπται διήκειν ξυμβαίνει. ταῦτα μὲν οὖν τῇδέ πῃ ἔχει.

ζ'. Ἐπέκεινα δὲ κατ' αὐτὸ μάλιστα τοῦ κόλπου τὸ στόμα Εἰρήνης μάρτυρος νεὼς ἵδρυται. ὃς δὴ οὕτω μεγαλοπρεπῶς τῷ βασιλεῖ ὅλος ἐξείργασται
2 ὡς οὐκ ἂν ἔγωγε φράσαι ἱκανῶς ἔχοιμι. ἀντιφιλοτιμούμενος γὰρ τῇ θαλάσσῃ ἀμφὶ τοῦ κόλπου τῇ εὐπρεπείᾳ, ὥσπερ ὅρμῳ περιφερεῖ ἐγκαλλώπισμα τὰ ἱερὰ ταῦτα ἐντέθεικεν. ἀλλ' ἐπεὶ τούτου δὴ τοῦ τῆς Εἰρήνης νεὼ ἐπεμνήσθην, καὶ τὸ ἐκείνῃ ξυνενεχθὲν [3] οὔ μοι ἀπὸ τρόπου τῇδε

[1] εἶτα V: om. A. [2] δὴ V: δὴ τὸν A.

Across the bay the Emperor built a martyr's shrine which had not existed before, by the very strand of the bay, and dedicated it to the martyr Anthimus. The foundations of the shrine are washed by the caressing flow of the sea in an altogether charming manner. For the incoming waves do not rise up with a roar and break on the stones there, nor do the breakers thunder aloud like those of the sea and divide and break up in a foaming mass, but the water comes forward gently, and silently touches the land and then quietly draws back. And extending back from the beach is a smooth and very level court (*aulê*), adorned on all sides with marbles and with columns and glorying in its view over the sea. Beyond this is a stoa with the church inside rising in the form of a quadrangle to a great height and made beautiful by the charm of its stones and by the gold applied to them. And the length exceeds the width only by the extent of the sanctuary, where alone the sacred mysteries may be performed, along the side which faces towards the east. So much, then, for this.

vii. Beyond this, just about at the opening of the bay, was built a Church of the Martyr Eirenê. This entire church was constructed by the Emperor on such a magnificent scale that I, at least, could not possibly do it justice. For seeking to rival the sea in lending beauty to the land about the gulf, he set all these shrines, as in an encircling necklace, round about it. But since I have mentioned this Church of Eirenê, it will not be amiss for me at this point to recount also the incident which happened there.

---

[3] ξυνενεχθὲν Hoeschel: ξυνεχθὲν V.

3 γεγράψεται. ἐνταῦθα ἔκειτο λείψανα ἐκ παλαιοῦ ἀνδρῶν ἁγίων οὐχ ἧσσον ἢ τεσσαράκοντα· οἳ στρατιῶται μὲν Ῥωμαῖοι ἐτύγχανον ὄντες, ἐν λεγεῶνι δὲ δυοδεκάτῃ[1] ἐτάττοντο, ἣ ἐν πόλει Μελιτηνῇ τῆς Ἀρμενίας τὸ παλαιὸν ἵδρυτο.
P 19 4 ἡνίκα τοίνυν οἱ λιθοδόμοι διώρυσσον οὗπερ ἐπεμνήσθην ἀρτίως, κιβώτιον εὗρον γράμμασι σημαῖνον ὡς λείψανα ἔχοι τούτων δὴ τῶν ἀνδρῶν.
5 ὅπερ ἐξήνεγκε λεληθὸς τέως ἐξεπίτηδες ὁ θεός, ἅμα μὲν πιστούμενος ἅπαντας ὡς τὰ βασιλέως ἀσμενέστατα ἐνδέδεκται δῶρα, ἅμα δὲ καὶ τοῦ ἀνδρὸς τὴν ἀγαθοεργίαν ἀμείψασθαι διατεινό-
6 μενος χάριτι μείζονι. ἐτύγχανε γὰρ Ἰουστινιανὸς βασιλεὺς χαλεπῶς ἄγαν τοῦ σώματος ἔχων, ἐπεὶ ῥεύματος δεινόν τι χρῆμα κατὰ τὸ γόνυ ἐπιπεσὸν συντριβῆναι ταῖς ὀδύναις τὸν ἄνδρα ἐποίει· οὗπέρ
7 οἱ αὐτὸς αἰτιώτατος ἦν. ἐν γὰρ ταῖς ἡμέραις ἁπάσαις αἵπερ τὴν Πασχαλίαν ἑορτὴν προτερεύουσαι νηστεῖαι καλοῦνται, σκληράν τινα βιοτὴν ἔσχε μὴ ὅτι βασιλεῖ ἀλλόκοτον οὖσαν, ἀλλὰ καὶ
B 196 ἀνθρώπῳ ἀμηγέπη τῶν πολιτικῶν ἁπτομένῳ.
8 δυοῖν γὰρ ἡμέραιν διεγεγόνει ἐς ἀεὶ ἀπόσιτος ὤν, καὶ ταῦτα μὲν ὄρθρου βαθέος διηνεκὲς[2] ἐκ τῶν στρωμάτων ἐξανιστάμενος καὶ προεγρηγορὼς τῆς πολιτείας, ἀεί τε αὐτῆς ἔργῳ καὶ λόγῳ διαχειρίζων τὰ πράγματα, ὄρθριός τε καὶ μεσημβρινός,
9 καὶ οὐδέν τι ἧσσον ἐπινυκτίδιος. πόρρω γὰρ τῶν νυκτῶν ἐς κοίτην ἰὼν ἐξανίστατο αὐτίκα δὴ μάλα, ὥσπερ χαλεπῶς τοῖς στρώμασιν ἔχων.
10 καὶ ἡνίκα δέ που τροφὴν αἵροιτο, οἴνου μὲν καὶ

[1] δυοδεκάτῃ Haury: δυοδεκάτω or δυωδεκάτω.
[2] διηνεκὲς om. A.

Here from ancient times were buried the remains of no fewer than forty holy men; these had chanced to be Roman soldiers who served in the Twelfth Legion, which in ancient times had been posted in the city of Melitenê in Armenia. So when the masons were excavating in the place which I have just mentioned, they found a chest shewing by an inscription that it contained the remains of these very men. And God brought to light this chest, which thus far had been forgotten, with an express purpose, partly to assure all men that He had accepted the Emperor's gifts most gladly, and partly because He was eager to repay this great man's beneficence with a greater favour. It chanced that the Emperor Justinian was suffering from a grievous affliction, since a dangerous discharge had set in at the knee and caused him to be tortured with pain; and for this he himself was chiefly responsible. For during all the days which precede the Feast of Easter, and which are called days of fasting, he observed a severe routine which was unfit not only for an Emperor, but for any man who was concerned in any way with state affairs.[1] Indeed he had gone two whole days quite without food, and that too while rising regularly from his bed at early dawn and keeping watch over the State, and constantly managing its affairs by word and deed from early dawn to midday and equally into the night. And although he went to his couch late in the night, he immediately rose again, as if he could not endure his bed. And when he did take nourishment, he

[1] *Cf.* the description of the Emperor's observances and habits in the *Secret History*, xii. 27, xiii. 28–33.

ἄρτου καὶ τῶν ἄλλων ἐδωδίμων ἐκτὸς ἔμενε, βοτάνας δὲ ἤσθιε μόνον, καὶ ταύτας ἀγρίας ἐπὶ χρόνου μῆκος τεταριχευμένας ἁλσί τε καὶ ὄξει,
11 ὅ τε πότος αὐτῷ τὸ ὕδωρ ἐγίνετο μόνον. οὐ μέντοι οὐδὲ τούτοις κατακορὴς γέγονε πώποτε, ἀλλὰ καὶ ἡνίκα δαῖτα αἴροιτο, ἀπογευσάμενος τούτων δὴ τῶν αὐτῷ ἐδωδίμων, εἶτα μεθίει, οὔπω
12 ἐδηδοκὼς τὰ αὐτάρκη. ἐντεῦθεν τοίνυν τὸ πάθος ἀκμάσαν τὴν ἀπὸ τῶν ἰατρῶν ἐπικουρίαν ἐνενικήκει, καὶ χρόνος τῷ βασιλεῖ πολὺς ἐν ταύταις δὴ
13 ταῖς ὀδύναις ἐτρίβη. μεταξὺ δὲ τὰ περὶ τῶν δεδηλωμένων λειψάνων ἀκούσας, τῆς ἀνθρωπείας ἀφέμενος τέχνης, ἐπὶ ταῦτα τὸ πρᾶγμα ἦγε, τὴν ὑγείαν ἐπισπώμενος τῇ ἐς αὐτὰ πίστει, καὶ δόξης τῆς ἀληθοῦς ἐν τοῖς ἀναγκαιοτάτοις ἀπώνατο.
14 οἱ μὲν γὰρ ἱερεῖς τὸν δίσκον ἐπὶ τὸ τοῦ βασιλέως ἐτίθεντο γόνυ, ἀφανίζεται δὲ τὸ πάθος εὐθύς, σώμασι δεδουλωμένοις θεῷ βιασθέν. ὅπερ ἀμφίλεκτον ὁ θεὸς οὐ ξυγχωρῶν εἶναι, σημεῖον τῶν
15 πραττομένων ἐνδέδεικται μέγα. ἔλαιον γὰρ ἐξαπιναίως ἐπιρρεῦσαν μὲν ἐκ τούτων δὴ τῶν ἁγίων λειψάνων, ὑπερβλύσαν δὲ τὸ κιβώτιον, τώ τε πόδε καὶ τὴν ἐσθῆτα τοῦ βασιλέως κατ-
B 197 16 έκλυσεν ὅλην ἁλουργὸν οὖσαν. διὸ δὴ ὁ χιτὼν οὕτω καταβεβρεγμένος διασώζεται ἐν τοῖς βασιλείοις, μαρτύριον μὲν τῶν τηνικάδε γεγενημένων, σωτήριον δὲ τοῖς ἐς τὸ ἔπειτα πάθεσι περιπεσουμένοις τισὶν ἀνηκέστοις.

P 20 η΄. Οὕτω μὲν οὖν ὑπογέγραπται Ἰουστινιανῷ βασιλεῖ τὸ Κέρας ὁ κόλπος. καὶ πορθμοῖν δὲ τοῖν ἄλλοιν δυοῖν, ὧνπερ ἐπεμνήσθην ἀρτίως, οἰκοδομίαις τὰς ἠϊόνας ἐς μέγα τι κάλλος ἐξείρ-

abstained from wine and bread and other foods and ate only herbs, and those, too, wild ones thoroughly pickled with salt and vinegar, and his only drink was water. Yet he never took a sufficiency even of these, but whenever he did take a meal, he merely tasted these foods he liked and then left them before he had eaten enough. Hence, then, his malady gathered strength and got beyond the help of the physicians, and for a long time the Emperor was racked by these pains. But during this time he heard about the relics which had been brought to light, and abandoning human skill, he gave the case over to them, seeking to recover his health through faith in them, and in a moment of direst necessity he won the reward of the true belief. For as soon as the priests laid the reliquary on the Emperor's knee, the ailment disappeared instantly, driven out by the bodies of men who had been dedicated to the service of God. And God did not permit this to be a matter of dispute, for he shewed a great sign of what was being done. For oil suddenly flowed out from these holy relics, and flooding the chest poured out over the Emperor's feet and his whole garment, which was purple. So this tunic, thus saturated, is preserved in the Palace, partly as testimony to what occurred at that time, and also as a source of healing for those who in future are assailed by any incurable disease.

viii. Thus was the bay called the Horn given distinction by the Emperor Justinian. And by erecting buildings he elaborated into a thing of great beauty the shores of the other two straits which I have just mentioned, in the following

2 γασται τρόπῳ τοιῷδε. ἱερὰ δύο τῷ ἀρχαγγέλῳ Μιχαὴλ ἀνειμένα καταντικρὺ ἀλλήλοιν ἑστῶτα τοῦ πορθμοῦ ἑκατέρωθι ξυνέβαινεν εἶναι, θάτερον μὲν ἐν χώρῳ καλουμένῳ Ἀνάπλῳ ἐν ἀριστερᾷ εἰσπλέοντι τὸν Εὔξεινον Πόντον, τὸ δὲ δὴ ἕτερον
3 ἐν τῇ ἀντιπέρας ἀκτῇ· Προόχθους μὲν ἐκάλουν οἱ παλαιοὶ ἄνθρωποι τὴν ἀκτήν, ὅτι δὴ προβέβληται, οἶμαι, κατὰ πολὺ τῆς ταύτῃ ἠϊόνος, νῦν δὲ Βρόχοι ἐπικαλεῖται, διαφθειρούσης τὰ ὀνόματα τῆς τῶν ἐπιχωρίων ἀγνοίας τῷ μήκει τοῦ χρόνου.
4 ταῦτα δὲ τὰ δύο [1] τεμένη οἱ μὲν αὐτῶν ἱερεῖς κατερρακωμένα ὑπὸ τοῦ χρόνου θεώμενοι καὶ περίφοβοι γεγενημένοι ὡς μὴ αὐτίκα δὴ μάλα σφίσιν ἐμπέσοιεν, βασιλέως ἐδέοντο ἀνοικοδομήσασθαι ἄμφω ἐφ᾽ οὗπερ σχήματος τὸ παλαιὸν
5 ἦν. οὐ γὰρ οἷόν τε ἦν ἐπὶ τούτου βασιλεύοντος ἐκκλησίαν τινὰ ἢ γίνεσθαι πρῶτον, ἢ καταπεπονηκυῖαν ἐπανορθοῦσθαι, ὅτι μὴ ἐκ χρημάτων βασιλικῶν, οὐκ ἐν Βυζαντίῳ μόνον, ἀλλὰ καὶ
6 πανταχόθι τῆς Ῥωμαίων ἀρχῆς. βασιλεὺς δὲ αὐτίκα τῆς προφάσεως τυχὼν τῆσδε καθεῖλε μὲν ἑκάτερον ἐς τὸ ἔδαφος,[2] ὡς μή τι αὐτοῖς τῆς προτέρας ἀκοσμίας ἀπολειφθῆναι. ἀνῳκοδομήσατο δὲ τὸν μὲν ἐπὶ τοῦ Ἀνάπλου τρόπῳ
B 198 7 τοιῷδε. πετρῶν ἐμβολῇ τὴν ἐκείνῃ ἀκτὴν εἴσω περιελίξας ἐς σκέπας λιμένος, τὴν τῆς θαλάττης
8 ἠϊόνα ἐς μεταμόρφωσιν ἀγορᾶς ἤνεγκεν. ἡσύχιος γὰρ ὑπεράγαν ἐνταῦθα ἡ θάλασσα οὖσα τῇ γῇ
9 ἐπικοινοῦται συναλλαγάς. ταῖς τε ἀκάτοις οἱ τῶν ἐμπόρων θαλάσσιοι παρὰ τὴν ἐμβολὴν τῶν

[1] δύο omitted by A.
[2] ἐς τὸ ἔδαφος V: ἕως ἐδάφους A.

manner. There happened to be two sanctuaries dedicated to the Archangel Michael, standing opposite one another on either side of the strait, the one at the place called Anaplus,[1] on the left bank as one sails toward the Euxine Sea, the other on the opposite shore. The men of ancient times called this point Proöchthi,[2] because, I suppose, it projects far out from the shore-line there, but now it is called Brochi,[3] for with the passage of time names are corrupted through the ignorance of local residents. And the priests of these two shrines, seeing them utterly dilapidated by time and having become fearful that they would fall in upon them at any moment, petitioned the Emperor to restore both of them to their ancient form. For it was not possible, during the reign of this Emperor, for any church either to be built for the first time or to be restored when it had fallen into disrepair except with imperial funds, not alone in Byzantium, but in every part of the Roman Empire.[4] So the Emperor no sooner had found this pretext than he at once tore them both down to the foundations, so that none of their previous untidiness was left. He rebuilt the one at Anaplus in the following way. By a stone quay he made the shore-line there curve inward to form a sheltered harbour and he transformed the sea-beach into a market. For the sea at that point is very calm, and makes possible trading with the land. And the sea-traders tie up their skiffs along the

[1] Modern Arnautkeuy, about four miles up the Bosporus from Byzantium. Procopius has slipped away from the "three straits" of the city.

[2] Literally, "projecting banks."

[3] "Knots," perhaps from the many fishing nets used there.

[4] *Cf.* Justinian, *Novellae*, LXVII.

πετρῶν ὁρμισάμενοι συμβάλλονται τοῖς ἐγγείοις
10 ἀπὸ τῶν καταστρωμάτων τὰ ἐμπολήματα. αὐλὴ
μετὰ τὴν παραλίαν ἀγορὰν τοῦ νεὼ πρόκειται.
καὶ μαρμάροις μὲν ὡραίοις τε καὶ χιόσιν[1] ἡ
11 αὐλὴ τὸ χρῶμα ὁμοιοῖ. οἱ δὲ τοὺς περιπάτους
τῇδε ποιούμενοι εὐπρεπείᾳ μὲν ἥδονται λίθων,
γεγήθασι δὲ θαλάσσης ὄψει, ἐναβρύνονται δὲ
κοιναῖς ταῖς αὔραις ἔκ τε τοῦ ῥοθίου ἐπεγειρο-
12 μέναις καὶ λόφων ἐπανεστηκότων τῇ γῇ. στοὰ
τὸν νεὼν περιβάλλει ἐγκύκλιος ἐς τὰ πρὸς ἕω
διαλιποῦσα μόνον. ἐπὶ μέσης τὸ ἱερὸν χρώμασι
13 μυρίοις πεποίκιλται λίθων. ὄροφος ἐν θόλῳ
μετάρσιος ὑπερῃώρηται. τί ἂν τις διαριθμη-
σάμενος ἐπαξίως τοῦ ἔργου φράσοι, τὰς ᾐωρη-
P 21 μένας στοάς, τὰς ὑπεσταλμένας οἰκοδομίας, τὸ
τῶν μαρμάρων ἐπίχαρι, οἷς δὴ οἵ τε τοῖχοι καὶ
14 τὰ ἐδάφη παντάπασι περιβέβληνται; πρὸς ἐπὶ
τούτοις δὲ καὶ χρυσοῦ πλῆθος ἐξαίσιον πανταχόσε
τοῦ ἱεροῦ καθάπερ αὐτῷ πεφυκὸς περικέχυται.
15 τοσαῦτα εἰπόντι καὶ τὸ Ἰωάννου τοῦ Βαπτιστοῦ
τέμενός μοι δεδήλωται, ὅπερ αὐτῷ βασιλεὺς Ἰουστινιανὸς[2] ἔναγχος ἐν τῷ Ἑβδόμῳ καλουμένῳ
16 ἀνέθηκεν. ἐμφερέστατα γὰρ ἄμφω ἀλλήλοιν τὰ
τεμένη τυγχάνει ὄντα, πλήν γε δὴ ὅτι οὐκ ἐπι-
θαλάσσιον τὸ τοῦ Βαπτιστοῦ ξυμβαίνει εἶναι.
17 Ὁ μὲν οὖν ἐν τῷ Ἀνάπλῳ καλουμένῳ τοῦ
18 ἀρχαγγέλου ναὸς τῇδε πεπόνηται. κατὰ δὲ
B 199 τὴν ἀντιπέρας ἀκτὴν ὀλίγῳ τῆς θαλάσσης διέχει
τις χῶρος, ὁμαλὸς μὲν φύσιν, συνθέσει δὲ λίθων
19 ὑψοῦ ἀνέχων. ἐνταῦθα τὸ τοῦ ἀρχαγγέλου δε-

[1] χιόσιν Maltretus: κίοσιν V.
[2] ἰουστινιανὸς V: οὗτος A.

stone quay and from their decks exchange their merchandise for the products of the land. Behind this shore-market extends the court (*aulê*) in front of the church. In colour this court resembles beautiful marbles and snow. Those who promenade here delight in the beauty of the stones, while they rejoice in the view of the sea and revel alike in the breezes wafted from the water and in those that descend from the hills which tower over the land. A circular (*enkyklios*) stoa surrounds the church and is lacking only on the side towards the east. In the centre stands the church, adorned with stones of an infinite variety of colours. The roof soars aloft in the form of a dome (*tholos*). How could any man do justice to the work in describing the lofty stoas, the secluded buildings within the enclosure, the charm of the marbles with which both walls and pavements are everywhere arranged? In addition to these an extraordinary amount of gold has been applied to every part of the shrine and looks just as if it had grown upon it. This same description can be applied equally well to the shrine of John the Baptist, which the Emperor Justinian recently dedicated to him at Hebdomum,[1] as it is called. For these two shrines happen to resemble each other closely, except that the shrine of the Baptist chances not to be on the sea.

Now the Church of the Archangel in the place called Anaplus was built in this way. And on the opposite bank is a site somewhat removed from the sea, naturally level and raised to a height by courses of stone. There has been built the other shrine of the

[1] Modern Macrikeuy, see p. 55, n. 3.

δημιούργηται τέμενος, εὐπρεπείᾳ μὲν ἐξαίσιον, μεγέθει δὲ πρῶτον, πολυτελείᾳ δὲ ἀνακεῖσθαι μὲν τῷ Μιχαὴλ πρέπον, ἀναθεῖναι δὲ Ἰουστινιανῷ
20 βασιλεῖ. τούτου δὲ δὴ οὐ πολλῷ ἄποθεν τοῦ νεὼ τέμενος ἅγιον τῇ θεοτόκῳ ἀνενεώσατο τρόπῳ τῷ αὐτῷ καταπεπονηκὸς πολλῷ πρότερον, οὗ δὴ τὸ σεμνὸν μακρὸν ἂν εἴη καὶ διερευνήσασθαι καὶ λόγῳ σημῆναι· ἐκδέχεται δὲ ἡ πάλαι τῆς ἱστορίας προσδοκωμένη μοῖρα.

θʹ. Ἐπὶ ταύτης δὴ τῆς ἀκτῆς ἀξιοθέατα ἐκ παλαιοῦ βασίλεια ἐτύγχανεν ὄντα. ταῦτα βασιλεὺς Ἰουστινιανὸς ἀνατέθεικε [1] τῷ θεῷ ἅπαντα, τὸν ἐνθένδε τῆς εὐσεβείας καρπὸν τῆς παραυτίκα
2 παραψυχῆς ἀλλαξάμενος τρόπῳ τοιῷδε. ὅμιλος ἦν ἐπὶ Βυζαντίου γυναίων ἐν μαστροπείῳ λελαγνευμένων οὐχ ἑκούσιον, ἀλλὰ βιαίαν τινὰ μισητίαν.
3 τῆς γὰρ πενίας τῷ ὑπερβάλλοντι ὑπὸ πορνοβοσκῷ τρεφομέναις ἀεὶ καὶ καθ' ἑκάστην ἀκολασταίνειν ἐπάναγκες ἦν, ἀνδράσι τε ἀγνῶσι καὶ παραπεπτωκόσιν ἐξαπιναίως ἐσποδιοῦντο συν-
4 δυαζόμεναι. πορνοβοσκῶν γὰρ ἐνταῦθα ἦν ἐκ παλαιοῦ ἑταιρία πολλή, ἐπ' ἐργαστηρίου τὸ τῆς ἀκολασίας διαχειριζόντων ἐμπόλημα, ἔν τε τῷ δημοσίῳ τῆς ἀγορᾶς ὥραν ἀποδιδομένων τὴν
5 ἀλλοτρίαν καὶ δουλαγωγούντων τὸ σῶφρον. βασιλεὺς δὲ Ἰουστινιανὸς καὶ βασιλὶς Θεοδώρα (τὴν γὰρ εὐσέβειαν ἀλλήλοις ἐπικοινούμενοι ἅπαντα
6 ἔπρασσον) ἐπενόουν τάδε. τὴν μὲν πολιτείαν τοῦ τῶν μαστροπείων ἄγους ἐκάθηραν, ἐξελάσαντες
B 200 τὸ τῶν πορνοβοσκῶν ὄνομα, τῶν δὲ [2] γυναικῶν

[1] ἀνατέθεικε V : ἀνέθηκε A. [2] δὲ Maltretus : τε.

[1] That is, men's violent lust.

Archangel, a work of extraordinary beauty and unrivalled in size, and because of its magnificence worthy both of Michael, to whom it is dedicated, and of the Emperor Justinian, who dedicated it. Not far from this place he restored in the same way a holy shrine of the Virgin which had fallen into disrepair a long time before, and it would be a long task to study this building and describe in words its majesty. But here follows the long-awaited portion of my narrative.

ix. On this shore there chanced to have been from ancient times a remarkable palace. This the Emperor Justinian has dedicated wholly to God, exchanging immediate enjoyment for the reward of piety thereby obtained, in the following manner. There was a throng of women in Byzantium who had carried on in brothels a business of lechery, not of their own free will, but under force of lust.[1] For it was because of their extreme poverty that they were maintained by brothel-keepers, and inmates of such houses were obliged at any and all times to practise lewdness, and pairing off at a moment's notice with strange men as they chanced to come along, they submitted to their embraces. For there had been a numerous body of procurers in the city from ancient times, conducting their traffic in licentiousness in brothels and selling others' youth in the public market-place and forcing virtuous persons into slavery. But the Emperor Justinian and the Empress Theodora, who always shared a common piety in all that they did, devised the following plan. They cleansed the state of the pollution of the brothels, banishing the very name of brothel-keepers, and they set free from a licentiousness fit only for

P 22 τὰς πενίᾳ ταλαιπωρουμένας πολλῇ ἀκολασίας τῆς δουλοπρεποῦς ἠλευθέρωσαν, βίοτον μὲν σφίσιν αὐτόνομον, ἐλευθέραν[1] δὲ τὴν σωφροσύνην πεπορισμένοι. ταῦτα μὲν οὖν διῳκήσαντο τῇδε. 7 παρὰ ταύτην δὴ[2] τοῦ πορθμοῦ τὴν ἀκτὴν[3] ἥ ἐστιν ἐν δεξιᾷ εἰσπλέοντι τὸν Εὔξεινον καλούμενον Πόντον, βασίλεια πρότερον ὄντα μοναστήριον μεγαλοπρεπὲς κατεστήσαντο καταγώγιον ταῖς μεταμελουμέναις γυναιξὶν ἐπὶ τῷ προτέρῳ 8 βίῳ ἐσόμενον· ἐφ᾽ ᾧ τῇ ἐνταῦθα περί τε τὸν θεὸν καὶ τὴν εὐσέβειαν ἀσχολίᾳ γενησομένῃ περικαθῆραι τὰς ἁμαρτάδας δυναταὶ εἶεν τῆς ἐν 9 μαστροπείῳ διαίτης. διὸ δὴ καὶ Μετάνοιαν τοῦτο δὴ τῶν γυναικῶν τὸ διαιτητήριον ὁμωνύμως τῷ 10 ἔργῳ ἐπονομάζουσι. καὶ πολλαῖς μὲν χρημάτων προσόδοις οἱ βασιλεῖς οὗτοι τὸ μοναστήριον δεδώρηνται τοῦτο, πολλὰ δὲ οἰκία κάλλει τε καὶ πολυτελείᾳ διαφερόντως ἐξαίσια, ταῖς γυναιξὶ παραψυχὴν ἐσόμενα,[4] ᾠκοδομήσαντο, ὡς μηδενὶ ἀναγκασθεῖσαι πρὸς τὰ τῆς σωφροσύνης ἐπιτηδεύματα τρόπῳ ὁτῳοῦν ἀποκνήσουσι. ταῦτα μὲν οὖν τῇδέ πῃ ἔχει.

11 Ἐς δὲ τὸν Εὔξεινον Πόντον ἐνθένδε ἰόντι ἄκρα τις ἀπορρὼξ παρὰ τὴν τοῦ πορθμοῦ προβέβληται ἠϊόνα, ἐφ᾽ ἧς μαρτύριον Παντελεήμονος ἁγίου εἱστήκει, ἀρχήν τε ἀπημελημένως πεποιημένον καὶ χρόνῳ μακρῷ πεπονηκὸς ἄγαν· ὅπερ ἐνθένδε περιελὼν Ἰουστινιανὸς βασιλεύς, τοῦτόν τε μεγαλοπρεπῶς τὰ μάλιστα οἰκοδομησάμενος

[1] ἐλευθέραν Haury: ἐλευθερίαν. Hoeschel proposed δόντες, ἐλευθέραν.
[2] δὴ Dewing: δὲ.

slaves the women who were struggling with extreme poverty, providing them with independent maintenance, and setting virtue free. This they accomplished as follows. Near that shore of the strait which is on the right as one sails toward the Sea called Euxine, they made what had formerly been a palace into an imposing convent designed to serve as a refuge for women who repented of their past lives, so that there through the occupation which their minds would have with the worship of God and with religion they might be able to cleanse away the sins of their lives in the brothel. Therefore they call this domicile of such women "Repentance," in keeping with its purpose. And these Sovereigns have endowed this convent with an ample income of money, and have added many buildings most remarkable for their beauty and costliness, to serve as a consolation for the women, so that they should never be compelled to depart from the practice of virtue in any manner whatsoever. So much, then, for this.[1]

As one goes on from there toward the Euxine Sea, a certain sheer promontory is thrust out along the shore-line of the strait, on which stands a martyr's shrine of St. Panteleëmon, which had been carelessly built to begin with and had suffered greatly from the long passage of time; this the Emperor Justinian removed completely from the spot and in its place built in a very magnificent manner the church which now

[1] The reader should compare the very different account of this foundation given by Procopius in the *Secret History*, xvii. 5, 6.

[3] παρὰ . . . ἀκτὴν V: ἐπὶ ταύτης δὲ τῆς ἀκτῆς A.
[4] ἐσόμενα l: ἐσομένην VA.

τὸν ἐκείνῃ τανῦν ὄντα νεών, τῷ τε μάρτυρι διεσώσατο τὴν τιμὴν καὶ τῷ πορθμῷ κάλλος ἐντέθεικεν, ἑκατέρωθι τὰ ἱερὰ ταῦτα πηξάμενος.

12 τούτου δὲ τοῦ τεμένους ἐπίπροσθεν ἐν χώρῳ τῷ καλουμένῳ Ἀργυρωνίῳ πτωχῶν ἦν ἐκ παλαιοῦ B 201 καταγώγιον οἷσπερ ἡ νόσος τὰ ἀνήκεστα ἐλωβή-

13 σατο. ὅπερ τῷ χρόνῳ διερρωγὸς ἤδη τὰ ἔσχατα προθυμίᾳ τῇ πάσῃ ἀνενεώσατο, γενησόμενον τοῖς οὕτω ταλαιπωρουμένοις ἀνάπαυλαν. ἀκτὴ δέ τίς ἐστι Μωχάδιον ὄνομα τοῦ χώρου

14 ἐγγὺς ὃ καὶ νῦν Ἱερὸν ὀνομάζεται. ἐνταῦθα νεὼν τῷ ἀρχαγγέλῳ ἄλλον ἐδείματο ἱεροπρεπῆ τε διαφερόντως, καὶ τῶν τοῦ ἀρχαγγέλου ἱερῶν ὧνπερ ἐπεμνήσθην ἀρτίως, οὐδενὸς ἀξιώματι ἀποδέοντα.

15 Καὶ Τρύφωνι δὲ ἀνέθηκεν ἱερὸν μάρτυρι, πόνῳ τε καὶ χρόνῳ πολλῷ ἐς κάλλος ἀποτετορνευμένον ἀμύθητον ὅλως, ἐν τῇ τῆς πόλεως ἀγυιᾷ ἣ τοῦ

16 Πελαργοῦ ἐπώνυμός ἐστιν. ἔτι δὲ Μηνᾷ καὶ Μηναίῳ μάρτυσιν ἕδος ἐν τῷ Ἑβδόμῳ ἀνέθηκεν. ἐν ἀριστερᾷ δὲ εἰσιόντι ἐς τὰς Χρυσᾶς καλουμένας Πύλας Ἴας ἁγίας μαρτύριον εὑρὼν κατα-

17 πέπτωκός,[1] πολυτελείᾳ τῇ πάσῃ ἀνενεώσατο. τὰ μὲν οὖν ἀμφὶ τοῖς ἐν Βυζαντίῳ ἱεροῖς εἰργασμένα Ἰουστινιανῷ βασιλεῖ τοιαῦτά ἐστι, τὰ δὲ ἀνὰ πᾶσαν διαπεπονημένα τὴν Ῥωμαίων ἀρχὴν ἕκαστα διαριθμεῖσθαι χαλεπόν τέ ἐστι καὶ λόγῳ παντελῶς

18 ἄπορον. ἀλλ' ἡνίκα ἡμῖν δεήσει πόλεως ἢ χωρίου

[1] καταπεπτωκός V: καταπεπονηκός A.

---

[1] See above, Chap. iii. 10, and the description of Hieron in *Wars*, III. i. 8 and *Secret History*, xv. 36.

stands on this site, and he thus preserved to the martyr his honour and at the same time added beauty to the strait by setting these shrines on either side of it. Beyond this shrine, in the place called Argyronium, there had been from ancient times a refuge for poor persons who were afflicted with incurable diseases. This, with the passage of time, had already fallen into a state of extreme disrepair, but he restored it with all enthusiasm, so that it should provide a lodging for those who suffered in this way. And there is a certain promontory named Mochadium near the place which is now called Hieron.[1] There he built another church to the Archangel, one of peculiar sanctity and inferior in esteem to none of the shrines of the Archangel which I have just mentioned.

He also dedicated a shrine to the martyr Tryphon which was finely built at a great cost of labour and of time so that it became an object of altogether indescribable beauty, in a street of the city which is named Pelargus.[2] Furthermore he dedicated a shrine to the martyrs Menas and Menaeus in the Hebdomum.[3] And on the left as one enters the gate which is known as the Golden Gate, this Emperor found a martyr's shrine of St. Ia, fallen in ruins, which he restored with all sumptuousness. Such were the labours accomplished by the Emperor Justinian in connection with the holy places in Byzantium; but to enumerate all the sacred edifices which he built through the length and breadth of the whole Roman Empire is a difficult, nay, an altogether impossible task. However, when it becomes necessary for us to mention any city or

[2] "Stork." [3] Modern Macrikeuy.

του πρὸς ὄνομα ἐπιμνησθῆναι, καὶ τὰ ἐνταῦθα ἱερὰ ἐν ἐπιτηδείῳ γεγράψεται.

P 23 ι΄. Τὰ μὲν οὖν ἀμφὶ τοῖς ἱεροῖς ἔν τε Κωνσταντινουπόλει καὶ τοῖς τῇδε προαστείοις οὕτως 2 Ἰουστινιανῷ δεδημιούργηται βασιλεῖ· τῶν δὲ δὴ ἄλλων αὐτῷ οἰκοδομημάτων πεποιημένων ἕκαστον μὲν ἐπελθεῖν οὐ ῥᾴδιον λόγῳ, ὡς ἐν κεφαλαίῳ δὲ φράσαι, τά τε πλεῖστα καὶ ἀξιολογώτατα τῆς τε ἄλλης πόλεως καὶ τῶν βασιλείων καταφλεχθέντα τε καὶ καθῃρημένα ἐπ᾽ ἔδαφος ἀνοικοδομησάμενος ἅπαντα ἐπὶ τὸ εὐπρεπέστερον B 202 μετεστήσατο· ἅπερ μοι ἐν τῷ παρόντι λεπτο- 3 λογεῖσθαι οὔτι ἀναγκαῖον ἔδοξεν εἶναι· ἅπαντα γάρ μοι ἐς τὸ ἀκριβὲς ἐν τοῖς ὑπὲρ τῶν πολέμων δεδήλωται λόγοις. τοσοῦτον δὲ μόνον ἔν γε τῷ παρόντι γεγράψεται, ὡς τῶν βασιλείων τά τε προπύλαια καὶ ἡ καλουμένη Χαλκῆ μέχρι ἐς τὸν Ἄρεως[1] καλούμενον οἶκον, ἔκ τε τῶν βασιλείων τό τε βαλανεῖον ὁ Ζεύξιππος αἵ τε μεγάλαι στοαὶ καὶ τὰ ἑκατέρωθεν ἑξῆς ἅπαντα μέχρι ἐς τὴν ἀγορὰν ἣ Κωνσταντίνου ἐπώνυμός ἐστι, τούτου δὴ ἔργα τοῦ βασιλέως τυγχάνει 4 ὄντα. πρὸς ἐπὶ τούτοις δὲ τὴν Ὁρμίσδα ἐπώνυμον οἰκίαν, ἄγχιστα οὖσαν τῶν βασιλείων, παραλλάξας τε καὶ ὅλως ἐς τὸ ἐπιφανέστερον μεθαρμοσάμενος, ὡς τοῖς βασιλείοις ἐπιεικῶς πρέπειν, τῷ Παλατίῳ ἐντέθεικεν, εὐρύτερόν τε αὐτὸ καὶ πολλῷ ἔτι μᾶλλον ἀξιώτερον ταύτῃ ἐξείργασται.

5 Ἔστι δέ τις ἀγορὰ πρὸ τῶν βασιλείων περί-

[1] Ἄρεως Haury, cf. *Wars* I. xxiv. 9: Ἄρεος Maltretus, ἀρέας V, ἀραιᾶς A.

district by name, the sanctuaries in that place shall be recorded at the proper point.

x. So the churches, both in the city of Constantinople and in its suburbs, were built as stated by the Emperor Justinian; but it is not easy to recount in my narrative each one of the other buildings erected by him. But to speak comprehensively, the majority of the buildings and the most noteworthy structures of the rest of the city, and particularly of the Palace area, had been burned and razed to the ground when he undertook to rebuild them and to restore them all in more beautiful form. Yet it has seemed to me not at all necessary at the present time to recount these in detail, for they have all been described with care in my Books on the Wars. At this point, only this shall be set down, that this Emperor's work includes the propylaea (*propylaia*) of the Palace and the so-called Bronze Gate [1] as far as what is called the House of Ares, and beyond the Palace both the Baths of Zeuxippus and the great colonnaded stoas and indeed everything on either side of them as far as the market-place which bears the name of Constantine. And besides these he remodeled the building known as the House of Hormisdas, which is close by the Palace, so altering and transforming it altogether into a more noble structure as to be really in keeping with the royal residence, to which he joined it, making it greater in width and consequently much more admirable.[2]

And there is before the Palace a certain market-

[1] See n. 1, p. 85.
[2] See above, Chap. iv. 2.

στυλος. Αὐγουσταῖον καλοῦσι τὴν ἀγορὰν οἱ Βυζάντιοι. ταύτης ἐν λόγοις ἐπεμνήσθην τοῖς ἔμπροσθεν, ἡνίκα τῆς Σοφίας περιηγησάμενος τὸν νεὼν τὴν ἐπὶ τῷ ἔργῳ χαλκῆν εἰκόνα τῷ βασιλεῖ ἐπὶ κίονος ὑψηλοτάτου καὶ λίθοις συν- 6 θέτου ἀνατεθεῖσαν δεδήλωκα. ταύτης ἐς τὰ πρὸς ἕω τῆς ἀγορᾶς τὸ Βουλευτήριον ἵδρυται, λόγου μὲν τῇ τε πολυτελείᾳ καὶ τῇ κατασκευῇ τῇ πάσῃ κρεῖττον, Ἰουστινιανοῦ δὲ βασιλέως 7 ἔργον. ἔνθα δὴ ξυνιοῦσα ἔτους ἀρχομένου ἡ Ῥωμαίων βουλὴ σύγκλητος ἐνιαύσιον ἑορτὴν ἄγει, τὰ τῆς πολιτείας ὀργιάζουσα ἐς ἀεὶ νόμιμα. 8 ἓξ δὲ αὐτοῦ κίονες ἐπίπροσθεν ἑστᾶσιν, οἱ μὲν δύο τὸν τοῦ βουλευτηρίου τοῖχον ἐν μέσῳ ἔχοντες ὃς πρὸς δύοντα ἥλιον τέτραπται, οἱ δὲ τέσσαρες B 203 ὀλίγῳ ἐκτός, τὸ μὲν εἶδος λευκοὶ ἅπαντες, μέγεθος δὲ πρῶτοι τῶν ἐν γῇ, οἶμαι, κιόνων τῇ 9 πάσῃ. στοὰν δὲ ποιοῦσιν οἱ κίονες ὄροφον ἐν θόλῳ ἑλίττουσαν, τὰ δὲ ἄνω τῆς στοᾶς ἅπαντα μαρμάρων μὲν κάλλει διακεκόσμηται τοῖς κίοσι τὸ εἶδος ἴσων, ἀγαλμάτων δὲ πλήθει ὑπεράνω ἑστώτων θαυμασίως ὡς ὑπογέγραπται.

10 Ταύτης δὲ τῆς ἀγορᾶς οὐ πολλῷ ἄποθεν τὰ βασιλέως οἰκία ἐστί, καὶ νέα μὲν τὰ βασίλεια σχεδόν τι πάντα, Ἰουστινιανῷ δέ, ᾗπέρ μοι εἴρηται, δεδημιούργηται βασιλεῖ, φράσαι δὲ αὐτὰ λόγῳ ἀμήχανά ἐστιν, ἀλλ᾽ ἀποχρήσει μὲν τοὺς γενησομένους εἰδέναι ὅτι δὴ ἅπαντα τούτου δὴ

---

[1] *Cf.* Chap. ii. 1.

[2] The description, while not clear, seems to imply a structure tetrastyle, prostyle, with one column on the return at each

place surrounded by columns (*peristylos*), which the people of Byzantium call the Augustaeum. This I have mentioned previously[1] when in the account of the Church of Sophia I described the bronze statue of the Emperor commemorating the work, set upon a very tall column made of fitted blocks. To the east of this market-place stands the Senate House, surpassing description by reason of its costliness and every element of its construction, the work of the Emperor Justinian. There the Senate of the Romans assembles at the beginning of the year and celebrates an annual festival, observing always the ancient tradition of the State. Six of its columns stand in front of it, two of which have between them the wall of the Senate House which faces the west, while the four others stand a little beyond it; all of them are white in colour, and in size, I believe, they are the largest of all columns in the whole world. And the columns form a porch (*stoa*) which carries a roof curving into a vault (*tholos*), and the whole upper portion of the colonnade is adorned with marbles which rival the columns in their beauty, and the roof is wonderfully set off by a great number of statues which stand upon it.[2]

Not far from this market-place is the residence of the Emperor, and practically the whole Palace is new, and, as I have said, was built by the Emperor Justinian; but it is impossible to describe it in words and it must suffice for future generations to know

side and the doorway between the two rear columns. The ambiguity of the word *tholos*, which may mean either a dome or a vault, makes it impossible to determine from this passage whether there was a dome over the porch or a tunnel vault extending back from the central intercolumniation.

B 24 11 ἔργον τοῦ βασιλέως τυγχάνει ὄντα. ὥσπερ δέ φασι, τὸν λέοντα ἐξ ὄνυχος ἴσμεν, καὶ τούτων δὴ οὕτω τῶν βασιλείων τὴν δύναμιν ἐκ τοῦ προτεμενίσματος οἱ τάδε ἀναλεγόμενοι εἴσονται. τοιοῦτον δὲ τὸ προτεμένισμά ἐστιν ὃ καλοῦσι 12 Χαλκῆν. ὄρθιοι τοῖχοι οὐρανομήκεις ἐν τετραγώνῳ ἑστᾶσι τέσσαρες, τὰ μὲν ἄλλα ἰσοστάσιοι ἀλλήλοις ὄντες, μήκει δὲ ἄμφω, ὅ τε πρὸς μεσημβρίαν τετραμμένος καὶ βορρᾶν ἄνεμον, τῶν 13 ἑτέρων οὐ παρὰ πολὺ ἀποδέοντες. προβέβληται δέ τις ἀμφὶ τὴν γωνίαν αὐτῶν ἑκάστου λίθων εὖ μάλα εἰργασμένων ἀνάστασις, τῷ τοίχῳ ἐς τὴν ὑπερβολὴν ἐξ ἐδάφους συναναβαίνουσα, τετράπλευρος μέν, ἐνημμένη δὲ κατὰ τὴν μίαν τῷ τοίχῳ πλευράν, οὐ διακόπτουσα τοῦ χώρου τὸ κάλλος, ἀλλά τι καὶ κόσμου[1] αὐτῷ ἐντιθεῖσα 14 τῇ τοῦ ἐμφεροῦς ἁρμονίᾳ. ὑπερῃώρηνται δὲ αὐτῶν ἀψῖδες ὀκτώ, τέσσαρες μὲν ἀνέχουσαι τὸν ἐν μέσῳ τοῦ παντὸς ὄροφον ἐν σφαιροειδεῖ μεταρσίῳ ἐπικυρτούμενον, αἱ δὲ δὴ ἄλλαι δύο μὲν πρὸς νότον, δύο δὲ πρὸς βορρᾶν ἄνεμον τῷ B 204 γειτνιῶντι ἐναπερειδόμεναι τοίχῳ, τὸ μεταξὺ 15 τέγος ἐν θόλῳ ᾐωρημένον ἐξαίρουσιν. ἐναβρύνεται δὲ ταῖς γραφαῖς ἡ ὀροφὴ πᾶσα, οὐ τῷ κηρῷ ἐντακέντι τε καὶ διαχυθέντι ἐνταῦθα παγεῖσα, ἀλλ' ἐναρμοσθεῖσα ψηφῖσι λεπταῖς τε καὶ χρώμασιν ὡραϊσμέναις παντοδαποῖς· αἳ δὴ τά τε ἄλλα πάντα καὶ ἀνθρώπους ἀπομιμοῦνται. 16 ὁποῖα δὲ αὐτῶν τὰ γράμματά ἐστιν ἐγὼ δηλώσω.

[1] κόσμου A: κόσμον V.

---

[1] *Cf.* Libanius, *Orat.* XI. 232.

that it happens to be entirely the work of this Emperor. We know the lion, as they say, by his claw, and so those who read this will know the impressiveness of the Palace from the vestibule (*protemenisma*).[1] So this entrance, which they call Chalkê,[2] is of the following sort. Four straight walls stand in a quadrangle (*tetragonos*) rising heaven-high, equal to each other in all respects except that those which face south and north, respectively, are both slightly shorter than the others. At each corner there projects a sort of structure (*anastasis*) of very carefully worked stones, ascending with the wall from the ground to its very top, having four sides, to be sure, but joined to the wall on one side, not detracting from the beauty of the structure, but actually adding a sort of grace to it by the harmony of the similar proportions. Above them rise eight arches, four of which support the roof which curves over the centre of the whole structure in the form of a suspended dome (*sphairoeidês*), while the others, two toward the south and two toward the north, rest upon the adjoining walls and lift on high the vaulted (*tholos*) roof which is balanced between them.[3] And the whole ceiling boasts of its pictures, not having been fixed with wax melted and applied to the surface,[4] but set with tiny cubes of stone beautifully coloured in all hues, which represent human figures and all other kinds of subjects. The subjects of these pictures I will now describe. On either side

[2] The Bronze (Gate); mentioned also in *Wars*, I. xxiv. 47.

[3] Presumably this structure had four impost piers at the walls on the interior near the corners. These piers carried transverse and longitudinal arches which formed an interior cruciform plan, supporting a dome over the centre.

[4] *I.e.* by the encaustic method of painting.

ἐφ' ἑκάτερα μὲν πόλεμός τέ ἐστι καὶ μάχη, καὶ ἁλίσκονται πόλεις παμπληθεῖς, πῇ μὲν Ἰταλίας, πῇ δὲ Λιβύης· καὶ νικᾷ μὲν βασιλεὺς Ἰουστινιανὸς ὑπὸ στρατηγοῦντι Βελισαρίῳ, ἐπάνεισι δὲ παρὰ[1] τὸν βασιλέα, τὸ στράτευμα ἔχων ἀκραιφνὲς ὅλον ὁ στρατηγός, καὶ δίδωσιν αὐτῷ λάφυρα βασιλεῖς τε καὶ βασιλείας, καὶ πάντα τὰ ἐν ἀνθρώποις ἐξαίσια.

17 κατὰ δὲ τὸ μέσον ἑστᾶσιν ὅ τε βασιλεὺς καὶ ἡ βασιλὶς Θεοδώρα, ἐοικότες ἄμφω γεγηθόσι τε καὶ νικητήρια ἑορτάζουσιν ἐπί τε τῷ[2] Βανδίλων καὶ Γότθων βασιλεῖ,[3] δορυαλώτοις τε καὶ ἀγωγί-

18 μοις παρ' αὐτοὺς ἥκουσι. περιέστηκε δὲ αὐτοὺς ἡ Ῥωμαίων βουλὴ σύγκλητος, ἑορτασταὶ πάντες. τοῦτο γὰρ αἱ ψηφῖδες δηλοῦσιν ἐπὶ τοῖς προσώ-

19 ποις ἱλαρὸν αὐτοῖς ἐπανθοῦσαι. γαυροῦνται οὖν καὶ μειδιῶσι τῷ βασιλεῖ νέμοντες ἐπὶ τῷ ὄγκῳ τῶν πεπραγμένων ἰσοθέους τιμάς· ἠμφίασται δὲ μαρμάρων εὐπρεπείᾳ τὰ ἐντὸς ἅπαντα μέχρι ἐς τὰς ὑπεράνω ψηφῖδας, οὐχ ὅσα ἐπανέστηκε

20 μόνον, ἀλλὰ καὶ τὸ ἔδαφος ἐφεξῆς ὅλον. τῶν δὲ μαρμάρων ἔνια μὲν λίθου Σπαρτιάτου ἐκεῖ σμαράγδῳ ἴσα, ἔνια δὲ πυρὸς φλόγα μιμοῦνται· λευκὸν δὲ τῶν πλειόνων τὸ εἶδος, οὐ λιτὸν μέντοι, ἀλλ' ὑποκυμαίνει κυαναυγεῖ ὑπογεγραμμένον μεταξὺ χρώματι. ταῦτα μὲν οὖν τῇδέ πῃ ἔχει.

B 205
P 25

ια'. Ἐκ δὲ τῆς Προποντίδος ἐσπλέοντι ἐς τὰ πρὸς ἕω τῆς πόλεως, βαλανεῖον ἐν ἀριστερᾷ ἐν δημοσίῳ ἐστίν. ὅπερ Ἀρκαδιαναὶ μὲν ἐπικαλεῖται, Κωνσταντινούπολιν δὲ πηλίκην οὖσαν

2 ἐπικοσμεῖ. αὐλὴν ἐνταῦθα ὁ βασιλεὺς οὗτος

[1] παρὰ A: περὶ V. [2] τῷ V: τῶν A.
[3] βασιλεῖ: βασιλεῦσι Maltretus.

is war and battle, and many cities are being captured, some in Italy, some in Libya; and the Emperor Justinian is winning victories through his General Belisarius, and the General is returning to the Emperor, with his whole army intact, and he gives him spoils, both kings and kingdoms and all things that are most prized among men. In the centre stand the Emperor and the Empress Theodora, both seeming to rejoice and to celebrate victories over both the King of the Vandals and the King of the Goths, who approach them as prisoners of war to be led into bondage. Around them stands the Roman Senate, all in festal mood. This spirit is expressed by the cubes of the mosaic, which by their colours depict exultation on their very countenances. So they rejoice and smile as they bestow on the Emperor honours equal to those of God, because of the magnitude of his achievements. And the whole interior of the building, as far as the mosaics above, is clothed with handsome marbles, not only the upright surfaces, but the whole of the pavement as well. Some of these marbles are of Spartan stone [1] which rivals the emerald, while some simulate the flame of fire; but the most of them are white in colour, yet the white is not plain, but is set off with wavy lines of blue which mingle with the white. So much, then, for this.

xi. As one sails from the Propontis [2] up toward the eastern side of the city, there is on the left a public bath. This is called Arcadianae, and it is an ornament to Constantinople, large as the city is. There this Emperor built a court (*aulê*) which lies

[1] Verd-antique.

[2] Modern Sea of Marmara.

ἐδείματο, τῆς μὲν πόλεως προβεβλημένην, καὶ τοῖς μὲν ἐκείνῃ διατριβὴν ἔχουσιν ἐς περιπάτους ἀεὶ ἀνειμένην, ἐς δὲ τὸ ἐνορμίσασθαι τοῖς περι-
3 πλέουσι. ταύτην ἥλιος καταλάμπει μὲν ἀνίσχων τῇ αἴγλῃ, ἐκτρεπόμενος δὲ ἀμφὶ τὰ πρὸς ἑσπέραν ἐν ἐπιτηδείῳ ἐπισκιάζει. ταύτην ἡ θάλασσα περιρρεῖ ἀτρεμὴς ἐν ἡσυχίᾳ περιχεομένη τῷ ῥείθρῳ, ποταμοῦ τρόπον ἐκ Πόντου ἰοῦσα· ὥστε καὶ προσδιαλέγονται τοῖς περι-
4 πλέουσιν οἱ τοὺς περιπάτους ποιούμενοι. ἡ γὰρ θάλασσα κατατείνουσα μὲν ἐς ἄβυσσον μέχρι ἐς τῆς αὐλῆς τὴν κρηπῖδα πλώιμος ἐνταῦθα ταῖς ναυσὶ γίνεται, τῆς δὲ γαλήνης τῷ ὑπερβάλλοντι τοὺς ἑκατέρωθι ὄντας ἐπιμίγνυσιν ἐς τοὺς δια-
5 λόγους ἀλλήλοις. τὰ μὲν οὖν κατὰ τῆς θαλάσσης τὸ γειτόνημα τῇ αὐλῇ τῇδέ πῃ ἔχει, καλλωπιζομένῃ μὲν τῇ ἐς αὐτὴν ὄψει, περιπνεομένῃ δὲ ἁπαλαῖς οὔσαις ταῖς ἀπ' αὐτῆς αὔραις.
6 καὶ κιόνων δὲ καὶ μαρμάρων κάλλει ὑπερφυεῖ τά τε αὐτῆς ἐδάφη καὶ τὰ ὕπερθεν καλύπτεται πάντα· ὧν ἡ αἴγλη ὑπεράγαν λευκή τίς ἐστι, ταῖς τοῦ ἡλίου αὐγαῖς ἐπιεικῶς ἀπαστράπτουσα.
7 καὶ μὴν καὶ εἰκόνες αὐτὴν κοσμοῦσι παμπληθεῖς, αἱ μὲν χαλκαῖ, αἱ δὲ τῷ λίθῳ ἐπιξυσθεῖσαι, θέαμα λόγου πολλοῦ ἄξιον. εἰκάσαις ἂν ἢ Φειδίου τοῦ Ἀθηναίου ἢ τοῦ Σικυωνίου Λυσίππου ἔργον ἢ Πραξιτέλους αὐτὰς γεγονέναι.
8 ἐνταῦθα καὶ Θεοδώρα ἡ βασιλὶς ἐπὶ κίονος ἕστηκε·[1] τοῦτο γὰρ ἀνατέθεικεν ἡ πόλις αὐτῇ
B 206 9 ὑπὲρ τῆς αὐλῆς χαριστήριον. καὶ ἡ μὲν εἰκὼν εὐπρόσωπος, ἀλλὰ τῆς βασιλίδος τῷ κάλλει[2] ἐλάσσων, ἐπεὶ αὐτῆς τὴν εὐπρέπειαν λόγῳ τε

outside the city, and it is always open to those who tarry there for promenades and to those who anchor there as they are sailing by. This is flooded with light when the sun rises, and when it passes on toward the west it is pleasantly shaded. And the unruffled sea flows quietly about this court, encircling it with its stream, coming in from the Pontus like a river, so that those who are promenading can actually converse with those who are sailing by. For the sea preserves its depth even though it reaches up to the very foundations of the court and so is navigable there for ships, and by reason of the deep calm which prevails it brings together those on land and those on the sea so that they can converse with each other. Such, then, is the side of the court which borders on the sea, adorned by the view over it, and breathed upon by the gentle breezes which come from it. Columns and marbles of surpassing beauty cover the whole of it, both the pavement and the parts above. And from these gleams an intensely brilliant white light as the rays of the sun are flashed back almost undimmed. Nay more, it is adorned with great numbers of statues, some of bronze, some of polished stone, a sight worthy of a long description. One might surmise that they were the work of Pheidias the Athenian, or of the Sicyonian Lysippus or of Praxiteles. There also the Empress Theodora stands upon a column, which the city in gratitude for the court dedicated to her. The statue is indeed beautiful, but still inferior to the beauty of the Empress; for to express her loveliness in words or to portray it

[1] ἕστηκε V: ὑψηλοῦ ἵσταται A.
[2] τῶ κάλλει: τὸ κάλλος Maltretus.

φράσαι καὶ ἰνδάλματι ἀπομιμεῖσθαι ἀνθρώπῳ γε ὄντι παντάπασιν ἀμήχανα ἦν· ἁλουργὸς δὲ ὁ κίων καὶ πρὸ τοῦ ἐκτυπώματος ὅτι δὴ βασιλίδα φέρει διαφανῶς ἐνδεικνύμενος.

10 Ὅπερ δὲ ὕδατος εὐπορίας πέρι ἐνταῦθα διαπεπόνηται τῷ βασιλεῖ τούτῳ αὐτίκα δηλώσω. θέρους ὥρᾳ ἡ βασιλὶς πόλις ὕδατος ὑπεσπάνιζεν ἐκ τοῦ ἐπὶ πλεῖστον, καίπερ ἐς τοὺς ἄλλους 11 καιροὺς διαρκὲς ἔχουσα. τοῦ γὰρ καιροῦ τηνικάδε αὐχμοὺς ἔχοντος ἐλασσόνως ἢ κατὰ τὰς ἄλλας ὥρας αἱ πηγαὶ τὸ ὕδωρ ἀποβλυστάνουσαι καταδεεστέραν παρείχοντο τὴν ὀχεταγωγίαν τῇ 12 πόλει. διὸ δὴ ὁ βασιλεὺς ἐπενόει τοιάδε. κατὰ τὴν βασιλέως στοάν, ἵνα δὴ τὰς δίκας παρασκευάζονται οἵ τε ῥήτορες καὶ εἰσαγωγεῖς καὶ εἴ τινες ἄλλοι τοῦ ἔργου τούτου ἐπιμελοῦνται, αὐλή τίς P 26 ἐστιν ὑπερμεγέθης, περιμήκης μὲν καὶ εὔρους ἱκανῶς ἔχουσα, ἐν τετραπλεύρῳ δὲ περίστυλος οὖσα,[1] οὐκ ἐπὶ γεώδους ἐδάφους τοῖς αὐτὴν 13 δειμαμένοις,[2] ἀλλ' ἐπὶ πέτρας πεποιημένη. στοαί τε τὴν αὐλὴν περιβάλλουσι τέσσαρες, κατὰ πλευρὰν ἑκάστην ἑστῶσαι. ταύτην τε οὖν καὶ τῶν στοῶν μίαν, ἥπερ αὐτῆς τέτραπται πρὸς ἄνεμον νότον, ἐς βάθους μέγα τι χρῆμα κατορύξας Ἰουστινιανὸς βασιλεύς, ἀποβαλλομένοις τῇ περιουσίᾳ κατὰ τὰς ἄλλας ὥρας τοῖς ὕδασιν 14 ἐς θέρος ἐν ἐπιτηδείῳ θησαυρὸν ἔθετο. δεχόμενα γὰρ τὰ ἔλυτρα τάδε τοῦ ὀχετοῦ τὴν ἐπιρ-

[1] *οὖσα* Maltretus for *ὅσα*.
[2] *δειμαμένοις* Maltretus for *δημαμένοις*.

[1] Mentioned also in the *Secret History*, xiv. 13 (see the note there). The cistern which Justinian dug under a part of the

in a statue would be, for a mere human being, altogether impossible. The column is purple, and it clearly declares even before one sees the statue that it bears an Empress.

I shall now describe the labours which were carried out here by this Emperor to ensure an abundant water-supply. In the summer season the imperial city used to suffer from scarcity of water as a general thing, though at the other seasons it enjoyed a sufficiency. Because that period always brings droughts, the springs, running less freely than at the other seasons, used to deliver through the conduits a less abundant flow of water to the city. Wherefore the Emperor devised the following plan. At the Imperial Portico,[1] where the lawyers and prosecutors prepare their cases, as well as all others who are concerned with such matters, there is a certain very large court (*aulê*), very long, and broad in proportion, surrounded by columns (*peristylos*) on the four sides (*tetrapleuron*), not set upon a foundation of earth by those who constructed it, but built upon living rock. Four colonnaded stoas surround the court, standing one on each side. Excavating to a great depth this court and one of the stoas (that which faces toward the south), the Emperor Justinian made a suitable storage reservoir for the summer season, to contain the water which had been wasted because of its very abundance during the other seasons. For receiving this overflow of the aqueduct

building is probably the one now called Yeri Batan Serai, a short distance west of the Church of St. Sophia. *Cf.* also Downey, "The Architectural Significance of the Use of the Words *Stoa* and *Basilikê* in Classical Literature," *American Journal of Archaeology*, xli, 1937, pp. 204 f.

ῥοὴν ὑπερβλύζοντος στενοχωρουμένοις μὲν τοῖς ὕδασι τότε χαρίζεται χώραν, ποθεινῶν δὲ αὐτῶν γινομένων ἐπὶ καιροῦ τοῖς δεομένοις παρέχεται

B 207 15 πόρον. οὕτω μὲν μὴ προσδεῖν Βυζαντίοις ποτίμων ὑδάτων βασιλεὺς Ἰουστινιανὸς διεπράξατο.

16 Καὶ βασίλεια δὲ ἀλλαχόθι δεδημιούργηκεν αὐτὸς καινουργήσας ἔν τε τῷ Ἡραίῳ, ὃ νῦν Ἱερὸν ὀνομάζουσι, καὶ Ἰουκουνδιάναις ταῖς καλουμέναις· ὧν δὴ οὔτε τὸ μεγαλοπρεπὲς σὺν τῷ ἐς τέχνην ἠκριβωμένῳ, οὔτε τὸν ὄγκον ἂν σὺν τῷ εὐπρεπεῖ λόγῳ φράσαι ποτὲ ἱκανῶς

17 ἔχοιμι. ἀλλ' ἀποχρήσει ταῦτα εἰπεῖν βασίλειά τε εἶναι καὶ πρὸς Ἰουστινιανοῦ γεγονέναι παρόντος τε καὶ ἐπιτεχνωμένου, καὶ οὐδενὸς ἀπεριόπτου, ὅτι μὴ χρημάτων, καθισταμένου. ταῦτα γὰρ οὐχ οἷόν τέ ἐστι μὴ καὶ λόγου κρατεῖν.

18 Ἐνταῦθα δὲ καὶ λιμένων [1] σκέπας ἀποτετόρνευται οὐ πρότερον ὄν. ἀκτὴν γὰρ εὑρὼν ἑκατέρωθι τοῖς τε ἀνέμοις καὶ ταραχῇ τοῦ ῥοθίου [2] ἀποκειμένην, σωτήριον εἶναι τοῖς πλέουσι

19 κατεστήσατο ὧδε. τὰς κιβωτοὺς καλουμένας ἀναρίθμους τε καὶ παμμεγέθεις πεποιημένος, ἀμφοτέρωθέν τε αὐτὰς τῆς ἠϊόνος ἐπὶ πλεῖστον ἐγκαρσίας ἀπορριψάμενος, ἀεί τε τῶν προτέρων καθύπερθεν ἑτέρων ἐν τάξει ἐπιβολὴν [3] ἐντιθέμενος, τοίχους πλαγίους ἀπ' ἐναντίας ἀλλήλων ἀνέστησε δύο ἐκ τῶν τῆς ἀβύσσου κρηπίδων μέχρι ἐς τὸ ὕδωρ ᾧ δὴ αἱ νέες ἐναπερειδόμεναι

[1] λιμένων V: om. A.
[2] ταραχῇ τοῦ ῥοθίου V: τῷ ῥοθίῳ A.
[3] ἐπιβολὴν V: ὑπερβολὴν A.

when its stream is spilling over, this cistern both furnishes a place for the water which for the moment can find no space, and provides a supply for those who need it when water becomes scarce. Thus the Emperor Justinian made provision that the people of Byzantium should not be in want of fresh water.

He has also built palaces at various places, completely new ones, one at the Heraeum, which they now call Hieron, and another at the place called Jucundianae.[1] But I could never adequately describe in fitting words either their magnificence and their exquisitely detailed workmanship or their massive bulk. It will be sufficient to say simply that they are regal and that they were built under the personal supervision of the Emperor and with the help of his skill, while nothing was disregarded, excepting only money. The sum of this indeed was so great that it cannot be computed by any reckoning.

There too he skilfully contrived a sheltered harbour which had not existed before. Finding a shore which lay open to the winds from two directions and to the beating of the waves, he converted it into a refuge for voyagers in the following way. He prepared great numbers of what are called "chests" or cribs, of huge size, and threw them out for a great distance from the shore along oblique lines on either side of the harbour, and by constantly setting a layer of other chests in regular courses upon those underneath he erected two very long walls,[2] which lay at an angle to each other on the opposite sides of the harbour, rising from their foundations deep in the water up to

[1] Both on the Bosporus; cf. *supra*, p. 41.
[2] *i.e.* breakwaters.

20 πλέουσι. πέτρας τε τὸ λοιπὸν ἀποτόμους ταύτῃ ἐμβέβληται. ὧν δὴ πρὸς τοῦ ῥοθίου ἀρασσομένων, ἀποκρουομένων τε τὴν τοῦ κλυδωνίου ἐπίθεσιν, καὶ ἀνέμου χειμῶνος ὥρᾳ καταβάντος σκληροῦ, διαμένει τὰ ἐντὸς ἥσυχῇ ἅπαντα τῶν τοίχων, μεταξὺ μιᾶς ἀπολελειμμένης ἐπὶ τὸν 21 λιμένα τοῖς πλοίοις εἰσόδου. ἐνταῦθα δὲ καὶ ἱερὰ τεμένη πεποίηται, ᾗπέρ μοι ἔμπροσθεν B 208 δεδιήγηται, καὶ στοάς τε καὶ ἀγορὰς[1] καὶ λουτρῶνας ἐν δημοσίῳ καὶ τὰ ἄλλα σχεδόν τι πάντα· ὥστε δὴ ταῦτα τῶν ἐν τῇ πόλει βασιλείων 22 ἐλασσοῦσθαι μηδέν. καὶ λιμένα δὲ ἄλλον ἐτεκτήνατο ἐν τῇ ἀντιπέρας ἠπείρῳ, ἐν τοῖς Εὐτροπίου ἐπωνύμοις, τοῦ Ἡραίου τοῦδε οὐ πολλῷ ἄποθεν, κατὰ ταὐτὰ εἰργασμένον τοῖς ἄλλοις ὧνπερ ἐπεμνήσθην ἀρτίως.

23 Τὰ μὲν οὖν Ἰουστινιανῷ βασιλεῖ ἐν πόλει δεδημιουργημένα τῇ βασιλίδι, ὡς διὰ βραχυτάτων εἰπεῖν, ταύτῃ πῃ ἔχει. ὃ δὲ μόνον ἡμῖν ἐνταῦθα 24 δὴ ἀπολέλειπται αὐτίκα δηλώσω. τῇδε τοῦ βασιλέως τὰ διαιτητήρια ἔχοντος, διὰ μέγεθος τῆς βασιλείας, ἐκ πάσης γῆς ὅμιλος ἀνθρώπων P 27 25 τῇ πόλει παντοδαπὸς ἐπεισέρχεται. παραγίνεται δὲ αὐτῶν ἕκαστος ἢ πράξει τινὶ ποδηγούμενος ἢ ἐλπίδι ἢ τύχῃ, πολλοὶ δέ τινες, οἷς δὴ τὰ κατὰ τὴν οἰκίαν[2] οὐκ ἐν καλῷ κεῖται, βασιλέως δεησόμενοι, τῇ πόλει ἔνδημοι γίνονται διὰ βίαν

[1] ἀγορὰς V: ἀγυιὰς A. [2] οἰκίαν A: οἰκείαν V.

the surface on which the ships float.[1] Then upon these walls he threw rough-cut stones, which are pounded by the surf and beat back the force of the waves; and even when a severe storm comes down in the winter, the whole space between the walls remains calm, a single entrance being left between the breakwaters for the ships to enter the harbour. In that place also he erected holy shrines, as I have already recounted,[2] and stoas and markets and public baths, and practically all the other types of buildings, so that this quarter is in no way inferior to the Palace-quarter within the city. And he also constructed another harbour on the opposite mainland, in the place which bears the name of Eutropius, not far distant from this Heraeum, executed in the same manner as the harbour which I have just mentioned.

Now the building operations carried out by the Emperor Justinian in the imperial city, to describe them in the briefest terms, were about such as I have recounted. The one detail which remains to be mentioned here I shall straightway set forth. Since the Emperor maintains his residence here, it results from the very magnitude of the Empire that a throng of men of all conditions comes to the city from the whole world. Each of them is led to come either by some errand of business or by some hope or by chance; and many indeed come whose affairs are not in a happy state at home, in order to petition the Emperor; and all these become residents of the city because of some compulsion which is either urgent

[1] Procopius's description indicates that the "chests" were caissons, in this case probably boxes without lids, which were weighted with stones and sunk.

[2] Chap. iii. 10.

τινὰ ἢ πιέζουσαν ἢ ἐγκειμένην ἢ μέλλουσαν.
26 οἷσπερ συμβαίνει πρὸς τῇ ἄλλῃ ἀμηχανίᾳ καὶ οἰκίας ὑποσπανίζειν, οὐχ οἵοις τε οὖσι τὴν ὑπὲρ
27 τῆς ἐνταῦθα διατριβῆς προέσθαι μίσθωσιν. ταύτην δὲ αὐτοῖς βασιλεύς τε Ἰουστινιανὸς καὶ ἡ βασιλὶς Θεοδώρα τὴν ἀπορίαν διέλυσαν. τῆς γὰρ θαλάσσης ὡς ἀγχοτάτω, ἵνα δὴ Στάδιον [1] ὁ χῶρος καλεῖται (ἀγῶσι γάρ, οἶμαι, τὸ παλαιὸν ἀνεῖτό τισι) ξενῶνας [2] ὑπερμεγέθεις ἐδείμαντο, τοῖς τὰ τοιαῦτα ταλαιπωρουμένοις ἐπὶ καιροῦ γενησομένους καταλυτήρια.

B 209

ΛΟΓΟΣ Β΄.

P 28

α΄. Ὅσα μὲν δὴ ἐπί τε Κωνσταντινουπόλεως καὶ τῶν ἐκείνῃ προαστείων ἱερὰ τεμένη βασιλεὺς Ἰουστινιανὸς νέα ἱδρύσατο, καὶ ὅσα καταπεπονηκότα διὰ χρόνου μῆκος ἀνενεώσατο, τά τε ἄλλα οἰκοδομήματα, ὅσα δὴ ἐνταῦθα πεποίηται, ἐν
P 29 2 τῷ ἔμπροσθεν λόγῳ δεδήλωται. τὸ δὲ λοιπὸν ἐπὶ τὰ ἐρύματα ἡμῖν ἰτέον, οἷσπερ [3] τὰς ἐσχατιὰς περιέβαλε Ῥωμαίων τῆς γῆς. ἔνθα δὴ καὶ ταλαιπωρεῖσθαι τῷ λόγῳ τὰ μάλιστα ἐπάναγκες
3 ἂν εἴη καὶ τὰ ἀμήχανα διαπονεῖσθαι. οὐ γὰρ τὰς πυραμίδας ἀφηγησόμεθα, τοῦτο δὴ τῶν ἐν Αἰγύπτῳ βεβασιλευκότων τὸ διαθρυλλούμενον ἐπιτήδευμα, ἐς χάριν ἀποκεκριμένον ἀνόνητον, ἀλλὰ τὰ ὀχυρώματα σύμπαντα, οἷς ὁ βασιλεὺς οὗτος τὴν βασιλείαν ἐσώσατο, τειχισάμενός τε αὐτὴν

[1] στάδιον V: om. A.

imminent, or threatening. And in addition to their other difficulties, it comes about that these persons are also in want of quarters, being unable to pay the hire of any stay here. This difficulty the Emperor Justinian and the Empress Theodora solved completely for them. For very close to the sea, in the place called Stadium (for in ancient times, I suppose, it was given over to games of some kind), they built a very large hospice, destined to serve as a temporary lodging for those who should find themselves thus embarrassed.

BOOK II

i. All the new churches which the Emperor Justinian built both in Constantinople and in its suburbs, and all those which, having been ruined by the passage of time, he restored, as well as all the other buildings which he erected here, have been described in the preceding Book. From this point we must proceed to the defences with which he surrounded the farthest limits of the territory of the Romans. Here indeed my narrative will be constrained to halt painfully and to labour with an impossible subject. For it is not the pyramids which we are about to describe, those celebrated monuments of the rulers of Egypt, on which labour was expended for a useless show, but rather all the fortifications whereby this Emperor preserved the Empire, walling it about

[2] ξενῶνας A: καὶ ξενῶνας V.
[3] οἶσπερ Maltretus: καὶ οἶσπερ V, καὶ οἷς A.

καὶ ἀμήχανον τοῖς βαρβάροις καταστησάμενος
B 210 τὴν ἐς Ῥωμαίους ἐπιβουλήν. ἐκ δὲ ὁρίων
τῶν Μηδικῶν ἄρξασθαι οὔ μοι ἀπὸ τρόπου
ἔδοξεν εἶναι.

4 Ἐπειδὴ Μῆδοι ἀνεχώρησαν ἐκ Ῥωμαίων τῆς
γῆς, πόλιν αὐτοῖς Ἄμιδαν ἀποδόμενοι, ᾗπερ ἐν
λόγοις τοῖς ὑπὲρ τῶν πολέμων δεδήλωται, βασιλεὺς μὲν Ἀναστάσιος ἄγχιστά πη τῶν Περσικῶν
ὅρων κώμην ἄδοξόν τινα τὰ πρότερα οὖσαν,
Δάρας ὄνομα, τείχει περιβαλεῖν διὰ σπουδῆς
ἔσχε, πόλιν τε αὐτὴν ἐπιτείχισμα ἐσομένην[1]
5 τοῖς πολεμίοις ἐργάσασθαι. ἐν δὲ ταῖς σπονδαῖς
ἀπειρημένον, ἅσπερ ποτὲ βασιλεὺς Θεοδόσιος
ἔθετο πρὸς τὸ Περσῶν γένος, μηδετέρους ἐν χωρίῳ
οἰκείῳ ἐν γειτόνων που τοις τῶν ἑτέρων ὁρίοις
κειμένῳ ὀχύρωμα νεώτερόν τι ἐπιτεχνᾶσθαι,
προτεινόμενοι Πέρσαι τὰς ἐπὶ τῇ εἰρήνῃ ξυν-
θήκας ἐμπόδιοι τῷ ἔργῳ σπουδῇ τῇ πάσῃ ἐγίνοντο,
καίπερ Οὐννικοῦ πολέμου πιεζόμενοι τῇ ἀσχολίᾳ.
6 Ῥωμαῖοι δὲ αὐτοὺς ἀπαρασκεύους διὰ ταῦτα
ὁρῶντες ὀξύτερον τῆς οἰκοδομίας ἀντελαμβάνον-
το, προτερῆσαι διὰ σπουδῆς ἔχοντες πρὶν οἱ
πολέμιοι τὴν πρὸς Οὔννους ἀγώνισιν διαλύ-
7 σαντες ἐπὶ σφᾶς ἴωσιν. ὑποψίᾳ οὖν τῇ ἐκ τῶν
πολεμίων περίφοβοι ὄντες καὶ καραδοκοῦντες ἀεὶ
τὰς ἐφόδους, οὐκ ἐς τὸ ἀκριβὲς τὴν οἰκοδομίαν
ἐξῆγον, τοῦ τάχους αὐτοῖς τῷ ὑπερβάλλοντι τῆς
σπουδῆς παραιρουμένου τὴν ἐς τὸ ἔργον ἀσφά-
8 λειαν. τῷ γὰρ συντόμῳ τό γε ἀσφαλὲς οὐδαμῆ
εἴωθε ξυνοικίζεσθαι, οὐδὲ τῷ ὀξεῖ τὸ ἀκριβὲς
9 φιλεῖ ἕπεσθαι. οὕτω τοίνυν ἐπισπερχῶς ἀπειργάσαντο τὴν τοῦ περιβόλου ἀνάστασιν οὐκ

and frustrating the attacks of the barbarians on the Romans. And it seems to me not amiss to start from the Persian frontier.

When the Persians retired from the territory of the Romans, selling to them the city of Amida, as I have related in the Books on the Wars,[1] the Emperor Anastasius selected a hitherto insignificant village close to the Persian boundary, Daras by name, and urgently set about enclosing it with a wall and making it into a city which should serve as a bulwark against the enemy. But since it was forbidden in the treaty which the Emperor Theodosius once concluded with the Persian nation, that either party should construct any new fortress on his own land where it bordered on the boundaries of the other nation, the Persians, citing the terms of the peace, tried with all their might to obstruct the work, though they were hard pressed by being involved in a war with the Huns. So the Romans, observing that they were for this reason unprepared, pressed on the work of building all the more keenly, being anxious to get ahead of the enemy before they should finish their struggle with the Huns and come against them. Consequently, being fearful by reason of suspicion of the enemy, and continually expecting their attacks, they did not carry out the building with care, since the haste inspired by their extreme eagerness detracted from the stability of their work. For stability is never likely to keep company with speed, nor is accuracy wont to follow swiftness. They therefore carried out the construction of the circuit-wall in great

[1] I. ix. 20.

[1] ἐσομένην V : ἐσόμενον A.

ἀνανταγώνιστον τοῖς πολεμίοις πεποιημένοι, ἀλλ' ὅσον αὐτῷ ἀναγκαῖον ὕψος ἐνθέμενοι, οὐ μὴν οὐδὲ αὐτοὺς ἐμβεβλημένοι ἐν ἐπιτηδείῳ τοὺς B 211 λίθους, ἢ αὐτῶν ἐν δέοντι εἰργασμένοι[1] τὴν σύνθεσιν, ἢ τῷ τέλματι τῆς τιτάνου κατὰ λόγον 10 ἐναρμοσάμενοι. χρόνου οὖν ὀλίγου (χιόσι τε γὰρ καὶ ἡλίου θέρμῃ τῷ τῆς οἰκοδομίας σφαλερῷ ἀντέχειν οἱ πύργοι ὡς ἥκιστα εἶχον) διερρωγέναι αὐτῶν τοῖς πλείστοις ξυνέβη. οὕτω μὲν τὰ πρότερα ἐν πόλει Δάρας τὰ τείχη ἀνέστη.

11 Ἔννοια δὲ Ἰουστινιανῷ βασιλεῖ γέγονεν ὡς οὐ περιόψονται Πέρσαι ὅσα γε δυνατὰ τοῦτο δὴ τὸ κατ' αὐτῶν ἐπιτείχισμα Ῥωμαίοις ἑστάναι, ἀλλὰ πανοικεσίᾳ μὲν προσβαλοῦσι, τέχνας δὲ κινήσουσι πάσας ἐξ ἀντιπάλου τειχομαχήσειν τῆς πόλεως, καὶ ὅμιλος μὲν αὐτοῖς ἐλεφάντων P 30 ἕψεται, οἴσουσι δὲ ξυλίνους ἐπὶ τῶν ὤμων οἱ ἐλέφαντες πύργους, οἷς ὑποκείμενοι ἀντὶ θεμελίων ἑστήξουσι, καὶ τὸ δὴ χαλεπώτερον ἐν ἐπιτηδείῳ τοῖς πολεμίοις περιαγόμενοι καὶ φέροντες τεῖχος γνώμῃ τῶν κεκτημένων ὅπῃ παρατύχοι ἑπόμενον· 12 ἐπεμβαίνοντες δὲ οἱ πολέμιοι βαλοῦσι μὲν κατὰ κορυφὴν τοὺς ἔνδον Ῥωμαίους, ἐκ δὲ ὑπερδεξίων ἐπιθήσονται, ἀλλὰ καὶ λόφους χειροποιήτους ἐπαναστήσουσι, καὶ μηχανὰς τὰς ἑλεπόλεις ἐπάξ- 13 ονται πάσας. ἢν δέ τι τῇ πόλει Δάρας ἀξύμφορον ἐπιγένηται, πάσης μὲν προβεβλημένῃ τῆς Ῥωμαίων ἀρχῆς, ἀντιτεταγμένῃ δὲ τῇ πολεμίᾳ διαφανῶς, οὐκ ἄχρι τοῦδε ἡμῖν κείσεται

[1] εἰργασμένοι A: πεποιημένοι V.

haste, not having made it fit to withstand the enemy, but raising it only to such a height as was barely necessary; indeed they did not even lay the stones themselves carefully, or fit them together as they should, or bind them properly at the joints with mortar. So within a short time, since the towers could not in any way withstand the snows and the heat of the sun because of their faulty construction, it came about that the most of them fell into ruin. So were the earlier walls built at the city of Daras.[1]

The Emperor Justinian perceived that the Persians, as far as lay in their power, would not permit this outpost of the Romans, which was a menace to them, to stand there, but they would of course assault it with all their might, and would use every device to conduct siege operations on even terms with the city; and that a great number of elephants would come with them, and these would bear wooden towers on their shoulders, under which they would stand, supporting them like foundations; and worse still, that they would be led about wherever the enemy needed them and would bear a fortress which would follow along wherever, according to the judgement of their masters, it should happen to be needed; and that the enemy would mount these towers and shoot down upon the heads of the Romans inside the city, and attack them from a higher level; that, furthermore, they would raise up artificial mounds against them, and would bring up all manner of siege-engines. And if any misfortune should befall the city of Daras, which was thrown out like an earthwork before the whole Roman Empire and was obviously placed as a threat to the enemy's land, the disaster for us would

[1] See W. Ensslin, *Byz.-neugr. Jbb.*, V, 1926–7, pp. 342–347.

τὸ κακόν, ἀλλ' ἡ πολιτεία κατασεισθήσεται ἐκ τοῦ ἐπὶ πλεῖστον. ἐβούλετό τε διὰ ταῦτα ὀχύρωμα τῷ χωρίῳ περιβαλεῖν ἐπαξίως τῆς χρείας.

14 Πρῶτα μὲν οὖν τὸ τεῖχος (κολοβόν τε γὰρ ἦν κομιδῇ, ᾗπέρ μοι εἴρηται, καὶ τοῖς ἐπιοῦσι διὰ ταῦτα ἐπιμαχώτατον) ἀπρόσοδόν τε καὶ ἄμαχον 15 ὅλως τοῖς πολεμίοις ἐσκευάσατο εἶναι. τὰς B 212 μὲν γὰρ ἐπάλξεις πρότερον οὔσας λίθων ἐνθήκῃ ξυναγαγὼν ἀπέσφιγξεν ἐν στενῷ μάλιστα, ἴχνη αὐταῖς μόνα ἐς θυρίδων ἀπολιπὼν σχῆμα, τοσοῦτον δὲ αὐτῶν συγκεχωρηκὼς ἀνεῳγέναι, ὅσον δὴ καὶ χεῖρα διεῖναι, καὶ τῶν τοξευμάτων ἐξόδους 16 ἐπὶ τοὺς ἐνοχλοῦντας ἐνθένδε λελεῖφθαι. ὕπερθεν δὲ αὐτῶν ὕψος τῷ περιβόλῳ ἐπετεχνήσατο ἐς τριάκοντα μάλιστα πόδας, οὐχ ὅλον ἐνθέμενος τὸ πάχος τῷ τείχει, ὡς μὴ τῶν θεμελίων τῇ τῶν ἐγκειμένων περιουσίᾳ βαρυνομένων ἀνήκεστόν τι τῷ ἔργῳ ξυμβαίη,[1] ἀλλὰ τὸν ἐκείνῃ ἀέρα λίθων περιβολῇ περιελίξας, στοάν τε ἐν κύκλῳ τοῦ περιβόλου περίδρομον ἐργασάμενος, ὑπέρ τε τὴν στοὰν τὰς ἐπάλξεις ἐπιβαλών, ὥστε διώροφον μὲν πανταχόσε τὸ τεῖχος εἶναι, κατὰ δὲ τοὺς πύργους καὶ τρεῖς γεγονέναι τὰς χώρας τῶν τε ἀμυνομένων τοῦ περιβόλου καὶ τὰς ἐπ' 17 αὐτὸν ἀποκρουομένων ἐφόδους. κατὰ μέσους γάρ πη τοὺς πύργους σφαιρικὸν σχῆμα ἐνθέμενος αὖθις ἐνταῦθα ἐντέθεικεν ἐπάλξεις ἑτέρας, τριώροφον ταύτῃ τὸ τεῖχος ἀπεργασάμενος.

[1] ξυμβαίη V : ξυμβαίνοι A.

---

[1] The type of fortifications erected under Justinian here and at other places on the eastern frontier is illustrated by the drawings of the defences of Rusafa reproduced on pp. 104, 105.

not stop there, but a great part of the State would be seriously shaken. For these reasons he wished to surround the place with defences in keeping with its practical usefulness.

First of all he rendered the wall (which, as I have said, was very low and therefore very easy for an enemy to assault) both inaccessible and wholly impregnable for an attacking force.[1] For he contracted the original apertures of the battlements by inserting stones and reduced them to very narrow slits, leaving only traces of them in the form of tiny windows, and allowing them to open just enough for a hand to pass through, so that outlets were left through which arrows could be shot against assailants. Then above these he added to the wall a height of about thirty feet,[2] not building the addition upon the whole thickness of the wall, lest the foundations should be overloaded by the excessive weight which bore upon them, so that the whole work would suffer some irreparable damage, but he enclosed the space at that level with courses of stones on the outside and constructed a colonnaded stoa (*stoa*) running all around the wall, and he placed the battlements above this portico, so that the wall really had a double roof throughout; and at the towers there were actually three levels for the men who defended the wall and repelled attacks upon it. For at about the middle of each tower he added a rounded structure (*sphairikon schêma*) upon which he placed additional battlements, thus making the wall three-storeyed.

[2] In *Wars*, II. xiii. 17 Procopius says that when Chosroes attacked Daras in A.D. 540 the circuit-wall of the city was sixty feet high, and each of its towers one hundred feet in height.

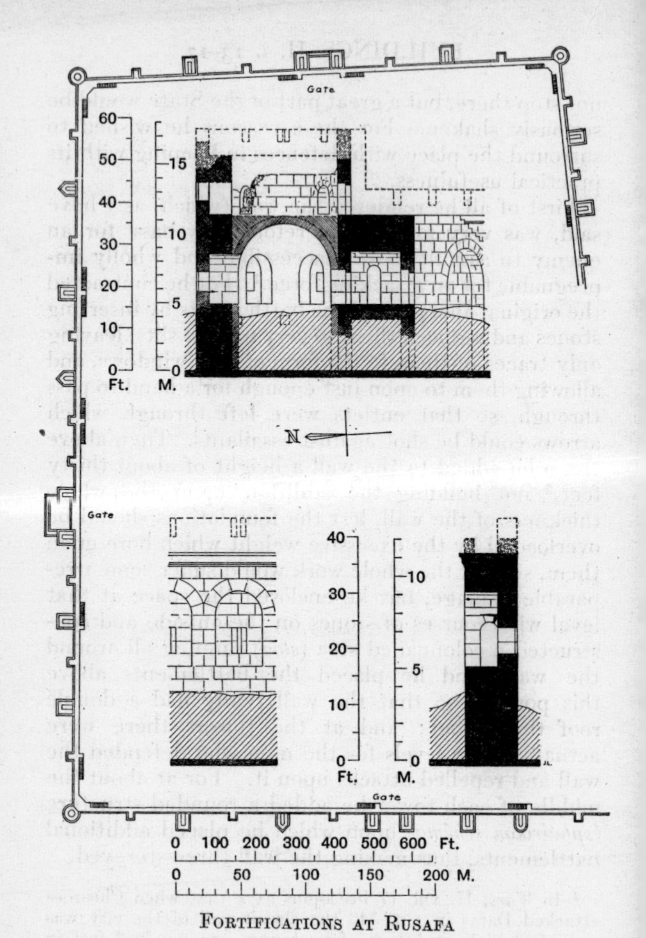
Gate
60
50
40
30
20
10
0
Ft.
15
10
5
0
M.
N
Gate
40
30
20
10
0
Ft.
10
5
0
M.
Gate
0 100 200 300 400 500 600 Ft.
0 50 100 150 200 M.

FORTIFICATIONS AT RUSAFA

Plan of part of the circuit-wall. Above, section of a tower. Below, elevation and section of part of the circuit-wall.

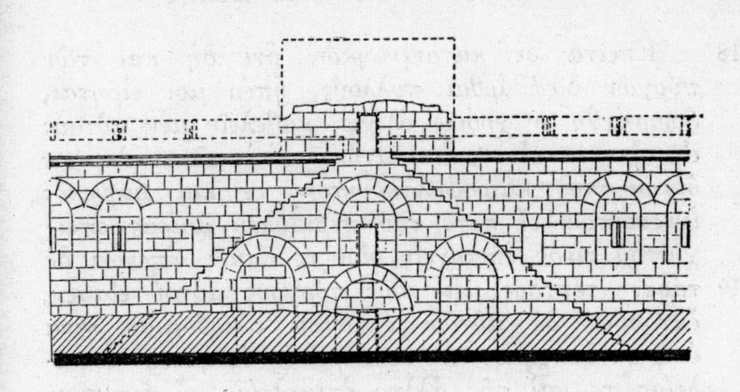

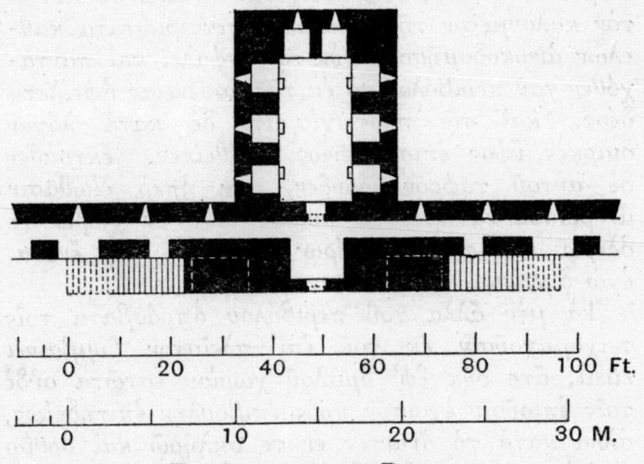
0 20 40 60 80 100 Ft.
0 10 20 30 M.

FORTIFICATIONS AT RUSAFA

Elevation and plan of a part of the circuit-wall, with stairs and a projecting tower.

18 Ἔπειτα δὲ κατανενοηκὼς ὅτι δὴ καὶ τῶν πύργων διεφθάρθαι πολλούς, ᾗπέρ μοι εἴρηται, ξυνηνέχθη ἐν χρόνῳ ὀλίγῳ, καθελεῖν μὲν αὐτοὺς ὡς ἥκιστα εἶχεν, ἐν γειτόνων ἀεὶ τῶν πολεμίων ὄντων καὶ καιροφυλακούντων τε καὶ διηνεκὲς ἰχνευόντων εἴ ποτε τοῦ περιβόλου μοίρας ἀτειχίστου τινὸς ἐπιτυχεῖν οἷοί τε ὦσιν· ἐπενόει δὲ 19 τάδε. τούτους μὲν τοὺς πύργους αὐτοῦ εἴασεν, ἔκτοσθεν δὲ αὐτῶν ἑκάστου οἰκοδομίαν τινὰ ἑτέραν ἐμπείρως ἐν τετραγώνῳ ἐδείματο ἀσφαλείας τε καὶ τῆς ἄλλης ἐπιμελείας εὖ ἔχουσαν, ταύτῃ τε τοὺς πεπονηκότας τῶν τοίχων ἐρύματι 20 ἑτέρῳ ἐς τὸ ἀσφαλὲς ἐτειχίσατο. ἕνα δὲ αὐτῶν B 213 τὸν καλούμενον τῆς Φρουρᾶς ἐπικαιριώτατα καθελὼν P 31 ἀνῳκοδομήσατο ξὺν τῷ ἀσφαλεῖ καὶ πανταχόθεν τοῦ περιβόλου τὸ ἐκ τῆς ἀσθενείας ἀφείλετο 21 δέος. καὶ τῷ προτειχίσματι δὲ κατὰ λόγον 22 διαρκὲς ὕψος ἐπισταμένως ἐντέθεικεν. ἔκτοσθεν δὲ αὐτοῦ τάφρον ὤρυξεν, οὐχ ᾗπερ εἰώθασιν ἄνθρωποι τὰ τοιαῦτα ποιεῖν, ἀλλ' ἐν χώρῳ τε ὀλίγῳ καὶ τρόπῳ ἑτέρῳ· ὅτου δὲ δὴ ἕνεκα, ἐγὼ δηλώσω.

23 Τὰ μὲν ἄλλα τοῦ περιβόλου ἀπρόσβατα τοῖς τειχομαχοῦσιν ἐκ τοῦ ἐπὶ πλεῖστον ξυμβαίνει εἶναι, ἅτε οὐκ ἐφ' ὁμαλοῦ χωρίου ἑστῶτα οὐδὲ τοῖς ἐπιοῦσιν ἔχοντος πρὸς ἐπιβουλὴν ἐπιτηδείως, ἀλλὰ κατὰ τὸ ἄναντες ἔν τε σκληρῷ καὶ ὀρθίῳ κειμένου, ἔνθα οὔτε διώρυχα οἷόν τέ ἐστιν οὔτε 24 προσβολὴν γενέσθαι τινά. ᾗ δὲ αὐτοῦ πρὸς ἄνεμον νότον ἡ πλευρὰ τέτραπται, μαλθακή τε οὖσα καὶ γεώδης ἡ χώρα καὶ πρὸς διώρυχας εὔκολος ἄγαν, εὐέφοδον ταύτῃ ποιεῖ τὴν πόλιν.

Then he observed that it had come about that many of the towers, as I have said, had fallen into ruin in a short time, yet it was entirely out of the question to pull them down, since the enemy were constantly in the neighbourhood watching their opportunity and continually scouting to see whether they might not find some part of the defences dismantled at any time. But he hit upon the following plan. He left these towers in place, and outside each of them he cleverly erected another structure in the form of a rectangle, which was built securely and with every possible care, and thus, by means of a second set of defences, he safely enclosed those parts of the wall which had suffered. But one of the towers, called the "Tower of the Guard," he pulled down at a favourable moment and rebuilt so that it was safe, and everywhere he removed the fear which had arisen from the weakness of the circuit-wall. He also wisely added sufficient height, in due proportion, to the outworks. And outside these he dug a moat, not in the way in which men are wont to make them, but only for a short distance and in a novel manner; and the reason for this I shall explain.

The greater part of the defences, as it happens, are in general unapproachable for an attacking party, since they do not stand on level ground and offer no favourable opportunity for assault to an approaching force; but they stand along a steep slope of a rough and precipitous character, where it is not possible for a mine to be dug or for any attack to be made. But on the side which is turned toward the south, the soil is deep and soft and consequently easy to mine, so that it makes the city assailable on this side. So in

25 τάφρον οὖν ἐνταῦθα μηνοειδῆ, εὔρους τε καὶ βάθους ἱκανῶς ἔχουσαν ἐπὶ μακρῷ κατορύξας, ἑκάτερον αὐτῆς τῷ προτειχίσματι τὸ πέρας ἐνῆψεν, ὕδατος μὲν αὐτὴν διαρκῶς ἐμπλησάμενος, ἄβατόν τε παντάπασι τοῖς πολεμίοις καταστησάμενος, ἐν μοίρᾳ δὲ αὐτῆς τῇ ἐντὸς προτείχισμα θέμενος ἕτερον· ᾧ δὴ ἐφεστῶτες ἐν πολιορκίᾳ φρουροῦσι Ῥωμαῖοι, τοῦ τε περιβόλου καὶ προτειχίσματος τοῦ ἑτέρου ἀφροντιστήσαντες,
26 ὅπερ τοῦ τείχους προβέβληται. ἐτύγχανε δὲ τοῦ τε τείχους καὶ τοῦ προτειχίσματος μεταξὺ κατὰ τὰς πύλας αἳ καταντικρὺ τοῦ Ἀμμώδιος χωρίου εἰσί, μέγα τι χρῆμα χώματος κείμενον, καὶ ἀπ' αὐτοῦ οἱ πολέμιοι λανθάνειν ἐκ τοῦ ἐπὶ πλεῖστον οἷοί τε ἦσαν ἐπὶ τῇ πόλει διώρυχας
27 ἔνερθεν τοῦ περιβόλου ποιούμενοι. ὅπερ ἐνθένδε
B 214 περιελὼν καὶ περικαθήρας εὖ μάλα τὸν χῶρον, ταύτῃ τοῖς πολεμίοις τὴν ἐς τὸ τεῖχος ἐπιβουλὴν ἀνεχαίτισε.

β'. Τὰ μὲν οὖν τοῦ ὀχυρώματος αὐτῷ τῇδέ πῃ πεποίηται. καὶ ὕδατος δὲ εἰργάσατο ἔλυτρα πῇ μὲν τοῦ περιβόλου καὶ τοῦ προτειχίσματος μεταξύ, πῇ δὲ ἄγχιστα τοῦ νεὼ ὃς Βαρθολομαίῳ ἀποστόλῳ ἀνεῖται πρὸς δύοντά που τὸν ἥλιον.
2 ῥεῖ δὲ καὶ ποταμὸς ἐκ προαστείου τῆς πόλεως διέχοντος αὐτῆς[1] σημείοιν[2] δυοῖν, ὃ δὴ Κόρδης
3 ἐπικαλεῖται. ἐφ' ἑκάτερα δὲ αὐτοῦ σκοπέλω δύο ἀνέχετον ὑπεράγαν σκληρώ· πρόεισί τε μεταξὺ τῆς ἑκατέρου ὑπωρείας ἄχρι ἐς τὴν πόλιν ὁ ποταμὸς οὗτος, παρὰ τοὺς πρόποδας φερό-

[1] αὐτῆς Maltretus: αὐτὴν.

that place he dug a crescent-shaped moat, with sufficient breadth and depth and extending to a great distance, and joined either end of this to the outworks and filled it amply with water, rendering it altogether impassable for the enemy; and on its inner side he set up another outwork. On this the Romans take their stand and keep guard in time of siege, freed from anxiety for the circuit-wall and the other outwork which is thrown out before the main wall. And it happened that between the main wall and the outwork, at the gate which faces toward the village of Ammodius,[1] there lay a great mound of earth, under cover of which the enemy were able to be in large measure unobserved while making mines against the city under the circuit-wall. This mound he removed from the spot and he cleared up the place thoroughly, and thus frustrated any secret attack on the wall by the enemy.

ii. Thus did he construct these fortifications. He likewise made reservoirs for water both in the space between the circuit-wall and the outworks and also close by the church which is dedicated to the Apostle Bartholomew, situated toward the west. And a river also flows from a suburb of the city which is two miles distant from it and is called Cordes.[2] On either side of it rise two cliffs which are exceedingly rugged. This river flows down between the heights on either side of it all the way to the city, carried along the bases of the mountains, and for

[1] Modern Amudah, about twelve miles south of Daras.

[2] *Cf.* the description of this river, and of its entrance into the city, in *Wars*, VIII. vii. 6–9.

[2] σημείοιν Dewing; *cf.* for the dative § 16 *infra*: σημείων.

μενος τῶν ὀρῶν, μάλιστά τε καὶ δι᾽ αὐτὸ τοῖς
4 πολεμίοις ἄτρεπτός τε καὶ ἀνέπαφος ὤν· οὐ γὰρ
ἔχουσι βιάζεσθαί πη αὐτὸν ἐν ὑπτίῳ τῆς γῆς.
ἐπιαπῶνται δὲ αὐτὸν ἐς τὴν πόλιν τρόπῳ τοιῷδε.
P 32 5 ὀχετὸν μὲν ἐκ τοῦ περιβόλου πεποίηνται μέγαν,
ὀβελοῖς δὲ σιδηροῖς τὸ τοῦ ὀχετοῦ στόμα συχνοῖς τε καὶ ὡς παχυτάτοις καταλαβόντες, τοῖς
μὲν ὀρθοῖς, τοῖς δὲ ἐγκαρσίοις, διεπράξαντο τῷ
ὕδατι ἐς τὴν πόλιν εἰσιτητὰ εἶναι, οὐχ ἐπὶ πονηρῷ
6 τοῦ ὀχυρώματος. οὕτω τοίνυν ἐς τὴν πόλιν
ἐσιὼν καὶ τὰ ἐκείνῃ ἔλυτρα ἐμπλησάμενος,
περιαγόμενός τε ὅποι ποτὲ δοκοίη τοῖς τῇδε
ἀνθρώποις, εἶτα ἐκβάλλει ἐς ἑτέραν τινὰ τῆς
πόλεως χώραν, ἐμφεροῦς αὐτῷ τῇ ἐς τὴν πόλιν
7 εἰσαγωγῇ πεποιημένης τῆς ἐκβολῆς. περιιὼν
τε τὰ ταύτῃ[1] πεδία ἐς πολιορκίαν εὐπετῆ
ἐποιεῖτο τὴν πόλιν. ἐνταῦθα γὰρ ἐνστρατο-
πεδεύεσθαι τοῖς πολεμίοις τῇ τοῦ ὕδατος περιουσίᾳ
8 οὐ χαλεπὸν ἦν. ὅπερ ἵνα μὴ γένηται λογισά-
B 215 μενος Ἰουστινιανὸς βασιλεὺς τὰ παρόντα ἐν
βουλῇ ἐποιεῖτο, διασκοπούμενος εἴ τινα τῷ πράγ-
9 ματι ἄκεσιν εὕροι. ὁ δὲ θεὸς αὐτῷ τὴν ἀμηχα-
νίαν ἰώμενος, ἀπαυτοματίσας τὴν πρᾶξιν μελλήσει
τὴν πόλιν οὐδεμιᾷ διεσώσατο. ἐγίνετο δὲ δὴ ὧδε.
10 Τῶν τις ἐκείνῃ στρατευσαμένων, εἴτε τινὰ
ὄψιν ὀνείρου ἰδὼν[2] εἴτε αὐτόματος εἰς τοῦτο
ἠγμένος, τῶν περὶ τὰς οἰκοδομίας τεχνιτῶν
ἑταιρισάμενος πολὺν ὅμιλον, διώρυχα ἐκέλευε
μακρὰν ἐντὸς τοῦ περιβόλου γεγενῆσθαι, δείξας
τι χωρίον αὐτοῖς· ὕδωρ γὰρ πότιμον ἐνταῦθα
11 εὑρήσειν ἐκ μυχῶν ἀποβλύζον τῆς γῆς. κυκλο-

[1] ταύτῃ V: ταύτης A. [2] ἰδὼν V: εἰδὼς A.

just this reason it cannot be turned aside or tampered with by the enemy; for there is no flat ground where they might be able to turn it from its course. And it is drawn into the city in the following way. They have constructed a large channel extending out from the circuit-wall, and covered the mouth of the conduit with a great number of the thickest possible iron bars, some upright and some horizontal; and thus they have arranged that the water can enter the city without endangering the fortifications. In this way the water flows into the city and fills its reservoirs and then is conducted wherever the inhabitants wish, and finally flows out at another part of the city, the opening for its discharge being made like that by which it enters the city. And winding about the plain near by, it used to make the city easy to besiege; for it was not a difficult matter, thanks to the bountiful supply of water, for the enemy to encamp there. So in order that this should not happen the Emperor Justinian took the situation under careful consideration, seeking diligently to find some remedy for the condition. And God provided the solution for the impossible problem which confronted him, settling the matter out of hand and saving the city without the least delay. This took place as follows.

One of the men serving in the army in this place, either in consequence of a dream or led to do it of his own accord, gathered a great throng of the workmen who were engaged in the building operations and bade them dig a long trench within the circuit-wall, shewing them a certain spot where he said that they would find sweet water welling up from the recesses of the earth. He made the pit in the form

τερῆ τε τὴν διώρυχα ἐς ποδῶν μῆκος πεντεκαίδεκα ποιησάμενος ἐπὶ πλεῖστον τὸ βάθος κατῆγε.
12 τοῦτο τῇ πόλει σωτήριον, οὐκ ἐκ προνοίας τῶν τεχνιτῶν τούτων πεποίηται, ἀλλ' ὅπερ ἐνταῦθα ξυμβήσεσθαι κακὸν ἔμελλεν, ἐς πᾶν ξυμφέρον διὰ
13 τῆς κατώρυχος ἀπεκρίθη Ῥωμαίοις. ὄμβρων γὰρ μεταξὺ ἐξαισίων καταρραγέντων, ὁ ποταμὸς οὗπερ ἐπεμνήσθην ἀρτίως πρὸ τοῦ περιβόλου μορμύρων ἀρθείς τε ἐπὶ μέγα κατὰ τὰ ξυνειθισμένα οὐκέτι ἐχώρει, οὐ δεχομένων αὐτὸν τηλικόνδε γεγενημένον οὔτε τῶν εἰσόδων οὔτε τοῦ ὀχετοῦ
14 ᾗπερ τὰ πρότερα. ξυνίστατο οὖν ἐπὶ τὸ τεῖχος ξυνάγων τὸν ῥοῦν, ἐς ὕψος τε καὶ βάθος κατατείνων πολύ, καὶ πὴ μὲν λιμνάζων, πὴ δὲ κυρτού-
15 μενός τε καὶ κυματίας γεγενημένος. τὸ μὲν οὖν προτείχισμα βιασάμενος καθεῖλεν εὐθύς, κατασείσας δὲ καὶ πολλήν τινα τοῦ τείχους μοῖραν καὶ τὰς πύλας ἀναπετάσας πολύς τε ῥεύσας τὴν πόλιν καταλαμβάνει σχεδόν τι ὅλην, καὶ αὐτῆς τήν τε ἀγορὰν καὶ τοὺς στενωποὺς καὶ οὐδέν τι ἧσσον τὰς οἰκίας περιπολήσας, ἐπίπλων τε ἐνθένδε καὶ
B 216 ξυλίνων τευχῶν καὶ ἄλλων τοιούτων φορτὸν μέγαν ἐπαγόμενος, ἐς ταύτην τε τὴν διώρυχα
16 ἐμπεσὼν ἀφανίζεται ὑπόγειος γεγενημένος. ἡμέραις δὲ οὐ πολλαῖς ὕστερον ἄγχιστά πη τῶν Θεοδοσιουπόλεως ὁρίων ἐκδούς, ἐν χώρῳ ἐφάνη σημείοις τεσσαράκοντα διέχοντι μάλιστα Δάρας πόλεως, οἷσπερ ἐπηγάγετο ἐκ τῶν τῇδε οἰκίων γνωσθείς· διεφάνη γὰρ ἐνταῦθα ὁ συρφετὸς
17 ὅλος. καὶ τὸ λοιπὸν ἐν μὲν εἰρήνῃ καὶ ἀγαθοῖς πράγμασιν ἐν μέσῃ πόλει γινόμενος ὁ ποταμὸς οὗτος, περιπλέους τε τοῦ ὕδατος τοὺς θησαυροὺς

of a circle fifteen feet across and drove it down to a great depth. This pit proved to be the salvation of the city, not indeed by any foresight of these workmen, but an event here, which would have been a disaster, turned out entirely to the advantage of the Romans, all on account of the pit. For during this time extraordinarily heavy rains fell, and the river, which I just mentioned, rose in high flood before the circuit-wall and no longer flowed in its usual bed, and it became so swollen that neither the opening by which it entered the city nor the conduit could contain it as formerly. So it backed up and gathered its stream against the wall, rising to a great height and depth; in some places it was stagnant, but elsewhere it was rough and turbulent. Consequently it broke through the outer defences and levelled them at once, and it also carried away a great portion of the main wall, and forcing open the gates and flowing in a mighty stream it spread over practically the whole city, and it circulated through the market-place and the streets and even through the houses, sweeping onward a great mass of furniture and wooden utensils and other such objects; then plunging into this pit it disappeared underground. Not many days later it emerged near the confines of Theodosiopolis, reappearing in a place about forty miles from the city of Daras, and it was recognised by the objects which it had carried off from the houses of that city; for the whole of the rubbish came to light there. And since then, in times of peace and in prosperity, this river has flowed into the centre of the city and filled the storage-reservoirs with water

ἐργασάμενος, φέρεται μὲν τῆς πόλεως ἔξω διὰ τῶν ἐξόδων αἵπερ αὐτῷ πεποίηνται ἐξεπίτηδες πρὸς τῶν δειμαμένων τὴν πόλιν, ὥσπερ μοι P 33 18 ἔναγχος δεδιήγηται. ἀρδεύων δὲ τὰ ἐκείνῃ χωρία ποθεινὸς ἅπασι τοῖς περιοικοῦσιν ἐς ἀεὶ γίνεται. ἐπειδὰν δὲ πολεμίων στρατὸς ὡς πολιορκήσων τὴν πόλιν ἐνταῦθα ἴοι, τὰς μὲν διὰ τῶν σιδηρῶν ὀβελῶν ἐξόδους ἐπιβύσαντες τοῖς καταράκταις καλουμένοις, αὐτίκα τε τὸν ποταμὸν μεταπεφυκέναι καὶ τὴν ἐκβολὴν μεταπορεύεσθαι βιασάμενοι ἀνάγκῃ χειροποιήτῳ, ἐπί τε τὴν διώρυχα καὶ τὸ 19 ἐνθένδε περιάγουσι χάος. καὶ ἀπ' αὐτοῦ οἱ πολέμιοι πιεζόμενοι τοῦ ὕδατος τῇ ἀπορίᾳ διαλύειν ἀναγκάζονται τὴν πολιορκίαν εὐθύς. Μιρράνης ἀμέλει ὁ Περσῶν στρατηγὸς ἐπὶ Καβάδου βασιλεύοντος ἐπὶ πολιορκίᾳ ἐνταῦθα ἥκων, τούτοις τε πᾶσιν ἀναγκασθείς, ἄπρακτος οὐκ εἰς μακρὰν 20 ἀνεχώρησε. καὶ Χοσρόης αὐτὸς πολλῷ ὕστερον ἐπ' αὐτῷ τούτῳ ἀφικόμενος στρατῷ μεγάλῳ ἐγκεχεί21 ρηκε τῇ ἐς τὴν πόλιν ἐπιβουλῇ. ὕδατός τε ἀπορίας πέρι ἀμηχανῶν, καὶ ἀποσκοπούμενος τὴν τοῦ περιβόλου ὑπερβολήν, ἄμαχόν τε αὐτὴν διαρκῶς ὑπώπτευεν εἶναι, καὶ τὰ βεβουλευμένα B 217 μεταγνούς, εὐθυωρὸν[1] ἐς τὰ Περσῶν ἤθη ἀπιὼν ᾤχετο, τῇ τοῦ Ῥωμαίων αὐτοκράτορος καταστρατηγηθεὶς προμηθείᾳ.

[1] εὐθυωρὸν Haury: εὐθύωρος V.

---

[1] *I.e.* Perozes. In *Wars*, I. xiii. 16 Procopius uses the word *Mirrhanes* as the title of Perozes; actually it was the name of a distinguished Persian family (*cf.* Pauly-Wissowa, XV. 2029, *s.v.* Mirrhanes).

to overflowing and then has been borne out of the city by the exits made for this purpose by those who built the city, as I have just explained. And it waters the land in that region and is always eagerly welcomed by all those who dwell round about. But whenever a hostile army comes up to besiege the city, they close the exits through the iron bars by means of sluice-gates (*katarraktais*), as they are called, straightway forcing the river, by this artificial constraint, to alter its course and change its exit, and they conduct it to the pit and the chasm which leads away from it. And as a result of this the enemy are hard pressed by lack of water and are compelled immediately to abandon the siege. Indeed Mirrhanes,[1] the Persian general during the reign of Cabades, came there to lay a siege, but was compelled by all these difficulties to retire after no long time without having accomplished anything. And Chosroes himself, a long time later, came there for the same purpose with a great army and undertook to attack the city. But finding himself in straits for want of water, and viewing the imposing height of the circuit-wall, which he suspected was quite impregnable, he changed his purpose and departed, marching straight for the Persian territory, outwitted by the foresight of the Roman Emperor.[2]

[2] In the last book of the *Wars*, published six years or more before the *Buildings*, Procopius gives a different account of the course of the river (VIII. vii. 8, 9): "But as soon as this river gets inside the circuit-wall, it flows about the entire city, filling its cisterns, and then flows out, and very close to the circuit-wall it falls into a chasm, where it is lost to sight. And where it emerges from there has become known to no man up to this time. Now this chasm was not there in ancient times, but, a long time after the Emperor Anastasius built

γʹ. Ταῦτα μὲν οὖν ἐν πόλει Δάρας οὕτω δὴ βασιλεὺς Ἰουστινιανὸς κατεστήσατο· ὅντινα δὲ προσεποίησε τρόπον τῇ πόλει μηκέτι αὐτῇ πάθος πρὸς τοῦ ποταμοῦ ξυμβῆναι τοιοῦτον, τοῦ θεοῦ διαρρήδην αὐτῷ ξυνεπιλαμβανομένου τὸ σπούδασμα 2 τοῦτο, ἐγὼ δηλώσω. Χρύσης ἦν τις Ἀλεξανδρεύς, μηχανοποιὸς δεξιός, ὅσπερ βασιλεῖ τὰ ἐς τὰς οἰκοδομίας ὑπηρετῶν, τὰ πλεῖστα τῶν τε ἐν πόλει Δάρας καὶ τῇ ἄλλῃ χώρᾳ γεγονότα 3 ἐξείργασται. οὗτος ὁ Χρύσης ἀπεδήμει μὲν ἡνίκα δὴ ἐν πόλει Δάρας τὸ ἐκ τοῦ ποταμοῦ πάθος ξυνέπεσεν· ἀκηκοὼς δὲ καὶ περιαλγήσας τῇ συμφορᾷ ἐς κοίτην τὴν αὑτοῦ ἀπεχώρησεν. ὄψιν 4 δὲ ὀνείρου τοιάνδε εἶδεν· ἐδόκει οἱ ἐν τῷ ὀνείρῳ τις ὑπερφυής τε καὶ τὰ ἄλλα[1] κρείσσων ἢ ἀνθρώπῳ εἰκάζεσθαι μηχανήν τινα ἐπαγγέλλειν τε καὶ ἐνδείκνυσθαι, ᾗ ἂν διακωλύειν τὸν ποταμὸν ἱκανὴ εἴη ἐπὶ πονηρῷ τῆς πόλεως μηκέτι μορμύ-5 ρειν. καὶ ὁ μὲν αὐτίκα θεῖον ὑποτοπήσας τὸ πρᾶγμα εἶναι, τήν τε μηχανὴν καὶ τὴν τοῦ ὀνείρου ὄψιν ἐς βασιλέα γράψας ἀνήνεγκε, σκια-6 γραφήσας τὴν ἐκ τοῦ ὀνείρου διδασκαλίαν. ἐτύγχανε δὲ οὐ πολλῷ πρότερον ἄγγελος ἥκων ἐς βασιλέα ἐκ Δάρας πόλεως, ὅσπερ αὐτῷ τὰ ἐκ τοῦ ποταμοῦ 7 ξυνενεχθέντα πάντα ἐσήγγειλε. βασιλεὺς δὲ τότε P 34 τοῖς ξυμπεπτωκόσι ξυνταραχθεὶς καὶ περιώδυνος γεγονώς, τοὺς τὰ μηχανικὰ εὐδοκιμοῦντας εὐθὺς

[1] ἄλλα Braun: ἄκρα.

---

this city, nature unaided fashioned and placed it there, and for this reason it comes about that those desiring to draw a

iii. These projects, then, were carried out as I have said by the Emperor Justinian at the city of Daras. I shall now relate how he brought it about that this city should never again suffer such damage from the river, a matter in which God manifestly assisted his effort. There was a certain Chryses of Alexandria, a skilful master-builder, who served the Emperor in his building operations and built most of the structures erected in the city of Daras and in the rest of the country. This Chryses was away at the time when the disaster caused by the river befell the city of Daras, and after he heard the news he went to his bed in distress over the misfortune. And he saw a vision as follows. It seemed in his dream that a certain creature of enormous size and in other respects too mighty to resemble a man,[1] prescribed and gave directions for a certain device which would be able to prevent the river from again running wild to the ruin of the city. He immediately surmised that the suggestion came from God, and wrote an account of the device and of the vision and sent it to the Emperor, shewing by a sketch the instructions received from the dream. It chanced that not long before this a messenger had come to the Emperor from the city of Daras, who reported to him all the damage which had been caused by the river. Thereupon the Emperor was greatly perturbed and deeply grieved by what had happened, and he straightway summoned the emi-

siege about the city of Daras are very hard pressed by scarcity of water." Evidently Procopius learned the account given in the present passage only after he had published Book VIII of the *Wars*.

[1] *Cf.* the description of a vision in the *Secret History*, vi. 6.

μετεκάλει, Ἀνθέμιόν τε καὶ Ἰσίδωρον, ὧνπερ
8 ἔμπροσθεν ἐπεμνήσθην. καὶ τὰ ξυμβεβηκότα
B 218 ἐπικοινούμενος ἀνεπυνθάνετο τῶν ἀνδρῶν ὁποία
ποτὲ μηχανὴ γένοιτο, ὡς μή τι περαιτέρω τῇ
πόλει ξυμβαίη· καὶ αὐτῶν μὲν ἑκάτερος ὑποθήκην
τινὰ ἔφραζε τήν οἱ δοκοῦσαν ἐπιτηδείως ἐς τοῦτο
ἔχειν· βασιλεὺς δέ, θείας δηλονότι ἐπινοίας αὐτῷ
γενομένης τινός, οὔπω τὰ Χρύσου ἰδὼν γράμματα,
ἐπενόει τε καὶ ἐσκιαγράφει αὐτογνωμονήσας ἐκ
τοῦ παραδόξου ὃ δὴ τοῦ ὀνείρου ἐκτύπωμα ἦν.
9 ἔτι δὲ τῆς βουλῆς ᾐωρημένης καὶ τοῦ πρακτέου
σφίσιν ἐν ἀδήλῳ ὄντος, διέλυσαν τὸν διάλογον.
10 ἡμέραις τε[1] τρισὶν ὕστερον ἧκέ τις βασιλεῖ τήν
τε τοῦ Χρύσου ἐπιστολὴν καὶ τῆς τοῦ ὀνείρου
11 μηχανῆς τὸ ἐκμαγεῖον ἐνδεικνύμενος. καὶ ὃς
μεταπεμψάμενος τοὺς μηχανικοὺς αὖθις ἀνα-
νεοῦσθαι τῇ μνήμῃ ἐκέλευεν ὅσα δὴ σφίσιν ἀμφὶ τῷ
12 ἔργῳ τὸ πρότερον δοκοῦντα εἴη. οἱ δὲ ἀπεστομά-
τιζον ἐφεξῆς ἅπαντα, ὅσα τε αὐτοὶ τεχνάζοντες
εἶπον καὶ ὅσα βασιλεὺς ἀπαυθαδιασάμενος ἐπήγ-
13 γειλε γενέσθαι. καὶ τότε δὴ βασιλεὺς τόν τε
πρὸς τοῦ Χρύσου σταλέντα καὶ τὰ γράμματα
ἐπιδείξας, ἔτι δὲ καὶ τὴν ἐκ τοῦ ὀνείρου γεγονυῖαν
ἐπὶ τῷ ἐσομένῳ ὄψιν τε καὶ σκιαγραφίαν, κατεστήσατο αὐτοὺς ἐν θαύματι μεγάλῳ, ἐν νῷ ποιου-
μένους ὡς ἅπαντα ὁ θεὸς συνδιαπράσσεται τῷ
14 βασιλεῖ τούτῳ τὰ τῇ πολιτείᾳ ξυνοίσοντα. ἐκράτει
τοίνυν ἡ τοῦ βασιλέως ἐπίταξις, ὑποχωρούσης
15 μηχανοποιῶν σοφίας καὶ τέχνης. καὶ γίνεται ὁ
Χρύσης αὖθις ἐν πόλει Δάρας, ἐπιτεταγμένον οἱ
πρὸς τοῦ βασιλέως ὑποτελέσαι τὰ γεγραμμένα

[1] τε MSS.: δὲ Hoeschel.

nent master-builders Anthemius and Isidorus, whom I have mentioned previously.[1] And he communicated the details of what had happened and enquired of the men what contrivance could possibly be made, so that no such calamity might again befall the city. Each of them gave some suggestion which seemed to himself well adapted to the situation. But the Emperor, obviously moved by a divine inspiration which came to him, though he had not yet seen the letter of Chryses, devised and sketched out of his own head, strange to say, the very plan of the dream. However, while their opinion was still unsettled, and it was not clear to them what should be done, they adjourned the conference. And three days later there came a man who shewed to the Emperor the letter of Chryses and the drawing of the device of the dream. The Emperor again summoned the master-builders, and bade them to call to mind their previous thoughts on this problem. And they repeated all the details in order, both what they had devised themselves and what the Emperor had daringly proposed should be done. Then the Emperor shewed them the man who had been sent by Chryses, and his letter, and told them of the vision of what was to be done which had been seen in the dream, and the sketch which had been made, and caused them to marvel greatly, as they considered how God becomes a partner with this Emperor in all matters which will benefit the State. So the Emperor's plan won the day, while the wisdom and skill of the master-builders yielded place to it. And Chryses again went to the city of Daras, with instructions from the Emperor to carry out with all zeal the scheme

[1] *Buildings*, I. i. 24, 50, 70.

σπουδῇ τῇ πάσῃ, καθάπερ ἡ τοῦ ὀνείρου ὑποθήκη ἐπήγγελλεν. ἐποίει τε τὰ ἐπιτεταγμένα[1] τρόπῳ τοιῷδε.

16 Ἐν χώρῳ διέχοντι τοῦ τῆς πόλεως προτειχίσματος ἐς τεσσαράκοντα μάλιστα πόδας, μεταξὺ σκοπέλου ἑκατέρου, ὧν δὴ κατὰ μέσον ὁ ποταμὸς
B 219 προϊὼν φέρεται, ἀντιτείχισμα ἐτεκτήνατο ὕψους
17 τε καὶ εὔρους ἱκανῶς ἔχον. οὗπερ τὰ πέρατα οὕτω δὴ ὄρει ἑκατέρῳ πανταχόθι ἐνῆψεν, ὡς τῷ ὕδατι τοῦ ποταμοῦ, ἢν καὶ σφοδρότατα ἐπιρ-
18 ρεύσειεν, ἐνταῦθα ἐσιτητὰ μηδαμῆ ἔσεσθαι. τοῦτο δὲ τὸ ἔργον οἱ περὶ ταῦτα σοφοὶ φράκτην ἢ ἀρίδα
19 καλοῦσιν, ἢ ὅ τί ποτε ἄλλο ἐθέλουσιν. οὐκ ἐπ' εὐθείας δὲ τὸ ἀντιτείχισμα πεποίηται τοῦτο, ἀλλ' ἐπὶ τὸ μηνοειδὲς τετραμμένον, ὅπως ἂν τὸ κύρτωμα πρὸς τῇ τοῦ ποταμοῦ ἐπιρροῇ κείμενον ἔτι μᾶλλον ἀντέχειν τῷ ῥείθρῳ βιαζομένῳ δυνατὸν
20 εἴη. θυρίδας δὲ ἐς τὸ ἀντιτείχισμα ἔς τε τὰ κάτω καὶ τὰ ἄνω πεποίηται, ὥστε τῷ ποταμῷ πλημμυροῦντι ἐξαπιναίως, ἂν οὕτω τύχοι, ξυνίστασθαι μὲν ἐνταῦθα ἐπάναγκες εἴη καὶ μὴ παντὶ τῷ ῥοθίῳ περαιτέρω χωρεῖν, ἐκροὴν δὲ κατὰ τὰς ὀπὰς ἀφιέντι βραχεῖάν τινα τοῦ μὲν ὑπερβάλλοντος ὄγκου κατὰ μικρὸν ἀπολήγειν ἀεί, τῷ δὲ τείχει[2]
21 λελυμασμένῳ μηδέποτε εἶναι. ἡ γὰρ ἐκροὴ ἐν τῷ χώρῳ ξυνισταμένη ὅσπερ ἐς τεσσαράκοντα διήκων πόδας, ἧπέρ μοι εἴρηται, τῆς τε ἀρίδος καὶ τοῦ προτειχίσματος μεταξύ ἐστιν, οὐδαμῆ τὸ
P 35 παράπαν βιαζομένη, ἀλλ' ἐς τὰς ξυνειθισμένας εἰσόδους κατὰ λόγον χωροῦσα ἐς τὴν ὀχεταγωγίαν
22 ἐνθένδε εἰσβάλλει. καὶ τὰς πύλας, ἅσπερ τὸ πρό-

[1] ἐπιτεταγμένα V: ὑποτεταγμένα A.

which had been described, just as the intimation of the dream had dictated. And he carried out the instructions in the following manner.

At a place about forty feet removed from the outer fortifications (*proteichisma*) of the city, between the two cliffs between which the river runs, he constructed a barrier (*antiteichisma*) of proper thickness and height. The ends of this he so mortised into each of the two cliffs, that the water of the river could not possibly get by that point, even if it should come down very violently. This structure is called by those skilled in such matters a dam (*phraktes*) or flood-gate (*aris*), or whatever else they please. This barrier (*antiteichisma*) was not built in a straight line, but was bent into the shape of a crescent, so that the curve, by lying against the current of the river, might be able to offer still more resistance to the force of the stream. And he made sluice-gates (*thyrides*) in the dam, in both its lower and its upper parts, so that when the river suddenly rose in flood, should this happen, it would be forced to collect there and not go on with its full stream, but discharging through the openings only a small volume of the excess accumulation, would always have to abate its force little by little, and the city-wall would never suffer damage. For the outflow collects in the space which, as I have said, extends for forty feet between the dam and the outer fortifications, and is under no pressure whatever, but it goes in an orderly fashion into the customary entrances and from there empties into the conduit (*ochetagogia*). And the city gate itself, which the river

[2] τείχει l, Hoeschel: τείχη V.

τερον βιασάμενος ἐξαπιναίως ὁ ποταμὸς ἀνεπέτασε, περιελὼν ἐντεῦθεν, λίθοις μὲν παμμεγέθεσι τὴν προτέραν αὐτῶν ἐφράξατο χώραν, ἐπεὶ ἐφ' ὁμαλοῦ κείμεναι τῷ ποταμῷ ὑπερβλύζοντι εὐέφοδ-

23 οι ἦσαν. ἄγχιστα δέ πη ἐν χώρῳ ἀνάντει κατὰ τὸ κρημνῶδες τοῦ περιβόλου αὐτὰς ἔθετο, οὗ δὴ τῷ ποταμῷ βάσιμα ὡς ἥκιστα ἦν. ταῦτα μὲν οὖν οὕτω διαπεπόνηται τῷ βασιλεῖ τούτῳ.

B 220 24 Ἦν δέ τις ἐν πόλει πολλὴ ὕδατος πέρι ἀμηχανία τοῖς τῇδε ἀνθρώποις. οὔτε[1] γὰρ ἀναβλυστάνουσαν εἶχον ἐνταῦθά πη κρήνην, οὔτε[1] ὀχετῷ περιαγομένην ἐς τὰς ἀγυιὰς αἳ τῇδέ εἰσιν, οὔτε τισὶ θησαυριζομένην ἐκείνῃ ἐλύτροις, ἀλλ' οἷς μὲν ἀγχοτάτω ὁ ποταμὸς κατὰ τὰς ἀμφόδους ἐφέρετο, οἵδε ἀταλαιπώρως ἀρυόμενοι τῷ γειτονήματι[2] ῥᾷστα ἔπινον, οἷς δὲ[3] ὡς ἀπωτάτω τῆς τοῦ ποταμοῦ ἐκροῆς τὰ οἶκοι[4] ἐτύγχανεν ὄντα, τούτοις δυοῖν τὸ ἕτερον ἐπάναγκες ἦν, ἢ τὰ ἔσχατα πονουμένοις πιεῖν, ἢ δίψει ἐχομένοις

25 ἀπολωλέναι. ἀλλ' ὀχετὸν βασιλεὺς Ἰουστινιανὸς ἐτεκτήνατο μέγαν, ᾧ δὴ τὸ ὕδωρ περιαγαγὼν πανταχόσε τῆς πόλεως τὴν ἀπορίαν τοῖς τῇδε

26 ᾠκημένοις διέλυσεν. ἀλλὰ καὶ ἱερὰ πεποίηται δύο, τήν τε μεγάλην ἐκκλησίαν καλουμένην καὶ τὸν τοῦ ἀποστόλου Βαρθολομαίου νεών. ἔτι μέντοι καὶ τοῖς στρατιώταις καταλυτήρια ἐδείματο παμπληθῆ, ὅπως δὴ τοὺς τῇδε ᾠκημένους μηδαμῶς ἐνοχλοῖεν.

27 Καὶ Ἀμίδης δὲ πόλεως τό τε τεῖχος καὶ τὸ προτείχισμα ἐν τοῖς ἄνω γενόμενα χρόνοις καὶ ἀπ' αὐτοῦ ὕποπτα ὄντα ἐξίτηλα γενήσεσθαι, οὐ

[1] οὔτε . . . οὔτε Haury: οὐδὲ . . . οὐδέ.
[2] τῷ γειτονήματι om. A.

had earlier burst open by its sudden pressure, he removed from that place, and he walled up with very large stones the place which it had formerly occupied, because lying on level ground, as it did, it was easily reached by the river when it was in flood. And he set this gate near by at a place higher up where the circuit-wall was on a steep slope, to which the river could not possibly come. Thus were these works carried out by this Emperor.

And there was a great difficulty regarding water for the people living in this city. For they had neither any spring welling up there, nor water conveyed about the streets of the city by a conduit (*ochetos*); neither was it stored there in any cisterns; but those very near whose streets the river flowed drew their drinking-water without any trouble because of its proximity, those whose homes [1] chanced to be very far from the river's course, were obliged to choose one of these two alternatives—either to take a vast deal of trouble in order to obtain drinking-water at all, or to perish of thirst. But the Emperor Justinian built a great conduit by which he led the water about to every part of the city, and thus relieved the straits of the inhabitants. Furthermore, he constructed two shrines, both the Great Church, as it is called, and the Church of the Apostle Bartholomew. He also built numerous barracks for the soldiers, in order that they might cause no annoyance whatever to the inhabitants.

Likewise both the wall and the outworks of the city of Amida, which had been built long before, and, because of their age, seemed likely to fall

[1] Literally "the domestic concerns."

[3] δὲ A: μέντοι V. [4] οἶκοι V: οἰκία A.

πολλῷ ὕστερον νέᾳ τινὶ καταλαβὼν οἰκοδομίᾳ τῇ 28 πόλει τὴν ἀσφάλειαν ἀνεσώσατο. ὅσα δὲ κἂν[1] τοῖς φρουρίοις αὐτῷ εἴργασται, ἅπερ ἐν τοῖς ὁρίοις τούτων δὴ τυγχάνει τῶν πόλεων ὄντα, ἐρῶν ἔρχομαι.

δʹ. Ἐκ Δάρας πόλεως ἰόντι ἐς τὰ Περσῶν ἤθη χώρα τις ἐν ἀριστερᾷ ἐστιν ἀναμάξευτός τε καὶ ἄφιππος ὅλως, κατατείνουσα μὲν ἐς ἡμέραιν ὁδὸν δυοῖν εὐζώνῳ ἀνδρὶ μάλιστα, τελευτῶσα δὲ ἐς χῶρον σιμὸν καὶ ἀπόκρημνον, Ῥάβδιος ὄνομα. B 221 2 ταύτης δὲ τῆς ἐπὶ τὸ Ῥάβδιος φερούσης ὁδοῦ ἐφ᾽ ἑκάτερα τὰ Περσῶν ὅρια ἐπὶ μακρότατον 3 ξυμβαίνει εἶναι. ὅπερ μοι κατ᾽ ἀρχὰς ἀγαμένῳ καὶ τῶν ἐπιχωρίων ἀναπυνθανομένῳ ὅντινα τρόπον P 36 Ῥωμαίοις προσήκουσα ὁδός τε καὶ χώρα γῆν ἑκατέρωθι τὴν πολεμίαν διακεκλήρωται, ἀπήγγελλόν τινες ὡς εἴη μὲν Περσῶν τὸ χωρίον ποτέ, δεομένῳ δὲ τῷ[2] Περσῶν βασιλεῖ τῶν τις Ῥωμαίων αὐτοκρατόρων ἀμπέλοις τινὰ κατακορῆ κώμην ἐπὶ Μαρτυροπόλεως οὖσαν δώσειε, τοῦτο δὴ 4 αὐτῆς τὸ χωρίον ἀνταλλαξάμενος. τὸ μὲν οὖν Ῥάβδιος ἐπὶ πετρῶν οἰκεῖται ἀποτόμων τε καὶ ὅλως ἀγρίων αἵπερ ἐνταῦθα ἐπανεστήκασι θαυμά-5 σιον ὅσον. ἔνερθεν δὲ αὐτοῦ χωρίον ἐστὶν ὅπερ καλοῦσι Ῥωμαίων ἀγρόν, ἀγασθέντες, οἶμαι, τὸ ἐξ ἀρχῆς, ὅτι δὴ ἐν μέσῳ[3] χωρίων Περσικῶν 6 κείμενον Ῥωμαίοις προσήκει. οὗτος δὲ ὁ Ῥωμαίων ἀγρὸς κεῖται μὲν τῆς γῆς ἐν ὑπτίῳ,

[1] κἂν V: καὶ A.
[2] τῷ Haury: τῶν.
[3] μέσῳ A: μέσων V.

in ruins, he not long afterwards replaced by new structures and thus restored the safety of the city. All else that he did in the fortresses which chance to be within the territory of these cities I shall now proceed to relate.

iv. As one goes from Daras into the Persian country there lies on the left a territory which cannot be traversed at all by waggons or even by horses, extending to a distance of about two days' journey for an unencumbered traveller [1] and ending in a steep and precipitous bluff which is called Rhabdios.[2] And on both sides of this road leading to Rhabdios the Persian territory stretches out to a very great distance. At first I was amazed at this, and I made enquiry of the natives how it came about that a road and district which belonged to the Romans had land of the enemy on either side of it; and some of them explained that the place had belonged to the Persians at one time, but that at the petition of the Persian King one of the Roman Emperors had handed over a certain vine-producing village near Martyropolis [3] and had received this place in exchange for it. Rhabdios stands on precipitous and wholly wild rocks, which rise there to an astonishing height. And beneath it is a place which they call the Field of the Romans, I suppose because they marvelled, at first, that though this lies in the midst of Persian territory, it belongs to the Romans. This Field of the Romans lies on flat ground, and is very productive

[1] In his *Wars*, III. i. 17, Procopius defines this rough measure of distance, which was in common use: "One day's journey extends two hundred and ten stades, or as far as from Athens to Megara." 210 stades is about 24 English miles.

[2] Apparently the modern Kalat Hatim Tai.

[3] Modern Mejafarkin; *cf.* below, III. iii. 1 ff.

ἀγαθῶν δέ ἐστι τῶν ἐν τοῖς ληίοις κομιδῇ εὔπορος. 7 τεκμηριώσειε δ᾽ ἄν τις καὶ τοῖσδε, ὅτι δὴ πανταχόθεν τὸν χῶρον περιβάλλουσι [1] τὰ Περσῶν ὅρια.

8 Πόλισμά ἐστιν ἐν Πέρσαις ἐπιφανὲς ἄγαν, ὄνομα Σισαυράνων, ὅπερ ποτὲ Ἰουστινιανὸς βασιλεὺς ἐξελὼν ἐς ἔδαφος καθεῖλεν, ὅμιλον πολὺν τῶν ἐν Πέρσαις ἱππέων ξὺν Βλησχάμῃ τῷ σφῶν 9 ἡγεμόνι δορυαλώτους πεποιημένος. τοῦτο πόλεως μὲν Δάρας ὁδῷ ἡμέραιν διέχει δυοῖν εὐζώνῳ ἀνδρί· τούτου δὲ τοῦ Ῥάβδιος σημείοις διέστηκε 10 τρισὶ μάλιστα. πρότερον μὲν οὖν ἀφύλακτός τε ἦν ὁ χῶρος ὅδε καὶ Ῥωμαίοις παντελῶς ἄσημος. οὐκοῦν οὔτε [2] φρουρᾶς οὔτε [2] ὀχυρώματος οὔτε [2] ἄλλου ὁτουοῦν ἀγαθοῦ πρὸς αὐτῶν ἔλαχε πώποτε. 11 Πέρσαις ἀμέλει οἱ τὸν ἀγρὸν γεωργοῦντες, οὗπερ B 222 ἐπεμνήσθην ἀρτίως, ὥσπερ ἄλλο τι ἀγγαροφοροῦντες, πεντήκοντα ἐπετείους χρυσοῦς ἔφερον,[3] ἐφ᾽ ᾧ ἀδεέστερον κεκτήσονται τὰ αὐτῶν ἴδια καὶ καρπῶν δύνωνται τῶν τῇδε φυομένων ὀνίνασθαι. 12 βασιλεὺς δὲ Ἰουστινιανὸς ἅπαντα αὐτοῖς μεταπεφυκέναι διεσκευάσατο. τειχίσματι γὰρ τὸ Ῥάβδιος περιβαλὼν κατὰ τῶν πετρῶν τὴν ὑπερβολήν, αἵπερ ἐκείνῃ ἀνέχουσιν, ἀπρόσοδον αὐτὸ τοῖς πολεμίοις πεποίηται τὸ χωρίον, δηλονότι ξυλλαμ13 βανούσης τῆς φύσεως. ἐπεὶ [4] δὲ ὕδατος οἱ τῇδε ᾠκημένοι ἐσπάνιζον, ἐν τῇ τῶν σκοπέλων ἀκρωρείᾳ πηγῆς ὡς ἥκιστα οὔσης, ταμιεῖά τε ὑδάτων εἰργάσατο δύο καὶ τὰς ἐκείνῃ πέτρας πολλαχῇ διορύξας παμπληθεῖς ὑδάτων θησαυροὺς διεπράξατο

[1] περιβάλλουσι V : περιβάλλει A. [2] οὔτε Haury : οὐδὲ.
[3] ἔφερον Haury : ἔφερον Πέρσαις.
[4] ἐπεὶ V : ἐπειδὴ A.

of the crops which grow on corn-lands. One might conjecture this also from the circumstance that Persian territory surrounds the place on every side.

There is a fortress in Persia of very great note, Sisauranon [1] by name, which the Emperor Justinian once captured and levelled to the ground, taking captive a great throng of Persian horsemen along with their leader Bleschames.[2] This is separated from the city of Daras by a journey of two days for an unencumbered traveller, and is about three miles distant from Rhabdios. At first this region was unguarded and was of no consequence whatever to the Romans. For it had never been garrisoned nor had it been fortified, and it had not received any other care from them. Indeed it was to the Persians that those who farmed the "Field" which I just mentioned paid fifty staters annually, just as though they were paying ordinary taxes,[3] on condition that they might possess their own lands free from fear and be able to profit by the crops which grew upon them. But the Emperor Justinian arranged to alter all this for their benefit. He encircled Rhabdios with a wall built along the crest of the rocks which rise there, thus making the place inaccessible for the enemy, that is, with the assistance of nature. Then, since those who dwelt there had a scanty supply of water—for no spring was to be found on the summit of the rocks—he constructed two cisterns and dug channels into the rock there in many directions, so that he made many reservoirs for water, in

[1] Other sources call this place Sarbanê, or use variant forms of the name; the site is apparently represented by the modern Serwan.

[2] *Cf. Wars*, II. xix. 24.

[3] On the collection of taxes under Justinian see *Secret History*, xxiii. i–24.

εἶναι, ὅπως δὴ ξυρρεόντων ὑετίων ἐνταῦθα ὑδάτων ἀδεέστερον αὐτοῖς οἱ τῇδε ἄνθρωποι δύνωνται χρῆσθαι, ὡς μὴ τοῦ ὕδατος πιεζόμενοι τῇ ἀπορίᾳ εὐάλωτοι εἶεν.

14 Καὶ τὰ ἄλλα δὲ φρούρια πάντα ἐν ὄρει κείμενα, ἅπερ ἐνθένδε τε καὶ ἐκ Δάρας πόλεως ἄχρι ἐς Ἄμιδαν διήκειν ξυμβαίνει, τό τε Κιφὰς καὶ Σαυρὰς καὶ Μάργδις τε καὶ Λούρνης τό τε Ἰδριφθὸν καὶ Ἀταχὰς καὶ Σίφριός τε καὶ Ῥιπαλθὰς καὶ Βανασυμέων, ἔτι μέντοι καὶ Σινὰς καὶ Ῥάσιος, καὶ Δαβανάς, καὶ ὅσα ἄλλα ἐνταῦθα ἐκ παλαιοῦ ἐστι, γελοιότατα δῆθεν τῷ σχήματι ἀποτεθριγκωμένα τὸ πρότερον ἀνοικοδομησάμενος σὺν τῷ ἀσφαλεῖ ἔς τε τὸ νῦν P 37 φαινόμενον κάλλος τε καὶ ὀγύρωμα μεταθέμενος ἀνάλωτα εἶναι καὶ προβεβλῆσθαι Ῥωμαίων τῆς γῆς 15 βεβαιότατα κατεστήσατο. ἐνταῦθα ὄρος οὐρανόμηκες ἀποκρέμαται, ἀπόκρημνόν τε καὶ προσελθεῖν 16 ἀμήχανον ὅλως. ἐν πεδίῳ δὲ ὑπόκειται χώρα γεώδης τε καὶ μαλθακὴ λίαν, ἀγαθὴ μὲν ἀρόσαι, B 223 θρέμμασι δὲ ἀτεχνῶς εὔνομος.[1] ἐπιεικῶς γὰρ 17 τῇ πόᾳ χλοάζει. παμπληθεῖς δὲ κῶμαι παρὰ τοὺς πρόποδας τοῦ ὄρους εἰσίν. οἰκοῦσί τε αὐτὰς ἄνθρωποι τὰ μὲν ἐς κτῆσιν τῶν ἐπιτηδείων 18 εὐδαίμονες, εὐάλωτοι δέ, εἴ τις προσίοι. ὅπερ αὐτοῖς ἐπηνώρθωσεν Ἰουστινιανὸς βασιλεύς, φρούριον ἐπὶ τοῦ ὄρους τῇ ἀκρωνυχίᾳ δειμάμενος, ἵνα δὴ τὰ σφίσιν ἐναποθέμενοι τιμιώτατα, ἐπειδὰν προσίοιεν οἱ πολέμιοι, ἀνατρέχοντες διασώζωνται· 19 Βασιλέων δὲ τὸ φρούριον ἐπωνόμασται. καὶ μὴν

[1] εὔνομος Maltretus: ἔννομος.

order that when the rain-water collected in these the inhabitants might be able to use them in security, and then they might not be captured easily when hard pressed for lack of water.

And all the other forts which lie in the mountains, forming a line from there and from the city of Daras all the way to Amida, namely Ciphas and Sauras and Margdis and Lournês and Idriphthon and Atachas and Siphriŭs and Rhipalthas and Banasymeôn, and also Sinas and Rhasios and Dabanas, and all the others which have been there from ancient times, and which had previously been fenced about in most ridiculous fashion, he rebuilt and made safe, transforming them to their present aspect as to both beauty and strength, and making them impregnable, so that actually they are thrown out as a mighty bulwark to shield the land of the Romans. In that place there is a lofty mountain towering to the sky, exceedingly steep and altogether inaccessible. And in the plain below the soil lies deep and soft, an excellent surface for plowing and extremely good for pasture, for it is covered with a great abundance of forage. There are numerous villages along the foot-hills of the mountain, inhabited by people who are indeed happy in their possession of the necessities of life, but would be easy to capture, if anyone should attack them. This situation the Emperor Justinian corrected for them by building a fort on the very tip of the mountain, so that they might store their most valuable property there and also, fleeing thither, save themselves whenever the enemy should come against them; and this fort is named Basileôn.[1] Furthermore, he carefully rebuilt the

[1] "Emperors' Fort."

καὶ τὰ ἀμφὶ πόλιν Ἄμιδαν φρούρια, πηλῷ τε περιβεβλημένα καὶ τοῖς πολεμίοις βάσιμα παντάπασιν ὄντα, ἐς τὸ ἀκριβὲς ἀνοικοδομησάμενος ἅπαντα ἐς τῆς ἀσφαλείας τὸ ἀκριβέστατον μετεστή-
20 σατο. ἐν οἷς τό τε Ἀπάδνας καὶ τὸ Βιρθὸν πολίχνιόν ἐστιν. ἅπαντα γὰρ [1] ἀκριβολογεῖσθαι
21 πρὸς ὄνομα οὐκ εὐπετές ἐστι. συνελόντα δὲ εἰπεῖν ἅπαντα πρότερον τοῖς ἐπιβουλεύουσιν ὑποκείμενα [2] τανῦν ἀνανταγώνιστα πεποίηκεν εἶναι. καὶ ἀπ᾽ αὐτοῦ ἡ Μεσοποταμία τῷ Περσῶν γένει ἄβατος διαφανῶς ἐστιν.

22 Οὐ σιωπητέον δὲ οὐδὲ ὅπερ ἐν τῷ Βάρας φρουρίῳ ἐξεῦρεν, οὗπερ ἐπεμνήσθην ἀρτίως. τὰ μὲν γὰρ τοῦ φρουρίου ἐντὸς ἄνυδρα τὸ παράπαν ὄντα ἐτύγχανεν, ἐν ὄρει δὲ ὑψηλῷ μάλιστα κατὰ
23 τὸ κρημνῶδες τὸ Βάρας τοῦτο πεποίηται. ἔκτοσθεν δὲ αὐτοῦ ὡς ἀπωτάτω ἐν τῇ ὑπωρείᾳ μετὰ τὸ πρανὲς κρήνη ἦν,[3] ἥνπερ ἐδόκει ἀξύμφορον εἶναι τῷ τειχίσματι τοῦ φρουρίου περιβαλεῖν, ὡς μή τις αὐτοῦ μοῖρα ἐν ὑπτίῳ κειμένη εὐάλωτος εἴη.
24 ἐπενόει δὲ τάδε· τὰ ἐντὸς τοῦ περιβόλου διορύσσειν ἐκέλευεν ἕως ἐς τὸ ὁμαλὲς μάλιστα ἵκωνται. ὅπερ ἐπεὶ ὑπετελέσθη κατὰ τὴν τοῦ βασιλέως
B 224 ἐπίταξιν, ἐπιρρέον ἐνταῦθα τὸ ὕδωρ ἐκ τῆς πηγῆς παρὰ δόξαν ἐφάνη. οὕτω τε [4] καὶ τὸ φρούριον δεδημιούργηται ξὺν τῷ ἀσφαλεῖ καὶ ὕδατος πέρι ἐν ἐπιτηδείῳ φαίνεται κείμενον.

ε΄. Οὕτω δὲ καὶ Θεοδοσιουπόλεως, τῆς παρὰ

[1] ἅπαντα γὰρ V, πάντα μὲν οὖν A.
[2] ὑποκείμενα V, ἀποκείμενα A.
[3] κρήνη ἦν added by Haury, πηγὴ ἦν Maltretus.

forts about the city of Amida which had been enclosed by mud walls and were entirely at the mercy of the enemy, and he so transformed them all that they were perfectly secure. Among these are Apadnas and the little town of Virthon; for it is not easy to mention all separately by name. But, to speak briefly, he has made impregnable at the present time all the places which previously lay exposed to assailants. And as a result of this, Mesopotamia is manifestly inaccessible to the Persian nation.

But I must not pass by in silence the device which he hit upon in the fort Baras which I have just mentioned.[1] It so happened that inside the fort there was no water at all, for this Baras was built on the steep slope of a very high mountain. Outside the fort, however, at a very great distance, there was a spring at the foot of the mountain, beyond the slope; but it had seemed inadvisable to enclose this within the fortifications of the stronghold, so that no part of the defences might lie on level ground and so be easy to capture. Therefore he devised the following plan. He bade them dig within the fortifications until they came approximately to the level of the plain. And when this work was completed according to the Emperor's instructions, water was found there, contrary to all expectation, running in from the spring. Thus not only is the fortress placed in a position of safety, but it proves to be properly situated as regards water also.

v. In the same way he restored the circuit-wall of

[1] Not previously mentioned; but Haury suggests that it is identical with the Sauras mentioned above in section 14.

[4] τε V, δὴ A, δὲ Dindorf.

ποταμὸν Ἀβόρραν γῆς τῆς Ῥωμαίων προβεβλημένης, τὸν περίβολον, ὅνπερ ὁ χρόνος κατεργάσασθαι μάλιστα ἴσχυσε, καὶ ἀπ' αὐτοῦ τοῖς τῇδε ἀνθρώποις οὐχ ὑπὲρ τῆς ἀσφαλείας ἐδίδου θαρρεῖν, ἀλλὰ διηνεκὲς ἅπαντας ἐξέπλησσε, δεδισσόμενος ὅτι δὴ οὐκ εἰς μακρὰν αὐτοῖς ἐμπεσεῖται, ἀνοικοδομησάμενος ἐκ τοῦ ἐπὶ πλεῖστον ὁ βασιλεὺς οὗτος διακωλύειν τάς γε κατὰ Μεσοποταμίαν Περσῶν ἐσβολὰς ἱκανῶς ἔσχεν.

2 Οἷα δὲ καὶ ἐν Κωνσταντίνῃ ἐπιδέδεικται εἰπεῖν ἄξιον. ἦν μὲν τὰ πρότερα ὁ Κωνσταντίνης περίβολος τό τε ὕψος κλίμακι ἁλωτὸς τήν τε ἄλλην κατασκευὴν εὐέφοδος ἄγαν, ὥσπερ τι πάρεργον γεγενημένος τοῖς πάλαι ἀνθρώποις. 3 τοσούτῳ γὰρ διειστήκεσαν οἱ πύργοι ἀλλήλων ὥστε εἰ προσβαλοῦντές τινες ἐς τὴν μεταξὺ χώραν προσίοιεν, οὐκ εἶχον οἱ κατὰ τοὺς πύργους ἑστῶτες καθ' ὅτι ἂν αὐτοὺς ἀμυνόμενοι ἀποκρούοιντο. ἀλλὰ μὴν καὶ χρόνου μήκει πεπονηκὼς ἐκ τοῦ ἐπὶ πλεῖστον τοῦ καταπεπτωκέναι οὐ 4 μακράν που ἐγένετο. πρὸς δὲ καὶ τοιοῦτο τῇ πόλει προτείχισμα ἦν οἷον ἐπιτείχισμα κατ' αὐτῆς γεγονέναι δοκεῖν. οὐ πλέον γὰρ αὐτοῦ ἢ ἐς πόδας τρεῖς ἐγεγόνει τὸ πάχος, καὶ αὐτὸ μέντοι πηλῷ σύνθετον, τὰ μὲν κάτω ἐς ὀλίγον ἐκ λίθου μυλίτου ἀνεστηκός, τὰ δὲ ὕπερθεν ἐκ τοῦ λευκολίθου καλουμένου, σφαλεροῦ τε ὄντος καὶ μαλακοῦ λίαν. ὥστε δὴ ὅλον ἦν τοῖς ἐπιοῦσιν 5 εὐάλωτον. βασιλεὺς δὲ Ἰουστινιανὸς τὰ μὲν

---

[1] Originally called Resaina; modern Ras el Ain.

[2] Modern Khabour.

Theodosiopolis,[1] which stands on the River Aborrhas [2] as a bulwark of the Roman Empire; for time had succeeded most completely in breaking it down, so that it afforded no assurance of safety to the people there, but rather kept them all in a constant state of terror for fear that it would fall upon them in the not distant future. But this Emperor rebuilt the greater part of the wall and thus succeeded effectually in checking the inroads of the Persians at least on the Mesopotamian border.

The work that he carried out in Constantina is also worthy of mention. Formerly the circuit-wall of this city was of such a height that it could be scaled with a ladder, and its whole method of construction made it easy to attack, built as it was by men of former times in a casual sort of way. Indeed the towers were so widely separated that if any attackers advanced to make an assault upon the space between them, the defenders posted on the towers had no means of driving them back. Moreover the wall had suffered from the passage of time, and for the most part had come to be not very far from a state of collapse. Furthermore, the outworks (*proteichisma*) protecting the city were of such a sort that they looked like a wall built for the purpose of attacking it (*epiteichisma*). In fact their thickness had not been made more than three feet, and even that was held together with mud, the lower courses for a short space being built of hard stone suitable for making mill-stones (*lithos mylites*), but the upper portion consisting of so-called "white stone" (*leukolithos*), which is untrustworthy and very soft. So the whole place was easy for assailants to capture. But the Emperor Justinian rebuilt with new masonry

πεπονηκότα τοῦ περιβόλου νέᾳ τινὶ ἀνεσώσατο οἰκοδομίᾳ, καὶ διαφερόντως τὰ πρὸς ἥλιον δύοντα
6 τετραμμένα καὶ βορρᾶν ἄνεμον. τοῦ δὲ δὴ ἐρύματος πανταχῇ μεταξὺ πύργοιν δυοῖν ἄλλον ἐντέθεικε, καὶ ἀπ᾽ αὐτοῦ πύργοι ἅπαντες ὡς ἀγχοτάτω ἀλλήλοις ὄντες τοῦ περιβόλου προ-
7 βέβληνται. ὅλῳ δὲ τῷ τείχει καὶ πᾶσι πύργοις μέγα τι χρῆμα ὕψους ἐνθέμενος ἄμαχον τοῖς πολεμίοις τὸ τῆς πόλεως ὀχύρωμα κατεστήσατο.
8 ἀλλὰ καὶ ἀνόδους τοῖς πύργοις κεκαλυμμένας πεποιημένος, τριωρόφους τε αὐτοὺς λίθων ἐπιβολαῖς τεκτηνάμενος κυρτώμασι γεγονυίαις[1] θόλων, πυργοκάστελλον αὐτῶν ἕκαστον εἶναί τε[2] καὶ
9 καλεῖσθαι πεποίηκε. καστέλλους γὰρ τὰ φρούρια τῇ Λατίνων καλοῦσι φωνῇ. ἀλλὰ καὶ ἀμφὶ τοῖς ὕδασιν ἡ Κωνσταντίνα τὰ ἀνήκεστα ἔπασχε
10 πρότερον. τὰ μὲν γὰρ ἐκτός, ὅσον ἐκ σημείου ἑνός, πηγαί τέ εἰσι ποτίμων ὑδάτων καὶ ἄλσος ἐνθένδε φύεται ἐπιεικῶς μέγα, οὐρανομήκεσι κατάφυτον δένδροις· τὰ μέντοι ἐντός, ἵνα δὴ οὐκ ἐφ᾽ ὁμαλοῦ, ἀλλ᾽ ἐν τῷ ἀνάντει τὰς ἀγυιὰς συμβαίνει εἶναι, ἄνυδρός τε ἦν ἡ πόλις ἐκ παλαιοῦ καὶ δίψῃ τε καὶ ἀμηχανίᾳ πολλῇ οἱ τῇδε ᾠκημένοι
11 ἐς ἀεὶ εἴχοντο. βασιλεὺς δὲ Ἰουστινιανὸς ὀχετῷ τὸ ῥεῖθρον μεταβιβάσας τοῦ τείχους ἐντός, κρήναις τε τὴν πόλιν ἀειρρύτοις διακοσμήσας, οἰκιστὴς ἂν αὐτῆς[3] δικαίως καλοῖτο. τὰ μὲν οὖν ἐς τάσδε τὰς πόλεις ταύτῃ Ἰουστινιανῷ βασιλεῖ εἴργασται.

P 39 ϛʹ. Ἦν δὲ Ῥωμαίων φρούριον παρὰ ποταμὸν Εὐφράτην ἐν τοῖς Μεσοποταμίας ἐσχάτοις, ἵνα

[1] γεγονυίαις V, γεγονόσι A. [2] τε added by Maltretus.

those portions of the circuit-wall which had suffered, particularly the parts which faced the west and the north. And in all parts of the defences he inserted a new tower between each pair of towers, and consequently all the towers stood out from the circuit-wall very close to one another. Also he added greatly to the height of the whole wall and of all the towers, and thus made the defences of the city impregnable to the enemy. And he also built covered approaches (*anodoi*) to the towers, and made them three-storied (*triôrophoi*) by adding courses of stones curved in the form of vaults (*tholoi*); thus he made each one of them a *pyrgo-castellum*,[1] as it was called and as it actually was. For they call forts *castella* in the Latin tongue. Furthermore, Constantina in former times used to suffer terribly for want of water. Outside the city, about a mile away, there are springs of sweet water and then a very large grove planted with trees which reach to the sky; but within the walls, where the streets happen to be sloping, and not level, the city had been without water from early times, and the inhabitants always suffered from thirst and from the great difficulty of obtaining water. But the Emperor Justinian brought the stream within the wall by means of an aqueduct, and adorned the city with ever-flowing fountains, so that he might justly be called its founder. All this, then, is what was done by the Emperor Justinian for these cities.

vi. And there was a Roman fortress beside the Euphrates River on the frontier of Mesopotamia

[1] A hybrid Greek and Latin expression: "tower-fortress."

[3] αὐτῆς V, αὐτῶν A.

δὴ Ἀβόρρας ποταμὸς τῷ Εὐφράτῃ ἀναμιγνύμενος
2 τὴν ἐκβολὴν ἐνταῦθα ποιεῖται. τοῦτο Κιρκήσιον
B 226 μὲν ὀνομάζεται, βασιλεὺς δὲ αὐτὸ Διοκλητιανὸς
3 ἐν τοῖς ἄνω χρόνοις ἐδείματο. Ἰουστινιανὸς δὲ
τανῦν βασιλεὺς χρόνου τε μήκει εὑρὼν συντριβὲς
γεγονός, ἀπημελημένον δὲ καὶ ἄλλως ἀφύλακτον
ὄν, ἐς ὀχύρωμα βεβαιότατον μετεστήσατο, πόλιν
τε διεπράξατο μεγέθει καὶ κάλλει περιφανῆ εἶναι.
4 Διοκλητιανὸς μὲν γὰρ τηνικάδε τὸ φρούριον
πεποίηται τοῦτο οὐχ ὅλον ἐν κύκλῳ τείχει
περιβαλών, ἀλλὰ μέχρι μὲν ἐς ποταμὸν Εὐφράτην
ἐπεξαγαγὼν τὴν τοῦ περιβόλου οἰκοδομίαν καὶ
πύργον ἑκατέρωθι ἀπεργασάμενος ἔσχατον, ἀπολιπὼν
δὲ τὴν ἐνθένδε τοῦ χωρίου πλευρὰν ἀτείχιστον
ὅλως, ἀποχρῆναι, οἶμαι, τὸ τοῦ ποταμοῦ
ὕδωρ ἐς τὸ τοῦ φρουρίου ὀχύρωμα τῆδε ἡγούμενος.
5 προϊόντος δὲ χρόνου τὸν ἔσχατον πύργον, ὃς δὴ
ἐτέτραπτο πρὸς ἄνεμον νότον, τὸ τοῦ ποταμοῦ
ῥόθιον παραξύον ἐνδελεχέστατα κατέσεισεν [1] ὅλον,
ἔνδηλός τε ἦν ὡς, εἰ μὴ βοηθοίη τις ὅ τι τάχιστα,
6 καταπεσεῖται αὐτίκα δὴ μάλα. ἐφάνη τοίνυν
Ἰουστινιανὸς βασιλεὺς τοῦτο πρὸς τοῦ θεοῦ
κεκομισμένος ἀξίωμα, πάσης ἐπιμελεῖσθαι καὶ
ὡς ἔνι μάλιστα μεταποιεῖσθαι τῆς Ῥωμαίων
7 ἀρχῆς· ὃς δὴ οὐ μόνον τὸν πεπονθότα πύργον
ἐσώσατο, ἀνοικοδομησάμενος αὐτὸν μυλίῳ λίθῳ
καὶ φύσει σκληρῷ, ἀλλὰ καὶ τοῦ φρουρίου τὴν
ἀτείχιστον πλευρὰν ξύμπασαν ὀχυρωτάτῳ περιβέβληκε
τείχει, διπλασιάσας αὐτῇ πρὸς τῷ ποταμῷ
8 τὴν ἐκ τοῦ περιβόλου ἀσφάλειαν. πρὸς ἐπὶ
τούτοις δὲ καὶ προτείχισμα ἐχυρώτατον προσ-

[1] κατέσεισεν V, κατέσειεν A.

at the point where the Aborrhas River mingles with the Euphrates, into which it empties. This is called Circesium,[1] and was built by the Emperor Diocletian in ancient times. And our present Emperor Justinian, finding it dilapidated through the passage of time and neglected besides and in general unguarded, transformed it into a very strong fortress and brought it about that it became a city conspicuous for its size and beauty. For Diocletian, when he constructed this fortress, did not surround it with a wall on all sides, but carried out the construction of the circuit-wall only as far as the River Euphrates, and he finished off the work at each of the two ends with a terminal tower, but after that he left that side of the site wholly unwalled, believing, I suppose, that the water of the river would serve as a protection for the fort on that side. However, as time went on, the terminal tower which faced toward the south was undermined by the ceaseless wash of the water, and entirely wrecked, and it became evident that, unless someone brought help with the greatest speed, it would collapse immediately. Then appeared the Emperor Justinian, entrusted by God with this commission, to watch over the whole Roman Empire and, so far as was possible, to remake it. Indeed he not only preserved the damaged tower by rebuilding it with hard stone, such as would be suitable for making mill-stones, but he also enclosed the entire unwalled side of the fortress with a wall of the greatest strength, thus doubling its stability by adding the protection given by the circuit-wall to that afforded by the river. In addition to this, he added very strong outworks to the defences

[1] Marked the eastern limit of the Roman Empire.

ἐποίησεν αὐτὸς τῇ πόλει, καὶ διαφερόντως οὗ δὴ τοῖν ποταμοῖν ἡ ἐς ἀλλήλους ἐπιμιξία τρίγωνον ἀποτελεῖ σχῆμα, ταύτῃ τε τὰς ἐνθένδε τῶν 9 πολεμίων ἐπιβουλὰς ἀπεκρούσατο. καὶ στρατιω- B 227 τικῶν δὲ καταλόγων ἄρχοντα τῇδε καταστησάμενος, ὃν δοῦκα καλοῦσι, διηνεκὲς ἐνταῦθα καθιζησόμενον, ἀποχρῶν φυλακτήριον πεποίηκεν 10 εἶναι τῇ τῆς πολιτείας ἀρχῇ. καὶ τὸ βαλανεῖον δέ, ὅπερ δημοσίᾳ τὴν χρείαν τοῖς τῇδε ᾠκημένοις παρέχεται, ἀνόνητον ὅλως τῇ τοῦ ποταμοῦ ἐπιρροῇ γεγενημένον ἐνεργεῖν τε τὰ ξυνειθισμένα οὐκέτι ἔχον, ἐς τὸν νῦν ὄντα μετέθηκε κόσμον. 11 ὅσα μὲν γὰρ αὐτοῦ ἀπεκρέματο πρότερον ἐπὶ στερρᾶς τῆς οἰκοδομίας ἑστῶτα κατὰ τὸ τῶν λουτρῶν [1] τῇ χρείᾳ συνοῖσον (ὧν δὴ ἔνερθε τὸ P 40 πῦρ καίεται, χυτρόποδάς [2] τε καλεῖν αὐτὰ νενομίκασι), ταῦτα δὴ ἅπαντα τῇ τοῦ ὕδατος ἐπιρροῇ ἀποκείμενα πρόσθεν εὑρών, καὶ ἀπ' αὐτοῦ τὴν χρείαν τῷ βαλανείῳ διεφθαρμένην, λίθων μὲν αὐτὸς ἐμπεδώσας ἐπιβολαῖς ὅσα πρότερον ἀπεκρέματο,[3] ᾗπέρ μοι εἴρηται, ἑτέραν καθύπερθεν ἀποκρεμάσας οἰκοδομίαν, ἵνα δὴ ἀπρόσοδα τῷ ποταμῷ ἐστιν, ἀνεσώσατο τὴν ἐνθένδε εὐπάθειαν τοῖς τῇδε φρουροῖς. τὰ μὲν δὴ τοῦ Κιρκησίου ἐς τόνδε τὸν τρόπον δεδημιούργηται τῷ βασιλεῖ τούτῳ.

12 Μετὰ δὲ τὸ Κιρκήσιον φρούριόν ἐστι παλαιόν, Ἀννούκας ὄνομα, οὗπερ ἐρείπιον τὸ τεῖχος εὑρὼν οὕτω δὴ μεγαλοπρεπῶς ἀνῳκοδομήσατο Ἰουστινιανὸς βασιλεὺς ὡς μηδὲ τῶν τινος ἐπι-

[1] τῶν λουτρῶν Braun: τῶ λουτρῶ V.
[2] χυτρόποδάς Maltretus: κυθρόποδας V.

of the city, and especially where the junction of the two rivers forms a triangle he thus made any attack by the enemy impossible. And he stationed here a commander of select troops, one whom they call a Duke or "leader," who was to be stationed there permanently, and he thus constituted the place an adequate bulwark of the government of the State. The bath, too, which serves the common use of all the people living in the city, had become entirely useless because of the incursion of the river, with the result that it was no longer capable of providing its usual service; and so he transformed it to its present state of splendour. For all the receptacles which previously were poised on solid masonry and were destined to serve the purposes of the bath (it is beneath these that the fire is kept burning, and they are wont to call them cauldrons [1])—all these, he found, had already been exposed to the invasion of the water, and consequently the bath had been rendered useless; so he strengthened with courses of stone all that had formerly been poised there, as I have explained, and built another structure above it, where the river cannot reach it, and thus he restored to the troops there the enjoyment which they gained from the bath. In such a way was the work at Circesium carried out by this Emperor.

Beyond Circesium is an ancient fort, Annoucas [2] by name, whose wall, which he found a ruin, the Emperor Justinian rebuilt in such magnificent style

[1] Literally "pots with legs." Here the "legs" were apparently the pillars upon which the pots were poised.
[2] Modern Khanukah.

---

[3] ἀπεκρέματο Maltretus: ἀποκρέμαται V.

φανεστάτων πόλεων ὀχυρώματος πέρι τὰ δευτερεῖα
13 τὸ λοιπὸν φέρεσθαι. τρόπῳ δὲ τῷ αὐτῷ καὶ τὰ
φρούρια, ὅσα δὴ ἀμφὶ πόλιν Θεοδοσιούπολιν κεῖται, τὰ μὲν ἀτείχιστα τὸ πρότερον ὄντα, τὰ δὲ
πηλῷ τε καὶ τῇ ἐνθένδε γελωτοποιίᾳ τετειχισμένα
αἱμασιᾶς τρόπον, φοβερά τε τανῦν καὶ τὸ παράπαν
14 ἀπρόσβατα τοῖς ἐπιοῦσιν εἰργάσατο· τό τε
Μαγδαλαθὼν σὺν ἑτέροιν δυοῖν ἅπερ αὐτοῦ
ἑκατέρωθεν τυγχάνει ὄντα, καὶ Θαννούριος δύο,
B 228 μικρόν τε καὶ μέγα, καὶ Βιμισδεὼν καὶ Θήμερες,
ἔτι δὲ Βιδάμας καὶ Δαυσαρὼν καὶ Θιόλλα,
Φιχάς τε καὶ Ζαμαρθὰς καὶ τὰ λοιπά, ὡς εἰπεῖν,
15 ἅπαντα. ἦν δέ τις χῶρος παρὰ Θαννούριος τὸ
μέγα, ᾧ δὴ ἐπιχωριάζειν Σαρακηνοῖς τοῖς πολεμίοις διαβαίνουσι ποταμὸν Ἀβόρραν πολλὴ ἐξουσία
ἐγίνετο, ἔνθεν δὲ ὁρμωμένοις διασκεδάννυσθαι
μὲν ἀνά τε τὴν ὕλην δασεῖάν τε καὶ ἀμφιλαφῆ
οὖσαν καὶ τὸ ὄρος ὃ ταύτῃ ἀνέχει, καταθεῖν τε[1]
ἀδεέστερον τοὺς ᾠκημένους ἀμφὶ τὰ ἐκείνῃ χω-
16 ρία Ῥωμαίους. ἀλλὰ νῦν πύργον κομιδῇ μέγαν
ἐκ λίθου σκληροῦ Ἰουστινιανὸς βασιλεὺς ἐν τῷ
χώρῳ τούτῳ δειμάμενος ἐνταῦθά τε φρουρὰν
ἀξιολογωτάτην καταστησάμενος ἀναστέλλειν τὰς
τῶν πολεμίων ἐπιδρομὰς παντελῶς ἴσχυσε, τοῦτον
ἐπιτεχνησάμενος κατ᾽ αὐτῶν πρόβολον.

ζʹ. Τὰ μὲν ἐπὶ Μεσοποταμίας τῇδε Ἰουστινιανῷ βασιλεῖ εἴργασται. ἀναγκαῖον δέ μοι
ἐνταῦθα τοῦ λόγου Ἐδέσσης[1] τε καὶ Καρρῶν και
Καλλινίκου καὶ τῶν ἄλλων πολιχνῶν ἁπασῶν

[1] τε V, δὲ A.

[1] Modern Urfa.

that thereafter it took second place in point of strength to no single one of the most notable cities. In the same way those forts which lie about the city of Theodosiopolis, some of which had previously been without walls, while some were walled with mud and the ridiculous construction that goes with mud-work, like a wall made of loose stones, he made truly formidable, as they now are, and altogether unapproachable for their assailants; these include Magdalathôn with two others which chance to be on either side of it, and two named Thannourios, one large and one small, and Vimisdeôn, and Themeres, as well as Vidamas, Dausarôn, Thiolla, Phichas and Zamarthas, and, one may say, all the rest. And there was a certain spot near the larger Thannourios at which the hostile Saracens, after crossing the Aborrhas River, had complete freedom to resort, and making that their headquarters they would scatter through the thick leafy forest and over the mountain which rises there, and then they would descend with impunity upon the Romans who lived in the places round about. But now the Emperor Justinian has built a very large tower of hard stone at this point, in which he has established a very considerable garrison, and thus has succeeded completely in checking the inroads of the enemy by devising this bulwark against them.

vii. Such were the works of the Emperor Justinian in Mesopotamia. And it is necessary for me at this point in my narrative to mention Edessa [1] and Carrhae [2] and Callinicum [3] and all the other towns which

[2] Modern Harran, a few miles south of Edessa near the ruins of Rakkah.

[3] Originally named Nicephorium.

ἐπιμνησθῆναι, ὥσπερ ἐκείνῃ ξυμβαίνει εἶναι, ἐπεὶ
2 καὶ αὗται τοῖν ποταμοῖν μεταξὺ κεῖνται. τὴν
Ἔδεσσαν ποταμὸς παραρρεῖ τὸ ῥεῦμα βραχύς,
Σκιρτὸς ὄνομα, ὃς δὴ ἐκ χωρίων πολλῶν ξυνάγων
3 τὸ ῥεῖθρον ἐπὶ τὴν πόλιν φέρεται μέσην. ἐνθένδε
P 41 τε ἐξιὼν ἐπίπροσθεν ἵεται, ἐπειδὰν αὐτάρκη
παρέχηται τῇ πόλει τὴν χρείαν τῶν τε εἰσόδων
αὐτοῦ καὶ ἐκβολῶν δι' ὀχεταγωγίας κατὰ τὸ
4 τεῖχος πεποιημένων τοῖς πάλαι ἀνθρώποις. οὗτός
ποτε ὁ ποταμός, ὄμβρων οἱ ἐπιγενομένων πολλῶν,
ὑπερπεφυκώς τε ὕψου ἀνεῖχε καὶ ὡς καταλύσων
5 τὴν πόλιν ἐπῄει. τοῦ τοίνυν προτειχίσματος
καὶ τοῦ περιβόλου καθελὼν ἐς τὸ ἔδαφος πολλήν
B 229 τινα μοῖραν τὴν πόλιν περιεβάλετο σχεδόν τι
ὅλην, ἔργα τε ἀνήκεστα τῇδε εἰργάσατο. τῶν τε
γὰρ οἰκοδομημάτων τὰ κάλλιστα ἐξίτηλα ἐξαπιναίως πεποίηται καὶ τῶν ἀνθρώπων τὸ τριτημόριον
6 διεχρήσατο. βασιλεὺς δὲ Ἰουστινιανὸς μὴ ὅτι
ἀνεσώσατο τῇ πόλει τὰ καθῃρημένα εὐθὺς ἅπαντα,
ἐν οἷς ἥ τε τῶν Χριστιανῶν ἐκκλησία καὶ ὁ
καλούμενος Ἀντίφορος ἦν, ἀλλὰ καὶ ὅπως μή τι
αὐτῇ καὶ αὖθις τοιοῦτο ξυμβαίη διεπράξατο
7 σπουδῇ τῇ πάσῃ. πορείαν γὰρ ἑτέραν πρὸ τοῦ
περιβόλου τῷ ποταμῷ νεοχμοῦν ἴσχυσε, τοιᾷδε
8 αὐτὸν περιελθὼν τέχνῃ. τὰ μὲν ἐν δεξιᾷ τοῦ
ποταμοῦ ὕπτιά τε καὶ χθαμαλὰ πρότερον ἦν, τὰ
δὲ δὴ ἐν ἀριστερᾷ ὄρος ἀπότομον, οὐκ ἐπιχωροῦν
αὐτῷ ἐπικλίνειν που ἢ ἐκτρέπεσθαι τῆς ξυνειθισ-

[1] The flood is mentioned also in the *Secret History*, xviii. 38, where Procopius seems to allude to his intention of writing the *Buildings*: "Thus the Scirtus River, by overflowing Edessa, became the author of countless calamities to the

chance to lie in that region, for these too are situated between the two rivers. The city of Edessa is situated on a river of small volume, Scirtus by name, which collects its water from a wide area and flows into the middle of the city. And after leaving the city, it flows on further, after it has furnished the city with an abundant supply, effecting its entrance and its exit through channels in the wall constructed by men of former times. On one occasion this river, swollen by heavy rains, rose to an altogether extraordinary height and came upon the city as if bent upon destroying it.[1] Consequently it levelled to the ground a large part of the outworks and of the circuit-wall and covered practically the whole city, doing irreparable damage. For in a moment it wiped out completely the finest of the buildings and caused the death of one third of the population. But the Emperor Justinian immediately not only restored all the ruined parts of the city, including the church of the Christians and the structure called Antiphorus,[2] but also made effective provision that such a calamity should not occur again. For he succeeded in making a new channel for the river before the circuit-wall, circumventing it by the following device. The land on the right of the river was formerly both flat and low, while on the left stood a steep hill, which did not permit the stream to turn aside at all or deviate from

people of that region, as will be written by me in a following Book."

[2] Mentioned also in the *Chronicle* of Joshua the Stylite, Chap. xxvii. ed. Wright. An Antiphorus at Antioch is mentioned by Malalas, p. 397 Bonn ed., and by Evagrius, *Hist. Eccl.*, III. 28. Du Cange, *s.v.*, points out that a structure might be so called either because it stood "opposite a forum" or served "instead of a forum."

μένης ὁδοῦ, ἀλλ' ἐπὶ τὴν πόλιν αὐτὴν διωθούμενον ἀνάγκῃ τῇ πάσῃ. οὐ γὰρ ἦν τι αὐτὸν ἐπὶ δεξιᾷ ξυμποδίζον, ἡνίκα ἂν τῆς πόλεως εὐθὺ

9 φέροιτο. τοῦτο οὖν τὸ ὄρος ἀποτεμὼν ὅλον κοῖλα μὲν τοῦ ποταμοῦ τὰ ἐν ἀριστερᾷ καὶ γλαφυρώτερα τῆς αὐτοῦ πορείας κατεσκεύαστο, ἐν δεξιᾷ δὲ τοῖχον ὑπερμεγέθη ἐκ λίθων ἁμαξιαίων συνέστησεν, ὥστε, εἰ μὲν κατὰ τὰ εἰωθότα ὁ ποταμὸς μέτριος φέρηται, μήποτε ἀποστεροῖτο τῆς ἐνθένδε ὠφελείας ἡ πόλις, ἐπειδὰν δὲ τύχῃ τινὶ ἐς ὕψος ἀρθεὶς ὑπερβλύζοι, μετρία μέν τις αὐτοῦ ἐκροὴ ἐπὶ τὴν πόλιν κατὰ τὰ ξυνειθισμένα χωροίη, τοῦ δὲ ῥοθίου τὸ ἐπιγινόμενον ἐς τὴν Ἰουστινιανοῦ ἐπιτέχνησιν ἀναγκαστὸν ἴοι, ἐς τοῦ ἱπποδρόμου τὰ ὄπισθεν οὐ μακράν που ὄντος, τέχνῃ τε ἀνθρωπείᾳ καὶ γνώμῃ προμηθεῖ παρὰ δόξαν μεμηχανημένον

10 ἀλλὰ καὶ τῷ ποταμῷ τῆς πόλεως γινομένῳ ἐντὸς ὀρθήν τινα πορείας ἀνάγκην ἀπεργασάμενος, ὕπερθέν τε οἰκοδομίαν ἑκατέρωθι ἐπικρεμάσας, ὡς

B 230 μὴ ἐκτρέπεσθαι τῆς ὁδοῦ δύναιτο, καὶ τὴν χρείαν τῇ πόλει ἐσώσατο καὶ δέους αὐτὴν τοῦ ἐνθένδε

11 ἀπήλλαξεν. ἐτύγχανε δὲ[1] τὸ Ἐδέσσης τεῖχος καὶ προτείχισμα οὐδέν τι ἧσσον διὰ χρόνου μῆκος ἐν τοῖς ἐρειπίοις ταττόμενον ἐκ τοῦ ἐπὶ

12 πλεῖστον. διὸ δὴ ἄμφω ἀνοικοδομησάμενος βασιλεύς, νέα τε αὐτὰ κατεστήσατο καὶ πολλῷ

13 ἐχυρώτερα ἢ πρότερον ἦν. μοῖρα δέ τις τοῦ Ἐδέσσης περιβόλου φρούριον κέκτηται, ἧς δὴ ἔκτοσθέν τις ἐπανειστήκει λόφος ὡς πλησιαίτατα

14 ὑποκειμένῃ ἐπικύπτων ἐνταῦθα τῇ πόλει· ὅνπερ ἐκ παλαιοῦ καταλαβόντες ἐπιτείχισμά τι οἱ

[1] δὲ V, γὰρ A.

its customary course, but drove it against the city by sheer compulsion; for on the right there was nothing to check it when it rushed straight towards the city. So he cut down this whole hill, and while making the land on the left of the river hollow and deeper than its own bed, on the right he set up a huge wall of stones, each a load for a waggon, so that as long as the river flowed with its usual temperate stream, the city would never be deprived of its benefit, but whenever by any chance it rose to a great height and overflowed, a moderate portion of it would flow as usual into the city, while the excess of the stream would pass under constraint into the channel devised by Justinian and be led behind the hippodrome which is not far away, thus being vanquished, contrary to all expectation, by human skill and foresight. In addition to this, he also compelled the river to follow a practically straight course after it gets inside the city, and above it he raised a structure resting on either bank so that it could not be diverted from its course, and he thus not only preserved the benefit which the city gained from the river, but also freed the city from the fear of it. Moreover, it happened that the main wall of Edessa and its outworks had suffered from the passage of time no less than they had from the flood and for the most part were fit only to be called ruins. Therefore the Emperor rebuilt both of them and made them new and much stronger than they had been formerly. And a certain section of the circuit-wall of Edessa contains a fort outside of which rose a hill, which stood very close by and commanded the city spread out beneath it. The inhabitants of early times, perceiving that this hill

ἐπιχώριοι ἐντὸς τοῦ περιβόλου πεποίηνται, ὡς
15 μὴ ἐπίμαχον ποιοίη τὴν πόλιν. ἀλλὰ ταύτῃ
ἐπιμαχωτέραν αὐτὴν παρὰ πολὺ ἀπειργάσαντο·
διατείχισμα γὰρ ὡς βραχύτατον ἐπὶ τῷ ἀνειμένῳ[1]
τῆς γῆς κείμενον καὶ παιδαρίοις τειχομαχίαν
P 42 16 ἐμμελετῶσιν ἁλώσιμον ἦν. οὗ δὴ ἐνθένδε καθῃρη-
μένου ἕτερον ἐν τῇ τοῦ ὄρους ὑπερβολῇ τεῖχος
ἀνέστη, βασιλέως Ἰουστινιανοῦ διαπόνημα, δέος
μὲν ἐξ ἐπιθέσεως καθύπερθε γενησομένης οὐδαμῆ
ἔχον, συγκαταβαῖνον δὲ τῇ ὑπωρείᾳ μέχρι ἐς τὸ
πρανὲς ἑκατέρωθεν καὶ τῷ περιβόλῳ ἐναρμοζό-
μενον.

17 Ἀλλὰ μὴν καὶ Καρρῶν καὶ Καλλινίκου πόλεως
τά τε τείχη καὶ τὰ προτειχίσματα καθελών, ἅπερ
ὁ πολὺς αἰὼν μεταξὺ ἐπιρρεύσας διέφθειρε,
ταῦτά τε ἀκραιφνῆ ἀπεργασάμενος, ἀμαχώτατα
18 κατεστήσατο. ἔτι μέντοι καὶ φρούριον ὃ ἐν
Βάτναις ἦν, ἀτείχιστόν τε καὶ ἀπημελημένον τὰ
πρότερα ὄν, τείχεσιν ἐχυρωτάτοις περιβαλὼν ἐς
τὸν νῦν φαινόμενον μετήνεγκε κόσμον.

η΄. Ταῦτα μὲν οὖν τρόπῳ, ᾧπέρ μοι ἐρρήθη,
ἐπί τε Μεσοποταμίας καὶ Ὀσροηνῆς τῆς καλου-
B 231 2 μένης Ἰουστινιανῷ βασιλεῖ πεποίηται. ὅντινα δὲ
τρόπον Εὐφράτου ποταμοῦ τὰ ἐν δεξιᾷ ξυμβαίνει
εἶναι, ἐγὼ δηλώσω. τὰ μὲν ἄλλα Ῥωμαίων τε
3 καὶ Περσῶν ὅρια τῇδέ πῃ ἔχει· γειτονοῦσιν
ἑκατέρων ἀλλήλοις χωρία, ὁρμώμενοί τε ἀπὸ
τῶν οἰκείων ἀμφότεροι καὶ διαμάχονται καὶ
συμβάλλουσι τὰς συναλλαγάς, οἷά γε τὰ ἀνθρώ-

[1] ἀνειμένῳ Haury : ἀνεσταμένωι V, ἀνατεταμένῳ Hoeschel, comparing *infra* V. v. 3.

constituted a threat to the city-wall, had brought it inside the circuit-wall, so that it might not render the city vulnerable. But by this they caused the city to be actually much more vulnerable, for a very small cross-wall,[1] lying on the exposed ground, was an easy thing to capture even for children playing at storming a wall. So after this had been torn down, another wall was built on the crest of the hill, the work of the Emperor Justinian, which did not have to fear any attack to be made from a higher position, and this descended along the slope as far as the level ground at either end and was joined to the circuit-wall.

Furthermore, he also took down the walls and the outworks of Carrhae and of the city of Callinicum, which were falling into ruin because of their great age, and once more made them, as they now are, entire and completely invulnerable. He also surrounded with very strong walls the fortress at Batnae [2] which previously had been unwalled and neglected, and transformed it into the fine condition in which it is now seen.

viii. So these structures were erected by the Emperor Justinian in the manner which I have described in Mesopotamia and in Osroenê, as it is called. And I shall describe the fashion in which his work was carried out on the right of the Euphrates River. The other boundaries between the Romans and the Persians are in general of such a sort that the territories of the two peoples are adjacent to each other, and both peoples push out from their own territory and either fight with each other or compose

[1] *I.e.* the additional wall by which the hill was brought inside the fortifications.

[2] Modern Tell Butnan.

πεια, ὁπηνίκα τοῖς τε ἤθεσι καὶ ταῖς πολιτείαις
4 διάφοροι ὄντες χώραν τινὰ ὅμορον ἔχουσιν. ἐν
δέ γε τῇ πάλαι μὲν Κομμαγηνῇ χώρᾳ, τανῦν δὲ
καλουμένῃ Εὐφρατησίᾳ, οὐδαμῇ ἀλλήλων ἄγχιστα
ᾤκηνται. χώρα γὰρ ἔρημος καὶ ἄγονος ὅλως
διορίζει ἐπὶ μακρότατον τὰ Ῥωμαίων τε καὶ
Περσῶν ὅρια, περιμάχητόν τε οὐδὲν ἔχουσα.
5 ἑκάτεροι μέντοι ἐν ἐρήμῳ ἥπερ ἄγχιστα γῆς τῆς
πρὸς αὐτῶν οἰκουμένης τυγχάνει οὖσα φρούρια
6 παρέργως ᾠκοδομήσαντο ἐκ πλίνθου ὠμῆς· ἅπερ
ἐπιβουλῆς οὐδεμιᾶς παρὰ τῶν πέλας ἔτυχε
πώποτε, ἀλλ' ἀνεπιφθόνως ἀμφότεροι τῇδε ᾠκήσαντο,[1] ἐπεὶ οὐκ εἶχον οὐδὲν ὅτου ἂν καὶ οἱ
7 ἐναντίοι ἐφεῖντο. βασιλεὺς δὲ[2] Διοκλητιανὸς
τρία φρούρια τὸν τρόπον τοῦτον ἐν τῇ ἐρήμῳ
ταύτῃ ἐδείματο, ὧνπερ ἕν, Μαμβρὶ ὄνομα,
καταπεπονηκὸς τῷ μακρῷ χρόνῳ Ἰουστινιανὸς
ἀνενεώσατο βασιλεύς.

8 Τούτου δὲ τοῦ φρουρίου ἐκ σημείων μάλιστα
πέντε ἐς τὰ Ῥωμαίων ἤθη ἰόντι Ζηνοβία ποτὲ
Ὀδονάθου γυνὴ τῶν ἐκείνῃ Σαρακηνῶν ἄρχοντος
πόλιν ᾤκισέ[3] που ἐνταῦθά τινα ἐν τοῖς ἄνω
χρόνοις βραχεῖαν, καὶ τὸ ὄνομα ἀφῆκε τῇ πόλει.
9 Ζηνοβίαν γὰρ αὐτήν, ὡς τὸ εἰκός, ἐπωνόμασεν.
ἀλλὰ πολὺς ἄγαν μετὰ ταῦτα ἐπιρρεύσας ὁ χρόνος
P 43 ἐρείπιον αὐτῆς τὸν περίβολον κατεστήσατο, ἅτε
Ῥωμαίων αὐτῆς ἐπιμελεῖσθαι οὐδαμῇ ἀξιούντων,
ἔρημόν τε αὐτὴν τῶν ἐνοικούντων παντάπασι
B 232 10 διειργάσατο. παρῆν οὖν Πέρσαις κατ' ἐξουσίαν,

[1] ἅπερ . . . ᾠκήσαντο V, ἄγχιστα γῆς τῆς πρὸς αὐτῶν οἰκου μένης ἑκάτεροι A.
[2] δὲ V, οὖν A.

their differences, as people will whenever nations differing in customs and in government hold any land on a common boundary. However, in the territory anciently called Commagenê, but now known as Euphratesia, they do not live close to each other at all. For a land which is altogether bare and unproductive separates the Roman and the Persian territory for a great distance, and this contains nothing worth fighting for. Both of them, however, have built forts carelessly of unbaked brick in the desert which chances to lie nearest to the land which they inhabit; these forts never suffered attack from their neighbours, for both peoples lived there without enmity, since they possessed nothing which their adversaries might desire. The Emperor Diocletian had built three forts, such as I have described, in this desert, one of which, Mambri[1] by name, had fallen into decay in the long course of time and was restored by the Emperor Justinian.

At a distance of about five miles from this fort on the road to Roman territory, Zenobia, wife of Odonathus, who was ruler of the Saracens in that district, once founded a small city in earlier times and gave her name to it; for the name she gave it was Zenobia, as was fitting.[2] But the long period of time that had elapsed since those events had reduced its circuit-wall to a ruin, since the Romans were quite unwilling to take care of it, and thus it had come to be altogether destitute of inhabitants. So it was possible for the

[1] Possibly the modern Tabus, above Deir ez Zor.
[2] Modern Zelebiye.

---

[3] ᾤκισέ Hoeschel: ὤκησε.

ἡνίκα ἂν ᾖ βουλομένοις σφίσιν, ἐν μέσοις γενέσθαι Ῥωμαίοις, ἀνηκόοις ἔτι τῆς τῶν πολεμίων
11 ἐφόδου οὖσιν. ἀλλὰ τὴν Ζηνοβίαν Ἰουστινιανὸς βασιλεὺς ἀνοικοδομησάμενος σύμπασαν, οἰκητόρων τε κατακόρως ἐμπλησάμενος, ἄρχοντά τε στρατιωτικῶν καταλόγων καὶ διαρκὲς ἄγαν καταστησάμενος φυλακτήριον, πρόβολον μὲν εἶναι τῆς Ῥωμαίων ἀρχῆς, ἐπιτείχισμα δὲ διεπράξατο
12 Πέρσαις· ὅς γε οὐχ ὅσον τὸ πρότερον ἀπέδωκε σχῆμα, ἀλλὰ καὶ πλεῖστον ἐχυρωτέραν εἰργάσατο ἢ πρότερον ἦν. σκόπελοι γὰρ αὐτὴν περι-
13 βάλλουσιν ὡς ἀγχοτάτω· τοῖς τε πολεμίοις διὰ ταῦτα ἐξῆν τοὺς ἐκ τοῦ περιβόλου ἀμυνομένους
14 κατὰ κορυφὴν ἐνθένδε βάλλειν. ὅπερ ἀποκρούεσθαι διὰ σπουδῆς ἔχων οἰκοδομίαν τινὰ τῇ τοῦ περιβόλου ὑπερβολῇ ἑτέραν ἐνῆψε κατ' αὐτὸ μάλιστα τὸ τῶν σκοπέλων γειτόνημα, προκάλυμμα τοῖς ἐνθένδε μαχομένοις ἀεὶ ἐσομένην. πτερὰ τὴν οἰκοδομίαν καλοῦσι ταύτην, ἐπεὶ ὥσπερ
15 ἀποκρέμασθαι τοῦ τείχους δοκεῖ. ἅπαντα μὲν οὖν ὅσα βασιλεὺς ἐπὶ Ζηνοβίας εἰργάσατο φράσαι ἀμήχανον, ἐπεὶ ἐν χώρῳ ἐπὶ μακρότατον ἀγείτονι οὖσαν καὶ διὰ τοῦτο μὲν ἐν κινδύνοις ἀεὶ ἐσομένην, ἐπικουρίας δὲ τυχεῖν Ῥωμαίων πλησιοχώρων οὐκ ὄντων αὐτῇ οὐκ ἂν δυναμένην, βεβαιοτάτης, ὡς τὸ εἰκός, ἐπιμελείας μάλιστα πάντων ἠξίωσεν· ὀλίγα δέ μοι ἄττα τῶν τῇδε πεπραγμένων γεγράψεται.

16 Παραρρεῖ μὲν [1] τὴν Ζηνοβίαν Εὐφράτης ποταμὸς πρὸς ἀνίσχοντά που τὸν ἥλιον, ὡς ἀγχοτάτω τοῦ ἐκείνῃ περιβόλου ἰών, ὁρῶν δὲ παρ' αὐτὸν

[1] μὲν V, δὲ A.

Persians freely, whenever they wished, to get into the middle of Roman territory before the Romans had word of the hostile inroad. But the Emperor Justinian rebuilt Zenobia completely and filled it quite full of inhabitants, and he stationed there a commander of select troops and a thoroughly adequate garrison, and made it a bulwark of the Roman Empire and a frontier barrier against the Persians; indeed he did not simply restore its previous form, but he actually made it very much stronger than it was before. It is surrounded by cliffs which stand very close to the city, and for this reason it was possible for the enemy to shoot down from their summits upon the heads of the defenders of the circuit-wall. This he was anxious to prevent, and so he built a certain additional structure on the top of the circuit-wall, at precisely the place where the cliffs are nearest, designed to serve permanently as a shelter for the men fighting there. Such a structure they call "wings" (*ptera*), because it appears to droop, as it were, from the wall. However, it is impossible to describe all that the Emperor accomplished at Zenobia, since, seeing that it occupies a site far removed from any neighbour and on this account is sure to be always in danger, and that it is unable to secure succour because there are no Romans who live near at hand, the Emperor considered the city worthy, as well he might, of his unceasing attention above all other places. Nevertheless I shall describe a few of the things that were done there.

By the side of Zenobia flows the Euphrates River, passing to the east of it and coming very close to the circuit-wall on that side; but since high mountains

ὑψηλῶν ἀνεχόντων ἐν τούτῳ τῷ χώρῳ διασκεδάν-
B 233 νυσθαι οὐδαμῆ ἔχων, ἀλλ' ἀνάγκῃ τοῦ γειτονή-
ματος τῶν ἐνταῦθα ὀρῶν, ταῖς τε ὄχθαις
σκληραῖς οὔσαις πεπιεσμένος καὶ ἐν στενῷ μάλιστα ξυνάγων τὸ ῥεῦμα, ἐπειδὰν αὐτῷ ὄμβρων
ἐπιγενομένων ὑπερβλύζειν ξυνενεχθείη, ἐπιχυθεὶς
τῷ τείχει, εὐθὺς οὐκ ἀμφὶ τὰ θεμέλια μόνον, ἀλλ'
17 ἄχρι ἐς τὰς ἐπάλξεις ἐπέκλυζεν. οὗ δὴ τῷ
ῥοθίῳ καταβεβρεγμένου ξυνέβαινε τὰς ἐπιβολὰς
ξυγχεῖσθαι τῶν λίθων ἐπὶ σφαλερᾶς τε αὐτῶν
18 τὸ λοιπὸν τῆς ξυνθήκης ἑστάναι. ἀλλὰ [1] παμμεγέθη ἐκ λίθου μυλίου πρόβολον τῷ περιβόλῳ [2]
ἰσομήκη ἀπεργασάμενος ἐνταῦθα μὲν ἀεὶ ἐνοχλεῖν
τὸ τοῦ ποταμοῦ κλυδώνιον ὑπερβλύζοντος κατ-
ηνάγκασεν, ἐλεύθερον δὲ τὸ παράπαν τῆς ἐνθένδε
λώβης τὸ τεῖχος ἀφῆκεν, ἣν καὶ τὰ μάλιστα ὁ
ποταμὸς κυμαίνων [3] ἐς ὕψος ἐγείρηται μέγα.
19 ταύτης δὲ τῆς πόλεως τὸν περίβολον, ὃς δὴ
αὐτῆς ἐτέτραπτο πρὸς βορρᾶν ἄνεμον, πεπονηκότα
παντάπασι χρόνου μήκει εὑρών, παρέλυσε μὲν
σὺν τῷ προτειχίσματι ἐς τὸ ἔδαφος, ἀνῳκοδομήσατο δὲ οὐχ ᾗπερ τὸ πρότερον ἦν, ἐπεὶ ἐνταῦθα
P 44 αἱ τῆς πόλεως οἰκοδομίαι στενοχωρούμεναι μάλιστα
20 τοὺς ταύτῃ ᾠκημένους ἠνίων. ἀλλὰ τὴν προτέραν
ὑπερβὰς τῶν τε θεμελίων τοῦ περιβόλου καὶ τοῦ
προτειχίσματος χώραν, ἔτι μέντοι καὶ τὴν τάφρον
αὐτήν, ἐνταῦθα τὸ τεῖχος ἐδείματο ἀξιοθέατόν τε
καὶ διαφερόντως εὐπρόσωπον, ταύτῃ εὐρυτέραν
21 παρὰ πολὺ τὴν Ζηνοβίαν πεποιημένος. ἀλλὰ καὶ
λόφος τις ἄγχιστα [4] τῆς πόλεως εἱστήκει πρὸς

[1] ἀλλὰ Maltretus: ἀλλὰ λίθον.
[2] τῷ περιβόλῳ V, τοῦ περιβόλου A.

rise beside the river at this point, the stream cannot spread out at all, but by reason of the proximity of these mountains and because it is constrained by its banks, which are hard, it would gather its stream into an extraordinarily narrow space whenever it chanced that rains caused it to rise in flood, and would pour out against the wall and immediately rise, not only about the foundations but even as far as the battlements. And when the wall had once been soaked through by the water, the result was that the river loosened the courses of stones and thereafter the wall stood upon a dangerous conglomeration of stones. But he constructed a huge protective wall (*probolos*) of hard stone of equal length with the circuit-wall, and caused this to check at that point the turbulence of the river when it rose, and so freed the wall entirely from harm from this source, even should the river rise to a great height in its most violent state. He also found that portion of the city's circuit-wall which faces the north dangerously weakened by the passage of time; so he first took it down, along with the outworks, clear to the ground, and then rebuilt it, yet not as it had been before, for at that point the buildings of the city had been especially crowded, causing trouble to those who lived there. But he went beyond the place where the foundations of the circuit-wall and the outworks had formerly stood, even beyond the moat itself, and there he built the wall, which is a remarkable sight in itself and exceptionally beautiful, thus materially increasing the area of Zenobia. Furthermore, a certain hill stood very close to the city on the

[3] κυμαίνων A, κυματῶν V.
[4] πρὸ τῆς πόλεως before ἄγχιστα bracketed by Haury.

δύοντά που τὸν ἥλιον· ἐξ οὗ δὴ παρῆν τοῖς ἐπιοῦσιν ἀεὶ βαρβάροις βάλλειν κατὰ κορυφὴν ἀδεέστερον τούς τε ἀμυνομένους αὐτῆς καὶ οὐχ 22 ἥκιστα τοὺς ἐν μέσῃ πόλει ἑστῶτας. τούτῳ B 234 οὖν τῷ λόφῳ τείχισμα ἐνάψας Ἰουστινιανὸς βασιλεὺς ἑκατέρωθεν, ἐντός τε αὐτὸν τῆς Ζηνοβίας καταστησάμενος, ἔξυσε μὲν ὅλον ἐνδελεχέστατα, ὡς μή τις κακουργήσων ἐνθένδε ἀνίοι, τείχισμα δὲ ἄλλο τοῦ λόφου ὕπερθεν ἔθετο, ἀπρόσοδόν τε ὅλως τὴν πόλιν οὕτως τοῖς ἐπι- 23 βουλεύειν ἐθέλουσιν ἀπειργάσατο. τοῦ μὲν γὰρ λόφου ἐκτὸς κοίλην εἶναι τὴν γῆν ἐς ἄγαν συμβαίνει, καὶ διὰ τοῦτο ἐγγυτέρω ἰέναι τοὺς 24 πολεμίους ἀδύνατον. ὑπὲρ γῆν δὲ τὴν κοίλην εὐθὺς τὰ ὄρη ἀνέχει ἃ πρὸς ἥλιον δύοντα τέτραπται. οὐ μόνον δὲ τῇ πόλει τὰ ἐς τὴν ἀσφάλειαν οὗτος ὁ βασιλεὺς ἐπρυτάνευσεν, ἀλλὰ καὶ ἱερὰ ταύτῃ ἀνέθηκε καὶ στρατιωτικῶν σημείων οἰκίας. 25 ἔτι μέντοι λουτρῶνας καὶ στοὰς προσεποίησεν αὐτῇ δημοσίας. ἐς ταῦτα δὲ πάντα Ἰσίδωρός τε καὶ Ἰωάννης μηχανοποιοὶ τὴν ὑπουργίαν παρέσχοντο, Βυζάντιος μὲν Ἰωάννης, Ἰσίδωρος δὲ Μιλήσιος γένος, Ἰσιδώρου ἀδελφιδοῦς οὗπερ ἔμπροσθεν ἐπεμνήσθην, νεανίαι μὲν ἄμφω, δύναμιν δὲ φύσεως ὑπὲρ τὴν ἡλικίαν ἐπιδειξάμενοι καὶ τῇ ἐμπειρίᾳ τῶν τοῦ βασιλέως συνακμάσαντες ἔργων.

θʹ. Μετὰ δὲ τὴν [1] Ζηνοβίαν τὸ Σούρων πόλισμα, πρὸς τῷ Εὐφράτῃ ποταμῷ κείμενον, οὕτω δὴ εὐκαταφρόνητον τὸ τείχισμα εἶχεν ὥστε Χοσρόην

[1] τὴν V, om. A.

side toward the west, from which it was possible for the barbarians, whenever they attacked the city, to shoot down with impunity upon the heads of the defenders, and even upon the heads of those who stood in the middle of the city. So the Emperor Justinian connected the fortifications with this hill on both sides, and thus brought it inside Zenobia; and he escarped the whole hill throughout, so that no one might climb it to work harm from there, and placed another fortification on its summit and thus made the city altogether inaccessible to those who wished to assault it. For beyond the hill it chances that the ground is very low and for this reason it is impossible for the enemy to approach it at all closely. And immediately above the depression rise the mountains which face toward the west. Yet this Emperor did not provide only for the safety of this city, but he erected churches there and barracks for the military forces; nay more, he added to it public baths and stoas. For all these operations the master-builders Isidorus and John gave their assistance—John a Byzantine and Isidorus a Milesian by birth, nephew of the Isidorus whom I have mentioned before.[1] Both of them were young men, but they displayed a natural ability beyond their years, and they had come to their full maturity with their experience in the Emperor's undertakings.

ix. After Zenobia is the fortress of Sura,[2] situated on the Euphrates River, which had such contemptible defences that when Chosroes, on one occasion,

[1] *Buildings*, I. i. 24, 50, 70, II. iii. 7. It is possible that Isidorus the younger is mentioned in an inscription recording work done at Chalcis in A.D. 550–1; see the inscriptions cited in the note on II. xi. 1, below.

[2] Modern Suriya, near el Hammam, west of Callinicum.

προσβαλόντα ποτὲ οὐδὲ ὅσον ἡμιώριον ἀπεκρού-
2 σατο, ἀλλ' εὐθυωρὸν ἑάλω Πέρσαις. ἀλλὰ καὶ τοῦτο, ὥσπερ Καλλίνικον, Ἰουστινιανὸς βασιλεὺς ἀνοικοδομησάμενος τὸ πολίχνιον ὅλον τείχει τε ἐχυρωτάτῳ περιβαλὼν καὶ προτειχίσματι κρατυνάμενος μηκέτι εἴκειν[1] προσβάλλουσι πολεμίοις διεσκευάσατο.[2]

3 Ἔστι δέ τις νεὼς Σεργίῳ ἀνειμένος ἐν τῇ
B 235 Εὐφρατησίᾳ ἐπιφανεῖ ἁγίῳ, ὃν δὴ σέβοντές τε καὶ τεθηπότες οἱ πάλαι ἄνθρωποι Σεργιούπολίν τε ἐπωνόμασαν τὸ χωρίον, καὶ τειχίσματι βραχυτάτῳ περιβεβλήκεσαν, ὅσον τοὺς ἐκείνῃ[3] Σαρακη-
P 45 νοὺς ἀποκρούεσθαι οἷόν τε εἶναι ἐξ ἐπιδρομῆς
4 αὐτὸ ἐξελεῖν. ἀδύνατοι γὰρ τειχομαχεῖν εἰσι Σαρακηνοὶ φύσει, καί τι αὐτῶν, ἂν οὕτω τύχοι, τείχισμα φαυλότατον καὶ πηλῷ σύνθετον ἐμπόδιον
5 τῇ ὁρμῇ γίνεται. ἀλλ' ὕστερον ὁ νεὼς οὗτος κειμηλίων προσόδῳ δυνατός τε καὶ ἀπόβλεπτος
6 διὰ παντὸς ἦν. ὃ δὴ λογισάμενος Ἰουστινιανὸς βασιλεὺς τὸ πρᾶγμα εὐθὺς ἐν ἐπιμελείᾳ πεποίηται, τείχει τε ἀξιολογωτάτῳ ἐν τοῖς μάλιστα περιβέβληκε, καὶ ὑδάτων θησαυρίσας μέγα τι χρῆμα
7 πλήθειν αὐτοῖς ἐσκευάσατο. ἔτι μέντοι καὶ οἰκίας τε καὶ στοὰς καὶ τὰς ἄλλας οἰκοδομίας τῷ χωρίῳ ἐντέθεικεν ἃ δὴ πόλεως ἐγκαλλωπίσματα
8 γίνεσθαι εἴωθεν. ἀλλὰ καὶ φρουρὰν τῇδε στρατιωτῶν εἰς καιρὸν τοῦ περιβόλου ἀμυνομένων
9 ἱδρύσατο. Χοσρόης ἀμέλει ὁ Περσῶν βασιλεὺς

[1] εἴκειν V, ἥκειν A.
[2] διεσκευάσατο V, μετεσκευάσατο A.
[3] ἐκείνῃ V, ἐκεῖ A.

attacked it, it did not hold him off for so much as a half-hour, but was captured immediately by the Persians. This too, like Callinicum, was rebuilt by the Emperor Justinian, who surrounded the entire fortress with a very stout wall, which he strengthened by outworks and thus brought it about that it should no longer yield to the enemy's assaults.

There is a certain church in Euphratesia, dedicated to Sergius, a famous saint, whom men of former times used to worship and revere, so that they named the place Sergiopolis,[1] and they had surrounded it with a very humble wall, just sufficient to prevent the Saracens of the region from capturing it by storm. For the Saracens are naturally incapable of storming a wall, and the weakest kind of barricade, put together with perhaps nothing but mud, is sufficient to check their assault. At a later time, however, this church, through its acquisition of treasures, came to be powerful and celebrated. And the Emperor Justinian, upon considering this situation, at once gave it careful attention, and he surrounded the church with a most remarkable wall, and he stored up a great quantity of water and thus provided the inhabitants with a bountiful supply. Furthermore, he added to the place houses and stoas and the other buildings which are wont to be the adornments of a city. Besides this he established there a garrison of soldiers who, in case of need, defended the circuit-wall. Chosroes, indeed, the King of the Persians,

[1] Originally called Resapha, now Rusafa; south of Callinicum, on the road from Palmyra. Drawings of parts of its fortifications, which are typical of those built under Justinian on the eastern frontier, are reproduced on pp. 104, 105.

ἐν σπουδῇ πεποιημένος τὴν πόλιν ἑλεῖν στράτευμά τε αὐτῇ ἐπὶ πολιορκίᾳ [1] πολὺ ἐπιστήσας ἄπρακτος ἐνθένδε ὀχυρώματος ἰσχύϊ τὴν προσεδρείαν διέλυσε.

10 Καὶ πολίσματα δὲ καὶ φρούρια πάντα ἐν ἐσχατιαῖς τῶν Εὐφρατησίας ὁρίων ὄντα τῆς ὁμοίας ἐπιμελείας ἠξίωσε, Βαρβαλισσοῦ τε καὶ Νεοκαισαρείας καὶ τοῦ Γαβούλων καλουμένου καὶ τῆς πρὸς Εὐφράτῃ τῷ ποταμῷ Πεντακωμίας καὶ τοῦ Εὐρωποῦ· ἔτι μέντοι καὶ τοῦ καλουμένου Ἡμερίου τὰ τείχη εὑρὼν πῆ μὲν παρέργως τε καὶ ἐπὶ σφαλερᾶς τῆς οἰκοδομίας γεγενημένα, πῆ δὲ καὶ μόνῳ περιβεβλημένα πηλῷ, πιεζόμενα δὲ καὶ ὕδατος ἀπορίᾳ πολλῇ καὶ ἀπ᾽ αὐτοῦ τοῖς B 236 πολεμίοις εὐκαταφρόνητα παντάπασιν ὄντα, καθελὼν μὲν εἰς τὸ ἔδαφος, ἐς δὲ τὸ ἀκριβὲς λίθων ἐπιβολαῖς σκληρῶν μάλιστα δειμάμενος εὐθὺς ἅπαντα, εὔρους τε καὶ ὕψους μέγα τι χρῆμα τῷ ἔργῳ κατὰ λόγον ἐνθέμενος, καὶ ὑδάτων ταμιεῖα τεκτηνάμενος πανταχόσε τῶν ὀχυρωμάτων παμπληθῆ, ταῦτά τε κατακορῆ ὕδασιν ὀμβρίοις καταστησάμενος ἅπαντα· ἱδρυσάμενος δὲ καὶ φρουρῶν [2] ὅμιλον, ἐς τὴν νῦν φαινομένην ἀσφάλειαν καρτερώτατα τὴν αὐτοῦ ἐπικράτειαν μετεβίβασεν.

11 ἃ δὴ ἐπὶ μακρότατον ἄν τις διασκοπούμενος τάς τε ἄλλας ἁπάσας Ἰουστινιανοῦ βασιλέως ἀγαθοεργίας ὑπεριδών, τούτου δὴ μόνου φαίη ἂν εἵνεκα τὴν βασιλείαν παραλαβεῖν, τοῦ θεοῦ δηλονότι τὰ τῆς σωτηρίας Ῥωμαίων τῷ γένει διηνεκὲς πρυτανεύοντος.

[1] πολιορκίᾳ l, πολιορκίαν V.
[2] φρουρῶν Haury : φρουρὸν V.

made a great effort to capture the city, sending a great army to besiege it; but because of the strength of the defences he accomplished nothing and abandoned the investment.

The Emperor bestowed the same careful attention on all the towns and forts which lie on the farthest borders of Euphratesia, namely Barbalissus [1] and Neocaesarea,[2] and Gaboulôn,[3] as it is called, and the Pentacomia which is on the Euphrates River, and Europus.[4] Also he found the walls of the place called Hemerium [5] to be in part carelessly built and of unsafe construction and in part actually to consist of nothing but mud, while the place suffered from great scarcity of water, so that it was in every way an object of contempt to the enemy; so he razed it to the ground and immediately rebuilt it all carefully with courses of very hard stone, rightly giving the work generous proportions of both breadth and height, and he fashioned many cisterns for water in all parts of the defences, filling all these amply with rain-water; moreover, he established a large garrison there and so brought about the state of security which we now see there, and made the city's dominance sure. And if one should consider these fortresses very carefully, disregarding all the other useful works of the Emperor Justinian, he would say that it was solely for this purpose that he succeeded to the imperial power, since God unceasingly provides for the safety of the Roman people.

[1] Modern Balis, at Eski Meskenê on the Euphrates, between Beroea and Callinicum.
[2] On the Euphrates between Barbalissus and Sura.
[3] Modern Jabboul, south-east of Beroea.
[4] Modern Jerablus, the site of Carchemish, on the Euphrates.
[5] Near the Euphrates, close to Europus.

12 Πρὸς ἐπὶ [1] τούτοις δὲ καὶ τὴν Ἱεράπολιν,[2] ἥπερ ἁπασῶν πρώτη τῶν τῇδε πόλεων τυγχάνει οὖσα, λαβὼν ἀποκειμένην τοῖς ἐπιβουλεύειν ἐθέλουσι, 13 προμηθεῖ διεσώσατο γνώμῃ. χώραν τε γὰρ ἔρημον τὰ πρότερα περιβεβλημένην πολλὴν καὶ διὰ τοῦτο ἀφύλακτον οὖσαν, τῶν μὲν ἀνονήτων αὐτὴν περιόδων ἀπήλλαξεν,[3] ἐπιτομώτερον δὲ [4] σὺν τῷ ἀσφαλεῖ καταστησάμενος [5] τὸν περίβολον, ἔς τε τὸ τῆς χρείας ἀναγκαῖον ξυναγαγὼν ἐχυρωτάτην τανῦν ἐν τοῖς μάλιστα διεπράξατο 14 τὴν πόλιν εἶναι. οὗ δὴ καὶ τόδε ἀγαθὸν εἴργασται. πότιμον ὕδωρ ἐκ μυχῶν τῆς γῆς ἄνεισιν ἐν μέσῃ P 46 πόλει διηνεκῶς, λίμνην τέ τινα ἐνταῦθα εὐρεῖαν 15 ποιεῖται. τοῦτο πολεμίων μέν, ἂν οὕτω τύχοι, προσεδρευόντων γίνεται τῇ πόλει σωτήριον, ἐν δὲ ἀγαθοῖς πράγμασιν οὐκ ἀναγκαῖον αὐτῇ [6] ξυμβαίνει εἶναι, ἔξωθεν εἰσαγομένων ὑδάτων 16 πολλῶν· προϊόντος δὲ τοῦ χρόνου εἰρήνῃ μακρᾷ συμβεβιωκότες οἱ τῇδε ᾠκημένοι, ἀνάγκης δὲ οὐδεμιᾶς ἐς πεῖραν ἐλθόντες, ἐν ὀλιγωρίᾳ τοῦτο B 237 πεποίηνται. οὐ γὰρ οἶδεν ἀνθρώπου φύσις ὑπὲρ τῶν οὔπω [7] παρόντων κακῶν ἐν εὐδαιμονίᾳ βουλεύεσθαι. 17 ῥύπου τοίνυν τὴν λίμνην ἐνδελεχέστατα ἐνεπλήσαντο, νηχόμενοί τε καὶ πλυνοὺς ἐνταῦθα ποιούμενοι καὶ ἀπορριπτοῦντες φορυτοὺς ἅπαντας . . .

18 Ἔκειτο δὲ καὶ ἄλλα ἄττα ἐν ταύτῃ δὴ τῇ Εὐφρατησίᾳ χωρία, Ζεῦγμά τε καὶ Νεοκαισάρεια, ἃ δὴ πολίχναι μὲν ἄχρι ἐς τὸ ὄνομα ἦσαν, τείχεσι

[1] ἐπὶ V, om. A.
[2] Ἱεράπολιν Dindorf : ἱερὰν πόλιν.
[3] ἀπήλλαξεν V, ἀπαλλάξας A.
[4] δὲ V, τε A.

In addition to these he also found Hierapolis,[1] which happens to be the first of all the cities of that region, lying exposed to those who wished to attack it, and by his prudent foresight he assured its safety. Previously it had enclosed a large tract of barren land, and consequently was undefended; so he relieved it of this senseless expanse and made the circuit-wall shorter as well as more safe, reducing it to a measure calculated to meet the actual need of the situation, and thus bringing it about that the city is among the strongest of the present day. Here too he conferred the following benefit. An unfailing supply of drinking-water springs up from the recesses of the earth in the midst of the city and makes a broad lake there. And whenever an enemy chances to lay siege to the place, this water proves the salvation of the city; but in good times the lake becomes unnecessary to it, because abundant water is brought in from outside. And as time went on, the inhabitants of the place, having enjoyed a long-continued peace and experiencing no need, treated this spring with neglect. For in times of prosperity human nature knows not how to take thought against ills not yet at hand. So they kept filling the lake constantly with pollution, both swimming and washing clothes in it and throwing all manner of rubbish into it. . . .

There were also two other towns in this district of Euphratesia, Zeugma and Neocaesarea, which went by the name of fortified towns, but were enclosed by

[1] Bambycê, modern Menbidj.

---

[5] καταστησάμενος V, κατασκευάσας A.
[6] αὐτῇ Maltretus: αὐτῷ.
[7] οὔπω (or οὐ) added by Capps.

19 δὲ περιεβέβλητο αἱμασιᾶς τρόπον. τῷ[1] μὲν γὰρ τῆς οἰκοδομίας κολοβῷ ἐσβατὰ πόνῳ οὐδενὶ[2] τοῖς πολεμίοις ἐγίνετο, ἀδεέστερον ἐς αὐτὰ ἐσπηδᾶν ἔχουσι, τῷ δὲ στενῷ λίαν ἀφύλακτα, οὐκ ἐχόντων τὸ παράπαν τῶν ἐνταῦθα φρουρῶν 20 ὅποι ἂν ἑστῶτες ἀμύνοιντο. ἀλλὰ καὶ ταῦτα Ἰουστινιανὸς βασιλεὺς τείχεσιν ἀληθέσι περιβαλὼν εὔρους τε καὶ ὕψους ἱκανῶς ἔχουσι, καὶ τῇ ἄλλῃ κατασκευῇ κρατυνάμενος, πόλεις τε διεπράξατο καλεῖσθαι δικαίως καὶ κρείσσους εἶναι τῆς τῶν πολεμίων ἐπιβουλῆς.

ι΄. Ἀλλὰ καὶ τῶν πόλεων τὰς Χοσρόῃ ἁλούσας (ἡνίκα ὁ βάρβαρος οὗτος ἀλογήσας τὰ παρ' αὐτοῦ ὀμωμοσμένα ἐν ταῖς ἀπεράντοις σπονδαῖς καὶ τὰ διδόμενά οἱ ἐπ' αὐταῖς χρήματα, καὶ βασκανίᾳ μὲν ἐς Ἰουστινιανὸν βασιλέα ἐχόμενος, οἷς δὴ Λιβύης τε καὶ Ἰταλίας τῷ πολέμῳ κύριος γέγονε, καὶ τὴν ἐς τὰ ὀμωμοσμένα πίστιν περὶ ἐλάσσονος τῆς ἐς ταῦτα λύσσης πεποιημένος. καιροφυλακήσας δὲ ἀπολελειμμένον ἐν τῇ ἑσπερίᾳ ἐκ τοῦ ἐπὶ πλεῖστον τὸν Ῥωμαίων στρατὸν[3] αὐτάγγελος ἐσβέβληκεν[4] ἐς Ῥωμαίων τὴν γῆν, ἀνηκόων ἔτι Ῥωμαίων ὄντων τῆς τῶν πολεμίων B 238 ἐφόδου), ἐς τοῦτο δὴ μετεστήσατο βασιλεὺς Ἰουστινιανὸς ἀσφαλείας καὶ κόσμου, ὥστε ἁπάσας εὐδαιμονεστέρας κατὰ πολὺ τανῦν ἢ πρότερον εἶναι, καὶ μηκέτι περὶ[5] τὰς τῶν κακουργησόντων

[1] τῷ Maltretus: ᾧι τῷ. [2] οὐδενὶ added by Hoeschel.
[3] ἀπολελειμμένον . . . τὸν ῥωμαίων στρατὸν A, ἀπολελειμμένου . . . τοῦ ῥωμαίων στρατοῦ V.
[4] ἐσβέβληκεν Haury: βέβληκεν V, ἐσβέβηκεν A.
[5] περὶ V, πρὸς A.

fortifications resembling walls of loose stones. And because these were made too low when they were built, they were accessible to the enemy without any effort, since they could leap upon them without fear, while their extreme narrowness made them impossible to defend, since the garrison of the town had no place whatever where they might stand and carry on the defence. But the Emperor Justinian surrounded these places too with real walls of adequate breadth and height, and he made them strong in their other equipment, and so brought it about that they are justly called cities and are too well built for hostile attacks.

x. He also turned his attention to the cities which had been captured by Chosroes. (This was when that barbarian ignored the oaths he had sworn at the time of the "endless peace" [1] and the money given him to secure this peace; when he was filled with malice against the Emperor Justinian because he had become master of Italy and of Libya by conquest, and was moved less by the obligation of his oaths than by his rage at the Emperor's successes. So he watched for the right time, and when the greater part of the Roman army was away in the West, he invaded the Roman territory without any previous notice, before the Romans could hear of the approach of the enemy). So the Emperor Justinian transformed these cities to such a state of safety and beauty that they are all much more prosperous at the present time than they were formerly, and no longer need either be fearful of the inroads of the

[1] Procopius has recounted these matters in the *Wars*: on the ἀπέραντος εἰρήνη, concluded in the year 532, see I. xxii. 17, on Chosroes' violation of it seven years later see II. iii. 55 ff.; on the towns of the Romans which Chosroes captured, consult the Index at the end of this volume.

βαρβάρων ἐφόδους περιδεεῖς εἶναι, μηδέ τινι μηχανῇ πρὸς τὰς ἐπιβουλὰς ὑπόπτως ἔχειν.

2 Μάλιστα δὲ ἁπασῶν Ἀντιόχειαν, ἣ νῦν Θεούπολις ἐπικέκληται,[1] κόσμου τε καὶ ὀχυρώματος ἐνεπλήσατο πολλῷ μείζονος ἢ πρότερον εἶναι 3 ξυνέβαινεν. ἦν μὲν γὰρ αὐτῆς τὸ παλαιὸν ὁ περίβολος μακρός τε ὑπεράγαν καὶ περιόδων πολλῶν ἀτεχνῶς ἔμπλεως, πὴ μὲν τὰ πεδία περιβάλλων οὐδενὶ λόγῳ, πὴ δὲ τὰς τῶν σκοπέλων ὑπερβολάς, καὶ ἀπ' αὐτοῦ πλείοσιν ἐπιβουλαῖς 4 ὑποκείμενος. συστείλας δὲ αὐτὸν Ἰουστινιανὸς βασιλεὺς κατὰ τὸ χρείᾳ ξυνοῖσον, οὐ ταῦτα φρουρεῖν ἅπερ καὶ πρότερον, ἀλλὰ τὴν πόλιν 5 ἐς τὸ ἀκριβὲς πεποίηκε μόνην. τὰ μὲν γὰρ κάτω τοῦ περιβόλου, ἔνθα ἡ πόλις ἐπικινδύνως εὐρύνετο, ἐν πολλῷ τε πεδίῳ κειμένη καὶ περιουσίᾳ τειχίσματος ἀφύλακτος οὖσα, μεταβιβάζει ὡς ἐνδοτάτω, ἐπικαιριώτατα στενοχωρήσας ἐνταῦθα τὴν πόλιν, περιστελλομένην τῷ πεπιέσθαι. 6 ποταμὸν δὲ Ὀρόντην, ὅσπερ αὐτὴν παρέρρει ἐν περιόδοις τὰ πρότερα οὖσαν, διωθήσατο μεταπορευθέντα τὸ ῥεῖθρον τῷ περιβόλῳ γειτονεῖν, 7 αὖθις ὀχεταγωγίᾳ τὸν ῥοῦν ὡς ἀγχοτάτω περιελίξας, ταύτῃ τε καὶ τὸ σφαλερὸν τῆς ἀμετρίας ἀνῆκε τῇ πόλει καὶ τὴν ἐκ τοῦ Ὀρόντου ἀσφά- 8 λειαν ἀνεσώσατο. ἐνταῦθά τε νεοχμώσας γεφύρας ἑτέρας ζεύγματα τῷ ποταμῷ νέα ἐντέθεικε, περιαγαγὼν δὲ ὡς πορρωτάτω τῆς χρείας αὐτόν,

P 47

[1] The name was officially changed after the earthquake of A.D. 528 (Malalas, p. 443 Bonn ed.), though the earlier name

villainous barbarians, or apprehensive for any reason of their attacks.

Above all he made Antioch, which is now called Theopolis,[1] both fairer and stronger by far than it had been formerly. In ancient times its circuit-wall was both too long and absolutely full of many turnings, in some places uselessly enclosing the level ground and in others the summits of the mountain, and for this reason it was exposed to attack in a number of places. But the Emperor Justinian, contracting this wall as would best serve the need, carefully remade it so as to guard, not the same districts as before, but only the city itself. As for the lower part of the circuit-wall, where the city was dangerously spread out (since it lay in a soft plain and could not be defended because of a superfluity of wall), he changed its course by drawing it inward as much as possible, most advantageously crowding the city at this point, it having gained protection by being compressed. And the River Orontes, which had flowed past the city, as it formerly was, in a winding course, he thrust over so that it ran in a new bed, hugging the circuit-wall. He did this by winding the stream round again by means of an artificial channel as near the wall as possible. In this way he both relieved the city of the danger arising from its excessive size and recovered the protection afforded by the Orontes. And by building other bridges there he furnished new means of crossing the river; and after changing its stream for as great a

continued in common use. On Procopius's description of the rebuilding of the city, see an article by Downey, "Procopius on Antioch: a Study of Method in the *De aedificiis*," which will be published in *Byzantion*, xiv, part 1.

εἶτα τὴν προτέραν ἀπέδωκε πορείαν τῷ ῥείθρῳ.
B 239 9 τὰ μέντοι ἄνω ἐς τὸ κρημνῶδες αὐτῷ κατὰ τάδε διαπεπόνηται. ἐν τῇ τοῦ ὄρους ὑπερβολῇ ἥνπερ Ὀροκασσιάδα καλοῦσι, πέτρα τις τοῦ τείχους ἐκτὸς ὡς ἀγχοτάτω ἐτύγχανεν οὖσα, ἐξ ἀντιπάλου τε τοῦ περιβόλου ἐνταῦθα κειμένη καὶ λίαν ἐπι- 10 μαχώτατον αὐτὸν τιθεμένη. Χοσρόῃ ἀμέλει ἐνθένδε ἡ πόλις ἑάλω, ᾗπέρ μοι ἐν λόγοις τοῖς ἐπιτηδείοις ἐρρήθη. τὰ δὲ τοῦ περιβόλου ἐντὸς ἔρημός τε χώρα ἐπὶ πλεῖστον καὶ δύσοδος ἦν· 11 πέτραι γὰρ ὑψηλαὶ καὶ χαράδραι ἀνέκβατοι διακεκλήρωνται τὸν χῶρον ἐκεῖνον, ἀδιεξόδους τὰς ἐνθένδε ποιούμεναι τρίβους, ὥσπερ ἀλλοτρίου ἐνταῦθά τινος, ἀλλ' οὐ[1] τῶν Ἀντιοχέων τοῦ 12 τείχους ὄντος. χαίρειν τοίνυν πολλὰ τῇ πέτρᾳ [illegible], ἥπερ ἐν [illegible] τῷ τείχει οὖσα εὐάλωτον αὐτὸ διαφανῶς ἐσκαιώρητο, ὡς πορρωτάτω αὐτῆς περιβάλλειν τὴν πόλιν ἔγνω, ἀβουλίας πέρι τῶν πρότερον αὐτὴν δειμαμένων ἀπὸ τῶν πραγμάτων 13 τῆς πείρας πεποιημένος τὴν μάθησιν. χώραν τε ὁμαλὴν μάλιστα τοῦ τείχους ἐντὸς τὴν τὰ πρότερα κρημνώδη οὖσαν ἀπεργασάμενος, ἀνόδους ταύτῃ πεποίηται οὐχ ὅσον ἀνδράσι πεζοῖς, ἀλλὰ δὴ καὶ ἱππεῦσι βασίμους, ἔτι μέντοι καὶ ἁμαξηλά- 14 τους τὸ λοιπὸν οὔσας. ἀλλὰ καὶ βαλανεῖα καὶ ὑδάτων ταμιεῖα ἐν τοῖς ὄρεσι πεποίηται τούτοις τοῦ τείχους ἐντός. φρέαρ τε ὤρυξεν ἐν πύργῳ ἑκάστῳ, τὴν πρότερον ἀνυδρίαν ἐνταῦθα οὖσαν ὕδασιν ὑετίοις ἰώμενος.

15 Ὅσα δὲ καὶ ἀμφὶ τῷ χειμάρρῳ πεποίηται, ὃς

[1] ἀλλ' οὐ Haury, ἄλλου.

distance as was necessary, he then restored it to its former course. The upper part,[1] in the mountainous portion, he managed as follows: on the summit of the mountain which they call Orocassias[2] there happened to be a rock outside the wall and very close to it, nearly matching in height the circuit-wall in this place and making it quite vulnerable. It was from this point in fact that the city was taken by Chosroes, as is related in my description of the event.[3] The region within the circuit-wall was for the most part bare and difficult to traverse, for high rocks and impassable ravines divide up that district, so that the paths from that place have no outlet. Thus the wall there is just as if it belonged to some other city and not to Antioch at all. So he bade a long farewell to the rock, which, being close to the wall, was fiendishly devised to make the wall easy to capture, and decided to build the defences of the city as far away from it as possible, having learned from the experience of events the folly of those who had built the city in former times. Moreover he made quite level the region within the wall, which formerly had been precipitous, building ascents there which would in the future be passable, not only for men on foot, but for cavalry, and would even serve as waggon-roads. He also built baths and reservoirs on these hills inside the wall. And he dug a cistern in each tower, remedying by means of rain-water the want of water which had previously existed there.

It is proper to describe also what he did with the

[1] *I.e.* of the circuit-wall.

[2] So named with reference to Mt. Casius, the principal peak of the range which comes to an end at Antioch.

[3] *Wars*, II. viii. 8 ff.

P 48 ἐκ τούτων δὴ τῶν ὀρέων κάτεισιν, εἰπεῖν ἄξιον. ὄρη μὲν ἀπότομα δύο τῇ πόλει ἐπῆρται, ἀλλήλοιν 16 ξυνιόντα ὡς ἀγχοτάτω. τούτων[1] θάτερον μὲν Ὀροκασσιάδα καλοῦσι, τὸ δὲ δὴ ἕτερον Σταυρὶν B 240 κέκληται. ἀπολήγοντα δέ πη αὐτὰ νάπη τις ζεύγνυσι καὶ χαράδρα μεταξὺ οὖσα, χειμάρρουν ἀποτελοῦσα, ἐπειδὰν ὕοι, Ὀνοπνίκτην ὄνομα, ὃς δὴ ἐξ ὑπερδεξίων κατιὼν ὕπερθέν τε τοῦ περιβόλου φερόμενος ἐπὶ μέγα τε, ἂν οὕτω τύχῃ, ἐξανιστάμενος, διεσκεδάννυτο μὲν ἐς τοὺς τῆς πόλεως στενωπούς, ἀνήκεστα δὲ κακὰ τοὺς 17 ταύτῃ ᾠκημένους εἰργάζετο. ἀλλὰ καὶ τούτου τὴν ἄκεσιν Ἰουστινιανὸς βασιλεὺς εὕρατο τρόπῳ τοιῷδε. πρὸ τοῦ περιβόλου ὅνπερ ἄγχιστα τῆς χαράδρας ξυμβαίνει εἶναι, ἐξ ἧς ὁ χειμάρρους ἐπὶ τὰ τείχη ἴοι, τοῖχον ἐδείματο ὑπερμεγέθη ἐκ κοίλης χαράδρας διήκοντα ἐς ἑκάτερον τοῖν ὀροῖν μάλιστα, ὡς μηκέτι περαιτέρω ἰέναι κυματοῦντι τῷ ποταμῷ δυνατὰ εἴη, ἀλλ' ἐπὶ 18 μακρότερον ξυνιστάμενος ἐνταῦθα λιμνάζοι. ἐν δὲ τῷ τοίχῳ θυρίδας ποιησάμενος ἐνθένδε ἀπορρέοντα ὑπολήγειν κατὰ βραχὺ ἀνάγκῃ χειροποιήτῳ τὸν χειμάρρουν διεσκευάσατο, οὐκέτι λάβρως τῷ παντὶ ῥεύματι τῷ περιβόλῳ προσβάλλοντα, καὶ διὰ τοῦτο ὑπερβλύζοντά τε καὶ τὴν πόλιν κατεργαζόμενον, ἀλλὰ πρᾴως τε καὶ προσηνῶς ὑπορρέοντα, ᾗπέρ μοι εἴρηται, ταύτῃ τε τῇ ἐκροῇ διὰ τῆς ὀχεταγωγίας ἰόντα ὅποι ἂν αὐτὸν βουλομένοις ᾖ περιάγειν οὕτω μέτριον γεγενημένον τοῖς πάλαι ἀνθρώποις.

[1] For τούτων Haury would prefer τούτοιν.

---

[1] "The Cross"; this name apparently originated from the vision of the holy cross which appeared over a part of the

torrent which comes down from these mountains. Two precipitous mountains rise above the city, approaching each other quite closely. Of these they call the one Orocassias and the other is called Staurin.[1] Where they come to an end they are joined by a glen and ravine which lies between them, which produces a torrent, when it rains, called Onopnictes.[2] This, coming down from a height, swept over the circuit-wall and on occasion rose to a great volume, spreading into the streets of the city and doing ruinous damage to those who lived in that district. But even for this the Emperor Justinian found the remedy, in the following way: Before that part of the circuit-wall which happens to lie nearest to the ravine out of which the torrent was borne against the fortifications, he built an immense wall or dam, which reached roughly from the hollow bed of the ravine to each of the two mountains, so that the stream should no longer be able to sweep on when it was at full flood, but should collect for a considerable distance back and form a lake there. And by constructing sluice-gates in this wall he contrived that the torrent, flowing through these, should lose its force gradually, checked by this artificial barrier, and no longer violently assault the circuit-wall with its full stream, and so overflow it and damage the city, but should gently and evenly glide on in the manner I have described and, with this means of outflow, should proceed through the channel wherever the inhabitants of former times would have wished to conduct it if it had been so manageable.

city after the earthquake of A.D. 526 (Malalas, p. 421 Bonn ed.).

[2] "Donkey-drowner," with reference to its violence. Other writers call the torrent Parmenius.

19 Τὰ μὲν οὖν ἀμφὶ τῷ Ἀντιοχείας περιβόλῳ τῇδε Ἰουστινιανῷ βασιλεῖ εἴργασται. καὶ ξύμπασαν δὲ πρὸς τῶν πολεμίων καταφλεχθεῖσαν
20 ἀνῳκοδομήσατο τὴν πόλιν αὐτός. τετεφρωμένων γὰρ πανταχόσε καὶ καθῃρημένων ἁπάντων, λόφων τε μόνον ἐκ πόλεως ἐξηνθρακωμένης ἐπανεστηκότων πολλῶν, ἄπορον τοῖς Ἀντιοχεῦσιν ἐγίνετο τήν τε χώραν ἐπιγνῶναι τῆς ἑκάστου ἰδίας οἰκίας [1] γενομένης τὰ πρῶτα ἐκφορήσασι [2] τὸ συμπτωθὲν ἅπαν, οἰκίας τε πυρκαϊᾶς περικαθῆραι τὰ λείψανα, ἔτι μέντοι δημοσίων στοῶν ἢ περιστύλων αὐλῶν οὐδαμῆ οὐσῶν, οὐδὲ ἀγορᾶς πη καθισταμένης, οὐδὲ τῶν στενωπῶν τὰς ἀγυιὰς διαιρούντων τῇ πόλει, οἰκίας τινὸς οἰκοδο-
B 241

21 μίαν ἀπαυθαδιάσασθαι. ἀλλὰ βασιλεὺς οὐδεμιᾷ μελλήσει ὡς ἀπωτάτω τῆς πόλεως τὰ καθῃρημένα μετενεγκών, ἐλεύθερόν τε τὸν ταύτῃ ἀέρα ξὺν τοῖς ἔνερθεν τῶν ἐνοχλούντων καταστησάμενος, πρῶτα μὲν τὰ ἐδάφη πανταχόθι τῆς πόλεως λίθοις
22 ἁμαξιαίοις ἐκάλυψεν· ἔπειτα δὲ στοαῖς τε καὶ ἀγοραῖς αὐτὴν διακρίνας, καὶ διελὼν μὲν τοῖς στενωποῖς ἀμφόδους ἁπάσας, ὀχετοὺς δὲ καὶ κρήνας καὶ ὑδροχόας καταστησάμενος, ὅσοις ἡ πόλις κεκόμψευται, θέατρά τε αὐτῇ καὶ βαλανεῖα πεποιημένος, καὶ ταῖς ἄλλαις δημοσίαις οἰκοδομίαις ἁπάσαις κοσμήσας, αἷσπερ εὐδαιμονία διαφαίνεσθαι πόλεως εἴωθε. τεχνιτῶν δὲ καὶ ἐπιδη-

[1] οἰκίας added by Haury.
[2] πρῶτα ἐκφορήσασι Haury for πρῶτα. ἐκφορήσας οὖν.

---

[1] For the meaning of the word, *cf. Secret History*, xxii. 14.

This, then, was what the Emperor Justinian accomplished concerning the circuit-wall of Antioch. He also rebuilt the whole city, which had been completely burned by the enemy. For since everything was everywhere reduced to ashes and levelled to the ground, and since many mounds of ruins were all that was left standing of the burned city, it became impossible for the people of Antioch to recognise the site of each person's house, when first they carried out all the debris, and to clear out the remains of a burned house; and since there were no longer public stoas or colonnaded courts in existence anywhere, nor any market-place remaining, and since the side-streets no longer marked off the thoroughfares of the city, they did not any longer dare to build any house. But the Emperor without any delay transported the debris as far as possible from the city, and thus freed the air and the ground of all encumbrances; then he first of all covered the cleared land of the city everywhere with stones each large enough to load a waggon. Next he laid it out with stoas and market-places, and dividing all the blocks of houses by means of streets, and making water-channels and fountains and sewers,[1] all those of which the city now boasts, he built theatres and baths for it, ornamenting it with all the other public buildings by means of which the prosperity of a city is wont to be shewn.[2] He also, by bringing in a multitude of

[2] *Cf.* Pausanias, X. iv. 1, translated by W. H. S. Jones in the Loeb Classical Library: "From Chaeroneia it is twenty stades to Panopeus, a city of the Phocians, if one can give the name of city to those who possess no government offices, no gymnasium, no theatre, no market-place, no water descending to a fountain, but live in bare shelters just like mountain cabins, right on a ravine."

P 49 μιούργων πλῆθος ἐπαγαγὼν ῥᾷόν τε καὶ ἀπονώτερον τοῖς ἐνοικοῦσι παρέσχετο δείμασθαι τὰς
23 αὐτῶν ἰδίας οἰκίας. οὕτω τε Ἀντιόχειαν ἐπιφανεστέραν γεγονέναι τανῦν ἢ πρότερον ἦν ξυν-
24 ηνέχθη. ἀλλὰ καὶ ἱερὸν ἐνταῦθα τῇ θεοτόκῳ πεποίηται μέγα, οὗ δὴ τό τε κάλλος καὶ τὸ ἐς ἅπαντα μεγαλοπρεπὲς ἐπελθεῖν λόγῳ ἀμήχανον· ὃ δὴ καὶ προσόδῳ ἐτίμησε χρημάτων μεγάλων.
25 ἔτι μέντοι καὶ Μιχαὴλ τῷ ἀρχαγγέλῳ νεὼν παμμεγέθη ἐδείματο. προὐνόησε δὲ καὶ τῶν ἀρρωστήμασι πονουμένων ἐνταῦθα πτωχῶν, οἰκία τε σφίσι καὶ τὰ ἐς τὴν ἐπιμέλειαν καὶ τῶν νοση-
B 242 μάτων ἀπαλλαγὴν ἐν ἐπιτηδείῳ καταστησάμενος ἅπαντα, χωρὶς μὲν ἀνδράσι, χωρὶς δὲ γυναιξί, καὶ οὐδέν τι ἧσσον τοῖς ξένοις ἐπὶ καιροῦ γενομένοις ἐνταῦθα ἐνδήμοις.

ια΄. Οὕτω δὲ καὶ Χαλκίδος πόλεως τὸν περίβολον, ἐπισφαλῶς τε ἀρχὴν γεγονότα καὶ ὑπὸ τῶν ἐτῶν κατερρακωμένον, σὺν τῷ προτειχίσματι[1] ἀνανεωσάμενός τε καὶ πολλῷ ἐχυρώτερον καταστησάμενος ἢ πρότερον ἦν, ἐς τὸν νῦν φαινόμενον πεποίηται τρόπον.

2 Ἦν δέ τι ἐπὶ Συρίας κομιδῇ ἀπημελημένον πολίχνιον, Κῦρος ὄνομα, ὅπερ Ἰουδαῖοι ἐν τοῖς

[1] προτειχίσματι V, τειχίσματι A.

---

[1] The restoration of the circuit-wall and the outworks of Chalcis is also described a little below, in section 8. One of the passages must refer to the Chalcis (modern Kinnesrin) which is south-west of Beroea (Aleppo), for two Greek inscriptions found at this Chalcis record extensive building operations executed there, evidently on the circuit-wall, in

artisans and craftsmen, made it more easy and less laborious for the inhabitants to build their own houses. Thus it was brought about that Antioch has become more splendid now than it formerly was. Moreover, he built there a great Church to the Mother of God. The beauty of this, and its magnificence in every respect, it is impossible to describe; he also honoured it with an income of a very large sum. Moreover, he built an immense Church for the Archangel Michael. He made provision likewise for the poor of the place who were suffering from maladies, providing buildings for them and all the means for the care and cure of their ailments, for men and women separately, and he made no less provision for strangers who might on occasion be staying in the city.

xi. In the same manner he also repaired the circuit-wall of the city of Chalcis, which had been faultily built in the first place and had been wrecked by the years; he restored this along with the outworks and rendered it much more defensible than before, and gave it the form which we now see.[1]

There was a certain utterly neglected fortress in Syria, Cyrus by name,[2] which the Jews built in early

A.D. 550–1; *cf.* W. K. Prentice, *Greek and Latin Inscriptions* (*Publ. of an Amer. Arch. Exp. to Syria*, III, New York, 1908), nos. 305–306, and Ch. Clermont-Ganneau, *Recueil d'archéologie orientale*, VII (1906), pp. 228–230, and VIII (1924), pp. 81–88. Another Chalcis (modern Andjar) lies between Beyrouth and Damascus. The passages may refer to the two places, which Procopius may have confused; or he may have intended to note the distinction, but neglected to do so. It is more likely that both passages refer to Kinnesrin; Procopius may have written the entry twice in his manuscript either intentionally or accidentally, neglecting later to delete one passage.

[2] Modern Chorres.

ἄνω χρόνοις ἐδείμαντο, δορυάλωτοι μὲν ἐκ Παλαιστίνης ἐς τὴν Ἀσσυρίαν ἀποκεκομισμένοι πρὸς[1] τοῦ Μήδων στρατοῦ, παρὰ Κύρου δὲ βασιλέως ἀφειμένοι πολλῷ ὕστερον· διὸ δὴ καὶ Κῦρον τὸ χωρίον ἐκάλεσαν,[2] ταῦτα τῷ εὐεργέτῃ
3 ἐκτίνοντες χαριστήρια. προϊόντος δὲ τοῦ χρόνου ἡ Κῦρος τά τε ἄλλα ὑπερῴφθη καὶ ἀτείχιστος
4 ὅλως μεμένηκεν. ἀλλὰ βασιλεὺς Ἰουστινιανὸς ἅμα μὲν πρόνοιαν τῆς πολιτείας ποιούμενος, ἅμα δὲ καὶ τοὺς ἁγίους Κοσμᾶν τε καὶ Δαμιανὸν τὰ μάλιστα σέβων, ὧν δὴ ἄγχιστά πη τὰ σώματα καὶ ἐς ἐμὲ κεῖται, πόλιν εὐδαίμονα καὶ λόγου ἀξίαν πολλοῦ, τείχους τε ἀσφαλείᾳ ἐχυρωτάτου καὶ φρουρῶν πλήθει καὶ οἰκοδομιῶν δημοσίων μεγέθει, καὶ τῆς ἄλλης κατασκευῆς τῷ ἐς ἄγαν
5 μεγαλοπρεπεῖ, πεποίηται Κῦρ[illegible] ταύτης δὲ τῆς πόλεως τὰ μὲν ἐντὸς ὕδατος ἄπορα ἐκ παλαιοῦ ἦν, ἔκτοσθε δὲ ὑπερφυής τις ἐγεγόνει πηγή, περιουσίᾳ μὲν πλήθουσα ποτίμων ὑδάτων, ἀνόνητος δὲ τοῖς τῇδε ᾠκημένοις παντάπασιν οὖσα, ἐπεὶ οὐκ εἶχον ὅθεν ἂν ἐνθένδε ἀρύοιντο ὕδωρ, ὅτι μὴ πόνῳ
6 τε καὶ κινδύνῳ μεγάλῳ. περιόδοις τε γὰρ
B 243 αὐτόσε ἰοῦσιν ἀναγκαῖον ἐγίνετο χρῆσθαι, κρημνώδους χωρίου καὶ ὅλως ἀβάτου μεταξὺ ὄντος· καὶ τοῖς πολεμίοις, ἂν οὕτω τύχῃ, ἐνεδρεύου-
P 50 7 σιν ὑποχείριοι ῥᾷστα ἐγίγνοντο. διώρυχα τοίνυν ἔκτοσθε τῆς πόλεως ἄχρι ἐς τὴν κρήνην οὐκ ἀπαρακαλύπτως, ἀλλὰ κεκρυμμένως ὡς ἔνι μάλιστα πεποιημένος, ἄπονόν τε αὐτοῖς καὶ ἀκίνδυνον τὴν τοῦ ὕδατος παρέσχετο χρείαν.

[1] πρὸς V, παρὰ A.
[2] ἐκάλεσαν V, ὠνόμασαν A.

times, when they had been carried off as captives from Palestine into Assyria by the army of the Medes and were released much later by King Cyrus;[1] and for this reason they named the place Cyrus, paying this tribute of gratitude to their benefactor. And as time went on this place came to be neglected in general and remained altogether without walls. But the Emperor Justinian, both out of his forethought for the safety of the State, and at the same time as shewing especial honour to the Saints Cosmas and Damian, whose bodies lie close by even up to my day, made Cyrus a flourishing city and one of great note through the safety afforded by the strongest possible wall, by the great strength of its garrison, by the size of its public buildings, and by the imposing scale of its other appointments. The interior of this city had been destitute of water from ancient times; outside of it there had been a certain extraordinary spring which provided a great abundance of water fit for drinking, yet it was utterly useless to the inhabitants of the city, since they had no means of drawing water from the spring except with great toil and danger. For it was necessary, in order to get to it, for them to make use of circuitous paths, since a steep and altogether impassable area lay between; thus they could casily fall into the hands of the enemy if they should happen to lie in ambush. So he dug a channel outside the city all the way to the spring, not allowing it to be seen, but concealing it as carefully as possible, and thus he provided the inhabitants with a supply of water without toil or risk.

[1] In 537 B.C.

8 Καὶ Χαλκίδος δὲ πόλεως τὸν περίβολον ὅλον, ἔς τε τὸ ἔδαφος καθειμένον καὶ ἄλλως ἀφύλακτον ὄντα ἐχυρῷ διαφερόντως ἀνενεώσατο οἰκοδομίᾳ, 9 καὶ προτειχίσματι ἐκρατύνατο.[1] ἔτι μέντοι καὶ τὰ ἄλλα Σύρων πολίσματά τε καὶ φρούρια τὸν αὐτὸν κεκοσμηκὼς τρόπον ζηλωτὰ ἐπιεικῶς κατεστήσατο.

10 Οὕτω μὲν Συρίαν Ἰουστινιανὸς βασιλεὺς ἐν τῷ ἀσφαλεῖ διεσώσατο. πόλις δέ πού ἐστιν ἐπὶ Φοινίκης τῆς παρὰ Λίβανον, Παλμύρα ὄνομα, ἐν χώρῳ μὲν πεποιημένη τοῖς πάλαι ἀνθρώποις ἀγείτονι, ἐν καλῷ δὲ τῆς τῶν πολεμίων Σαρακη- 11 νῶν διόδου κειμένη. τούτου γὰρ δὴ αὐτὴν ἕνεκα καὶ ᾠκοδομήσαντο πρότερον, ὡς μὴ λάθοιεν οἱ βάρβαροι οὗτοι ἐξάπινα ἐς τὰ Ῥωμαίων ἤθη 12 ἐμβάλλοιεν. [illegible] αὐτὴν βασιλεὺς Ἰουστινιανὸς διὰ χρόνου μῆκος ἔρημον ἐπὶ πλεῖστον γεγενημένην ὀχυρώμασί τε λόγου μείζοσιν ἐπιρρώσας, πρὸς δὲ καὶ ὑδάτων περιουσίας καὶ φυλακτηρίου στρατιωτῶν ἐμπλησάμενος, τὰς τῶν Σαρακηνῶν ἐπιδρομὰς ἀνεχαίτισεν.

B 244

ΛΟΓΟΣ Γ΄

P 51 α΄. Χώραν μὲν[2] τὴν ἑῴαν οὕτως Ἰουστινιανὸς βασιλεὺς ὀχυρώμασιν ἐκρατύνατο, ᾗπέρ μοι ἐν P 52 τῷ ἔμπροσθεν λόγῳ ἐρρήθη. ἀρξαμένῳ δέ μοι ἐκ τῶν παρὰ Πέρσας ὁρίων τῆς Ῥωμαίων ἀρχῆς

[1] καὶ . . . ἐκρατύνατο: Haury would delete as repetition of section 1 above.
[2] μὲν A, μέντοι V.

Also he restored the entire circuit-wall of the city of Chalcis, which had fallen down to the ground and anyhow was unsuitable for defence, by means of exceptionally stout masonry, and he strengthened it with outworks.[1] Furthermore, he improved the other towns and forts of the Syrians in the same manner and made them altogether objects of envy.

Thus did the Emperor Justinian assure the safety of Syria. And there is a city in Phoenicia by Lebanon,[2] Palmyra by name, built in a neighbourless region by men of former times, but well situated across the track of the hostile Saracens. Indeed it was for this very reason that they had originally built this city, in order, namely, that these barbarians might not unobserved make sudden inroads into the Roman territory. This city, which through lapse of time had come to be almost completely deserted, the Emperor Justinian strengthened with defences which defy description, and he also provided it with abundant water and a garrison of troops, and thus put a stop to the raids of the Saracens.

BOOK III

i. Thus the Emperor Justinian strengthened the territory of the East with fortifications, as I have set forth in the preceding Book. And since I began at the Persian frontier of the Roman Empire in

[1] See the note on section 1 above.
[2] *I.e.* in the province of Phoenicê Libanensis.

περιηγεῖσθαι τὰ πρὸς αὐτοῦ ἐρύματα γεγενημένα, οὔ μοι ἀπὸ καιροῦ ἔδοξεν εἶναι ἐπὶ τοὺς Ἀρμενίους ἐνθένδε ἰέναι, οἳ δὴ ἐκ πόλεως Ἀμίδης ἄχρι ἐς Θεοδοσιούπολιν τὴν ἑτέραν προσοικοῦσι

2 Πέρσαις. μέλλοντι δέ μοι τῶν ἐκείνῃ οἰκοδομημάτων ἐπιμνησθῆναι προυργιαίτατον φαίνεται εἶναι ὑπειπεῖν πρότερον ὅντινα δὴ τρόπον σφαλερῶς ἄγαν βιοτεύοντας τοὺς Ἀρμενίους ὁ βασιλεὺς οὗτος ἐς τὴν παροῦσαν ἀσφάλειαν βεβαιότατα

3 μεθηρμόσατο. οὐ γὰρ δὴ ὅσον οἰκοδομίαις τούτους τοὺς κατηκόους ἐσώσατο, ἀλλὰ καὶ τῇ ἄλλῃ προνοίᾳ, ᾗπέρ μοι αὐτίκα μάλα γεγράψεται. ἀρκτέον δὲ μικρὸν ἄνωθεν.

B 245 4 Βασιλεὺς μὲν ὁμογενὴς πάλαι τοῖς Ἀρμενίοις καθίστατο, ᾗπερ τοῖς ἀναγραψαμένοις τῶν ἱστοριῶν

5 τὰ ἀρχαιότατα δεδιήγηται. ἐπειδὴ δὲ Ἀλέξανδρος ὁ Μακεδὼν τὸν Περσῶν βασιλέα καθεῖλε, Πέρσαι μὲν δεδουλωμένοι ἡσυχῇ ἔμενον, Πάρθοι δὲ Μακεδόσιν ἐπαναστάντες καὶ τῷ πολέμῳ περιγενόμενοι ἐξήλασάν τε αὐτοὺς ἐνθένδε καὶ τὰ μέχρι ἐς Τίγριν ποταμὸν ἔσχον, ὑπ' αὐτοῖς τε τὸ λοιπὸν ἐς ἔτη πεντακόσια ἔκειτο τὰ Περσῶν πράγματα, ἕως Ῥωμαίοις ὁ Μαμαίας Ἀλέξανδρος

6 βασιλεὺς γέγονε. καί ποτέ τις τῶν ἐν Πάρθοις βασιλέων τὸν ἀδελφὸν τὸν αὐτοῦ[1] Ἀρμενίοις βασιλέα κατεστήσατο, Ἀρσάκην ὄνομα, ὥσπερ ἡ τῶν Ἀρμενίων ἱστορία φησί. μὴ γάρ τις Ἀρ-

7 μενίους τοὺς Ἀρσακίδας οἰέσθω εἶναι. εἰρήνη γοῦν αὐτοῖς ἐς ἔτη τὰ[2] πεντακόσια κατὰ τὸ

[1] τὸν αὐτοῦ Dindorf, τοῦ αὐτοῦ V, αὐτοῦ A.
[2] τὰ V, om. A.

describing the defences built by him, it has seemed to me not inappropriate to pass on from there to Armenia, which adjoins Persia from the city of Amida as far as the second Theodosiopolis.[1] But now that I am about to mention the buildings of that region, it seems to me highly opportune to describe first how this Emperor brought the Armenians out of a very precarious way of life into their present state of complete safety. For it was not by means of buildings alone that he saved these subjects of his, but also by his foresight in other matters, as I shall presently shew. But I must go back a little to begin.

The Armenians of ancient times used to have a king of their own race, as is recorded by those who have written the history of the earliest period. And when Alexander of Macedon overthrew the King of the Persians, the Persians remained quietly in subjection, but the Parthians rose against the Macedonians and overcoming them in the struggle, drove them out of the country and gained the territory as far as the Tigris River, and the Persian state remained subject to them after that for five hundred years, until Alexander, son of Mamaea,[2] became Emperor of the Romans. At one time, one of the kings of the Parthians appointed his brother, Arsaces by name, King of the Armenians, as the history of the Armenians declares. I say this lest anyone think the descendants of Arsaces are Armenians. At least peace continued between them for these five hundred years because of the kinship.

[1] *I.e.* as distinguished from the Theodosiopolis on the Aborrhas mentioned above, II. ii. 16, vi. 13; see further below, Chap. v. 2.

[2] Alexander Severus, A.D. 222–235.

8 ξυγγενὲς διαγέγονε. καὶ ὁ μὲν τῶν Ἀρμενίων βασιλεὺς ἐν Ἀρμενίᾳ τῇ μεγάλῃ καλουμένῃ καθῆστο, τῷ Ῥωμαίων αὐτοκράτορι ἐκ παλαιοῦ ὑποχείριος ὤν, χρόνῳ δὲ ὕστερον παῖδες ἐγένοντο Ἀρσάκῃ τινὶ Ἀρμενίων βασιλεῖ δύο, Τιγ-
9 ράνης τε καὶ Ἀρσάκης ὀνόματα. ὅσπερ, ἐπεὶ ἔμελλε τὸν βίον διαμετρήσασθαι, διαθήκας τιθείς, ἄμφω τὼ παῖδε ποιεῖται διαδόχους αὐτῷ τῆς ἀρχῆς, οὐκ ἰσοστάσιον διορίσας ἑκατέρῳ τὸ κράτος, ἀλλὰ τῷ[1] Τιγράνῃ τετραπλασίαν ἀπο-
10 λιπὼν μοῖραν. Ἀρσάκης μὲν οὖν ὁ πατὴρ οὕτω βασιλείαν διοικησάμενος ἐξ ἀνθρώπων ἠφάνιστο, Ἀρσάκης δὲ ὁ παῖς, ἐφ' οἷς δὴ αὐτῷ ἐλασσοῦσθαι ξυνέβη ἀγανακτῶν τε καὶ δυσφορούμενος ἐπὶ τὸν Ῥωμαίων αὐτοκράτορα τὸ πρᾶγμα ἦγε, τοῦ τε ἀδελφοῦ καταλῦσαι τὴν βασιλείαν

B 246 μηχανῇ πάσῃ ἐλπίδα ἔχων καὶ ἄδικον οὖσαν τὴν
11 πατρὸς γνώμην ἀβέβαιον καταστήσεσθαι. Θεοδόσιος δὲ τότε, Ἀρκαδίου υἱὸς ἔτι παῖς ὢν κομιδῇ, Ῥωμαίων ἦρχε. τίσιν τε δειμαίνων τὴν ἐκ βασιλέως Τιγράνης Πέρσαις αὑτὸν ἐνεχείρισε, τὴν βασιλείαν παραδιδούς, περὶ πλείονός τε πεποιημένος ἰδιώτης ἐν Πέρσαις εἶναι ἢ πρὸς τὸν ἀδελφὸν τὰ δίκαια θέσθαι καὶ συμβασιλεύειν

P 53 12 Ἀρμενίων αὐτῷ ὀρθῶς καὶ δικαίως. καὶ Ἀρσάκης δὲ οὐδέν τι ἧσσον τὴν ἐκ Περσῶν τε καὶ τ' ἀδελφοῦ ἐπιβουλὴν δείσας ἐξέστη τῆς βασιλείας τῆς αὐτοῦ Θεοδοσίῳ τῷ αὐτοκράτορι ἐπὶ ξυνθήκαις τισὶν αἵ μοι ἐν τοῖς ὑπὲρ τῶν πολέμων
13 δεδήλωνται λόγοις. καὶ χρόνον μέν τινα περιμάχητος Ῥωμαίοις τε καὶ Πέρσαις ἡ τῶν Ἀρμενίων

[1] τῷ V, om. A.

And the King of the Armenians had his seat in Greater Armenia, as it was called, being subject to the Roman Emperor from an early period; but at a later time two sons were born to a certain Arsaces, King of Armenia, Tigranes and Arsaces by name. When this king was about to reach the end of his life, he made a will in which he made both of the boys his successors in the kingdom, not assigning an equal weight of power to each of them, but leaving to Tigranes a four-fold portion. So the father Arsaces, having made this disposition of the royal power, departed from the world, but his son Arsaces, being resentful and angry because his portion proved to be inferior, laid the matter before the Roman Emperor, hoping that by using every device he might destroy the power of his brother and nullify his father's purpose as being unjust. At that time Theodosius, son of Arcadius,[1] who was still quite a boy, was ruling over the Romans. And Tigranes, fearing the vengeance of the Emperor, placed himself in the power of the Persians and handed over his kingdom to them, considering it preferable to live as a private individual among the Persians, than to make a fair settlement with his brother and with him to rule over the Armenians righteously and justly. Arsaces meanwhile still feared the hostility of the Persians and of his brother and resigned his own kingship in favour of the Emperor Theodosius, on certain conditions which I have described in the Books on the Wars.[2] And for a time the territory of the Armenians was fought over by the Romans and the Persians, but at length

[1] Ascended the throne in 408 after Christ.
[2] II. iii. 35.

γεγένηται χώρα, ἐν ὑστάτῳ δὲ ξυνέβησαν, Πέρσας μὲν τὴν Τιγράνου μοῖραν, Ῥωμαίους δὲ τὴν
14 Ἀρσάκου ἔχειν. ἐπὶ τούτοις τε σπονδαὶ ἀμφοτέροις ξυνετελέσθησαν, καὶ τὸ λοιπὸν ὁ Ῥωμαίων βασιλεὺς ἄρχοντα τοῖς Ἀρμενίοις ἀεὶ καθίστη ὅντινά ποτε καὶ ὁπηνίκα ἂν αὐτῷ βουλομένῳ
15 εἴη. κόμητά τε Ἀρμενίας ἐκάλουν καὶ εἰς ἐμὲ τὸν ἄρχοντα τοῦτον.

16 Ἀλλ' ἐπεὶ οὐχ οἵα τε ἦν ἡ τοιαύτη ἀρχὴ ἀποκρούεσθαι τὰς τῶν πολεμίων ἐφόδους, οὐ παρόντων αὐτῇ [1] στρατιωτικῶν καταλόγων, κατανενοηκὼς Ἰουστινιανὸς βασιλεὺς οὕτως ἀτάκτως τὴν Ἀρμενίαν ἀεὶ φερομένην, ταύτῃ τε τοῖς βαρβάροις εὐάλωτον οὖσαν, ταύτην μὲν τὴν ἀρχὴν ἐνθένδε καθεῖλε, στρατηγὸν δὲ τοῖς Ἀρμενίοις ἐπέστησε, στρατιωτικῶν τε καταλόγων αὐτῷ κατεστήσατο πλῆθος ἀξιόχρεων ταῖς τῶν πολεμίων ἐπιδρομαῖς
17 ἀντιτάξασθαι. τὰ μὲν οὖν ἀμφὶ τῇ μεγάλῃ καλουμένῃ Ἀρμενίᾳ διῳκήσατο ὧδε, τῇ δὲ ἄλλῃ Ἀρμενίᾳ, ἥπερ ἐντὸς Εὐφράτου ποταμοῦ
B 247 οὖσα διήκει ἐς Ἄμιδαν πόλιν, σατράπαι ἐφειστήκεισαν Ἀρμένιοι πέντε, καὶ κατὰ γένος μὲν ἐς ἀεὶ ἐς [2] τὰς ἀρχὰς ἐκαλοῦντο ταύτας, ἐχόμενοι
18 αὐτῶν ἄχρι ἐς θάνατον. σύμβολα μέντοι αὐτῶν πρὸς τοῦ Ῥωμαίων βασιλέως ἐδέχοντο μόνον. ἄξιον δὲ τὰ σύμβολα ταῦτα δηλῶσαι λόγῳ, ἐπεὶ
19 οὐκέτι ἐς ἀνθρώπου ὄψιν ἀφίξεται. χλαμὺς ἡ ἐξ ἐρίων πεποιημένη, οὐχ οἷα τῶν προβατίων ἐκπέφυκεν, ἀλλ' ἐκ θαλάσσης συνειλεγμένων.
20 πίννους τὰ ζῷα καλεῖν νενομίκασιν, ἐν οἷς ἡ τῶν ἐρίων ἔκφυσις γίνεται. χρυσῷ δὲ ἡ τῆς πορφύρας

[1] αὐτῇ V, αὐτῷ A.

they reached an agreement that the Persians should hold the portion of Tigranes and the Romans that of Arsaces. On these conditions a truce was agreed upon by both sides and thereafter the Roman Emperor always appointed a ruler for the Armenians, whomever he wished and whenever he wished. And they used to call this ruler even to my time the Count of Armenia.

Such a government, however, was not able to repel the attacks of its enemies, since it had at its disposal no regular troops, and therefore the Emperor Justinian, observing that Armenia was always in a state of disorder and was, for this reason, an easy prey for the barbarians, abolished this form of administration and placed a general in charge of Armenia and assigned to him military forces sufficient to withstand the inroads of the enemy. Such was the disposition he made for Greater Armenia, as it is called, but in the other Armenia, which extends inside of the Euphrates River as far as the city of Amida,[1] five Armenian satraps held the power, and these offices were always hereditary and held for life. However, they received the symbols of office only from the Roman Emperor. It is worth while to describe these insignia, for they will never again be seen by man. There is a cloak made of wool, not such as is produced by sheep, but gathered from the sea. *Pinnos*[2] the creature is called on which this wool grows. And the part where the purple

[1] *I.e.* west and north of it.
[2] A bivalve which grows a silky beard. The usual form of word is *πίννα*.

[2] ἐς before τὰς added by Maltretus.

κατηλήλειπτο μοῖρα, ἐφ' ἧς εἴωθεν ἡ τῆς ἁλουργίδος ἐμβολὴ γίνεσθαι.[1] 21 περόνη χρυσῆ τῇ χλαμύδι ἐπέκειτο, λίθον ἐπὶ μέσης περιφράττουσά τινα ἔντιμον, ἀφ' οὗ δὴ ὑάκινθοι τρεῖς χρυσαῖς τε καὶ χαλαραῖς ταῖς ἁλύσεσιν ἀπεκρέμαντο. 22 χιτὼν ἐκ μετάξης ἐγκαλλωπίσμασι χρυσοῖς πανταχόθεν ὡραϊσμένος ἃ δὴ νενομίκασι πλούμια καλεῖν. 23 ὑποδήματα μέχρι ἐς γόνυ φοινικοῦ χρώματος, ἃ [1] δὴ βασιλέα μόνον Ῥωμαίων τε καὶ Περσῶν ὑποδεῖσθαι θέμις.

24 Στρατιώτης δὲ Ῥωμαῖος οὔτε τῷ Ἀρμενίων βασιλεῖ οὔτε σατράπαις ἤμυνε πώποτε, ἀλλὰ τὰ πολέμια κατὰ μόνας αὐτοὶ διῳκοῦντο. 25 χρόνῳ δὲ ὕστερον ἐπὶ Ζήνωνος βασιλεύοντος Ἰλλοῦ τε καὶ Λεοντίῳ τετυραννηκόσιν ἐπὶ βασιλέα διαφανῶς συντάσσεσθαί τινες τῶν σατραπῶν ἔγνωσαν. 26 (P 54) διὸ δὴ Λεόντιόν τε καὶ Ἰλλοῦν Ζήνων βασιλεὺς ὑποχειρίους πεποιημένος, σατράπην μὲν ἕνα φαυλοτάτην ἀρχὴν ἔχοντα καὶ ὡς ἥκιστα λόγου ἀξίαν ἐν χώρᾳ τῇ Βελαβιτίνῃ καλουμένῃ ἐπὶ τοῦ προτέρου σχήματος εἴασε, τοὺς δὲ λοιποὺς καθελὼν ἅπαντας οὐκέτι ἐς τοὺς κατὰ γένος σφίσι προσήκοντας ξυνεχώρησε τὰς ἀρχὰς φέρεσθαι, (B 248) ἀλλ' ἑτέρους ἀεὶ τὴν ἀρχὴν διαδέχεσθαι διώρισε ταύτην, οὓς ἂν βουλομένῳ βασιλεῖ εἴη, ὥσπερ ἐφ' ἁπάσαις ταῖς ἄλλαις διώρισται Ῥωμαίων ἀρχαῖς. 27 στρατιῶται μέντοι οὐδ' ὣς Ῥωμαῖοι αὐτοῖς εἵποντο, ἀλλὰ τῶν Ἀρμενίων τινές,

[1] ἃ Maltretus: ὅ.

---

[1] The description is obscure, and the precise meaning of ἐμβολή is unknown; see Haury's *Index Graecitatis*. But the

should have been, that is, where the insertion of purple cloth is usually made, is overlaid with gold.[1] The cloak was fastened by a golden brooch in the middle of which was a precious stone from which hung three sapphires by loose golden chains. There was a tunic of silk adorned in every part with decorations of gold which they are wont to call *plumia.*[2] The boots were of red colour and reached to the knee, of the sort which only the Roman Emperor and the Persian King are permitted to wear.

Roman soldiers, however, never fought under the orders of the king of the Armenians or of the satraps, but these rulers conducted their wars independently. But at a later time, during the reign of Zeno,[3] some of the satraps decided to array themselves openly with Illus and Leontius, who had revolted against the Emperor. Consequently, when the Emperor had reduced Leontius and Illus to subjection, he left in the former status only one satrap, who held a very inferior province which was not of any importance, in the region called Belabitinê; all the others he removed and no longer permitted them to transmit the office to those connected with them by kinship, but he ordained that on each occasion different men of the Emperor's choosing should succeed to these offices, just as is the rule in all the other offices of the Romans. Even so, these officials were not in command of Roman soldiers, but only of a few Armenians, as had been customary

general idea seems to be that where in the dress of high officials purple was normally used, this space was done in gold.

[2] Latin *plumeus*, "embroidered."

[3] A.D. 474–491.

ᾗπερ τὰ πρότερα εἴθιστο, καὶ ἀπ' αὐτοῦ πολεμίους
28 προσβάλλοντας ἀποκρούεσθαι ἀδύνατοι ἦσαν. ἃ
δὴ καταμαθὼν Ἰουστινιανὸς βασιλεὺς τὸ μὲν
τῶν σατραπῶν ὄνομα ἐξήλασεν ἐνθένδε εὐθύς,
δοῦκας δὲ τοὺς καλουμένους δύο τοῖς ἔθνεσιν
29 ἐπέστησε τούτοις· οἷς δὴ ξυνεστήσατο μὲν
Ῥωμαίων στρατιωτῶν καταλόγους παμπληθεῖς,
ἐφ' ᾧ τὰ Ῥωμαίων ξυμφυλάξουσιν αὐτοῖς ὅρια·
ὀχυρώματα δὲ δεδημιούργηκεν αὐτοῖς κατὰ τάδε.

β'. Ἄρξομαι δὲ ἀπὸ τῶν ἐν Μεσοποταμίᾳ
χωρίων, ὅπως δὴ ὁ λόγος τοῖς ἔμροσθέν μοι
δεδιηγημένοις προσεχῶς ἄγοιτο. τὸν μὲν οὖν
ἕνα, τὸν ἐν τοῖς Ἀρμενίων ἔθνεσιν ἄρχοντα, ὃν
δοῦκα καλοῦσιν, ἐν πόλει Μαρτυροπόλει καλουμένῃ ἱδρύσατο, τὸν δὲ δὴ ἕτερον ἐν φρουρίῳ
2 ὅπερ Κιθαρίζων καλοῦσιν. ὅπη ποτὲ δὲ τῆς
Ῥωμαίων ἀρχῆς τὰ χωρία τάδε ξυμβαίνει εἶναι,
ἐγὼ δηλώσω. ἐν Ἀρμενίᾳ τῇ Σοφανηνῇ καλουμένῃ πόλις ἐστί που Μαρτυρόπολις ὄνομα παρ'
αὐτὸν ποταμὸν Νύμφιον κειμένη καὶ τοῖς πολεμίοις
ὡς ἀγχοτάτω πρόσοικος οὖσα, ἐπεὶ ὁ Νύμφιος
ποταμὸς διορίζει ἐνταῦθα τὰ Ῥωμαίων τε καὶ
3 Περσῶν ἤθη. ἐπὶ θάτερα γὰρ τοῦ ποταμοῦ
Ἀρξανηνὴ [1] ἡ χώρα οἰκεῖται Περσῶν κατήκοος
ἐκ παλαιοῦ οὖσα. ἀλλὰ καὶ ὣς ἡ πόλις ἀπημελη-
μένη Ῥωμαίοις τούτοις δὴ ἀεὶ τοῖς βαρβάροις
4 ἀπέκειτο. ὥστε ἀμέλει Καβάδης ὁ Περσῶν
βασιλεὺς ἐπὶ Ἀναστασίου βασιλεύοντος ἐσέβαλε
B 249 Ῥωμαίων τὴν γῆν, διὰ Μαρτυροπόλεως τὸ

[1] Ἀρξανηνὴ Haury: ἀρξάνη.

---

[1] Modern Mejafarkin.

previously, with the result that they were unable to repel the attacks of an enemy. And when this came to the knowledge of the Emperor Justinian, he immediately did away with the title of Satrap and appointed over these provinces two Dukes, as they are called; and he put under them a very large force of regular Roman troops to assist them in guarding the Roman frontier. He also built strongholds for them as follows.

ii. I shall start from the places in Mesopotamia, so that my account may proceed in order from the points which I have described previously. One of the rulers of the Armenian provinces, whom they call Duke, he established in the city called Martyropolis,[1] and the other in a stronghold which they call Citharizôn.[2] And I shall make clear just where in the Roman Empire these places actually are. In the part of Armenia called Sophanenê there is a certain city known as Martyropolis which lies on the very bank of the Nymphius[3] River, quite close to the enemy, because the Nymphius River at that point divides the Roman from the Persian territory. For across the river lies the territory of Arxanenê, which has been subject to the Persians from early times. Even so the city had been neglected by the Romans and lay always exposed to these barbarians. In consequence of this, indeed, Cabades, King of the Persians, invaded[4] the Roman territory during the reign of Anastasius, directing his march by way of Martyropolis, since it lay a little more than

[2] Modern Köderidj.

[3] It is uncertain whether the name is accented Νύμφιος or Νυμφίος; Haury, *Index nominum*.

[4] In A.D. 502.

στράτευμα ἄγων, ἐπεὶ Ἀμίδης ὀλίγῳ πλέον
5 ἡμέρας ὁδῷ εὐζώνῳ ἀνδρὶ διειστήκει. ὥσπερ
δέ τι πάρεργον ὁδοῦ διαχειρίζων καὶ τῆς ἐφόδου
παρενθήκην τινὰ εὐθυωρὸν τὴν πόλιν ἐξεῖλεν, οὐ
τειχομαχήσας ἢ προσβολήν τινα ἢ προσεδρείαν
πεποιημένος, ἀλλὰ δηλώσας ὅτι δὴ ἀφίξεται
P 55 6 μόνον. εὖ γὰρ εἰδότες οἱ τῇδε ᾠκημένοι ὡς
οὐδὲ βραχεῖάν τινα χρόνου στιγμὴν τῷ στρατο-
πέδῳ ἀνθέξουσιν, ἐπειδὴ ἀγχοῦ τῶν Μήδων
στρατὸν ἥκοντα εἶδον, ἅμα Θεοδώρῳ τηνικάδε
Σοφανηνῆς σατραπεύοντι καὶ τῆς σατραπείας
ἐνδιδυσκομένῳ τὸ σχῆμα, Καβάδῃ προσῆλθον
εὐθύς,[1] σφᾶς τε αὐτοὺς καὶ Μαρτυρόπολιν αὐτῷ
ἐνδιδόντες, φόρους τε τοὺς δημοσίους ἐνιαυτοῖν
7 δυοῖν ἐν χερσὶν ἔχοντες. οἷς δὴ ὁ Καβάδης
ἡσθεὶς τῆς μὲν πόλεώς τε καὶ χώρας ἁπάσης, ὡς
τῇ Περσῶν ἀρχῇ προσηκούσης, ἀπέσχετο,[2] τοὺς
δὲ ἀνθρώπους ἀθῴους ἀφῆκεν, οὔτε τι λυμηνάμενος
οὔτε τι τῆς πολιτείας μεταβαλών, ἀλλὰ Θεόδωρον
αὐτὸν σατράπην αὐτοῖς ἐπιστήσας καὶ αὐτῷ ἅτε
οὐ γεγονότι ἀγνώμονι τὰ σύμβολα ἐγκεχειρικὼς
τῆς ἀρχῆς, ὡς τὴν χώραν φυλάξοντι Πέρσαις.
8 οὕτω τε τὸ στράτευμα πρόσω ἀπαγαγὼν πολιορκίᾳ τε Ἄμιδαν ἐξελὼν ἐς τὰ Περσῶν ἤθη
ἀπήλαυνεν, ᾗπερ ἐν λόγοις μοι τοῖς ὑπὲρ τῶν
9 πολέμων ἐρρήθη. βασιλεύς τε Ἀναστάσιος ἐξ-
επιστάμενος ὡς οὐχ οἷόν τε ἦν Μαρτυρόπολιν
ὀχύρωμα οὐδὲν ἔχουσαν ἐκ πολεμίων διασώσασθαι
προσβολῆς, οὐχ ὅπως ἐπὶ Θεόδωρόν τε καὶ
Σοφανηνοὺς ἠγανάκτησεν, ἀλλὰ καὶ χάριτας
αὐτοῖς τῆς πράξεως ἔχειν ὡμολόγει πολλάς.

[1] εὐθύς A, om. V. [2] ἀπέσχετο V, ἀντέσχετο A.

a one-day's journey from Amida for an unencumbered traveller. And as if he were dealing with some minor detail of his journey, an incidental task of his campaign, he captured this city out of hand, not by storming the wall or by making any kind of assault or siege, but simply by sending an announcement that he would arrive. For the inhabitants of the city, knowing well that they would not be able to hold out even for one short moment against the attacking force, when they learned that the army of the Medes had arrived close by, immediately approached Cabades in company with Theodorus, who at that time was Satrap of Sophanenê, clothed in his robes of office, and placed themselves and Martyropolis at his disposal, bearing in their hands the public taxes of two years. And Cabades was pleased with this and withheld his hand from the city and from the whole district, as belonging to the Persian Kingdom, and he let the people go unharmed, neither inflicting any damage nor changing the form of the government, but he appointed Theodorus himself their Satrap, entrusting to him, since he had shewn himself not indiscreet, the tokens of the office, with the intention that he watch over the land for the Persians. Then he led his army forward, captured Amida by siege, and marched back into the land of Persia, as I have related in the Books on the Wars.[1] And the Emperor Anastasius, understanding that it was not possible to defend Martyropolis from hostile assault, since it had no defences, not only shewed no resentment against Theodorus and the people of Sophanenê, but actually expressed deep gratitude to them for their action. Indeed the

[1] I. vii. 3.

10 ταύτης οὖν τῆς Μαρτυροπόλεως τοῦ περιβόλου
B 250 ἐτύγχανε τὸ μὲν πάχος διῆκον ἐς πόδας μάλιστα τέσσαρας, τὸ δὲ [1] ὕψος ἄχρι ἐς εἴκοσιν· ὥστε τοῖς πολεμίοις αὐτὸν οὐ τειχομαχοῦσιν οὐδὲ μηχανὰς προσβάλλουσι μόνον εὐέφοδον εἶναι, ἀλλὰ καὶ ἐσπηδῆσαι ἱκανῶς πρόχειρον.

11 Διὸ δὴ βασιλεὺς Ἰουστινιανὸς ἐπενόει τάδε· τοῦ περιβόλου ἐκτὸς τὴν γῆν διορύξας, θεμέλιά τε ταύτῃ ἐνθέμενος τείχισμα ᾠκοδομήσατο ἕτερον ἐς ποδῶν πάχος διῆκον τεττάρων, χώραν διαλιπὼν μεταξὺ τεττάρων ἑτέρων τὸ εὖρος, ἐς ὕψος δὲ καὶ τοῦτο ἀναστήσας ποδῶν εἴκοσιν, ἴσον τῷ
12 προτέρῳ παντάπασιν ἐσκευάσατο εἶναι. μετὰ δὲ λίθους τε καὶ τίτανον ἐς χῶρον τὸν μεταξὺ τείχους ἑκατέρου ἐμβεβλημένος ἐς μίαν τινὰ οἰκοδομίαν δυοκαίδεκα τὸ πάχος ποδῶν τὸ
13 ἔργον τοῦτο ἀποτετόρνευται. ὕπερθέν τε κατὰ πάχος τὸ αὐτὸ μάλιστα ἐς ὕψος τοσοῦτον ἐντέθει-
14 κεν, ὅσον ξυνέβαινε τὸ πρότερον εἶναι. ἀλλὰ καὶ προτείχισμα λόγου πολλοῦ ἄξιον τῇ πόλει δεδημιούργηκε καὶ τὰ ἄλλα ἁπλῶς ἅπαντα οἷς δὴ πόλεως ὀχύρωμα διασῴζεται.

P 56 γʹ. Ἐκ δὲ Μαρτυροπόλεως ἐς δύοντά που τὸν ἥλιον ἰόντι χωρίον ἐστὶ Φεισὼν ὄνομα ἐν Ἀρμενίᾳ μὲν καὶ αὐτὸ κείμενον τῇ Σοφανηνῇ καλουμένῃ, Μαρτυροπόλεως δὲ ὀλίγον ἔλασσον ἢ ὁδῷ ἡμέρας
2 διέχον. τούτου δὲ τοῦ χωρίου ἐπέκεινα, ὅσον ἐκ σημείων ὀκτὼ μάλιστα, ὄρη ἀπότομα καὶ παντάπασιν ἀδιέξοδα ξυνιόντα ἐς ἄλληλα στενωποὺς [2] ἀπεργάζονται δύο, ἄγχιστά πη ἀλλήλοιν ὄντας [3] οὕσπερ νενομίκασι Κλεισούρας καλεῖν.

[1] δὲ A, δέ γε V.

circuit-wall of this Martyropolis was really about four feet in thickness, while it was only twenty feet high. In consequence, the wall could not only be easily assaulted by the enemy if they stormed it or brought up their siege engines, but it was quite easy for them simply to scramble over it.

Therefore the Emperor Justinian devised the following plan: Outside the circuit-wall he dug a trench, and laying foundations there he built a second wall with a thickness of four feet, leaving a space of four feet between the two walls; and he raised the new wall also to a height of twenty feet and made it in all respects equal to the first. Then, by throwing stones and mortar into the space between the two walls, he brought this work to perfection by forming one solid structure with a thickness of twelve feet. Above this he added, in about the same thickness, the same height which the earlier wall had had. He also constructed admirable outworks for the city and all the other things without exception on which a city's defences are based.

iii. As one goes westerly from Martyropolis, there is a place called Pheisôn, which is also situated in Armenia, in the section called Sophanenê, a little less than a day's journey distant from Martyropolis. Beyond this place, at about the eighth milestone, precipitous and altogether impassable mountains come together to form two passes, very close to each other, which they are wont to call *cleisurae*.[1]

[1] Latin *clausura* or *clusura*, "a narrow shut-in road"; *cf. Wars*, II. xxix. 25, note, and *Jour. Hel. Stud.* xxi. 69 ff.

---

[2] στενωποὺς V, ποταμοὺς A.
[3] ὄντας V, ὄντα A.

3 τοὺς δὲ ἐκ Περσαρμενίας ἐπὶ Σοφανηνὴν πορευομένους, εἴτε ἐξ αὐτῶν τῶν Περσικῶν ὁρίων εἴτε διὰ τοῦ Κιθαρίζων φρουρίου ἴοιεν, ἀμήχανά ἐστιν ὅτι μὴ διὰ τούτων δὴ τῶν δύο στενωπῶν
B 251 4 ἐνταῦθα γενέσθαι. καλοῦσι δὲ αὐτῶν οἱ ἐπιχώριοι Ἰλλυρισὸν μὲν τὸν ἕτερον, τὸν δὲ ἄλλον
5 Σαφχάς. ὅπως μὲν οὖν ἀναστέλλοιτο τοῖς πολεμίοις ἡ ἐνταῦθα ὁδὸς ἀσφαλείας τε αὐτῆς καὶ τῆς ἄλλης ἐπιμελείας ἄξια ἐν τοῖς μάλιστα τὰ χωρία ταῦτα ὄντα ἐτύγχανεν. ἀλλὰ καὶ ὣς ἀφύλακτα τὸ παράπαν μεμένηκε τοῖς πρόσθεν
6 ἀνθρώποις. βασιλεὺς δὲ Ἰουστινιανὸς ἔν τε τῷ Φεισὼν κἀν τοῖς στενωποῖς ὀχυρώματά τε ἀξιοθέατα καὶ στρατιωτῶν φρουρὰν ἀνανταγώνιστον καταστησάμενος, ἄβατον βαρβάροις τὴν χώραν διεπράξατο παντάπασιν εἶναι. τὰ μὲν οὖν ἐπὶ χώρας τῆς Σοφανηνῆς καλουμένης τῇδε Ἰουστινιανῷ βασιλεῖ εἴργασται.

7 Ἐν δὲ τῷ Κιθαρίζων χωρίῳ, ὅπερ ἐπὶ Ἀσθιανίνης τῆς καλουμένης ἐστί, φρούριον οὐ πρότερον ὂν ἐν χώρῳ λοφώδει ὑπερφυές τε καὶ δαιμονίως
8 ἄμαχον κατεστήσατο· ἔνθα δὴ καὶ διαρκὲς ὕδωρ ἐσαγαγὼν τά τε ἄλλα πάντα τοῖς τῇδε ᾠκημένοις ἐν ἐπιτηδείῳ πεποιημένος, τὸν ἕτερον δοῦκα, ᾗπέρ μοι εἴρηται, ξὺν στρατιωτῶν ἐνταῦθα φρουρᾷ ἱκανωτάτῃ ἱδρύσατο. ταύτῃ τε τοῖς τῶν Ἀρμενίων ἔθνεσι τὴν ἀσφάλειαν ἀνεσώσατο.

9 Ἐκ δὲ Κιθαρίζων ἔς τε Θεοδοσιούπολιν καὶ Ἀρμενίαν τὴν ἑτέραν ἰόντι Χορζάνη μὲν ἡ χώρα καλεῖται, διήκει δὲ ἐς ὁδὸν τριῶν ἡμερῶν μάλιστα οὔτε λίμνης τινὸς ὕδατι οὔτε ποταμοῦ ῥείθρῳ οὔτε ὄρεσι τὴν δίοδον ἐν στενῷ εἴργουσι διοριζο-

And when travellers go from Persarmenia to Sophanenê, either from the Persian territory itself or by way of the fortress of Citharizôn, it is necessary for them to get there by way of these two passes. The natives call the one of them Illyrisum and the other Saphchae. And for the purpose of checking the enemy's advance in that region, these places were, as it happened, worth making thoroughly defended and well equipped in every way. Yet they remained altogether unguarded by the men of earlier times. But the Emperor Justinian, by establishing admirable forts at Pheisôn and in the passes and posting in them invincible garrisons, has made this region altogether inaccessible to the barbarians. Such were the things done by the Emperor Justinian in the territory called Sophanenê.

And at the place named Citharizôn, which is in Asthianinê, as it is called, he established a fortress which had not existed before, a huge and extraordinarily impregnable stronghold, situated in a hilly region. He also brought into it an abundant supply of water and made all other proper arrangements for the inhabitants, and stationed there the second of the Dukes, as I have said,[1] with a very numerous garrison of soldiers. And he thereby guaranteed the safety of the Armenian provinces.

As one goes from Citharizôn to Theodosiopolis and the other Armenia, the land is called Chorzanê; it extends for a distance of about three days' journey, not being marked off from the Persian territory by the water of any lake or by any river's stream or

[1] Chap. ii. 1.

μένη τῆς τῶν Περσῶν γῆς, ἀλλὰ τῶν ὁρίων
10 αὐταῖς ἀναμὶξ κειμένων. ὥστε οἱ ταύτῃ ᾠκημένοι, Ῥωμαίων ἢ Περσῶν ὄντες κατήκοοι, οὔτε τι ἀπ' ἀλλήλων δέος ἔχουσιν οὔτε ἀλλήλοις πη ἐς ἐπιβουλήν εἰσιν ὕποπτοι, ἀλλὰ καὶ γάμους ἀλλήλοις ἐπικηδεύουσι καὶ ἀγορὰν [1] τῶν ἐπιτηδείων συμβάλλονται καὶ τὰ ἐς γεωργίαν ἐπικοινοῦνται.
B 252 11 ἢν δέ ποτε οἱ τῶν ἑτέρων ἄρχοντες ἐπὶ τοὺς ἑτέρους στρατῷ ἴωσιν, ἐπιτεταγμένον σφίσι πρὸς τοῦ βασιλέως, ἀφυλάκτους ἀεὶ τοὺς πλησιοχώρους
12 εὑρίσκουσι. χωρία μὲν γὰρ ἑκατέροις πολυανθρωπότατα ὡς ἀγχοτάτω ἀλλήλων ἐστίν, ἔρυμα
P 57 13 δὲ οὐδετέροις πη ἐκ παλαιοῦ ἦν. παρῆν οὖν ἐνθένδε τῷ Περσῶν βασιλεῖ ῥᾷόν τε καὶ απονώτερον τὴν δίοδον ἐς τὰ Ῥωμαίων ἤθη ποιεῖσθαι, ἕως βασιλεὺς Ἰουστινιανὸς διακωλυτὴς αὐτῷ γέγονε τρόπῳ τοιῷδε. χωρίον ἦν ἐπὶ μέσης
14 τῆς χώρας Ἀρταλέσων ὄνομα. τοῦτο τείχει ἐχυρωτάτῳ περιβαλὼν φρούριόν τε ἀμαχώτατον ἐξειργάσατο καὶ στρατιωτικοὺς καταλόγους τῇδε ἱδρύσατο, οἷς δὴ ἄρχοντα ἐς ἀεὶ ἐφεστάναι διώρισεν, ὅνπερ δοῦκα Ῥωμαῖοι τῇ Λατίνων καλοῦσι φωνῇ. οὕτω τε τὴν ἐκείνῃ ἐσχατιὰν ἐτειχίσατο ξύμπασαν.

δ'. Ταῦτα μὲν οὖν βασιλεῖ ταύτῃ ἐξείργασται. ὅσα δὲ αὐτῷ ἐπὶ τῆς ἄλλης Ἀρμενίας διαπεπόνηται
2 ἐρῶν ἔρχομαι. Σάταλα πόλις ἐπὶ σφαλερᾶς τὸ παλαιὸν ἐλπίδος εἱστήκει. τῶν μὲν γὰρ πολεμίων

[1] ἀγορὰν V, ἀγορὰς A.

---

[1] That is, Lesser Armenia; cf. chap. i. 17 *supra*.

by a wall of mountains which pinch the road into a narrow pass, but the two frontiers are indistinct. So the inhabitants of this region, whether subjects of the Romans or of the Persians, have no fear of each other, nor do they give one another any occasion to apprehend an attack, but they even intermarry and hold a common market for their produce and together share the labours of farming. And if the commanders on either side ever make an expedition against the others, when they are ordered to do so by their sovereign, they always find their neighbours unprotected. Their very populous towns are close to each other, yet from ancient times no stronghold existed on either side. It was possible, therefore, for the Persian King to proceed by this route with comparative ease and convenience in passing through into Roman territory, until the Emperor Justinian blocked his way in the following manner. There was a town in the middle of this region named Artalesôn which he surrounded with a very strong wall and converted into an impregnable fortress; and he stationed there detachments of regular troops which by his orders were always to be commanded by an officer whom the Romans, in the Latin tongue, call a *Dux*. By these measures he fortified the whole of that remote frontier.

iv. These things were accomplished by the Emperor in the manner described. I shall now go on to tell about all the other works which by his diligence he executed in the other[1] Armenia. The city of Satala[2] had been in a precarious state in ancient times. For it is situated not far from the land of the enemy

[2] Modern Sadagh.

τῆς γῆς ὀλίγῳ διέχει, ἐν δαπέδῳ δὲ χθαμαλῷ κεῖται, λόφοις τε πολλοῖς ἀμφ' αὐτὴν ἐπανεστηκόσιν ὑπόκειται, περιβόλων τε αὐτῇ διὰ ταῦτα 3 ἔδει τοῖς ἐπιβουλεύουσιν ἀμηχάνων ἑλεῖν. ἀλλὰ καὶ τοιαύτῃ τοῦ χωρίου τὴν φύσιν οὔσῃ τὰ ἐκ τοῦ ἐρύματος σφαλερώτερα ἦν, φαύλως[1] τε ἀρχὴν τῇ κατασκευῇ καὶ παρέργως πεποιημένου καὶ τῷ μακρῷ χρόνῳ ἤδη τῆς οἰκοδομίας ἑκασ-4 ταχοῦ διερρωγότος. ἀλλὰ τοῦτο περιελὼν ὁ βασιλεὺς ὅλον, περίβολον ᾠκοδομήσατο ἐνταῦθα νέον, ὑψηλὸν μὲν ὅσον ὑπερπεφυκέναι τοὺς ἀμφ' αὐτὸν λόφους δοκεῖν, εὐρυνόμενον δὲ ὅσον ἐπ' ἀσφαλοῦς ἐπανεστηκέναι τό γε τοῦ ὕψους ὑπέρ-5 ογκον. καὶ προτείχισμα δὲ[2] πολλοῦ ἄξιον λόγου B 253 πηξάμενος ἐν κύκλῳ τοὺς πολεμίους κατέπληξε. καὶ[3] φρούριον δὲ Σατάλων οὐ πολλῷ ἄποθεν ἐχυρὸν ἄγαν ἐν χώρᾳ Ὀσροηνῶν καλουμένῃ ᾠκοδομήσατο.

6 Ἦν δέ τι φρούριον ἐν τῇδε τῇ χώρᾳ ἐν ἀκρωνυχίᾳ λόφου κατακρήμνου πεποιημένον[4] τοῖς πάλαι ἀνθρώποις, ὃ δὴ Πομπήιος ἐν τοῖς ἄνω χρόνοις ὁ Ῥωμαίων στρατηγὸς ἐξελὼν καὶ τῆς χώρας τῷ πολέμῳ κύριος γεγονὼς ἐκρατύνατό 7 τε ὡς μάλιστα καὶ Κολώνειαν ἐπωνόμασε· καὶ τοῦτο οὖν χρόνῳ πεπονηκὸς τοσούτῳ τὸ πλῆθος βασιλεὺς Ἰουστινιανὸς ἀνεσώσατο δυνάμει τῇ 8 πάσῃ. καὶ χρήματα μέντοι προέμενος ἀνάριθμα τοῖς τῇδε ᾠκημένοις, ἐρύματα ἑκασταχοῦ διεπράξατο ἐν τοῖς αὐτῶν ἰδίοις ἀγροῖς ἢ νέα δείμασθαι, 9 ἢ ἀνοικοδομήσασθαι σαθρὰ γεγονότα. ὥστε ἅπαντα σχεδόν τι τὰ ὀχυρώματα, ὅσα δὴ ἐνταῦθα

[1] φαύλως A, φαύλω V. [2] δὲ A, om. V.

and it also lies in a low-lying plain and is dominated by many hills which tower around it, and for this reason it stood in need of circuit-walls which would defy attack. Nevertheless, even though its surroundings were of such a nature as this, its defences were in a perilous condition, having been carelessly constructed with bad workmanship in the beginning, and with the long passage of time the masonry had everywhere collapsed. But the Emperor tore all this down and built there a new circuit-wall, so high that it seemed to overtop the hills around it, and of a thickness sufficient to ensure the safety of its towering mass. And he set up admirable outworks on all sides and so struck terror into the hearts of the enemy. He also built a very strong fortress not far from Satala in the territory called Osroenê.

There was a certain fortress in that region erected by men of ancient times on the crest of a precipitous hill, which in early times Pompey, the Roman general, captured; and becoming master of the land by his victories, he strengthened this town materially and named it Coloneia.[1] This also the Emperor Justinian, finding that it had suffered much through the ravages of so long a time, restored with all his resources. Furthermore, by granting great sums to the inhabitants of this region he brought it about that everywhere on their own land either new defences were built or those which had fallen into decay were restored. Thus practically all the fortifications which

[1] Modern Kara Hissar.

---

[3] καὶ V, om. A.
[4] κατακρήμνου πεποιημένον V, ἀποκρήμνου γεγενημένον A.

ξυμβαίνει εἶναι, Ἰουστινιανοῦ βασιλέως τυγχάνει
10 ἔργα ὄντα. ἐνταῦθα δὲ καὶ φρούρια ᾠκοδομήσατο τό τε Βαιβερδὼν καλούμενον καὶ τὸ Ἄρεων.
καὶ τὸ Λυσίορμον ἀνενεώσατο πεπονηκὸς ἤδη
P 58 11 σὺν τῷ Λυταραριζών. ἔν τε χωρίῳ, ὅπερ Γερ-
μανοῦ καλοῦσι Φοσσᾶτον, φρούριον ἐδείματο νέον.
ἀλλὰ καὶ Σεβαστείας καὶ Νικοπόλεως τῶν ἐν
Ἀρμενίαις πόλεων τὰ τείχη, ἐπεὶ καταπεσεῖσθαι
πάντα [1] ἔμελλον, τεταλαιπωρημένα τῷ μήκει τοῦ
12 χρόνου, ἀνοικοδομησάμενος πεποίηται νέα. καὶ
ἱερῶν δὲ καὶ μοναστηρίων ἐνταῦθα οἰκοδομίας
B 254 ἐξείργασται. ἔν τε γὰρ τῇ Θεοδοσιουπόλει νεὼν
τῇ θεοτόκῳ ἀνέθηκε, καὶ μοναστήρια ἔν τε
χωρίῳ τῷ καλουμένῳ Πέτριος, κἀν τῷ Κου-
13 καρίζων ἀνενεώσατο. ἔν τε Νικοπόλει τὸ τῶν
ἁγίων τεσσαράκοντα πέντε καλούμενον μοναστήριον, καὶ ἱερὸν Γεωργίῳ τῷ μάρτυρι ἐν Βιζανοῖς
14 ἐδείματο. τῆς τε Θεοδοσιουπόλεως ἄγχιστα μοναστήριον ἀνενεώσατο τῶν τεσσαράκοντα μαρτύρων
ἐπικαλούμενον.

15 Ἦν δέ τι χωρίον ἐν τοῖς Ἀρμενίοις τὸ παλαιὸν
μικροῖς καλουμένοις οὐ πολλῷ ἄποθεν ποταμοῦ
Εὐφράτου, ἐφ᾿ οὗ δὴ λόχος Ῥωμαίων στρατιω-
16 τῶν ἵδρυτο. Μελιτηνὴ μὲν τὸ χωρίον, λεγεὼν
δὲ ὁ λόχος ἐπωνομάζετο. ἐνταῦθά πη ἔρυμα ἐν
τετραγώνῳ ἐπὶ χώρας ὑπτίας ἐδείμαντο ἐν τοῖς
ἄνω χρόνοις Ῥωμαῖοι, τοῖς τε στρατιώταις
ἀποχρώντως ἐς καταλύσεις ἔχον καὶ ὅπως σφίσι
17 τὰ σημεῖα τῇδε ἐναποκείσονται. μετὰ δὲ Τραϊανῷ
τῷ Ῥωμαίων αὐτοκράτορι δεδογμένον, ἐς πόλεώς
τε ἀξίωμα [2] ὁ χῶρος ἀφῖκται καὶ μητρόπολις

[1] πάντα A, πάντως V. [2] ἀξίωμα V, ὀχύρωμα A.

can be found there are, as it happens, the work of the Emperor Justinian. In that region also he constructed the forts called Baiberdôn and Areôn. He likewise restored Lysiormum, which had already fallen into ruin, as well as Lytararizôn.[1] And at the place which they call Germani Fossatum [2] he built a new fort. Furthermore, he rebuilt the walls of Sebasteia [3] and Nicopolis,[4] cities of Armenia, for they were all on the point of collapsing, having suffered from the long passage of time, and he made them new. He also carried out the building of churches and monasteries there. In Theodosiopolis he dedicated a church to the Mother of God, and he restored monasteries in the place called Petrios and in Coucarizôn. In Nicopolis he built the monastery named after the Forty-five Saints, and in Bizani a church to the martyr George. And close to Theodosiopolis he restored a monastery named after the Forty Martyrs.

There was in antiquity a certain town in Lesser Armenia, as it is called, not far from the Euphrates River, in which a detachment of Roman soldiers was posted. The town was Melitenê,[5] and the detachment was called a "legion." In that place the Romans in former times had built a stronghold in the form of a square, on level ground, which served adequately as barracks for the soldiers and provided a place where they could deposit their standards. Later on, by decision of the Roman Emperor Trajan, the place received the rank of a city and became the

[1] The name appears elsewhere in a variety of forms, especially Olotoidariza.

[2] "The Trench of Germanus"; see below, Chap. vi. 23.

[3] At or near the modern town of Siwas.

[4] Modern Pjurk, near Enderes.

[5] Modern Malatia.

18 κατέστη τῷ ἔθνει. προϊόντος δὲ τοῦ χρόνου ἐγένετο ἡ τῶν Μελιτηνῶν πόλις μεγάλη καὶ πολυάνθρωπος. ἐπεί τε ἐρύματος ἐντὸς ἐνοικήσασθαι οὐκέτι εἶχον (ἐς γὰρ [1] ὀλίγον τινὰ ξυνῄει χῶρον, ᾗπέρ μοι εἴρηται) ἱδρύσαντο ἐν τῷ ταύτης πεδίῳ, ἵνα δὴ τὰ ἱερὰ σφίσι πεποίηται καὶ τὰ τῶν ἀρχῶν καταγώγια καὶ [2] τήν τε ἀγοράν ὅσα τε ἄλλα ἐμπολημάτων πωλητήριά ἐστι, τάς τε τῆς πόλεως ἀγυιὰς πάσας καὶ στοὰς καὶ βαλανεῖα καὶ θέατρα καὶ εἴ τι ἄλλο πόλεως
19 μεγάλης ἐς κόσμον διήκει. τῷ τε τρόπῳ τούτῳ Μελιτηνὴν ἀτείχιστον ἐκ τοῦ ἐπὶ πλεῖστον ξυνέβαινεν εἶναι. Ἀναστάσιος μὲν οὖν βασιλεὺς αὐτὴν ξύμπασαν τείχει περιβαλεῖν ἐγκεχείρηκεν·
20 οὔπω μέντοι τὸ βούλευμα ἀποτελέσας τὸν βίον συνεμετρήσατο. βασιλεὺς δὲ Ἰουστινιανὸς
B 255 πανταχόθεν αὐτὴν βεβαιότατα κατατειχισάμενος [3] μέγα τοῖς Ἀρμενίοις ὀχύρωμά τε καὶ ἐγκαλλώπισμα Μελιτηνὴν ἀπειργάσατο.

ε΄. Ταῦτα μὲν οὖν ἐν τῇ [4] Ἀρμενίᾳ ἥ ἐστιν ἐν δεξιᾷ Εὐφράτου ποταμοῦ εἰργάσατο· ὅσα δέ οἱ ἐν Ἀρμενίᾳ τῇ μεγάλῃ πεποίηται ἐρῶν ἔρχομαι.
2 ἡνίκα Θεοδόσιος ὁ Ῥωμαίων βασιλεὺς τὴν Ἀρσάκου ἐπικράτειαν ἔσχεν, ᾗπέρ μοι ἔναγχος δεδιήγηται, φρούριον ἐπί τινος τῶν λόφων [5]
P 59 ᾠκοδομήσατο τοῖς προσιοῦσιν εὐάλωτον, ὃ δὴ
3 Θεοδοσιούπολιν ἐπωνόμασε. τοῦτο Καβάδης τότε ὁ Περσῶν βασιλεύς, ἡνίκα δὴ Ἀμίδης εὐθὺ ἵετο,
4 παριὼν εἷλεν. Ἀναστάσιος δὲ ὁ Ῥωμαίων

[1] ἐς γὰρ V, ἐπεὶ ἐς A.
[2] καὶ V, om. A.
[3] βεβαιότατα κατατειχισάμενος V, τειχισάμενος A.

metropolis of the province. And as time went on, the city of Melitenê became large and populous. But since the people were no longer able to live inside the fortifications (for it was reduced to a small space, as I have said) they settled in the adjoining plain, and here their shrines have been erected and the residences of the magistrates and their market-place, and all the other places for the sale of goods, and all the streets and stoas and baths and theatres of the city, and whatever else contributes to the embellishment of a great city. In this way it came about that Melitenê was for the most part unwalled. Accordingly the Emperor Anastasius undertook to surround the whole of it with a wall; before, however, he had carried out his purpose he fulfilled the measure of his life. But the Emperor Justinian built about it on all sides a very strong wall and made Melitenê a mighty stronghold for the Armenians and a thing of beauty.

v. These works he built in the Armenia which is on the right of the Euphrates River; and I shall go on to tell what was done by him in Greater Armenia. When Theodosius, the Emperor of the Romans, took over the dominion of Arsaces, as I have just related,[1] he built on one of the hills a fort which was easy for assailants to capture, and he named it Theodosiopolis.[2] This city Cabades, who was then King of Persia, captured in passing when he was marching on Amida. The Roman Emperor Anastasius not

[1] *Cf.* Chap. i. 12 and note. [2] Modern Erzeroum.

[4] τῇ added by Capps.
[5] λόφων Maltretus: λίθων V.

αὐτοκράτωρ οὐ πολλῷ ὕστερον πόλιν ἐνταῦθα ἐδείματο, τὸν λόφον ἐντὸς τοῦ περιβόλου πεποιημένος, ἐφ᾽ οὗ δὴ φρούριον τὸ Θεοδοσίου εἱστήκει.
5 καὶ τὸ μὲν αὐτοῦ ὄνομα τῇ πόλει ἀφῆκεν, ἐξίτηλον δὲ τὸ Θεοδοσίου ποιεῖσθαι τοῦ πρότερον οἰκιστοῦ ἥκιστα ἴσχυσεν, ἐπεὶ νεοχμοῦσθαι μὲν τὰ καθωμιλημένα τοῖς ἀνθρώποις ἐς ἀεὶ πέφυκεν, ὀνομάτων δὲ τῶν πρόσθεν μεθίεσθαι οὐκ εὐπετῶς
6 ἔχει. τοῦτο δὲ τὸ Θεοδοσιουπόλεως τεῖχος εὐρύνετο μὲν ἱκανώτατα, οὐ κατὰ λόγον δὲ τοῦ
7 εὔρους ἀνεῖχε. τὸ γὰρ ὕψος αὐτῷ ἐς τριάκοντα ἐξικνεῖτο μάλιστα πόδας· ταύτῃ τε πολεμίοις τειχομαχοῦσιν, ἄλλως τε καὶ Πέρσαις, ἐγεγόνει
8 λίαν εὐάλωτον. ἦν δὲ καὶ ἄλλως ἐπίμαχον. οὔτε γὰρ προτείχισμα οὔτε τάφρος αὐτῷ ἤμυνεν.
9 ἀλλὰ καὶ χῶρός τις ὡς ἀγχοτάτω ἐπεμβαίνων τῇ πόλει τῷ περιβόλῳ ἐπανειστήκει. διὸ δὴ βασιλεὺς Ἰουστινιανὸς ἀντεμηχανήσατο τάδε. πρῶτα μὲν[1] τάφρον ὡς βαθυτάτην ἐν κύκλῳ ὀρύξας,
B 256 χαράδραις αὐτὴν ὀρῶν ἀποτόμων ἐμφερεστάτην
10 εἰργάσατο. ἔπειτα δὲ χῶρον τὸν ὑπερπεφυκότα κατατεμὼν ἔς τε ἀνεκβάτους κρημνοὺς[2] καὶ σήραγγας ἀδιεξόδους μετεστήσατο τὴν αὐτοῦ φύσιν· ὅπως δὲ τὸ τεῖχος ὑψηλόν τε εἴη διαφερόντως καὶ ὅλως ἀνανταγώνιστον, εἴ τις προσίοι, προσεπετεχνήσατο ἅπαντα ὅσα ἐν πόλει Δάρας
11 εἰργάσατο. τὰς γὰρ ἐπάλξεις ἀποσφίγξας ἐν στενῷ μάλιστα ὅσον ἐνθένδε βάλλειν τοὺς τειχομαχοῦντας δυνατὰ εἶναι, ἔμβολόν τε αὐταῖς λίθων ἐπιβολαῖς ἐν περιδρόμῳ περιελίξας, ἐντέθεικεν ἐμπείρως ἐπάλξεις ἑτέρας, προτειχίσματί τε αὐτὸ

[1] πρῶτα μὲν A, om. V.
[2] κρημνοὺς V, om. A

much later built a city there, enclosing within the circuit-wall the hill on which stood the fortress of Theodosius. And he gave his own name to the city, yet he was quite unable to obliterate that of Theodosius, the earlier founder; for although familiar names are wont constantly to be changed by men for new, nevertheless the older names cannot easily be relinquished. This wall of Theodosiopolis was of adequate extent, but it did not rise to a height proportionate to its thickness. In fact it attained a height of only about thirty feet, and for this reason it had proved to be very easy for an enemy to capture by assault, particularly for the Persians. In other ways too it was vulnerable; for it was protected neither by outworks nor by a moat. Indeed, there was actually a certain elevation which came very close to the city and overtopped the circuit-wall. Consequently the Emperor Justinian took the following measures to meet the situation. First of all he dug a very deep ditch all around, making it very like the ravines between lofty mountains. Next he sliced off the elevated ground, so transforming it as to make a series of impassable cliffs and of gulches affording no outlet. And in order that the wall might be exceptionally high and altogether impregnable, in case anyone should attack it, he added all the details which he had incorporated in the fortifications of Daras.[1] For he made the embrasures quite narrow, just wide enough for the defenders to be able to shoot from them, and by adding courses of stones he built thereon a storey like a gallery all round, and then cleverly added other embrasures above them;

[1] *Cf. Buildings*, II. i. 14 ff.

περιβαλὼν κύκλῳ ἐμφερέστατον τῷ ἐν πόλει Δάρας περιβόλῳ πεποίηται, πύργον ἕκαστον 12 φρούριον ἐχυρὸν τεκτηνάμενος. οὗ δὴ τὰς δυνάμεις ἁπάσας καὶ τὸν ἐν Ἀρμενίαις στρατηγὸν ἱδρύσασθαι καταστησάμενος κρείσσους τοὺς Ἀρμενίους διεπράξατο τὸ λοιπὸν εἶναι ἢ δεδιέναι τὴν Περσῶν ἔφοδον.

13 Ἐς μέντοι τὰ Βιζανὰ οὐδὲν εἴργασται τῷ βασιλεῖ τούτῳ ἐξ αἰτίας τοιᾶσδε. κεῖται μὲν ἐν τῷ ὁμαλῷ τὸ χωρίον, πεδία τε [1] ἀμφ᾽ αὐτὸ ἐπὶ μακρὸν ἱππήλατά ἐστιν, ὕδατος δὲ σηπεδόνες 14 πολλαὶ ξυνισταμένου ἐνταῦθά εἰσι. καὶ ἀπ᾽ αὐτοῦ τοῖς μὲν πολεμίοις ἐπιμαχώτατον, τοῖς δὲ οἰκήτορσι λοιμωδέστατον αὐτὸ [2] ξυμβαίνει εἶναι. 15 ὧν δὴ ἕνεκα τὸ χωρίον τοῦτο ὑπεριδὼν ἑτέρωθι πόλιν ἐδείματο αὐτοῦ βασιλέως ἐπώνυμον, ἀξιολογωτάτην τε καὶ ἄμαχον ὅλως ἐν χωρίῳ Τζουμινᾷ καλουμένῳ, ὅπερ σημείοις μὲν τρισὶ Βιζανῶν διέχει, ἐν κρημνώδει δὲ μάλιστα κείμενον εὐεξίας ἀέρων εὖ ἔχει.

B 257 P 60 ς´. Τὰ μὲν οὖν ἐν Ἀρμενίοις Ἰουστινιανῷ βασιλεῖ τῇδέ πη ἔχει. τὰ δὲ δὴ κατὰ τὰ Τζάνων ἔθνη ἀναγράψασθαί μοι ἐνταῦθα τοῦ λόγου οὔ τι ἀπὸ τρόπου ἔδοξεν εἶναι, ἐπεὶ καὶ πρόσοικοι 2 Ἀρμενίοις εἰσίν. αὐτόνομοι μὲν Τζάνοι ἐκ παλαιοῦ καὶ ἄναρχοι ᾤκουν, θηριώδη τινὰ βιοτὴν ἔχοντες, θεοὺς μὲν τά τε ἄλση καὶ ὄρνις καὶ ἄλλα ἄττα ζῷα ἡγούμενοί τε καὶ σέβοντες, ἐν ὄρεσι δὲ οὐρανομήκεσί τε καὶ ἀμφιλαφέσι τὸν πάντα αἰῶνα δίαιταν ἔχοντες, γῆν δὲ οὐδαμῇ γεωργοῦν-

[1] τε Maltretus for δὲ. [2] αὐτὸ V, om. A.

and surrounding the wall with outworks on all sides he made it much like the circuit-wall of Daras, fashioning each tower as a strong fortress. Here he stationed all the troops and the General of the two Armenias, and thus he made the Armenians thenceforth too strong to be afraid of the attacks of the Persians.

In Bizana, however, nothing was done by this Emperor, for the following reason. This town lies on level ground, and about it for a great distance stretch plains suitable for cavalry manoeuvres, and there are many pools of standing water there. Consequently it is not only very open to the enemy's attack, but most unhealthy for the inhabitants. For these reasons he passed over this town and in another situation built a city bearing the Emperor's own name, a very noteworthy and altogether impregnable place, in the district called Tzumina, which is three miles removed from Bizana, situated on very precipitous ground and enjoying excellent air.

vi. These, then, are the things which the Emperor Justinian did in Armenia. And it has seemed to me not inappropriate to record at this point in my account what he did for the Tzani, for they are neighbours of the Armenians. From ancient times the Tzani[1] have lived as an independent people, without rulers, following a savage-like manner of life, regarding as gods the trees and birds and sundry creatures besides, and worshipping them, and spending their whole lives among mountains reaching to the sky and covered with forests,[2] and cultivating

[1] In *Wars*, I. 15. 19 ff., Procopius places these people in Iberia, south of the Caucasus.

[2] But for the statement below in sec. 9 the adjective ἀμφιλαφής might be given the meaning "of stupendous mass."

τες, ἀλλὰ λῃστεύοντές τε καὶ τοῖς φωρίοις ἀεὶ
3 ἀποζῶντες. αὐτοί τε γὰρ ἀμελέτητοί εἰσιν ἐργάζεσθαι γῆν καὶ ἡ χώρα σφίσιν, ἔνθα δὴ μὴ ὄρη τά γε ἀποτομώτατα περιβέβληται, λοφώδης ἐστίν.
4 οὐ γήλοφοι δέ εἰσι τὰ ἐπανεστηκότα τῆς γῆς οὐδὲ γεώδη οὐδὲ οἷα καρποὺς ἀφεῖναι, εἴ τις αὐτῶν ἐπιμελοῖτο, ἀλλὰ τραχέα τε ὑπερβαλλόντως καὶ σκληρὰ ὑπεράγαν καὶ καρπῶν ἁπάντων
5 δεινῶς ἄφορα. καὶ οὔτε ἀρόσαι τὴν γῆν οὔτε ἀμήσασθαι λήιον οὔτε λειμῶνι ἐντυχεῖν ἐνταῦθά πῃ δυνατὰ γίνεται, ἀλλὰ καὶ τοῖς δένδροις, οἷσπερ ἡ Τζανικὴ τέθηλεν, ἀκάρποις τε οὖσιν ἀνθεῖ καὶ ὅλως ἀγόνοις, ἐπεὶ οὐδὲ ἀλλήλους ἐκδέχονται καιροὶ ἐκ τοῦ ἐπὶ πλεῖστον, οὐδὲ νῦν μὲν ἡ γῆ τῷ τῆς ὥρας ὑγρῷ τε καὶ ψυχρῷ βάλλεται, νῦν δὲ δὴ αὐτὴν ἡ τοῦ ἡλίου θέρμη ὀνίνησιν, ἀλλὰ χειμῶνί τε ἀπεράντῳ ξυνῴκισται ἡ χώρα καὶ
6 χιόσιν ἀϊδίοις κατάρρυτός ἐστι. διὰ ταῦτα μὲν αὐτόνομοι τὸ παλαιὸν οἱ Τζάνοι ἐβίουν, ἐπὶ τούτου δὲ Ἰουστινιανοῦ βασιλεύοντος ἡττήθησάν τε Ῥωμαίων τῇ μάχῃ, Τζίττα στρατηγοῦντος Ῥωμαίων, καὶ τὴν ἀγώνισιν ἀπογνόντες εὐθὺς προσεχώρησαν αὐτῷ ἅπαντες, πρὸ τῆς ἐπικινδύνου ἐλευθερίας τὴν ἄπονον δουλείαν ἑλόμενοι σφίσι.
B 258 7 καὶ τήν τε δόξαν ἐπὶ τὸ εὐσεβὲς αὐτίκα μετέθεντο ἅπαντες Χριστιανοὶ γεγενημένοι, τήν τε δίαιταν ἐπὶ τὸ ἡμερώτερον μεθηρμόσαντο, λῃστείας μὲν ἀφέμενοι πάσης, τοῖς δὲ Ῥωμαίοις συστρατεύοντες ἐπὶ
8 πολεμίους ἀεὶ τοὺς σφετέρους ἰοῦσι. δείσας δὲ Ἰουστινιανὸς βασιλεὺς μή ποτε Τζάνοι μεταπορευσάμενοι τὴν δίαιταν αὖθις τὰ σφέτερα ἤθη ἐπὶ τὸ ἀγριώτερον μεταστρέψωνται [1] ἐπενόει τοιάδε.

no land whatever, but robbing and living always on their plunder. For they themselves are not skilled in cultivating the soil, and their country, at least where it is not occupied by the steepest mountains, is hilly. These uplands are not rolling hills, neither do they provide soil such as would produce harvests, if one should cultivate them, but they are excessively rough and extremely hard and altogether unfavourable to any crops. It is not possible either to irrigate the land or to harvest corn; one cannot find meadow-land in that region, indeed even the trees which grow in Tzanica bear no fruit and are entirely unproductive, for seasons do not regularly follow one another, and the earth is not visited at one period by a cold wet season, while at another the sun's heat quickens it, but the land is held in the grip of an endless winter and buried under everlasting snows. For this reason the Tzani in ancient times used to live in independence, but during the reign of the present Emperor Justinian they were defeated in battle by the Romans under the general Tzittas, and abandoning the struggle they all straightway yielded to him, preferring the toilless servitude to the dangerous liberty. And they immediately changed their belief to piety, all of them becoming Christians, and they altered their manner of life to a milder way, giving up all brigandage and always marching with the Romans whenever they went against their enemies. And the Emperor Justinian, fearing that the Tzani at some time might alter their way of life and change their habits back to the wilder sort, devised the following measures.

---

[1] *μεταστρέψωνται* Hoeschel: *μεταστρέψονται.*

9 Δύσοδος ἦν ἡ Τζανικὴ λίαν καὶ ἄφιππος ὅλως, κρημνοῖς τε πανταχόθεν καὶ χώροις περικεκλεισμένη ἐκ τοῦ ἐπὶ πλεῖστον ὑλώδεσιν, ᾗπέρ μοι
10 εἴρηται. καὶ ἀπ' αὐτοῦ Τζάνοις ἐπιμίγνυσθαι τοῖς πλησιοχώροις ἀμήχανον ἦν, ἀλλὰ κατὰ
P 61 μόνας ἐν σφίσιν αὐτοῖς ἀπηγριωμένοι θηρίων
11 τρόπον τὴν δίαιταν εἶχον. τὰ τοίνυν δένδρα ἐκτεμὼν ἅπαντα, οἷσπερ τὰς ὁδοὺς ξυνέβαινε ξυμποδίζεσθαι, καὶ τὰς ἐκείνῃ δυσχωρίας μεθαρμοσάμενος, εὐπετεῖς τε αὐτὰς καὶ ἱππασίμους καταστησάμενος, ἐπιμίγνυσθαι αὐτοὺς κατὰ ταὐτὰ τοῖς ἄλλοις ἀνθρώποις καὶ προσχωρεῖν τῇ ὁμιλίᾳ
12 τῶν πλησιοχώρων πεποίηκεν. ἔπειτα δὲ αὐτοῖς ἐκκλησίαν ἐν χωρίῳ Σχαμαλινίχων καλουμένῳ δειμάμενος, ἱερᾶσθαί τε διεπράξατο καὶ μυστηρίων μεταλαμβάνειν[1] λιταῖς τε τὸν θεὸν ἱλεοῦσθαι, καὶ τὰ ἄλλα ἐξοσιοῦσθαι, συνιέντες ὡς ἄνθρωποι
13 εἶεν. καὶ φρούρια δὲ οἰκοδομησάμενος πανταχόθι τῆς χώρας φρουρούς τε ἐνταῦθα Ῥωμαίων στρατιωτῶν ἱδρυσάμενος βεβαιότατα, Τζάνοις ἐς τοὺς ἄλλους ἀνθρώπους τὰς ἐπιμιξίας ἀκωλύτους
14 πεποίηκεν. ὅπη ποτὲ δὲ Τζανικῆς τὰ φρούρια ταῦτα ἐδείματο ἐρῶν ἔρχομαι.

B 259 15 Χώραν ἐνταῦθά τινα ἐς τρίοδον ἀποκεκριμένην ξυμβαίνει εἶναι. Ῥωμαίων τε γὰρ καὶ Περσαρμενίων τὰ ὅρια καὶ Τζάνων αὐτῶν τῇδε ἀρξάμενα
16 ἐνθένδε διασκεδάννυται. ἐνταῦθα φρούριον ἐχυρώτατον, οὐ πρότερον ὄν, ὄνομα Ὀρονῶν, ἐξείργασται, κεφάλαιον αὐτὸ τῆς εἰρήνης πεποιημένος.
17 ἔνθεν γὰρ τὰ πρῶτα Ῥωμαίοις ἡ Τζανικὴ ἐσβατὴ γέγονεν· οὗ δὴ καὶ ἄρχοντα στρατιωτῶν κατεστή-
18 σατο, ὃν δοῦκα καλοῦσιν. ἐν χωρίῳ δὲ ὁδῷ

Tzanica was a very inaccessible country and altogether impossible for horses, being shut in on all sides by cliffs and for the most part by forests, as I have said. As a result of this it was impossible for the Tzani to mingle with their neighbours, living as they did a life of solitude among themselves in the manner of wild beasts. Accordingly he cut down all the trees by which the routes chanced to be obstructed, and transforming the rough places and making them smooth and passable for horses, he brought it about that they mingled with other peoples in the manner of men in general and consented to have intercourse with their neighbours. After this he built a church for them in a place called Schamalinichôn, and caused them to conduct services and to partake of the sacraments and propitiate God with prayers and perform the other acts of worship, so that they should know that they were human beings. And he built forts in all parts of the land, assigned to them very strong garrisons of Roman soldiers, and gave the Tzani unhampered intercourse with other peoples. I shall now tell where in Tzanica he built these forts.

It happens that a certain point in that land forms the meeting-place of three roads; for the boundaries of the Romans and the Persarmenians and the Tzani themselves begin here and extend out from this point. Here he constructed a very strong fortress which had not existed previously, Horonôn by name, making it the mainstay of the peace of the region. For the Romans were first able to enter Tzanica from that point. Here too he established a military commander called a Duke. And at a place two

---

[1] μεταλαμβάνειν V, μεταλαγχάνειν A.

ἡμέραιν δυοῖν Ὀρονῶν διέχοντι, οὗ δὴ Τζάνων τῶν Ὠκενιτῶν καλουμένων τὰ ὅριά ἐστιν (ἐπεὶ ἐς ἔθνη πολλὰ διακέκρινται Τζάνοι), ἐνταῦθά τι ὀχύρωμα πεποιημένον ἦν τοῖς πάλαι ἀνθρώποις, ἐρείπιον ἤδη πολλῷ πρότερον τῷ ἀπημελῆσθαι

19 γεγενημένον, Χαρτὼν ὄνομα. ὅπερ ἀνανεωσάμενος Ἰουστινιανὸς βασιλεύς, ἐνοικεῖν τε ἀνθρώπων ἐνταῦθα διεπράξατο μέγα τι χρῆμα καὶ τὰ ἐς τὴν

20 εὐκοσμίαν τῇ χώρᾳ φρουρεῖν. τῷ δὲ ἐνθένδε ἰόντι πρὸς ἀνίσχοντα ἥλιον φάραγξ ἐστὶ κρημνώδης, κατατείνουσα μέχρι ἐς τὰ πρὸς βορρᾶν ἄνεμον· οὗ δὴ φρούριον, Βαρχὼν ὄνομα, ἐδείματο νέον.

21 ἐπέκεινα δὲ κατὰ τοῦ ὄρους τὴν ὑπώρειαν ἐπαύλεις εἰσίν, ἵνα δὴ οἱ Τζάνων τῶν Ὠκενιτῶν καλουμένων βόες αὐλίζονται, οὕσπερ ἐκτρέφουσιν οὐ τοῦ ἀροῦν τὴν γῆν ἕνεκα, ἐπεὶ ἀργοί τε τὸ παράπαν οἱ Τζάνοι εἰσὶ καὶ γεωργικῶν ἀλλότριοι πόνων, ᾗπέρ μοι εἴρηται, καὶ οὔτε ἀρόματά ἐστιν αὐτοῖς οὔτε ἄλλα τῆς γεωργίας διαπονήματα, ἀλλὰ τοῦ γε γάλα ἐς ἀεὶ βδάλλειν [1] καὶ σιτίζεσθαι τοῖς

22 αὐτῶν κρέασι. μετὰ δὲ τοῦ ὄρους τὸν πρόποδα, οὗ Κενὰ τὸ χωρίον ἐν τῷ ὁμαλῷ ξυμβαίνει εἶναι, ἐνθένδε τοι ἰόντι ἐπὶ δύοντά που τὸν ἥλιον, τὸ

B 260 Σισιλισσῶν ὄνομα φρούριόν ἐστιν, ὅπερ ἐκ παλαιοῦ μὲν πεποιημένον, ἔρημον δὲ διὰ χρόνου μῆκος γεγενημένον ἀνανεωσάμενος Ἰουστινιανὸς βασιλεὺς διαρκὲς Ῥωμαίων στρατιωτῶν, ὥσπερ κἀν τοῖς

23 ἄλλοις ἅπασι, φυλακτήριον κατεστήσατο. ἔνθεν δὲ ἰόντι ἐν ἀριστερᾷ πρὸς βορρᾶν ἄνεμον χῶρός τίς ἐστιν, ὅνπερ καλοῦσιν οἱ ἐπιχώριοι Λογγίνου

P 62 φοσσᾶτον, ἐπεὶ Λογγῖνος ἐν τοῖς ἄνω χρόνοις

[1] βδάλλειν A, βάλλει V.

days' journey distant from Horonôn, where the territory of the Tzani who are called Ocenitae commences (for the Tzani are divided into many tribes), there was a sort of stronghold built by men of former times, Chartôn by name, which long before had already become a ruin through neglect. This the Emperor Justinian restored, and he caused a large population to live there and to preserve order in the country. And as one goes from there towards the east, there is a precipitous ravine which extends around to the north; here he built a new fortress, Barchôn by name. Beyond this at the foot of the mountain are folds where the cattle of the Ocenite Tzani, as they are called, find shelter; and they breed these cattle, not in order to plough the earth—for the Tzani are altogether indolent and averse to the tasks of husbandry, as I have said,[1] and they neither plough nor perform the other labours of husbandry—but in order to have a constant supply of milk and to eat their flesh. Beyond the foothills of the mountain, where the place called Cena lies in the level country, as one goes approximately westward there is a fort named Sisilissôn; this had been built in ancient times, but, with the passage of time, had come to be deserted; so the Emperor Justinian restored it and established there a sufficient garrison of Roman soldiers, just as in all the others. And as one goes on from that fort, there is a certain place on the left, towards the north, which the natives call Longini Fossatum,[2] because in earlier times Longinus, a Roman general,

[1] *Cf.* III. vi. 2.
[2] "The Trench of Longinus."

Ῥωμαίων στρατηγός, Ἴσαυρος γένος, στρατεύσας ἐπὶ Τζάνους ποτὲ τῇδε πεποίηται τὸ
24 στρατόπεδον. ἐνταῦθα φρούριον ὁ βασιλεὺς οὗτος ὄνομα Βουργουσνόης δεδημιούργηκεν, ἡμέρας ὁδῷ
25 Σισιλισσῶν διέχον. ὅπερ Σισιλισσῶν φρούριόν ἐστι καὶ αὐτὸ ὑπ᾽ αὐτοῦ τοῦ βασιλέως, ὡς μικρὸν ἐρρήθη ἔμπροσθεν, ἐξειργασμένον βεβαιό-
26 τατα. ἐντεῦθεν ὅρια τῶν Τζάνων τῶν Κοξυλίνων καλουμένων ἐστίν· οὗ δὴ φρούρια νῦν πεποίηται δύο, τό τε Σχαμαλινίχων καλούμενον καὶ ὅπερ Τζανζάκων ἐπονομάζουσιν· ἔνθα δὴ καὶ ἄλλον ἄρχοντα στρατιωτῶν κατεστήσατο.

ζ'. Ταῦτα μὲν οὖν ἐν Τζάνοις Ἰουστινιανῷ βασιλεῖ εἴργασται. ἐν δὲ δὴ τῇ μετ᾽ αὐτοὺς χώρᾳ, ᾗ παρὰ τὸν Εὔξεινον οἰκεῖται Πόντον, πόλις ἐστί που, Τραπεζοῦς ὄνομα· οὗ δὴ ἀπορίας ὑδάτων οὔσης, ὀχετὸν ἐτεκτήνατο Ἰουστινιανὸς βασιλεὺς ὅνπερ Εὐγενίου καλοῦσι μάρτυρος, ταύτῃ τε τὴν ἀπορίαν τοῖς τῇδε ᾠκημένοις διέλυσεν.
2 ἐνταῦθα δὲ κἀν τῇ Ἀμασείᾳ τὰ πλεῖστα τῶν ἱερῶν ἀνενεώσατο, χρόνῳ πεπονηκότα πολλῷ.
3 μετὰ δὲ τοὺς Τραπεζουντίων ὅρους χωρίον ἐστὶ Ῥιζαῖον ὄνομα, ὃ δὴ καινουργήσας αὐτὸς ὀχύρωμα περιβέβληκε [1] λόγου τε καὶ ἀκοῆς κρεῖσσον.
4 πόλεων γὰρ τῶν Πέρσαις ὁμόρων οὐδεμιᾶς ἧσσον μεγέθους πέρι καὶ ἀσφαλείας δεδημιούργηται.
B 261 5 Καὶ φρούριον δὲ ᾠκοδομήσατο ἐπὶ Λαζικῆς Λοσόριον ὄνομα, καὶ τοὺς ἐν τῇ χώρᾳ στενωποὺς ἐτειχίσατο οὕσπερ Κλεισούρας καλεῖν νενομίκασιν, ὅπως δὴ ἀποκεκλεισμένοι τῆς ἐπὶ Λαζικὴν

[1] περιβέβληκε A, περιβέβληται V.

an Isaurian by birth, had made an expedition against the Tzani on one occasion and built his camp there. In that place this Emperor built a fortress called Bourgousnoes, one day's journey distant from Sisilissôn. This fort of Sisilissôn too was rendered very strong by this same Emperor, as was stated a little above. From there begins the territory of the Coxyline Tzani, as they are called; and here he has now made two forts, one called Schamalinichôn and the other is the one they call Tzanzacôn; and here he posted another military commander.

vii. These things, then, were done by the Emperor Justinian in Tzanica. In the land beyond this which lies along the Euxine Sea there is a city named Trapezus;[1] and since there was a scarcity of water in that city, the Emperor Justinian built an aqueduct which they call the Aqueduct of the martyr Eugenius, and thus he put an end to the scarcity for the inhabitants of this place. Both there and in Amaseia he restored most of the churches, which had been damaged by the long passage of time. And beyond the confines of Trapezus there is a place called Rhizaeum[2] which he restored himself, throwing about it a novel system of defences which surpass any description or report of them. For it was so fashioned as to be inferior in point of size and safety to no one of the cities on the Persian frontier.

He also built a fortress in Lazica named Losorium, and he fortified the mountain-passes of the country which they are wont to call *cleisurae*,[3] with the purpose, of course, that the enemy might be shut off

[1] Modern Trebizond.
[2] Modern Risê, a port on the Black Sea.
[3] See above, Chap. iii. 2, note.

6 εἰσόδου οἱ πολέμιοι εἶεν. ἀλλὰ καὶ τὴν ἐν Λαζοῖς τῶν Χριστιανῶν ἐκκλησίαν, ἀρχαίαν τε οὖσαν καὶ σαθρὰν τῇ οἰκοδομίᾳ γεγενημένην, ἀνενεώσατο.
7 οὕτω καὶ Πέτραν ἐν Λαζοῖς πόλιν ἀξιοθέατον κατεστήσατο, ἥνπερ Λαζοὶ μὲν ἀβουλίᾳ τῇ σφετέρᾳ παρέδοσαν Πέρσαις, Χοσρόην ἐνταῦθα στρατῷ μεγάλῳ ἐπαγαγόμενοι, Ῥωμαῖοι δὲ Περσῶν καθυπέρτεροι τῷ πολέμῳ γενόμενοι καὶ τοὺς μὲν κτείναντες τοὺς δὲ δορυαλώτους πεποιημένοι, ἐς τὸ ἔδαφος τὴν πόλιν καθεῖλον, ὡς μὴ αὖθις οἱ βάρβαροι κακουργεῖν ἔχοιεν ἐνταῦθα ἰόντες, ᾗπέρ μοι ἅπαντα ἐν τοῖς ὑπὲρ τῶν πολέμων δεδήλωται
8 λόγοις· ἵνα δὴ καὶ τοῦτό μοι δεδιήγηται, ὡς ἐν τῇ ἀντιπέρας ἠπείρῳ ἐκ Λαζικῆς ἐπὶ τὴν Μαιῶτιν ἰόντι λίμνην φρούρια δύο, Σεβαστούπολίν τε καὶ
P 63 Πιτυοῦντα, καθεῖλον Ῥωμαῖοι, Χοσρόην ἀκούσαντες στράτευμα στέλλειν ἐνταῦθα διὰ σπουδῆς ἔχειν τούς τε [1] τὰ φρούρια ταῦτα καθέξοντας.
9 ἀλλὰ νῦν Ἰουστινιανὸς βασιλεὺς ταύτην δὴ τὴν Σεβαστούπολιν [2] ἀνανεωσάμενος ξύμπασαν, καὶ τῷ μὲν περιβόλῳ τοῖς τε ἄλλοις ὀχυρώμασι πεποιημένος ἀνάλωτον, ταῖς δὲ ἀγυιαῖς καὶ ταῖς ἄλλαις οἰκοδομίαις διακοσμήσας, τῷ τε κάλλει καὶ τῷ μεγέθει πόλιν τανῦν ἀξιολογωτάτην ἐν τοῖς μάλιστα κατεστήσατο.
10 Καὶ μὴν καὶ Βοσπόρου καὶ Χερσῶνος πόλεων, [3] αἵπερ κατὰ τὴν ἐκείνῃ ἀκτὴν ἐπιθαλασσίδιαι μετὰ λίμνην τε τὴν Μαιώτιδα καὶ τοὺς Ταύρους καὶ Ταυροσκύθας ἐν ἐσχάτῳ οἰκοῦνται [4] τῆς
B 262 Ῥωμαίων ἀρχῆς, πεπονηκότα παντάπασι τὰ

[1] τούς τε Haury: τοὺς.
[2] After Σεβαστούπολιν A adds φρούριον οὖσαν τὸ πρότερον.
[3] πόλεων Maltretus: πόλεως.

from the entrance into Lazica. Nay more, he restored the Christian church in Lazica, which was old and had become weakened in its masonry. He likewise founded Petra in Lazica, an admirable city, which the Lazi through their own folly handed over to the Persians, bringing Chosroes there with a great army; but the Romans prevailed over the Persians in the struggle and killed a part of the enemy and made the rest captive and razed the city, so that the barbarians might not again be able, by coming there, to work mischief, all of which has been set forth by me in the Books on the Wars.[1] In the same place I have explained how the Romans dismantled two fortresses, Sebastopolis [2] and Pityûs,[3] on the opposite coast as one goes from Lazica to the Maeotic Lake,[4] because they had heard that Chosroes was eager to send an army with men to take possession of these fortresses. But at a later time the Emperor Justinian restored the whole of Sebastopolis and made it impregnable by means of its circuit-wall and other defences, adorned it with streets and with various buildings besides, and produced the present city, which is remarkable among the cities of the world for its beauty and its size.

Moreover, in the case of the coastal cities Bosporus [5] and Chersôn,[6] which lie on the shore there beyond the Maeotic Lake and the Taurians and Tauroscythians, at the extremity of the Roman Empire, he found that the walls had fallen completely into ruin,

[1] VIII. xii. 28. [2] Near the older city of Dioscurias.
[3] Modern Pitzunda. [4] Modern Sea of Azov.
[5] Generally called Panticapaeum; modern Kertsch.
[6] Modern Sevastopol.

---

[4] οἰκοῦνται V, οἰκοῦντας A.

τείχη εὑρὼν ἐς μέγα τι κάλλους τε καὶ ἀσφα-
11 λείας κατεστήσατο χρῆμα. ἔνθα δὴ καὶ φρούρια
πεποίηται τό τε Ἀλούστου καλούμενον καὶ τὸ
12 ἐν Γορζουβίταις. διαφερόντως δὲ τὴν Βόσπορον
τῷ ἐρύματι ἐκρατύνατο, ἥνπερ ἐκ παλαιοῦ βεβαρ-
βαρωμένην καὶ ὑπὸ τοῖς Οὔννοις κειμένην ἐς τὸ
13 Ῥωμαίων αὐτὸς μετήνεγκε κράτος. ἔστι δέ τις
ἐνταῦθα χώρα κατὰ τὴν παραλίαν, Δόρυ ὄνομα,
ἵνα δὴ ἐκ παλαιοῦ Γότθοι ᾤκηνται οἱ Θευδερίχῳ
ἐς Ἰταλίαν ἰόντι οὐκ ἐπισπόμενοι, ἀλλ' ἐθελούσιοι
αὐτοῦ μείναντες, Ῥωμαίων καὶ εἰς ἐμέ εἰσιν
ἔνσπονδοι· ξυστρατεύουσί τε αὐτοῖς ἐπὶ πολεμίους τοὺς σφετέρους ἰοῦσιν, ἡνίκα ἂν βασιλεῖ
14 βουλομένῳ εἴη. ἐξικνοῦνται δὲ ἐς τρισχιλίους,
καὶ τά τε πολέμια ἔργα εἰσὶν ἄριστοι τά τε ἐς
τὴν γεωργίαν αὐτουργοὶ δεξιοί, καὶ φιλοξενώ-
15 τατοι δέ εἰσιν ἀνθρώπων ἁπάντων. αὐτὴ δὲ ἡ
χώρα τὸ Δόρυ τῆς μὲν γῆς ἐν ὑψηλῷ κεῖται, οὐ
μέντοι οὔτε [1] τραχεῖα οὔτε [1] σκληρά ἐστιν, ἀλλ'
ἀγαθή τε καὶ εὔφορος καρπῶν τῶν ἀρίστων.
16 πόλιν μὲν οὖν ἢ φρούριον οὐδαμῆ τῆς χώρας ὁ
βασιλεὺς ἐδείματο ταύτης, κατείργεσθαι περιβόλοις τισὶν οὐκ ἀνεχομένων τῶν τῇδε ἀνθρώπων,
17 ἀλλ' ἐν πεδίῳ ἀσμενέστατα ᾠκημένων ἀεί. ὅπη
ποτὲ δὲ τῶν ἐκείνῃ χωρίων βάσιμα εὐπετῶς τοῖς
ἐπιοῦσιν ἐδόκει εἶναι, ταύτας δὴ τειχίσμασι
μακροῖς τὰς εἰσόδους περιβαλών, τὰς ἐκ τῆς
ἐφόδου φροντίδας ἀνέστειλε Γότθοις. ταῦτα μὲν
οὖν τῇδέ πη ἔχει.

18 Πόλιν δέ τινα ἐπιθαλασσίαν οἰκοῦσι Θρᾷκες
παρὰ τὴν ἠϊόνα τοῦ Εὐξείνου Πόντου, Ἀγχίαλον
ὄνομα, ἧσπερ ἐν ἐπιτηδείῳ μνησθείημεν ἄν,

and he made them remarkably beautiful and thoroughly safe. In that region he built two fortresses, that called Aloustou and the one among the Gorzoubitae. He strengthened the defences of Bosporus particularly, which in ancient times had been a barbarous city lying under the power of the Huns, but which he himself had brought under Roman sway. And there is a certain region along the coast there called Dory, where Goths have lived from ancient times, those namely who had not followed Theoderic when he went into Italy, but remained there of their own accord, and even up to my day they are on terms of alliance with the Romans. And they march with the Romans against their enemies whenever the Emperor so wishes. Their number comes to three thousand, and they are both excellent soldiers and skilful tillers of the soil, and the most hospitable people in the world. The land of Dory itself lies on high ground, yet it is neither rough nor hard, but good soil and productive of the best crops. However, the Emperor built no city or fortress in any part of this land, since the men of the country would not suffer themselves to be confined in any fortified places but always lived most happily in an open plain. But wherever the region seemed easily accessible to assailants, he shut off these approaches with long walls and thereby freed the Goths from fear of invasion. So much, then, for this.

There is a certain city on the coast of the Euxine Sea, inhabited by Thracians, Anchialus [1] by name, which properly we should mention in describing the

[1] Modern Ankhialo.

---

[1] οὔτε . . . οὔτε Dindorf: οὐδὲ . . . οὐδὲ.

19 περιηγούμενοι τὰ ἐπὶ τῆς Θρᾴκης χωρία. ἐπεὶ B 263 δὲ τανῦν ὁ λόγος ἡμῖν διελήλυθεν ὅσα παρὰ τὴν ἀκτὴν τοῦ Εὐξείνου Πόντου δεδημιούργηται τῷ βασιλεῖ τούτῳ, οὐδέν τι χεῖρον ἀφηγήσασθαι ἐνταῦθα τοῦ λόγου ὅσα δὴ ἐπὶ τῆς Ἀγχιάλου 20 ταύτης ἐδείματο. ἐνταῦθα οὖν πηγαὶ θερμῶν φύσει ὑδάτων ἀναβλυστάνουσι, τῆς πόλεως οὐ πολλῷ ἄποθεν ἀπαυτοματίζουσαι βαλανεῖα τοῖς 21 τῇδε ἀνθρώποις· τοῦτον δὲ τὸν χῶρον ἀτείχιστον ἐκ παλαιοῦ ὄντα ὑπερεώρων οἱ προβεβασιλευκότες τὰ πρότερα, καίπερ ἐν γειτόνων ᾠκημένων P 64 αὐτῷ βαρβαρικῶν ἐθνῶν τοσούτων τὸ πλῆθος. 22 ἐπεχωρίαζόν τε αὐτῷ οἱ νενοσηκότες τὰ σώματα, μετὰ κινδύνων τὴν παραψυχὴν κομιζόμενοι.[1] 23 τειχήρη τοίνυν αὐτὸν ἐν τῷ παρόντι πεποιημένος Ἰουστινιανὸς βασιλεύς, ἀκίνδυνον διεπράξατο σφίσι 24 τὴν ἄκεσιν εἶναι. τὰ μὲν οὖν γῆς τῆς ἑῴας, ἔτι μέντοι καὶ Ἀρμενίας καὶ Τζανικῆς ὀχυρώματα καὶ τά γε ἀμφὶ τὸν Εὔξεινον Πόντον[2] τῇδε 25 Ἰουστινιανῷ βασιλεῖ εἴργασται. ἡμῖν δὲ ἐνθένδε ἐπὶ τὰς οἰκοδομίας ἰτέον ὥσπερ ἐν Εὐρώπῃ τῇ ἄλλῃ πεποίηται.

B 264

ΛΟΓΟΣ Δʹ

P 65 αʹ. Πέλαγος μέγα νηὶ διαπλεῦσαι ἀπαρασκεύῳ μοχθηρόν τε ἡγοῦμαι εἶναι καὶ κινδύνων μεγάλων ἀτεχνῶς ἔμπλεων. ταὐτὸ δέ ἐστι τὰς[3] Ἰουστινιανοῦ βασιλέως οἰκοδομίας λόγῳ φαυλοτάτῳ 2 διαμετρήσασθαι. ψυχῆς γὰρ μεγέθει ὁ βασιλεὺς

[1] κομιζόμενοι V, ποριζόμενοι A.
[2] πόντον A, καλούμενον πόντον V.

land of Thrace. But since in the present place our treatise has enumerated the buildings of this Emperor along the shore of the Euxine Sea, it is in no way inappropriate to describe at this point in our narrative what he built at this town of Anchialus. At that place, then, natural springs of warm water bubble forth, not far from the city, providing natural baths for the people there. The Emperors of earlier times used to allow this place to remain unwalled from ancient times, though such a host of barbarians dwelt near by; and sick persons used to visit the place, gaining relief at the cost of danger. Therefore the Emperor Justinian made it a walled city, as it now is, and thus made the cure free from danger. So the strongholds of the East, as well as those of Armenia and Tzanica, and those on both shores of the Euxine Sea, were thus built by the Emperor Justinian. From this point we must proceed to the buildings which he erected in the rest of Europe.

BOOK IV

i. To cross a great sea in an ill-appointed ship is a miserable task, I think, beset with the greatest dangers. And it is the same thing to recount the buildings of the Emperor Justinian with impotent words. For through the greatness of his mind this

---

[3] τὰς V, τὰς τοῦ A.

οὗτος τά τε ἄλλα, ὡς εἰπεῖν, ἅπαντα καὶ τὰ ἐς
P 66 τὰς οἰκοδομίας οὐδέν τι ἧσσον λόγου διαπέ-
3 πρακται κρείσσω. ἐν δὲ δὴ τῇ Εὐρώπῃ καὶ τὴν
ὑπουργίαν ἐναρμόσασθαι τῷ τῆς χρείας ἀξιώματι
διὰ σπουδῆς ἔχων ἔργα οὐκ εὐδιήγητα οὐδὲ εἰς
4 συγγραφὴν διαπεπόνηται πρόχειρα. γεγένηται
γὰρ ἐπαξίως τῷ τε γειτονήματι ποταμοῦ Ἴστρου
καὶ τῇ ἐνθένδε διὰ τοὺς ἐγκειμένους τῇ χώρᾳ
5 βαρβάρους ἀνάγκῃ. ἔθνη γὰρ αὐτῇ γειτονοῦντα
διακεκλήρωται [1] Οὐννικά τε καὶ Γοτθικά, καὶ τὰ
ἐν Ταύροις καὶ τὰ ἐν Σκύθαις ἀνταίρει, καὶ ὅσα
B 265 Σκλαβηνοὶ καὶ ὅσα ἄττα,[2] εἴτε Σαυρομάτας
Ἁμαξοβίους εἴτε Μετανάστας ταῦτα δὴ ἐκάλουν
τὰ ἔθνη οἱ τῶν ἱστοριῶν ἀναγραψάμενοι τὰ
ἀρχαιότατα, καὶ εἴ τι ἄλλο θηριῶδες ἀνθρώπων
γένος ἢ νέμεσθαι, ἢ ἵδρυσθαι ἐνταῦθα ξυμβαίνει.
6 οἷς δὴ ἀπέραντα πολεμησείουσιν ὑπαντιάζειν
διατεινομένῳ Ἰουστινιανῷ βασιλεῖ πάρεργόν τε
οὐδὲν ποιουμένῳ ἐπάναγκες ἦν ἐρύματά τε
περιβάλλεσθαι ἀνάριθμα καὶ στρατιωτῶν ἀμύθητα
φυλακτήρια καταστήσασθαι, καὶ ὅσα ἄλλα πολεμίοις ἀνεπικηρυκεύτοις τε καὶ ἀνεπιμίκτοις ἐμπόδια
7 εἴη. οἷς δὴ τοῖς πολεμίοις τὸν πόλεμον οὐκ ἐξ
αἰτίας ἐγειρομένοις [3] ποιεῖσθαι νόμος, οὐδὲ μετὰ
πρεσβείαν ἐπενεγκεῖν, οὐδὲ μὴν οὐδὲ ξυνθήκαις
διαλῦσαί τισιν, ἢ κατὰ χρόνον ἀνακωχεῦσαι, ἀλλ'

[1] γειτονοῦντα διακεκλήρωται V, γειτονοῦσιν A.
[2] ἄττα V, ἄλλα Maltretus.
[3] ἐγειρομένοις Hoeschel: ἐγειρομένης.

---

[1] For the Sauromatae *cf.* Herodotus, IV. xxi, etc. Both

Emperor has accomplished things which surpass description, in buildings no less than in practically all other matters. And in Europe, being consumed by the desire to make his services fit the magnitude of the need which existed for them, he has carried out works which are not easy to enumerate or simple to describe in writing. For these works have been executed with due regard for the nearness of the Ister River and for the consequent necessity imposed by the barbarians who threaten the land. For it has as neighbours nations of Huns and of Goths, and the regions of Taurus and of Scythia rise up against it, as well as the haunts of the Sclaveni and of sundry other tribes—whether they are called by the writers of the most ancient history Hamaxibian or Metanastic Sauromatae,[1] and whatever other wild race of men really either roams about or leads a settled life in that region. And in his determination to resist these barbarians who were endlessly making war, the Emperor Justinian, who did not take the matter lightly, was obliged to throw innumerable fortresses about the country, to assign to them untold garrisons of troops, and to set up all other possible obstacles to an enemy who attacked without warning and who permitted no intercourse. Indeed it was the custom of these peoples to rise and make war upon their enemies for no particular cause, and to open hostilities without sending an embassy, and they did not bring their struggles to an end through any treaty or cease operations for any specified

epithets of the Sauromatians ("Living in waggons" and "Migraters") describe their mode of life. A Scythian race, their habitat included European Russia and westward to the Vistula River.

ἐγχειρῆσαι μὲν ἀπροφασίστως, καταλῦσαι δὲ σιδήρῳ μόνῳ. ἀλλὰ καὶ ὥς ἐπὶ τῆς ἱστορίας τὰ
8 λειπόμενα βαδιούμεθα. ἔργου γὰρ[1] ἀρξαμένους[2] τρόπῳ ὁτῳοῦν ἐς πέρας ἀφῖχθαι ξυνοίσει μᾶλλον ἢ ἀτελεύτητον ἀπολιπόντας ὀπίσω ἰέναι.
9 ἐπεὶ καὶ ἄλλως ἂν οὐκ ἔξω κατηγορίας τὸ πρᾶγμα εἴη, βασιλέα μὲν τὸν ἡμέτερον εἰργάσθαι τὰ ἔργα, ἡμᾶς δὲ τοὺς ὑπὲρ αὐτῶν ἀποκνεῖν λόγους.
10 μέλλοντας δὲ τὰ Εὐρωπαῖα τούτου δὴ τοῦ βασιλέως διαριθμεῖσθαι οἰκοδομήματα, ὀλίγα ἄττα ἀμφὶ τῇδε τῇ χώρᾳ ὑπειπεῖν ἄξιον.

11 Ἐκ τοῦ Ἀδριατικοῦ καλουμένου πελάγους ἐπιρροή τις διωθουμένη τε καὶ ἀποσαλεύουσα τῆς ἄλλης θαλάσσης ἐπὶ τὴν ἤπειρον ἀναβαίνει, καὶ σχίζουσα τὴν γῆν ἐπὶ πλεῖστον ποιεῖται τὸν Ἰόνιον κόλπον, ἐν δεξιᾷ μὲν Ἠπειρώτας τε καὶ τὰ ἐκείνῃ ἔθνη, ἐν ἀριστερᾷ δὲ Καλαβροὺς
B 266 ἔχουσα, ἔν τε πορθμῷ ἐπὶ μακρότατον θλιβομένη περιλαμβάνει τὴν ἤπειρον σχεδόν τι πᾶσαν.
12 καθύπερθε δὲ ἀντιπρόσωπος τῇ θαλάσσῃ φερόμενος ποταμὸς Ἴστρος γῆς τῆς Εὐρώπης νησοειδῆ τὴν
13 γῆν τίθεται. ἐνταῦθα οἰκοδομήματα πολλά τε καὶ ἀξιολογώτατα ὁ βασιλεὺς οὗτος πεποίηται.
14 πᾶσαν γὰρ Εὐρώπην ἐς τὸ ἀσφαλὲς τειχισάμενος ἀπρόσβατον κατεστήσατο βαρβάροις εἶναι[3] οἳ δὴ ὑπὲρ Ἴστρου ποταμοῦ ᾤκηνται.
15 Ἀλλά μοι ἀπὸ τῆς τοῦ βασιλέως ἀρκτέον πατρίδος, ᾗ πασῶν μάλιστα τά τε πρωτεῖα ἐν πᾶσι τοῖς ἄλλοις καὶ τοῦδε τὰς ἀπαρχὰς τοῦ

[1] ἔργου γὰρ A, ἔργω οὖν V.
[2] ἀρξαμένους Haury: ἀρξαμένου.
[3] εἶναι V, om. A.

period, but they made their attacks without provocation and reached a decision by the sword alone. But still we must proceed to the remainder of our story. For when we have begun a task it will be better to go through to the end in any fashion whatever than to depart leaving it unfinished. Certainly my action would not be free from blame, if, after our Emperor has performed the work, I for my part, should shrink from telling of what he has done. But now that we are on the point of enumerating the buildings of this Emperor in Europe, it is proper first to make a few observations regarding this land.

There is a narrow arm or bight which is pushed out from the Adriatic Sea, as it is called, and strays away from the remainder of the sea and goes up into the mainland, and dividing the continent for a great distance it forms the Ionian Gulf, having on the right the Epirotes and the other peoples of that region and on the left Calabria; then, being compressed into a narrow inlet for a very long way, the sea bounds practically the whole continent.[1] And the River Ister, flowing higher up,[2] and opposite the sea, makes the land of Europe an island, as it were. In that region this Emperor built many noteworthy buildings. Indeed he fortified the whole of Europe so safely that he rendered it inaccessible to the barbarians who live beyond the Ister River.

But I must commence from the native land of the Emperor, to which of all places must be given first rank in all other respects, and with this I must begin

[1] See the description of the Adriatic Sea in *Wars*, V. xv. 16, and the note there. By "Adriatic" here is meant a part of the Mediterranean; Procopius' "Ionian Gulf" is our Adriatic Sea.

[2] *I.e.* farther to the north.

P 67 16 λόγου δοτέον. αὐτῇ γὰρ ἂν μόνῃ ὀγκοῦσθαί τε καὶ διαθρύπτεσθαι καὶ ἀποσεμνύνεσθαι πρέποι βασιλέα Ῥωμαίοις θρεψαμένῃ τε καὶ παρασχομένῃ τοιοῦτον, οὗ δὴ τὰ ἔργα καὶ λόγῳ εἰπεῖν καὶ γραφῇ παρακαταθέσθαι ἀμήχανον.[1]

17 Ἐν Δαρδάνοις που τοῖς Εὐρωπαίοις, οἳ δὴ μετὰ τοὺς Ἐπιδαμνίων ὅρους ᾤκηνται, τοῦ φρουρίου ἄγχιστα ὅπερ Βεδερίανα ἐπικαλεῖται, χωρίον Ταυρίσιον ὄνομα ἦν, ἔνθεν Ἰουστινιανὸς βασιλεὺς ὁ τῆς οἰκουμένης οἰκιστὴς ὥρμηται. 18 τοῦτο μὲν οὖν τὸ χωρίον ἐν βραχεῖ τειχισάμενος κατὰ τὸ τετράγωνον σχῆμα καὶ γωνίᾳ ἑκάστῃ πύργον ἐνθέμενος Τετραπυργίαν εἶναί τε καὶ 19 καλεῖσθαι πεποίηκε. παρ' αὐτὸ δὲ μάλιστα τὸ χωρίον πόλιν ἐπιφανεστάτην ἐδείματο, ἥνπερ Ἰουστινιανὴν ὠνόμασε Πρῖμαν (πρώτη δὲ τοῦτο τῇ Λατίνων φωνῇ δύναται) ταῦτα τῇ θρεψαμένῃ 20 τροφεῖα ἐκτίνων. καίτοι Ῥωμαίους ἐχρῆν ἅπαντας τοῦτο δὴ ἀλλήλοις ἐπικοινοῦσθαι τὸ ὄφλημα, ἐπεὶ καὶ σωτῆρα ἐθρέψατο ἡ χώρα κοινὸν ἅπασιν. B 267 21 ἐνταῦθα δὲ καὶ ὀχετὸν τεκτηνάμενος ὕδασι τὴν πόλιν ἀειρρύτοις διεπράξατο ἐπιεικῶς πλήθειν. 22 πολλὰ δὲ καὶ ἄλλα τῷ τῆς πόλεως οἰκιστῇ ὑπέρογκά τε καὶ λόγου πολλοῦ διαπεπόνηται 23 ἄξια. θεοῦ μὲν τεμένη διαριθμεῖσθαι οὐ ῥᾴδια, καταγώγια δὲ ἀρχόντων φράζεσθαι λόγῳ ἀμήχανα, στοῶν μεγέθη, ἀγορῶν κάλλη, τὰς κρήνας, τὰς 24 ἀγυιάς, τὰ βαλανεῖα, τὰ πωλητήρια. πόλις ἁπλῶς μεγάλη καὶ πολυάνθρωπος καὶ τὰ ἄλλα

[1] ἀμήχανον V, ἀμήχανα A.

my present account. For to this land alone is it given to rejoice and swell with pride and enjoy the solemn dignity of having bred and presented to the Romans an Emperor whose works it is impossible to tell in words or to record in writing.

Among the Dardanians of Europe who live beyond the boundaries of the Epidamnians, close to the fortress which is called Bederiana, there was a hamlet named Taurisium, whence sprang the Emperor Justinian, the founder of the civilised world.[1] He therefore built a wall of small compass about this place in the form of a square, placing a tower at each corner, and caused it to be called, as it actually is, Tetrapyrgia.[2] And close by this place he built a very notable city which he named Justiniana Prima[3] (this means "first" in the Latin tongue), thus paying a debt of gratitude to the home that fostered him. Yet all Romans should have shared this debt among themselves, for this land nourished a common saviour for all of them. In that place also he constructed an aqueduct and so caused the city to be abundantly supplied with ever-running water. And many other enterprises were carried out by the founder of this city—works of great size and worthy of especial note. For to enumerate the churches is not easy, and it is impossible to tell in words of the lodgings for magistrates, the great stoas, the fine market-places, the fountains, the streets, the baths, the shops. In brief, the city is both great and

[1] *Cf.* N. Vulić, "L'Origine ethnique de l'empereur Justinien," *Actes du IVe congrès international des études byzantines, Sofia,* 1934 (*Bull. de l'Inst. arch. Bulgare,* ix. 1935), pp. 400–405.

[2] "Four Towers," modern Ochrida.

[3] Modern Scupi.

εὐδαίμων καὶ οἵα τῆς χώρας ἁπάσης μητρόπολις[1] 25 εἶναι· εἰς ἀξιώματος γὰρ τοσόνδε ἥκει. πρὸς δὲ καὶ τὸν[2] Ἰλλυριῶν ἀρχιερέα διακεκλήρωται, τῶν ἄλλων πόλεων αὐτῇ, ἅτε πρώτῃ τὸ μέγεθος οὔσῃ, ἐξισταμένων. ὥστε καὶ ἀνθυπούργηκε τῷ 26 βασιλεῖ κλέος· ἡ μὲν γὰρ τροφίμῳ ἀποσεμνύνεται βασιλεῖ, ὁ δὲ ἀντιφιλοτιμεῖται δεδημιουργηκέναι τὴν πόλιν. καί μοι ἄχρι τοῦδε εἰπεῖν ἀποχρήσει. 27 ἅπαντα γὰρ ἐς τὸ ἀκριβὲς λεπτολογεῖσθαι ἀμήχανον, ἐπεὶ τῷ βασιλεῖ προσηκούσης τῆς πόλεως ἐλασσοῦσθαι αὐτῆς ἅπαντα λόγον ἐπάναγκες.

28 Ἔτι μέντοι καὶ Βεδερίανα τὸ φρούριον ἀνοικοδομησάμενος ὅλον πολλῷ ὀχυρώτερον κατεστήσατο. ἦν δέ τις ἐν Δαρδάνοις ἐκ παλαιοῦ πόλις 29 ἥπερ Οὐλπιᾶνα ὠνόμαστο. ταύτης τὸν περίβολον καθελὼν ἐκ τοῦ ἐπὶ πλεῖστον (ἦν γὰρ σφαλερὸς ἐς τὰ μάλιστα καὶ ὅλως ἀχρεῖος) ἄλλα τε αὐτῇ παμπληθῆ ἐγκαλλωπίσματα ποιησάμενος, ἔς τε τὴν νῦν μεταθέμενος εὐκοσμίαν, Σεκοῦνδαν αὐτὴν 30 Ἰουστινιανὴν ἐπωνόμασε. σεκοῦνδαν γὰρ τὴν P 68 δευτέραν Λατῖνοι λέγουσι.[3] καὶ ἄλλην δὲ αὐτῇ πλησίον ἐδείματο πόλιν οὐ πρότερον οὖσαν, ἥνπερ Ἰουστινούπολιν τῷ θείῳ ὁμωνύμως ἐκάλεσεν. B 268 31 ἀλλὰ καὶ Σαρδικῆς καὶ Ναϊσουπόλεως, ἔτι μέντοι Γερμαῆς τε καὶ Πανταλείας διερρωγότα τῷ χρόνῳ τὰ τείχη εὑρὼν οἰκοδομησάμενός τε ξὺν τῷ ἀσφαλεῖ ἄμαχα τοῖς πολεμίοις διεπράξατο 32 εἶναι. καὶ πολίχνια δὲ τούτων δὴ μεταξὺ ἐδεί-

[1] μητρόπολις V, μητρόπολιν A. [2] τὸν A, τῶν V.
[3] Λατῖνοι λέγουσι V, καλοῦσι A.

---

[1] Modern Lipljan.
[2] Called Triaditza in medieval times; modern Sofia.

populous and blessed in every way—a city worthy to be the metropolis of the whole region, for it has attained this rank. It has also been allotted to the Archbishop of Illyricum as his seat, the other cities conceding this honour to it, as being first in point of size. Thus this city has won honour for the Emperor in requital for his favour; for while it prides itself upon its foster-son, he for his part takes a corresponding pride in that he built the city. But this will be enough for me to tell; indeed it is impossible to describe everything in detail, for since the city is the Emperor's own, any account of it necessarily falls short of the reality.

He also rebuilt the entire fortress of Bederiana and made it much stronger. And there was a certain city among the Dardanians, dating from ancient times, which was named Ulpiana;[1] he tore down most of its circuit-wall, for it was seriously damaged and altogether useless, and he added a very great number of improvements to the city, changing it to its present fair aspect; and he named it Justiniana Secunda (*secunda* is the Latin word for second). Near it he built another city where none had existed before, which he called Justinopolis from his uncle's name. Furthermore, he found the walls of Sardica[2] and Naïsopolis,[3] as well as those of Germaê and of Pantalia,[4] in ruins from the passage of time, and he built them up securely and made them such that they could defy the enemy. Between these he built

[3] Naïssus, modern Nish.

[4] A mistake for Pautalia; the place is mentioned again in the list below, Chap. iv, ὑπὸ πόλιν Παυτά. *Cf.* A. Salač, "The City of Pautalia in Procopius, περὶ κτισμάτων," *Listy filologické*, lviii. 1931, pp. 392–395, in Czech, with French summary, p. 487.

ματο τρία, Κρατίσκαρά τε καὶ Κουιμέδαβα καὶ Ῥουμισίανα. οὕτω μὲν οὖν τάσδε τὰς πόλεις 33 ἐκ θεμελίων ἀνέστησε. πρόβολον δὲ ἰσχυρότατον αὐτῶν τε καὶ πάσης Εὐρώπης Ἴστρον ποταμὸν ποιεῖσθαι ἐθέλων, ἐρύμασι τοῦ ποταμοῦ τὴν ἠϊόνα περιβάλλει συχνοῖς, ὥσπερ μοι γεγράψεται οὐ πολλῷ ὕστερον, φυλακτήριά τε στρατιωτῶν πανταχόθι τέθειται τῆς ἀκτῆς, ἀναχαιτίσοντα τὴν διάβασιν βεβαιότατα τοῖς τῇδε 34 βαρβάροις. ἀλλὰ καὶ τούτων οἱ ἐξειργασμένων, ὑπόπτως ἐς τῆς ἀνθρωπείας ἐλπίδος τὸ σφαλερὸν ἔχων, λογισάμενός τε ὡς εἰ τοῖς πολεμίοις ὅτῳ δή ποτε τρόπῳ διαπορθμεύσασθαι δυνατὰ εἴη, ἐπιθήσονται ἀφυλάκτοις τὸ παράπαν τοῖς ἀγροῖς οὖσι, καὶ ἀνθρώπους μὲν ἐξανδραποδιοῦσιν ἡβηδὸν ἅπαντας, χρήματα δὲ λῄσονται[1] πάντα, οὐκ ἐπὶ κοινῆς αὐτοῖς μόνον τὴν ἀσφάλειαν ἐν τοῖς κατὰ τὸν ποταμὸν ὀχυρώμασιν ἀπέλιπεν εἶναι, 35 ἀλλὰ καὶ ἰδίαν πεποίηται· οὕτω συνεχῆ τὰ ἐρύματα ἐν τοῖς χωρίοις ἀπεργασάμενος ὥστε ἀγρὸς ἕκαστος ἢ φρούριον ἀποτετόρνευται, ἢ τῷ τετειχισμένῳ πρόσοικός ἐστιν, ἐνταῦθά τε κἀν τῇ Ἠπείρῳ τῇ τε νέᾳ καὶ τῇ παλαιᾷ καλουμένῃ. 36 οὗ δὴ καὶ πόλις αὐτῷ πεποίηται Ἰουστινιανούπολις, ἡ πρότερον Ἀδριανούπολις καλουμένη.

37 Ἀνενεώσατο δὲ Νικόπολίν τε καὶ Φωτικὴν καὶ τὴν Φοινίκην ὠνομασμένην. αἱ δύο αὗται πολίχναι, ἥ τε Φωτικὴ καὶ ἡ Φοινίκη, ἐν τῷ χθαμαλῷ τῆς γῆς ἔκειντο, ὕδασι περιρρεόμεναι τῇδε λιμ-38 νάζουσι. διὸ δὴ λογισάμενος Ἰουστινιανὸς βασι-B 269 λεὺς εἶναι ἀμήχανα ἐπὶ στερρᾶς θεμελίων συνθήκης

[1] λῄσονται V, λῄσοιντο A.

three small forts, Cratiscara and Quimedaba and Roumisiana. Thus he raised these cities from their foundations. And wishing, as he did, to make the Ister River the strongest possible line of first defence before them and before the whole of Europe, he distributed numerous forts along the bank of the river, as I shall soon describe, and he placed garrisons of troops everywhere along the shore, in order to put the most rigid check upon the crossing of the barbarians there. But even after he had completed all these precautions, he was still uneasy because of the uncertainty of human plans; and since he reflected that if it should ever be possible for the enemy to break through somehow, they would then fall upon fields which would be entirely unguarded, would enslave the whole population, from the youths upwards, and would plunder all their property, he did not leave their common safety to depend upon the forts along the river alone, but he also provided individual safeguards for them; for he made the defences so continuous in the estates that each farm either has been converted into a stronghold or lies adjacent to one which is fortified; and he did this both here and in New Epirus, as it is called, and in Old Epirus.[1] Here too he built the city of Justinianopolis, which formerly was called Adrianopolis.[2]

And he restored Nicopolis and Photicê and the place called Phoenicê. These two towns, namely Photicê and Phoenicê, stood on low-lying ground and were surrounded by stagnant water which collected there. Consequently the Emperor Justinian, reasoning that it was impossible for walls to be built about

[1] *Cf.* page 250, note 2. [2] Modern Adrianople or Edirne.

περιβόλους αὐταῖς ἀναστῆναι, αὐτὰς μὲν ἐπὶ σχήματος τοῦ αὐτοῦ εἴασε, φρούρια δὲ αὐτῶν ἀγχοτάτω ἔν τε ἀνάντει καὶ ἰσχυρῶς ὀρθίῳ
39 ἐδείματο. ἦν δέ τις ἐνταῦθα πόλις ἀρχαία, ὕδασιν ἐπιεικῶς κατακορὴς οὖσα, ὀνόματός τε τῆς τοῦ χωρίου φύσεως ἀξίου ἐπιτυχοῦσα·[1]
40 Εὔροια γὰρ ἀνέκαθεν ὠνομάζετο. ταύτης δὲ τῆς Εὐροίας οὐ πολλῷ ἄποθεν λίμνη κέχυται καὶ νῆσος κατὰ[2] μέσον ἀνέχει καὶ λόφος αὐτῇ
41 ἐπανέστηκε. διαλείπει δὲ ἡ λίμνη τοσοῦτον, ὅσον τινὰ ἐν εἰσόδου μοίρᾳ τῇ νήσῳ λελεῖφθαι.
42 ἔνθα δὴ βασιλεὺς τοὺς τῆς Εὐροίας μεταβιβάσας οἰκήτορας, πόλιν ὀχυρωτάτην οἰκοδομησάμενος ἐτειχίσατο.

P 69 β΄. Μετὰ δὲ τὴν Ἤπειρον ὅλην Αἰτωλούς τε καὶ Ἀκαρνᾶνας παραδραμόντι ὅ τε Κρισαῖος[3] ἐκδέχεται[4] κόλπος καὶ ὅ τε Ἰσθμὸς ἥ τε Κόρινθος καὶ τὰ ἄλλα τῆς Ἑλλάδος χωρία. ἔνθα δὴ τῆς παρ᾽ αὐτοῦ τὰ μάλιστα προνοίας ἠξίωνται.
2 μάλιστα δὲ[5] πάντων θαυμάσειεν ἄν τις ὁπόσοις περιβόλοις ἐτειχίσατο τὴν Ῥωμαίων ἀρχήν. τῶν τε γὰρ ἄλλων προὐνόησε πάντων καὶ οὐχ ἥκιστα
3 τῶν ἐν Θερμοπύλαις ἀνόδων. πρῶτα μὲν οὖν τὰ τείχη ἐς ὕψος αὐτῷ ἀνέστη μέγα. ἦν γάρ, εἴ τις προσίοι, εὐπετῶς ἁλωτὰ καὶ οὐ τετειχισμένα τὰ ὄρη, ἃ ταύτῃ ἀνέχει, ἀλλ᾽ ἀποτετριγχωμένα ἐδόκει
4 εἶναι. οἷς δὴ καὶ διπλᾶς τὰς ἐπάλξεις ἐντέθειται πάσας. κατὰ ταὐτὰ δὲ κἀν τῷ φρουρίῳ ἐξείρ-

[1] ἀξίου ἐπιτυχοῦσα added by Haury.
[2] κατὰ V, om. A.
[3] Κρισαῖος Dindorf: σκρησαῖος.
[4] ἐκδέχεται Maltretus: ἐδέχετο.
[5] δὲ added by Hoeschel.

them on foundations of solid construction, left them just as they were, but close to them he built forts on rising ground which is exceedingly steep. There was a certain ancient city in this region, abundantly supplied with water and endowed with a name worthy of the place; for it was called Euroea [1] from ancient times. Not far from this Euroea a lake spreads out with an island in its midst upon which rises a hill. And a break is left in the lake just large enough so that a kind of approach to the island remains. The Emperor moved the inhabitants of Euroea to this place, built a very strong city, and put a wall about it.[2]

ii. Beyond [3] the whole of Epirus and Aetolia and Acarnania, as one skirts the coast, one comes to the Crisaean Gulf [4] and the Isthmus and Corinth and the other parts of Greece. These regions made demands upon his very utmost wisdom. And above all else one might wonder at the number of walled cities with which he fortified the Roman Empire. For he made provision for all of them and especially for the by-paths up the mountains at Thermopylae. First of all he raised the walls there to a very great height. For the mountains which rise in that region were easy to capture, if one should assault them, they being not really walled, but simply supplied with what appeared to be a cornice of masonry. On all these walls he even placed double battlements, and he likewise carried out this same improvement

[1] "Fair-flowing."

[2] Euroea was probably on the site of the modern village of Gardiki, near the city and lake of Ioannina.

[3] To the south.

[4] A northern arm of the Gulf of Corinth.

γασται, ὅπερ ἐνταῦθα ἐκ παλαιοῦ ἦν παρέργως
5 οὕτω πεποιημένον τοῖς πάλαι ἀνθρώποις. διαρκές
τε γὰρ αὐτῷ ὕψος ἐντέθεικε καὶ διπλοῦς τοὺς
6 προμαχῶνας πεποίηται. πρὸς ἐπὶ τούτοις δὲ καὶ
ἀνύδρῳ παντάπασιν ὄντι ταμιεῖον ὑετίων ὑδάτων
B 270 7 ἐπετεχνήσατο. ἔπειτα δὲ καὶ ἀνόδους πολλὰς
ἀφυλάκτους τε καὶ ἀτειχίστους τὰ πρότερα οὔσας
8 ἐς τὸ ἀκριβὲς ἐτειχίσατο. θαυμάσειεν ἄν τις
εἰκότως τὸν Περσῶν βασιλέα, ὅτι δὴ χρόνον
ἐνταῦθα κατατρίψας πολύν, μίαν τινὰ στενὴν
ἀτραπὸν εὕρατο, καὶ ταῦτα προδοτῶν Ἑλλήνων
τυχών, ὁδῶν τε ἀτειχίστων ἐκείνῃ πολλῶν καὶ
9 ἁμαξιτῶν σχεδόν τι οὐσῶν. ἥ τε γὰρ θάλασσα
τοὺς πρόποδας ἐπικλύζουσα τῶν ὀρῶν, ἀνεστο-
μωμένας ἐκ τοῦ ἐπὶ πλεῖστον ἐποιεῖτο εἶναι τὰς
ἐνθένδε ἀνόδους, καὶ σηράγγων τε καὶ χαραδρῶν
ἀδιεξόδων ἐνταῦθα οὐσῶν, ἀμήχανα ἔδοξεν εἶναι
τοῖς πάλαι ἀνθρώποις τειχίσμασιν ἐς τὸ ἀκριβὲς
περιβαλέσθαι τὰ διῃρημένα τῇ φύσει, τῇ τε πρὸς
τὰ χαλεπώτατα τῶν ἔργων ὀκνήσει ἀταλαίπωρον
ἀφέμενοι τὴν ἀσφάλειαν ἐπὶ τῇ τύχῃ κατέλιπον,
ἐς τὴν ἐσομένην βαρβάροις τῆς ὁδοῦ ἄγνοιαν
10 ἀποθέμενοι τὰς τῆς σωτηρίας ἐλπίδας. ἐπεὶ
πρὸς τὴν ταλαιπωρίαν ἀπολέγοντες ἀεὶ ἄνθρωποι,
τὰ σφίσιν αὐτοῖς δυσκολώτατα δόξαντα εἶναι
11 οὐδὲ ἄλλοις τισὶν οἴονται ῥᾴδια ἔσεσθαι. διὸ δὴ
οὐκ ἄν τις ἔτι φιλονεικοίη μὴ οὐχὶ ἀνθρώπων
ἁπάντων οἳ δὴ ἐς τὸν πάντα αἰῶνα γεγένηνται,
Ἰουστινιανὸν βασιλέα προμηθέστατον γεγονέναι
καὶ διαφερόντως ἐπιμελέστατον, ᾧ γε οὐδὲ
θάλασσα χαλεπὴ γέγονε, γειτνιῶσά τε τοῖς ὄρεσι
καὶ περιχεομένη καὶ ἐπικλύζουσα, ἐν κλυδωνίῳ

in the fortress which had stood there from an ancient date, carelessly constructed, as it was, by men of former times. For he built it up to an adequate height and made the ramparts double. In addition to this he also devised for the fort, which was entirely without water, a storage-cistern for rain-water. Furthermore, he carefully walled off many paths up the mountains which previously had been both unguarded and unwalled. One might marvel with good reason at the Persian King for spending so much time there and finding only a single narrow path, and that too with the help of Grecian traitors, while in fact there are many unwalled routes there which are practically waggon-roads. The sea, washing the base of the mountains, continually made new ascents from this point; and since glens and impassable ravines abound there, it seemed to the men of ancient times impossible to close up thoroughly with walls the openings which had been made by nature; and because of their reluctance to undertake a difficult task, they carelessly abandoned their safety to chance, basing their hope of salvation on the assumption that the barbarians would be ignorant of the road. For since men always shrink from hard work, they imagine that what has seemed very difficult to them will not be easy for any others. So no man will any longer dispute the assertion that the Emperor Justinian has shewn himself most provident and most exceptionally careful as compared with all other men who have ever lived, seeing that even the sea, though it comes close to the mountains and surrounds them and beats against them, has not proved

P 70 τε καὶ ψάμμῳ ὑγρᾷ τοῖς θεμελίοις στηρίζεσθαι, καὶ τοῖς ἐναντιωτάτοις διαφανῶς ἐναρμόζεσθαι, ἀνθρώπων τε προσχωρεῖν τέχνῃ καὶ βιαζομένοις 12 ὑπείκειν. οὐ μέντοι οὐδὲ τάς τε λόχμας καὶ νάπας ἀλλήλαις ἀνάψας, οὐδὲ τὴν θάλασσαν τῷ ὄρει ἐναρμοσάμενος ὁ βασιλεὺς οὗτος, ὅλην τε τὴν Ἑλλάδα περιβαλὼν τοῖς ὀχυρώμασι, κατέπαυσε B 271 τὴν ὑπὲρ τῶν κατηκόων σπουδήν, ἀλλὰ καὶ φρούρια πολλὰ τοῦ τείχους ἐντὸς ἐτεκτήνατο, ἄξια τύχης τῆς ἀνθρωπείας βεβουλευμένος, ᾗ βέβαιον [1] οὐδὲν οὐδὲ ἀκαταγώνιστον γίνεται. 13 ὥστε εἰ τοῖς τείχεσι τούτοις τρόπῳ ὁτῳοῦν ἢ χρόνῳ ἁλῶναι ξυμβαίη, ἐν τοῖς φρουρίοις τὰ 14 φυλακτήρια διασώζοιτο. καὶ μὴν καὶ σιτῶνας ἐν τῷ ἀσφαλεῖ καὶ ὑδάτων ἔλυτρα πανταχόθι πεποίηται, στρατιώτας τε φρουροὺς ἐς δισχιλίους μάλιστα τῇδε ἱδρύσατο· ὃ οὐδέ τις τῶν πρώην βασιλέων πώποτε ἐκ τοῦ παντὸς χρόνου πεποίηκεν. 15 ἀφύλακτα γὰρ τὸ παράπαν τὰ τείχη ταῦτα ἄνωθέν τε καὶ ἐς ἐμὲ ἦν, ἀγροίκων τε τῶν ἐπιχωρίων τινὲς τῶν πολεμίων καταθεόντων μεθαρμοσάμενοι τὴν δίαιταν ἐν τῷ παραυτίκα, ἐπὶ καιροῦ τε αὐτοσχεδιάζοντες τὰ πολέμια, ἐκ περιτροπῆς ἐνταῦθα ἐφρούρουν, ἁλώσιμοί τε τοῖς πολεμίοις ἀπειρίᾳ τοῦ ἔργου ῥᾷστα ξὺν τῇ Ἑλλάδι ἐγίνοντο, ταύτῃ τε τῇ σμικρολογίᾳ ἡ χώρα ἐπὶ μακρότατον ἀπέκειτο ἐπιοῦσι βαρβάροις.

16 Οὕτω μὲν Ἰουστινιανὸς βασιλεὺς τὰ ἐν Θερμοπύλαις [2] ἐρύματα ἐκρατύνατο. καὶ πόλεων δὲ ἁπασῶν, αἵπερ αὐτῶν ἐκτὸς τῇ χώρᾳ ἐξικανοῦσιν

[1] βέβαιον A, βέβαιον γὰρ V.
[2] θερμοπύλαις V, τῇ ἑλλάδι A.

an obstacle sufficient to prevent the foundations from being securely laid in the midst of the surging water and on the wet sand, or to forestall the most striking union of the most opposite elements, which are thus forced to yield to man's skill and to bow to his superior power. Yet this Emperor, even after joining the forests and the glens to each other, and fastening the sea to the mountain, and encircling all Greece with strongholds, did not stop his zeal for his subjects, but he also constructed many forts inside the wall, planning for all the contingencies which sway man's fortune, wherein nothing is fixed or unconquerable, so that if these walls in any manner or at any time chanced to be captured, the garrisons might still be maintained in the fortresses. Furthermore, he placed granaries and reservoirs of water in safe places everywhere and established there about two thousand soldiers as a garrison, a thing which not one of the former Emperors has done in all time.[1] For these walls were entirely unguarded from early times even to my day, and some of the peasants from the neighbourhood, when the enemy came down, would suddenly change their mode of life, and becoming makeshift soldiers for the occasion, would keep guard there in turn; and because of their inexperience in the business they, together with Greece itself, proved an easy prey to the enemy, and on account of this niggardliness the country through its whole extent lay open to the oncoming barbarians.

Thus did the Emperor Justinian secure the defences at Thermopylae. And in all the cities outside the pass, which in that region are sufficiently numerous,

[1] *Cf. Secret History*, xxvi. 31–33 for a very different statement of the case.

οὖσαι, ξὺν ἐπιμελείᾳ πολλῇ τείχη ᾠκοδομήσατο ἰσχυρά, ἔν τε Σάκκῳ καὶ Ὑπάτῃ καὶ Κορακίοις καὶ Οὐννῷ καὶ Βαλέαις καὶ τῷ καλουμένῳ 17 Λεονταρίῳ. ἐν δὲ τῇ Ἡρακλείᾳ πεποίηται τάδε. ἐξ Ἰλλυριῶν ἐς Ἑλλάδα ἰόντι, ὄρη δύο ἐπὶ μακρότατον ἀλλήλοιν ὡς ἀγχοτάτω ξυνίασι, στενωπὸν ἐν βραχεῖ ἀπεργαζόμενα τὴν μεταξὺ χώραν (κλεισούρας νενομίκασι τὰ τοιαῦτα καλεῖν)· B 272 18 πηγὴ δὲ κατὰ μέσον κάτεισιν, ἐν μὲν ὥρᾳ θερινῇ πότιμον ἀποβλύζουσα καὶ καθαρὸν[1] ὕδωρ ἀπὸ τῶν ὀρῶν ἃ ταύτῃ ἀνέχει, ἐς ῥύακά τε ἀποκεκριμένη βραχύν. 19 ἐπειδὰν δὲ ὕοι,[2] χειμάρρους ἐνταῦθα ἐπικυρτοῦται ὑψηλός τε ὑπερφυῶς καὶ δεινῶς ἄγριος ἐπὶ πλεῖστον τῶν ἐκείνῃ σκοπέλων ἀπὸ τῶν χαραδρῶν συνάγων τὸ ῥεῦμα. 20 ἐνθένδε τοῖς βαρβάροις εὐπετὴς ἐπί τε Θερμοπύλας οὐδενὶ πόνῳ ἐγίνετο καὶ τὴν ταύτῃ Ἑλλάδα. 21 τοῦ δὲ στενωποῦ ἐφ' ἑκάτερα δύο ἐκ παλαιοῦ ὀχυρώματα ἦν, πῇ μὲν Ἡράκλεια πόλις, ἧσπερ ἐπεμνήσθην ἀρτίως, πῇ δὲ ὁ Μυροπώλης καλούμενος, οὐκ ὀλίγῃ διεστηκὼς χώρᾳ. 22 ταῦτα δὲ ἄμφω τὰ ὀχυρώματα ἐν ἐρειπίοις ἐκ παλαιοῦ ὄντα Ἰουστινιανὸς ἀνῳκοδομήσατο βασιλεὺς καὶ διατειχίσματι τὸν στενωπὸν ὀχυρωτάτῳ περιβαλών, τούτῳ τε συνάψας ὄρος ἑκάτερον τοῖς μὲν P 71 βαρβάροις τὴν δίοδον ἀνεχαίτισε, τῷ δὲ χειμάρρῳ ἐπάναγκές ἐστι λιμνάζοντι τοῦ τείχους ἐντός, εἶτα ἐφύπερθεν αὐτοῦ φερομένῳ ὅπῃ παρατύχοι ἰέναι.

[1] καθαρὸν V, γαληνὸν A.
[2] ὕοι V, ὕῃ A.

he very carefully built strong walls, both at Saccus and Hypatê and Coracii and Unnum and Baleae and at Leontarium, as it is called. At Heraclea he did as follows. As one descends from Illyricum into Greece, one is confronted by two mountains which rise very close together for a long distance, forming between them a narrow pass of the sort which they are wont to call *cleisurae*.[1] A small stream comes down between them, in the summer season flowing with pure drinking-water from the mountains which rise there and forming a tiny brook. Whenever it rains, however, an exceedingly deep and very violent torrent billows down, gathering its volume chiefly from the streams which course down from the mountain peaks thereabout. At that point it was possible for the barbarians with no difficulty to effect an entrance both against Thermopylae and into that part of Greece. But on either side of the pass there had been two fortresses from early times, on the one side the city of Heraclea, which I have just mentioned, and on the other, separated by no small distance, Myropoles, as it is called.[2] Both these fortresses had lain in ruin from ancient times, so the Emperor Justinian rebuilt them and closed the pass with a very strong cross-wall which he made fast to each of the two mountains, thus blocking the entrance for the barbarians, and the stream when it is in flood is now forced to form a pond inside the wall and then to flow over it and go on wherever it chances.

[1] See above, III. iii. 2, note.

[2] Possibly the route indicated was by way of the valley of the Sperchius, the upper portion of which might be characterised as a *cleisura*; in its lower reaches, however, near which Heraclea Trachinia is situated, the valley is wide and open.

23 Καὶ πόλεις δὲ τῆς Ἑλλάδος ἁπάσας αἵπερ ἐντός εἰσι τῶν ἐν Θερμοπύλαις τειχῶν, ἐν τῷ βεβαίῳ κατεστήσατο εἶναι, τοὺς περιβόλους ἀνα-
24 νεωσάμενος ἅπαντας. κατερηρίπεσαν[1] γὰρ πολλῷ πρότερον, ἐν Κορίνθῳ μὲν σεισμῶν ἐπιγενομένων ἐξαισίων, Ἀθήνησι δὲ καὶ Πλαταιᾶσι κἂν τοῖς ἐπὶ Βοιωτίας χωρίοις χρόνου μὲν[2] μήκει πεπονηκότες,[3] ἐπιμελησαμένου[4] δὲ αὐτῶν
25 οὐδενὸς τῶν πάντων ἀνθρώπων. ἐπίμαχον δὲ ἢ ἀφύλακτον οὐδὲν εἴασεν, ἐπεὶ αὐτῷ προεγρηγορότι τῶν κατηκόων ἔννοια γέγονεν ὡς οἱ βάρβαροι καταθέοντες, ἂν οὕτω τύχῃ, τά γε ἀμφὶ Θερμοπύλας χωρία, ἐπειδὰν τάχιστα πύθωνται οὐδὲν αὐτοῖς ὄφελος ἔσεσθαι ὑπερβεβηκόσι τὸ ἔρυμα τοῦτο, τειχήρους πανταχόθι γεγενημένης τῆς
B 273 ἄλλης Ἑλλάδος, ἐθελοκακήσουσιν αὐτίκα δὴ μάλα ἐξεπιστάμενοι ὡς πολιορκεῖν σφίσι πόλιν ἑκάστην
26 ἐπάναγκες ἔσται. προσδοκία γὰρ μηκυνομένη ταλαιπωρεῖν οὐκ ἀνέχεται, οὐδὲ ἀναβαλλομένης[5] ὠφελείας ἐφίεται, ἀλλ' ἀποδίδοται τῆς περὶ ταῦτα ὀκνήσεως τὴν μέλλουσαν τύχην.

27 Ταῦτα διαπεπραγμένος Ἰουστινιανὸς βασιλεύς, ἐπεὶ τὰς ἐν Πελοποννήσῳ πόλεις ἁπάσας ἀτειχίστους ἐμάνθανεν εἶναι, λογισάμενος ὅτι δή οἱ πολὺς τετρίψεται χρόνος, εἰ κατὰ μιᾶς ἐπιμελοῖτο, τὸν Ἰσθμὸν[6] ὅλον ἐν τῷ ἀσφαλεῖ ἐτειχίσατο,
28 ἐπεὶ αὐτοῦ καταπεπτώκει τὰ πολλὰ ἤδη. φρούριά τε ταύτῃ ἐδείματο καὶ φυλακτήρια κατεστήσατο. τούτῳ δὲ τῷ τρόπῳ ἄβατα τοῖς πολεμίοις ἅπαντα

[1] κατερηρίπεσαν Haury: καταρερείπεσαν V, κατερείπεσαν A.
[2] μὲν V, om. A.
[3] πεπονηκότες Haury: πεπο|ηκόσι V, πεπονηκότα A.

He also rendered secure all the cities of Greece which are inside the walls at Thermopylae, renewing their circuit-walls in every case. For they had fallen into ruin long before, at Corinth because of terrible earthquakes which had visited the city; and at Athens and Plataea and the towns of Boeotia they had suffered from the long passage of time, while no man in the whole world took thought for them. But he left nothing vulnerable or unguarded, for after vigilantly caring for the safety of his subjects, he felt convinced that even if the barbarians should chance to overrun the country about Thermopylae, they would, as soon as they learned that after surmounting this obstacle they would have gained no advantage (the rest of Greece having been fortified at every point), give up immediately in despair, knowing that it would be necessary for them to besiege each individual city. For when expectation is prolonged, it cannot endure the strain, nor does it even desire a profit which is delayed; but it simply abandons the contingent chance of success through waiting.

When the Emperor Justinian, after he had accomplished all this, learned that all the cities of the Peloponnesus were unwalled, he reasoned that obviously a long time would be consumed if he attended to them one by one, and so he walled the whole Isthmus securely, because much of the old wall had already fallen down. And he built fortresses there and established garrisons. In this manner he

---

[4] ἐπιμελησαμένου Maltretus: ἐπιμελησαμένων V.
[5] ἀναβαλλομένης V, ἀναβαλλομένη A.
[6] ἰσθμὸν V, πορθμὸν A.

πεποίηκεν εἶναι τὰ ἐν Πελοποννήσῳ χωρία, εἴ καί τι ἐς τὸ ἐν Θερμοπύλαις ὀχύρωμα κακουργήσοιεν. ἀλλὰ ταῦτα μὲν τῇδε κεχώρηκε.

γʹ. Πόλις δὲ ἦν τις ἐπὶ Θεσσαλίας, Διοκλητιανούπολις ὄνομα, εὐδαίμων μὲν τὸ παλαιὸν γεγενημένη, προϊόντος δὲ τοῦ χρόνου βαρβάρων οἱ ἐπιπεσόντων καταλυθεῖσα καὶ οἰκητόρων ἔρημος γεγονυῖα ἐπὶ μακρότατον· λίμνη δέ τις αὐτῇ ἐν γειτόνων τυγχάνει οὖσα, ᾗ Καστορία ὠνόμασται. καὶ νῆσος κατὰ μέσον τῆς λίμνης τοῖς ὕδασι 2 περιβέβληται. μία δὲ εἰς αὐτὴν εἴσοδος ἀπὸ τῆς λίμνης ἐν στενῷ λέλειπται, οὐ πλέον ἢ[1] ἐς πεντε- 3 καίδεκα διήκουσα πόδας. ὄρος τε τῇ νήσῳ ἐπανέστηκεν ὑψηλὸν ἄγαν, ἥμισυ μὲν τῇ λίμνῃ 4 καλυπτόμενον, τῷ δὲ λειπομένῳ ἐγκείμενον. διὸ δὴ ὁ βασιλεὺς οὗτος τὸν Διοκλητιανουπόλεως ὑπεριδὼν χῶρον ἅτε που διαφανῶς εὐέφοδον ὄντα καὶ πεπονθότα πολλῷ πρότερον, ἅπερ ἐρρήθη, P 72 πόλιν ἐν τῇ νήσῳ ὀχυρωτάτην ἐδείματο, καὶ τὸ B 274 5 ὄνομα, ὡς τὸ εἰκός, ἀφῆκε τῇ πόλει. ἐπὶ μέντοι Ἐχιναίου τε καὶ Θηβῶν καὶ Φαρσάλου καὶ ἄλλων τῶν ἐπὶ Θεσσαλίας[2] πόλεων ἁπασῶν, ἐν αἷς Δημητριάς τέ ἐστι καὶ Μητρόπολις ὄνομα καὶ Γόμφοι καὶ Τρίκα, τοὺς[3] περιβόλους ἀνανεωσάμενος, ἐν τῷ ἀσφαλεῖ ἐκρατύνατο, χρόνῳ τε καταπεπονηκότας μακρῷ, εὐπετῶς τε ἁλωτοὺς ὄντας, εἴ τις προσίοι.

6 Ἀλλ' ἐπεὶ ἐς Θεσσαλίαν ἀφίγμεθα, φέρε δή, τῷ λόγῳ ἐπί τε τὸ ὄρος τὸ Πήλιον καὶ

[1] πλέον ἢ Maltretus: πλέον V.
[2] ἐπὶ θεσσαλίας V: ἐπιθαλασσίων A.
[3] Τρίκα, τοὺς Haury for τρικαττοὺς.

made all the towns in the Peloponnesus inaccessible to the enemy, even if somehow they should force the defences at Thermopylae. Thus were these things done.

iii. There was a certain city in Thessaly, Diocletianopolis by name, which had been prosperous in ancient times, but with the passage of time and the assaults of the barbarians it had been destroyed, and for a very long time it had been destitute of inhabitants; and a certain lake chances to be close by which was named Castoria.[1] There is an island in the middle of the lake, for the most part surrounded by water; but there remains a single narrow approach to this island through the lake, not more than fifteen feet wide. And a very lofty mountain stands above the island, one half being covered by the lake while the remainder rests upon it. Wherefore this Emperor passed over the site of Diocletianopolis, since it was manifestly easy of access and had long been in a state of collapse, as has been stated, and built a very strong city on the island, and, as was right, he allowed it to bear his own name. Furthermore, he restored the circuit-walls of Echinaeus and of Thebes and Pharsalus and of all the other cities of Thessaly, including Demetrias and Metropolis, as it is called, and Gomphi and Tricca,[2] making them safe and strong, since they had all suffered with the passage of time and could be captured easily, if anyone should attack them.

But now that we have reached Thessaly, let us direct our account at once to Mt. Pelion and the

[1] *Cf.* A. D. Keramopoullos, "'Ὀρεστικὸν Ἄργος—Διοκλητιανούπολις—Καστορία." *Byz.-neugr. Jahrbb.*, ix., 1930–2, pp. 55–63. [2] Later Trikala, Mod. Trikkala.

7 Πηνειὸν ποταμὸν ἴωμεν. ῥεῖ μὲν ἐξ ὄρους τοῦ Πηλίου πρᾴῳ τῷ ῥείθρῳ ὁ Πηνειός, ὡραΐσται δὲ αὐτῷ περιρρεομένη πόλις ἡ Λάρισσα, τῆς Φθίας ἐνταῦθα οὐκέτι οὔσης, τοῦτο δὴ τοῦ 8 μακροῦ χρόνου τὸ διαπόνημα. φέρεται δὲ ὁ ποταμὸς οὗτος εὖ μάλα προσηνῶς ἄχρι ἐς θάλασσαν. εὔφορός τε οὖν ἐστιν ἡ χώρα καρπῶν παντοδαπῶν καὶ ποτίμοις ὕδασι κατακορὴς ἄγαν, ὧνπερ ὀνίνασθαι ὡς ἥκιστα εἶχον περίφοβοι ὄντες οἱ τῇδε ᾠκημένοι διηνεκὲς καὶ καραδοκοῦντες ἀεὶ τοὺς βαρβάρους ἐγκείσεσθαι[1] σφίσιν· ἐπεὶ οὐδαμῆ τῶν ταύτῃ χωρίων ὀχύρωμα 9 ἦν, ὅπη ἂν καταφυγόντες σωθήσονται. ἀλλὰ καὶ Λάρισσαν καὶ Καισάρειαν, πεπονηκότων σφίσιν ὑπεράγαν τῶν ἐρυμάτων, σχεδόν τι 10 ἀτειχίστους εἶναι ξυνέβαινε. βασιλεὺς δὲ Ἰουστινιανὸς ἄμφω τείχη ἰσχυρότατα[2] ποιησάμενος 11 γνησίᾳ τὴν χώραν εὐδαιμονίᾳ ξυνῴκισεν. οὐ πολλῷ δὲ ἄποθεν ὄρη ἀνέχει ἀπόκρημνα, οὐρανομήκεσιν ἀμφιλαφῆ δένδροις· οἰκεῖα[3] δὲ Κενταύ-12 ροις τὰ ὄρη. καὶ γέγονε Λαπίθαις ἐν τῇδε τῇ χώρᾳ πρὸς τὸ Κενταύρων γένος ἡ μάχη, ὡς οἱ μῦθοι ἡμῖν ἐκ παλαιοῦ ἰσχυρίζονται, νεανιευόμενοι γεγονέναι ἀνθρώπων γένος ἐν τοῖς ἄνω χρόνοις ἀλλόκοτον καὶ ζῴων φύσιν τινὰ δυοῖν B 275 13 σύμμικτον. ἀφῆκε δέ τι καὶ τῷ μύθῳ ἐν προσηγορίᾳ μαρτύριον ὁ παλαιὸς χρόνος, φρουρίου ἐν τοῖς τῇδε[4] ὄρεσιν ὄντος. Κενταυρόπολις

[1] ἐγκείσεσθαι A, ἐγκεῖσθαι V.
[2] τείχη ἰσχυρότατα V, τειχήρεις A.
[3] οἰκεῖα A, οἰκία V.
[4] τοῖς τῇδε V, τοῖσδε τοῖς A.

Peneus River. This river flows from Mt. Pelion [1] with a gentle stream which encircles and beautifies the city of Larissa; Phthia[2] is no longer in existence, this being the work of the long passage of time. And this river flows on with a very easy descent all the way to the sea. The country is indeed productive of all kinds of crops and has a surfeit of drinking-water, yet the inhabitants of the region could not derive the least enjoyment from these things because they were in a state of constant terror and ever expected the barbarians to fall upon them, since there was no stronghold anywhere in this district where they might take refuge and find safety. Even Larissa and Caesarea,[3] since their defences had suffered excessively, had come to be practically unwalled. But the Emperor Justinian made the defences of both very strong, and in this way brought the blessings of true prosperity to the region. And not far away rise precipitous mountains, covered with lofty trees—the home of the Centaurs. This was the spot where the battle of the Lapiths took place against the race of the Centaurs, as our myths have it from of old, childishly pretending that in early times a strange race of men existed, compounded of the nature of two creatures. Ancient times have also left a certain testimony to the myth in a name applied to a fort in the mountains there; for the place is called Cen-

[1] In fact its principal source arises in northwestern Thessaly; it is a small tributary that rises in Mt. Pelion and passes Larissa.

[2] The reputed home of Achilles.

[3] In western Macedonia, on the river Haliacmon. *Cf.* A. D. Keramopoullos, "Wo lag die Καισάρεια des Procopius?" *Actes du IVe congrès international des études byzantines, Sofia,* 1934 (*Bull. de l'Inst. arch. Bulgare,* ix. 1935), pp. 407–413.

14 γὰρ τὸ χωρίον καὶ εἰς ἐμὲ ὀνομάζεται. οὗπερ τὸ τεῖχος Ἰουστινιανὸς βασιλεὺς καταπεπτωκὸς ἤδη σὺν Εὐρυμένῃ τῷ φρουρίῳ ἐνταῦθά πη ὄντι καὶ ταὐτὸ πεπονθότι ἀνοικοδομησάμενος ἐκρατύ-

15 νατο. πολλὰ δὲ καὶ ἄλλα φρούρια ἐπὶ Θεσσαλίας ὁ βασιλεὺς οὗτος ἀνενεώσατο, ὧνπερ τὰ ὀνόματα σὺν τοῖς ἐν Μακεδονίᾳ τετειχισμένοις ἐν καταλόγῳ γεγράψεταί μοι οὐ πολλῷ ὕστερον.

16 Ἀλλὰ νῦν, ἵνα μηδὲν τῆς Ἑλλάδος ἀπολειφθείη μένον ἄρρητον, ἐς Εὔβοιαν ἡμῖν τὴν νῆσον ἰτέον, ἐπεὶ Ἀθηνῶν τε καὶ Μαραθῶνος ἄγχιστα

17 ἕστηκεν. Εὔβοια τοίνυν ἡ νῆσος ἥδε προβέβληται μὲν τῆς Ἑλλάδος εἰς θάλασσαν, δοκεῖ δέ που ἀπενεχθῆναι, μιᾶς μὲν οὔσης τῆς γῆς πρό-

18 τερον ἀποσχισθείσης δὲ πορθμῷ ὕστερον· ῥήγνυσι γάρ τις τὴν ἤπειρον ἐνταῦθα τῆς θαλάσσης ἐπιρροὴ ἀμφὶ Χαλκίδα πόλιν, ἐν στενῷ τε ξυνιοῦσα καὶ ταῖς ὄχθαις ἑκατέρωθι σφιγγομένη ἐς ῥύακος

19 εὖρος. καὶ νῆσος μὲν τὸ ἀποτετμημένον τῆς γῆς γέγονεν· Εὔριπος δὲ ὁ πορθμὸς ἐπωνό-

P 73 20 μασται. τοιαύτη μὲν οὖν τις ἡ Εὔβοια τυγχάνει οὖσα· ζεῦγμα δὲ τῷ πορθμῷ μία τις ἐγκειμένη ποιεῖται δοκός· ἥνπερ ἐπιτιθέντες μέν, ἡνίκα ἂν ᾖ βουλομένοις σφίσιν, οἱ ἐπιχώριοι ἠπειρῶται [1] δοκοῦσιν εἶναι καὶ εἰς γῆν τὴν ἀντιπέρας πεζοὶ ἴασιν, ἀφαιρούμενοι δὲ ταῖς τε ἀκάτοις διαπορθμεύονται τὸν ἀνάπλουν καὶ νησιῶται γίνονται αὖθις, ἑνός τε ξύλου ἐπιβολῇ καὶ ἀφαιρέσει καὶ πεζεύουσι καὶ ναυτίλλονται·[2] . . . ἐντὸς καθειργ-

21 μένην καλοῦσι Παλλήνην. τὴν μέντοι εἴσοδον

[1] ἠπειρῶται . . . ναυτίλλονται A, om. V.
[2] Lacuna indicated by Stewart and Haury.

tauropolis even to my day. The wall of this fort, which had already fallen down, as well as the fortress of Eurymenê, near by, which was in the same state, was rebuilt and strengthened by the Emperor Justinian. This Emperor restored also many other forts in Thessaly, the names of which I shall include a little further on in the list of towns in Macedonia which have been provided with walls.

But now, in order that no portion of Greece may be left unmentioned, we must go to the island of Euboea, for it stands close to Athens and Marathôn. This island of Euboea is thrown out into the sea in front of Greece, and it looks as if it had been cut off somehow from the mainland, having been one with the continent formerly, but later split off by a strait. An arm of the sea breaks the continent there near the city of Chalcis, collecting itself in a narrow stream and being compressed by its banks to the breadth of a brook. The portion of land which is thus cut off forms an island, and the strait is called Euripus. Such then is Euboea; and a bridge over the strait is formed by a single timber laid across it. This the natives put in place whenever they wish, and thus they seem to be mainlanders when they cross on foot to the opposite shore; but when they remove it and cross the strait in boats, they become islanders again, so that by the placing or removal of one timber they may either walk or go in boats[1] . . . they call the enclosed portion Pallenê.

[1] A lacuna of considerable extent must be assumed here. The author must have told of Justinian's fortifications at Chalcis and elsewhere in Euboea before passing to Macedonia, where he has mentioned Chalcidicê, on the westernmost of whose three peninsulas was Pallenê. The cross-wall, which

διατειχίσματι τὸ παλαιὸν καταλαβόντες οἱ ἐπιχώριοι, ταύτῃ τε τὴν ἑκατέρωθι συζεύξαντες
B 276 θάλασσαν, πόλιν ἐνταῦθα ἐδείμαντο, ἣν πάλαι μὲν Ποτίδαιαν, τανῦν δὲ Κασανδρίαν ὀνομά-
22 ζουσιν. οὕτω δὲ τὰς ἐνταῦθα οἰκοδομίας ὁ χρόνος διέφθειρε πάσας ὥστε δὴ Οὐννικόν τι ἔθνος οὐ πολλῷ πρότερον καταθέοντες τὰ ἐκείνῃ χωρία, ὥσπερ τι διαχειρίζοντες οἷόν τι πάρεργον, τό τε ξύναμμα[1] τοῦτο καὶ τὴν πόλιν ἄφοβοι ἐξεῖλον, καίπερ ἐξ οὗ γεγόνασιν ἄνθρωποι οὐ
23 τειχομαχήσαντες πώποτε. ἀλλὰ καὶ τοῦτο Ἰουστινιανῷ βασιλεῖ γέγονε πρόφασις ἀρετήν τε
24 καὶ μεγαλοφροσύνην ἐνδείξασθαι. τοῖς γὰρ ξυμπίπτουσι χαλεποῖς ἀντίξουν ποιούμενος ἀεὶ τὴν αὑτοῦ πρόνοιαν, τῶν ξυμβεβηκότων τὰ πονηρότατα ταῖς ἐπιγινομέναις ἀγαθοεργίαις εὐθὺς μετα-
25 βιβάζεται ἐς τύχην ἀμείνω. καὶ Παλλήνης ἀμέλει πόλιν τε τὴν προβεβλημένην τῆς χώρας ἁπάσης καὶ τὸ κατὰ τὴν εἴσοδον διατείχισμα τοῖς ἐπιβουλεύειν ἐθέλουσιν ἄμαχόν τε καὶ
26 ἀνανταγώνιστον διεπράξατο διαφανῶς εἶναι. ταῦτα μὲν οὖν ἐν πράξεσιν αὐτῷ ταῖς ἐπὶ Μακεδονίαν διαπεπόνηται.

27 Ῥεῖ δέ τις ποταμὸς Θεσσαλονίκης οὐ πολλῷ ἄποθεν, Ῥήχιος ὄνομα· ὃς δὴ χώραν ἀγαθήν τε καὶ γεώδη περιερχόμενος τὰς ἐκβολὰς εἰς
28 θάλασσαν τὴν ἐκείνῃ ποιεῖται. προσηνὴς δὲ ὁ ποταμός ἐστι, γαληνὸν τὸ ὕδωρ καὶ πότιμον, ἡ γῆ χθαμαλή, ἀρόματα πολλά, ἕλος εὔνομον.
29 καὶ ταύτῃ μὲν εὐδαιμονίας ἡ χώρα εὖ ἔχει,

[1] ξύναμμα Maltretus: ξύμβαμα

The natives in ancient times had closed the entrance with a cross-wall, with which they had linked together the two seas; and they had built there a city which in former times they called Potidaea, but now Cassandria. But time so ruined all the buildings in this place that a Hunnic tribe, in overrunning that region not long ago, destroyed the city and the wall without fear, quite as if they were doing something just by the way, though since the world began they had never stormed a wall. But this too provided the Emperor Justinian with an opportunity to display his skill and his magnanimity. For, by always bringing his wisdom to bear in circumventing the difficulties he meets with, he straightway uses beneficent measures, thus transforming the greatest disasters into a happier state of affairs. So in this way he brought it about that both the city of Pallenê, which stands as a bulwark of the whole region, and the cross-wall at the entrance of the peninsula, became manifestly impregnable and able to defy any who should wish to attack them. These things, then, were done by him as his service to Macedonia.

Not far from Thessalonica flows a certain river, Rhechius by name,[1] which wanders through a goodly land of deep soil and then empties into the sea near by. The river flows with a steady current, the water is calm and drinkable, and the ground is level with many ploughed fields and bottom-lands with good pasturage. In these respects the land is blessed, but

made the lower part of this peninsula "the enclosed portion," seems to have been built across the narrow neck of this peninsula, thus "connecting" the Thermaic Gulf with the gulf east of Pallenê.

[1] The Axius, modern Vardar?

βαρβάροις δὲ λίαν εὐέφοδος οὖσα ἐτύγχανεν, οὔτε φρούριον ἐν σημείοις τεσσαράκοντα οὔτε ἄλλο
30 τι ἔρυμα ἔχουσα. διὸ δὴ ὁ βασιλεὺς παρά τε τὰς τοῦ Ῥηχίου ποταμοῦ ἐκβολὰς καὶ τὴν τῆς
B 277 θαλάσσης ἠϊόνα φρούριον ᾠκοδομήσατο ἐχυρώτατον, καινουργήσας αὐτός, ὅπερ Ἀρτεμίσιον ἐπωνόμασται.

P 74 δ΄. Ὅσα δὲ καὶ ἄλλα ὀχυρώματα ἐν τῇδε τῇ τῆς Εὐρώπης πεποίηται μοίρᾳ εἰπεῖν ἄξιον. καὶ εἰ μὲν παρ᾿ ἄλλοις ἀνθρώπων τισὶ μακράν τε ᾠκημένοις καὶ πολιτείαν ἑτέραν ἔχουσι τὸν κατάλογον ἐποιούμεθα τῶν τῇδε φρουρίων ἅπερ Ἰουστινιανῷ βασιλεῖ εἴργασται, ἵνα δὴ ἔμελλεν ὁ λόγος ἀμάρτυρος εἶναι, εὖ οἶδ᾿ ὅτι μυθολόγος τε ἂν τῶν ἔργων τῷ ἀριθμῷ ἔδοξεν εἶναι καὶ ἄπιστος
2 ὅλως. νῦν δὲ (ἥ τε γὰρ ὄψις[1] οὐ μακράν που τυγχάνει οὖσα καὶ παμπληθεῖς ἄγαν οἱ ἐκεῖθεν ἐπιχωριάζοντες ἡμῖν ἄνθρωποι) φέρε δὴ νεανιευσάμενοι τὴν ἀλήθειαν ἐχέγγυον οὖσαν, ἀπαριθμησώμεθα μηδεμιᾷ ὀκνήσει τὰ ὀχυρώματα, ὅσα δὴ ἀμφὶ τὰς χώρας τάς μοι ἔναγχος δεδηλωμένας πεποίηται Ἰουστινιανὸς βασιλεύς, ἢ τὰ πεπονηκότα ἐρυμάτων ἀνανεούμενος, ἢ νέα τείχη ἐπιτεχνώ-
3 μενος. οὐδὲν δὲ χεῖρον ὡς ἐν καταλόγῳ ἐπελθεῖν ἅπαντα, ὡς μὴ τῶν ὀνομάτων ἐπιμιξίᾳ ὄχλος τις ἐπιγένηται τῷ λόγῳ πολύς.

[1] γὰρ ὄψις Haury, πάροψις.

[1] With the list which follows, especially the headings, *cf.* ch. viii of this Book, where Procopius, recapitulating his enumeration of the fortifications up to that point, speaks of Dardania, Epirus, and Macedonia as belonging to Illyricum;

it used to be completely exposed to the barbarians, having neither fortress nor any other defence in a space of forty miles. Consequently the Emperor built a new fort of great strength beside the mouth of the Rhechius River, near the shore of the sea, and it has been named Artemisium.

iv. It is proper to tell also how many other strongholds he constructed in this part of Europe. If we were making this catalogue of the forts in this region—those namely which were constructed by the Emperor Justinian—for the benefit of some other nations of men who lived far away, with a different form of government, in some place where the record would lack the testimony of witnesses, I know well that my account would seem fabulous and altogether incredible because of the mere number of the forts built. But as matters stand, since these things are to be seen at no great distance, and visitors from these regions are very numerous in our midst, let us, boldly telling the truth, well vouched for as it is, proceed with unbounded confidence to enumerate without any hesitation all the forts which the Emperor Justinian has built throughout the regions which I have just described, either by restoring those fortifications which were in ruins or by contriving new walls. It will be preferable to set them all down together in catalogue form so that my narrative may not become utterly irksome by interspersing a crowd of place-names here and there in it.[1]

he has treated of those in Moesia also as far as the Danube. It would seem as if Illyricum extended in his time as far east as the Danube, as far north as the River Savê, and as far west as the Julian Alps.

Φρούρια μὲν οὖν νέα πρὸς τοῦ βασιλέως ἐν Ἠπείρῳ νέᾳ[1] γεγένηται τάδε·

Now the following new forts were built by the Emperor in New Epirus:[2]

Βουλπιανσός.	Boulpiansus
Ἐπίστερβα.	Episterba
Σκημινίτης.	Sceminites
Ἄονα.	Aona
Στεφανιακόν.	Stephaniacum
Ἄργος.	Argus
Ἀλίουλα.	Aliula
Δυρράχιν.	Dyrrachin
Ὁ ἅγιος Σαβιανός.	St. Sabianus
Γέμενος.	Gemenus
Βακουστή.	Bacustê
Ἄλιστρος.	Alistrus
Πάταπα.	Patapa
Ἐπιδοῦντα.	Epidunta
Βάκουστα.	Bacusta
Μάρτις.	Martis
B 278 Εἰρήνη.	Eirenê
Σπερέτιον.	Speretium
Ἀοιών.	Aoiôn
Στρέδην.	Stredên
Γυναικομίτης.	Gynaecomites

[1] νέᾳ added by Hoeschel.

[2] Nova Epirus or Illyris Graeca extended from the Drilô (Mod. Drina) River on the north to the Ceraunian Mts. on the south, thus comprising a large part of modern Albania. Immediately to the south of it to the Ambracian Gulf (Mod. Gulf of Arta) lay what is here called Old Epirus, approximately identical with the Epirus of modern Greece.

Λάβελλος.	Labellus
Ἐπίλεον.	Epileum
Πισκιναί.	Piscinae
Δεύφρακος.	Deuphracus
Δολέβιν.	Dolebin
Ἡδονία.	Hedonia
Τιτιάνα.	Titiana
Κιθινάς.	Cithinas
Οὐλίβουλα.	Ulibula
Βρεβατή.	Brebatê
Θησαυρός.	Thesaurus
Ἀνενεώθη δὲ τάδε·	The following were restored:
Τοῦ ἁγίου Στεφάνου.	St. Stephen's
Κεθρέων.	Cethreôn
Ἄπις.	Apis
75 Πήλεον.	Peleum
Κώμη.	Comê
Πακούε.	Pacuê
Σκυδρέων πόλις.	The city of Scydreŏn
Ἀντίπαγραι.	Antipagrae
Τίθυρα.	Tithyra
Βρέβετα.	Brebeta
Βοῦπος.	Bupus
Ἐνδύνεια.	Endyneia
Διόνυσος.	Dionysus
Τοῦ Πτωχείου.	Ptocheiou
Τυρκανός.	Tyrcanus
Κάπαζα.	Capaza
Πούψαλος.	Pupsalus
Γάβραιον.	Gabraeum

Διόνοια.	Dionoia
Κλημεντιανά.	Clementiana
Ἰλλύριν.	Illyrin
Κιλικαί.	Cilicae
Ἀργυάς.	Argyas
Θέρμα.	Therma
Ἀμάντεια.	Amanteia
Παρέτιον.	Paretium

Ἐν δὲ Ἠπείρῳ παλαιᾷ, νέα μὲν φρούρια ἐγένοντο τάδε·

And in Old Epirus the following new forts were built:

Παρμός.	Parmus
Ὄλβος.	Olbus
Κιόνιν.	Cionin
D 279 Μαρκιανά.	Marciana
Ἄλγος.	Algus
Κείμενος.	Ceimenus
Ξηροπόταμος.[1]	Xeropotamus
Εὐρώπη.	Europê
Χίμαιραι.	Chimaerae
Ἡλέγα.	Helega
Ὁμόνοια.	Homonoia
Ἄδανον.	Adanum

Ἀνενεώθη δὲ τάδε·

And the following forts were restored:

Μουρκίαρα.	Murciara
Κάστινα.	Castina
Γενύσιος.	Genysius

[1] Ξηροπόταμος Haury for ξηροπο τμ'

Πέρκος.	Percus
Μαρμάρατα.	Marmarata
Λίστρια.	Listria
Πετρωνιανά.	Petroniana
Κάρμινα.	Carmina
Τοῦ ἁγίου Σαβίνου.	St. Sabinus'
Καὶ ἐν φρουρίῳ Κώμῃ κινστάρνα.[1]	And a cistern in the fort of Comê
Μάρτιος.	Martius
Πέζιον.	Pezium
Ὄναλος.	Onalus
Καὶ ἀπὸ Ἰουστινιανοπόλεως καὶ Φωτικῆς· φρούρια δύο τοῦ ἁγίου Δονάτου.	And from Justinianopolis[2] and Photicê, two forts of St. Donatus
Συμφύγιον.	Symphygium
Προνάθιδον.	Pronathidum
Ἥδωνες.	Hedones
Κάστελλος.	Castellus
Βουλιβάς.	Bulibas
Πάλυρος.	Palyrus
Τράνα.	Trana
Ποσειδών.	Poseidôn
Κολοφωνία.	Colophonia

Ἐπὶ Μακεδονίας·	In Macedonia:
Κάνδιδα.	Candida
Κολοβῶνα.	Colobona

[1] In Byzantine writers commonly spelt *κινστέρνα*. Cisterns are also often referred to by the name of the maker.

[2] Formerly called Adrianopolis (modern Adrianople or Edirne); mentioned above, IV. i. 36.

Βασιλικὰ Ἀμύντου.	Basilica Amyntou [1]
Μελίχιζα.	Melichiza
Πασκᾶς.	Pascas
Αὐλών.	Aulon
Βολβός.	Bolbus
Βριγίζης.	Brigizes
Ὀπτᾶς.	Optas
Πλευρόν.	Pleurum
Κάμινος.	Caminus
Θέρμα.	Therma [2]
Βογᾶς.	Bogas
Νεάπολις.	Neapolis [3]
Κάλαρνος.	Calarnas
Μουσεῖον.	Museum
B 280 Ἀκρέμβα.	Acremba
Ἀδριάνιον.	Adrianium
Ἔδανα.	Edana
Σίκλαι.	Siclae
Νύμφιον.	Nymphium
Μέτιζος.	Metizus
Ἀργικιανόν.	Argicianum
Βάζινος.	Bazinus
Κασσωπᾶς.	Cassopas
Παρθίων.	Parthiôn
Γεντιανόν.	Gentianum

[1] Procopius has moved northeastward into the land of the Dardani and of Moesia Superior (southern Jugoslavia of to-day), though he seems to consider this region as still in Epirus and Epirus still in Illyricum.

[2] The ancient name of the settlement at the head of the Thermaic Gulf, transformed by Cassander into an important seaport and named Thessalonicê.

[3] On the Strymonic Gulf, modern Kavalla.

Πρινίανα.	Priniana
Θήστεον.	Thesteum
76 Κύρρου.	Cyrrou
Γουρασσών.	Gourassôn
Κουμαρκίανα.	Cumarciana
Λιμνηδήριον.	Limnederium
Βουρβοώδην.	Bourboöden
Βάβας.	Babas
Κρυνίανα.	Cryniana
Πέλεκον.	Pelecum
Λάγης.	Lagês
Κραταιά.	Crataea
Φασκίαι.	Phasciae
Πλακιδιανά.	Placidiana
Ὑγεά.	Hygea
Λιμνααί.	Limnaae
Ὄπτιον.	Optium
Χάραδρος.	Charadrus
Κάσσωπες.	Cassopes

Ἀνενεώθη καὶ ἐπὶ Θεσσαλίας φρούρια τάδε·

And these forts were restored in Thessaly:

Ἀλκών.	Alcôn
Λόσσονος.	Lossonus
Γεροντική.	Geronticê
Πέρβυλα.	Perbyla
Κερκινέου.	Cercineou
Σκιδρεοῦς.	Scidreûs
Φράκελλαν.	Phracellan

Ἐπὶ Δαρδανίας δὲ πεποίηται τάδε. νέα μέν·	In Dardania the following were built. New:
Λαβέριον.	Laberium
Κάστιμον.	Castimum
Ῥαβεστόν.	Rhabestum
Καστέλλιον.	Castellium
Ἀκρένζα.	Acrenza
Τεριάς.	Terias
Δροῦλλος.	Drullus
Βικτωρίας.	Victorias
Ἀνενεώθη δὲ τάδε·	And the following were restored:
Κεσίανα.	Cesiana
Τεζούλη.	Tezulê
B 281 Οὐσιανά.	Usiana
Βεσίανα.	Besiana
Μασκᾶς.	Mascas
Λίστη.	Listê
Κελλιριανά.	Celliriana
Ζυσβάες.	Zysbaes
Γένζανα.	Genzana
Πετρίζην.	Petrizên
Εὐτυχιανά.	Eutychiana
Μουλατώ.	Mulatô
Βελάς.	Belas
Κάτταρος.	Cattarus
Κατταρηκός.	Cattarecus
Πέντζα.	Pentza
Κατταφέτερος.[1]	Cattapheterus

[1] κάτταφ' ἕτερος V: Haury conjectured Κάτταρος ἕτερος.

Δάβανος.	Dabanus
Κούβινος.	Cubinus
Γέρματζα.	Germatza
Βικτωριανά.	Victoriana
Ἄζετα.	Azeta
Δουρβουλιανά.	Durbuliana
Σούρικον.	Suricum
Κούσινες.	Cusines
Τουττιανά.	Tuttiana
Βαλλεσιανά.	Ballesiana
Βήλλα.	Bella
Κατρέλατες.	Catrelates
Κασύελλα.	Casyella
Μανίανα.	Maniana
Πρισκούπερα.	Priscupera
Μιλετής.	Miletês
Δαρδάπαρα.	Dardapara
Κέσουνα.	Cesuna
Βερινιανά.	Beriniana
Λάσβαρος	Lasbarus
Καστελλοβρέταρα.	Castellobretara
Ἐδετζίω.	Edetziô
Δίνιον.	Dinium
Κέκωλα.	Cecola
Ἔμαστος.	Emastus
Καστελῶνα.	Castelona
Καπόμαλβα.	Capomalba
Σέρετος.	Seretus
Πτωχεῖον.	Ptocheium
Κουινώ.	Cuinô
Βέρζανα.	Berzana
Βεσαΐανα.	Besaïana

	Ἄρσα.	Arsa
	Βλεζώ.	Blezô
	Λάβουτζα.	Labutza
	Κυίντου.	Quintou
	Βερμέζιον.	Bermezium
	Κατράσεμα.	Catrasema
	Ῥοτοῦν.	Rhotun
	Κοβέγκιλες.	Cobenciles
P 77	Μαρκελλιανά.	Marcelliana
	Πριμονιανά.	Primoniana
B 282	Παμίλινος.	Pamilinus
	Ἀρία.	Aria

Ὑπὸ πόλιν Σαρδικήν·

Near the city Sardicê:

Σκούπιον.	Scupium
Στενες.	Stenes
Μαρκίπετρα.	Marcipetra
Βρίπαρον.	Briparum
Ῥωμανιανά.	Romaniana
Στρούας.	Struas
Πρωτίανα.	Protiana
Μακκουνιανά.	Maccuniana
Σκοπέντζανα.	Scopentzana

Ἐν δὲ τῇ Καβετζῷ χώρᾳ, νέον μὲν Βαλβαί. ἀνενεώθη δὲ τάδε·

And in the district of Cabetzus, Balbae was built new, and the following were restored:

Βυρσία.	Byrsia
Σταμαζώ.	Stamazô
Κλεσβέστιτα.	Clesbestita
Δουΐανα.	Duiana

Τούρικλα.	Turicla
Μέδεκα.	Medeca
Πεπλαβιός.	Peplabius
Κοῦναι.	Cunae
Βίνεος.	Bineüs
Τρισκίανα.	Trisciana
Παρνοῦστα.	Parnusta
Τζίμες.	Tzimes
Βιδζώ.	Bidzô
Στενεκόρτα.	Stenecorta
Δανεδέβαι.	Danedebae
Ἀρδεία.	Ardeia
. . . νέα μέν·	. . . the following new:
Βουγάραμα.	Bugarama
Βέτζας.	Betzas
Βρεγεδάβα.	Bregedaba
Βόρβρεγα.	Borbrega
Τουροῦς.	Turûs
Ἀνενεώθη δέ·	And the following were restored:
Σαλεβρίες.	Salebries
Ἀρκοῦνες.	Arcunes
Δουρίες.	Duries
Βουτερίες.	Buteries
Βαρβαρίες.	Barbaries
Ἀρβατίας.	Arbatias
Κουτζούσουρα.	Cutzusura
Ἐταιρίες.	Etaeries
Ἰταβερίες.	Itaberies
Βόττες.	Bottes

Βιτζιμαίας.
Βαδζιάνια.
B 283 Βάνες.
Βιμηρός.
Τουσουδεάας.
Σκουάνες.
Σκεντουδίες.
Σκάρες.
Τουγουρίας.
Βεμάστες.
Στραμεντίας.
Λίγνιος.
Ἰταδεβά.

Ὑπὸ πόλιν Γέρμεννε, νέον μὲν Σκαπλιζώ· ἀνενεώθη δέ·

Γερμάς.
Κανδαράς.
Ῥολλιγεράς.
Σκινζερίες.
Ῥιγινοκάστελλον.
Σουεγωγμένσε.

Ὑπὸ πόλιν Παυτά·

Τάρπωρον.
Σουάβαστας.
Χερδούσκερα.
Βλέβοις.
Ζεαπουρίες.

Bitzimaeas
Badziania
Banes
Bimerus
Tusudeaas
Scuanes
Scentudies
Scares
Tugurias
Bemastes
Stramentias
Lignius
Itadeba

Near the city Germenne, Scaplizo was built new, and the following were restored:

Germas
Candaras
Rolligeras
Scinzeries
Rhiginocastellum
Suegogmense

Near the city Pauta:

Tarporum
Suabastas
Cherduscera
Blebois
Zeapuries

Ἐν χώρᾳ Σκασσετάνᾳ·

Ἄλαρον.
Μαγιμιάς.
Λουκουννάντα.
Βάλαυσον.
Βούττις.

P 78 Ὑπὸ πόλιν δὲ . . . νέα μέν·

Καλβεντία.
Φαράνορες.
Στρανβάστα.
Ἄλδανες.
Βαραχτέστες.
Σάρματες.
Ἄρσενα.
Βράρκεδον.
Ἐραρία.
Βερκάδιον.
Σαβινίριβες.
Τιμίανα.
Κάνδιλαρ.
Ἄρσαζα.
Βικούλεα.
284 Καστέλλιον.
Γρόφφες.
Γάρκες.
Πίστες.
Δούσμανες.
Βράτζιστα.

In the district of Scassetana:

Alarum
Magimias
Lucunanta
Balausum
Buttis

Near the city . . . the following were built new:

Calbentia
Pharanores
Stranbasta
Aldanes
Barachtestes
Sarmates
Arsena
Brarcedum
Eraria
Bercadium
Sabiniribes
Timiana
Candilar
Arsaza
Biculea
Castellium
Groffes
Garces
Pistes
Dusmanes
Bratzista

Ὁλόδορις.	Holodoris
Κασσία.	Cassia
Γράνδετον.	Grandetum
Οὐρβρίανα.	Urbriana
Νώγετο.	Nogeto
Γούρβικον.	Gurbicum
Λαύτζονες.	Lautzones
Δουλίαρες.	Duliares
Μεδίανα.	Mediana
Τιούγκωνα.	Tiuncona
Καστέλλιον.	Castellium

Ἀνενεώθη δέ· — And the following were restored:

Ἕρκουλα.	Hercula
Μουτζιανικάστελλον.	Mutzianicastellum
Βούρδωπες.	Burdopes
Κάλις.	Calis
Μιλλάρεκα.	Millareca
Δέδβερα.	Dedbera
Χεσδούπαρα.	Chesdupara

Ἐν χώρᾳ Ῥεμισιανισίᾳ· — In the district of Remisianisia:

Βρίττουρα.	Brittura
Σούβαρας.	Subaras
Λαμπωνίανα.	Lamponiana
Στρόγγες.	Stronges
Δάλματας.	Dalmatas
Πριμίανα.	Primiana
Φρερραρία.	Phrerraria
Τόπερα.	Topera

Τόμες.	Tomes
Κούας.	Cuas
Τζερτζενούτζας.	Tzertzenutzas
Στένες.	Stenes
Αἰάδαβα.	Aeadaba
Δέστρεβα.	Destreba
Πρετζουρίες.	Pretzouries
Κουμούδεβα.	Cumudeba
Δευριάς.	Deurias
Λούτζολο.	Lutzolo
Ῥεπόρδενες.	Rhepordenes
Σπέλογκα.	Spelonca
Σκοῦμβρο.	Scumbro
Βρίπαρο.	Briparo
Τουλκόβουργο.	Tulcoburgo
Λογγίανα.	Longiana
Λουποφαντάνα.[1]	Lupophantana
Δαρδάπαρα.	Dardapara
Βουρδόμινα.	Burdomina
285 Γριγκιάπανα.	Grinciapana
Γραῖκος.	Graecus
Δρασίμαρκα.	Drasimarca

Ἐν χώρᾳ Ἀκυενισίῳ, νέον μὲν Τιμαθοχιώμ. τὰ δὲ ἀνανεωθέντα·

In the district of Aquenisium, Timathochiôm was built new, and the following were restored:

Πέτρες.	Petres
Σκουλκόβουργο.	Sculcoburgo
Βινδιμίολα.	Vindimiola

[1] That is, Lupi Fontana.

Βραίολα.[1]	Braeola
Ἀργανόκιλι.	Arganocili
Καστελλόνοβο.	Castellonovo
Φλωρεντίανα.	Florentiana
Ῥωμυλίανα.	Romyliana
Σεπτέκασαι.[2]	Septecasae
Ἀργένταρες.	Argentares
Αὐριλίανα.	Auriliana
Γέμβερο.	Gembero
Κλέμαδες.	Clemades
Τουρρίβας.	Turribas
Γρίβο.	Gribo
Χάλαρο.	Chalaro
T 79 Τζούτρατο.	Tzutrato
Μουτζίπαρα.	Mutzipara
Στένδας.	Stendas
Σκαρίπαρα.	Scaripara

ε'. Οὕτω μὲν σύμπασαν τὴν μεσόγειον Ἰουστινιανὸς βασιλεὺς ἐν Ἰλλυριοῖς ἐτειχίσατο. τρόπον δὲ ὅντινα καὶ τὴν ἠϊόνα ποταμοῦ Ἴστρου, ὃν καὶ Δανούβιον[3] ὀνομάζουσιν, ἐρύμασί τε καὶ φυλακτηρίοις στρατιωτῶν ἐκρατύνατο, ἐγὼ δηλώσω. B 286 2 οἱ Ῥωμαίων τὸ παλαιὸν αὐτοκράτορες τοῖς ἐπέκεινα ᾠκημένοις βαρβάροις τὴν τοῦ Δανουβίου διάβασιν ἀναστέλλοντες ὀχυρώμασί τε κατέλαβον τούτου δὴ τοῦ ποταμοῦ τὴν ἀκτὴν ξύμπασαν, οὐ δὴ ἐν δεξιᾷ τοῦ ποταμοῦ μόνον, ἀλλὰ καὶ αὐτοῦ ἐνιαχῇ ἐπὶ θάτερα πολίσματά 3 τε καὶ φρούρια τῇδε δειμάμενοι. ταῦτα δὲ τὰ ὀχυρώματα ἐξειργάσαντο οὐκ ἀμήχανα προσελθεῖν,

[1] Probably the same as the Braeola of page 265, line 11.

Ὀδρίουζο.	Odriuzo
Κιπίπενε.	Cipipene
Τρασίανα.	Trasiana
Πότες.	Potes
Ἄμουλο.	Amulo
Σέτλοτες.	Setlotes
Τιμακίολον.	Timaciolum
Μερίδιο.	Meridio
Μεριοπόντεδε.	Meriopontede
Τρεδετετιλίους.	Tredetetilious
Βραίολα.	Braeola
Μώτρεσες.	Motreses
Βικάνοβο.	Vicanovo
Κουαρτίανα.	Quartiana
Ἰουλιόβαλλαι.	Julioballae
Πόντζας.	Pontzas
Ζάνες.	Zanes

v. Thus did the Emperor Justinian fortify the whole interior of Illyricum. I shall also explain in what manner he fortified the bank of the Ister River, which they also call the Danube, by means of strongholds and garrisons of troops. The Roman Emperors of former times, by way of preventing the crossing of the Danube by the barbarians who live on the other side, occupied the entire bank of this river with strongholds, and not the right bank of the stream alone, for in some parts of it they built towns and fortresses on its other bank. However, they did not so build these strongholds that they were impossible to attack, if anyone should come against them, but

[2] Σεπτέκασαι (*i.e.*, Septem Casae) Haury : Σεπτέκασας.
[3] Δανούβιον Haury : δάνουβιν.

εἴ τις προσίοι, ἀλλ᾽ ὅσον δὴ μὴ ἀνδρῶν ἔρημον τὴν τοῦ ποταμοῦ ἠιόνα λελεῖφθαι· ἐπεὶ τειχομαχεῖν τοῖς ἐκείνῃ βαρβάροις οὐδαμῇ ἔγνωστο.
4 τὰ πολλὰ τῶν ἐρυμάτων αὐτοῖς ἀμέλει ἀπεκέκριτο ἐς πύργον ἕνα, μονοπύργιά τε, ὡς τὸ εἰκός, ἐπεκαλεῖτο, ἄνθρωποί τε ὀλίγοι κομιδῇ ἐν αὐτοῖς
5 ἵδρυντο. καὶ τοῦτο τηνικάδε ἀπέχρη τὰ τῶν βαρβάρων δεδίσσεσθαι γένη, ὥστε δὴ ἀναδύ-
6 εσθαι τὴν ἐς Ῥωμαίους ἐπίθεσιν. χρόνῳ δὲ ὕστερον Ἀττίλας στρατῷ μεγάλῳ ἐσβεβληκώς, τά τε ὀχυρώματα πόνῳ οὐδενὶ ἐς ἔδαφος καθεῖλε, καὶ γῆν Ῥωμαίων ὑπαντιάζοντός οἱ οὐδενὸς
7 ἐληΐσατο τὴν πολλήν. ἀλλ᾽ Ἰουστινιανὸς βασιλεὺς ἀνῳκοδομήσατό τε τὰ καθῃρημένα, οὐχ ᾗπερ τὰ πρότερα ἦν, ἀλλ᾽ ἐς τοῦ ὀχυρώματος τὸ καρτερώτατον μάλιστα, καὶ πλεῖστα ἔτι ἐπετεχνήσατο
8 καινουργήσας αὐτός. ταύτῃ τε παντάπασιν ἀνεσώσατο [1] ἀπολωλυῖαν ἤδη τὴν ἀσφάλειαν τῇ Ῥωμαίων ἀρχῇ. ἅπερ ἅπαντα ὅντινα γεγένηται τρόπον, ἐγὼ δηλώσω.

9 Κάτεισι μὲν ἐξ ὀρέων [2] τῶν ἐν Κελτοῖς ποταμὸς Ἴστρος, οὓ τανῦν Γάλλοι ἐπικαλοῦνται· χώραν δὲ περιβάλλει πολλήν, ἐκ μὲν τοῦ ἐπὶ πλεῖστον παντελῶς ἔρημον, ἐνιαχῇ δὲ βαρβάρους οἰκήτορας ἔχουσαν, θηριώδη τέ τινα δίαιταν ἔχοντας καὶ
B 287 10 ἀνεπίμικτον τοῖς ἄλλοις ἀνθρώποις. Δακίας δὲ
P 80 ὡς ἀγχοτάτω γενόμενος, ἐνταῦθα διορίζων φαίνεται πρῶτον τούς τε βαρβάρους, οἳ δὴ αὐτοῦ τὰ ἐπ᾽ ἀριστερᾷ ἔχουσι, τήν τε Ῥωμαίων γῆν ἐν δεξιᾷ
11 οὖσαν. διὸ δὴ Ῥιπησίαν καλοῦσι Ῥωμαῖοι τὴν

[1] ἀνεσώσατο V, ἀνενεώσατο A.

they only provided that the bank of the river was not left destitute of men, since the barbarians there had no knowledge of storming walls. In fact the majority of these strongholds consisted only of a single tower, and they were called appropriately "lone towers," and very few men were stationed in them. At that time this alone was quite sufficient to frighten off the barbarian clans, so that they would not undertake to attack the Romans. But at a later time [1] Attila invaded with a great army, and with no difficulty razed the fortresses; then, with no one standing against him, he plundered the greater part of the Roman Empire. But the Emperor Justinian rebuilt the defences which had been torn down, not simply as they had been before, but so as to give the fortifications the greatest possible strength; and he added many more which he built himself. In this way he completely restored the safety of the Roman Empire, which by then had been lost. And I shall explain how all this was accomplished.

The River Ister flows down from the mountains in the country of the Celts, who are now called Gauls; and it passes through a great extent of country which for the most part is altogether barren, though in some places it is inhabited by barbarians who live a kind of brutish life and have no dealings with other men. When it gets close to Dacia, for the first time it clearly forms the boundary between the barbarians, who hold its left bank, and the territory of the Romans, which is on the right. Consequently the Romans apply the term Ripesia to this part of

[1] A.D. 441.

[2] ὀρέων Maltretus: ὁρίων.

ταύτῃ Δακίαν· ῥίπα γὰρ ἡ ὄχθη τῇ Λατίνων
12 καλεῖται φωνῇ. πόλιν οὖν παρὰ τὴν ἐκείνῃ
ἀκτήν, ὄνομα Σιγγηδόνον, ἐν τοῖς ἄνω χρόνοις
13 ἐδείμαντο πρώτην. ταύτην δὲ βάρβαροι προϊόντος τοῦ χρόνου ἑλόντες ἔς τε τὸ ἔδαφος καθελόν-
τες εὐθύς, ἔρημον ἀνθρώπων παντάπασι κατεστή-
14 σαντο. τρόπῳ δὲ τῷ αὐτῷ καὶ τῶν ἄλλων
15 ὀχυρωμάτων κατεστήσαντο τὰ πλεῖστα. βασιλεὺς
δὲ Ἰουστινιανὸς ἀνανεωσάμενος ξύμπασαν καὶ
τειχίσματι ὀχυρωτάτῳ περιβαλών, πόλιν περιφανῆ
τε καὶ λόγου πολλοῦ ἀξίαν πεποίηκεν αὖθις.
16 φρούριόν τε ἄλλο διαφερόντως ἐχυρὸν ἀνέστησε
νέον, πόλεως Σιγγηδόνου[1] ὀκτὼ μάλιστα σημείοις
διέχον, ὅπερ Ὀκταβου λόγῳ τῷ εἰκότι καλοῦσιν.
17 ἐπίπροσθεν δὲ αὐτοῦ πόλις ἦν ἀρχαία τὸ Βιμινά-
κιον, ἥνπερ ὁ βασιλεὺς (ἐκ θεμελίων γὰρ ἀπωλώλει
τῶν ἐσχάτων πολλῷ πρότερον) ἀνοικοδομησάμενος
ξύμπασαν ἀπέδειξε νέαν.

ϛ′. Ἐκ δὲ Βιμινακίου προϊόντι ὀχυρώματα
τρία πρὸς τῇ τοῦ Ἴστρου ἠϊόνι ξυμβαίνει εἶναι,
2 Πιγκούς τε καὶ Κούπους καὶ Νοβάς. οἷς[2] δὴ
πρότερον ἥ τε οἰκοδομία μία[3] καὶ τὸ ὄνομα ἐπὶ
πύργου ἑνὸς ἔκειτο. ἀλλὰ νῦν Ἰουστινιανὸς
βασιλεὺς τά τε οἰκία καὶ τὰ ἐρύματα ἔς τε πλῆθος καὶ μέγεθος ἐν τούτοις δὴ τοῖς χωρίοις
ἀνενεγκὼν μέγα, πόλεων αὐτοῖς ἀξιώματα οὐκ
3 ἀπὸ τοῦ εἰκότος ἐντέθεικε. Νοβῶν δὲ καταντικρὺ ἐν τῇ ἀντιπέρας ἠπείρῳ πύργος ἐκ παλαιοῦ
ἀπημελημένος ἑστήκει, ὄνομα Λιτερατά· ὅνπερ
4 οἱ πάλαι ἄνθρωποι Λεδέρατα ἐκάλουν. ὃν δὴ

[1] πόλεως Σιγγηδόνου Haury: πόλεως σιγγηδονίου V, ταύτης τῆς πόλεως A.

Dacia, for *ripa* signifies bank in the Latin tongue. Accordingly they had made a beginning by building on the bank there in ancient times a city, by name Singidunum.[1] This the barbarians captured in time, and they immediately razed it, leaving the place quite destitute of inhabitants. They did precisely the same thing to most of the other strongholds. But the Emperor Justinian restored the entire city and surrounded it with a very strong fortification, and thus made it once more a famous and important city. And he set up another new fortress of exceptional strength about eight miles distant from Singidunum, which they call by the appropriate name of Octavus. Beyond it was the ancient city of Viminacium,[2] which the Emperor rebuilt entire and made new, for it had long before been ruined down to its uttermost foundations.

vi. As one goes on from Viminacium there chance to be three strongholds on the bank of the Ister, Pinci and Cupi and Novae. These were formerly both single in construction and when named were single towers[3]. But now the Emperor Justinian has greatly increased the number of the houses and enlarged the defences at these places, and thereby has properly given them the rank of cities. And opposite Novae in the mainland on the other side of the river, had stood from ancient times a neglected tower, by name Literata; the men of former times used to call this Lederata.

[1] Modern Belgrade. [2] Modern Kostolatz.
[3] See above, Chap. v. 4.

[2] καὶ Νοβάς. οἷς Haury, καὶ Νοβαί. οἷς Maltretus: καινοβασαῖς.
[3] μία added by Capps.

B 288 ἐς φρούριον μέγα τε καὶ διαφερόντως ἐχυρώτατον
5 ὁ καθ' ἡμᾶς βασιλεὺς μετεστήσατο. μετὰ Νοβὰς δὲ φρούρια Κανταβαζά τε καὶ Σμόρνης τε καὶ Κάμψης καὶ Τανάτα καὶ Ζέρνης καὶ Δουκεπράτου. ἐν δὲ τῇ ἀντιπέρας ἠπείρῳ ἄλλα τε πολλὰ φρούρια
6 ἐκ θεμελίων[1] τῶν ἐσχάτων ἐδείματο. μετὰ δὲ Καπούτβοες ὠνόμασται, τοῦ Ῥωμαίων αὐτοκράτορος Τραϊανοῦ ἔργον, καὶ πολίχνιον ἐφεξῆς
7 παλαιόν, Ζάνες ὄνομα. οἷσπερ ἅπασιν ἐρύματα περιβαλὼν ἐχυρώτατα προβόλους εἶναι τῆς πολι-
8 τείας ἀνανταγωνίστους πεποίηται. τούτου δὲ τοῦ Ζάνες οὐ πολλῷ ἄποθεν φρούριον μέν ἐστι, Πόντες ὄνομα· ὁ δὲ ποταμὸς ἐκροήν τινα ἐνταῦθα ἐκβάλλων, ταύτῃ τε περιπολῶν ὀλίγην τινὰ τῆς ἀκτῆς μοῖραν, ἐπιστρέφει αὖθις ἐς ῥοῦν τὸν
P 81 9 οἰκεῖον καὶ ἐφ' ἑαυτὸν ἀναμίγνυται. ποιεῖ δὲ ταῦτα οὐκ αὐτόματος, ἀλλ' ἀνθρώπων ἐπινοίαις
10 ἀναγκασθείς. ὅτου δὲ δὴ ἕνεκα Πόντες τε ὁ χῶρος ἐκλήθη καὶ ἀναγκαστὸν περιάγουσιν αὐτόσε τὸν Ἴστρον, ἐγὼ δηλώσω.

11 Ὁ Ῥωμαίων αὐτοκράτωρ Τραϊανός, θυμοειδής τε ὢν καὶ δραστήριος, ὥσπερ ἀγανακτοῦντι ἐῴκει, ὅτι δὴ οὐκ ἀπέραντος αὐτῷ ἡ βασιλεία εἴη, ἀλλὰ
12 ποταμῷ Ἴστρῳ ὁρίζεται. ζεῦξαι οὖν αὐτὸν[2] γεφύρᾳ διὰ σπουδῆς ἔσχεν, ὡς διάβατός τε αὐτῷ καὶ οὐδαμῇ ἐμπόδιος εἴη ἐς τοὺς ἐπέκεινα
13 βαρβάρους ἰόντι. ὅπως μὲν οὖν τὴν γέφυραν ἐπήξατο ταύτην, ἐμοὶ μὲν οὐκ ἂν ἐν σπουδῇ γένοιτο, Ἀπολλόδωρος δὲ ὁ Δαμασκηνός, ὁ καὶ παντὸς γεγονὼς ἀρχιτέκτων τοῦ ἔργου, φραζέτω.

[1] καὶ ταῦτα after θεμελίων deleted by Haury.

This the present Emperor transformed into a great fortress of exceptional strength. After Novae are the forts of Cantabaza, Smornês, Campsês, Tanata, Zernês, and Ducepratum. And on the opposite side he built a number of other forts from their lowest foundations. Farther on is the so-called Caput Bovis,[1] the work of the Roman Emperor Trajan, and beyond this an ancient town named Zanes. And he placed very strong defences around all these and so made them impregnable bulwarks of the State. And not far from this Zanes there is a fort, Pontes by name. The river throws out a sort of branch there, and after thus passing around a certain small portion of the bank, it turns again to its own stream and is reunited with itself. It does this, not of its own accord, but compelled by human devices. The reason why the place was called Pontes, and why they made this forced diversion of the Ister at this point, I shall now make clear.

The Roman Emperor Trajan, being of an impetuous and active temperament, seemed to be filled with resentment that his realm was not unlimited, but was bounded by the Ister River. So he was eager to span it with a bridge that he might be able to cross it and that there might be no obstacle to his going against the barbarians beyond it. How he built this bridge I shall not be at pains to relate, but shall let Apollodorus of Damascus, who was the master-builder of the whole work, describe the

[1] "Ox-head."

---

[2] *αὐτὸν* A, om. V.

14 οὐ μέντοι τις τὸ λοιπὸν γέγονεν ὄνησις ἐνθένδε Ῥωμαίοις, ἀλλὰ καὶ τὴν γέφυραν ὅ τε Ἴστρος ἐπιχυθεὶς ὕστερον καὶ ὁ χρόνος ἐπιρρεύσας
15 καθεῖλον. πεποίηται δὲ Τραϊανὸς τότε καὶ φρούρια δύο τοῦ ποταμοῦ ἐφ' ἑκάτερα, καὶ
B 289 αὐτοῖν Θεοδώραν μὲν ἐπωνόμασαν τὸ ἐν τῇ ἀντιπέρας ἠπείρῳ, Πόντες δὲ τὸ ἐπὶ Δακίας
16 ὁμωνύμως τῷ ἔργῳ ἐκλήθη. πόντην γὰρ τὴν γέφυραν Ῥωμαῖοι τῇ Λατίνων καλοῦσι φωνῇ. ἀλλ' ἐπεὶ ἐνταῦθα γινομέναις ναυσὶν ἄπλους τὸ λοιπὸν ὁ ποταμὸς ἦν, τῶν τῆς γεφύρας αὐτόθι ἐρειπίων τε καὶ θεμελίων[1] κειμένων, τούτου δὴ ἕνεκα τὸν ποταμὸν ἀναγκάζουσι μεταπορεύεσθαι τὸν αὐτοῦ δρόμον καὶ τὴν πορείαν ἀνακυκλεῖν αὖθις, ὅπως ἂν πλώϊμον καὶ τὸ ἐνθένδε αὐτὸν
17 ἔχοιεν. ἄμφω μὲν οὖν καταπεπονηκότα τὰ φρούρια ταῦτα διά τε χρόνου μῆκος καὶ οὐχ ἥκιστα ἐπισκηψάντων ἐνταῦθα βαρβάρων[2] δι-
18 εφθάρθαι ξυνέβη. βασιλεὺς δὲ Ἰουστινιανὸς Πόντην μέν, ὅπερ ἐστὶ τοῦ ποταμοῦ ἐπὶ δεξιᾷ, νέᾳ τε καὶ ἀμάχῳ ἐπιεικῶς ἀνανεωσάμενος οἰκοδομίᾳ, τὴν ἀσφάλειαν Ἰλλυριοῖς ἀνεσώσατο· τοῦ δὲ αὐτοῦ ἐπὶ θάτερα ὄντος, ὅπερ Θεοδώραν καλοῦσιν, ἅτε ἀποκειμένου τοῖς ἐκείνῃ βαρβάροις, προσήκειν οἱ[3] ἐπιμελεῖσθαι οὐδαμῇ ᾤετο· τὰ δὲ νῦν ἑστῶτα μετὰ τὴν Πόντην ὀχυρώματα ᾠκοδομήσατο καινουργήσας αὐτός,[4] ἅπερ καλεῖται Μαρεβούργου τε

[1] ἐνταῦθα after θεμελίων deleted by Maltretus.
[2] οὐχ . . . βαρβάρων V, βαρβάρων ἐπίθεσιν A, καὶ βαρβάρων ἐπίθεσιν corrector of V in margin.
[3] οἱ Maltretus: ᾗ V.

operation.[1] However, the Romans derived no profit from it subsequently, because later on the bridge was completely destroyed by the floods of the Ister and by the passage of time. At the same time Trajan built two forts, one on either side of the river; the one on the opposite bank they named Theodora, while the one in Dacia was called Pontes from the work—for the Romans call a bridge *pontem* in the Latin tongue.[2] But when boats reached that point, the river was no longer navigable, since the ruins and the foundations of the bridge lay in the way; and it is for this reason that they compel the river to change its course and to go about in a detour, so that they may keep it navigable even beyond that point. Both these forts had suffered so much from the passage of time, and more still from the assaults of the barbarians, that they had come to be utterly destroyed. And the Emperor Justinian restored Pontes, which is on the right of the river, providing it with new and thoroughly impregnable defences, and thus re-established the safety of Illyricum. However, the fort on the other side of the river, the one which they call Theodora, he considered in no way worthy of his attention, exposed as it was to the barbarians there. But the strongholds which now stand beyond Pontes he himself built new; these are named

[1] The reference is to a treatise of Apollodorus which is no longer extant. This Apollodorus was active in Rome for a time, having among his other undertakings done the Forum of Trajan and Trajan's column.

[2] It bore the name Pons Traiani.

---

[4] After *αὐτὸς* A has *ἄλλα τε πλεῖστα, ἅπερ ἀμήχανον λόγῳ διεξελθεῖν*, "and very many others, which it is impossible to enumerate."

καὶ Σουσίανα, Ἁρμάτα τε καὶ Τιμένα, καὶ Θεοδωρούπολίς τε καὶ Στιλιβούργου καὶ Ἁλικανιβούργου.

19 Ἦν δέ τι πολίχνιον ἐγγὺς κείμενον, Ἀκυὲς ὄνομα, οὗπερ ὀλίγα ἄττα σαθρὰ γεγονότα ὁ
20 βασιλεὺς ἐπηνώρθωσε. καὶ μετ' ἐκεῖνο Βουργονόβορε καὶ Λακκόβουργο, καὶ τὸ Δορτικὸν ἐπικαλούμενον φρούριον, ὅπερ τῷ χρόνῳ ἐξίτηλον γεγενημένον ἐς ὀχύρωμα νῦν ἐχυρώτατον κατ-
21 εστήσατο. καὶ πύργον ἕνα, Ἰουδαῖος καλούμενον, φρούριον διεσκευάσατο κεκαλλιστευμένον καλεῖσθαί
22 τε[1] καὶ εἶναι. καὶ τὸ δὴ Βουργουάλτου[2]
B 290 ὠνομασμένον, ἔρημόν τε καὶ παντάπασιν ἀοίκητον τὰ πρότερα ὄν,[3] ἀλλὰ καὶ χῶρον ἕτερον περιβόλῳ
23 ἐτειχίσατο νέῳ ὅνπερ ἐπικαλοῦσι Γόμβες. καὶ τὸ Κρίσπας ἔρυμα καταπεπονηκὸς τῷ μήκει τοῦ χρόνου, ἔτι μέντοι καὶ Λογγινιάνα καὶ Ποντεσέ-
24 ριον[4] ἐδείματο, ἔργον διαφερόντως ἐξαίσιον. ἐν δὲ Βονωνίᾳ τε καὶ Νοβῷ[5] προμαχεῶνας διερρυηκότας ἀνενεώσατο. καὶ Ῥατιαρίας πόλεως ὅσα
25 καταπεπτώκει ὀρθὰ ἐστήσατο. καὶ πολλὰ δὲ ἄλλα κατὰ τὸ χρείᾳ ξυνοῖσον ἢ βραχέα κομιδῇ
P 82 ὄντα ἐπὶ μέγα ἐξῆρεν, ἢ συνέστειλε τὸ περιττὸν ἀφελόμενος, ὅπως δὴ μὴ τοῖς πολεμίοις ἢ τῷ ὑπεράγαν βραχεῖ ἢ τῷ ἀμέτρῳ εὐέφοδα εἴη· ὥσπερ ἀμέλει Μωκατίανα μὲν πύργον ἕνα κατὰ μόνας τὰ πρότερα ὄντα φρούριον τανῦν τελεώ-
26 τερον κατεστήσατο. τὸ δέ γε Ἀλμοῦ, χώραν

[1] τε added by Maltretus.
[2] δὴ Βουργουάλτου Maltretus for διβουργουάλτου.
[3] A lacuna after ὄν noted by Capps, who suggests, *e.g.*, οὐκ ἐν ὀλιγωρίᾳ ἐποίησεν.

Mareburgou and Susiana, Harmata and Timena, and Theodoropolis, Stiliburgou and Halicaniburgou.

There was a certain small town near by, Acues by name, which had partly fallen into decay; this the Emperor put in order. Beyond that lay Burgonobore and Laccoburgo, and the fortress called Dorticum, utterly effaced by time, which he made into a fort now very strong. And he remodelled a stronghold called Judaeus, which had consisted of a single tower, and made it a splendid fortress in name and in fact. [Nor did he neglect] the fort named Burgualtu, which previously was desolate and wholly without inhabitants, but also surrounded with a new circuit-wall another place which they call Gombes. Also he rebuilt the defences of Crispas, which had suffered with the passage of time, likewise Longiniana and Ponteserium,[1] an exceptionally fine piece of work. In Bononia and Novus he restored the parapets which had crumbled. And all the parts of the city Ratiara[2] which had collapsed he re-erected. He improved many other places in accordance with their particular needs, either making very small places large, or curtailing their size where it was excessive, so that they might not be easy for an enemy to attack either because of excessive smallness or because of too great size; thus, for example, Mocatiana, which previously was a single tower standing alone, he converted into the more complete fortress which it now is. On the other hand, the fortress of Almou, which used

[1] Cf. modern Pontresina.
[2] Modern Arzar Palanka in Bulgaria.

[4] Ποντεσέριον Maltretus for *πόντες ἔριον*.
[5] Νοβῷ Haury: *νοβῶ* V.

περιβεβλημένον πολλήν, ἐς ὀλίγον ξυναγαγὼν σὺν τῷ ἀσφαλεῖ ἄμαχον εἶναι τοῖς πολεμίοις
27 εἰργάσατο. καὶ πολλαχῇ δὲ πύργον ἕνα κατὰ μόνας ἑστῶτα εὑρὼν καὶ διὰ τοῦτο εὐκαταφρόνητον τοῖς ἐπιοῦσιν ὄντα, φρούριον ἐχυρώτατον
28 κατεστήσατο. ὃ δὴ περί τε Τρίκεσαν καὶ Πούτεδιν πεποίηκε. καὶ μὴν καὶ ὀχυρώματα τοῦ ἐν Κεβρῷ τὰ καταπεπονηκότα θαυμασίως ὡς ἐπηνώρθωσε· φρούριόν τε οὐ πρότερον ὂν ἐν Βιγραναῇ δεδημιούργηκε, καὶ αὐτοῦ ἄγχιστα ἕτερον ἐν χωρίῳ, ἐφ᾽ οὗ δὴ πύργος εἷς τὰ πρότερα
29 ὢν εἱστήκει μόνος, ὄνομα Ὄνος. ἐλέλειπτο δὲ μόνα πόλεως ἐδάφη οὐ πολλῷ ἄποθεν· Αὐγοῦστες
30 ὠνομάζετο ἐν τοῖς ἄνω χρόνοις ἡ πόλις. νῦν δὲ τὸ μὲν παλαιὸν ὄνομα ἔχουσα, νέα δὲ καὶ ἀκραιφνὴς ὅλη πρὸς Ἰουστινιανοῦ βασιλέως γεγενημένη,
31 ὁμιλεῖ[1] οἰκητόρων ἐπιεικῶς πλήθει. ἀλλὰ καὶ τὰ πεπονθότα τοῦ ἐν Ἀεδάβῃ ἐρύματος ἐπηνώρθωσε,
B 291 καὶ Βαριάνα πόλιν ἐκ παλαιοῦ κειμένην ἀνέστησεν. ἔτι μέντοι καὶ Βαλεριάναν, ἔρυμα πρότερον οὐδὲν ἔχουσαν, ἐτειχίσατο.

32 Πρὸς ἐπὶ τούτοις δὲ καὶ χωρίων οὐ παρὰ τοῦ ποταμοῦ κειμένων τὴν ὄχθην, ἀλλὰ κατὰ πολὺ ἄποθεν ὄντων ἐπεμελήσατο, πεσουμένων ἐκ τοῦ ἐπὶ πλεῖστον, τειχίσμασί τε αὐτὰ περιβέβληκεν
33 ἀμάχοις τισί. Κάστρα Μάρτις[2] τε καὶ Ζητνουκόρτου καὶ Ἰσκὸς τὰ χωρία ἐπικαλεῖται ταῦτα. παρὰ δὲ τοῦ ποταμοῦ τὴν ὄχθην φρούριον παλαιόν, Οὔννων[3] ὄνομα, ἐπιμελείας ἠξίωσε τά τε ἄλλα καὶ
34 ἀμφὶ τῷ περιβόλῳ πολλῆς. ἔστι δέ τις χῶρος

[1] ὁμιλεῖ Capps: ὁμίλῳ.
[2] Καστράμαρτίς Maltretus: καὶ στραμάρτις.

to cover a large area, he brought into small compass and thus made it safe and able to defy the assaults of the enemy. In many places, finding a single tower standing by itself and therefore an easy prey for assailants, he converted it into a very strong fortress; this he did, for example, with Tricesa and Putedis. Furthermore, he restored in a marvellous way the damaged defences at Cebrus. At Bigranaê he constructed a fortress which had not existed before, and very close to it a second one, Onus by name, where a single tower had previously stood. And not far away there were the bare foundations of a city which in early times used to bear the name of Augustes. But now, still bearing its ancient name, though all made over new by the Emperor Justinian and quite complete, it knows [1] a rather numerous population. Also he restored the damaged portion of the defences of Aëdabê, and put in order the city of Variana which had long lain in ruins. In addition, he built a wall around Valeriana, which previously had no defences.

Furthermore, he gave his attention to towns which do not lie upon the bank of the river but stand at a great distance from it—towns which were about to fall in ruins for the most part—and he encircled them with walls which are practically impregnable. These places are named Castra Martis and Zetnucortou and Iscus. And an ancient fort named Hunnôn, on the bank of the river, he treated as worthy of attention in all respects and particularly in the matter of its circuit-wall. There is a certain place not far re-

[1] A use of ὁμιλεῖν very common in Procopius; *cf.* Haury's *Index Craecitatis* and Herwerden's *Lexicon Suppletorium*.

[3] Οὔννων Maltretus: οὖννον V.

οὐ πολλῷ ἄποθεν τούτου δὴ τοῦ Οὔννων φρουρίου, ἔνθα δὴ ὀχυρώματα δύο Ἴστρου ποταμοῦ ἐφ' ἑκάτερα ἦν, ἐν μὲν Ἰλλυριοῖς Παλατίολον ὄνομα, 35 ἐπὶ θάτερα δὲ Συκίβιδα. ταῦτα καθῃρημένα τῷ χρόνῳ ἀνανεωσάμενος Ἰουστινιανὸς βασιλεὺς τῶν ταύτῃ βαρβάρων τὰς ἐπιδρομὰς ἀνεχαίτισεν, ἐπέκεινά τε φρούριον ᾠκοδομήσατο, παλαιὸν 36 ἔρυμα, ὅπερ Οὔτως[1] ὠνόμασται. ἐν ὑστάτῳ δὲ τῶν Ἰλλυρικῶν ὁρίων φρούριον ἀνῳκοδομήσατο, Λαπιδαρίας ὄνομα, καὶ πύργον ἕνα ἑστῶτα μόνον, Λουκερναριαβούργου[2] καλούμενον, ἐς φρούριον 37 ἀξιοθέατον μετεστήσατο. ταῦτα μὲν Ἰουστινιανὸς βασιλεὺς ἐν Ἰλλυριοῖς διαπέπρακται. οὐ μόναις δὲ ταῖς οἰκοδομίαις τὴν χώραν ἐτειχίσατο ταύτην, ἀλλὰ καὶ στρατιωτῶν φρουρὰς ἐν τοῖς ὀχυρώμασι πᾶσιν ἀξιολογωτάτας καταστησάμενος τὰς τῶν βαρβάρων ἐπιβουλὰς ἀπεκρούσατο.

P 83 ζ'. Τὰ μὲν οὖν Ἰλλυριῶν ὀχυρώματα παρὰ ποταμὸν Ἴστρον ταύτῃ πη ἔχει. ἐπὶ Θρᾴκης δὲ νῦν ἰτέον ἡμῖν τὰ ἐρύματα, ὅσα δὴ παρὰ τὴν 2 ἐκείνῃ ἀκτὴν Ἰουστινιανῷ βασιλεῖ εἴργασται. οὐ B 292 γάρ μοι ἀπὸ τρόπου ἔδοξεν εἶναι, ἅπασαν πρότερον περιηγησαμένῳ τὴν ταύτῃ ἠϊόνα οὕτω δὴ ἐπελθεῖν καὶ τὰ κατὰ τὴν μεσόγαιαν αὐτῷ πεπραγ-3 μένα. πρῶτον μὲν οὖν ἐπὶ Μυσοὺς ἐνθένδε ἴωμεν, οὕσπερ ἀγχεμάχους οἱ ποιηταὶ καλοῦσιν· ἐπεὶ 4 καὶ χώραν τὴν Ἰλλυριοῖς ὅμορον ἔχουσι. μετὰ τὸν χῶρον οὖν ὅνπερ Λουκερναριαβοῦργον καλοῦσι, Σεκούρισκα τὸ φρούριον ᾠκοδομήσατο Ἰουστι-5 νιανὸς βασιλεύς, καινουργήσας αὐτός. ἐπέκεινά

[1] Οὔτως Haury (Uto in *Itin. Ant.* 221) : οὕτως V.

moved from this fort of Hunnôn where there are two fortresses, one on either side of the Ister River, the one in Illyricum named Palatiolum, and the one on the other side, Sycibida. These, which had been ruined by time, the Emperor Justinian restored and thereby checked the incursions of the barbarians of that region; and beyond them he built a fort at an ancient stronghold which was named Utôs. And at the extremity of the Illyrian territory he built a fort named Lapidarias, and he transformed into a notable fortress a single tower which had stood alone, called Lucernariaburgou. These then were the works executed by the Emperor Justinian in Illyricum. Yet it was not with buildings alone that he fortified this land, but he also established very considerable garrisons of troops in all the strongholds and thereby warded off the assaults of the barbarians.

vii. Such, then, are the strongholds of Illyricum along the Ister River. But we must now go on to the fortified towns of Thrace, those namely which were built by the Emperor Justinian along the river-bank there. For it has seemed to me not improper, after first describing the coast of that region, then to take up also the record of what he did in the interior. First, then, let us proceed to Mysia,[1] the home of men whom the poets call hand-to-hand fighters,[2] for their country borders upon Illyricum. So beyond that place which they call Lucernaria-burgou the Emperor Justinian built the fortress Securisca, a new work of his own. Beyond this he

[1] That is, Moesia, which is here confused with Mysia in Asia Minor; *cf.* Dio Cassius, XLIX. 36.
[2] Homer, *Iliad*, XIII. 5.

---

[2] So Maltretus: λουκερναρία βουργοῦ V.

τε τὰ πεπονηκότα ἐν Κυντοδήμου ἀνενεώσατο. καὶ μετὰ τοῦτο πόλιν ἐδείματο οὐ πρότερον οὖσαν, ἥνπερ ὁμωνύμως τῇ βασιλίδι Θεοδωρό-
6 πολιν ἐπωνόμασεν. ἔτι μέντοι φρουρίων τοῦ τε Ἰατρῶν καλουμένου καὶ Τιγᾶς τὰ πεπονθότα νέᾳ τινὶ διεσώσατο οἰκοδομίᾳ, καὶ τοῖς Μαξεντίου[1] πύργον ἐντέθεικεν, ἐπεὶ αὐτοῦ προσδεῖν ᾤετο.
7 καὶ τὸ Κυντῶν[2] ἐδείματο φρούριον οὐ πρότερον ὄν. μεθ' ὃ δὴ τὸ Τρασμαρίσκας[3] ὀχύρωμά ἐστιν· οὗπερ καταντικρὺ ἐν τῇ ἀντιπέρας ἠπείρῳ Κωνσταντῖνός ποτε Ῥωμαίων βασιλεὺς φρούριον οὐκ ἀπημελημένως ᾠκοδομήσατο, Δάφνην ὄνομα, οὐκ ἀξύμφορον νενομικὼς εἶναι φυλάσσεσθαι
8 ταύτῃ τὸν ποταμὸν ἑκατέρωθεν. ὃ δὴ προϊόντος τοῦ χρόνου βάρβαροι μὲν ἀφανίζουσι τὸ παράπαν, Ἰουστινιανὸς δὲ ἀνῳκοδομήσατο βασιλεὺς
9 ἐκ θεμελίων ἀρξάμενος. μετὰ δὲ Τρασμαρίσκαν ἔρυμά τε τὸ Ἀλτηνῶν, καὶ ὅπερ καλοῦσι Κανδιδιάνα, καθῃρημένον πρὸς αὐτῶν πολεμίων πολλῷ πρότερον, ἐπιμελείας ἠξίωσε κατὰ λόγον τῆς
10 χρείας. ἔστι δὲ τρία ἑξῆς ὀχυρώματα παρὰ τὴν τοῦ Ἴστρου ἠϊόνα, Σαλτουπύργος τε καὶ Δο-
11 ρόστολος καὶ Συκιδάβα. ὧν δὴ ἑκάστου τὰ πεπονθότα[4] οὐκ ἀπημελημένως ὁ βασιλεὺς ἐπ-
B 293 12 ηνώρθωσε. καὶ Κούηστρις δέ, ὅπερ κεῖται τῆς ἀκτῆς ἔκτοσθεν, ἐπιμέλειαν τὴν ὁμοίαν πεποίηται. καὶ Πάλματις ἐν στενῷ κείμενον μεῖζόν τε κατεστήσατο καὶ διαφερόντως εὐρύτερον, καίπερ
13 οὐ παρὰ τὴν ἀκτὴν τοῦ ποταμοῦ ὄν. οὗ δὴ ἄγχιστα καὶ φρούριον Ἄδινα καινουργήσας ἐδείματο, ἐπεὶ διηνεκὲς διαλανθάνοντες Σκλαβηνοὶ

[1] So Maltretus: Μαζεντίου V.

restored the parts of Cyntodemus which had suffered. And still further on he built a city which had not existed previously, and this he named Theodoropolis, after the Empress. Furthermore, he preserved the fortresses called Iatrôn and Tigas by building anew the parts which had suffered, and to the fort of Maxentius he added a tower, which he thought it needed. And he built the fort of Cyntôn which had not existed before. Beyond this is the stronghold Trasmariscas. Just opposite this, on the other bank of the river, Constantine, Emperor of the Romans, once built with no small care a fort, Daphnê by name, thinking it not inexpedient that the river should be guarded on both sides at this point. As time went on, the barbarians destroyed this entirely; but the Emperor Justinian rebuilt it, beginning at the foundations. And beyond Trasmariscas is the stronghold Altenôn and one which they call Candidiana, destroyed long before by the same enemy, which he repaired with all the care that they deserved. And there are three forts, Saltupyrgus, Dorostolus and Sycidaba, one after the other along the bank of the Ister, which the Emperor put in order by carefully repairing such parts of each one as had suffered. He displayed a similar care in the case of Questris, which lies back from the river. And Palmatis, which was cramped for space, he enlarged and made very much broader, though it is not on the bank of the river. Close to this he built also a new fort named Adina, because the barbarian Sclaveni were constantly laying con-

---

[2] Κυντῶν Haury : Κυιντόν.
[3] So Haury : *τρασμακαρίσκας* V, *τρισμακαρίας* A.
[4] *πεπονθότα* V : *πεπονηκότα* A.

βάρβαροι ἐνταῦθα ἐνεδρεύοντές τε κεκρυμμένως ἀεὶ τοὺς τῇδε ἰόντας ἄβατα ἐποίουν τὰ ἐκείνῃ
14 χωρία. καὶ φρούριον δὲ τὸ Τιλικίων ᾠκοδομήσατο, καὶ αὐτοῦ ἐν ἀριστερᾷ κείμενον ἔρυμα.
15 Οὕτω μὲν καὶ Μυσοῖς τὰ ὀχυρώματα ἐπί τε τῆς ἀκτῆς ποταμοῦ Ἴστρου ἔσχε καὶ ταύτης πλησίον.
16 ἐπὶ Σκύθας δὲ τὸ λοιπὸν βαδιοῦμαι· ἔνθα δὴ φρούριον πρῶτον Κυρίλλου ἁγίου ἐπώνυμόν ἐστιν, οὗπερ τὰ πεπονηκότα τῷ χρόνῳ ἀνῳκοδομήσατο
P 84 17 οὐκ ἀπημελημένως Ἰουστινιανὸς βασιλεύς. ἐπέκεινά τε αὐτοῦ ἦν μὲν ἐκ παλαιοῦ ὀχύρωμα, Οὐλμιτῶν ὄνομα, βαρβάρων δὲ Σκλαβηνῶν ἐπὶ χρόνου μῆκος ἐκείνῃ τὰς ἐνέδρας πεποιηκότων, διατριβήν τε αὐτόθι ἐπὶ μακρότατον ἐσχηκότων, ἔρημόν τε παντάπασι γέγονε, καὶ οὐδὲν αὐτοῦ ὅτι
18 μὴ τὸ ὄνομα ἐλέλειπτο ἔτι. ὅλον τοίνυν ἐκ θεμελίων δειμάμενος, ἐλεύθερα τῆς[1] τῶν Σκλαβηνῶν ἐπιθέσεώς τε καὶ ἐπιβουλῆς κατεστήσατο
19 εἶναι τὰ ἐκείνῃ χωρία. ἔστι δέ που μετὰ τοῦτο Ἰβιδὰ πόλις, ἧς δὴ τοῦ περιβόλου πολλὰ ἐπεπόνθει, ἅπερ ἀνανεωσάμενος οὐδεμιᾷ μελλήσει ἐχυρωτάτην
20 διεπράξατο εἶναι. φρούριόν τε δεδημιούργηκε νέον αὐτὸς μετ᾽ αὐτὴν ὅπερ Αἴγισσον ὀνομάζουσι.[2] καὶ ἄλλο δὲ φρούριον Σκυθίας ἐν ὑστάτῳ κεῖται, Ἅλμυρις ὄνομα, οὗ δὴ τὰ πολλὰ σαθρὰ γεγονότα
21 διαφανῶς ἀνοικοδομησάμενος διεσώσατο. ὅσα δὲ καὶ ἄλλα ὀχυρώματα ἐν τῇ τῆς Εὐρώπης μοίρᾳ εἰπεῖν ἄξιον.

B 294 η΄. Ὅσα μὲν δὴ ἔν τε Δαρδάνοις καὶ Ἠπειρώταις καὶ Μακεδόσι καὶ τοῖς ἄλλοις Ἰλλυριῶν

[1] τῆς V, τε A.
[2] ὀνομάζουσι V, ὀνομάζεται A.

cealed ambuscades there against travellers,[1] thus making the whole district impassable. He likewise built the fortress of Tiliciôn [2] and a stronghold which lies to its left.

Such was the condition of the fortresses of Mysia [3] on the bank of the Ister River, as well as of those near it. Next I shall proceed to Scythia; there the first fortress is the one named for St. Cyril, of which the Emperor Justinian rebuilt with care those portions which had suffered with time. Beyond this from ancient times there was a stronghold, Ulmitôn by name, but since the barbarian Sclaveni had been making their ambuscades there for a great length of time and had been tarrying there very long, it had come to be wholly deserted and nothing of it was left except the name. So he built it all up from the foundations and thus freed that region from the menace and the attacks of the Sclaveni. Beyond this is the city of Ibida, whose circuit-wall had suffered in many places; these he renewed without delay and made the city very strong. And beyond it he built a new fortress, a work of his own, which they call Aegissus.[4] At the extremity of Scythia lies another fortress, Halmyris by name, a great part of which had become manifestly insecure, and this he saved by rebuilding it. All the other strongholds also within the bounds of Europe are worthy of mention.

viii. All the building that was done by the Emperor Justinian in Dardania, Epirus, Macedonia and the

[1] *Cf. Wars*, VI. xxvi. 18, 19.

[2] Teglicio in *Itin. Ant.* 223.

[3] Moesia.

[4] Aegissus (Aegyso in *Itin. Ant.* 226) is placed by cartographers at the head of the Danube's delta, Halmyris (Salmorudê or Salmoridê in *Itin. Ant.* 226) near its right mouth.

ἔθνεσιν, ἔτι μέντοι καὶ ὅσα ἐπί τε τῆς Ἑλλάδος, καὶ ἀμφὶ ποταμὸν Ἴστρον οἰκοδομήματα Ἰουστινιανῷ βασιλεῖ εἴργασται, ἤδη μοι ἔμπροσθεν 2 δεδιήγηται. ἐπὶ τὴν Θρᾴκην δὲ τὸ λοιπὸν ἴωμεν, ἀρίστην πηγνύμενοί τινα τοῦ λόγου κρηπῖδα τὰ ἐπὶ Βυζαντίου χωρία, ἐπεὶ καὶ τῆς Θρᾴκης ἡ πόλις οὐ τῷ κράτει μόνον, ἀλλὰ καὶ χωρίων προέστηκε φύσει, τῇ μὲν Εὐρώπῃ ὥσπερ τις ἀκρόπολις ἐπεμβαίνουσα, φραττομένη δὲ τῆς διοριζούσης αὐτὴν ἀπὸ τῆς Ἀσίας θαλάσσης τὸ 3 πέρας. ἤδη μὲν οὖν τάς τε ἄλλας ἁπάσας τῆς πόλεως κτίσεις, καὶ ὅσα δὴ ἐπὶ τοῖς ἱεροῖς ἐντός τε καὶ ἐκτὸς τοῦ Κωνσταντινουπόλεως περιβόλου δεδημιούργηκεν, ἐν τοῖς ἔμπροσθεν δεδήλωκα λόγοις. τὰ δὲ δὴ ἐνθένδε ἐρῶν[1] ἔρχομαι.

4 Φρούριόν ἐστιν ἐν προαστείῳ τῆς πόλεως, ὅπερ Στρογγύλον ὁμωνύμως τῇ τοῦ ἐρύματος 5 συνθέσει καλοῦσιν. ἐντεῦθεν ἡ ἐς τὸ Ῥήγιον ὁδὸς ἄγουσα, ἐκ τοῦ ἐπὶ πλεῖστον ἀνώμαλος οὖσα, ὄμβρων, ἂν οὕτω τύχοι, ἐπιπεσόντων, τελματώδης τε καὶ δυσπάριτος τοῖς τῇδε ἰοῦσιν 6 ἐγίνετο. νῦν δὲ λίθοις αὐτὴν καταστρώσας ἁμαξιαίοις ὁ βασιλεὺς οὗτος[2] εὐπετῆ τε κατεστήσατο 7 καὶ ἄπονον ὅλως. μῆκος μὲν τῇ ὁδῷ τῇδε ἄχρι ἐς Ῥήγιον· εὐρύνεται δὲ τοσοῦτον ἐς ὅσον ἁμάξας οὐ στενοχωρεῖν δύο ἀπ' ἐναντίας ἀλλήλαις ἰούσας. 8 τραχεῖς οἱ λίθοι διαφερόντως· εἰκάσαις ἂν αὐτοὺς μυλίτας[3] εἶναι· εὐμεγέθεις τέ εἰσι μάλιστα. ὥστε δὴ ἕκαστος γῆν μὲν ἐπικαλύπτει πολλήν, P 85 9 ἐς ἄγαν δὲ ὑψοῦ ἀνέχει. ἐς δὲ τό τε ὁμαλὲς καὶ

[1] ἐρῶν V, λέξων A. [2] οὗτος A, οὕτως V.
[3] μυλίτας Haury: μυλίας V, om. A.

other parts of Illyricum,[1] also in Greece and along the Ister River has already been described by me. Next let us go to Thrace, laying down as the fairest foundation, as it were, for our narrative the environs of Byzantium, since this city is preëminent in Thrace not only because of its power, but also by reason of its natural site, planted as it is on Europe like a kind of acropolis and finally setting a guard over the sea which divides it from Asia. I have already described in the preceding narrative all the buildings of the city itself, including the work which was done for the shrines, both inside and outside the walls of Constantinople. I shall now proceed from that point.

In a suburb of the city there is a fortress which they call Strongylum[2] from the form in which it is built. The road which leads from that point to Rhegium[3] was for the most part uneven; and if rain chanced to fall it became a bog and was difficult for travellers to get through. But now this Emperor has paved it with blocks of stone each large enough to load a waggon and so has made it altogether practicable and easy. In length, this road extends all the way to Rhegium and its breadth is such that two waggons, going in opposite directions, have no lack of room. The paving-stones are exceptionally coarse, so that you would suppose them to be mill-stones; and they are of goodly size. Consequently each one covers much ground and stands very high. They are very

[1] See note 1, p. 248.

[2] "Round."

[3] This would be the famous Via Egnatia which ran west to the Adriatic and terminated at a point near modern Valona. On the situation of Rhegium, see E. Mamboury in *Byzantion*, xiii., 1938, pp. 308–310.

τό γε λεῖον ἐπιεικῶς ἐξειργασμένοι, οὐκ ἐνῆφθαι
B 295 τῇ συνθέσει, οὐδέ πη ἐς τὸ ἀκριβὲς μεμυκέναι,
ἀλλὰ συμπεφυκέναι δοκοῦσιν ἀλλήλοις. ταῦτα μὲν
οὖν τοιαῦτά ἐστι.

10 Λίμνην δέ τινα εἶναι ἄγχιστα τοῦ Ῥηγίου
καλουμένου ξυμβαίνει ἐς ἣν τὰς ἐκβολὰς ἔχουσι
ποταμοὶ ἐκ χωρίων τῶν ὕπερθεν τῇδε φερόμενοι.
11 διακέχυται δὲ ἡ λίμνη αὕτη μέχρι ἐς θάλασσαν·
ὥστε μία τις ἀμφοτέραιν ἀκτὴ ἐν στενῷ μάλιστα
12 τυγχάνει οὖσα. ταύτην δὲ ἄμφω ἐπικλύζουσι
τὴν ἀκτὴν ἀντικυματοῦσαι, καὶ ἀλλήλοις ἀντι-
μυκώμεναι, ἀεί τε ἀλλήλαις εὐθὺ ἵενται τὴν
ἠϊόνα ἐπικοινούμεναι. ἐπειδὰν δὲ ὡς πλησιαίτατα
ἵκωνται, ἀναχαιτίζουσι τὴν ἐπιρροήν, ἐφ' ἑαυτὰς
ἐπιστρέφουσαι, ὥσπερ ἐνταῦθα τὰ ὅρια σφίσι
13 πηξάμεναι. ἔστι δὲ καὶ ἀλλήλαις οὐ ἀναμίγνυν-
ται, πορθμόν τινα μεταξὺ ἔχουσαι, ἄδηλον ὂν
ὁποτέρα ποτὲ αὐτῶν τὸ τοῦ πορθμοῦ ὕδωρ
14 διακεκλήρωται. οὔτε γὰρ ἡ τῆς θαλάσσης ἐπιρροὴ ἐς τὴν λίμνην[1] ἀεὶ φέρεται οὔτε διηνεκὲς ἐς
τὴν θάλασσαν ἡ λίμνη[2] ἐκβάλλει, ἀλλ' ὄμβρων
μὲν ἐπιγενομένων πολλῶν, ἐπιπνεύσαντός τε
ἀνέμου νότου, ἐκ τῆς λίμνης ὁ πορθμὸς προϊὼν
15 φαίνεται. ἢν δὲ ἀπὸ βορρᾶ τὸ πνεῦμα ἴοι, ἡ
θάλασσα τὴν λίμνην ἐπικλύζειν δοκεῖ. ἐν τούτῳ
μέντοι ἡ θάλασσα τῷ χώρῳ ἐς βράχος κατατείνει
παμμέγεθες, ὀλίγης τινὸς ἀπολελειμμένης μεταξὺ
16 χώρας ἥπερ διήκει ἐς ἄβυσσον· ἐς τόσον δὲ
στενὴ[3] τυγχάνει οὖσα, ὥστε δὴ καὶ Μύρμηξ
ὠνόμασται. οὗτος δὲ ὁ πορθμός, ὅ τε τὴν

[1] λίμνην V, ἠιόνα A. [2] ἡ λίμνη A, τὴν λίμνην V.
[3] τόσον δὲ στενὴ A, τοσόνδε V.

carefully worked so as to form a smooth and even surface, and they give the appearance not simply of being laid together at the joints, or even of being exactly fitted, but they seem actually to have grown together.[1] So much, then, for this.

There chances to be a kind of lake very close to this place called Rhegium, into which pour streams that flow from the adjacent uplands. This lake extends as far as the sea so that in the very narrow tongue of land between them they have a common shore. Both sea and lake wash against this shore as their waters roll against its opposite sides, and they bellow against each other as they constantly rush straight on towards one another, sharing a common beach. But when they come very close, they check their flow and turn upon themselves, just as if they had fixed their limits there. However, there is a place where the waters mingle, having a sort of strait between them, and it is uncertain to which of them belongs the water of the strait. Neither does the current of the sea always flow into the lake nor does the lake continuously empty into the sea; but when heavy rains have fallen, and when the south wind has been blowing, the water of the channel seems to flow out from the lake, but if the wind comes from the north, the sea seems to be flooding into the lake. At this point, moreover, the sea is shallow for a considerable distance, with the exception of a very small space where the depth is great. Indeed this is so narrow that it is called Myrmex.[2] This strait which joins the sea and the

[1] *Cf.* the description of the Appian Way in *Wars*, V. xiv. 6–11.

[2] "Ant."

θάλασσαν καὶ τὴν λίμνην ζευγνύων,[1] ἧπέρ μοι εἴρηται, πάλαι μὲν γεφύρᾳ ξυλίνῃ διαβατὸς ἦν ἐπὶ κινδύνῳ μάλιστα τοῖς τῇδε ἰοῦσιν, ἐπεὶ τοῖς
17 ξύλοις, ἂν οὕτω τύχοι, ξυνδιεφθείροντο·[2] νῦν δὲ αὐτὴν Ἰουστινιανὸς βασιλεὺς λίθοις λογάδην
B 296 ἐμβεβλημένοις ἐς ἁψῖδος μετεωρίσας μέγα τι χρῆμα, τὴν ἐκείνῃ διάβασιν ἀκίνδυνον κατεστήσατο.
18 Τοῦ δὲ Ῥηγίου ἐπέκεινα πόλις ἐστί που, Ἀθύρας ὄνομα, ἧσπερ τοὺς οἰκήτορας δίψῃ δεινοτάτῃ ἐχομένους εὑρὼν τὴν ἀπορίαν διέλυσε σφίσιν, ἔλυτρον ἐνταῦθα δειμάμενος, θησαυρίζων μὲν ἐπικαιριώτατα τὴν τῶν ὑδάτων οὐκ ἀναγκαίαν περιουσίαν, πρυτανεύων δὲ αὐτὴν ἐν ἐπιτηδείῳ τοῖς τῇδε ἀνθρώποις. ἀνῳκοδομήσατο δὲ καὶ τὰ πεπονθότα[3] τοῦ περιβόλου.
19 Ἔστι δὲ μετὰ τὴν Ἀθύραν τις χῶρος, ὅνπερ
20 Ἐπισκοπεῖα καλοῦσιν οἱ ἐπιχώριοι. ὃν δὴ κατανενοηκὼς Ἰουστινιανὸς βασιλεὺς ταῖς τῶν πολεμίων ἐπιδρομαῖς ὑποκείμενον,[4] ἐπὶ πλεῖστον δέ, ὡς οὐδαμῇ ὀχυρώματος ὄντος, ἀφύλακτα παντάπασιν ὄντα τὰ ἐκείνῃ χωρία, φρούριον ἐνταῦθα ἐδείματο· οὗ δὴ τοὺς πύργους πεποίηται οὐχ ᾗπερ εἰώθει,
21 ἀλλὰ τρόπῳ τοιῷδε. προὔχει τις ἐκ τοῦ περιβόλου οἰκοδομία, στενωτάτη μὲν κατ' ἀρχὰς οὖσα, τελευτῶσα δὲ ἐς εὖρος μέγα· ἐφ' οὗ δὴ
22 ἕκαστος ἐξείργασται πύργος. ταύτῃ τε τοῖς πολεμίοις ἄγχιστά πη τοῦ τείχους ἰέναι ἀμήχανά
P 86 ἐστιν, ἐπεὶ τῶν πύργων κατὰ μέσον γινόμενοι ἐν ἀμφιβόλῳ κατὰ κορυφὴν πρὸς τῶν ἐκείνῃ φρουρῶν
23 ῥᾷστα βαλλόμενοι διαφθείρονται. τάς τε πύλας

[1] ζευγνύων V, ξυνδέων A.
[2] ξυνδιεφθείροντο Haury : διεφθείροντο.

lake, as I have said, was crossed in ancient times by a wooden bridge, with great danger for those passing that way, because they were often destroyed together with the bridge-timbers if they happened to collapse. But now the Emperor Justinian has carried the bridge on a huge arch built of picked stones, and thus he has made the crossing there free from danger.

Beyond Rhegium is a certain city named Athyras, whose inhabitants he found suffering from extreme scarcity of water; this difficulty he remedied for them by building a reservoir there, in which by storing at just the right time the unnecessary excess of water, he dispensed it as needed to the inhabitants. He also rebuilt such parts of the circuit-wall as had suffered.

Beyond Athyras is a certain place which the inhabitants call Episcopia. The Emperor Justinian, perceiving that this lay exposed to the assaults of the enemy, and that a large expanse of country here was altogether unguarded, since no stronghold at all existed, built a fortress in that place; and he built the towers there, not in the customary manner, but as follows. At regular intervals a structure is built out from the circuit-wall, very narrow at first, but finally spreading out to a great breadth; on this in each case a tower was erected. Thus it is impossible for the enemy to get close to the wall anywhere, because when they get into a precarious position between the towers they are easily shot at from both sides and from above by the guards there and are destroyed. The gates too he did not place in the

---

[3] πεπονθότα V : πεπονηκότα A.
[4] ὑποκείμενον V : ἀποκείμενον A.

ἐνταῦθα οὐ κατὰ τὰ ξυνειθισμένα τῶν πύργων[1] μεταξὺ ἔθεντο, ἀλλ' ἐκ πλαγίας κατὰ τὸ ἐν στενῷ προὖχον τοῦ τείχους, οὐχ ὁρωμένας τοῖς
24 πολεμίοις, ἀλλ' ὄπισθεν διαλανθανούσας. ἐνταῦθα Θεόδωρος βασιλεῖ τὴν ὑπουργίαν παρέσχετο,
25 σιλεντιάριος τὴν ἀρχήν,[1] συνετὸς μάλιστα. τοῦτο
B 297 μὲν οὖν τὸ ἔρυμα τῇδε πεποίηται. ἐπὶ τείχη δὲ τὰ μακρὰ ἐνθένδε ἰόντας ὀλίγα ὑπειπεῖν ἄξιον.

θ'. Ἡ θάλασσα ἐξ ὠκεανοῦ καὶ Ἰσπανίας γῆν τὴν Εὐρωπαίαν ἐν ἀριστερᾷ ποιουμένη μέχρι μὲν ἐς Θρᾴκην κατὰ ταὐτὰ[2] χωρεῖ πρὸς ἀνίσχοντά που τὸν ἥλιον, ἔνθεν δὲ σχιζομένη πὴ μὲν ἐπὶ τὴν ἑῴαν στέλλεται μοῖραν, πὴ δὲ κατὰ βραχὺ ἐγκαρσία γεγενημένη τὸν Εὔξεινον καλούμενον
2 ἀποτελεῖ πόντον. ἐς Βυζάντιον δὲ ἀφικομένη ὥσπερ ἐπὶ νύσσης τινὸς καμπὴν ποιεῖται ἀμφὶ τὰ πρὸς ἕω τῆς πόλεως,[2] πλαγία τε πολλῷ ἔτι μᾶλλον γιγνομένη ἐν πορθμῷ ἵεται, ἰσθμὸν τῆς Θρᾴκης τά τε πρόσω καὶ ὀπίσω, ὡς τὸ εἰκός, ἐργαζομένη.
3 οὐχ ὅτι ἐς ἐκροὰς ἐνταῦθα ἡ θάλασσα μερίζεται δύο, ᾗπερ ἐν τοῖς ἄλλοις ἰσθμοῖς εἴωθεν, ἀλλὰ περιστρεφομένη τε θαυμασίως ὡς καὶ περιβαλλομένη ἑκατέρωθεν Θρᾴκην τε τὴν ἄλλην καὶ διαφερόντως τὰ ἐπὶ Βυζαντίου προάστεια πάντα.
4 οἰκοδομοῦνται δὲ καὶ περιστέλλουσιν οἱ ταύτῃ ἄνθρωποι τὰ προάστεια οὐχ ὅσον ἐς χρείαν, ἀλλ' ἐς ὕβριν τε καὶ τρυφὴν ὅρον οὐκ ἔχουσαν, καὶ ὅσα ἄλλα πλούτου ἐξουσία ἐς τοὺς ἀνθρώπους

[1] πύργων V : ἔργων A. [2] ταὐτὰ Haury : ταῦτα.

[1] Privy counsellor; *cf. Wars* II. xxi. 2.
[2] Of Constantinople.

customary position between the towers, but at an angle, in the narrow part of the projection which runs out from the wall, where they could not be seen by the enemy but were masked behind the towers. In that place Theodore, a very clever man who held the office of silentiarius,[1] was of service to the Emperor. Thus were these fortifications built. And it is proper, proceeding thence to the long walls,[2] to explain them briefly.

ix. The Sea,[3] commencing from the Ocean and from Spain, goes on in a single direction, approximately eastward, keeping Europe on its left as far as Thrace, but at that point it divides itself and while one portion goes towards the East, another part of it turns gradually, at an oblique angle,[4] and forms the Euxine Sea, as it is called. When it reaches Byzantium, it makes a bend about the eastern portion of the city, as if rounding a turning-post, and bending much more obliquely,[5] it runs in the form of a strait,[6] turning the front and back portions of Thrace into an isthmus, as one would expect. This does not mean that the sea is divided here into two separate bays,[7] as is wont to happen at other isthmuses, but it circles round in a marvellous way, from two sides surrounding Thrace and especially all the suburbs of Byzantium. The people there build and adorn their suburbs, not only to meet the actual needs of life, but they display an insolent and boundless luxury and all the other vices that the power of wealth brings

[3] The Mediterranean. [4] North-eastward.

[5] That is, turning toward the north-west.

[6] The Bosporus.

[7] Procopius uses the term "outlets" (or "mouths") for the recesses of the sea which, opposite each other, make an isthmus between them, which is not the case here.

5 ἰοῦσα ποιεῖ. ἔπιπλά τε κατατίθενται ἐνταῦθα πολλὰ καὶ διαπονήματα ἐν αὐτοῖς ἐνδελεχέστατα ἔχουσιν. ἐπειδὰν οὖν καταθεῖν τινας τῶν πολεμίων γῆν τὴν Ῥωμαίων ἐξαπιναίως ξυνενεχθείη, οὐδὲν ὁμοίως τοῖς ἄλλοις χωρίοις προστρίβεσθαι τὴν ζημίαν ἐνταῦθα ξυμβαίνει, ἀλλὰ κακοῖς ἄγαν τοῖς 6 ἀνηκέστοις βαρύνεσθαι τὰ ἐκείνῃ χωρία.[1] ὃ δὴ ἀναστέλλειν Ἀναστάσιος βασιλεὺς διὰ σπουδῆς ἔχων ἐν χώροις οὐχ ἧσσον ἢ σημείοις τεσσαράκοντα τοῦ Βυζαντίου διέχουσι μακρὰ οἰκοδομησάμενος τείχη, ἄμφω τῆς θαλάσσης τὰς ἀκτὰς ἔζευξεν, οὗ δὴ ἀλλήλαιν διεστήκασιν ὁδῷ ἡμέραιν δυοῖν[2] μάλιστα· ταύτῃ τε ἅπαντα ἐν τῷ ἐχυρῷ 7 καθεστάναι τὰ ἐντὸς ᾤετο. ἦν δὲ ἄρα μειζόνων τοῦτο συμφορῶν αἴτιον. οὐδὲ[3] γὰρ οἷόν τε ἦν οἰκοδομίαν τοσαύτην τὸ μέγεθος ἢ ἐς τὸ ἀσφαλὲς ἐξειργάσθαι, ἢ φρουρεῖσθαι ξὺν τῷ ἀκριβεῖ. 8 ἐπειδάν τε μοίρᾳ τινὶ τούτων δὴ τῶν μακρῶν τειχῶν ἐπισκήψαιεν οἱ πολέμιοι, καὶ τοὺς φρουροὺς ἅπαντας ὑποχειρίους ἐποιοῦντο οὐδενὶ πόνῳ, τοῖς τε ἄλλοις ἐπιπίπτοντες ἀπροσδόκητοι κακὰ οὐκ εὐδιήγητα ἐξειργάζοντο.

B 298 · P 87

9 Ἀλλὰ βασιλεὺς τά τε πεπονθότα τούτων δὴ ἀνοικοδομησάμενος τῶν τειχῶν, τά τε σφαλερὰ ἐπὶ τὸ ἐχυρώτατον κρατυνάμενος τῶν φρουρῶν 10 ἕνεκα, προσεπετεχνήσατο τάδε. τὰς μὲν ἐξόδους, αἵπερ ἐκ πύργου ἑκάστου ἐς τοὺς αὐτοῦ ἐχομένους 11 ἐξάγουσιν, ἐφράξατο πάσας. ἄνοδον δὲ καθ᾽ ἕκαστον ἐκ τοῦ ἐδάφους ἔντοσθεν ἐτεκτήνατο μίαν·[4] ἥνπερ ἐπὶ καιροῦ καθειργνύντες οἱ ταύτῃ φρουροὶ τοὺς πολεμίους περιφρονοῦσι τοῦ περι-

[1] χωρία V: χωρία ξυμβαίνει A.

when it comes to men. And they accumulate much furniture in their houses and make it a point to keep costly objects in them. Thus, when it comes about that any of the enemy overrun the land of the Romans suddenly, the damage caused there is much greater than in other places, and the region is then overwhelmed with irreparable calamities. The Emperor Anastasius had determined to put a stop to this and so built long walls [1] at a distance of not less than forty miles from Byzantium, uniting the two shores of the sea on a line where they are separated by about a two-days' journey.[2] By this means he thought that everything inside was placed in security. But in fact this was the cause of greater calamities. For neither was it possible to make safe a structure of such great length nor could it be guarded rigorously. And whenever the enemy descended on any portion of these long walls, they both overpowered all the guards with no difficulty, and falling unexpectedly upon the other people they inflicted loss not easy to describe.

But the Emperor rebuilt those portions of these walls which had suffered, and making the weak parts very strong for the sake of the guards, he added the following devices. He blocked up all the exits from each tower leading to those adjoining it; and he built from the ground up a single ascent inside each individual tower, which the guards there can close in case of emergency and scorn the enemy if

[1] *Cf. Wars*, VII. xl. 43, and note.
[2] Forty miles.

---

[2] δυοῖν Haury: δυεῖν.
[3] οὐδὲ Haury: οὔτε.
[4] So V; ἐτεκτήνατο μίαν ἐκ τοῦ ἐδάφους A.

βόλου ἐντὸς γενομένους· ἐπεὶ πύργος ἐς ἀσφάλειαν ἕκαστος αὐτὸς κατὰ μόνας τοῖς φρουροῖς ἀπόχρη.[1]
12 καὶ τούτων δὴ τῶν τειχῶν ἐντὸς [2] τὰ ἐς ἀσφάλειαν ἐνδελεχέστατα διεπράξατο, τά τε ἄλλα πεποιημένος ᾗπέρ μοι ἔναγχος εἴρηται καὶ πόλεως Σηλυβρίας [3] ἀνανεωσάμενος ὅσα πεπονθότα τοῦ περιβόλου
13 ἐτύγχανεν. ἐπὶ μὲν οὖν τῶν μακρῶν τειχῶν ταῦτα Ἰουστινιανῷ βασιλεῖ εἴργασται.

14 Ἡράκλεια δὲ ἡ πόλις ἥδε, ἡ παραλία, ἡ ἐν γειτόνων, ἡ Πέρινθος (ᾗ πάλαι μὲν τὰ πρωτεῖα τῆς Εὐρώπης ἐδίδοσαν, νῦν δὲ δὴ μετά γε Κων-
B 299 σταντινούπολιν τὰ δευτερεῖα παρέχονται) διψῶσά τε καὶ λίαν αὐχμῶσα ἔναγχος ἔκειτο, οὐχ ὅτι ἄνυδρος ἦν [4] ἡ ἀμφ' αὐτὴν χώρα, οὐδὲ ὅτι ἀπημέλητο ταῦτα τοῖς ἐκ παλαιοῦ δειμαμένοις τὴν πόλιν (ἐπεὶ καὶ κατάρρυτος Εὐρώπη ταῖς κρήναις, καὶ ποιεῖσθαι τοῖς πάλαι ἀνθρώποις ὀχετοὺς ἔμελεν), ἀλλὰ τὰ ξυνειθισμένα ποιῶν ὁ χρόνος τῇ πόλει τὴν ὀχεταγωγίαν ἀνῄρηκεν, ἢ καταγεγηρακυῖαν τὴν οἰκοδομίαν ὑπεριδών, ἢ τῷ μὴ ἐπιμελεῖσθαι τοὺς Ἡρακλεώτας αὐτῆς ἐπὶ τὴν φθορὰν ποδηγούμενος. ὀλίγου τε ἀοίκητος διὰ
15 τοῦτο Ἡράκλεια ἐλέλειπτο εἶναι. ταὐτὸ δὲ τοῦτο καὶ τὰ ἐκείνῃ βασίλεια ὁ χρόνος ἐποίει
16 ἀξιοθέατα ἐπιεικῶς ὄντα. βασιλεὺς δὲ Ἰουστινιανὸς οὐ παρέργως, ἀλλὰ βασιλικῶς μάλιστα, τὴν πόλιν ἰδών, ὕδασί τε αὐτὴν ποτίμοις καὶ

[1] ἀπόχρη V : ἀπέχρη A.
[2] ἐντὸς V : om. A.
[3] σηλυβρίας V : μεσημβρίας A.
[4] ἦν added by Haury.

they have penetrated inside the circuit-wall, since each tower by itself was sufficient to ensure safety for its guards. Also inside these walls he diligently made provision for safety, not only doing what has just been mentioned, but also restoring all the parts of the circuit-wall of the city of Selymbria [1] which happened to have been damaged. These things then were done by the Emperor Justinian at the long walls.

The well-known city of Heraclea [2] which is situated on the coast near by, the ancient Perinthus—which in former times men regarded as the first city of Europe, though it now takes a place second to Constantinople —suffered cruelly from lack of water in recent times. This was not because the country about it had no water, nor yet because this matter was neglected by the ancient builders of the city (for Europe has an abundance of springs and the men of ancient times were careful to build aqueducts), but because Time, following its custom, had destroyed the city's aqueduct, since it either failed to notice that its masonry had become enfeebled by age, or else was leading the people of Heraclea to their own destruction through their neglect of it; [3] and the city was nearly left depopulated for this reason. And Time was having the same effect upon the palace there, a very admirable building. But when the Emperor Justinian saw the city, he in no careless fashion, but rather in a manner befitting an

[1] Modern Silivri, on the north shore of the Propontis.

[2] Modern Eregli, on a peninsula twenty-two miles west of Selymbria. It was founded in 559 B.C.

[3] The rendering reproduces the author's personification of Time, illogical as it is.

διειδέσιν ἐπέκλυσε, καὶ τῶν βασιλείων ἀποστερεῖσθαι τοῦ ἀξιώματος ὡς ἥκιστα ξυνεχώρησεν, ἀνοικοδομησάμενος ἅπαντα.

17 Ἡρακλείας δὲ ἄποθεν ἡμέρας ὁδὸν χωρίον ἐπιθαλασσίδιον ἦν, Ῥαιδεστὸς ὄνομα, παράπλου μὲν ἐφ' Ἑλλησπόντου καλῶς κείμενον, εὐλίμενον δὲ καὶ τῇ κατὰ θάλασσαν ἐργασίᾳ ἐπιτηδείως ἔχον τοῖς ἐπ'[1] ἐμπορίᾳ ναυτιλλομένοις καταίρειν τε καὶ ἀποφορτίζεσθαι προσηνῶς μάλιστα, καὶ αὖ πάλιν ἀνάγεσθαι οὐδενὶ πόνῳ ἐμπλησαμένοις τοῦ γόμου τὰ πλοῖα· βαρβάροις δὲ ἀποκείμενον καταθέουσιν, ἂν οὕτω τύχῃ,[2] ἐξαπιναίως τὰ ἐκείνῃ χωρία, τῷ μήτε ἀποτετριγχωμένον μήτε

P 88 18 τῇ φύσει δυσπρόσοδον εἶναι. ὥστε καὶ τοῖς ἐμπόροις δέει τοῦ κινδύνου ὑπεροφθὲν ἐν ὀλιγωρίᾳ

19 ἐγένετο. νῦν δὲ βασιλεὺς Ἰουστινιανὸς οὐχ ὅσον τῷ χωρίῳ τὴν ἀσφάλειαν προσεποίησεν,

20 ἀλλὰ καὶ τοὺς περιοίκους ἐσώσατο πάντας. ἐπὶ

B 300 Ῥαιδεστοῦ γὰρ ἀνέστησε πόλιν, τείχει μὲν

21 ἐρυμνήν, μεγέθει δὲ διαφερόντως ὑπέρογκον. οὗ δὴ βαρβάρων σφίσιν ἐγκειμένων οἱ πλησιόχωροι ἅπαντες εἰς καιρὸν καταφεύγοντες σὺν τοῖς χρήμασι διασώζονται.

ι'. Τὰ μὲν οὖν ἐπὶ Ῥαιδεστοῦ Ἰουστινιανῷ βασιλεῖ ταύτῃ πῃ ἔσχεν. ὅσα δὲ αὐτῷ ἀμφὶ

2 Χερρονήσῳ διαπεπόνηται, ἐρῶν ἔρχομαι. προβέβληται μὲν πάσης ἡ Χερρόνησος τῆς κατ' αὐτὴν Θρᾴκης. ἐπεμβαίνουσα γὰρ τῇ θαλάσσῃ καὶ ὥσπερ ἐχομένη τοῦ πρόσω, δόκησιν παρέχεται

[1] ἐπ' added by Haury.
[2] τύχῃ V : τύχοι A.

Emperor, flooded it with crystal-clear drinking water, and he, far from permitting the city to be deprived of the honour of its palace, rebuilt it throughout.

One day's journey distant from Heraclea was a town on the coast named Rhaedestus,[1] well situated for the voyage to the Hellespont, with a good harbour well adapted for the business of the sea, so that merchant vessels could put in and unload their cargoes very conveniently and then put out to sea again with no difficulty after loading their freight. But it lay exposed to the barbarians, who sometimes overran that region in unexpected raids, because it was not protected even by makeshift defences nor was it naturally difficult of access. Consequently the place came to be disregarded and neglected by the merchants through fear of the risk. But now the Emperor Justinian has not only provided for the safety of the place but has also saved all those who dwell round about. For he erected at Rhaedestus a city which is not only strongly defended by its wall, but is also of extraordinary size. Hither on occasion all those who dwell near by flee for refuge when the barbarians fall upon them, and they thus save themselves and their property.

x. Such were the works carried out by the Emperor Justinian at Rhaedestus. I shall go on to tell what he did in the region of the Chersonese.[2] The Chersonese extends out from all that portion of Thrace. It projects boldly into the sea and seems to be pressing onward, giving the impression that it is

[1] Modern Rodosto, west of Heraclea, on the north shore of the Propontis; its original name was Bisanthê.

[2] Modern Gallipoli Peninsula.

3 ὅτι δὴ ἐπὶ τὴν Ἀσίαν χωρεῖ. ἀκτὴ δὲ αὐτῆς ἀμφὶ πόλιν Ἐλαιοῦντα προὔχουσα μία, σχίζει τε εἰς δύο τὴν θάλασσαν μοίρας, καὶ αὐτὴ τῷ ῥοθίῳ ἀποτεμνομένη τῆς ἄλλης ἠπείρου, καὶ προσιούσῃ ἐπίπροσθεν τῇ θαλάσσῃ ὑποχωροῦσα, τὸν Μέλανα 4 καλούμενον ποιεῖ κόλπον. νῆσος δὲ τὸ λοιπὸν ὀλίγου δέοντος γίνεται, ὄνομα τῷ ποιουμένῳ προσῆκον κτωμένη. Χερρόνησος γάρ, ὡς τὸ εἰκός, ὀνομάζεται, ἰσθμῷ διειργομένη βραχεῖ μὴ 5 νῆσος παντάπασιν εἶναι. κατὰ τοῦτον οἱ πάλαι ἄνθρωποι τὸν ἰσθμὸν παρέργως τε καὶ λίαν ἀπημελημένως ἐδείμαντο διατείχισμα κλίμακι 6 ἁλωτόν. κῆπον γάρ πού τινα εἰκῇ κείμενον αἱμασιᾷ περιβάλλειν οἰόμενοι, ἰσχνόν τε αὐτὸ καὶ ὀλίγον τῆς γῆς ὑπερανεστηκὸς[1] ἐξειργάσαντο. 7 πρὸς δὲ καὶ τὴν ἑκατέρωθι τοῦ ἰσθμοῦ θάλασσαν προβόλους τεκτηνάμενοι βραχεῖς τε καὶ φαύλους, οὕσπερ καλεῖν νενομίκασι μώλους, τὴν μεταξὺ χώραν τοῦ τε ῥοθίου καὶ τοῦ περιβόλου ἐφράξαντο, οὐ ταύτῃ τοὺς ἐπιβουλεύσοντας ἀπωσόμενοι, ἀλλ' B 301 ἐπὶ τὰς εἰσόδους παρακαλέσοντες· οὕτω δὴ αὐτὸ εὐκαταφρόνητον ἐξειργάσαντο, καὶ τοῖς ἀποπειρα- 8 σομένοις εὐάλωτον. ἡγούμενοι δέ τι τοῖς πολεμίοις ἄμαχον πεποιῆσθαι ὀχύρωμα, τούτου δὴ τοῦ περιβόλου τὰ ἐντὸς ἅπαντα φυλακῆς οὐδεμιᾶς ἀξιοῦν ἔγνωσαν, ἐπεὶ οὔτε φρούριον οὔτε ἄλλο τι ἔρυμα ἐπὶ Χερρονήσου ξυνέβαινεν εἶναι, καίπερ ὀλίγου δέοντος ἐς τριῶν κατα- 9 τεινούσης ὁδὸν ἡμερῶν. ἔναγχος ἀμέλει γοῦν οἱ

[1] ὑπερανεστηκὸς V: ἐπανεστηκὸς A.

[1] *I.e.* in a south-westerly direction, toward the Troad.

advancing toward Asia.[1] It has a single projecting point at the city of Elaeus,[2] and this divides the sea into two parts, while the promontory itself is cut off from the rest of the mainland by the water, and curves inward before the advancing sea to form the so-called Gulf of Melas.[3] The remainder of it almost forms an island, acquiring a name appropriate to the shape which it assumes, for it is called Chersonese, most likely because it is prevented only by a tiny isthmus from being altogether an island. At this isthmus the men of former times built a cross-wall of a very casual and indifferent sort which could be captured with the help of a ladder, because, I suppose, they thought they were building an earthen wall around a casually placed garden-plot, and so built it of meagre dimensions and rising only slightly from the ground. And facing the sea at either side of the isthmus they constructed wretched little bastions, of the sort which people are wont to call "moles," and with these they closed the gap between the water and the circuit-wall, not with the expectation of repelling attacking forces at this point, but rather in order to invite them to effect an entrance; so contemptible did they make them and so easy to capture for any who should attack. But they thought they had set up a kind of invincible bulwark against the enemy and so decided to regard everything inside this circuit-wall as requiring no further protection, for there actually was neither fort nor any other stronghold on the Chersonese, though it extends to a length of almost three days' journey.[4] Indeed the enemy,

[2] At the southern tip of the peninsula.
[3] Modern Gulf of Saros.
[4] Sixty miles.

πολέμιοι καταθέοντες τὰ ἐπὶ τῆς Θρᾴκης χωρία ἐγκεχειρήκασι μὲν ὡς ἀποπειρασόμενοι τῆς κατὰ τὴν ἠϊόνα εἰσόδου, δεδιξάμενοι δὲ τοὺς ταύτῃ
P 89 φρουροὺς ἐσπεπηδήκασιν ὥσπερ τι ἄθυρμα παίζοντες, ἐντός τε τοῦ περιβόλου γεγένηνται οὐδενὶ πόνῳ.

10 Πολλὰ τοίνυν ἀμφὶ τῶν κατηκόων[1] τῇ σωτηρίᾳ διασκοπούμενος Ἰουστινιανὸς βασιλεὺς ἐποίει τάδε. 11 πρῶτα μὲν αὐτῷ[2] ἐξίτηλον τὸ παλαιὸν γεγένηται τεῖχος, οὐδὲ ὅσον ἴχνους οἱ ἀπολελειμμένου τινός. 12 ἕτερον δὲ αὐτίκα ἐπὶ τῆς αὐτῆς χώρας ἀνέστη, 13 ὅπερ ἐπιεικῶς εὐρυνόμενον ὕψοῦ ἀνέχει. ὑπεράνω τε τῶν ἐπάλξεων ἀνειλημμένη[3] θόλος ἐν στοᾶς τρόπῳ ὄροφον ποιεῖται, καλύπτουσα τοὺς τοῦ 14 περιβόλου ἀμυνομένους. ἄλλοι τε τῇ[4] θόλῳ προμαχῶνες ἐγκείμενοι διπλασιάζουσι τοῖς τῇδε τειχο-15 μαχοῦσι τὸν πόλεμον. ἔπειτα δὲ ἀμφοτέρωθι ἐς τοῦ περιβόλου τὰ πέρατα πρὸς αὐταῖς που τῆς θαλάσσης ταῖς ῥαχίαις μάλιστα, προβόλους πεποίηται,[5] ἐπὶ πλεῖστον μὲν τοῦ ῥοθίου διήκοντας, τῷ δὲ τείχει ξυναπτομένους, ὕψους δὲ πέρι τῷ 16 ἐρύματι ἐναμίλλους ὄντας. ἀλλὰ καὶ τὴν τάφρον τοῦ περιβόλου ἔκτοσθεν οὖσαν περικαθάρας τε καὶ κατορύξας ἐνδελεχέστατα μέγα τι αὐτῇ 17 εὔρους τε καὶ βάθους ἐντέθειται χρῆμα.[6] καὶ μὴν καὶ στρατιωτῶν καταλόγους ἐν τούτοις ἵδρύσατο
B 302 τοῖς μακροῖς τείχεσι πᾶσι βαρβάροις ἀντιτάξασθαι ἱκανοὺς ὄντας, ἤν τι τῆς Χερρονήσου ἀποπειρῶνται. 18 οὕτω δὲ ταῦτα ἐν τῷ βεβαίῳ τῆς ἀσφαλείας

[1] κατηκόων V, A: κατοικούντων corrector in V.
[2] αὐτῷ V: αὐτὸ A.

while overrunning the land of Thrace recently, did actually undertake to force the entrance by the beach, and frightening off the guards there they leaped inside just as if they were playing a game, and they got inside the defences with no trouble.

So the Emperor Justinian, with his constant solicitude for the safety of his subjects, did as follows. First of all he demolished completely the old wall, so that not so much as a trace of it was left. And he straightway erected another wall, upon the same ground, very broad and rising to a great height. Above the battlements a set-back [1] vaulted structure in the manner of a colonnaded stoa makes a roof to shelter those who defend the circuit-wall. And other breastworks resting upon the vaulted structure double the fighting for those who lay siege to the wall. Furthermore, at either end of the wall, at the very edge of the sea, he made bastions (*proboloi*) extending far out into the water, which were joined to the wall and rivalled its defences in height. He also cleared the moat outside the wall and dug it out very thoroughly, adding a great deal to its width and to its depth. Furthermore, he stationed detachments of soldiers on these long walls, sufficient to offer resistance to all the barbarians if they should make any attempt upon the Chersonese. And after he had made all this firm provision for its safety, he also

[1] This seems to be the meaning of ἀνειλημμένη.

---

[3] ἀνειλημμένη V: om. A.
[4] τῇ Haury: τῷ.
[5] οὓς μώλους καλοῦσιν after πεποίηται deleted by Haury.
[6] ἐντέθειται χρῆμα V: σχῆμα ἐντέθειται A.

καταστησάμενος καὶ τοῖς ἔνδον οὐδέν τι ἧσσον
19 ὀχυρώματα προσεποίησεν· ὥστε εἰ τοῖς μακροῖς
τείχεσιν (ἀπέστω δὲ τοῦ λόγου) παθεῖν τι ξυμβαίη,
οὐδέν τι ἧσσον Χερρονησιώτας ἐν ἀσφαλεῖ εἶναι.
20 πόλιν τε γὰρ Ἀφροδισιάδα ἐρύματι ἐχυρωτάτῳ
περιεβάλλετο, ἀτείχιστον ἐκ τοῦ ἐπὶ πλεῖστον τὰ
πρότερα οὖσαν, καὶ Κίβεριν πόλιν, ἐπ' ἐδάφους
21 κειμένην, τειχήρη πεποιημένος ξυνῴκισεν· ἔνθα
δὴ καὶ βαλανεῖα καὶ ξενῶνας ᾠκοδομήσατο
οἰκία τε παμπληθῆ καὶ ὅσα ἄλλα πέφυκεν ἐπιφανῆ
22 ἐνδείκνυσθαι πόλιν. ἀλλὰ καὶ τὴν Καλλίπολιν
καλουμένην βεβαιότατα ἐτειχίσατο, ἐλπίδι τῶν
μακρῶν τειχῶν ἀτείχιστον ἀπολελειμμένην τοῖς
23 πρόσθεν ἀνθρώποις. οὗ δὴ καὶ σιτῶνάς τε καὶ
οἰνῶνας ἐδείματο δαπάνῃ τῇ πάσῃ τῶν ἐπὶ Χερρονήσου στρατιωτῶν ἱκανῶς ἔχοντας.

24 Ἔστι δέ τις Ἀβύδου καταντικρὺ πόλις ἀρχαία,
Σηστὸς ὄνομα, καὶ αὐτὴ τὰ πρότερα παρέργως
25 κειμένη, ὀχύρωμά τε οὐδὲν ἔχουσα. λόφος δὲ
αὐτῇ τις ἰσχυρῶς ἀπότομος ἐπανέστηκεν· ἵνα
δὴ φρούριον ἐδείματο ἀπρόσβατον ὅλως, ἑλεῖν τε,
26 εἴ τις ἐγχειροίη, ἀμήχανον. Σηστοῦ δὲ οὐ
μακρὰν ἄποθεν τὴν Ἐλαιοῦντα ξυμβαίνει εἶναι.
πέτρα τε τῆς θαλάσσης ἀπορραγεῖσα ἐνταῦθα
ἀνέχει, ἄκραν οὐρανομήκη ἐξαίρουσα τειχήρη
27 φύσιν. φρούριον οὖν καὶ τῇδε ὁ βασιλεὺς οὗτος
ἐδείματο, δυσπάριτόν τε καὶ τοῖς προσιοῦσι
28 παντελῶς ἄμαχον. ἀλλὰ καὶ τὸ ἐν Θεσκῷ
φρούριον ἐπὶ θάτερα τοῦ μακροῦ τείχους ἱδρύσατο,
B 303 περιβόλῳ κρατυνάμενος ἐχυρῷ μάλιστα· ταύτῃ

[1] Modern Gallipoli.

built additional strongholds for the people inside; so that if (God forbid) any mischance should befall the long walls, the inhabitants of the Chersonese would none the less be in safety. For he surrounded the city of Aphrodisias with very strong defences, though it had been unwalled for the most part before that, and he put walls around the city of Ciberis which was lying dismantled, and provided it with inhabitants. He also built there baths and guest-houses and numerous dwellings, and all the other things which make a city notable. Furthermore, he provided Callipolis,[1] as it is called, with a very strong wall, a city which had been left unwalled by the men of earlier times because of the faith which was placed in the long walls. There too he built storehouses for grain and for wine amply sufficient for all the wants of the soldiers in Chersonese.

There was a certain ancient city opposite Abydus,[2] Sestus [3] by name, which again had been carelessly planned in earlier times and had no defences. A certain very steep hill towers above it, on which he built an altogether inaccessible fortress, which cannot possibly be taken by any assailant. And it happens that at no great distance from Sestus is situated Elaeus, where a precipitous rock rises from the sea, culminating in a lofty headland which is a natural fortress. So this Emperor built a fort there too, which is hard to get past and altogether impregnable for assailants. Furthermore, he founded the fortress at Thescus on the other side of the long wall, strengthening it by means of an especially strong circuit-wall.

[2] On the Asiatic shore of the Hellespont.
[3] On the Chersonese.

τε τοῖς Χερρονησιώταις τὴν ἀσφάλειαν πανταχόθεν αὐτὸς προσεποίησε.

P 90 ια΄. Μετὰ δὲ Χερρόνησον Αἶνος οἰκεῖται πόλις, ἐπὶ τοῦ οἰκιστοῦ τῆς προσηγορίας ὠνομασμένη. Αἰνείας γὰρ ἦν, ὥσπερ λέγουσιν, ὁ τοῦ Ἀγχίσου. 2 ταύτης ὁ περίβολος εὐάλωτός τε ἦν τῷ χθαμαλὸς εἶναι· οὐδὲ ὅσον γὰρ ἐς τὸ ἀναγκαῖον ἀνεῖχεν 3 ὕψος· καὶ ἀναπεπταμένην τινὰ εἴσοδον κατὰ τῆς θαλάσσης τὸ γειτόνημα εἶχεν, ἀμηγέπη ἐπι- 4 ψαύοντος αὐτοῦ τοῦ ῥοθίου. ἀλλὰ βασιλεὺς Ἰουστινιανὸς ἀνέστησε μὲν αὐτὸν ἐς ὕψος, μὴ ὅτι ἁλῶναι, ἀλλὰ καὶ ἀποπειρᾶσθαι ἀμήχανον. 5 ἐπεξαγαγὼν δὲ καὶ πανταχόσε φραξάμενος ἀνάλω- 6 τον Αἶνον παντάπασι κατεστήσατο. καὶ ταύτῃ μὲν ἡ πόλις ἐν τῷ ἀσφαλεῖ ἐγεγόνει· ἔμεινε δὲ τοῖς βαρβάροις ἡ χώρα καταθεῖν εὐπετής· ἐπεὶ Ῥοδόπη ὀχυρωμάτων ἐκ παλαιοῦ ὑπεσπάνιζεν. 7 ἦν δέ τις κώμη ἐν τῇ μεσογείᾳ, Βέλλουρος ὄνομα, πλούτου μὲν δυνάμει καὶ πολυανθρωπίᾳ ἴσα καὶ πόλις, τῷ μέντοι τειχήρης οὐδαμῇ εἶναι ληϊζομένοις διηνεκὲς ἐπαρκοῦσα βαρβάροις, ἀγροῖς τε τοῖς ἀμφ᾽ αὐτὴν κειμένοις πολλοῖς γε οὖσι ταὐτὸ 8 πάσχουσα. καὶ αὐτὴν δὲ ὁ βασιλεὺς οὗτος πολίζει τε καὶ ἀποτειχίζει, καὶ αὐτοῦ[1] ἐπαξίαν 9 τίθεται εἶναι. καὶ μὴν καὶ ἄλλων τῶν ἐπὶ Ῥοδόπης πόλεων ὅσα δὴ ἐνδεῖν ἢ καταπεπονηκέναι ξυνηνέχθη τῷ χρόνῳ σπουδῇ τῇ πάσῃ ἀνέστησεν. 10 ἐν αἷς Τραϊανούπολίς τε καὶ Μαξιμιανούπολίς

Thus he ensured the safety of the inhabitants of the Chersonese from every side.

xi. Beyond the Chersonese stands the city of Aenus,[1] which bears the name of its founder; for he was Aeneas, as they say, son of Anchises. The circuit-wall of this place was easy to capture not only because of its lowness, since it did not rise even to the necessary height, but because it offered an exposed approach on the side toward the sea, whose waters actually touched it in places. But the Emperor Justinian raised it to such a height that it could not even be assailed, much less be captured. And by extending the wall and closing the gaps on every side he rendered Aenus altogether impregnable. Thus the city was made safe; and yet the district remained easy for the barbarians to overrun, since Rhodopê[2] from ancient times had been lacking in fortifications. And there was a certain village in the interior, Vellurus by name, which in wealth and population ranked as a city, but because it had no walls at all it constantly lay open to the plundering barbarians, a fate which was shared by the many fields lying about it. Our Emperor made this a city and provided it with a wall and made it worthy of himself. He also took great pains to put in order all such parts of the other cities in Rhodopê as had come to be defective or had suffered with time. Among these were Trajanopolis[3] and Maximianopolis,

[1] Modern Enos, near the mouth of the Hebrus.
[2] A district in western Thrace.
[3] Near the mouth of the Hebrus River.

---

[1] αὑτοῦ Dewing: αὐτοῦ MSS., editors.

εἰσιν,[1] ὧνπερ ἐπηνώρθωσε τὰ ἐν τοῖς προβόλοις[2] σαθρὰ γεγονότα. ταῦτα μὲν οὖν τῇδε πεποίηται.

11 Ἀναστασιούπολις δὲ ἡ τῇδε οὖσα τειχήρης μὲν B 304 καὶ πρότερον ἦν, ἐν δὲ τῇ παραλίᾳ κειμένη ἀφύλακτον εἶχε τὴν ταύτῃ ἠϊόνα. τὰ πλοῖα πολλάκις ἀμέλει ἐνταῦθα καταίροντα ὑποχείρια βαρβάροις Οὔννοις ἐξαπιναίως γεγένηται· ὥστε καὶ τὰς νήσους ἐνθένδε τὰς τῇ χώρᾳ ἐπικειμένας 12 ἠνώχλησαν. Ἰουστινιανὸς δὲ βασιλεὺς διατειχίσματι τὴν παραλίαν περιβαλὼν ὅλην, ταῖς τε ναυσὶ καὶ τοῖς νησιώταις τὴν ἀσφάλειαν ἀνεσώσατο. 13 ἀλλὰ καὶ τὸν τοῦ ὕδατος ὀχετὸν ἐκ τῶν ὀρῶν ἃ ταύτῃ ἀνέχει μέχρι ἐς τὴν πόλιν ἐς[3] ὑπέρογκον 14 ἀνέστησεν ὕψος. ἔστι δέ τις ἐν Ῥοδόπῃ πόλις ἀρχαία, Τόπερος ὄνομα, ἣ ποταμοῦ μὲν ῥεῖθρα περιβάλλεται ἐκ τοῦ ἐπὶ πλεῖστον, λόφον δὲ αὐτῇ ἐπανεστηκότα ὄρθιον εἶχεν. ἀφ'[4] οὗ δὴ οὐ πολλῷ ἔμπροσθεν Σκλαβηνοῖς βαρβάροις ἑάλω. 15 ἀλλὰ βασιλεὺς Ἰουστινιανὸς μέγα τῷ περιβόλῳ ὕψος ἐντέθεικεν· ὥστε ὑπεραίρει τοσούτῳ τὸν λόφον, ὅσῳ δὴ αὐτοῦ καταδεέστερος τὰ πρότερα 16 ἦν. καὶ στοὰν μὲν ἐπανέστησεν ἐν θολωτῷ P 91 τείχει, ὅθεν δὴ τοῖς τειχομαχοῦσιν οἱ τῆς πόλεως ἀμυνόμενοι ἐκ τοῦ ἀσφαλοῦς διαμάχονται, τῶν δὲ πύργων ἕκαστον φρούριον ἐρυμνὸν ἐσκευάσατο εἶναι. 17 ἀλλὰ καὶ τὰ ἐκ τοῦ περιβόλου μέχρι ἐς τὸν ποταμὸν διατειχίσματι περιβαλὼν ἐκρατύνατο. ταῦτα μὲν οὖν Ἰουστινιανῷ βασιλεῖ τῇδε πεποίηται.

18 Καὶ ὅσα δὲ αὐτῷ ὀχυρώματα εἴργασται ἀμφὶ

[1] εἰσιν Maltretus: ἐστιν V.
[2] προβόλοις: Haury would prefer περιβόλοις.

where he restored the parts of the bastions which had become weak. Thus were these things done.

The city of Anastasiopolis in this region was indeed walled even before this, but it lay along the shore and the beach was unprotected. Consequently the boats putting in there often fell suddenly into the hands of the barbarian Huns, who by means of them also harassed the islands lying off the coast there. But the Emperor Justinian walled in the whole sea-front by means of a connecting wall and thus restored safety both for the ships and for the islanders. Furthermore, he raised the aqueduct to an imposing height all the way from the mountains which rise here as far as the city. And there is a certain ancient town in Rhodopê, Toperus [1] by name, which is surrounded for the most part by the stream of a river, but had a steep hill rising above it. As a result of this it had been captured by the barbarian Sclaveni not long before. But the Emperor Justinian added a great deal to the height of the wall, so that it now overtops the hill by as much as it previously fell below its crest. And he set a colonnaded portico with a vaulted roof on its wall, and from this the defenders of the city fight in safety against those attacking the wall; and he equipped each one of the towers so as to be a strong fort. He also secured the interval between the circuit-wall and the river by shutting it off with a cross-wall. These things, then, were done by the Emperor Justinian as I have said.

And I shall describe all the fortresses which were

[1] On the Via Egnatia; once also called Rhousion.

---

[3] ἐς added by Haury.
[4] ἀφ' Braun: ὑφ'.

τε τὴν ἄλλην Θρᾴκην καὶ τὴν νῦν καλουμένην Αἱμίμοντον, ἐγὼ δηλώσω. 19 πρῶτα μὲν Φιλιππουπόλεώς τε καὶ Βεροίας, ἔτι μέντοι Ἀδριανουπόλεώς τε καὶ Πλωτινουπόλεως τά τε ἐνδέοντα καὶ καταπεπονηκότα σπουδῇ τῇ πάσῃ ᾠκοδομήσατο· ἐπεὶ αὐτὰς ἐπιμαχωτάτας ξυνέβαινεν εἶναι, καίπερ ἔθνεσι γειτονούσας βαρβάρων πολλοῖς. 20 καὶ φρούρια δὲ ἀνάριθμα ἐπὶ Θρᾴκης ἱδρύσατο πάσης, δι' ὧν τὴν χώραν, ἀποκειμένην[1] τὰ B 305 πρότερα ταῖς τῶν πολεμίων ἐπιδρομαῖς, παντάπασιν τανῦν ἀδῄωτον κατεστήσατο. ἔστι[2] δὲ τὰ φρούρια, ὅσα ἡμᾶς μεμνῆσθαι αὐτῶν, πρὸς ὄνομα τάδε.[3]

Ἐν Εὐρώπῃ·	In Europe:
Λυδικαί.	Lydicae
Ἐλαῖαι.	Elaeae
Ἐν Ῥοδόπῃ τὰ καινούργια·	In Rhodopê, new:
Κασεήρα.	Caseëra
Θεοδωρούπολις.	Theodoropolis
Τὸ τοῦ Θράσου.	Thrasou
Σουδανέλ.	Sudanel
Μούνδεπα.	Mundepa
Θαρσάνδαλα.	Tharsandala

[1] ἀποκειμένην V: ὑποκειμένην corrector in V.
[2] ἔστι V: ἔτι A.
[3] Here the MSS. except A have: Ὅσα φρούρια ὁ θειότατος ἡμῶν βασιλεὺς Ἰουστινιανὸς ἔκτισεν ἐν χώρᾳ τῇ καλουμένῃ Εὐρώπῃ καὶ Ῥοδόπῃ καὶ Θρᾴκῃ καὶ Αἱμιμόντῳ οὕτως. Haury and editors omit.

made by him through the rest of Thrace and through what is now called Haemimontum.[1] First of all he built with great pains those parts which were lacking, and those which had suffered, in Philippopolis [2] and Beroea,[3] and also at Adrianopolis [4] and Plotinopolis,[5] (for these happened to be very vulnerable), though they lay close to many tribes of barbarians. And in all parts of Thrace he established countless fortresses, by which he has now made entirely free from devastation a land which formerly lay exposed to the inroads of the enemy. These fortresses, so far as I recall them, are as follows:

Δένιζος.	Denizus
Τόπαρον.	Toparum
Δαλάταρβα.	Dalatarba
Βρέ.	Bre
Κουσκάβιρι.	Cuscabiri
Κούσκουλις.	Cusculis
Θρᾴκης.	Of Thrace:
Βόσπαρα.	Bospara
Βεσούπαρον.[6]	Besuparum
Καπιστούρια.	Capisturia
Βηρίπαρα.	Beripara
Ἰσγίπερα.	Isgipera
Ὀζόρμη.	Ozormê

[1] A region in northern Thrace, named from Mt. Haemus, now the Balkan range.

[2] Modern Philippopoli.

[3] Modern Stara Zagora.

[4] Modern Adrianople.

[5] On the Hebrus River.

[6] Bessapara *Itin. Ant.* 136. 3.

Βηρηΐαρος.	Bereiärus
Ταμονβαρί.	Tamonbari
Σκέμνας.	Scemnas
Καράσθυρα.	Carasthyra
Πίνζος.	Pinzus
Τουλεοῦς.	Tuleûs
Ἄρζον.	Arzum
Καστράζαρβα.[1]	Castrazarba
Ζωσίτερσον.	Zositersum
Βέργισον.	Bergisum
Δίγγιον.	Dingium
Σάκισσος.	Sacissus
Κουρτουξοῦρα.	Curtuxura
Ποταμουκάστελλον.	Potamùcastellum
Εἰσδίκαια.	Eisdicaea
Τὸ ἐμπόριον Ταυροκεφάλων.	The trading-port of the Taurocephali
Βηλαϊδίπαρα.	Belaïdipara
Σκίτακες.	Scitaces
Βέπαρα.	Bepara
Πουσινόν.	Pusinum
B 306 Ὑμαυπάρουβρι.	Hymauparubri
Σκαριωτασαλούκρα.	Scariotasalucra
Αὐγούστας.	Augustas
Οὐρδαούς.	Urdaûs
Τοῦ ἁγίου Τραϊανοῦ.	St. Trajan's
Δέρταλλος.	Dertallus
Σολβανοῦ.	Solbanû
Βάσκον.	Bascum
Ζίγκυρο.	Zincyro

[1] *Itin. Ant.* 231. 5.

	Αἱμιμόντου.	Of Haemimontum:
	Ζημάρκου.	Zemarcû
	Κηριπάρων.	Ceriparon
	Κασιβόνων.	Casibonon
	Τὸ Οὔκου.	Ucû
	Ἀντωῖνον.	Antoïnum
	Γεσιλαφοσσᾶτον.	Gesilafossatum
	Χεροῖνον.	Cheroenum
	Προβίνου.	Probinû
? 92	Τοῦ ἁγίου Θεοδώρου.	St. Theodore's
	Βουρδέπτω.[1]	Burdepto
	Ῥακούλη.	Raculê
? 92	Τοῦ ἁγίου Ἰουλιανοῦ.	St. Julian's
	Τζιταετοῦς.	Tzitaëtûs
	Βηλαστύρας.	Belastyras
	Γετρίνας.	Getrinas
	Βρέδας.	Bredas
	Βῆρος.	Verus
	Θωκύωδις.	Thocyodis
	Βία.	Via
	Ἀναγογκλί.	Anagoncli
	Σούρας.	Suras
	Αὐθιπάρου.	Authiparû
	Δορδᾶς.	Dordas
	Σαρμαθών.	Sarmathon
	Κλεισοῦρα.	Clisura
	Ὑλασιάναι.	Hylasianae
	Θρασαρίχου.	Thrasarichû
	Βαῖκα.	Baeca
	Χρύσανθος.	Chrysanthus

[1] Burdipta *Itin. Ant.* 137. 2.

	Μαρκέρωτα.	Marcerota
	Ζδεβρήν.	Zdebrên
	Τοῦ ἁγίου Θεοδώρου.	St. Theodore's
	Ἄσγαρζος.	Asgarzus
	Βουρτούδγιζ.[1]	Burtudgiz
	Ταυρόκωμον.	Taurocomum
	Νίκη.	Nicê
	Καβοτούμβα.	Cabotumba
	Δείξας.	Deixas
	Γητριστάους.[2]	Getristaus
	Δέβρη.	Debrê
	Προβίνου.	Probinû
	Κάρβερος.	Carberus
	Τηεσιμόντη.	Teësimontê
	Ἀσγίζους.	Asgizûs
	Δαλάταρβα.	Dalatarba
B 307	Θεοδωρούπολις.	Theodoropolis
	Τζυειδών.	Tzyeidon
	Τζονπολέγων.	Tzonpolegon
	Βασίβουνον.	Basibunum
	Ἀγχίαλος.	Anchialus
	Μαρκιανόν.	Marcianum
	Κυρίδανα.	Cyridana
	Βεκοῦλι.	Beculi

Τὰ Θρᾳκῶν λειπόμενα. Παρά τε τὸν Εὔξεινον πόντον καὶ ποταμὸν

The remaining Thracian fortresses; also those along the Euxine Sea

[1] Burtudizo *Itin. Ant.* 230. 4.
[2] Or Γητριστάοι MSS.

Ἴστρον, κἂν τῇ μεσογείᾳ, οὕτως·	and the Ister River, and in the interior, as follows:
Μυσίας παρὰ μὲν ποταμὸν Ἴστρον·	In Mysia,[2] on the Ister River:
Ἐρκούλεντε.	Erculente
Σκατρῖνα.	Scatrina
Ἀππίαρα.	Appiara
Ἐξεντάπριστα.	Exentaprista
Δεονίανα.	Deoniana
Λιμώ.	Limô
Ὀδυσσός.[1]	Odyssus [3]
Βίδιγις.	Vidigis
Ἀρῖνα.	Arina
Νικόπολις.	Nicopolis
Ζικίδεβα.	Zicideba
Σπίβυρος.	Spibyrus
Πόλις Κάστελλον.	The city Castellum
Κιστίδιζος.	Cistidizus
Βαστέρνας.	Basternas
Μέταλλος.	Metallus
Βηρίπαρα.	Beripara
Σπαθιζός.	Spathizus
Μαρκέρωτα.	Marcerota
Βόδας.	Bodas
Ζισνούδεβα.	Zisnudeba
Τουρούλης.	Turulês
Ἰουστινιανούπολις.	Justinianopolis
Θερμά.	Therma

[1] Odisso, *Itin. Ant.* 228. 3.
[2] Moesia.
[3] Or Odêssus; modern Varna.

	Γεμελλομοῦντες.	Gemellomontes
	Ἀσίλβα.	Asilba
	Κούσκαυρι.	Cuscauri
	Κούσκουλι.	Cusculi
	Φοσσᾶτον.	Fossatum
	Βισδίνα.	Bisdina
	Μαρκιανούπολις.[1]	Marcianopolis[3]
	Σκυθιάς.	Scythias
	Γραψώ.	Grapsô
	Νονώ.	Nonô
	Τροσμῆς.	Trosmês[4]
	Νεαϊοδουνώ.	Neaïodunô
	Ῥεσιδίνα.	Residina
	Κωνσταντιανά.	Constantiana
	Καλλάτις.	Callatis[5]
	Βασσίδινα.	Bassidina
B 308	Βελεδίνα.	Beledina
	Ἄβριττος.[2]	Abrittus
	Ῥουβοῦστα.	Rubusta
	Δινισκάρτα.	Diniscarta
	Μοντερεγῖνε.	Monteregine
	Βέκις.	Becis
P 93	Ἀλτῖνα.	Altina[6]
	Μανροβάλλε.	Manroballe
	Τίγρα.	Tigra

[1] Cf. *Itin. Ant.* 228. 4.
[2] Cf. Müller, *F.G.H.* III. 674.16.
[3] A short distance inland from Odyssus.
[4] On the lower Danube.
[5] Modern Collati, midway between Odyssus and Tomis.
[6] Haury conjectures that this is identical with Ἀλτηνῶν ἔρυμα, *supra* IV. vii. 9.

Σκεδεβά.	Scedeba
Νόβας.	Novas
Ἐν δὲ τῇ μεσογείᾳ·	In the interior:
Κοπούστορος.	Copustorus
Βιργινασώ.	Birginasô
Τιλλιτώ.	Tillitô
Ἀγκυριανά.	Ancyriana
Μουριδεβά.	Murideba
Ἴτζης.	Itzês
Καστελλόνοβο.	Castellonovo
Παδισάρα.	Padisara
Βισμαφά.	Bismapha
Βαλεντινιάνα.	Valentiniana
Ζάλδαπα.	Zaldapa
Ἀξίοπα	Axiopa
Καρσώ.[1]	Carsô
Γρατίανα.	Gratiana
Πρεΐδις.	Preïdis
Ἀργαμώ.	Argamô
Παυλίμανδρα.	Paulimandra
Τζάσκλις.	Tzasclis
Πούλχρα Θεοδώρα.	Pulchra Theodora
Τόμις.	Tomis [2]
Κρέας.	Creas
Κατασσοῦ.	Catassû
Νίσκονις.	Nisconis
Νοβεϊουστινιανά.	Novejustiniana
Πρεσιδίω.	Presidiô
Ἐργαμία.	Ergamia

[1] Cf. *Itin. Ant.* 224. 4.
[2] Tomi, the place of Ovid's banishment.

B 309

ΛΟΓΟΣ Ε′

P 94

α′. Τὰ μὲν δὴ ἐν πάσῃ Εὐρώπῃ δεδημιουργημένα Ἰουστινιανῷ βασιλεῖ ἐς ὅσον οἷόν τε ἦν ἐν τῷ ἔμπροσθεν λόγῳ ἐρρήθη. ἐς δὲ τῆς Ἀσίας 2 τὰ λειπόμενα ἰτέον ἡμῖν. ὅσα μὲν οὖν πόλεών τε καὶ φρουρίων ἐρύματα, ἑτέρας τε οἰκοδομίας κατὰ τὴν ἑῴαν πεποίηται χώραν, ἐξ ὁρίων τῶν Μηδικῶν P 95 ἄχρι που ἐς Παλμύραν πόλιν, ἣ ἐν Φοίνιξι τοῖς ἐπὶ Λιβάνου τυγχάνει οὖσα, ἤδη μοι ἔμπροσθεν 3 δεδηλῶσθαι οἶμαι. ἐν δέ γε τῷ παρόντι καὶ ὅσα κατὰ τὴν ἄλλην Ἀσίαν καὶ Λιβύην αὐτῷ εἴργασται ἢ τειχιζομένῳ ἢ τὰ[1] κατὰ τὰς ὁδοὺς ἐπανορθοῦντι δυσπάριτα καὶ κινδύνων ἀτεχνῶς ἔμπλεα (πῇ μὲν ὀρῶν ἐπικειμένων κρημνώδη ὄντα, πῇ δὲ ποταμοῦ γειτονήματι τοὺς παραπίπτοντας ἀποπνίγοντα), ἢ πόλεων ἰωμένῳ παθήματα πάντα, ἐρῶν ἔρχομαι ἀρχόμενος ἐνθένδε.

B 310 4 Χῶρόν τινα πρὸ τῆς Ἐφεσίων πόλεως ἐν ὀρθίῳ κείμενον ξυνέβαινεν εἶναι, λοφώδη οὐ γεώδη[2] οὐδὲ δυνατὸν ἀφεῖναι καρπούς, εἴ τις πειρῷτο, ἀλλὰ 5 σκληρόν τε καὶ τραχὺν ὅλως. ἐνταῦθα νεὼν οἱ ἐπιχώριοι ἐν τοῖς ἄνω χρόνοις Ἰωάννῃ τῷ ἀποστόλῳ ἀνέθηκαν, θεολόγος δὲ τὴν ἐπίκλησιν ὁ ἀπόστολος οὗτος ὠνόμασται, ἐπεὶ τά γε ἀμφὶ τῷ θεῷ ἄμεινον αὐτῷ ἢ κατὰ ἀνθρώπου δεδιήγηται 6 φύσιν. τοῦτον δὴ τὸν νεὼν Ἰουστινιανὸς βασιλεὺς βραχύν τε ὄντα καὶ καταπεπονηκότα τῷ μήκει τοῦ

[1] ἢ τὰ Capps: τὰ V, ἢ A.
[2] λοφώδη οὐ γεώδη Capps, *cf.* V. vi. 2: οὐ γήλοφον.

---

[1] *I.e.* in the province of Phoenicê Libanensis.

BOOK V

i. The buildings erected by the Emperor Justinian in all Europe have been recorded, as far as possible, in the preceding Book. We must now go on to the remaining parts of Asia. All the fortifications of cities and the fortresses, as well as the other buildings which he erected throughout the East, from the boundary of Persia as far as the city of Palmyra, which chances to be in Phoenicia by Lebanon[1]—these, I think, have been sufficiently described by me above.[2] So at present I shall tell also of all that was done by him in the rest of Asia and in Libya, either in fortifying, or in repairing the roads where they were difficult to travel and wholly beset with dangers (sometimes, because mountains towered above them, where they were too steep, sometimes where, since there was a river near by, travellers were caught in it and drowned), or, finally, in repairing all the parts of cities which had become defective—all this I shall proceed to tell, beginning at this point.

There chanced to be a certain place before the city of Ephesus, lying on a steep slope hilly and bare of soil and incapable of producing crops, even should one attempt to cultivate them, but altogether hard and rough. On that site the natives had set up a church in early times to the Apostle John; this Apostle has been named "the Theologian," because the nature of God was described by him in a manner beyond the unaided power of man. This church, which was small and in a ruined condition because of its great age, the Emperor Justinian tore

[2] Books II, III.

χρόνου καθελὼν ἐς τὸ ἔδαφος, ἐς τοσόνδε μεθηρμόσατο μεγέθους καὶ κάλλους, ὥστε δή, ξυνελόντα εἰπεῖν, ἐμφερέστατος καὶ παντάπασιν ἐνάμιλλος τῷ ἱερῷ ἐστιν ὅπερ ἐν πόλει τῇ βασιλίδι τοῖς ἀποστόλοις ἀνέθηκε πᾶσιν, ὥσπερ μοι ἐν τοῖς ἔμπροσθεν δεδήλωται[1] λόγοις.

7 Ταῦτα μὲν ἐν Ἐφέσῳ ἐξείργασται τῷ βασιλεῖ τούτῳ. ἐν Τενέδῳ δὲ ταύτῃ τῇ νήσῳ σωτήριόν τι πόλει τε τῇ βασιλίδι καὶ τοῖς κατὰ θάλασσαν ἐργαζομένοις πεποίηται, ὅπερ ἐγὼ αὐτίκα δηλώσω, τοσοῦτον ὑπειπών· ἡ θάλασσα ἐφ' Ἑλλησπόντου 8 ἐν στενῷ μάλιστα φέρεται· ἄμφω γὰρ αἱ ἤπειροι ἀλλήλαις ὡς ἀγχοτάτω ἐνταῦθα ἰοῦσαι τὴν τοῦ πορθμοῦ ποιοῦνται ἀρχὴν ἀμφὶ Σηστόν τε καὶ Ἄβυδον, ἐπειδάν τε αἱ νέες ἐνταῦθα ἵκωνται, ὅσαι δὴ Κωνσταντινουπόλεως εὐθὺ ἵενται, τῇδε 9 ὁρμίζονται. ἀνάγεσθαι δὲ αὐταῖς ἐνθένδε ἀμήχανά ἐστιν, ὅτι μὴ νότου ἐπιπνεύσαντος ἀνέμου σφίσιν. 10 ἡνίκα οὖν ὁ σιταγωγὸς στόλος ἐκ πόλεως Ἀλεξανδρείας ἐνταῦθα ἴοι, εἰ μὲν ἐμπέσοι τὸ πνεῦμα ἐπίφορον σφίσι, δι' ὀλίγου μὲν οἱ ταύτην τὴν ἐργασίαν διαχειρίζοντες καταίρουσι ταῖς B 311 ναυσὶν ἐς τοὺς Βυζαντίους λιμένας, ἀποφορτιζόμενοι δὲ ἀπαλλάσσονται αὐτίκα δὴ μάλα, ἐφ' ᾧ δὴ πρὸ τῆς τοῦ χειμῶνος ἅπαντες ὥρας δεύτερόν 11 τε καὶ τρίτον διαπεραιώσονται στόλον. ὅσοις δὲ αὐτῶν βουλομένοις ᾖ, καὶ ἄλλο τι τῶν ἐμπολημά-12 των ἐνθένδε ἀντιφορτισάμενοι ἀναστρέφουσιν. εἰ μέντοι ἀπ' ἐναντίας σφίσι τὸ πνεῦμα ἐφ' Ἑλλησπόντου ἴοι, ἐνταῦθα δὴ τῷ τε σίτῳ καὶ ταῖς 13 ναυσὶ σεσηπέναι συνέβαινεν. ἅπερ ἐν προνοίᾳ πεποιημένος Ἰουστινιανὸς βασιλεὺς διαφανῶς

down to the ground and replaced by a church so large and beautiful, that, to speak briefly, it resembles very closely in all respects, and is a rival to, the shrine which he dedicated to all the Apostles in the imperial city, which I have described above.[1]

This, then, was done at Ephesus by this Emperor. And on our neighbouring island of Tenedos he made provision for the welfare of the imperial city and of those who labour on the sea, which I shall describe immediately, with the following introductory observation. The sea at the Hellespont flows in a very narrow channel, since the two continents at that point approach very close to each other and form the beginning of the strait at Sestus and Abydus; and when ships which are holding a direct course for Constantinople reach that point, they cast anchor. And it is impossible for them to go further unless they have a wind blowing from the south. So when the grain fleet from Alexandria reaches that point, if the wind blows favourably for them, those having this business in charge bring their ships into the harbours of Byzantium in a short time; then, after discharging their cargoes, they depart with all speed, so that before the winter season they may complete a second or even a third voyage. And those of them who wish to do so, also take on a return cargo of merchandise from that place before they sail back. If, however, the wind blew against them at the Hellespont, it came about that both the grain and the ships had to lie there rotting. The Emperor Justinian took this situation under consideration, and made a clear demonstration

[1] I. iv. 9 ff. A plan of the Church of St. John is reproduced above, p. 47.

[1] δεδήλωται V: δεδιήγηται A.

ἐπιδέδεικται ὡς ἀνθρώπῳ ἂν ἀμήχανον οὐδὲν γένοιτο, οὐδ᾽ ἢν τοῖς χαλεπωτάτοις ἀνταγωνίζοιτο.
14 ἐν Τενέδῳ γὰρ τῇ νήσῳ, ἣ τοῦ πορθμοῦ ἄγχιστά
P 96 ἐστι, σιτῶνα ἐπετεχνήσατο τῷ παντὶ στόλῳ ἀποφορτίσασθαι διαρκῶς ἔχοντα, εὖρος μὲν οὐχ ἧττον ἢ ποδῶν ἐνενήκοντα, μῆκος δὲ ποδῶν ὀγδοήκοντα καὶ διακοσίων, ἐς ὕψος τε[1] ἄφατον
15 ἐπιεικῶς κατατείνοντα. οὗ δὴ τῷ βασιλεῖ ἐξειργασμένου, ὁπηνίκα ἂν τοῦ δημοσίου σίτου παραπομποὶ ἐνταῦθα ἰόντες ἀνέμων ἐναντιώμασι συμποδίζοιντο, οἵδε τὸν φόρτον ἐν τῷ σιτῶνι καταθέμενοι τούτῳ καὶ χαίρειν φράσαντες τῷ τε βορρᾷ καὶ ζεφύρῳ πολλά, καὶ εἴ τις ἄλλος ἀπ᾽ ἐναντίας αὐτοῖς ἐνταῦθα ἴοι, ἐς πλοῦν ἕτερον
16 συσκευάζονται. καὶ αὐτοὶ μὲν εὐθὺς εἰς τὰ οἰκεῖα κομίζονται, χρόνῳ δὲ ὕστερον, ὁπηνίκα ἂν τὸν ἐνθένδε ἀπόπλουν ἐς Βυζάντιον ἐν ἐπιτηδείῳ γενέσθαι ξυμβαίη, πλοίοις ἑτέροις τὸν σῖτον ἐκ Τενέδου διακομίζουσιν οἷς ἐπίκειται ἡ τιμὴ[2] αὕτη.

β΄. Ἔστι δέ τις ἐν Βιθυνοῖς πόλις, Ἑλένης ἐπώνυμος οὖσα τῆς Κωνσταντίνου βασιλέως μητρός. ἐκ ταύτης γὰρ τὴν Ἑλένην ὡρμῆσθαί φασι, κώμης οὐκ ἀξιολόγου τὰ πρότερα οὔσης.
2 ᾗπερ τὰ τροφεῖα Κωνσταντῖνος ἐκτίνων ὀνόματι
B 312 μὲν καὶ ἀξιώματι πόλεως τὸ χωρίον δεδώρηται τοῦτο, οὐ μέντοι οὐδὲν οὐδὲ βασιλικὸν οὐδὲ μεγαλοπρεπὲς τῇδε πεποίηται, ἀλλὰ τῇ μὲν κατασκευῇ ἐπὶ τῆς προτέρας διέμεινε τύχης, κεκόμψευται δὲ μόνῳ τῷ πόλις κεκλῆσθαι καὶ τῇ ἐπωνυμίᾳ τῆς
3 τροφίμου Ἑλένης ἀποσεμνύνεται. ὁ δὲ καθ᾽ ἡμᾶς βασιλεύς, ὥσπερ τὴν ἀγνωμοσύνην ἀπολογού-

that nothing could prove impossible for man, even though he have the greatest difficulties to contend with. For on the island of Tenedos, which is very close to the strait, he contrived a granary large enough to allow the whole fleet to unload, in breadth not less than ninety feet and in length two hundred and eighty feet, and rising to a very great height. And since the time when this was built by the Emperor, whenever the carriers of public grain reach that point and are impeded by adverse winds, they deposit their cargoes in this storehouse, and bidding a happy farewell to the north wind and the west, and to any other wind that might impede them there, they make ready for the next voyage. And they for their part go straightway about their business, and at a later time, when the voyage from there to Byzantium comes to be practicable, those who are assigned to this office convey the grain from Tenedos in other ships.

ii. There is a certain city in Bithynia which bears the name of Helen,[1] mother of the Emperor Constantine, for they say that Helen was born in this village, which formerly was of no consequence. But Constantine, by way of repaying the debt of her nurture, endowed this place with the name and dignity of a city. However, he has built there nothing in a style of imperial magnificence, but, though the place remained outwardly as it had been before, it will now boast merely of the title of city and pride itself in the name of its foster-child Helen. But our Emperor, as if seeking to excuse his imperial pre-

[1] Helenopolis; originally called Drepanon, now Hersek.

---

[1] τε Wahler: δὲ. [2] τιμῇ V: σπουδῇ A.

μενος τοῦ τῆς βασιλείας προπάτορος, πρῶτα μὲν ὕδατος ἀπορίᾳ πιεζομένην τὴν πόλιν ἰδὼν καὶ δίψῃ ἐπιεικῶς δεινῇ ἐχομένην, ὀχετὸν αὐτοσχεδιάζει[1] θαυμάσιον οἷον, ὕδωρ τε αὐτῷ παρέχεται ἀπροσδόκητον ἰδεῖν, τοῖς τῇδε ἀνθρώποις οὐ πιεῖν μόνον, ἀλλὰ καὶ λούεσθαι ἱκανῶς ἔχον, καὶ ὅσα ἄλλα τρυφῶσιν ἄνθρωποι εὐπορίαν[2] κατακόρως
4 ὕδατος ἔχοντες. πρὸς δὲ καὶ βαλανεῖον αὐτοῖς ἐν δημοσίῳ πεποίηται οὐ πρότερον ὄν, ἕτερόν τε ἀνῳκοδομήσατο διεφθαρμένον τε καὶ εἰκῆ κείμενον τῷ τε σπανίζειν, ᾗπέρ μοι ἐρρήθη, τοῦ ὕδατος καὶ
5 τῷ ἀπημελῆσθαι καταπεσὸν ἤδη. ἀλλὰ καὶ ἱερὰ καὶ βασίλεια καὶ στοὰς καὶ καταλυτήρια ταῖς ἀρχαῖς ἐδείματο τῇδε, καὶ τοῖς ἄλλοις ἐπιδέδεικται αὐτὴν πόλιν εὐδαίμονα.

6 Ταύτης δὲ ῥεῖ τῆς πόλεως ἄγχιστα ποταμός, ὅνπερ ὁμωνύμως τῷ σχήματι Δράκοντα καλοῦσιν
7 οἱ ἐπιχώριοι. περιστρέφεται γὰρ ἑλισσόμενος ἐφ᾽ ἑκάτερα καὶ ἀπ᾽ ἐναντίας αὐτῷ[3] ἀντιπεριάγων[4] τὰς δίνας, σκολιῷ τε τῷ ῥοθίῳ, πῇ μὲν ἐν δεξιᾷ,
P 97 πῇ δὲ ἐν ἀριστερᾷ προσιών· ὥστε ἀμέλει διαβαίνειν αὐτὸν πλεῖν ἢ εἰκοσάκις ἐπάναγκές ἐστι
8 τοῖς τῇδε ἰοῦσι.[5] πολλοῖς τε οὕτω διεφθάρθαι ξυνέβαινε τοῦ ποταμοῦ ἐξαπιναίως παρὰ τὰ
9 ξυνειθισμένα πλημμύροντος. πρὸς δὲ καὶ δάσος ἀμφιλαφὲς καὶ καλάμου τῇδε φυομένου μέγα τι χρῆμα συμποδίζον αὐτοῦ τὴν ἐπὶ τὴν θάλασσαν
B 313 ἐκβολὴν χαλεπώτερον αὐτὸν ἐσκευωροῦντο εἶναι
10 τοῖς ἐκείνῃ χωρίοις. χρόνῳ γοῦν οὐ πολλῷ πρότερον, ὄμβρων οἱ ἐπιγενομένων πολλῶν, λιμνάζων τε καὶ κυρτούμενος καὶ σκεδαννύμενος

[1] αὐτοσχεδιάζει Haury: αὐτὸς σχεδιάζει.

decessor's want of propriety, first of all observed that the city was suffering from shortage of water and was cruelly oppressed by thirst, and so he improvised a marvellous aqueduct and provided it with an unlooked-for supply of water, sufficient for the people there not only to drink but also to use for bathing and for all the other luxuries in which men indulge who have an unstinted supply of water. Besides this he made for them a public bath which had not existed before, and he rebuilt another which was damaged and lay abandoned, and already lay in ruin because of the scarcity of water which I have mentioned and because of neglect. Nay more, he built here churches and a palace and stoas and lodgings for the magistrates, and in other respects he gave it the appearance of a prosperous city.

Close to this city flows a river which the natives call Dracon from the course which it follows. For it twists about and winds from side to side, reversing its whirling course and advancing with crooked stream, now to the right and now to the left. Consequently it is actually necessary for visiting there to cross it more than twenty times. Thus it has come about that many have lost their lives when the river has risen in sudden flood. Furthermore, a dense wood and a great expanse of reeds which grew there used to obstruct its exit to the sea and made it more troublesome for the regions round about. Indeed, not long ago, when it had been swollen by heavy rains, it backed up and rose in flood and spread far out over

---

[2] *εὐπορίαν* V : *εὐπορίας* A.
[3] *αὑτῷ* Dewing : *αὐτῷ*.
[4] *ἀντιπεριάγων* A : *ἀντιρεῖ ἄγων* V.
[5] *ἰοῦσι* A : *οὖσι* V.

ἐπὶ πλεῖστον τῆς γῆς, ἀνήκεστα κακὰ εἴργασται.
11 χωρία τε γὰρ παμπληθῆ καθεῖλε προρρίζους τε ἀμπέλους, ἔτι μέντοι ἐλαίας τε καὶ δένδρων ἄλλων παντοδαπῶν ἀνάριθμα πρέμνα, πρὸς δὲ καὶ τὰς οἰκίας αἳ πρὸ τοῦ περιβόλου τῆς πόλεως ἐτύγχανον οὖσαι, πάθεσί τε ἄλλοις ὑπερμεγέθεσι
12 τοὺς ἐπιχωρίους ἐπέτριψεν. οὗσπερ ἐποικτισάμενος Ἰουστινιανὸς βασιλεὺς ἐπενόει[1] τοιάδε. τὰ μὲν ἄλση περικαθήρας καὶ τὸν κάλαμον ἐκτεμὼν ἅπαντα, ἐλευθέρας ποιεῖσθαι τῷ ποταμῷ ξυνεχώρησε τὰς ἐς τὴν θάλασσαν ἐκβολάς, ὡς μηκέτι αὐτῷ διασκεδάννυσθαι ἐπάναγκες εἴη· τὰ δὲ ὄρη κατὰ μέσον ἀποτεμὼν ἃ δὴ ἀνέχει ἀμφὶ τὰ ἐκείνῃ χωρία, ἐν ταῖς πρότερον ἀποτόμοις καὶ κρημνώδεσι χώραις ὁδὸν ἁμαξιτὸν ἐξειργάσατο.
13 ταύτῃ τε τοῦ ποταμοῦ τὴν διάβασιν οὐκ ἀναγκαίαν ἐκ τοῦ ἐπὶ πλεῖστον τοῖς ἐνταῦθα οὖσι πεποίηκεν εἶναι. καὶ γεφύρας δύο ἐς ἄγαν εὐρείας τῷ ποταμῷ τούτῳ ἐντέθειται, καὶ ἀπ᾿ αὐτοῦ ἀκινδύνως αὐτὸν διαβαίνουσι τὸ λοιπὸν ἅπαντες.

γʹ. Οἷα δὲ καὶ τὴν ἐν Βιθυνοῖς Νίκαιαν ἐξείργασται ἀγαθὰ εἰπεῖν ἄξιον. πρῶτα μὲν τὴν ὀχεταγωγίαν, παντάπασί τε διεφθαρμένην καὶ τὴν χρείαν ὡς ἥκιστα παρεχομένην, ἀνανεωσάμενος ἅπασαν,[2] ὕδασι τὴν πόλιν κατακορῆ διεπράξατο
2 εἶναι. ἔπειτα δὲ ἱερά τε καὶ μοναστήρια τὰ
3 μὲν γυναιξὶ τὰ δὲ ἀνδράσιν ἐδείματο. καὶ τὰ ἐκείνῃ βασίλεια, ἐκ μοίρας ἤδη καταπεπτωκότα τινός, ἀνενεώσατο σπουδῇ ἅπαντα, ἔτι μέντοι
B 314 καὶ βαλανεῖον ἐν τῷ καταλυτηρίῳ τῶν βερεδαρίων
4 καλουμένων ἐκ παλαιοῦ διεφθαρμένον. ταύτης δὲ τῆς πόλεως ἐς τὰ πρὸς δύοντα ἥλιον ὡς

the land and caused irreparable damage. For it ruined many districts, uprooted vines and even olive trees and countless other trees of all sorts, trunks and all, not sparing the houses which stood outside the circuit-wall of the city and inflicting other severe losses upon the inhabitants. And feeling compassion for them, the Emperor Justinian devised the following plan. He cleared off the woods and cut all the reeds, thus allowing the river a free outlet to the sea, so that it might no longer be necessary for it to spread out. And he cut off in the middle the hills which rise there, and built a waggon-road in places which formerly were sheer and precipitous; and in this way he made the crossing of the river for the most part unnecessary for those who dwelt there. Also he placed two very broad bridges over this river, and in consequence everyone now crosses it without danger.

iii. And it is proper to tell of the benefits which he also bestowed upon Nicaea in Bithynia. First of all, he restored the entire aqueduct, which was completely ruined and was not satisfying the need, and thus he provided the city with abundant water. Then he built churches and monasteries, some for women and some for men. And the palace there, which already had in part collapsed, he carefully restored throughout; and he also restored a bath at the lodgings of the *veredarii*, as they are called,[1] which had lain in ruin for a long time. To the west of this city and very close to it a torrent is wont to

[1] Couriers of the Public Post.

---

[1] ἐπενόει V: ἐποίει A. [2] ἅπασαν V: ξύμπασαν A.

ἀγχοτάτω χειμάρρους ὡς τὰ πολλὰ ἐπισκήπτειν φιλεῖ, ἄπορον ὅλως ἐργαζόμενος τὴν ταύτῃ ὁδόν.
5 καὶ γέφυρα μέν τις ἐνταῦθα πεποίηται τοῖς πάλαι ἀνθρώποις, ἣ προϊόντος χρόνου προσβάλλουσαν οὐδαμῆ ἐνεγκοῦσα τὴν τοῦ χειμάρρου ἐπιρροὴν (ἐπεὶ οὐκ ἐν ἐπιτηδείῳ διασκευασθεῖσα ἐτύγχανεν) ὑπεχώρησέ τε τῷ ῥοθίῳ βιαζομένῳ καὶ ἀπιοῦσα σὺν αὐτῷ ᾤχετο, οὐδὲ ἴχνος αὐτῆς
P 98 6 ἐν τῷ χώρῳ ἀπολιποῦσα, οὗ πρότερον ἦν. βασιλεὺς δὲ Ἰουστινιανὸς γέφυραν ἐπήξατο ἐνταῦθα ἑτέραν ἐς τόσον ὕψους τε καὶ εὔρους διήκουσαν, ὥστε δὴ αὐτῆς οὐδὲ κατὰ πολλοστημόριον τὴν προτέραν οὖσαν γεγονέναι δοκεῖν, ἣ τὸν χειμάρρουν, ἡνίκα μορμύρει, κατὰ πολὺ ὑπεραίρουσα ἐν τῷ βεβαίῳ διασώζεται τοὺς ταύτῃ ἰόντας.

7 Ἐν δὲ Νικομηδείᾳ τὸ βαλανεῖον τὸν Ἀντωνῖνον ἀνενεώσατο· μοῖρα γὰρ αὐτοῦ ἡ ἀξιολογωτάτη καταπεπτώκει, μεγέθει τοῦ ἔργου ἀπροσδόκητος
8 ὅτι δὴ ἀνοικοδομηθήσεται γεγενημένη. ὁ μέγας δὲ ποταμὸς οὗτος, ὅνπερ Σάγαριν καλοῦσι νῦν, σφοδρῷ μὲν κατιὼν ἐς ἄγαν τῷ ῥείθρῳ, ἐπὶ μέσης δὲ πεφυκὼς ἄβυσσος, εὐρυνόμενος δὲ θαλάσσῃ ἴσα, διαγέγονε μὲν τά γε εἰς γέφυραν ἀνέπαφος πᾶσιν, ἐξ οὗ γεγόνασιν ἄνθρωποι, ἀκάτων δὲ συνδέοντες πλῆθος καὶ φορμηδὸν αὐτὰς ἀλλήλαις ἐναρμοσάμενοι, ἐνταῦθα διαπορθμεύεσθαι τολμῶσι πεζοί, ὥσπερ ποτὲ δέει τοῦ Ξέρξου τὸν Ἑλλήσποντον ὁ τῶν Μήδων στρατός.
9 ἀλλὰ καὶ τοῦτο οὐκ ἀνεπικινδύνως αὐτοῖς γίνεται. πολλάκις γὰρ ὁμοῦ τοῖς δεσμοῖς συλλαβὼν τὰς ἀκάτους ἁπάσας, εἶτα τὴν διάβασιν ἀνεχαίτισε
B 315 10 τοῖς τῇδε ἰοῦσι. βασιλεὺς δὲ Ἰουστινιανὸς γέφυ-

smite almost everything, making the road there altogether impassable. A bridge had been built over it by the men of earlier times, which, as time went on, was quite unable to withstand the impact of the torrent, since it had not been properly constructed, as it chanced; and finally it yielded to the pressure of the surge and was swept away with it without leaving a trace in the spot where previously it had stood. But the Emperor Justinian planted another bridge there of such height and breadth, that the previous bridge seemed to have been only a fraction of the new one in point of size; and this bridge rises high above the torrent when it is in flood and keeps in perfect safety those passing that way.

In Nicomedia[1] he restored the bath called Antoninus, for the most important part of it had collapsed, and because of the great size of the building it had not been expected that it would be rebuilt. And that great river which they now call the Sagaris,[2] rushing down, as it does, with its impetuous stream and having a great depth at the centre and broadening out till it resembles a sea, had always been, since the world began, left untouched by a bridge; instead they lash together a great number of skiffs and fasten them together cross-wise, and people venture to cross these on foot, as once the Persian host, through fear of Xerxes,[3] crossed the Hellespont. But even this is not without danger for them, for many a time the river has seized and carried away all the skiffs, together with their cables, and thus put a stop to the crossing of travellers. But the Emperor Justinian has now under-

[1] Modern Ishmid.
[2] *I.e.* Sangarius; modern Sakaria.
[3] Cf. Herodotus VII. 56.

ραν αὐτῷ ἐγκεχείρηκεν ἐποικοδομεῖσθαι τανῦν. ἀρξάμενός τε τοῦ ἔργου ἤδη [1] πολλὴν ἐς αὐτὸ διατριβὴν ἔχει· ὅπερ εὖ οἶδα ὅτι [2] ὑποτελέσει οὐ πολλῷ ὕστερον, τεκμηριούμενος ὅτι δὴ αὐτῷ τὰ 11 ἔργα συνεπιλαμβάνεται ὁ θεὸς ἅπαντα. οὐκοῦν ἀπέραντον αὐτῷ ἐνθύμημα οὐδὲν ἔμεινεν ἐς τόδε τοῦ χρόνου, καίτοι ἐπὶ πλείστοις τὸ κατ' ἀρχὰς τοῖς ἀμηχάνοις ἐγχειρεῖν ἔδοξεν.

12 Ἔστι δέ τις ἐν Βιθυνοῖς ὁδὸς ἐς τὰ Φρυγῶν ἤθη ἐνθένδε ἰόντι, ἔνθα δὴ ἀνθρώποις τε ἀναρίθμοις καὶ ζῴοις ἑτέροις [3] χειμῶνος ὥρᾳ διολωλέναι 13 ξυνέβαινε· γεώδης γὰρ ὑπεράγαν ἡ χώρα οὖσα, μὴ ὅτι ὄμβρων ἐξαισίων καταρραγέντων ἢ χιόνων πολλῶν ἐπικεχυμένων τε καὶ διαλυθεισῶν ἐν εὐχώρῳ, ἀλλὰ καὶ ψεκάδων ἐπιπεπτωκυιῶν, ἂν οὕτω τύχῃ, ἐς τέλμα βαθὺ καὶ ἀπόρευτον ξυνισταμένη, τάς τε ὁδοὺς τεναγώδεις ἐργαζομένη, τοὺς 14 τῇδε ἰόντας ἐκ τοῦ ἐπὶ πλεῖστον ἀπέπνιγεν. ἀλλὰ καὶ τοῦτον αὐτός τε μεγαλοφροσύνῃ ψυχῆς καὶ ἡ βασιλὶς Θεοδώρα τὸν κίνδυνον τοῖς παριοῦσι 15 διέλυσαν. ἐς ἡμέρας γὰρ ὁδοῦ ἥμισυ εὐζώνῳ ἀνδρὶ λίθοις παμμεγέθεσι σκέπας τῇ λεωφόρῳ ἀπεργασάμενοι ἐπὶ στερρᾶς τῆς ὁδοῦ παριέναι διεσκευάσαντο τοὺς τῇδε ἰόντας. ταῦτα μὲν Ἰουστινιανῷ βασιλεῖ ταύτῃ ἐξείργασται.

16 Πηγαὶ δὲ θερμῶν φύσει ἐν Βιθυνοῖς ὑδάτων ἀναβλυστάνουσιν ἐν χώρῳ ὅνπερ ἐπονομάζουσι 17 Πύθια. ταύτας [4] ἔχουσι παραψυχὴν ἄλλοι τε

[1] ἤδη V: om. A.
[2] ὅτι V: om. A.
[3] ἑτέροις V: om. A.
[4] ταύτας A: ταύτην V.

taken the project of building a bridge over the river. Having already begun the task, he is now much occupied with it; and I know well that he will complete it not long hence, finding my assurance in this—that God coöperates with him in all his labours.[1] Indeed it is for this reason that no project of his has failed of fulfilment up to the present time, though in the beginning he has seemed in many cases to be undertaking impossible things.

There is a certain road in Bithynia leading from there into the Phrygian territory, on which it frequently happened that countless men and beasts too perished in the winter season. The soil of this region is exceedingly deep; and not only after unusual deluges of rain or the final melting of very heavy snows, but even after occasional showers it turns into a deep and impassable marsh, making the roads quagmires, with the result that travellers on that road were frequently drowned. But he himself and the Empress Theodora, by their wise generosity, removed this danger for wayfarers. They laid a covering of very large stones over this highway for a distance of one half a day's journey for an unencumbered traveller[2] and so brought it about that travellers on that road could get through on the hard pavement. These things, then, were done by the Emperor Justinian in this way.

A natural spring of hot water bubbles up in Bithynia, at a place known as Pythia.[3] This spring is used as a cure by many and particularly by the

[1] This work was done in A.D. 559–60; see the Introduction, p. ix, and an inscription published by H. Grégoire in *Byzantion*, iv., 1927–8, pp. 465–468.

[2] About ten miles.

[3] Modern Yalova.

πολλοὶ καὶ διαφερόντως Βυζάντιοι, ἄλλως τε
18 ὅσοις νοσώδεσι συμβαίνει εἶναι. ἔνθα δὴ πολυτέλειαν ἐπιδέδεικται βασιλεῖ πρέπουσαν· βασίλειά τε γὰρ ᾠκοδομήσατο οὐ πρότερον ὄντα καὶ λου-
P 99 19 τρῶνα ἐν δημοσίῳ τῶν ἐκεῖ φυομένων θερμῶν
B 316 ὑδάτων πεποίηται. πηγάς τε ποτίμων ὑδάτων ὡς ἑκαστάτω[1] ἀποβλυζούσας ἐς τόνδε τὸν χῶρον ὀχεταγωγίᾳ διακομίσας, τὸν πρότερον ἐνταῦθα
20 ἐπιχωριάζοντα περιεῖλεν αὐχμόν. ἀλλὰ καὶ τοῦ ἀρχαγγέλου τὸ τέμενος καὶ τὸ τῶν νοσούντων ἀναπαυστήριον, μείζω τε καὶ κατὰ πολὺ ἐπιφανέστερα κατεστήσατο.

δʹ. Ἔστι δὲ ποταμὸς ἐν Γαλάταις, ὅνπερ καλοῦσιν οἱ ἐπιχώριοι Σίβεριν, τῶν μὲν καλουμένων Συκεῶν ἄγχιστα, πόλεως δὲ Ἰουλιουπόλεως ἀπὸ σημείων μάλιστα δέκα ἐς τὰ πρὸς ἀνίσχοντα
2 ἥλιον. ὃς δὴ πολλάκις ἐξαπιναίως ἀρθεὶς ἐπὶ μέγα τῶν ἐκείνῃ ὁδῷ ἰόντων πολλοὺς ἔφθειρεν.
3 οἷσπερ ὁ βασιλεὺς ἀπαγγελλομένοις συνταραχθεὶς διακωλυτὴς τοῦ κακοῦ τὸ λοιπὸν γέγονε, τὸν μὲν ποταμὸν γεφυρώσας ἔργῳ ἰσχυρῷ καὶ οἵῳ πλημμύροντι ποταμῷ μάχεσθαι, ἕτερον δὲ τοῖχον ἐν προβόλου σχήματι τῆς γεφύρας ἐς τὰ πρὸς ἕω πεποιημένος· ὃν δὴ πρόμαχον[2] καλοῦσιν οἱ
4 ταῦτα σοφοί. καὶ νεὼν δὲ αὐτῆς ᾠκοδομήσατο ἐς τὰ πρὸς δύοντα ἥλιον τοῖς παριοῦσι σωτήριον
5 χειμῶνος ὥρᾳ ἐσόμενον. ταύτης δὲ Ἰουλιουπόλεως[3] τὸν περίβολον ἠνώχλει τε καὶ κατέσειε

[1] ἑκαστάτω V: ἑκάστω A.
[2] πρόμαχον V: πρόβολον A.
[3] ταύτης δὲ ἰουλιοπόλεως V: τῆς δὲ ἡλιουπόλεως A.

people of Byzantium, especially those who chance to be afflicted by disease. There indeed he displayed a prodigality befitting an Emperor. He built a palace which had not been there before, and made a public bath supplied by the hot water which rises there. And by means of an aqueduct he conveyed to this place springs of drinking-water which gush forth at a very great distance, and thus abated the lack of sweet water which previously had prevailed there. In addition to this, he enlarged and made much more notable both the Church of the Archangel and the infirmary for the sick.

iv. There is a river in Galatia which the natives call Siberis, close to the place called Syceae, about ten miles from Juliopolis[1] toward the east. This river often rose suddenly to a great height and caused the death of many of those travelling that way. The Emperor was disturbed when these things were reported to him, and he put a stop to the evil thenceforth by bridging the river with a strong structure capable of resisting the stream when in flood, and by adding another wall in the form of a jetty on the eastward side of the bridge; such a thing is called a *promachon* or breakwater by those skilled in these matters.[2] He also built a church to the west of the bridge to be a refuge for travellers in the winter season. As to this Juliopolis, its circuit-wall used to be disturbed and weakened by a river which

[1] Originally called Gordiucomê; the river is probably the Hierus.

[2] This structure was evidently a starling added to the pier to reduce the currents and eddies created by the presence of the pier which would wash the bed of the stream and endanger the foundations.

ποταμός, ἀμφὶ τὰ πρὸς ἑσπέραν παραρρέων.
6 ἀλλὰ καὶ αὐτὸν διεκώλυσεν ὁ βασιλεὺς οὗτος, ἀντιτείχισμα τῷ περιβόλῳ ἐπὶ πόδας οὐχ ἧσσον ἢ πεντακοσίους καταστησάμενος. ταύτῃ τε τὸ τῆς πόλεως ἔρυμα οὐκέτι ἐπικλυζόμενον διεσώσατο.

7 Ἐν δὲ Καππαδόκαις ἐποίει τάδε. Καισάρεια μὲν πόλις ἐνταῦθα μεγίστη τε καὶ πολυάνθρωπος ἐκ παλαιοῦ τυγχάνει οὖσα. τεῖχος δὲ αὐτὴν περιέβαλλε τῷ ὑπερβάλλοντι τῆς ἀμετρίας ἐπιμα-
8 χώτατόν τε ὂν καὶ ἀφύλακτον ὅλως. χώρας τε
B 317 γὰρ οὔ τι ἀναγκαίας τῇ πόλει περιεβάλλετο μέγα τι χρῆμα, καὶ τῇ ἐς ἄγαν περιουσίᾳ τοῖς ἐπιβουλεύ-
9 ουσιν εὐέφοδον ἦν. λόφοι γὰρ ἐνταῦθα ἐπανεστήκασιν ὑψηλοί, οὐκ ἄγχιστά πη ἀλλήλων, ἀλλὰ κατὰ πολὺ ἄποθεν· οὕσπερ ὁ τῆς πόλεως οἰκιστὴς ἐντὸς τοῦ περιβόλου καταλαβεῖν ἐν σπουδῇ ἔχων, ὡς μὴ ἐπιτείχισμα κατ' αὐτῆς εἶεν, τῷ τῆς ἀσφαλείας ὀνόματι τὰ σφαλερώτατα ἐξειργάσατο.
10 πεδία τε γὰρ πολλὰ καὶ κήπους ἐτειχίσατο, καὶ
11 σκοπέλους τε καὶ θρεμμάτων νομάς. ἔνθα δὴ οὐδὲ χρόνῳ ὕστερον οἰκοδομήσασθαί τι οἱ τῇδε ἄνθρωποι ἔγνωσαν, ἀλλ' ἐφ' οὗπερ ἦν σχήματος
12 ἔμεινεν. εἰ δέ που καὶ οἰκία τετύχηκεν εἶναι, ταῦτα δὴ[1] ἀγείτονα κατὰ μόνας ὄντα διαγεγόνασιν
13 ἐς τόδε τοῦ χρόνου. καὶ οὔτε τὰ φυλακτήρια κατὰ λόγον τοῦ περιβόλου ἐς τὴν αὐτοῦ ἐξικνεῖσθαι
P 100 φυλακὴν εἶχεν, οὔτε αὐτοῦ ἐπιμελεῖσθαι τοσοῦδε ὄντος ἐν δυνάμει ἐγίνετο τοῖς τῇδε ἀνθρώποις. ἀτείχιστοί τε δοκοῦντες εἶναι περίφοβοι διηνεκὲς
14 ἦσαν. ἀλλὰ βασιλεὺς Ἰουστινιανὸς τὰ μὲν οὐκ

[1] δὴ Haury: δέ.

flows along its western side. This Emperor, however, put a stop to that, by setting up a wall flanking the circuit-wall for a distance of not less than five hundred feet, and in this way he preserved the defences of the city, which were no longer deluged by the stream.

In Cappadocia he did the following. The city of Caesarea[1] there has been from ancient times very large and populous. But it was surrounded by a wall which, by reason of its immoderate extent, was very easy to attack and altogether impossible to defend. For it embraced a great expanse of land which was not at all necessary to the city, and by reason of its excessive size it was easily assailable by an attacking force. High hills rise there, not standing very close together, but far apart. These the founder of the city was anxious to enclose within the circuit-wall so that they might not be a threat against the city; and in the name of safety he did a thing which was fraught with danger. For he enclosed within the walls many open fields and gardens as well as rocky cliffs and pasture-lands for flocks. However, even at a later time the inhabitants of the place decided not to build anything in this area, but it remained exactly as it had been. Even such houses as did chance to be in this district have continued to be isolated and solitary up to the present day. And neither could the garrison maintain a proper defence in keeping with the extent of the wall, nor was it possible for the inhabitants to keep it in repair, seeing that it was so large. And because they seemed to be unprotected, they were in constant terror. But the Emperor Justinian tore down the unneces-

[1] Originally Mazica, near Mt. Argaeus.

ἀναγκαῖα τοῦ περιβόλου περιελών, τὴν δὲ πόλιν ὡς ἀληθῶς ἐρύματι ἐς τὸ ἀσφαλὲς περιστείλας, ὀχύρωμα μὲν κατεστήσατο ἀμαχώτατον εἴ τις προσίοι, διαρκεῖ δὲ αὐτὸ φυλακτηρίῳ ἐπέρρωσε. Καισαρεῦσι μὲν οὖν τοῖς ἐν Καππαδόκαις οὕτω τὴν ἀσφάλειαν διεσώσατο.

15 Ἦν δέ τι φρούριον ἐν Καππαδόκαις Μωκησὸς ὄνομα, ἐν μὲν τῷ ὁμαλεῖ κείμενον, σαθρὸν δὲ οὕτω γεγενημένον ὥστε δὴ αὐτοῦ τὰ μὲν κατα-16 πεπτώκει, τὰ δὲ ἔμελλεν. ὅπερ Ἰουστινιανὸς βασιλεὺς καθελὼν τεῖχος ᾠκοδομήσατο κομιδῇ μέγα ἐς τὰ πρὸς ἑσπέραν τοῦ πάλαι φρουρίου ἐν χωρίῳ ἀνάντει τε καὶ λίαν ὀρθίῳ καὶ ἀμηχάνῳ 17 προσελθεῖν, εἴ τις προσίοι. ἔνθα δὴ καὶ ἱερὰ B 318 τεμένη πολλὰ καὶ ξενῶνας καὶ λουτρῶνας ἐν δημοσίῳ ἐδείματο καὶ ὅσα ἄλλα ἐνδείκνυται 18 πόλιν εὐδαίμονα. ἐξ οὗ δὴ καὶ εἰς μητροπόλεως ἀξίωμα ἦλθεν· οὕτω γὰρ πόλιν τὴν πρώτην τοῦ ἔθνους καλοῦσι Ῥωμαῖοι. τὰ μὲν οὖν ἐν Καππαδόκαις τοιαῦτα ἐγεγόνει.

ε'. Ἐκ πόλεως δὲ Ἀντιοχείας, ἣ νῦν Θεούπολις ἐπικέκληται, ἐς Κιλικίαν ἰόντι παρ' αὐτὴν μάλιστα τὴν ὁδὸν προάστειόν ἐστι, Πλατανὼν ὄνομα· ταύτης δὴ τῆς πόλεως οὐ πολλῷ ἄποθεν τρίβος τε ἦν ἐκ παλαιοῦ σφιγγομένη ἐκ τῶν παρατεταμένων ὀρῶν ἐν στενῷ μάλιστα, ὄμβρων δὲ αὐτὴν ἐς χρόνου μῆκος ἐπικλυσάντων ἐξίτηλος ἐκ τοῦ ἐπὶ πλεῖστον γεγενημένη μετὰ κινδύνων τὰς διεξόδους παρείχετο ποιεῖσθαι τοῖς τῇδε 2 ἰοῦσιν. ἅπερ ἐπεὶ Ἰουστινιανὸς βασιλεὺς ἀκοῇ

[1] It became the capital of Cappadocia Tertia.

sary portions of the circuit-wall and surrounded the city with a wall which was truly safe, and made defences which would be thoroughly impregnable in case of attack; and then he made the place strong by the addition of a sufficient garrison. Thus did he guarantee the safety of the inhabitants of Caesarea in Cappadocia.

There was a certain fortress in Cappadocia, Mocesus by name, situated on level ground, but it had sunk into such a state of disrepair that part of it had fallen down and the rest was on the point of doing so. All this the Emperor Justinian pulled down, and he built a very strong wall to the west of the old fortress, on a site which lay above a very steep slope and was quite inaccessible if anyone should try to attack it. There too he built many churches and hospices and public baths and all the other structures that are the mark of a prosperous city. Consequently it rose even to the rank of a metropolis,[1] for thus the Romans call the leading city of a province. These things, then, were done in Cappadocia.

v. As one goes from the city of Antioch, which is now called Theopolis, into Cilicia, there is a suburb lying very close to the road, Platanôn by name;[2] and not far from this city lay a path which had long been compressed into a very narrow track by the overhanging mountains; and after being washed by rains for a long time it was destroyed for the most part and afforded only dangerous passage to travellers. When the Emperor Justinian heard of this, he

[2] This place is mentioned also by Theophanes, A.M. 6004, I, p. 156, 15 De Boor. Procopius evidently refers to work done in the Beilan Pass, though this is so far from Antioch that Platanôn could not properly be called a suburb of the city.

ἔλαβεν, ἐν βουλῇ τε καὶ προνοίᾳ πάσῃ πεποιημένος,
3 ἄκεσιν εὐθὺς τοῦ κακοῦ εὕρετο. χρήματα γὰρ προέμενος ἀριθμοῦ κρείττονα, ὄρη τε τὰ ἐκείνῃ ἀνέχοντα ἐπὶ μακρότατον ἐκτεμὼν ἅπαντα καὶ νενικηκὼς τὰ ἀμήχανα, ὁδὸν ἁμαξήλατον ἐκ τοῦ παραλόγου καὶ τοῦ παραδόξου καὶ τὰ[1] πρόσθεν ἀπόκρημνα ἔν τε τῷ ὑπτίῳ καὶ τῷ ἀνειμένῳ διεσκευάσατο, διαφανῶς ἐνδειξάμενος ὡς γνώμῃ προμηθεῖ καὶ χρημάτων ὑπερορώσῃ οὐδὲν ἀνθρώπῳ ἄπορον γένοιτο. τοῦτο μὲν οὖν ταύτῃ ἐξείργασται.

4 Πόλις δέ πού ἐστιν ἐν Κίλιξιν ἡ Μοψουεστία, τοῦ μάντεως, ὥς φασιν, ἐκείνου τοῦ παλαιοῦ
P 101 ἔργον. ταύτην ποταμὸς παραρρεῖ Πύραμος, τῇ μὲν πόλει γινόμενος ἐγκαλλώπισμα, γεφύρᾳ δὲ
5 μόνῃ διαβατὸς ὤν. χρόνου δὲ πολλοῦ ἐπιρρεύσαντος πεπονηκέναι τῆς γεφύρας τὰ πλεῖστα ξυνέβη. ἐῴκει τε πεσουμένοις αὐτίκα δὴ μάλα, καὶ τοῖς διαβαίνουσι διὰ τοῦτα ὁ θάνατος ἐν
B 319 6 ὀφθαλμοῖς ἦν. πρᾶγμά τε εἰς σωτηρίαν ἐπινενοημένον τοῖς πάλαι ἀνθρώποις, τῇ τῶν προεστηκότων ὀλιγωρίᾳ ἐγίνετο κινδύνου τε πολλοῦ καὶ
7 φόβου αἰτία. ὁ δὲ καθ᾽ ἡμᾶς βασιλεὺς τὰ διερρυηκότα ἐπανορθώσας σπουδῇ ἅπαντα τῇ τε γεφύρᾳ καὶ τοῖς παριοῦσι τὴν ἀσφάλειαν ἀνεσώσατο, τήν τε πόλιν ἀπέδειξεν αὖθις τὴν ἐκ τοῦ ποταμοῦ ἀκινδύνως ἀναδουμένην εὐπρέπειαν.

8 Ἔστι δέ τις μετ᾽ αὐτὴν Ἄδανα πόλις, ἧς δὴ ἐς τὰ πρὸς ἀνίσχοντα ἥλιον ποταμὸς φέρεται

[1] καὶ τὰ V: κατὰ A.

---

[1] Mopsus, who made an oracle at Mallus; the city lies near modern Missis.

took the matter under careful consideration and straightway found a remedy for the trouble. He spent a sum of money past reckoning, cutting through, for a great distance, all the mountains which rose there to a great height and overcoming impossible obstacles; and he constructed a waggon-road, contrary to all reason and expectation, making flat and open ground of what had previously been broken by precipices, thereby clearly demonstrating that nothing could prove impossible for a man of discerning judgment who was ready to disregard expense. This, then, was done as I have said.

There is in Cilicia a certain city called Mopsuestia, said to be the work of that ancient seer.[1] Alongside this flows the Pyramus River, which, while it adds beauty to the city, can be crossed only by a bridge. But as much time passed it came about that the greater part of the bridge had suffered; indeed it seemed to be on the point of falling at any moment and for this reason death faced those who crossed it. Thus a structure which was devised by the men of former times for the preservation of life came, by reason of the negligence of the authorities, to be a source of great danger and a thing to be feared. But our Emperor with great care set right all the damaged parts and once more restored the safety of the bridge and of those who crossed it, and caused the city to plume itself[2] again, and without risk, on the river's beauty.

Beyond it there is a certain city named Adana,[3] on the eastern side of which the Sarus[4] River flows,

[2] Literally " bind its brow," as with a wreath.
[3] Also its modern name.
[4] The Sagrus, now called Sangro.

Σάρος ὄνομα, ἐκ τῶν ἐν Ἀρμενίοις ὀρῶν κατιών.
9 ναυσίπορος δὲ ὁ Σάρος ἐστὶ καὶ ἀνδράσι πεζοῖς οὐδαμῇ ἐσβατός. γέφυρα οὖν ἐκ παλαιοῦ τῇδε ὑπερφυής τε ἀποτετόρνευται καὶ λόγου ἀξία.
10 γεγένηται δὲ τρόπῳ τοιῷδε. λίθων μὲν εὐμεγέθων οἰκοδομίαι πολλαχῇ τοῦ ποταμοῦ ἐκ τῆς γῆς ἐπανεστήκασιν ἐς μέγα τι πάχος διήκουσαι, καὶ τῷ ποταμῷ κατὰ μὲν τὸ εὖρος ξυνεξικνούμεναι, τὸ δέ γε ὕψος πολλῷ ὑπερβάλλουσαι τῷ ὑπεραίροντι.
11 ὕπερθέν τε δυοῖν[1] κατὰ μέσον ἁψῖδες ἐν τῷ μετεώρῳ ἐπηρμέναι ἀνέχουσιν ὕψους ἐς μέγα τι χρῆμα. ταύτης δὲ τῆς τῶν λίθων ξυνθήκης, ἣ κατὰ τὸ ὕδωρ οὖσα ἐτύγχανεν, ἅτε ῥοθίῳ μαχομένης πολλῷ, ἐπὶ χρόνου μῆκος ἀπέραντον
12 ὅσον διεφθάρθαι τὰ πλεῖστα ξυνέβη οὐκ εἰς μακράν τε ἡ γέφυρα πᾶσα τῷ ποταμῷ ἐμπεσεῖσθαι ἐπίδοξος ἦν. ἐγίνετό τε ἀεὶ ἐν εὐχῇ τῶν διαβαινόντων ἑκάστῳ ἐν τῇ κατ᾽ αὐτὸν διαβάσει τὴν τοῦ χρόνου στιγμὴν διαμεῖναι μόνον ἐν τῷ
13 βεβαίῳ τὴν γέφυραν. ἀλλὰ βασιλεὺς Ἰουστινιανὸς ἑτέραν τινὰ τῷ ποταμῷ πορείαν ὀρύξας, ἐκεῖσε μὲν αὐτὸν ἐπὶ καιροῦ μεταπορεύεσθαι διωθήσατο, ὕδατος δὲ χωρὶς τὴν οἰκοδομίαν λαβών, ἧσπερ ἐπεμνήσθην ἀρτίως, καὶ αὐτῆς τὰ
B 320 πεπονθότα περιελὼν ἀνῳκοδομήσατο οὐδεμιᾷ μελλήσει, τόν τε ποταμὸν αὖθις ἐς τὴν πρόσθεν ὁδὸν ἐπανήγαγεν, ἣν κοίτην καλοῦσι. ταῦτα μὲν οὖν τῇδε κεχώρηκε.

14 Κύδνος δὲ ποταμὸς κατὰ πόλιν μέσην Ταρσὸν φέρεται. καὶ χρόνον μὲν τὸν ἄλλον οὐδὲν ἄχαρι διαπεπραγμένος φαίνεται πώποτε, ἅπαξ δὲ αὐτῷ ξυνηνέχθη ποτὲ τὰ ἀνήκεστα διεργάσασθαι ἐξ

coming down from the mountains of Armenia. The Sarus is navigable and quite impossible for men on foot to ford. So in ancient times an enormous and very notable bridge was constructed here. It was built in the following fashion. At many points in the river piers of massive blocks of stone were reared upon its bed, built to a great thickness and forming a line extending across the entire width of the stream and in height rising far above high water. Above each pair of piers spring arches which rise to a great height, spanning the open space between them. The portion of this masonry which chanced to be below the water and so was constantly battered by its powerful current had, in a space of time beyond reckoning, come to be mostly destroyed. So the whole bridge appeared likely after no long time to fall into the river. It had come to be always the prayer of each man who crossed the bridge that it might remain firm if only during the moment of his crossing. But the Emperor Justinian dug another channel for the river and forced it to change its course temporarily; and then getting the masonry which I have just mentioned free from the water and removing the damaged portions, he rebuilt them without any delay and then returned the river to its former path, which they call the "bed." Thus then were these things done.

At Tarsus, the Cydnus River flows through the middle of the city. It appears that in general it had caused no damage at any time, but on one occasion it chanced that it did cause irreparable loss, for the

---

[1] δυοῖν Dindorf: δυεῖν.

15 αἰτίας τοιᾶσδε. τοῦ μὲν καιροῦ ἀμφὶ τροπὰς ἐαρινὰς ἦν·[1] νότος δὲ ἄνεμος ἐξαπιναίως ἐπιπνεύσας πολὺς τὰς χιόνας διέλυσε πάσας, αἷς δὴ χειμῶνος ὥρᾳ ἐπιπεσούσαις τὸ ὄρος ὁ Ταῦρος
16 ἐκεκάλυπτο σχεδόν τι ὅλον. ῥύακες οὖν ὑδάτων πανταχόθεν ξυνέρρεον τῶν ἐκείνῃ σκοπέλων, αἵ τε χαράδραι χειμάρρους ἀφίεσαν πᾶσαι, καὶ κρήναις πολλαῖς αἵ τε ὑπώρειαι καὶ οἱ πρόποδες ὀρῶν τῶν
17 Ταυρείων κατάρρυτοι ἦσαν. τούτοις οὖν ὁ Κύδνος τοῖς ὕδασι κυματίας γεγενημένος, ἐπεὶ ἐς αὐτὸν ἐν γειτόνων ὄντα ἐπεσέβαλλον,[2] ἅμα δέ οἱ καὶ ὄμβρων ἐπιγενομένων πολλῶν, τὰ μὲν Ταρσέων προάστεια πάντα, ὅσα πρὸς μεσημβρίαν τετραμ-
P 102 μένα ἐτύγχανε, κατακλύσας εὐθὺς ἐξίτηλα τὸ παράπαν ἐποίει· ἐπὶ τὴν πόλιν δὲ μορμύρων ᾔει καὶ τὰς γεφύρας βραχείας οὔσας περιελὼν τάς τε ἀγορὰς συνεῖχεν ἁπάσας τάς τε ἀγυιὰς ὑπερέβλυζε καὶ τοῖς οἴκοις καὶ ὑπερῴοις ἐπιπολάζων ἐπὶ
18 μέγα ἐχώρει. νύκτα τε καὶ ἡμέραν ἡ πόλις ὅλη ἐν κινδύνῳ διαγέγονε καὶ σάλῳ τοιούτῳ, καὶ μόλις ἐν ὑστάτῳ ὁ ποταμὸς οὗτος κατὰ βραχὺ ἀπολωφή-
19 σας ἐν τοῖς εἰωθόσι γέγονεν αὖθις. ἅπερ ἐπεὶ βασιλεὺς Ἰουστινιανὸς ἤκουσεν, ἐπενόει τοιάδε. πρῶτα μὲν ἑτέραν πρὸ τῆς πόλεως διεσκευάσατο τῷ ποταμῷ κοίτην, ὅπως ἐνταῦθα διασχιζόμενος
B 321 ἑκατέρωθί τε μερίζων τὸν ῥοῦν κατὰ ἥμισυ
20 γεγονὼς μάλιστα ἐπὶ Ταρσὸν ἴοι. ἔπειτα δὲ τὰς γεφύρας παρὰ πολὺ εὐρυτέρας πεποιημένος κρείσσους ἀπειργάσατο εἶναι ἢ πλημμύροντι βιασθῆναι

[1] ἦν ἡ ὥρα A.
[2] ἐπεσέβαλλον V: ἐσέβαλλον A.

following reason.[1] It was about the time of the spring equinox, and a strong south wind which arose suddenly had melted all the snow which had fallen through the winter season, blanketing practically the whole Taurus range. Consequently streams of water were pouring down from the heights everywhere and each of the ravines discharged a torrent, and both the summits and the foothills of the Taurus mountains were deluged. So by reason of this water the Cydnus rose in flood, for the streams kept pouring their water into it, since it was close to the mountains, and it was further swollen by heavy rains which fell at the same time; consequently the river flooded and immediately wiped out completely all the suburbs which were situated to the south of the city. Then it went roaring against the city itself, and tearing out the bridges, which were small, it covered all the market-places, flooded the streets, and wrought havoc by entering the houses and rising even to their upper storeys. Night and day the whole city continued in this critical and uncertain situation, and it was only tardily and at length that the river subsided little by little and returned once more to its accustomed level. When the Emperor Justinian learned of this, he devised the following plan. First he prepared another bed for the river above the city, in order that the stream might be separated there into two parts and might divide its volume so that only about half of it should flow toward Tarsus. Then he made the bridges very much broader and so strong that the Cydnus in flood could not sweep them away.

[1] This flood is mentioned in the *Secret History*, xviii. 40.

τῷ Κύδνῳ. ταύτῃ τε διεπράξατο φόβου καὶ κινδύνου ἐκτὸς ἐς πάντα τὸν χρόνον οἰκεῖσθαι τὴν πόλιν.

ϛʹ. Τὰ μὲν οὖν ἐν Κίλιξιν Ἰουστινιανῷ βασιλεῖ ταύτῃ πη ἔσχεν. ἐν δὲ Ἱεροσολύμοις ἱερὸν τῇ θεοτόκῳ ἀνέθηκεν, ᾧπερ ἄλλο εἰκασθῆναι οὐδὲν 2 οἷόν τέ ἐστι. νέαν ἐκκλησίαν καλοῦσι τὸ ἱερὸν οἱ ἐπιχώριοι· ὅπερ δὴ ὁποῖόν ποτέ ἐστιν, ἐγὼ δηλώσω, τοσοῦτον ὑπειπών, ὡς ἡ πόλις ἥδε λοφώδης μέν ἐστιν ἐκ τοῦ ἐπὶ πλεῖστον, οὐ γεώδεις δὲ οἱ λόφοι εἰσίν, ἀλλ' ἔν τε τραχεῖ καὶ ἀποκρήμνῳ ἐπανεστήκασι, τὰς ἀμφόδους ἐν κλίμακος τρόπῳ ἀπὸ τοῦ ὀρθίου ἐς τὸ πρανὲς κατα- 3 τείνοντες. τὰ μὲν οὖν ἄλλα τῆς πόλεως οἰκοδομήματα ἅπαντα ἐφ' ἑνὸς χωρίου συμβαίνει εἶναι, ἢ ἐπὶ λόφου πεποιημένα, ἢ ἐν τῷ χθαμαλῷ κατὰ τὸ ἀναπεπταμένον τῆς γῆς, τοῦτο δὲ μόνον 4 τὸ ἱερὸν οὐ ταύτῃ πη ἔχει.[1] ἐπέστελλε γὰρ αὐτὸ Ἰουστινιανὸς βασιλεὺς ἐν τῷ προὔχοντι γενέσθαι τῶν λόφων, δηλώσας ὁποῖον τά τε ἄλλα δεήσει 5 καὶ τὸ εὖρος αὐτῷ καὶ μῆκος εἶναι. οὐκ ἀπέχρησέ τε κατὰ τὴν βασιλέως ἐπίταξιν πρὸς τοῦ ἔργου τὴν χρείαν ὁ λόφος, ἀλλὰ τοῦ ἱεροῦ τὸ τεταρτημόριον ἀπελέλειπτο πρός τε ἄνεμον νότον καὶ ἀνίσχοντά που τὸν ἥλιον, ἵνα δὴ ὀργιάζειν τοῖς 6 ἱερεῦσι θέμις. διὸ δὴ ἐπενόουν τάδε οἷς τὸ ἔργον τοῦτο ἐπέκειτο. ἀπορριψάμενοι τὰ θεμέλια εἰς γῆς τῆς ὑπτίας τὰ ἔσχατα, οἰκοδόμημα 7 πεποίηνται συνεπανεστηκὸς τῷ σκοπέλῳ. ἐπειδή τε ἄνω κατὰ τὴν ἀκρωνυχίαν ἐγένοντο, τῶν

[1] ἔχει V : ἀνέχει A.

Thus he brought it about that the city stands forever freed from fear and from danger.

vi. Such were the works of the Emperor Justinian in Cilicia. And in Jerusalem he dedicated to the Mother of God a shrine with which no other can be compared.[1] This is called by the natives the "New Church"; and I shall explain of what sort it is, first making this observation, that this city is for the most part set upon hills; however these hills have no soil upon them, but stand with rough and very steep sides, causing the streets to run straight up and down like ladders. All the other buildings of the city chance to lie in one group, part of them built upon a hill and part upon the lower level where the earth spreads out flat; but this shrine alone forms an exception. For the Emperor Justinian gave orders that it be built on the highest of the hills, specifying what the length and breadth of the building should be, as well as the other details. However, the hill did not satisfy the requirements of the project, according to the Emperor's specifications, but a fourth part of the church, facing the south and the east, was left unsupported, that part in which the priests are wont to perform the rites. Consequently those in charge of this work hit upon the following plan. They threw the foundations out as far as the limit of the even ground, and then erected a structure which rose as high as the rock. And when they had raised this up level with

[1] While it has not been possible to identify the site of this church with certainty, traces of such a building have been found on a site between the eastern side of the Jewish quarter and the Haram which corresponds closely with that described by Procopius; see H. Vincent and F.-M. Abel, *Jérusalem*, II (Paris, 1922), pp. 912–919.

τοίχων καθύπερθε θόλους ἐνθέμενοι συνάπτουσι τὴν οἰκοδομίαν τῷ ἄλλῳ τοῦ τεμένους ἐδάφει.
B 322 8 ταύτῃ τε ὁ νεὼς πὴ μὲν ἐπὶ πέτρας ἰσχυρᾶς ἵδρυται, πὴ δὲ ᾐώρηται, τῆς τοῦ βασιλέως δυνάμεως μέγεθος ἄλλο ἐπιτεχνησαμένης τῷ 9 λόφῳ. ταύτης δὲ δὴ τῆς οἰκοδομίας οἱ λίθοι οὐ P 103 10 τοιοίδε εἰσὶ μέγεθος, ὁποίους ἴσμεν. πρὸς γὰρ τοῦ χωρίου τὴν φύσιν οἱ ἐπιδημιουργοὶ τοῦ ἔργου τοῦδε διαμαχόμενοι ὕψος τε ἀντιτεταγμένον τῷ σκοπέλῳ διαπονούμενοι, τῶν ξυνειθισμένων ὠλιγωρηκότες ἁπάντων ἐπὶ τὰ παράδοξα καὶ ὅλως 11 ἀγνῶτα τῶν ἐπιτηδευμάτων ἐχώρουν. πέτρας οὖν ὑπερμεγέθεις ἐκ τῶν ὀρῶν ὑποτεμνόμενοι ἅπερ οὐρανομήκη ἐν τοῖς πρὸ τῆς πόλεως χωρίοις ἀνέχει, ξύσαντές τε αὐτὰς ἐπισταμένως, ἐνταῦθα 12 ἦγον τρόπῳ τοιῷδε. ἁμάξας μὲν ταῖς πέτραις ἐτεκτήναντο μεγέθει ἴσας, ἕνα δὲ λίθον ἐνετίθεντο ἁμάξῃ ἑκάστῃ, βόες τε ἀριστίνδην πρὸς βασιλέως ξυνειλεγμένοι [1] κατὰ τεσσαράκοντα σὺν τῇ ἁμάξῃ 13 τὸν λίθον ἐφεῖλκον. ἀλλ' ἐπεὶ τὰς ἐς τὴν πόλιν φερούσας ὁδοὺς ταύτας δὴ φέρειν τὰς ἁμάξας ἀμήχανα ἦν, ἐκτέμνοντες ἐπὶ πλεῖστον τὰ ὄρη ἐσιτητὰ ταῖς ἐπιγενομέναις ἁμάξαις ἐποίουν, οὕτως τε περιμήκη ἀπειργάσαντο τὸν νεών, ᾗπερ 14 βουλομένῳ τῷ βασιλεῖ ἦν. εὖρός τε αὐτῷ κατὰ λόγον πεποιημένοι, τέγος ἐπιθεῖναι τῷ ἱερῷ ὡς 15 ἥκιστα εἶχον. δρυμούς τε οὖν καὶ δάση πάντα περιιόντες, καὶ εἴ πού τι χωρίον ἠκούετο οὐρανομήκεσι κατάφυτον δένδροις, ὕλην τινὰ εὗρον ἀμφιλαφῆ, κέδρους φέρουσαν ἐς ὕψος ἐξικνουμένας ἀπέραντον ὅσον, αἷς δὴ τὴν ὀροφὴν τῷ νεῷ

the rock they set vaults upon the supporting walls, and joined this substructure to the other foundation of the church. Thus the church is partly based upon living rock, and partly carried in the air by a great extension artificially added to the hill by the Emperor's power. The stones of this substructure are not of a size such as we are acquainted with, for the builders of this work, in struggling against the nature of the terrain and labouring to attain a height to match the rocky elevation, had to abandon all familiar methods and resort to practices which were strange and altogether unknown. So they cut out blocks of unusual size from the hills which rise to the sky in the region before the city, and after dressing them carefully they brought them to the site in the following manner. They built waggons to match the size of the stones, placed a single block on each of them, and had each waggon with its stone drawn by forty oxen which had been selected by the Emperor for their strength. But since it was impossible for the roads leading to the city to accommodate these waggons, they cut into the hills for a very great distance, and made them passable for the waggons as they came along there, and thus they completed the length of the church in accordance with the Emperor's wish. However, when they made the width in due proportion, they found themselves quite unable to set a roof upon the building. So they searched through all the woods and forests and every place where they had heard that very tall trees grew, and found a certain dense forest which produced cedars of extraordinary height, and by means of these they

---

[1] ξυνειλεγμένοι V: ἐξειλεγμένοι A.

ἔθεντο, ὕψος αὐτῷ κατὰ μέτρον πεποιημένοι, ἐς ὅσον τε εὐρύνεται καὶ ἐς τὸ μῆκος ἐξάγεται.

16 Ταῦτα μὲν οὖν δυνάμει τε ἀνθρωπείᾳ καὶ τέχνῃ βασιλεὺς Ἰουστινιανὸς ἐξειργάσατο. ἐπέδωκε δὲ καὶ ἡ τῆς εὐσεβείας ἐλπὶς ἀμειβομένη αὐτὸν τῇ τιμῇ, καὶ ξυνεπιλαμβάνουσα τὸ σπούδασμα 17 τοῦτο. τῷ μὲν γὰρ ἱερῷ πανταχόσε κιόνων ἔδει τό τε εἶδος οὐκ ἀποδεόντων τοῦ ἀμφὶ τὸ τέμενος κάλλους καὶ τοιούτων τὸ μέγεθος οἷοι δὴ ὄντες ἀντέχειν ἐς τὸ ἄχθος τῶν ἐγκειμένων 18 σφίσιν ἔμελλον. ἡ δὲ χώρα ἐν τῇ μεσογείᾳ κειμένη τῆς θαλάσσης πολλῷ ἄποθεν, ὄρεσί τε πανταχόθεν ἀποπεφραγμένη ἀποτόμοις τισίν, ᾗπέρ μοι εἴρηται, ἄπορον τοῖς τεκταινομένοις τὸ ἔδαφος ἐποίει κίονας ἑτέρωθεν εἰσκομίζεσθαι. 19 ἀλλὰ βασιλέως δυσφορουμένου τῇ τοῦ ἔργου ἀμηχανίᾳ, λίθου φύσιν ὁ θεὸς ἐπιτηδείως ἐς τοῦτο ἔχουσαν ἐν τοῖς ἄγχιστα ὄρεσιν ἔδειξεν, ἢ οὖσάν τε καὶ κρυπτομένην τὰ πρότερα, ἢ νῦν γενομένην. 20 ἐπ᾽ ἀμφότερα δὲ πιστὸς ὁ λόγος τὴν αἰτίαν ἐπὶ [1] 21 τὸν θεὸν ἀναφέρουσιν. ἡμεῖς μὲν γὰρ ἀνθρωπείᾳ δυνάμει πάντα σταθμώμενοι πολλὰ ἐς τὸ ἀδύνατον ἀποκεκρίσθαι οἰόμεθα, τῷ δὲ θεῷ τῶν πάντων οὐδὲν οὔτ᾽ ἂν ἄπορον οὔτ᾽ ἀμήχανον γένοιτο. 22 κιόνων τοίνυν ἐνθένδε μέγα τι χρῆμα ὑπερμεγεθῶν τε καὶ ἀπομιμουμένων τῷ χρώματι πυρός τινα φλόγα, πανταχόθεν ὑποστηρίζουσι τὸν νεών, οἱ μὲν ἔνερθεν, οἱ δὲ ὕπερθεν, οἱ δὲ ἀμφὶ τὰς στοὰς αἳ περιβάλλουσι τὸ ἱερὸν ὅλον, πλὴν τῆς πρὸς ἕω τετραμμένης πλευρᾶς· ὧνπερ δύο ἑστᾶσι πρὸ τῆς τοῦ νεὼ θύρας ὑπερφυεῖς ἄγαν καὶ τῶν ἐν γῇ 23 τῇ πάσῃ κιόνων ἴσως οὐδενὸς δεύτεροι. στοά

B 323 · P 104

put the roof upon the church, making its height in due proportion to the width and length of the building.

These things the Emperor Justinian accomplished by human strength and skill. But he was also assisted by his pious faith, which rewarded him with the honour he received and aided him in this cherished plan. For the church required throughout columns whose appearance would not fall short of the beauty of the building and of such a size that they could resist the weight of the load which would rest upon them. But the site itself, being inland very far from the sea and walled about on all sides by quite steep hills, as I have said, made it impossible for those who were preparing the foundations to bring columns from outside. But when the impossibility of this task was causing the Emperor to become impatient, God revealed a natural supply of stone perfectly suited to this purpose in the near by hills, one which had either lain there in concealment previously, or was created at that moment. Either explanation is credible to those who trace the cause of it to God; for while we, in estimating all things by the scale of man's power, consider many things to be wholly impossible, for God nothing in the whole world can be difficult or impossible. So the church is supported on all sides by a great number of huge columns from that place, which in colour resemble flames of fire, some standing below and some above and others in the stoas which surround the whole church except on the side facing the east. Two of these columns stand before the door of the church, exceptionally large and probably second to no column in the whole world. Here is added another

[1] ἐπὶ V: ἐς A.

τις ἐκδέχεται ἐντεῦθεν ἑτέρα ἐπὶ τοῦ νάρθηκος
24 ὠνομασμένη, οἶμαι, τῷ μὴ εὐρύνεσθαι. αὐλὴ
μετὰ ταύτην κίοσιν ὁμοίοις ἐν τετραπλεύρῳ
ἀνεχομένη· θύραι μέταυλοι ἱεροπρεπεῖς οὕτως,
B 324 ὥστε μηνύουσι τοῖς ἔξω ἰοῦσιν ὁποίῳ ποτὲ
θεάματι ἐντυχεῖν μέλλουσι. προπύλαια[1] τὸ
ἐνθένδε θαυμάσια οἷα, καί τις ἐπὶ κιόνων δυοῖν[2]
25 ἐπαιρομένη ἀψὶς ἐς ἄφατον ὕψος. προϊόντι δὲ
πρόσω ἡμίκυκλα δύο, ἀλλήλοις ἀντιπρόσωπα
ἑκατέρωθεν τῆς ἐπὶ τὸ ἱερὸν ὁδοῦ ἑστᾶσι· ξενῶνες
δὲ τῆς ἑτέρας ἐφ' ἑκάτερα δύο, Ἰουστινιανοῦ
βασιλέως ἔργον· ἅτερος μὲν ξένοις ἐνδημοῦσι
καταλυτήριον, ὁ δὲ δὴ ἕτερος ἀναπαυστήριον
26 νοσοῦσι πτωχοῖς. τοῦτον δὲ τὸν τῆς θεοτόκου
νεὼν Ἰουστινιανὸς βασιλεὺς καὶ προσόδῳ ἐτίμησε
χρημάτων μεγάλων. τὰ μὲν οὖν ἐν Ἱεροσολύμοις
Ἰουστινιανῷ βασιλεῖ πεπραγμένα[3] ταύτῃ πῃ ἔσχεν.

ζ'. Ἔστι δὲ πόλις ἐπὶ Παλαιστίνης, Νεάπολις
ὄνομα· ἐφ' ἧς δὴ ὄρος ὑψηλὸν ἀνέχει, Γαριζὶν
2 ὄνομα. τοῦτο δὲ τὸ ὄρος κατ' ἀρχὰς μὲν οἱ
Σαμαρεῖται εἶχον· ὡς εὐξόμενοί τε ἀνέβαινον ἐς
τὴν τοῦ ὄρους ὑπερβολήν, οὐδένα ἀνιέντες καιρόν·
οὐχ ὅτι νεών τινα ἐνταῦθα ᾠκοδομήσαντο πώποτε,
ἀλλὰ τὴν ἀκρώρειαν αὐτὴν σεβόμενοι ἐτεθήπεσαν
3 πάντων μάλιστα. ἡνίκα δὲ Ἰησοῦς ὁ τοῦ θεοῦ
παῖς ἐν σώματι ὢν τοῖς τῇδε ἀνθρώποις ὡμίλει,

[1] After προπύλαια Maltretus added δὲ.
[2] δυοῖν Haury: δυεῖν.
[3] πεπραγμένα added by Hoeschel.

colonnaded stoa which is called the narthex, I suppose because it is not broad.[1] Beyond this is a court with similar columns standing on the four sides. From this there lead doors to the interior (*metauloi thyrai*) which are so stately that they proclaim to those walking outside what kind of sight they will meet within. Beyond there is a wonderful gateway (*propylaia*) and an arch (*apsis*), carried on two columns, which rises to a very great height. Then as one advances there are two semi-circles (*hemikykla*) which stand facing each other on one side of the road which leads to the church, while facing each other on the other side are two hospices, built by the Emperor Justinian. One of these is destined for the shelter of visiting strangers, while the other is an infirmary for poor persons suffering from diseases. And the Emperor Justinian endowed this Church of the Mother of God with the income from a large sum of money. Such were the activities of the Emperor Justinian in Jerusalem.

vii. In Palestine there is a city named Neapolis,[2] above which rises a high mountain, called Garizin. This mountain the Samaritans originally held; and they had been wont to go up to the summit of the mountain to pray on all occasions, not because they had ever built any temple there, but because they worshipped the summit itself with the greatest reverence. But when Jesus, the Son of God, was in the body and went among the

[1] *Cf.* above, I. iv. 7 and note.
[2] Modern Nablous.

γέγονεν αὐτῷ πρὸς γυναῖκα τῶν τινα ἐπιχωρίων διάλογος· ταύτῃ τε ἐπὶ τῷ ὄρει πυνθανομένῃ ὑπεῖπεν ὡς χρόνῳ ὕστερον οὐχ οἱ Σαμαρεῖται προσκυνήσουσιν ἐν τούτῳ τῷ ὄρει, ἀλλ' ἐνταῦθα αὐτὸν οἱ ἀληθινοὶ προσκυνηταὶ προσκυνήσουσι, τοὺς Χριστιανοὺς παραδηλώσας· ἐγένετό τε 4 προϊόντος τοῦ χρόνου ἔργον ἡ πρόρρησις. οὐ γὰρ οἷόν τε ἦν μὴ οὐχὶ ἀψευδεῖν τὸν ὄντα[1] θεόν. 5 ἐγένετο δὲ τρόπῳ τοιῷδε· ἐπὶ Ζήνωνος βασιλεύον- B 325 τος ἀθρόοι ἐξαπιναίως οἱ Σαμαρεῖται γενόμενοι ἐπεισπηδῶσιν ἐν Νεαπόλει τοῖς Χριστιανοῖς ἐν τῇ ἐκκλησίᾳ τὴν Πεντηκοστὴν καλουμένην ἑορτὴν ἄγουσι, καὶ αὐτῶν τε πολλοὺς διαχρῶνται, καὶ ὅσπερ ἦν αὐτοῖς ἐπίσκοπος τότε, Τερεβίνθιος P 105 ὄνομα, καταλαβόντες ἐπὶ τῆς ἱερᾶς ἑστῶτα τραπέζης, καὶ ἱερουργοῦντα τὰ ἄρρητα ξίφεσι παίοντες, ἄλλως τε συγκόπτουσι καὶ τοὺς τῶν χειρῶν ἀφαιροῦνται δακτύλους, ἔς τε τὰ μυστήρια ὕβρισαν, ὡς δρᾶσαι μὲν Σαμαρείταις προσήκει, 6 σιωπᾶν δὲ ἡμῖν. ὁ δὲ ἱερεὺς οὗτος αὐτίκα ἐν Βυζαντίῳ γενόμενος, τῷ τότε βασιλεῖ ἐς ὄψιν ἥκων, ἐπέδειξέ τε τὸ πάθος καὶ τὰ ξυνενεχθέντα σημάνας καὶ τοῦ Χριστοῦ τῆς προρρήσεως ὑπομνήσας, τιμωρὸν αὐτὸν ἐφ' ἅπασιν ἐδεῖτο 7 γενέσθαι. Ζήνων δὲ βασιλεὺς τοῖς ξυμπεπτωκόσι ξυνταραχθείς, κόλασίν τε ἀποχρώντως ἐς τοὺς τὰ δεινὰ δεδρακότας πεποίηται οὐδεμιᾷ ὀκνήσει· ἔκ τε ὄρους τοῦ Γαριζὶν τοὺς Σαμαρείτας ἐξελάσας, εὐθὺς Χριστιανοῖς τε αὐτὸ παραδίδωσιν, ἐκκλησίαν

[1] ὄντα V: ὄντως A.

---

[1] *Gospel of John*, IV.

people there, He had a conversation with a certain woman who was a native of the place.[1] And when this woman questioned Him about the mountain, He replied that thereafter the Samaritans would not worship on this mountain, but that the true worshippers (referring to the Christians), would worship Him in that place; and as time went on the prediction became a fact. For it was not possible that He who was God should not utter truth. And it came about as follows. During the reign of Zeno,[2] the Samaritans suddenly banded together and fell upon the Christians in Neapolis in the church while they were celebrating the festival called the Pentecost, and they destroyed many of them, and they struck with their swords the man who at that time was their Bishop, Terebinthius by name, finding him standing at the holy table as he performed the mysteries; and they slashed at him and cut off the fingers from his hand; and they railed at the mysteries, as is natural for Samaritans to do, while we honour them with silence. And this priest straightway came to Byzantium and appeared before the ruling Emperor and displayed what he had suffered, setting forth what had happened and reminding the Emperor of the prophecy of Christ; and he begged him to avenge all that had been done. The Emperor Zeno was greatly disturbed by what had happened, and with no delay inflicted punishment in due measure upon those who had done the terrible thing. He drove out the Samaritans from Mt. Garizin and straightway handed it over to the Christians, and building a church

[2] A.D. 474–491.

τε ἄνω δειμάμενος τῇ θεοτόκῳ ἀνέθηκε, τειχισάμενος τὸ ἱερὸν τοῦτο[1] δῆθεν τῷ λόγῳ, τὸ δὲ
8 ἀληθὲς ἀποτριγχώσας. καὶ φρουρὰν στρατιωτῶν κατεστήσατο, κάτω μὲν ἐν τῇ πόλει πολλῶν, ἐν δὲ τῷ τειχίσματι καὶ τῇ ἐκκλησίᾳ οὐ πλέον ἢ
9 δέκα. οἷς δὴ Σαμαρεῖται ἀχθόμενοι ἤσχαλλον μὲν ἐς τὰ μάλιστα καὶ δυσφορούμενοι ἀπηξίουν τὰ σφίσι παρόντα, δέει δὲ τῷ ἐκ βασιλέως
10 δυσωπούμενοι σιωπῇ εἴχοντο. προϊόντος δὲ χρόνου, Ἀναστασίου τὴν αὐτοκράτορα ἀρχὴν ἔχοντος,
11 τοιόνδε τι ξυνηνέχθη γενέσθαι. τινὲς τῶν Σαμαρειτῶν, γυναικὸς ὑποθήκῃ ἀναπεισθέντες, ἀναβαίνουσι μὲν παρὰ δόξαν κατὰ τὸ τοῦ ὄρους κρημνῶδες, ἐπεὶ τῆς ἀνόδου ᾗ ἐκ τῆς πόλεως ἐνταῦθα ἄγει
B 326 ἐς τὸ ἀκριβὲς φυλασσομένης, ἐνθένδε αὐτοῖς
12 ἀποπειρᾶσθαι τῆς ἀναβάσεως ἀδύνατα ἦν. ἐν δὲ τῇ ἐκκλησίᾳ ἐξαπιναίως γενόμενοι κτείνουσι μὲν τοὺς ἐνταῦθα φρουρούς, μετακαλοῦσι δὲ τοὺς ἐν
13 τῇ πόλει Σαμαρείτας φωνῇ ἐξαισίᾳ. οἱ δὲ τοὺς στρατιώτας δειμαίνοντες συνεπιτίθεσθαι τοῖς ἐγκε-
14 χειρηκόσιν οὐδαμῇ ἤθελον. οὐ πολλῷ τε ὕστερον ὁ τὴν χώραν ἐπιτροπεύων (Προκόπιος δὲ ἦν ἐξ Ἐδέσσης πόλεως, ἀνὴρ λόγιος) τοὺς τὰ δεινὰ
15 δεδρακότας συλλαβὼν ἔκτεινε. τοῦ μέντοι ὀχυρώματος οὐδ᾽ ὥς[2] τις λόγος ἢ πρόνοια παρὰ τοῦ
16 βασιλέως τηνικάδε γεγένηται. ἀλλὰ νῦν Ἰουστινιανὸς βασιλεύς, καίπερ τοὺς Σαμαρείτας ἐκ τοῦ ἐπὶ πλεῖστον ἐπὶ τὸ εὐσεβέστερον μεταθέμενος καὶ καταστησάμενος Χριστιανοὺς εἶναι, τὸ μὲν

[1] τοῦτο Maltretus: τούτῳ.
[2] οὐδ᾽ ὥς Maltretus: οὐχ ὥς V, οὐδ᾽ ὅς A.

on the summit he dedicated it to the Mother of God, putting a barrier, as it was made to appear, around this church, though in reality he erected only a light wall of stone. And he established a garrison of soldiers, placing a large number in the city below, but not more than ten men at the fortifications and the church. The Samaritans resented this, and chafed bitterly in their vexation and deplored their condition, but through fear of the Emperor they bore their distress in silence. But at a later time, when Anastasius[1] was holding the imperial office, the following happened. Some of the Samaritans, incited by a woman's suggestion, unexpectedly climbed the steep face of the mountain, since the path which leads up from the city was carefully guarded and it was impossible for them to attempt the ascent by that route. Entering the church suddenly, they slew the guards there and with a mighty cry summoned the Samaritans in the city. They, however, through fear of the soldiers, were by no means willing to join the attempt of the conspirators. And not long afterwards the governor of the district (he was Procopius of Edessa, a man of learning) arrested the authors of the outrage and put them to death. Yet even after that no thought was taken for the fortifications, and no provision for proper defence was made at that time by the Emperor. But during the present reign, although the Emperor Justinian has converted the Samaritans for the most part to a more pious way of life and has made them Christians, he

[1] A.D. 491–518.

παλαιὸν τῆς ἐν τῷ Γαριζὶν ἐκκλησίας τείχισμα[1] ἐφ᾽ οὗπερ ἦν σχήματος εἴασεν ἀποτετριγχωμένον, ᾗπέρ μοι εἴρηται, ἑτέρῳ δὲ αὐτὸ ἔκτοσθεν τείχει περιβαλὼν ἄμαχον διεπράξατο παντάπασιν εἶναι. 17 ἐνταῦθα δὲ καὶ ἱερὰ πέντε Χριστιανῶν ἀνενεώσατο πρὸς τῶν Σαμαρειτῶν καταφλεχθέντα. ταῦτα μὲν οὖν τῇδε εἴργασται.

P 106 η΄. Ἐν δὲ τῇ πάλαι μὲν Ἀραβίᾳ, νῦν δὲ Παλαιστίνῃ τρίτῃ καλουμένῃ, χώρα μὲν ἔρημος ἐπὶ μακρὸν κατατείνει, καρπῶν τε καὶ ὑδάτων καὶ πάντων ἀγαθῶν ἄφορος. καὶ ὄρος ἀπότομόν τε καὶ δεινῶς ἄγριον ἀποκρέμαται ἄγχιστά πη τῆς Ἐρυθρᾶς καλουμένης θαλάσσης, Σινὰ ὄνομα. 2 οὐδὲν δέ μοι ἀμφὶ τοῖς ἐκείνῃ χωρίοις ἀναγράψασθαι ἀναγκαῖον ἐνταῦθα τοῦ λόγου, ἐπεὶ ἅπαντά μοι τά τε κατὰ τὴν Ἐρυθρὰν θάλασσαν καὶ τὸν Ἀραβικὸν καλούμενον κόλπον,[2] Αἰθίοπάς τε τοὺς B 327 Αὐξωμίτας καὶ τὰ τῶν Ὁμηριτῶν Σαρακηνῶν γένη ἀκριβολογουμένῳ ἐν τοῖς ὑπὲρ τῶν πολέμων δεδήλωται λόγοις· ἵνα δὴ καὶ τοῦτό μοι διδιήγηται, ὄντινα τρόπον Ἰουστινιανὸς βασιλεὺς τὸν Φοινι- 3 κῶνα προσεποίησε τῇ Ῥωμαίων ἀρχῇ. ταῦτα μὲν οὖν τούτου δὴ ἕνεκα λέγειν ἀφίημι, ὡς μὴ 4 ἀπειροκαλίας ἀνενέγκοιμι δόξαν. ἐν τούτῳ δὲ τῷ Σινᾷ ὄρει μοναχοὶ ᾤκηνται, οἷς ἐστιν ὁ βίος ἠκριβωμένη τις μελέτη θανάτου, ἐρημίας τῆς 5 σφίσι φιλτάτης ἀδεέστερον ἀπολαύουσι. τούτοις δὴ τοῖς μοναχοῖς Ἰουστινιανὸς βασιλεὺς (ἐπεὶ οὐκ εἶχον[3] οὐδὲν ὅτου ἐφεῖντο, ἀλλὰ κρείσσους τῶν

[1] τείχισμα V : προτείχισμα A.
[2] κόλπον V : πόντον A.
[3] εἶχον Hoeschel : εἶχεν.

left the old fortification around the church on Garizin in the form in which it was, that is, merely a barrier, as I have said; but by surrounding this with another wall on the outside he made the place absolutely impregnable. There too he restored five shrines of the Christians which had been burned down by the Samaritans. Thus, then, have these things been done.

viii. In what was formerly called Arabia and is now known as "Third Palestine,"[1] a barren land extends for a great distance, unwatered and producing neither crops nor any useful thing. A precipitous and terribly wild mountain, Sina[2] by name, rears its height close to the Red Sea, as it is called. There is no need at this point in my account to write a description of that region because everything has been set forth in the Books on the Wars,[3] where I gave a full description of the Red Sea and what is called the Arabian Gulf, as well as of the Ethiopians and Auxomitae and the tribes of the Homerite Saracens. At that point I shewed also in what manner the Emperor Justinian added the Palm Groves[4] to the Roman Empire. Therefore I omit mention of these things, that I may not acquire a reputation for bad taste. On this Mt. Sina live monks whose life is a kind of careful rehearsal of death,[5] and they enjoy without fear the solitude which is very precious to them. Since these monks had nothing to crave—for they are superior to all

[1] Under Constantine three provinces were set up, Palaestina Prima in the centre, Secunda in the north, and Tertia in the south.

[2] Or Sinaï, now Jebel-et-Tur.

[3] I. xix. 8.

[4] Inhabited by the Saracens, *Wars*, *loc. cit.* and II. iii. 41.

[5] *Cf.* Plato, *Phaedo* 81.

ἀνθρωπείων ἁπάντων εἰσίν, οὐδέ τι κεκτῆσθαι οὐδὲ θεραπεύειν τὰ σώματα, οὐ μέντοι οὐδὲ ἄλλου ὁτουοῦν ὀνίνασθαι ἐν σπουδῇ ἔχουσιν) ἐκκλησίαν ᾠκοδομήσατο, ἥνπερ τῇ θεοτόκῳ ἀνέθηκεν, ὅπως δὴ αὐτοῖς ἐνταῦθα ἐξῇ εὐχομένοις τε καὶ ἱερω-
6 μένοις διαβιῶναι. ταύτην δὲ τὴν ἐκκλησίαν οὐ κατὰ τοῦ ὄρους ἐδείματο τὴν ὑπερβολήν, ἀλλὰ
7 παρὰ πολὺ ἔνερθεν· ἀνθρώπῳ γὰρ ἐν τῇ ἀκρωρείᾳ διανυκτερεύειν ἀμήχανά ἐστιν, ἐπεὶ κτύποι τε διηνεκὲς καὶ ἕτερα ἄττα θειότερα νύκτωρ ἀκούονται, δύναμίν τε καὶ γνώμην τὴν ἀνθρωπείαν
8 ἐκπλήσσοντα. ἐνταῦθά ποτε τὸν Μωσέα φασὶ πρὸς τοῦ θεοῦ τοὺς νόμους παραλαβόντα ἐξενεγ-
9 κεῖν. ἐς δὲ τοῦ ὄρους τὸν πρόποδα καὶ φρούριον ἐχυρώτατον ὁ βασιλεὺς οὗτος ᾠκοδομήσατο, φυλακτήριόν τε στρατιωτῶν ἀξιολογώτατον κατεστήσατο, ὡς μὴ ἐνθένδε Σαρακηνοὶ βάρβαροι ἔχοιεν ἅτε τῆς χώρας ἐρήμου οὔσης, ᾗπέρ μοι εἴρηται, ἐσβάλλειν ὡς λαθραιότατα ἐς τὰ ἐπὶ Παλαιστίνης χωρία.

10 Ταῦτα μὲν οὖν τῇδε πεποίηται. ὅσα δὲ κἂν τοῖς μοναστηρίοις πεποίηται τοῖς τῇδέ τε καὶ[1] κατὰ τὴν ἄλλην ἑῴαν οὖσιν, αὐτίκα δή μοι ὡς ἐν κεφαλαίῳ γεγράψεται.

B 328
P 107
θʹ. Μοναστήρια μὲν οὖν ἐν Ἱεροσολύμοις ἀνενεώσατο τάδε.

1 τὸ τοῦ ἁγίου Θαλελαίου.
2 τὸ τοῦ ἁγίου Γρηγορίου.
3 τὸ τοῦ ἁγίου Παντελεήμονος ἐν τῇ ἐρήμῳ τοῦ Ἰορδάνου.
4 ξενῶνα ἐν Ἱεριχῷ.

human desires and have no interest in possessing anything or in caring for their bodies, nor do they seek pleasure in any other thing whatever—the Emperor Justinian built them a church which he dedicated to the Mother of God, so that they might be enabled to pass their lives therein praying and holding services. He built this church, not on the mountain's summit, but much lower down. For it is impossible for a man to pass the night on the summit, since constant crashes of thunder and other terrifying manifestations of divine power are heard at night, striking terror into man's body and soul. It was in that place, they say, that Moses received the laws from God and published them. And at the base of the mountain this Emperor built a very strong fortress and established there a considerable garrison of troops, in order that the barbarian Saracens might not be able from that region, which, as I have said, is uninhabited, to make inroads with complete secrecy into the lands of Palestine proper.

Thus, then, were these things done. All that he did in the monasteries of this region and throughout the rest of the East I shall now record in the form of a summary.

ix. These, then, were the monasteries restored in Jerusalem:

The Monastery of St. Thalelaeus.
The Monastery of St. Gregory.
Also St. Panteleëmôn's in the Desert of Jordan.
A hospice in Jerichô.

---

[1] *καὶ* added by Hoeschel.

5 ἐκκλησίαν τῆς θεοτόκου ἐν Ἱεριχῷ.
6 τὸ τῶν Ἰβήρων ἐν Ἱεροσολύμοις.
7 τὸ τῶν Λαζῶν ἐν τῇ ἐρήμῳ Ἱεροσολύμων.
8 τὸ τῆς ἁγίας Μαρίας ἐν τῷ ὄρει τῶν Ἐλαιῶν.
9 τὸ τῆς πηγῆς τοῦ ἁγίου Ἐλισσαίου ἐν Ἱεροσολύμοις.
10 τὸ Σιλέθεως.
11 τὸ τοῦ ἀββᾶ Ῥωμανοῦ.
12 ἐν Βηθλεὲμ τὸ τεῖχος ἀνενέωσε.
13 τὸ τοῦ ἀββᾶ Ἰωάννου ἐν Βηθλεέμ.

14 Φρέατα δὲ ἢ δεξαμενὰς ᾠκοδομήσατο οὕτως·

15 εἰς τὸ τοῦ ἁγίου Σαμουὴλ φρέαρ καὶ τεῖχος.
16 εἰς τὸ τοῦ ἀββᾶ Ζαχαρίου φρέαρ.
17 εἰς τὸ Σωσάννης φρέαρ.
18 εἰς τὸ Ἀφελίου φρέαρ.
19 εἰς τὸ τοῦ ἁγίου Ἰωάννου ἐν τῷ Ἰορδάνῃ φρέαρ.
20 εἰς τὸ τοῦ ἁγίου Σεργίου ἐν ὄρει καλουμένῳ Κισσερῶν φρέαρ.
21 τὸ τεῖχος Τιβεριάδος.
22 τὸ ἐν Βόστρᾳ πτωχεῖον.

23 Φοινίκης·

τὸν οἶκον τῆς θεοτόκου ἐν Πορφυρεῶνι.
24 μοναστήριον τοῦ ἁγίου Φωκᾶ ἐν ὄρει.
25 τὸν οἶκον τοῦ ἁγίου Σεργίου ἐν Πτολεμαΐδι.
26 ἐν Δαμασκῷ οἶκον τοῦ ἁγίου Λεοντίου.
27 ὑπὸ Ἀπάμειαν πτωχεῖον τοῦ ἁγίου Ῥωμανοῦ ἀνενεώσατο.
28 τεῖχος τοῦ μακαρίου Μάρωνος.

A Church of the Mother of God in Jerichô.
The Monastery of the Iberians in Jerusalem.
The Monastery of the Lazi in the Desert of Jerusalem.
The Monastery of St. Mary on the Mount of Olives.
The Monastery of the Spring of St. Elissaeus in Jerusalem.
The Monastery of St. Siletheus.
The Monastery of the Abbot Romanus.
At Bethlehem he restored the wall.
The Monastery of the Abbot John in Bethlehem.

He also built wells or cisterns as follows:

at the Monastery of St. Samuel, a well and a wall;
at that of the Abbot Zacharias, a well;
at that of Susanna, a well;
at that of Aphelius, a well;
at St. John's on the Jordan, a well;
at St. Sergius' on the mountain called Cisserôn, a well;
the wall of Tiberias;
the Poor-house in Bostra.

In Phoenicia, the following:

the House of the Virgin in Porphyreôn;
the Monastery of St. Phocas on the Mount;
the House of St. Sergius in Ptolemaïs;
in Damascus, the House of St. Leontius;
near Apamea,[1] he restored the Poor-house of St. Romanus;
the wall of the Blessed Marôn;

[1] Modern Famieh.

29 ὑπὸ Θεούπολιν τὴν ἐκκλησίαν Δάφνης ἀνενέωσεν.
30 ἐν Λαοδικείᾳ τὸν ἁγίου Ἰωάννου ἀνενέωσε.

31 Μεσοποταμίας·

μοναστήριον τοῦ ἁγίου Ἰωάννου ἀνενέωσε.
32 μοναστήρια Δέλφραχις, Ζηβίνου, Θεοδότου, Ἰωάννου, Σαρμαθῆς, Κυρήνου, Βεγαδαίου.
33 μοναστήριον εἰς τὸ Ἀπάδνας ἐν Ἰσαυρίᾳ.
34 πόλεως Κουρίκου λουτρὸν καὶ[1] πτωχεῖον ἀνενέωσε.
B 329 35 τὸ πτωχεῖον τοῦ ἁγίου Κόνωνος.
36 τὸν ἀγωγὸν αὐτοῦ ἀνενέωσεν ἐν Κύπρῳ.
37 οἶκον τοῦ ἁγίου Κοσμᾶ καὶ Δαμιανοῦ ἐν Παμφυλίᾳ.
38 πτωχεῖον τοῦ ἁγίου Μιχαὴλ ἐν Ἐμπορίῳ ἐπίκλην ἐπινείου πόλεως Πέργης τῆς Παμφυλίας.

B 330

ΛΟΓΟΣ Σʹ.

P 108

αʹ. Ταῦτα μὲν Ἰουστινιανῷ βασιλεῖ τῇδε πεποίηται. ἐν δὲ Ἀλεξανδρείᾳ ἐξείργασται τάδε. Νεῖλος ποταμὸς οὐκ ἄχρι ἐς τὴν Ἀλεξάνδρειαν φέρεται, ἀλλ' ἐπὶ πόλισμα ἐπιρρεύσας ὃ δὴ Χαιρέου ἐπονομάζεται, ἐπ' ἀριστερὰ τὸ λοιπὸν 2 ἵεται, ὅρια τά γε Ἀλεξανδρέων ἀπολιπών. διὸ P 109 δὴ οἱ πάλαι ἄνθρωποι, ὡς μὴ ἀμοιροίη τὸ παράπαν ἡ πόλις, διώρυχα ἐκ τῆς Χαιρέου κατορύξαντες βαθεῖάν τινα βραχείᾳ τοῦ ποταμοῦ ἐς αὐτὴν ἐκροῇ διεπράξαντο ἐσιτητὰ εἶναι. οὗ δὴ καὶ

[1] καὶ added by Maltretus.

near Theopolis, he restored the Church of Daphnê;[1]
in Laodicea, he restored St. John's.

In Mesopotamia:
he restored a Monastery of St. John; the Monasteries of Delphrachis, Zebinus, Theodotus, John, Sarmathê, Cyrenus, Begadaeus;
A Monastery of Apadnas in Isauria;
At the city of Curicum, he restored a Bath and a Poor-house;
the Poor-house of St. Conôn;
He renewed the aqueduct of the same in Cyprus;
The House of Sts. Cosmas and Damian in Pamphylia;
The Poor-house of St. Michael in the Emporium, as it is called, of the harbour-city of Perga in Pamphylia.

BOOK VI

i. Thus were these things done by the Emperor Justinian. And at Alexandria he did the following. The Nile River does not flow all the way to Alexandria, but after flowing to the town which is named from Chaereüs, it then turns to the left, leaving aside the confines of Alexandria. Consequently the men of former times, in order that the city might not be entirely cut off from the river, dug a very deep canal from Chaereüs and thus by means of a short branch made the river accessible to it. There too, as it

[1] The famous suburb of Antioch, *i.e.* Theopolis; *cf. Buildings*, II. x. 2.

ἄλλας τινὰς[1] ἐκροὰς ἐκ λίμνης Μαρίας ἐσβάλλειν
3 ξυμβαίνει. ἐπὶ ταύτης δὲ τῆς διώρυχος μεγάλαις μὲν ναυσὶ πλώϊμα οὐδαμῇ γίνεται, ἐς λέμβους δὲ τὸν Αἰγύπτιον σῖτον ἐκ τῆς Χαιρέου μεταβιβάσαντες[2] οὕσπερ καλεῖν διαρήματα νενομίκασιν, ἔς τε τὴν πόλιν διακομίζουσιν, ἵνα δὴ ἐξικνεῖσθαι δυνατά ἐστι τῷ κατὰ τὴν διώρυχα ποταμῷ, καὶ
B 331 κατατίθενται ἐν χώρῳ ὅνπερ Ἀλεξανδρεῖς καλοῦσι
4 Φιάλην. ἀλλ᾽ ἐπειδὴ τῷ δήμῳ ἐς στάσιν πολλάκις καθισταμένῳ ἐνταῦθα διολωλέναι τῷ σίτῳ ξυνέβη, βασιλεὺς Ἰουστινιανὸς τειχίσματι τόνδε τὸν χῶρον περιβαλὼν τὴν ἐπὶ τῷ σίτῳ ἐπιβουλὴν
5 ἀνεχαίτισε. ταῦτα μὲν οὖν Ἰουστινιανῷ βασιλεῖ ταύτῃ ἐξείργασται.

Ἀλλ᾽ ἐπειδὴ ἐπ᾽ Αἰγύπτου ἡμᾶς ἤγαγε τῆς Λιβύης ὁμόρου τανῦν ὁ λόγος, φέρε δὴ καὶ ὁπόσα διαπέπρακται αὐτῷ ἐνταῦθα δηλώσωμεν, ἐπεὶ καὶ Λιβύην ξύμπασαν ὁ βασιλεὺς οὗτος ὑπὸ βαρβάροις κειμένην εὑρὼν τῇ ἄλλῃ ἐνῆψε Ῥωμαίων ἀρχῇ.

6 Νεῖλος μὲν ὁ ποταμὸς ἐξ Ἰνδῶν ἐπ᾽ Αἰγύπτου φερόμενος δίχα τέμνει τὴν ἐκείνῃ γῆν ἄχρι ἐς θάλασσαν. ἡ δὲ σχιζομένη τῷ ῥείθρῳ καὶ
7 ὀνόμασι διακέκριται τὸ ἐνθένδε δυοῖν.[3] τὰ μὲν

[1] ἐκροῇ . . . τινας, omitted in V, supplied in its margin.
[2] μεταβιβάσαντες V : καταβιβάσατες A.
[3] δυοῖν A : δυεῖν V.

---

[1] Modern Mariut, the ancient Lacus Mareotis.
[2] Trans-shipment of grain in Egypt is mentioned in several papyri, which call it the διέρασις (or διαίρασις) τοῦ δημοσίου πυροῦ; in the documents in which reference is made to the vessels into which the grain was transferred, they are called

chances, are the mouths of certain streams flowing in from Lake Maria.[1] In this canal it is by no means possible for large vessels to sail, so at Chaereüs they transfer the Egyptian grain to boats which they are wont to call *diaremata*,[2] and thus convey it to the city, which they are enabled to reach by way of the canal-route, and they deposit it in the quarter of the city which the Alexandrians call Phialê. But since it often came about that the grain was destroyed in that place by the people rising in sedition, the Emperor Justinian surrounded this district with a wall and so prevented the damage to the grain. Thus were these things done by the Emperor Justinian.

But inasmuch as our account has now led us to Egypt, the close neighbour of Libya, let us now set forth how many things were done by him there also, since this Emperor found all Libya too lying under the power of barbarians and joined it to the remainder of the Roman Empire.

The Nile River, flowing out of India into Egypt, divides that land into two parts as far as the sea. The land, thus divided by the stream, is thenceforth designated by two separate names[3]: the region on

διεράματα (*cf.* F. Oertel, *Die Liturgie*, Leipzig, 1917, p. 130). The spelling in the present passage may be an error of the author or of a copyist. Procopius' evidence, which has not been used in connection with that of the papyri, confirms Oertel's interpretation against the belief of Preisigke (*Wörterbuch*, *s.v.*, followed by Liddell–Scott–Jones, *Lexicon*, *s.v.*) that a διέραμα was a hopper for lading grain into a vessel. The references to the evidence of the papyri have been supplied by Professor H. C. Youtie.

[3] In *Wars*, VIII. vi. 2, Procopius, saying that opinions differ as to the boundaries between Asia and Europe, states that some people maintain that the Nile flows between Asia and Libya.

γὰρ ἐν δεξιᾷ τοῦ ποταμοῦ Ἀσία ὠνόμασται μέχρι που ἐς Φᾶσιν τὸν Κόλχον, ὅσπερ Ἀσίαν τε διορίζει καὶ γῆν τὴν Εὐρώπην, ἢ μέχρι ἐς πορθμεῖα
8 τὰ Κιμμέρια καὶ ποταμὸν Τάναϊν. τούτων γὰρ δὴ ἕνεκα διαμάχονται πρὸς ἀλλήλους οἱ ταῦτα σοφοί, ἧπερ ἐν λόγοις μοι τοῖς ὑπὲρ τῶν πολέμων δεδήλωται περιηγουμένῳ τὸν Εὔξεινον καλούμενον
9 πόντον. τὰ δὲ δὴ ἐν ἀριστερᾷ τοῦ Νείλου Λιβύη ἐκλήθη μέχρι ἐς ὠκεανόν, ὅσπερ ἐς δύοντά που τὸν ἥλιον ἑκατέραν ἤπειρον διορίζει, ἐκροήν τε
10 ἀφιεὶς τινα καὶ θάλασσαν τήνδε ποιούμενος. ἡ μὲν οὖν ἄλλη Λιβύη ξύμπασα ὀνόματα κατὰ χώραν ἑκάστην ἕτερα ἄττα διακεκλήρωται, ἐκ τῶν ἐκείνῃ ἐπιγενομένων, ὡς τὸ εἰκός, ἐπικληθεῖσα.
11 ἣ μέντοι ἐκ τῶν Ἀλεξανδρείας ὁρίων ἄχρι ἐς πόλιν Κυρήνην διήκουσα ἐπὶ Πενταπόλεώς ἐστιν, ἐπὶ τούτου δὴ μόνου τοῦ ὀνόματος Λιβύη καὶ νῦν
B 332 12 ἐπικέκληται. ἐνταῦθα πόλις ἐστὶν ἡμέρας ὁδῷ Ἀλεξανδρείας διέχουσα, Ταφόσιρις ὄνομα, ἵνα δὴ ταφῆναι τὸν τῶν Αἰγυπτίων θεὸν Ὄσιριν λέγου-
13 σιν. ἐν ταύτῃ τῇ πόλει ἄλλα τε πολλὰ καὶ τὰ τῶν ἀρχόντων καταλυτήρια καὶ λουτρῶνας ἐδείματο Ἰουστινιανὸς βασιλεύς.

P 110 β′. Ταύτης δὲ τῆς Λιβύης ἔρημα μὲν τὰ πολλὰ τετύχηκεν εἶναι, ἀπημελημένα ἐκ τοῦ ἐπὶ πλεῖστον.
2 καὶ αὐτῆς δὲ προεγρηγορὼς ὁ καθ' ἡμᾶς βασιλεὺς προμηθεῖ γνώμῃ, ὡς μή τι αὐτῇ παθεῖν ἐξ ἐπιδρομῆς πρὸς Μαυρουσίων τῶν πλησιοχώρων ξυμβαίη, ὀχυρώματά τε δύο καὶ φυλακτήρια κατεστήσατο, ὧν θάτερον μὲν Παρατόνιον ὀνομά-

---

[1] Modern Don. [2] VIII. vi.

the right of the river is called Asia as far as the Colchian Phasis, which divides Asia from the continent of Europe, or even all the way to the Cimmerian Strait and the River Tanaïs.[1] In regard to this question those who are learned in these matters are in conflict with one another, as has been made clear in the Books on the Wars [2] in the course of my description of the sea called Euxine. And the land on the left of the Nile bears the name of Libya as far as the Ocean, which on the west marks the boundary between the two continents by sending out a certain arm [3] which opens out into this sea of ours. All the rest of Libya has received several different names, each region being designated, presumably, by the name of the people who dwell there. However, the territory extending from the confines of Alexandria as far as the city of Cyrenê, comprising the Pentapolis, is now the only region which is called by the name of Libya. In that territory is a city one day's journey distant from Alexandria, Taphosiris by name, where they say that the god of the Egyptians, Osiris, was buried. In this city the Emperor Justinian built many things, and in particular the residences of the magistrates and baths.

ii. The greatest part of this land of Libya chances to have been desert, which was in general neglected. Yet our Emperor takes thought for this land also with watchful care, so that it might not have the ill fortune to suffer anything from inroads of the Moors who inhabit the adjoining country; and to this end he established there two strongholds with garrisons, one of which they call Paratonium,[4] while the other,

[3] The Strait of Gibraltar. [4] Also called Ammonia.

ζουσιν, Ἀντίπυργον δὲ τὸ ἕτερον ἐπικέκληται, οὐ
3 πόρρω Πενταπόλεως κείμενον. διέχει δὲ ἡ
Πεντάπολις Ἀλεξανδρείας ὁδῷ ἡμερῶν εἴκοσιν
4 εὐζώνῳ ἀνδρί. ἐν ταύτῃ δὲ τῇ Πενταπόλει καὶ
βασιλεὺς Ἰουστινιανὸς Τεύχειραν τὴν πόλιν ἐρύματι
5 ἐτειχίσατο ἐχυρωτάτῳ. καὶ Βερνίκης τὸν περίβολον ἐκ θεμελίων ἀνῳκοδομήσατο τῶν ἐσχάτων.
6 οὗ δὴ καὶ βαλανεῖον πεποίηται, δημοσίᾳ παρεχό-
7 μενον τῇ πόλει τὴν χρείαν. ἀλλὰ κἀν ταῖς Πενταπόλεως ἐσχατιαῖς, αἵπερ εἰσὶ τετραμμέναι πρὸς
ἄνεμον νότον, ὀχυρώματα ἐν δυοῖν μοναστηρίοιν
ἐξείργασται, οἷσπερ Ἀγριολώδη τε καὶ Δινάρθι-
σον ὀνόματά ἐστιν· ἅπερ ἐπιτειχίσματα κεῖται
8 τοῖς ταύτῃ βαρβάροις, τῷ μὴ καταθέοντας ὡς
λαθραιότατα ἐπισκήπτειν ἐξαπιναίως ἐς γῆν τὴν
Ῥωμαίων.

9 Ἔστι δέ τις ἐνταῦθα πόλις, Πτολεμαΐς ὄνομα,
τὸ μὲν παλαιὸν εὐδαίμων τε γεγενημένη καὶ
πολυάνθρωπος, προϊόντος δὲ τοῦ χρόνου ὕδατος
ἀπορίᾳ πολλῇ ἐς ὀλιγανθρωπίαν ἀποκριθεῖσα.
B 333 10 τῶν γὰρ οἰκητόρων ὁ πολὺς ὅμιλος δίψει ἐχόμενοι
πολλῷ ἔμπροσθεν ἐνθένδε ἐξαναστάντες ἀπεχώρη-
11 σαν ὅπῃ ἑκάστῳ δυνατὰ γέγονεν. ἀλλὰ νῦν ὁ
βασιλεὺς οὗτος ἀνανεωσάμενος τὴν ὀχεταγωγίαν
τῇ πόλει τὸ πρότερον αὐτῇ τῆς εὐδαιμονίας
ἀπέδωκε σχῆμα. Πενταπόλεως δὲ πόλις ἐσχάτη
ἐστὶ πρὸς δύοντά που τὸν ἥλιον, Βόρειον ὄνομα.
12 οὗ δὴ τὰ ὄρη συννενευκότα τε πρὸς ἄλληλα, καὶ
τῇ ἐνθένδε στενοχωρίᾳ ξυμπεφραγμένα, τῶν ἐπὶ
τὴν χώραν εἰσόδων ἀποκεκλεῖσθαι τοὺς πολεμίους
13 διασκευάζονται. ταύτην ὁ βασιλεὺς τὴν πόλιν
ἀτείχιστον οὖσαν ἐρύματι ἐχυρωτάτῳ περιβαλών,

which lies not far from the Pentapolis, has received the name Antipyrgum. And the Pentapolis is removed from Alexandria by a twenty days' journey for an unencumbered traveller.[1] In this region of Pentapolis the Emperor Justinian surrounded the city of Teuchira [2] with very strong fortifications. The circuit-wall of Bernicê [3] he rebuilt from its lowest foundations. In that city he also built a bath for the use of the people. Furthermore, on the extreme boundary of the Pentapolis which faces the south, he constructed fortresses in two monasteries which bear the names Agriolodê and Dinarthisum; and these stand as bulwarks against the barbarians of that region, so that they may not come down stealthily into Roman territory and suddenly fall upon it.

There is a certain city there, Ptolemaïs [4] by name, which in ancient times had been prosperous and populous, but as time went on it had come to be almost deserted owing to extreme scarcity of water. For the great majority of the population, driven by thirst, had moved from there long ago and gone wherever each one could. Now, however, this Emperor has restored the city's aqueduct and thus brought back to it its former measure of prosperity. The last city of Pentapolis towards the west is named Boreium.[5] Here the mountains press close upon one another, and thus forming a barrier by their crowding, effectively close the entrance to the enemy. This city, which had been without a wall, the Emperor enclosed with very strong defences, thus making it

[1] About four hundred miles. [2] Modern Tokra.
[3] Or Hesperus, modern Benghazi.
[4] On the coast of Cyrenaica, modern Tolometa.
[5] On the coast; probably modern Tabilbê.

ἐν τῷ ἀσφαλεῖ τὸ λοιπὸν βεβαιότατα σὺν πάσῃ τῇ ἀμφ' αὐτὴν χώρᾳ διεπράξατο εἶναι.

14 Πόλεις δέ πού εἰσι δύο ἐπ' ὀνόματος ἑνὸς 15 ᾠκημέναι· Αὐγίλα γὰρ ἑκατέρα ἐκλήθη. αὗται τοῦ Βορείου διέχουσιν ὁδῷ τεττάρων ἡμερῶν μάλιστα εὐζώνῳ ἀνδρί, τετραμμέναι μὲν αὐτοῦ πρὸς ἄνεμον νότον, ἀρχαῖαι δὲ οὖσαι καὶ τῶν οἰκητόρων ἀρχαιότροπα τὰ ἐπιτηδεύματα ἔχουσαι· θρησκείαν γὰρ πάντες καὶ εἰς ἐμὲ τὴν τῆς πολυ-16 θεΐας ἐνόσουν. ἐνταῦθα ἐκ παλαιοῦ τῷ τε Ἄμμωνι καὶ Ἀλεξάνδρῳ τῷ Μακεδόνι ἀνέκειτο P 111 17 ἕδη. οἷς δὴ καὶ ἐσφαγιάζοντο μέχρι ἐς τὴν 18 Ἰουστινιανοῦ βασιλείαν οἱ ἐπιχώριοι. ἦν δὲ καὶ ὅμιλος αὐτοῖς τῶν ἱεροδούλων καλουμένων πολύς. νῦν δὲ δὴ ὁ βασιλεὺς οὗτος οὐχ ὅσον ἐς τὰ σώματα τοῖς κατηκόοις ἐκποριζόμενος τὴν ἀσφάλειαν, ἀλλὰ καὶ τὰς ψυχὰς διασώσασθαι ἐν ἐπιμελείᾳ ποιούμενος, καὶ τῶν ταύτῃ ᾠκημένων ἀνθρώπων 19 κατὰ πάντα προὐνόησε τρόπον. τά τε γὰρ ἄλλα διαφερόντως αὐτῶν ἐπιμελεῖσθαι οὐδαμῇ ἀπηξίωσε καὶ τὴν τῆς εὐσεβείας ἐδίδαξε δόξαν Χριστιανοὺς B 334 πανοικεσίᾳ πεποιημένος[1] καὶ μεταπορευόμενος[2] 20 λελυμασμένα σφίσι τὰ πάτρια ἤθη. οἷς δὴ καὶ νεὼν τῆς θεοτόκου ἐδείματο, φυλακτήριον ταῖς πόλεσι τῆς τε σωτηρίας καὶ τῆς ἀμφὶ τῇ δόξῃ ἀληθείας ἐσόμενον. ταῦτα μὲν οὖν τῇδέ πη ἔσχε.

21 Βόρειον δὲ ἡ πόλις Μαυρουσίοις γειτνιῶσα βαρβάροις φόρου ὑποτελὴς οὐ γεγένηται ἐς τόδε τοῦ χρόνου· οὐδέ τινες πώποτε δασμολόγοι[3] ἢ

[1] πεποιημένος V: πεποιημένους A.

as safe as possible for the future, together with the whole country round about it.

And there are two cities which are known by the same name, each of them being called Augila. These are distant from Boreium about four days' journey for an unencumbered traveller,[1] and to the south of it; and they are both ancient cities whose inhabitants have preserved the practices of antiquity, for they all were suffering from the disease of polytheism even up to my day. There from ancient times there have been shrines dedicated to Ammon and to Alexander the Macedonian. The natives actually used to make sacrifices to them even up to the reign of Justinian. In this place there was a great throng of those called temple-slaves. But now the Emperor has made provision, not alone for the safety of the persons of his subjects, but he has also made it his concern to save their souls, and thus he has cared in every way for the people living there. Indeed he by no means neglected to take thought for their material interests in an exceptional way, and also he has taught them the doctrine of the true faith, making the whole population Christians and bringing about a transformation of their polluted ancestral customs. Moreover he built for them a Church of the Mother of God to be a guardian of the safety of the cities and of the true faith. So much, then, for this.

The city of Boreium, which lies near the barbarian Moors, has never been subject to tribute up to the present time, nor have any collectors of tribute or

[1] About eighty miles.

---

[2] μεταπορευόμενος Maltretus: μεταπορευομένους.
[3] δασμολόγοι A: δασμοφόροι V.

φορολόγοι ἐς αὐτὴν ἵκοντο, ἐξ οὗ γεγόνασιν
22 ἄνθρωποι. οἱ δὲ Ἰουδαῖοι ᾤκηντο ἐκ παλαιοῦ
αὐτῶν ἄγχιστα· οὗ δὴ καὶ νεὼς ἦν ἀρχαῖος
αὐτοῖς, ὅνπερ ἐσέβοντό τε καὶ ἐτεθήπεσαν μάλιστα, δειμαμένου τοῦτο Σολομῶνος,[1] ὥσπερ φασί,
23 βασιλεύοντος Ἑβραίων τοῦ ἔθνους. ἀλλὰ καὶ
αὐτοὺς ἅπαντας Ἰουστινιανὸς βασιλεὺς μεταγνῶναί
τε τὰ πάτρια ἤθη, καὶ Χριστιανοὺς γεγονέναι
διαπραξάμενος, τοῦτον δὴ τὸν νεὼν ἐς ἐκκλησίας
μεθηρμόσατο σχῆμα.

γʹ. Μετὰ τούτους αἱ Σύρτεις εἰσὶν αἱ μεγάλαι
ὠνομασμέναι. ἐφ᾽ οὗ δέ εἰσι σχήματος αὗται,
καὶ ὅτου δὴ ἕνεκα τούτου μεταλαγχάνουσι τοῦ
2 ὀνόματος, ἐγὼ δηλώσω. προβέβληταί τις ἐνταῦθα
ἠϊών· σχιζομένη δὲ αὐτὴ τῇ τῆς θαλάσσης
ἐπιρροῇ, τῷ τε ῥοθίῳ ἀφανιζομένη, ἀποβαίνειν
δοκεῖ, καὶ ἐφ᾽ ἑαυτὴν[2] ὑποχωροῦσα ὀπίσω ἰέναι·
ἐς κόλπον δὲ μηνοειδῆ ἐπὶ μακρότατον τέτραπται.
3 καὶ ὁ μὲν ἀρχομένης πλευρᾶς διάπλους ἐς τετ-
ρακοσίους διήκει σταδίους· τοῦ δὲ μηνοειδοῦς τὸ
4 περίμετρον ἐς ἡμερῶν ἓξ ὁδὸν κατατείνει. ταύτης
γὰρ ἡ θάλασσα πεπιεσμένη τῆς ἠπείρου ἐντὸς τὸν
5 κόλπον ποιεῖται. ἐπειδάν τε ναῦς ἀνέμῳ ἢ
κλύδωνι βιαζομένη τοῦ διάπλου ἐντὸς ὑπὲρ τοῦ
B 335 μηνοειδοῦς τὴν ἀρχὴν γένηται, τὸ ἐνθένδε αὐτῇ
ἐπανιέναι ἀμήχανά ἐστιν, ἀλλὰ συρομένῃ τὸ
λοιπὸν ἔοικε, καὶ διαφανῶς ἐπίπροσθεν ἀεὶ

taxes come to it since the creation of man. The Jews had lived close by from ancient times, and they had an ancient temple there also, which they revered and honoured especially, since it was built, as they say, by Solomon, while he was ruling over the Hebrew nation. But the Emperor Justinian brought it about that all these too changed their ancestral worship and have become Christians, and he transformed their temple into a church.

iii. Beyond these lie the Great Syrtes, as they are called. And I shall explain what their form is and why they are given this name. A sort of shore projects there, but is itself divided by the influx of the sea, and being hidden by the water it seems to disappear and to retreat back into itself; and it forms by its curve a very long crescent-shaped gulf.[1] The chord of the crescent extends to a distance of four hundred stades,[2] but the perimeter of the crescent amounts to a six-days' journey,[3] for the sea, thrusting itself inside of this arm of the mainland, forms the gulf. When a ship driven by wind or wave gets inside the opening and beyond the chord of the crescent, it is then impossible for it to return, but from that moment it seems "to be drawn" (*suresthai*) [4] and appears distinctly to be dragged steadily forward.

[1] Modern Gulf of Sidra. [2] About fifty miles.
[3] About 120 miles.
[4] A modern etymology connects the name with the Arabic *sert* "desert," a term now applied to the whole coast here bordering the Sahara. On the danger to sailors, cf. St. Paul's narrative of his experience, *Acts* 27. 17.

---

[1] Σολομῶνος Maltretus: σολομῶντος V.
[2] ἑαυτὴν V: ἑαυτῆς A.

6 ἑλκομένῃ. καὶ ἀπ' αὐτοῦ, οἶμαι, τὸν χῶρον οἱ πάλαι ἄνθρωποι τοῦ πάθους τῶν νεῶν ἕνεκα 7 Σύρτεις ὠνόμασαν. οὐ μὴν οὐδὲ διανεῦσαι τοῖς πλοίοις ἄχρι ἐς τὴν ἠϊόνα δυνατὰ γεγένηται. πέτραι γὰρ ὕφαλοι διακεκληρωμέναι τὰ πλεῖστα τοῦ κόλπου πλώϊμα οὐ ξυγχωροῦσιν ἐνταῦθα εἶναι, ἀλλ' ἐν τοῖς βράχεσι τὰς ναῦς διαχρῶν- P 112 8 ται. μόνοις δὲ τοῖς λέμβοις οἱ πλωτῆρες τούτων δὴ τῶν νηῶν οἷοί τέ εἰσι διασώζεσθαι, ἂν οὕτω τύχοι, μετὰ κινδύνων τὰς διεξόδους ποιούμενοι.

9 Τριπόλεως τῇδε τῆς καλουμένης τὰ ὅριά ἐστι. Μαυρούσιοί τε βάρβαροι ἐνταῦθα οἰκοῦσι, Φοινικικὸν ἔθνος. οὗ δὴ καὶ πόλις ἐστὶ Κιδαμὴ 10 ὄνομα. ἐνταῦθά τε Μαυρούσιοι ᾤκηνται Ῥωμαίων ἔνσπονδοι ἐκ παλαιοῦ ὄντες· οἵπερ ἅπαντες πεισθέντες Ἰουστινιανῷ βασιλεῖ, δόγματι τῷ Χριστιανῶν ἐθελούσιοι προσεχώρησαν. 11 Πακᾶτοι δὲ οὗτοι τανῦν οἱ Μαυρούσιοι ἐπικαλοῦνται, ἐπεὶ πρὸς Ῥωμαίους ἀεὶ σπονδὰς ἔχουσι· πάκεν[1] γὰρ τὴν εἰρήνην τῇ Λατίνων καλοῦσι 12 φωνῇ. Πενταπόλεως δὲ Τρίπολις ἡμερῶν διέχει ὁδῷ εἴκοσιν εὐζώνῳ ἀνδρί.

δ'. Πόλις ἐνθένδε ἡ Λεπτιμάγνα ἐκδέχεται, μεγάλη μὲν καὶ πολυάνθρωπος τὸ παλαιὸν οὖσα, ἔρημος δὲ χρόνῳ ὕστερον γεγενημένη ἐκ τοῦ ἐπὶ πλεῖστον, ψάμμου τε πλήθει τὰ πολλὰ τῷ 2 ἀπημελῆσθαι καταχωσθεῖσα. καὶ ταύτης δὲ[2] τὸν περίβολον ἐκ τῶν θεμελίων ὁ καθ' ἡμᾶς ᾠκοδομή- B 336 σατο βασιλεύς, οὐ τοσοῦτον μέντοι, ὅσος τὸ

[1] πάκεν V: πάκα A.

From this fact, I suppose, the men of ancient times named the place Syrtes because of the fate of the ships. On the other hand, it is not possible for the ships to make their way to the shore, for submerged rocks scattered over the greater part of the gulf do not permit sailing there, since they destroy the ships in the shoals. Only in small boats are the sailors of such ships able to save themselves, with good luck, by picking their way amid perils through the outlets.

Here are the boundaries of Tripolis,[1] as it is called. It is inhabited by the barbarian Moors, a Phoenician race. Here too is a city, Cidamê [2] by name; and in it live Moors who have been at peace with the Romans from ancient times. All these were won over by the Emperor Justinian and voluntarily adopted the Christian doctrine. These Moors are now called *pacati*, because they have a permanent treaty with the Romans; for peace they call *pacem* in the Latin tongue. Tripolis is a twenty-days' journey from the Pentapolis for an unencumbered traveller.[3]

iv. Next after this comes the city of Leptis Magna,[4] which in ancient times was large and populous, though at a later time it came to be deserted for the most part, being through neglect largely buried in sand. Our Emperor built up the circuit-wall of this city from the foundations, not however on as large a scale as it was formerly, but much smaller, in order

[1] That is, Tripolitana.
[2] Modern Ghadames.
[3] About four hundred miles.
[4] Modern Lebida.

[2] καὶ ταύτης δὲ V: ἀλλὰ καὶ ταύτης A.

πρότερον ἦν, ἀλλὰ κατὰ πολὺ ἥσσονα, ὡς μὴ τῷ μεγέθει σφαλερὰ καὶ αὖθις ἡ πόλις εἴη, καὶ 3 πολεμίοις μὲν ἁλωτή, ψάμμῳ δὲ πρόχειρος. νῦν δὲ δὴ τῆς πόλεως τὸ μὲν καταχωσθὲν ἐφ' οὗπερ ἦν σχήματος εἴασεν οὕτω δὴ ψάμμῳ ἐς λόφους συνειλεγμένῃ κεκαλυμμένον, τὴν δὲ λοιπὴν ἐτειχί- 4 σατο ἐν τῷ τῆς οἰκοδομίας ἐχυρῷ μάλιστα. καὶ ἱερὸν μὲν ἀξιοθέατον τῇ θεοτόκῳ τῇδε ἀνέθηκεν, 5 ἐκκλησίας δὲ τέτταρας ἐδείματο ἄλλας. πρὸς δὲ καὶ ἀνῳκοδομήσατο τὰ τῇδε γεγονότα ἐν τοῖς ἄνω χρόνοις καὶ καταπεπτωκότα βασίλεια, Σεβή- ρου βασιλέως τοῦ παλαιοῦ ἔργον· ὃς δὴ ἐνθένδε ὁρμώμενος μνημεῖα τῆς εὐδαιμονίας τὰ βασίλεια τάδε ἀπέλιπεν.

6 Ἀλλὰ γὰρ ἐνταῦθα γενόμενος τοῦ λόγου τὸ ξυνενεχθὲν ἐπὶ Λεπτιμάγνης ἐν χρόνῳ τῷ καθ' ἡμᾶς ὡς ἥκιστα σιωπήσομαι. ἤδη μὲν Ἰουστι- νιανοῦ τὴν βασιλείαν παραλαβόντος, οὔπω δὲ πόλεμον τὸν Βανδιλικὸν ἀνῃρημένου, Μαυρούσιοι βάρβαροι, οἳ Λευάθαι καλούμενοι, βιασάμενοι τοὺς Λιβύης τότε κυρίους Βανδίλους, ἔρημον ἀνθρώπων 7 τὴν Λεπτιμάγναν παντάπασι κατεστήσαντο. ἐν χώροις δὲ λοφώδεσι ξὺν τοῖς ἡγεμόσι διατριβήν τινα ἔχοντες Λεπτιμάγνης οὐ πολλῷ ἄποθεν, φλόγα πυρὸς ἐξαπιναίως ἐν μέσῃ τῇ πόλει 8 τεθέανται. πολεμίους τε ὑποτοπήσαντες ἐνδήμους ἐνταῦθα γενέσθαι, δρόμῳ ἐπ' αὐτοὺς ἐβοήθουν 9 πολλῷ. ἀνθρώπων τε οὐδένα εὑρόντες ἐπὶ τοὺς P 113 μάντεις τὸ πρᾶγμα ἦγον, οἳ δὴ τῷ ξυμβεβηκότι τεκμηριούμενοι τὴν Λεπτιμάγναν οὐκ εἰς μακρὰν 10 οἰκισθήσεσθαι προὔλεγον. οὐ πολλῷ τε ὕστερον ἀφικόμενος ὁ τοῦ βασιλέως στρατὸς Λιβύην τε τὴν

that the city might not again be weak because of its very size, and liable to capture by the enemy, and also be exposed to the sand. At present, indeed, he has left the buried portion of the city just as it was, covered by the sand heaped up in mounds, but the rest of the city he has surrounded with a very strongly built wall. Here he dedicated to the Mother of God a very notable shrine, and built four other churches. Furthermore, he rebuilt the palace, which had been built here in early times and now lay in ruins, the work of the ancient Emperor Severus,[1] who was born in this place and so left this palace as a memorial of his good fortune.

Now that I have reached this point in the narrative, I cannot pass over in silence the thing which happened in Leptis Magna in our time. When the Emperor Justinian had already taken over the imperial authority, but had not yet undertaken the Vandalic War, the barbarian Moors, those called Leuathae, overpowered the Vandals, who were then masters of Libya, and made Leptis Magna entirely empty of inhabitants. While they were tarrying for a time with their leaders on hilly ground not far from Leptis Magna, they suddenly saw a flame of fire in the middle of the city. Supposing that local enemies had got in there, they ran to the rescue with great speed. Finding no one there, they took the matter to the soothsayers, who, by an inkling of what has since happened, predicted that Leptis Magna would soon be inhabited again. Not long after that the Emperor's army came and occupied both Tripolis and

[1] Lucius Septimius Severus, A.D. 193–211.

B 337 ἄλλην καὶ Τρίπολιν ἔσχε, Βανδίλων τε καὶ Μαυρουσίων καθυπέρτερος τῷ πολέμῳ γεγενημένος. ἐγὼ δὲ ὅθεν τὴν ἐκβολὴν τοῦ λόγου ἐποιησάμην ἐπάνειμι.

11 Ἐν ταύτῃ τῇ πόλει βασιλεὺς Ἰουστινιανὸς καὶ λουτρῶνας ἐν δημοσίῳ πεποίηται, τόν τε περίβολον τῆς πόλεως ἐκ θεμελίων τῶν ἐσχάτων ᾠκοδομήσατο, καὶ τοῖς τε βαλανείοις τοῖς τε ἄλλοις πᾶσιν ἐς πόλεως αὐτὴν κατεστήσατο σχῆμα. 12 τούς τε πλησιοχώρους αὐτῇ βαρβάρους, οἳ Γαδαβιτανοὶ ἐπικαλοῦνται,[1] κατακόρως ἐς τόδε τοῦ χρόνου τὴν Ἑλληνικὴν καλουμένην ἀθεΐαν δοξάζοντας, Χριστιανοὺς διεπράξατο γενέσθαι 13 τανῦν προθυμίᾳ τῇ πάσῃ. ἀλλὰ καὶ Σαβραθὰν ἐτειχίσατο πόλιν, οὗ δὴ καὶ λόγου ἀξίαν πολλοῦ ἐκκλησίαν ἐδείματο.

14 Πόλεις δὲ δύο εἰσὶ ταύτης ἐν ἐσχάτῳ τῆς χώρας, Τάκαπά τε καὶ Γίργις, ὧν δὴ κατὰ μέσον Σύρτεις 15 τὰς μικρὰς ξυμβαίνει εἶναι. ἐνταῦθα γίνεταί τι ἐς ἡμέραν ἑκάστην θαυμάσιον ἡλίκον. ἡ θάλασσα ἐν στενῷ θλιβομένη ἀπεργάζεται μηνοειδῆ κόλπον, ᾗπερ γίνεσθαι καὶ κατὰ[2] τὰς ἄλλας Σύρτεις 16 ἐρρήθη. ἀναβαίνει δὲ εἰς τὴν ἤπειρον πλέον ἢ ὁδῷ ἡμέρας εὐζώνῳ ἀνδρί, ἀμφί τε τὰ πρὸς ἑσπέραν ἐπάνεισιν αὖθις, ἐπιλιποῦσα ἐπὶ ξηροῦ τὴν ἠϊόνα ταύτην κατὰ ταὐτὰ ταῖς ἄλλαις 17 ἀκταῖς. οἵ τε ναῦται εἰς τὴν ἤπειρον ἀναγόμενοι θάλασσαν ἐπὶ καιροῦ γεγενημένην, τῆς μὲν ἡμέρας ὡς πορρωτάτω τὰ εἰωθότα ναυτίλλονται, ἀμφὶ δείλην δὲ πάντως ὀψίαν ὡς ἐν γῇ αὐλισόμενοι συσκευάζονται, κοντούς τινας ἐν παρασκευῇ 18 μακροὺς ἔχοντες. ἐπειδάν τε τάχιστα τοῦ ῥοθίου

the rest of Libya, gaining ascendancy over both the Vandals and the Moors in the war. However, I shall return to the point at which I digressed from my account.

In this city the Emperor Justinian also built public baths, and he erected the circuit-wall of the city from its lowest foundations, and by means both of the baths and of all the other improvements gave it the character of a city. The barbarians who live close by, those called Gadabitani, who up to that time were exceedingly addicted to what is called the Greek [1] form of atheism, he has now made zealous Christians. He also walled the city of Sabrathan,[2] where he also built a very noteworthy church.

There are two cities at the extremity of this land, Tacapa [3] and Girgis, between which lie the Lesser Syrtes. There a thing happens every day which is truly wonderful. The sea, compressed into a narrow space, forms a crescent-shaped gulf, just as I have said happens at the other Syrtes. The sea comes up on the mainland more than a day's journey for an unencumbered traveller,[4] but towards evening it returns again, leaving the shore there dry as on other coasts. The sailors put out over the mainland, which is temporarily transformed into a sea, and during the day they sail as far as possible by the usual means, but in the late afternoon they make preparations to bivouac as if on land, having certain long poles in readiness. As soon as they observe

[1] *I.e.* pagan. [2] Modern Tripoli Vecchia.
[3] Modern Cabes. [4] About twenty miles.

---

[1] ἐπικαλοῦνται V: καλοῦνται A.
[2] κατὰ added by Haury, κατὰ for καὶ Maltretus.

αἴσθωνται ὑπόπτως ἐς τὴν ἀναχώρησιν ἔχοντος,
B 338 οἵδε τοὺς κοντοὺς ἔχοντες καὶ διαχειρίζοντες ἐκ-
19 πηδῶσιν ὀκνήσει[1] οὐδεμιᾷ ἐκ τῆς νεώς. νηχόμενοι
δὲ πρῶτον, εἶτα ἑστήκασιν, ἡνίκα ἂν σφίσι
20 τὸ ὕδωρ οὐχ ὑπεραίροι τὰ πρόσωπα. ἔκ τε
τῶν ἄκρων τοὺς κοντοὺς ἐπὶ τῆς γῆς προσ-
ουδίσαντες ἐν ξηρῷ ἤδη γεγενημένης ἢ ἐσομένης
αὐτίκα δὴ μάλα, ὀρθοὺς ἱστᾶσιν, ὑποκεισομένους
τῷ πλοίῳ καὶ μετεωρίσοντας ἑκατέρωθεν, ὡς μὴ
21 ἐπικλῖναν ἐπὶ θάτερα συντριβὲς γένηται. τῇ
δὲ ὑστεραίᾳ ὄρθρου βαθέος ἡ μὲν ἤπειρος μετ-
αμφιασαμένη τὴν θάλασσαν ἐπικυρτοῦται κυμαί-
22 νουσα, τὰ δὲ πλοῖα ἐπαιρόμενα πλεῖ. οἵ τε
ναῦται περιελόντες ἐπικαιριώτατα τοὺς κοντοὺς
23 ναυτίλλονται αὖθις. παράλλαξίν τε οὐδεμίαν τοῦ
ἔργου γενέσθαι ξυμβαίνει, ἀλλ' ἐς ἡμέραν ἑκάστην
ἡ τῶν στοιχείων διαδοχὴ ἐπιγίνεται.

P 114 ε'. Μετὰ δὲ Τρίπολίν τε καὶ Σύρτεις ἡμεῖς
2 ἐπὶ Λιβύην τὴν ἄλλην ἴωμεν. ἀρκτέον δὲ ἡμῖν
ἐκ Καρχηδόνος, ἣ μεγίστη τε καὶ ἀξιολογωτάτη
τῶν τῇδε πόλεων τυγχάνει οὖσα, τοσοῦτον πρότερον ὑπειποῦσιν, ὡς ἡνίκα Γιζέριχός τε καὶ
Βανδίλοι Λιβύην ἔσχον, ἐνθύμημα ἐπιγέγονεν
αὐτοῖς ἀξιώλεθρόν τε καὶ πρέπον βαρβάροις.
3 ἄμεινον γὰρ ἐλογίσαντο σφίσι τὰ πράγματα
ἕξειν ἀτειχίστων ὄντων τῶν τῇδε χωρίων, ὡς
μή τι καταλαβόντες αὐτῶν Ῥωμαῖοι Βανδίλους
4 κακουργεῖν ἔχοιεν. ἅπαντα οὖν τὰ τείχη ἐς
τὸ ἔδαφος καθεῖλον εὐθύς. βάρβαροι γὰρ ἅπαντες ἐκ τοῦ ἐπὶ πλεῖστον ἐπὶ πονηρῷ τῷ[2] Ῥωμαίων
βουλεύονται μὲν ὡς ὀξύτατα, ἐπιτελοῦσι δὲ ὡς
5 ταχύτατα ὅσα ἂν αὐτοῖς δοκοῦντα εἴη. μόνον

that the water is threatening to draw back, with no delay they leap out of the ships holding the poles and dragging them along. At first they swim, and then they stand as soon as the water does not rise above their faces. And they plant the ends of their poles in the earth as soon as it has become dry or is on the point of becoming so, and they set them upright so as to prop up the boat from both sides and keep it upright, in order that it may not fall over to either side and be crushed. On the following day, at early dawn, the mainland again transforms itself into the sea with its rolling waves, and the boats are lifted and float away. The sailors meanwhile remove the poles at just the right moment and proceed to sail once more. This goes on without any variation, but every day the alternation of the elements takes place.

v. After Tripolis and the Syrtes, let us go on to the rest of Libya. We must begin from Carthage, which chances to be the largest and the most noteworthy of the cities in this region, prefacing our account with the remark that when Gizeric and the Vandals acquired Libya, a device occurred to them which was both pernicious and worthy of barbarians. They reasoned that they would be better off if all the towns of the region should be without walls, so that the Romans might not capture any of them and thus be able to harm the Vandals. So they immediately tore down all the walls to the ground. All the barbarians, as a general thing, are very keen in planning damage to the Romans, and they are very swift in executing whatever they decide upon. Only Car-

[1] ἐν before ὀκνήσει deleted by Braun.
[2] τῷ A: τῶν V.

δὲ αὐτοῖς[1] τό τε Καρχηδόνος καὶ ὀλίγα ἄττα ἐφ' οὗπερ ἦσαν σχήματος ἔμειναν, ὧνπερ ἐπιμελεῖσθαι ἀπαξιοῦντες, διαφθορεῖν[2] αὐτὰ τῷ χρόνῳ ἀφῆκαν.

B 339 6 βασιλεὺς δὲ Ἰουστινιανὸς (ἀνθρώπων μὲν οὐδενὸς ἐπαινοῦντος, ἀλλὰ καὶ πεφρικότων τὸ ἔργον ἁπάντων, μόνου δὲ τοῦ θεοῦ εἰσηγουμένου τε καὶ ἐπαγγελλομένου καὶ ξυλλαμβάνοντος) Βελισάριόν τε καὶ στράτευμα ἐπὶ Λιβύην πέμψας, Γελίμερά τε καὶ δύναμιν τὴν[3] Βανδίλων καθεῖλε, πολλοὺς μὲν κτείνας τοὺς δὲ λοιποὺς δορυαλώτους πεποιημένος, ἧπέρ μοι ἐν λόγοις τοῖς ὑπὲρ τῶν 7 πολέμων δεδήλωται. καὶ τὰ μὲν καθῃρημένα τῶν ἐν Λιβύῃ ὀχυρωμάτων ἀνενεώσατο ἅπαντα, ἕτερα δὲ παμπληθῆ ἐπετεχνήσατο[4] νεοχμώσας αὐτός.

8 Πρῶτα μὲν οὖν Καρχηδόνος, τῆς νῦν καὶ Ἰουστινιανῆς, ὡς τὸ εἰκός, καλουμένης ἐπεμελήσατο, διερρυηκότα μὲν τὸν περίβολον ἀνοικοδομησάμενος ἅπαντα, καὶ τάφρον ἐν περιδρόμῳ 9 διορύξας οὐ πρότερον οὖσαν. ἀνέθηκε δὲ καὶ ἱερὰ τεμένη, τῇ μὲν θεοτόκῳ, ὅπερ ἐν Παλατίῳ ἐστί, καὶ τούτου ἐκτὸς τῶν τινι ἐπιχωρίων 10 ἁγίων[5] ἁγίᾳ Πρίμῃ. ἔτι μέντοι καὶ στοὰς ἑκατέρωθι τῆς Μαριτίμου ἀγορᾶς καλουμένης ἐδείματο, καὶ βαλανεῖον ἐν δημοσίῳ ἀξιοθέατον, ὅπερ ἐπωνύμως[6] τῇ βασιλίδι Θεοδωριανὰς ἐπω-11 νόμασαν. ἐδείματο δὲ καὶ μοναστήριον τοῦ περιβόλου ἐντὸς ἐπιθαλασσίδιον, ἄγχιστα τοῦ λιμένος ὅπερ Μανδράκιον ὀνομάζουσιν, ἐρύματί τε αὐτὸ ἐχυρωτάτῳ περιβαλὼν φρούριον ἀνανταγώνιστον ἀπειργάσατο.

[1] After αὐτοῖς V has καὶ αὐτὰ δὲ διεφθάρη τῷ χρόνῳ.

thage and a few other places were left by them just as they were, for they declined to concern themselves with these, and left them for time to destroy. But the Emperor Justinian (although no man approved of his purpose [1] and all actually shuddered at the undertaking, and only God furthered the project and promised help and support) sent Belisarius and an army against Libya; and he broke the power of Gelimer and the Vandals, killing many and making the rest captives, as I have recounted in the Books on the Wars.[2] He restored all the dismantled strongholds in Libya, every one of them, and he also added a great many new ones himself.

First, then, he cared for Carthage, which now, very properly, is called Justinianê, rebuilding the whole circuit-wall, which had fallen down, and digging around it a moat which it had not had before. He also dedicated shrines, one to the Mother of God in the palace, and one outside this to a certain local saint, Saint Prima. Furthermore, he built stoas on either side of what is called the Maritime Forum, and a public bath, a fine sight, which they have named Theodorianae, after the Empress. He also built a monastery on the shore inside the circuit-wall, close to the harbour which they call Mandracium, and by surrounding it with very strong defences he made it an impregnable fortress.

[1] *Cf. Wars*, III. x. 2. [2] Book III.

---

[2] διαφθορεῖν Maltretus: διαφθορεῖ.
[3] τὴν Haury: τῶν.
[4] ἐπετεχνήσατο V: μετετεχνήσατο A.
[5] ἁγίων added by Maltretus.
[6] ἐπωνύμως V: ὁμωνύμως A.

12 Ταῦτα μὲν οὖν[1] ἐπὶ Καρχηδόνος τῆς νέας Ἰουστινιανῷ εἴργασται. ἐν δὲ χώρᾳ τῇ ἀμφ' αὐτήν, ἣ Προκονσουλαρία ὠνόμασται, πόλις
P 115 ἀτείχιστος ἦν, Βάγα ὄνομα, μὴ ὅτι βαρβάροις ἐπιοῦσιν, ἀλλὰ καὶ τύχῃ τινὶ παριοῦσιν ἁλωτὴ
B 340 13 οὖσα. ταύτην ἐρύματι ἐχυρωτάτῳ περιβαλὼν Ἰουστινιανὸς βασιλεὺς πόλιν τε διεπράξατο εἶναι καὶ τοὺς οἰκήτορας ἐν τῷ ἀσφαλεῖ διασώσασθαι
14 οἷάν τε εἶναι.[2] οἳ δὴ τετυχηκότες τῆς χάριτος ἐς τὴν τῆς βασιλίδος τιμὴν Θεοδωριάδα καλοῦσι
15 τὴν πόλιν. φρούριον δὲ ᾠκοδομήσατο ἐν ταύτῃ τῇ χώρᾳ ὃ Τούκκα καλοῦσιν.

ς'. Ἐν Βυζακίῳ δὲ πόλις, Ἀδράμυτος ὄνομα, ἐν τῇ παραλίᾳ οἰκεῖται, μεγάλη καὶ πολυάνθρωπος ἐκ παλαιοῦ οὖσα, καὶ δι' αὐτὸ τὸ τῆς μητροπόλεως ὄνομά τε καὶ ἀξίωμα κληρωσαμένη ἐν ταύτῃ τῇ χώρᾳ, ἐπεὶ πρώτην αὐτὴν μεγέθει τε
2 καὶ τῇ ἄλλῃ εὐδαιμονίᾳ ξυμβαίνει εἶναι. ταύτης Βανδίλοι μὲν τὸν περίβολον ἐς ἔδαφος καθεῖλον, ὡς μή ποτε Ῥωμαῖοι αὐτῆς ἀντιλαβέσθαι δυνατοὶ εἶεν· Μαυρουσίοις τε καταθέουσι τὰ ἐκείνῃ
3 χωρία ἐν ἐπιτηδείῳ ἀπέκειτο. Λίβυες δὲ κατὰ ταύτην οἰκήτορες, ὅσα γε δυνατὰ τῆς σφῶν σωτηρίας ἐπιμελούμενοι, τὰ διῃρημένα τῶν τοίχων ἀποτριγχώσαντες τὰς οἰκίας ἀλλήλαις ἐνῆψαν·
4 ἐξ ὧν δὴ τοῖς ἐπιοῦσι διαμαχόμενοι ἔν τε τῷ σφαλερῷ τῆς ἐλπίδος καὶ τῷ ἐπικινδύνῳ ἠμύνοντο.
5 ἦν δὲ αὐτοῖς ἐπὶ τριχὸς ἡ σωτηρία διηνεκὲς καὶ ἐπὶ θατέρου σκέλους ἑστῶσα, πολεμουμένοις μὲν ὑπὸ τῶν Μαυρουσίων, ὑπὸ δὲ τῶν Βανδίλων ἀμε-

[1] οὖν A: αὐτῶι V.
[2] διασώσασθαι οἷάν τε εἶναι V: διεσώσατο A.

These things, then, were done by Justinian at modern Carthage. In the surrounding region, which is called Proconsularis,[1] there was an unwalled city, Vaga by name, which could be captured not only by a planned attack of the barbarians, but even if they merely chanced to be passing that way. This place the Emperor Justinian surrounded with very strong defences and made it worthy to be called a city, and capable of affording safe protection to its inhabitants. And they, having received this favour, now call the city Theodorias in honour of the Empress. He also built in this district a fortress which they call Tucca.

vi. In Byzacium there is a city on the coast, Adramytus by name,[2] which has been large and flourishing from ancient times, and for this reason it won the name and the rank of metropolis of the region, since it chances to be first in point of size and, in general, of prosperity. The Vandals had torn the circuit-wall of this city down to the ground, so that the Romans might not be able to use it against them. And it lay conveniently exposed to the Moors when they overran that region. Nevertheless, the Libyans who lived there tried to make provision, so far as they could, for their own safety, and so they made a barricade out of the ruins of the walls and joined their houses together; and from these they would fight against their assailants and try to defend themselves, though their hope was slight and their position precarious. So their safety always hung by a hair and they were kept standing on one leg, being exposed to the attacks of the Moors and to the

[1] *I.e.* the province Africa Proconsularis.
[2] Hadrumetum; modern Susa.

6 λουμένοις. ἀλλ' ἡνίκα Λιβύης κύριος τῷ πολέμῳ βασιλεὺς Ἰουστινιανὸς γέγονε, τεῖχός τε τῇ πόλει εὐμέγεθες ἄγαν περιβαλὼν καὶ φρουρὰν ἐνταῦθα στρατιωτῶν καταστησάμενος ἀξιόχρεων θαρσεῖν τε ὑπὲρ ἀσφαλείας τοὺς τῇδε ᾠκημένους πεποίηται ἀφροντιστῆσαί τε πολεμίων ἁπάντων.
7 διὸ δὴ αὐτὴν καὶ Ἰουστινιανὴν καλοῦσι τανῦν, σῶστρα τῷ βασιλεῖ ταῦτα ἐκτίνοντες, μόνῃ B 341 τοῦ ὀνόματος τῇ παρενθήκῃ τὴν εὐγνωμοσύνην ἐπιδεικνύμενοι, ἐπεὶ ἄλλο οὐδὲν ὅτῳ ἂν καὶ βασιλέως τὴν ἀγαθοεργίαν ἀμείβοιντο οὔτε αὐτοὶ εἶχον οὔτε οὗτος[1] ἐβούλετο.

8 Ἦν δέ τι καὶ ἄλλο ἐν τῇ τοῦ Βυζακίου παραλίᾳ χωρίον ὅπερ ἐκάλουν Καπούτβαδα οἱ ἐπιχώριοι. ἐνταῦθα καταπλεύσας τὰ πρῶτα ὁ τοῦ βασιλέως στόλος Λιβύων τῆς γῆς ἐπεβάτευεν, ἡνίκα ἐπὶ
9 Γελίμερά τε καὶ Βανδίλους ἐστράτευεν. οὗ δὴ καὶ τὸ θαυμάσιον ἐκεῖνο καὶ λόγου κρεῖσσον ἐς τὸν βασιλέα ἐπιδέδεικται ὁ θεὸς δώρημα, P 116 ὅπερ μοι ἐν τοῖς ὑπὲρ τῶν πολέμων δεδήλωται
10 λόγοις. ἀνύδρου γὰρ τοῦ χωρίου τὰ μάλιστα ὄντος, ὕδατός τε ἀπορίᾳ πολλῇ πιεζομένου τοῦ Ῥωμαίων στρατοῦ, ἡ γῆ, πρότερον ἐπὶ ξηροῦ βεβαιότατα οὖσα, πηγὴν ἀνῆκεν οὗ δὴ τὸ χαρά-
11 κωμα οἱ στρατιῶται εἰργάζοντο. οἱ μὲν γὰρ ὤρυσσον, ἡ δὲ ἀνεβλύστανεν. ἥ τε γῆ αὐχμὸν ἀποβαλοῦσα τὸν ἐπιχώριον καὶ μεθαρμοσαμένη τὴν αὐτῆς φύσιν ὕδατι ποτίμῳ ὑγρὰ ἐγεγόνει.
12 ταύτῃ τε τὸ λοιπὸν ἐν ἐπιτηδείῳ στρατοπεδεύ-

[1] οὗτος V: αὐτὸς A.

neglect of the Vandals. However, when the Emperor Justinian became master of Libya by conquest, he put an exceedingly massive wall about the city and stationed there an adequate garrison of troops, thus giving the inhabitants assurance of safety and enabling them to disdain all enemies. For this reason they now call the place Justinianê, thus repaying the Emperor for their deliverance and displaying their gratitude simply by the adoption of the name, since they had no other means by which they could requite the Emperor's beneficence, nor did he himself wish other requital.

There was also a certain other town on the coast of Byzacium which the inhabitants used to call Caputvada.[1] At that point the Emperor's fleet landed and there the troops first set foot on the land of Libya, when they made the expedition against Gelimer and the Vandals. In that place also God revealed that marvellous and indescribable gift to the Emperor which I have described in the Books on the Wars.[2] For although the locality was exceedingly arid, so that the Roman army was very hard pressed by lack of water, the ground, which previously had been completely dry, sent up a spring at the place where the soldiers were building their stockade, for as they dug, the water began to gush forth. So the earth threw off the drought which prevailed there, and transforming its own character became saturated with drinking-water. Because of this circumstance they built a satisfactory camp in that place and

[1] Modern Ras Kaboudia; in *Wars*, III. xiv. 17 Procopius explains the name as meaning "Shoal's Head."

[2] III. xv. 34, 35; the account given there is repeated in the present passage.

σαντές τε καὶ αὐλισάμενοι, καὶ τῇ ὑστεραίᾳ ὡς ἐς τὴν μάχην συσκευασάμενοι, ἵνα τὰ ἐν μέσῳ συντέμω, Λιβύην ἔσχον. 13 μαρτυρίῳ τοίνυν διηνεκεῖ τὸ τοῦ θεοῦ δῶρον πιστούμενος Ἰουστινιανὸς βασιλεύς, ᾧ δὴ βουλομένῳ τὰ ἀμηχανώτατα εὔκολα γίνεται, ἐς πόλιν αὐτίκα μεταβιβάσαι τὸ χωρίον τοῦτο βεβούλευται, τείχει μὲν ἐρυμνήν, τῇ δὲ ἄλλῃ κατασκευῇ ἐς πόλεως ὄγκον ὑπογεγραμμένην εὐδαίμονος, καὶ γέγονεν ἔργον τὸ τοῦ βασιλέως ἐνθύμημα. 14 τεῖχός τε γὰρ ἀποτετόρνευται καὶ πόλις,[1] καὶ ἀγροῦ τύχη ἐξαπιναίως ἀμείβεται. 15 οἵ τε ἄγροικοι τὴν ἐχέτλην ἀπορριψάμενοι πολιτικῶς βιοτεύουσιν, οὐκ ἄγροικον δίαιταν ἔτι, ἀλλ᾽ ἀστείαν διαχειρίζοντες. B 342 16 ἐπεὶ καὶ ἀγοράζουσιν ἐνταῦθα διημερεύοντες, καὶ ὑπὲρ τῶν σφίσιν ἀναγκαίων ἐκκλησιάζουσι, καὶ ἀγορὰν ἀλλήλοις συμβάλλουσι, τἄλλα τε ἅπαντα πράσσουσιν ὅσα δὴ ἐς πόλεως ἀξίωμα ἥκει.

17 Ταῦτα μὲν ἐν Βυζακίῳ τῷ ἐπιθαλασσίῳ πεποίηται. κατὰ δὲ τὴν μεσόγειαν ἐς τῆς χώρας τὰ ἔσχατα, ἵνα δὴ αὐτὴν βάρβαροι προσοικοῦσι Μαυρούσιοι, ἐπιτειχίσματα κατ᾽ αὐτῶν πεποίηται δυνατώτατα, ἐξ ὧν δὴ οὐκέτι οἷοί τέ εἰσι καταθεῖν τὴν Ῥωμαίων ἀρχήν. 18 πόλεις τε γὰρ τὰς ἐνταῦθα οὔσας ἐν ἐσχατιᾷ τῆς χώρας ἑκάστην[2] τείχεσιν ἐχυροῖς ἄγαν περιβαλών, αἷς αἱ προσηγορίαι Μάμμης τε καὶ Τελεπτὴ καὶ Κούλουλις, καὶ φρούριον τειχισάμενος, ὅπερ καλοῦσιν οἱ ἐπιχώριοι Αὐμέτρα, ἐχεγγύους ἐνταῦθα φρουροὺς στρατιωτῶν κατεστήσατο.

[1] πόλις A: πόλιν V. [2] ἑκάστην Haury: ἑκάστη.

spent that night there; and on the next day they prepared for battle and, to omit what intervened, took possession of Libya. So the Emperor Justinian, by way of bearing witness to the gift of God by means of a permanent testimony—for the most difficult task easily yields to his wish—conceived the desire to transform this place forthwith into a city which should be made strong by a wall and distinguished by its other appointments as worthy to be counted an impressive and prosperous city; and the purpose of the Emperor has been realized. For a wall has been brought to completion and with it a city, and the condition of a farm land is being suddenly changed. And the rustics have thrown aside the plough and lead the existence of a community, no longer going the round of country tasks but living a city life. They pass their days in the market-place and hold assemblies to deliberate on questions which concern them; and they traffic with one another, and conduct all the other affairs which pertain to the dignity of a city.

This then was done in Byzacium on the sea. In the interior of this land and to its farthest parts, where barbarian Moors live hard by, he built very powerful outposts against them, because of which they are no longer able to overrun the Roman dominion. He surrounded each one of the cities with very strong walls, since they stand on the rim of the territory; these bear the names Mammes, Teleptê and Cululis.[1] He also constructed a fort which the natives call Aumetra, and in these places he stationed trustworthy garrisons of troops.

[1] Cululis (or Collops Magna, modern Collo) was on the coast near the western boundary of Numidia.

ζʹ. Τρόπῳ δὲ τῷ αὐτῷ Νουμιδίων τῇ χώρᾳ τειχίσματί τε καὶ στρατιωτῶν φυλακτηρίοις τὴν ἀσφάλειαν προσεποίησεν, ὧνπερ ἕκαστα ἐρῶν 2 ἔρχομαι. ὄρος ἐστὶν ἐν Νουμιδίᾳ, ὅπερ Αὐράσιον[1] P 117 ἐπικέκληται, οἷον δὴ γῆς τῆς οἰκουμένης ἑτέρωθι 3 ὡς ἥκιστα ξυμβαίνει εἶναι. τοῦτο γὰρ τὸ ὄρος οὐρανόμηκες μὲν ἐν τῷ ἀποτόμῳ ἀνέχει, ἐς περίμετρον δὲ ἡμερῶν μάλιστα διήκει ὁδῷ τριῶν. καὶ προσιόντι μὲν ἀπρόσβατόν ἐστιν, ἀνάβασιν οὐδεμίαν ὅτι μὴ ἐν ἀποκρήμνῳ ἔχον. 4 ἄνω δὲ γενομένῳ γεώδης τε ἡ χώρα καὶ ὁμαλῆ τὰ πεδία καὶ ὁδοὶ προσηνεῖς, λειμῶνες εὔνομοι, παράδεισοι κατάφυτοι δένδροις, ἀρόματα πάντα. 5 καὶ πηγαὶ μὲν ἀποβλύζουσαι τῶν τῇδε σκοπέλων, γαληνὰ δὲ τὰ ὕδατα, καὶ ποταμοὶ πλήθει μυθίου ἐπικυρτούμενοι, καὶ τὸ δὴ πάντων παραδοξότατον, τά τε λήϊα καὶ τὰ δένδρα ἐν τούτῳ τῷ B 343 ὄρει διπλάσιον μεγέθους πέρι τὸν καρπὸν φέρουσιν ἢ ἐν Λιβύῃ τῇ ἄλλῃ πέφυκε γίνεσθαι. τὰ μὲν 6 οὖν ὄρους τοῦ Αὐρασίου ταύτῃ πη ἔχει. Βανδίλοι δὲ αὐτὸ σὺν πάσῃ Λιβύῃ τὸ κατ᾽ ἀρχὰς εἶχον, οὓς δὴ Μαυρούσιοι ἀφελόμενοι τῇδε 7 ἱδρύσαντο. Μαυρουσίους δὲ καὶ Ἰαῦδαν, ὃς αὐτῶν ἦρχεν, ἐξελάσας ἐνθένδε Ἰουστινιανὸς βασιλεύς, τῇ ἄλλῃ προσεποίησε Ῥωμαίων ἀρχῇ. 8 προνοήσας τε ὡς μὴ καὶ αὖθις οἱ βάρβαροι κακουργοῖεν ἐνταῦθα ἰόντες, πόλεις μὲν ἀμφὶ τὸ ὄρος ἐρήμους τε καὶ ἀτειχίστους τὸ παράπαν εὑρὼν ἐτειχίσατο, Πεντεβαγάην τε λέγω καὶ Φλωρεντιανὴν καὶ Βάδην τε καὶ Μήλεον καὶ Ταμουγάδην,

[1] Modern Jebel Auress.

vii. In the same way he assured the safety of the land of Numidia by means of fortifications and garrisons of soldiers, each one of which I shall now mention. There is a mountain in Numidia which is called Aurasius,[1] such as chances to be found nowhere else at all in the civilized world. For this mountain rises steeply to a towering height and its perimeter extends to a distance of about three days' journey.[2] It offers no path as one approaches it, having no ascent except over cliffs. But after one gets to the top there is deep soil and level plains and easy roads, meadows good for pasture, parks full of trees and plough-land everywhere. Springs bubble out from the cliffs there, their waters are placid, there are rippling rivers which flow chattering along, and strangest of all, the grain-fields and the trees on this mountain produce crops which are double in size compared with those which are wont to grow in the rest of Libya. Such is the condition of Mt. Aurasius. The Vandals held it originally along with the rest of Libya, but the Moors wrested it from them and settled there. The Emperor Justinian, however, expelled from there the Moors, and Iaudas who ruled over them,[3] and added this mountain to the rest of the Roman Empire. As a precaution in order that the barbarians might not again make trouble by getting a foothold there, he fortified cities about the mountain which he found deserted and altogether unwalled. I refer to Pentebagae and Florentianae and Badê and Meleum and Tamugadê,

[2] About sixty miles; actually it is larger than Procopius indicates.

[3] *Cf. Wars*, IV. xiii. 22 ff.

ἔτι μέντοι καὶ φρούρια δύο Δάβουσίν τε καὶ Γαιανά, φυλακτήρια δὲ στρατιωτῶν διαρκῆ ἐνταῦθα καταστησάμενος, οὐδεμίαν τοῖς ἐκείνῃ βαρβάροις ἐλπίδα τῆς ἐπὶ τὸ Αὐράσιον ἐπιβουλῆς
9 ἀπελίπετο.[1] καὶ χώραν δὲ τὴν ὑπὲρ τὸ Αὐράσιον ὑπὸ Βανδίλοις ὡς ἥκιστα οὖσαν τοὺς Μαυρουσίους ἀφείλετο. πόλεις τε ἐνταῦθα ἐτειχίσατο
10 δύο, τήν τε Φρίκην καὶ Σίτιφιν. ἐν δὲ δὴ πόλεσι ταῖς ἐπὶ Νουμιδίας τῆς ἄλλης κειμέναις ἀνανταγώνιστα ἐρύματα κατεστήσατο. αἷς αἱ προσηγορίαι αἵδε εἰσί· Λαριβουζουδούων, Παρατουρῶν, Κιλανά, Σικκαβενερία,[2] Τίγισις, Λαμ-
11 φουαομβά, Καλαμάα, Μέδαρα, Μέδελα. ἔτι μέντοι καὶ φρούρια δύο, ἥ Σκιλή τε καὶ Φώσαλα. ταῦτα μὲν ὧδέ πῃ ἔχει.

12 Πόλις δέ πού ἐστιν ἐν τῇ νήσῳ Σαρδοῖ, ἣ νῦν Σαρδινία καλεῖται, Τραϊανοῦ Φόρον[3] αὐτὴν
13 καλοῦσι Ῥωμαῖοι. ταύτην τειχήρη πεποίηται Ἰουστινιανός, οὐ πρότερον οὖσαν, ἀλλὰ Μαυρουσίοις τοῖς νησιώταις, οἳ Βαρβαρικῖνοι ἐπικαλοῦνται, ὁπηνίκα ἂν ληΐζεσθαι βουλομένοις ᾖ, ἐν προχείρῳ κειμένην.

14 Ἐν δὲ Γαδείροις, κατὰ θάτερα τῶν Ἡρακλέους στηλῶν, ἣ τοῦ πορθμοῦ ἐν δεξιᾷ ἐστι, κατὰ τὴν Λιβύης ἀκτὴν φρούριον ἦν ποτε Σέπτον ὄνομα, ὅπερ ἐδείμαντο μὲν ἐν τοῖς ἄνω χρόνοις Ῥωμαῖοι, Βανδίλων δὲ οὐκ ἐπιμελουμένων καθεῖλεν ὁ
15 χρόνος. ὁ δὲ καθ' ἡμᾶς βασιλεὺς Ἰουστινιανὸς τείχει μὲν ἐρυμνόν, φυλακτηρίῳ δὲ ἰσχυρὸν
16 κατεστήσατο. οὗ δὴ καὶ νεὼν ἀξιοθέατον τῇ

[1] ἀπελίπετο V : ἀπελείπετο A. [2] So Haury : βενερία V.
[3] φρούριον before Φόρον deleted by Haury.

as well as two forts, Dabusis and Gaeana; also he established there sufficient garrisons of soldiers, thus leaving to the barbarians there no hope of attacking Aurasius. The district beyond Aurasius, which had not been under the Vandals at all, he wrested from the Moors. There he walled two cities, Fricê and Sitifis.[1] At the cities situated in the rest of Numidia, the names of which follow, he set up impregnable defences: Laribuzuduôn, Paraturôn, Cilana, Siccaveneria,[2] Tigisis, Lamfouaomba, Calamaa, Medara,[3] Medela; besides these, two forts, Scilê and Foscala. So much, then, for this.

There is a city on the island Sardô, which is now named Sardinia, called by the Romans Traiani Forum. This Justinian has supplied with a wall which it did not have before, but instead it lay exposed to the island[4] Moors, who are called Barbaricini,[5] whenever they wished to plunder it.

And at Gadira,[6] at one side of the Pillars of Heracles, on the right side of the strait, there had been at one time a fortress on the Libyan shore named Septum;[7] this was built by the Romans in early times, but being neglected by the Vandals, it had been destroyed by time. Our Emperor Justinian made it strong by means of a wall and strengthened its safety by means of a garrison. There too he con-

[1] Modern Setif. [2] Or Sicca Veneris, modern Keff.

[3] Or Admedera.

[4] The Moors living in Sardinia; *cf. Wars*, IV. xiii 44.

[5] The region in the interior of Sardinia called Barbargia or Barbagia still preserves the name Barbaricini, but Procopius's explanation of the origin of the barbarian settlers has not been generally accepted. See *Wars*, IV. xiii. 44. The name survives in our Berbers.

[6] Gades; modern Cadiz. [7] Modern Ceuta.

θεοτόκῳ ἀνέθηκεν, ἀναψάμενος μὲν ἐπ' αὐτῆς τὰ τῆς πολιτείας προοίμια, παντὶ δὲ ἀνθρώπων τῷ γένει ταύτῃ ἄμαχον τὸ φρούριον τοῦτο ποιούμενος.

17 Ἀλλὰ ταῦτα μὲν τοιαῦτά ἐστιν. ἀμφίλεκτον δὲ οὐδὲν[1] γέγονεν, ἀλλ' ἔνδηλον ἀνθρώποις διαφανῶς B 344 πᾶσιν, ὡς ἐκ τῶν ἑῴων ὁρίων ἄχρι ἐς δύοντά που τὸν ἥλιον, ἃ δὴ πέρατά ἐστι τῆς Ῥωμαίων ἀρχῆς, οὐκ ἐρύμασι μόνοις, ἀλλὰ καὶ στρατιωτῶν φυλακτηρίοις Ἰουστινιανὸς βασιλεὺς τὴν πολιτείαν 18 ἐκρατύνατο. ὅσα μὲν οὖν τῶν Ἰουστινιανοῦ οἰκοδομημάτων μαθεῖν ἴσχυσα ἢ αὐτόπτης γεγενημένος ἢ τῶν θεασαμένων αὐτήκοος, ὅση δύναμις 19 τῷ λόγῳ ἐπῆλθον. ἐξεπίσταμαι δὲ ὡς πολλά με καὶ ἄλλα παρῆλθεν εἰπεῖν ἢ ὄχλῳ λαθοντα ἢ P 118 20 παντάπασιν ἄγνωστα μείναντα. ὥστε εἴ τῳ[2] διὰ σπουδῆς ἔσται διερευνήσασθαί τε ἅπαντα καὶ τῷ λόγῳ ἐνθεῖναι, προσέσται αὐτῷ τά τε δέοντα πεπραχέναι[3] καὶ φιλοκάλου κλέος ἀπενεγκεῖν.

[1] οὐδὲν V : οὐδενὶ A.
[2] εἴ τῳ V : ὅτῳ A.
[3] πεπραχέναι corrector in V : πεπραγέναι or πεποιηκέναι.

secrated to the Mother of God a noteworthy church, thus dedicating to her the threshold[1] of the Empire, and making this fortress impregnable for the whole race of mankind.

So much for these things. There can be no dispute, but it is abundantly clear to all mankind, that the Emperor Justinian has strengthened the Empire, not with fortresses alone, but also by means of garrisons of soldiers, from the bounds of the East to the very setting of the sun, these being the limits of the Roman dominion. As many, then, of the buildings of the Emperor Justinian as I have succeeded in discovering, either by seeing them myself, or by hearing about them from those who have seen them, I have described in my account to the best of my ability. I am fully aware, however, that there are many others which I have omitted to mention, which either went unnoticed because of their multitude, or remained altogether unknown to me. So if anyone will take the pains to search them all out and add them to my treatise, he will have the credit of having done a needed work and of having won the renown of a lover of fair achievements.[2]

[1] *Cf.* Libanius *Or.* lix. 37: ἐμβιβάσας γὰρ αὐτοὺς εἰς τὸ προοίμιον τῆς βασιλείας.

[2] The achievements, that is, of Justinian.

[illegible] the Mother of God a most worthy church, thus dedicating to her the threshold of the Empire and making this fortress impregnable for the whole race of mankind.[1]

So much for these things. There can be no dispute but it is abundantly clear to all mankind, that the Emperor Justinian has strengthened the Empire, not with fortresses alone, but also by means of garrisons of soldiers from the bounds of the East to the very setting of the sun, these being the limits of the Roman dominion. As many, then, of the buildings of the Emperor Justinian as I have succeeded in discovering, either by seeing them myself or by hearing about them from those who have seen them, I have described in my account to the best of my ability. I am well aware that there are many others which I have omitted to mention, which either went unnoticed because of their multitude, or remained altogether unknown to me. So if anyone shall take the pains to search them all out and add them to my treatise, he will have the credit of having done a useful work and of having won the renown of a lover of fair achievements.[2]

[1] [illegible]

[2] The achievements, that is, of Justinian.

APPENDIX

THE EQUESTRIAN STATUE OF JUSTINIAN IN THE AUGUSTAEUM (*Buildings*, I. ii. 5–12)

A DRAWING of this statue, made at the behest of the traveller and antiquary Cyriacus of Ancona when the monument still existed in the early fifteenth century, is preserved in Budapest; it has been published and discussed most recently by G. Rodenwaldt in the *Archäologischer Anzeiger*, 1931, Sp. 331–334 (the reproduction used as the frontispiece of the present volume was made from his illustration). Rodenwaldt sees, in the description of the statue as σχῆμα Ἀχίλλειον and in Procopius's comment that it represented the Emperor ἡρωϊκῶς, evidence of the interest in the antique conception of the Roman Empire which can be perceived in Justinian's legal policy and in his various efforts for the *renovatio* of the Imperium Romanum.[1] Justinian, however, can hardly, in Rodenwaldt's opinion, have actually been accustomed to wear the costume in which he was depicted.

There may be a question as to precisely what the significance of the statue may have been, beyond

[1] On this aspect of Justinian's reign, see, in addition to Rodenwaldt's paper, F. Pringsheim, " Die archaistische Tendenz Justinians," *Studi in onore di Pietro Bonfante* (Milan, 1930), I, pp. 551–587.

the interpretation of it which Procopius gives. Was the statue intended simply to shew the Emperor in the *costume* of Achilles, or was it designed to depict him in the *character* of Achilles? The word σχῆμα which Procopius uses would favour the second interpretation, though it could support the first also; but his use of this word might easily have been purely fortuitous, and the point cannot be pressed too far. There is also the question whether the representation of Justinian in this fashion reflects only the Emperor's own personal interest in antiquity, expressing itself in a conscious revival of ancient imperial symbolism, or whether the statue represents instead a particular expression of an official conception of the Emperor and his functions which was current at that time. It is always possible, of course, that the statue simply represents an artistic tradition, so that in this case it would be this tradition (possibly even the artist's choice) which was chiefly or solely responsible for the way in which the Emperor was depicted.

Without further knowledge it does not seem proper to adopt any one of these interpretations to the exclusion of the others. There happens to be evidence (unknown to Rodenwaldt) that at least on one occasion, half a century previously, an "Achilles costume" was actually worn, in rather unusual circumstances. The usurper Basiliscus, who reigned as Emperor for twenty months in A.D. 475–476, was persuaded by his wife the Augusta Zenonis to give preferment and high office to her lover Armatus, a young fop who was the Emperor's nephew.[1] A

[1] On the episode see J. B. Bury, *History of the Later Roman Empire* (London, 1923), I, p. 392.

historian of the time tells how this advancement elated the young man beyond all measure, so that he imagined himself to be a man of valour and rode about in the costume of Achilles.[1] This episode may or may not be taken to shew that the "costume of Achilles" was considered to be specifically an imperial dress; it is to be noted that the word used to describe it is σκευή, "dress," and not σχῆμα as in the case of Justinian. The incident certainly indicates that the costume was thought to be especially appropriate to a brave commander; our knowledge does not seem sufficient, however, to permit us to find in the episode a definitive explanation of Justinian's appearance in this manner in the statue.

The origin of the costume, the characteristic part of which seems to be the headdress, is not clear, though further evidence on this point may eventually come to light.[2] The evidence that an "Achilles costume" was worn by Armatus helps to eliminate a difficulty which Rodenwaldt encountered in this connection. The elder Pliny (*Nat. Hist.*, XXXIV. 18) states that "nude statues holding a spear, modelled after young men in the gymnasia, were called Achillean." Rodenwaldt thought it necessary

[1] His conduct is described by Suidas, s.v. Ἀρμάτιος. The passage was formerly thought to represent a fragment of Malchus of Philadelphia, and is attributed to him in the *Fragmenta Historicorum Graecorum*, IV, p. 117; it now seems more likely that it comes from Candidus the Isaurian (see Bury, *loc. cit.*, nn. 1–2). The costume is mentioned as follows: καὶ τοσοῦτον αὐτοῦ ἤδε ἡ ἄλη ἐπεκράτει, ὡς σκευὴν ἀναλαμβάνειν Ἀχιλλέως, οὕτω τε περιβαίνειν εἰς ἵππον . . .

[2] On the appearance of Roman emperors in the costumes of gods and heroes, reference may be made to A. Alföldi, "Insignien und Tracht der römischen Kaiser," *Römische Mitteilungen*, L. 1935, pp. 105–110.

to suppose that the term " Achillean " indicated that there was some connection between the nude statues described by Pliny and the armed costume described by Procopius, but he had to admit that it is difficult to see precisely what such a connection might be. The episode of Armatus now indicates that the passage in Pliny has nothing to do with the matter, and that the origin of the costume is to be sought elsewhere.

LIST OF LATIN WORDS[1]

Place-names are included only when Procopius indicates that they are Latin, and explains their meaning. S.H. (*Secret History*), B. (*Buildings*); other references are to the *Wars*.

ἄγεστα, *aggestus*, II. xxvi. 29
ἀντίφορος, (from *forum*), B. II. vii. 6
ἀσηκρῆτις, *a secretis*, II. vii. 15, S.H. xiv. 4

βαλλίστρα, *ballista*, V. xxi. 14 (*cf.* note on § 18), VIII. xxxv. 9
βάνδον, *bandum*, IV. ii. 1
βανδοφόρος, *bandifer*, IV. x. 4
Βενεβεντός, *bene* + *ventus* (meaning explained), V. xv. 4
Βένετοι, *Veneti* (circus faction), I. xxiv. 2, XX. xi. 32, S.H. vii. 1, 2, 6, 17, 22, ix. 33, x. 16, 18, 19, xii. 28, xvii. 2, 3, xxix. 27, 30, 32, 33 (twice), 36
βέντος, *ventus*, V. xv. 4
βερεδάριος, *veredarius*, III. xvi. 12, B. V. iii. 3
βέρεδος, *veredus*, II. xx. 20
βιβάριον, *vivarium*, V. xxii. 10, xxiii. 14, 18, 19
βοῦστα, *busta*, VIII. xxix. 5
Βουσταγαλλώρων, *Busta Gallorum*, VIII. xxix. 5

Δεκέμβριος, *December*, IV. iii. 28, V. xiv. 14 (*cf.* critical note)
Δεκεννόβιον, *Decennovium* (*decem* + *novem*), V. xi. 2
Δέλφιξ, *Delphicus* (Procopius believed that this was a Greek word which had been taken over into Latin), II. xxi. 2, 3
δομέστικος, *domesticus*, III. iv. 7, xi. 6, S.H. xxiv. 24, xxvi. 28
δοῦξ, *dux*, I. xvii. 46, B. II. vi. 9, III. i. 28, ii. 1, iii. 8, 14, vi. 17

ἐξκουβίτωρ, *excubitor*, IV. xii. 17

κανδιδᾶτος, *candidatus*, VII. xxxviii. 5
κασοῦλα, *casula* (*casa*), IV. xxvi. 26
κάστελλος, *castellum*, B. II. v. 9
κεντηνάριον, *centenarium*, I. xxii. 3, 4, II. iii. 7, v. 29, vi. 25, viii. 4, x. 24, xxviii. 44, VIII. xv. 3 (twice), 17, S.H. i. 33, iv. 31, xix. 7, 8, xxiv. 31, xxv. 19, xxvi. 13, 21, xxvii. 21, xxviii. 5, 11, xxx. 19
κέντον, *centum*, I. xxii. 4
κινστάρνα, *cisterna*, B. IV. iv. 3
κλείσουρα, *clausura*, II. xxix. 25, B. III. iii. 2, vii. 5, IV. ii. 17
κοιαισίτωρ, *quaesitor*, S.H. xx. 9, 11
κοιαίστωρ, *quaestor*, I. xxiv. 11, 18, V. xiv. 5, VII. xl. 23, S.H. vi. 13, ix. 41, xx. 15
κόμης, *comes*, B. III. i. 15
Κυιντίλιος, *Quintilis*, V. xxiv. 31

λεγεών, *legio*, B. I. vii. 3, III. iv. 16
λιμιτάναιος, *limitaneus*, S.H. xxiv. 12
λῶρος, *lorum*, VI. v. 18, B. I. i. 68, 75

μάγιστρος, *magister*, I. viii. 2, VI. xxii. 24, VIII. xi. 2, S.H. xvi. 5, xvii. 32, xxii. 12, xxiv. 22, xxv. 3
Μαλεβεντός, *male* + *ventus* (meaning explained), V. xv. 4
μοῦνδος, *mundus*, V. vii. 8
μῶλος, *moles*, B. IV. x. 7 (*cf.* § 15, critical apparatus)

ὄκταβον, *octavum*, B. IV. v. 16
ὀλόβηρον, (from *verum*), S.H. xxv. 21
ὀπτίων, *optio*, III. xvii. 1, IV. xx. 12
οὐγκία, *uncia*, S.H. xxv. 21

[1] *Cf.* E. Schwyzer, "Die sprachlichen Interessen Prokops von Cäsarea," *Festgabe Hugo Blümner*, Zurich, 1914, pp. 303–327.

LIST OF LATIN WORDS

πακᾶτοι, *pacati*, B. VI. iii. 11
πάκεν, (acc.), *pacem*, B. VI. iii. 11
παλατῖνος, *palatinus*, S.H. xxii. 12, xxiv. 25 (*cf.* critical note)
παλάτιον, *palatium*, I. viii. 2, xxvi. 11, III. xxi. 3, 4 (derivation from Pallas), S.H. xii. 26, xiv. 10, 13, 18, xvii. 34, xxiv. 8, 15, 25 (critical note), xxvi. 17, xxvii. 10, xxix. 36, 37, B. I. x. 4, VI. v. 9
πατρίκιος, *patricius*, I. viii. 5, xi. 24 (twice), xxiv. 18 (twice), IV. vi. 22, VI. vi. 16, VIII. xi. 2, S.H. xv. 25, 26, 27 (twice), 29, 32, 34, xxvii. 17, xxx. 21, 23, B. I. iii. 14
πατριμώνιον, *patrimonium*, V. iv. 1, vi. 26, S.H. xxii. 12
πένατες, *penates*, V. xxv. 19
πλούμια, *plumea*, B. III. i. 22
Πόντες, (from *pons*), B. IV. vi. 15
πόντην, (acc.), *pontem*, B. IV. vi. 16, 18 (twice)
πραίτωρ, *praetor*, III. x. 3, S.H. xx. 9, 10
πραιτώριον, *praetorium*, VI. xxii. 24, VII. vi. 9, S.H. xxi. 1
πριβᾶτα, *privata*, S.H. xxii. 12
πρῖμα, *prima*, B. IV. i. 19
προτίκτωρες, *protectores*, S.H. xxiv. 24
πυργοκάστελλος, (from *castellum*), B. II. v. 8

ῥεφερενδάριος, *referendarius*, II. xxiii. 6, S.H. xiv. 11, xvii. 32, xxix. 28
Ῥῆγες, *Reges*, V. xxiii. 3
ῥήξ, *rex*, V. i. 26, VI. xiv. 38
ῥίπα, *ripa*, B. IV. v. 12
Ῥιπησία, *Ripesia*, B. IV. v. 11

σεκοῦνδα, *secunda*, B. IV. i. 30
σενάτωρ, *senator*, B. I. iii. 14
σέπτον, *septem*, III. i. 6
σήκρητα, *secreta*, II. vii. 15
σιλεντιάριος, *silentiarius*, II. xxi. 2, xxix. 31, S.H. xxvi. 28, B. IV. viii. 24
στρᾶτα, *strata*, II. i. 6, 7
σχολάριοι, *scholares*, S.H. xxiv. 15, 21 (twice), xxvi. 28

ταβελλίων, *tabellio*, S.H. xxviii. 6

φαινόλης, *paenula*, II. xxx. 54
Φᾶτα, *Fata*, V. xxv. 19 (Τρία Φᾶτα)
φοίδερα, *foedera*, III. xi. 4, VIII. v. 14
φοιδερᾶτοι, *foederati*, III. xi. 2, 3, xix. 13, 14, IV. vii. 11, xv. 50, V. v. 2, VII. xxxi. 10, xxxiii. 13, VIII. v. 13
φόλλις, *follis*, S.H. xxv. 12
φοσσᾶτον, *fossatum*, B. III. vi. [illegible]

The following two oracles are quoted; in each case some of the readings are uncertain and reference should be made to the critical apparatus and notes:

Africa capta Mundus cum nato peribit, V. vii. 7

Quintili mense si regnum stat in urbe nihil Geticum iam (metuat?), V. xxiv. 30

INDEX

Abandanes, secretary of Chosroes, II. xxi. 1 ff.; his report, II. xxi. 13, 14
Abasgi, a people near the Caucasus, subject to the Lazi, II. xxix. 15, VIII. iii. 12, 13, iv. 1; friends of the Romans, II. xxix. 15; their religion, VIII. iii. 14; supplied eunuchs to Byzantium until the traffic was forbidden, VIII. iii. 15–20; converted to Christianity, III. xxix. 15, VIII. iii. 19; dethrone their kings, VIII. iii. 21, ix. 10; have a bishop sent by Justinian, VIII. iv. 12; revolt from the Romans, VIII. ix. 6, 9 ff.; their land protected by nature, VIII. ix. 15–18; outwitted and dispersed by the Romans, VIII. ix. 23 ff.; Mermeroes marches against them, VIII. xvii. 14
Abasgia, defended by a mountain pass, VIII. ix. 15
Abigas River, in Numidia, flowing down from Mt. Aurasius, IV. xiii. 20, xix. 7, 11; its many channels, IV. xix. 11–13; turned upon the Roman camp, IV. xix. 14
Abochorabus, ruler of the Saracens, presents the Palm Groves to Justinian, I. xix. 10 ff.
Aborrhas River, flows by Circesium, II. v. 2, and Theodosiopolis, II. xix. 29; B. II. v. 1; junction with the Euphrates, B. II. vi. 1; mentioned, B. II. vi. 15
Abramus, becomes king of the Homeritae, I. xx. 3; his servile origin, I. xx. 4; defeats two Ethiopian armies, I. xx. 5–7; pays tribute to the Ethiopians, I. xx. 8; his idle promises to Justinian to invade Persia, I. xx. 13
Abrittus, fortress in Moesia, B. IV. xi. 20
Abydus, city on the Hellespont; opposite Sestus, II. iv. 9, III. i. 8, B. IV. x. 24; Roman fleet delayed there, III. xii. 7, xiii. 5; Customs House established at, S.H. xxv. 2, 3, 5
Acacius, father of Adolius, II. xxi. 2; denounces Amazaspes to the Emperor, II. iii. 4; slays him treacherously, II. iii. 5; his shameless career as Governor of Armenia, II. iii. 6, 7; slain by the Armenians, II. iii. 7, IV. xxvii. 17
Acacius, Church of, restored by Justinian, B. I. iv. 25, 26
Acacius, priest of Byzantium, delivers over Basiliscus, III. vii. 22
Acacius, father of Theodora, Keeper of the Bears, S.H. ix. 2
Acampsis, the lower course of the Boas River, VIII. ii. 8
Acarnania, district north-west of Greece, B. IV. ii. 1; a Roman fleet winters there, V. xxiv. 20
Achaea, suffers from earthquakes, VIII. xxv. 16
Acherontia, Acherontis, fortress in Lucania; captured by Totila, VII. xxiii. 18; commanded by Moras, VIII. xxvi. 4; refuge of Ragnaris, VIII. xxxiv. 15
Achilles, name of a costume, B. I. ii. 7
Achilles, Baths of, in Byzantium, III. xiii. 16
Achilles, name applied to Hoamer, a Vandal leader, III. ix. 2
Aclas, suburb of Carthage, IV. vii. 13

INDEX

Acremba, fortress in Macedonia, B. IV. iv. 3

Acrenza, fortress in Dardania, B. IV. iv. 3

Acues, town on the Danube, B. IV. vi. 19

Adana, city near Mopsuestia, B. V. v. 8

Adanum, fortress in Epirus, B. IV. iv. 3

Adarbiganon, Chosroes halts there with his army, II. xxiv. 1; fire-sanctuary located there, II. xxiv. 2; abandoned by Chosroes, II. xxiv. 12

Adaulphus, King of the Visigoths, III. ii. 37

Addaeus, appointed to control shipping, S.H. xxv. 7–10

Adegis, bodyguard of Belisarius, VI. vii. 27

Adergoudounbades, made "chanaranges" by Chosroes, I. vi. 15, 18; saves Cabades from the hand of Chosroes, I. xxiii. 7 ff.; betrayed by his son, I. xxiii. 13; his death, I. xxiii. 21

Adina, fortress in Moesia; built by Justinian, B. IV. vii. 13

Adolius, son of Acacius, an Armenian, urges severe treatment of Armenians, II. iii. 10; commander of Roman cavalry, II. xxi. 2, 18, 20; commands a detachment in an army to invade Persia, II. xxiv. 13; killed by a stone, II. xxv. 35

Adonachus, commander in Chalcis, II. xii. 2

Adramytus *see* Hadrumetum

Adrastadaran Salanes, an office in Persia of high authority (*lit.* "Leader of the warriors"), I. vi. 18, xi. 25; held only by Seoses, I. vi. 19, xi. 38

Adrianium, fortress in Macedonia, B. IV. iv. 3

Adrianopolis, city in Thrace; restored by Justinian, B. IV. xi. 19; distance from Byzantium, VII. xl. 36

Adrianopolis, city in Epirus; renamed by Justinian, B. IV. i. 36

Adriatic Sea, including the modern Adriatic, V. xv. 16, B. IV. i. 11; divided from the Tuscan Sea by the islands Gaulus and Melite, III. xiv. 16; crossed by the Roman fleet, III. xiii. 21; the scene of one of Gizeric's atrocities, III. xxii. 18; crossed by Artabanes, VII. xl. 14; current thence seems to flow in the strait of Messina, VIII. vi. 21

Adulis, in Ethiopia, the city and harbour, distance from Auxomis, I. xix. 22; home of a certain Roman trader, I. xx. 4

Aeadaba, fortress in Remisianisia, B. IV. iv. 3

Aedabê, fortress on the Danube, restored by Justinian, B. IV. vi. 31

Aeetes, mythical king of Colchis, VIII. ii. 31; his legendary birthplace, VIII. xiv. 49

Aegean Sea, its meeting with the Euxine, B. I. v. 3

Aegisthus, name given to an infant reared by a goat, VI. xvii. 9, 11

Aeimachus, a butcher of Antioch; his encounter with a Persian horseman, II. xi. 8 ff.

Aelas, city on the "Red Sea," I. xix. 3. 19, 24

Aemilia, district in Northern Italy, on the right of the Po, V. xv. 30, VI. xviii. 25, xix. 8; recovered for the Romans by John, VI. xix. 22, xxi. 14; famine in, VI. xx. 17 ff.; not of great military importance, VI. xxi. 18, 22; invaded by a Roman army, VII. xi. 11; by the Goths, VII. xiii. 8; its cities, Caesena, VI. xxix. 40; Faventia, VII. iii. 22; and Placentia, VII. xiii. 8, 9

Aeneas, son of Anchises, VIII. xxii. 31; meets Diomedes at Beneventus, V. xv. 9; his reputed ship displayed at Rome, VIII. xxii. 7–16; reputed founder of Aenus, B. IV. xi. 1

Aenus, city near the Chersonese; its reputed founder, Aeneas, B. IV. xi. 1; strengthened by Justinian, B. IV. xi. 4, 5

Aeolian Islands, used as a naval station by the Goths, VII. xiii. 6

Aeschmanus, a Massagete, bodyguard of Belisarius, V. xvi. 1

Aeschylus, tragic poet; cited, VIII. vi. 15

INDEX

Aetius, Roman general; his splendid qualities, III. iii. 14, 15; rival of Boniface, III. iii. 15; whom he slanders to Placidia, III. iii. 17; writes a deceitful letter to Boniface, III. iii. 18, 28; spared by Placidia by reason of his great power, III. iii. 29; defeats Attila, III. iv. 24; Maximus plans to destroy him, III. iv. 24, 25; slandered to the Emperor, III. iv. 26; his death, III. iv. 27, vi. 7; a great loss to the Emperor, III. iv. 28

Aetna, volcanic mountain in Sicily, III. xiii. 22; compared with Vesuvius, VIII. xxxv. 2, 5

Aetolia, region north-west of Greece, B. IV. ii. 1; a Roman fleet winters there, V. xxiv. 20

Africa, mentioned in the oracle regarding Mundus, V. vii. 6, 7

Agamemnon, son of Atreus, VIII. xxii. 27; father of Iphigeneia, I. xvii. 11, VIII. v. 23; leader of the Trojan expedition, VIII. xxii. 28

Agesta, *i.e.* "agger," employed by the Persians in besieging Edessa, II. xxvi. 29

Agriolodê, monastery in Libya; fortified by Justinian, B. VI. ii. 7, 8

Aigan, Massagete chief; in the Roman army at the battle of Daras, I. xiii. 20, xiv. 39, 44; bodyguard of Belisarius, III. xi. 7, 9, IV. x. 4; commander of cavalry, III. xi. 7; on the right wing at the battle of Tricamarum, IV. iii. 4; makes a successful attack upon the Moors in Byzacium, IV. x. 5; his force in turn annihilated by the Moors, IV. x. 6 ff.; his death, IV. x. 10. xi. 22

Aigissus, fortress in Scythia; built by Justinian, B. IV. vii. 20

Air-tax, a surtax collected by Justinian, S.H. xxi. 2

Alamani, a barbarian people of Gaul, V. xii. 11

Alamundaras, son of Saccice, king of the Saracens, marches with the Persian army, I. xvii. 1; his character and services to the Persians, I. xvii. 40 ff.; advises Cabades to invade Roman territory south of the Euphrates River, I. xvii. 30 ff.; retires with Azarethes before Belisarius, I. xviii. 9 ff.; brings charge against Arethas of violating boundary lines, II. i. 3; war with Arethas, II. xxviii. 12–14; sacrifices the son of Arethas to Aphrodite, II. xxviii. 13; sought as an ally by Justinian, II. i. 13, iii. 47, S.H. xi. 12; accused by Justinian of violating the treaty, II. iv. 21; a menace to Syria and Phoenicia, II. xvi. 17; also to Lebanon, II. xix. 34; said to have suffered at the hands of the Saracens, VIII. xi. 10

Alani, a Gothic people, V. i. 3; allies of the Vandals in their migration, III. iii. 1; with the Vandals in Africa, III. v. 18, 19, xxiv. 3; lose their individuality as a people, III. v. 21; allied with the Romans; their mountainous country, II. xxix. 15, VIII. iii. 4; persuaded by Gubazes to ally themselves with him, II. xxix. 29; neighbours of the Sunitae, I. xv. 1; of the Bruchi, VIII. iv. 1; as allies in the Roman army, VIII. i. 4; fighting with the Persians, VIII. viii. 28, 34; one of them alone defends a camp, VIII. viii. 37; is killed by John, VIII. viii. 38

Alaric, King of the Visigoths, invades Europe, III. ii. 7, V. i. 3; captures Rome by a trick, III. ii. 14–23; plunders the city, III. ii. 24; deposits the plunder in Carcasiana, V. xii. 41; destroys Urvisalia, VI. xvi. 24; declares Attalus Emperor of the Romans, III. ii. 28; marches with Attalus against Ravenna, III. ii. 29; opposes sending of commanders to Libya by Attalus, III. ii. 30; quarrels with Attalus, and reduces him from the kingship, III. ii. 36; dies of disease, III. ii. 37

Alaric the Younger, ruler of the Visigoths; betrothed to Theodichusa, daughter of Theoderic, V. xii. 22; attacked by the Franks, V. xii. 33; appeals to Theoderic, V. xii. 34; meets the Franks in battle and is slain, V. xii. 35–40; father of Giselicus, V. xii. 43

Alarum, fortress in Scassctana, B. IV. iv. 3

Alba, town in Picenum, VI. vii. 25

Albani, a people near the Taurus, I. x. 1

Albani, a people north of Liguria, V. xv. 29

Albani, town near Rome, V. vi. 7; occupied by Gontharis, VI. iv. 8, vii. 20, 23

Albilas, Gothic commander of Urviventus, VI. xi. 1, xx. 14

Albis, a Goth sent as envoy to Belisarius, V. xx. 7

Alcon, fortress in Thessaly, B. IV. iv. 3

Aldanes, fortress in southern Europe, B. IV. iv. 3

Alexander of Macedon, son of Philip, fortified the Caspian Gates, I. x. 9; compared with Justinian, II. ii. 15; defeated the Persian King, B. III. i. 5; shrine of, in Libya, B. VI. ii. 16

Alexander Severus, Roman emperor, son of Mamaea, B. III. i. 5

Alexander, ambassador to the Persians, I. xxii. 1

Alexander, Roman Senator, envoy of Justinian, V. iii. 13, vi. 26; meets Amalasuntha in Ravenna, V. iii. 16; his report, V. iii. 29; brother of Athanasius, V. vi. 26

Alexander, commander of cavalry, VI. v. 1

Alexander, Logothete in Byzantium, VII. i. 28; his unscrupulous practices, VII. i. 29, 30, S.H. xxiv. 9; nicknamed "Snips" for clipping coins, VII. i. 30; sent to Italy, VII. i. 31, S.H. xxvi. 29; offends both Goths and Italians, VII. i. 32, 33, ix. 13; approved by Justinian, S.H. xxvi. 30, 34; in Ravenna, VII. iii. 2; oppresses inhabitants of Greece, S.H. xxvi. 31–33; shares chief command with Constantianus, VII. iii. 4

Alexandria, at the eastern limit of Libya, B. VI. i. 11; source of grain shipment, B. V. i. 10; distance from Pentapolis, B. VI. ii. 3; connected by canal with the Nile, B. VI. i. 1–4; visited by the pestilence, II. xxii. 6; its citizens accused by John the Cappadocian, I. xxv. 44; visited by Theodora, S.H. ix. 27; its Patriarch Paulus, S. H. xxvii. 3, 11, 22; Rhodon praefectus augustalis, S.H. xxvii. 3; heretics of, S.H. xxvii. 5; reached by Paulus and Arsenius, S.H. xxvii. 14; Liberius praefectus augustalis, S.H. xxvii. 17; home of Calonymus, III. xi. 14; and of Chryses, B. II. iii. 2

Alexandrians, oppressed by Hephaestus, S.H. xxvi. 35–44

Algedon, place near Rome, VII. xxii. 18; site of a Gothic camp, VII. xxiii. 9

Algus, fortress in Epirus, B. IV. iv. 3

Alistrus, fortress in Epirus, B. IV. iv. 3

Aliula, fortress in Epirus, B. IV. iv. 3

Almu, fortress on the Danube, B. IV. vi. 26

Aloustou, fortress built by Justinian on the Euxine, B. III. vii. 11

Alps, definition of the word "alp," V. xii. 3, 4; form boundary between Gaul and Liguria, V. xii. 4, 30; distance from Milan, VI. xii. 37, 38; crossed by the Franks, VI. xxv. 5, xxviii. 10

Altenon, fortress in Moesia; restored by Justinian, B. IV. vii. 9

Althias, commander of Roman auxiliaries, III. xi. 6; on the left wing at the battle of Tricamarum, IV. iii. 4; commander of the Huns in Numidia, IV. xiii. 2; his encounter with Iaudas, IV. xiii. 3–16; his fame from the deed, IV. xiii. 17

Altina, fortress in Moesia, B. IV. xi. 20

Aluith, an Erulian commander, VI. xiii. 18, xxii. 8

Amalaberga, daughter of Amalafrida, betrothed to Hermenefridus, V. xii. 22; sister of Theodatus, V. xiii. 2

Amalafrida, sister of Theoderic, III. viii. 11, V. iii. 1, VIII. xxv. 11; mother of Theodatus, V. iii. 1; and of Amalaberga, V. xii. 22; grandmother of Amalafridas, VIII. xxv. 11; given in marriage to Trasamundus, III. viii. 11, 12; presented with Lilybaeum, III. viii. 13; put under guard by the Vandals, III. ix. 4

Amalafridas, a Goth, commander of

INDEX

Roman troops sent to the Lombards, VIII. xxv. 11; grandson of Amalafrida, *ib.*; alone reaches the Lombards, VIII. xxv. 13; with the Lombards, VIII. xxv. 14

Amalaric, grandson of Theoderic and son of Theodichusa, V. xii. 43, 46; becomes King of the Visigoths, with Theoderic as regent, V. xii. 46; marries the daughter of the Frankish king, and divides Gaul with the Goths and his cousin Atalaric, V. xiii. 4; receives back the treasures of Carcasiana, V. xiii. 6; gives offence to Theudibert by his treatment of his wife, V. xiii. 9, 10; defeated by him in battle and slain, V. xiii. 11

Amalasuntha, daughter of Theoderic, V. ii. 23, xxiv. 25; her noble qualities, V. iv. 29; her ability and justice as a ruler, V. ii. 3–5; mother of Matasuntha, V. xi. 27; VII. xxxix. 14; and of Atalaric, V. ii. 1; acts as regent for him, V. ii. 3; appealed to by the Goths in regard to Lilybaeum, IV. v. 18; her conflict with the Gothic nobles, V. ii. 20–22; her plan for Atalaric's education frustrated by the Goths, V. ii. 6 ff.; allows him to be trained according to the ideas of the Goths, V. ii. 18 ff.; sends a ship to Epidamnus, V. ii. 26–28, iii. 14; later recalls it, V. ii. 29; her concern at the failing health of Atalaric, V. iii. 10, 11; plans to hand over Italy to Justinian, V. iii. 12; accused by Justinian, V. iii. 15–18; meets Alexander in Ravenna, V. iii. 16; receives Justinian's letter, V. iii. 16–18; her reply, V. iii. 19–27; makes an agreement with Justinian, III. xiv. 5; sends envoys to him agreeing to hand over all Italy, V. iii. 28, 29; courts his friendship to secure protection, III. xiv. 6; hears accusations against Theodatus, V. iv. 1; compels him to make restitution, V. iv. 2; attempts to gain his support, V. iv. 4 ff.; deceived by him, V. iv. 10; decides to go to Byzantium, S.H. xvi. 1; imprisoned, V. iv. 13–15; compelled to write Justinian, V. iv. 16; the envoy Peter sent to treat with her, V. iv. 18; championed by Justinian, V. iv. 22; her death, V. iv. 25–27, 31; slain by Theodatus, S.H. xvi. 5, 6; at the instigation of Peter, S.H. xxiv. 23; her death foreshadowed by the crumbling of a mosaic in Naples, V. xxiv. 25; the benefits of her reign, VII. ix. 10

Amanteia, fortress in Epirus, B. IV. iv. 3

Amantius, commander of the palace eunuchs; slain by Justinian, S.H. vi. 26

Amasia, city on the Euxine; its sanctuaries repaired by Justinian, B. III. vii. 2; destroyed by earthquake, S.H. xviii. 42

Amastris, city on the Euxine, VIII. ii. 2

Amazaspes, nephew of Symeon, made ruler of certain Armenian villages, II. iii. 3; denounced to the Emperor, II. iii. 4; treacherously slain, II. iii. 5

Amazons, their reputed home on the Thermodon, VIII. ii. 2; traditional account of their movements, VIII. iii. 5, 6; Procopius' explanation of the tradition, VIII. iii. 7–11

Ambazouces, a Hun; offers to sell to Anastasius the control of the Caspian Gates, I. x. 10; his death, I. x. 12

Ambrus, a Christian Saracen; saves Sergiopolis from capture by Chosroes, II. xx. 10, 14

Amida, a city on the border between Armenia and Mesopotamia, I. xvii. 24; B. III. i. 17; distance from Martyropolis, I. xxi. 6; B. III. ii. 4; distance from the Nymphius River, I. viii. 22; from Siphrios, I. viii. 10; from Endielon, I. vii. 5; from Thilasamon, I. ix. 14; besieged by Cabades, I. vii. 3, 12 ff., B. III. v. 3; bravely defended, I. vii. 4, 12 ff.; captured by Cabades, I. vii. 29; B. III. ii. 8; besieged by the Romans, I. ix. 1–4; recovered by the Romans by purchase, I. ix. 20, 23, B. II. i. 4; captives of, generously treated

by Chosroes, I. vii. 34; citizens relieved of taxes, I. vii. 35; made secure by Justinian, B. II. iii. 27; fortresses near; strengthened by Justinian, B. II. iv. 19; mentioned, B. II. iv. 14
Amisus, city on the Euxine, VIII. ii. 2; near the Thermodon River, VIII. iii. 5
Ammatas, brother of Gelimer; instructed to prepare to meet the Romans near Carthage, III. xvii. 11, xviii. 1; kills his kinsmen in prison, III. xvii. 12; his inopportune arrival at Decimum, III. xviii. 4, 5; on the day before Easter, III. xxi. 23; engages with John there and is defeated, III. xviii. 5, 6; his death, III. xviii. 6, xix. 30, xx. 6, xxv. 15; his body found by the Romans, III. xix. 14
Ammodios, place near Daras, I. xiii. 15, 38; II. xxviii. 35, B. II. i. 26
Ammon, shrine of, in Libya, B. VI. ii. 16
Amulo, fortress in Aquenisium, B. IV. iv. 3
Amyntou, Basilica, fortress in Macedonia, B. IV. iv. 3
Anagoncli, fortress in Haemimontum, B. IV. xi. 20
Anaplus, suburb of Byzantium; on the Bosporus, B. I. v. 1; site of a church of the Archangel Michael, B. I. viii. 2, 6, 17
Anasozadus, eldest son of Chosroes, VIII. x. 8; banished by him because of lawless conduct, VIII. x. 8-10; leads an uprising and is punished by mutilation, VIII. x. 17-xi. 1
Anastasia, sister of Theodora, S.H. ix. 3
Anastasiopolis, city in Rhodopê; strengthened by Justinian, B. IV. xi. 11-13
Anastasius, Roman Emperor, VI. xiv. 10, B. III. ii. 4; uncle of Hypatius, I. viii. 2, xi. 24; and of Probus, I. xii. 6; and of Pompeius, I. xxiv. 19; refuses offer of Ambazouces, I. x. 10, 11, xvi. 4; insurrection raised against him by Vitalianus, I. viii. 3, xiii. 10; refuses request of Cabades, I. vii. 1, 2; shews favour to citizens of Amida, I. vii. 35; sends succour to Amida, I. viii. 1; makes alliance with the Eruli, VI. xiv. 28, 32; fortifies Daras, I. x. 13, VIII. vii. 9, B. II. i. 4; placates Cabades, I. x. 17; fortifies Theodosiopolis, I. x. 18, 19, B. III. v. 4; begins wall around Melitenê, B. III. iv. 19; relinquishes Martyropolis, B. III. ii. 9; builds long walls of Byzantium, B. IV. ix. 6; keeps peace with the Vandals, III. vii. 26, viii. 14; at war with the Isaurians, S.H. vi. 4; blessings of his reign, VII. xxi. 23; succeeded by Justinus, S.H. vi. 11; left State Treasuries filled, S.H. xix. 5, 7; remitted taxes, S.H. xxiii. 7; mentioned, S.H. ix. 3; his death, I. xi. 1
Anastasius of Daras, puts down a rebellion there, I. xxvi. 8, II. iv. 10; bears a letter from Justinian to Chosroes, II. iv. 16; detained by Chosroes, II. iv. 26; dismissed by Chosroes, II. v. 27; present with Chosroes at the sack of Sura, II. ix. 10
Anastasius, grandson of Theodora; betrothed to Joannina, S.H. iv. 37; whom he marries irregularly and loves ardently, S.H. v. 20-22
Anatolius, eminent citizen of Ascalon, S.H. xxix. 17, 22, 24; his daughter, S.H. xxix. 18; his death, S.H. xxix. 21
Anatolius, General of the East; avoids danger to the Empire by courtesy to the Persian King, I. ii. 12-15, xvi. 6
Anazarbus, city in Cilicia; destroyed by earthquake, S.H. xviii. 41
Anchialus, Thracian town on the Euxine, B. III. vii. 18, 19; ravaged by the Goths, VIII. xxii. 31; its sanatorium, B. III. vii. 20-23
Anchialus, fortress in Haemimontum, B. IV. xi. 20
Anchises, father of Aeneas, V. xv. 9, VIII. xxii. 31, B. IV. xi. 1
Ancon, a dungeon in the royal resi-

INDEX

dence in Carthage, III. xx. 4; unexpected release of Roman merchants confined there, III. xx. 5-9
Ancon, fortress on the Ionian Gulf, VI. xi. 4, 21, VII. xxx. 17; its strong position, VI. xiii. 6; taken by Belisarius, VI. xi. 5; attacked by the Goths, VI. xiii. 5 ff., VIII. xxiii. 1 ff.; saved from them, VIII. xxiii. 39, 40; reinforced, VIII. xxiii. 41; used as a provision port by the Romans, VI. xxiv. 14; port of Auximus, VI. xiii. 7; distance from Ariminum, VI. xi. 4; and from Auximus, VI. xiii. 7
Ancyriana, fortress in **Moesia,** B. IV. xi. 20
Andreas, bishop of Ephesus, S.H. iii. 4
Andreas, of Byzantium; his exploits in single combat, I. xiii. 30 ff.
Andrew, the Apostle; his body revealed to Justinian, B. I. iv. 18, 21
Angili, one of the nations of Brittia, VIII. xx. 7, 12; sent as envoys by the Franks, VIII. xx. 10; attack and defeat the Varni, VIII. xx. 33, 34
Anglon, village in Persarmenia, II. xxv. 5; Roman armies routed there, II. xxv. 23 ff.
Aniabedes, sent by Chosroes to capture Petra, II. xvii. 4; impaled by Chosroes, II. xvii. 11
Annoucas, fortress in Mesopotamia, B. II. vi. 12
Ansilas, a Roman soldier; distinguished for valour, VIII. xxix. 22
Antae, a people settled near the Ister River; serve in the Roman army, V. xxvii. 2, VII. xxii. 3, 5, 21, VIII. iv. 9; good fighters on rough ground, VII. xxii. 3, 5; formerly called Spori, VII. xiv. 29; hold extensive territory, VII. xiv. 30, S.H. xviii. 20; their democratic government, VII. xiv. 22; religious beliefs, customs, language, VII. xiv. 23-28; force a man named Chilbudius to declare himself the Roman general of the same name, VII. xiv. 21, 31; treat with envoys from Justinian, VII. xiv. 32-34; neighbours of the Sclaveni, VII. xl. 5; defeated by them, VII. xiv. 7; invade Roman territory, VII. xiv. 2, 11, xl. 5, S.H. xi. 11; overrun Europe, S.H. xxiii. 6
Antaeus, the mythical wrestler, king in Libya, IV. x. 24
Antalas, ruler of the Moors in Byzacium, III. ix. 3; IV. xxv. 2; remains faithful to the Romans, IV. xii. 30; becomes hostile to Solomon, IV. xxi. 17; joins forces with the Leuathae, IV. xxi. 18; gathers almost all the Moors under him, IV. xxii. 5; writes a letter to Justinian, IV. xxii. 6-10; gathers his army again, IV. xxiii. 1; Areobindus sends an army against him, IV. xxiv. 6; makes an agreement with Gontharis for the destruction of Areobindus, IV. xxv. 6-10; Coutzinas agrees to turn against him, IV. xxv. 15, 18; hears of the plot of Coutzinas and keeps his knowledge secret, IV. xxv. 19-21; resents the sending of the head of Areobindus to him by Gontharis, IV. xxvii. 1, 2; decides to side with Justinian, IV. xxvii. 4; persuades Marcentius to come to him, IV. xxvii. 5, 6; Artabanes sent against him, IV. xxvii. 23; his quarrel with Coutzinas, IV. xxvii. 24; Artabanes marches against him, IV. xxvii. 25; his army spared by Artabanes, IV. xxvii. 28, 29; defeated by John, IV. xxviii. 46, 47, VIII. xvii. 21
Anthemius, a wealthy Senator; appointed Emperor of the West by Leon, III. vi. 5, S.H. xii. 1; killed by his son-in-law Rhecimer, III. vii. 1
Anthemius of Tralles, master-builder, B. I. i. 24, 50, 70, B. II. iii. 7
Anthium, coast-town of Italy; distance from Ostia, V. xxvi. 17; used as a harbour by the Romans *ib.*
Antinoüs, the city of (Antinopolis); in Egypt, I. xxv. 43, VIII. xxvii. 6
Antioch in Syria, principal city of the

INDEX

East, I. xvii. 36; II. viii. 23, ix. 3, x. 5; situation of, II. vi. 10, viii. 21; ease with which it might be captured, I. xvii. 38; character of the inhabitants, I. xvii. 37, II. viii. 6; distance from Beroea, II. vii. 2; from Seleucia, II. xi. 1; visited by an earthquake, II. xiv. 6, S.H. xviii. 41; the citizens propose to buy off Chosroes, II. vi. 16; besieged by Chosroes, II. viii. 1 ff.; the wall stormed by Chosroes, II. viii. 8 ff.; captured by Chosroes, II. viii. 20 ff., VIII. vii. 11; plundered by Chosroes, II. ix. 14 ff.; burnt, II. ix. 17, 18; young men of, check the victorious Persians in a street fight, II. viii. 28, 29, 32, ix. 5; citizens of, massacred by the Persians, II. viii. 34; church of, robbed of great treasures by Chosroes, II. ix. 15, 16; but spared in the burning of the city, II. ix. 18, x. 6; quarter called Cerateum also spared by the fire, II. x. 7; citizens of, [illegible] portent of coming misfortunes, II. x. 1 ff., xiv. 5; two women of, their fate at the capture of the city, II. viii. 35; captives of, offered for sale by Chosroes, II. xiii. 2 ff.; settled by Chosroes in a newly built city near Ctesiphon under special laws, II. xiv. 1 ff., S.H. ii. 25; called Theopolis, B. II. x. 2, B. V. v. 1, ix. 29; adorned and strongly fortified by Justinian, B. II. x. 2–25; church of St. Julian, II. x. 8; churches of the Virgin and of the Archangel Michael built by Justinian, B. II. x. 24, 25; the Blue Faction there, S.H. xii. 28; home of Macedonia, a dancer, *ib.* *See also* Daphne, Tretum, Platanon

Antioch of Chosroes, near Ctesiphon, founded for captives of Antioch in Syria, II. xiv. 1 ff., S.H. ii. 25; governed by special laws, II. xiv. 3, 4

Antiochus, a Syrian, resident in Naples; favours the Romans, V. viii. 21

Antipagrae, fortress in Epirus, B. IV. iv. 3

Antiphorus, structure in Edessa, restored by Justinian, B. II. vii. 6

Antipyrgum, fortress in Libya; built by Justinian, B. VI. ii. 2

Antoïnum, fortress in Haemimontum, B. IV. xi. 20

Antonina, wife of Belisarius, V. xviii. 43, S.H. i. 11–14; her lowly origin and her shameless character, S.H. i. 11–13, 36, 38, 39; tyrannizes over Belisarius, S.H. v. 27; her vindictive nature, S.H. i. 26; mother of Photius, V. v. 5, xviii. 18; mother-in-law of Ildiger, IV. viii. 24, VI. vii. 15; her magic arts, S.H. i. 26, ii. 2, iii. 2; brings about the downfall of John the Cappadocian, I. xxv. 13 ff., S.H. ii. 16, iii. 7; departs to the East, I. xxv. 23; falls in love with Theodosius, S.H. i. 16, 17; sets sail with Belisarius for Africa, III. xii. 2; preserves the drinking-water, III. xiii. 23, 24; with the army at Decimum, III. xix. 11, [illegible] departs for Naples, VI. iv. 6; arriving in Taracina, proceeds to Campania, VI. iv. 14; where she assists Procopius, VI. iv. 20; assists in shipping provisions from Ostia to Rome, VI. vii. 4 ff.; left by Belisarius in Portus, VII. xix. 7; who fears for her safety, VII. xix. 30; with him at Croton, VII. xxviii. 4; at Dryus, VII. xxx. 2; goes to Byzantium, VII. xxx. 3, 25; becomes hostile to Constantinus, S.H. i. 25; deceives Belisarius, S.H. i. 26; slays two slaves, S.H. i. 27; accuses Constantinus, S.H. i. 28, 29; in Byzantium, S.H. i. 31; drives Photius from Italy, *ib.*; returns to Byzantium with Belisarius and Theodosius, S.H. i. 35; rejoined by Theodosius, S.H. i. 42; remains in Byzantium, S.H. ii. 1; schemes to remove Photius, S.H. ii. 3, 4; accused by Photius, S.H. ii. 5; comes from Byzantium, S.H. ii. 14, 17; summoned to Byzantium, S.H. iii. 4; reconciled with Belisarius, S.H. iii. 12; surprised by Theodora, S.H. iii. 15–18; with whom she is on friendly terms, S.H. iv. 18, 19; hostile to Belisarius, S.H. iv. 23; blocks his reappointment, S.H. iv. 38; feared by John, S.H. v. 14; distrusted by Theodora, S.H. v. 20; her daughter courted by Sergius, S.H. v. 33; breaks up a match, S.H. v. 23; for which she is censured, S.H. v. 24

Antoninus, bath called at Nicomedia; restored by Justinian, B. V. iii. 7

Anzalas, spearman of Narses; answers the challenge of Coccas, VIII. xxxi. 13; and slays him, VIII. xxxi. 15

Aoion, fortress in Epirus, B. IV. iv. 3

Aona, fortress in Epirus, B. IV. iv. 3

Aordus, brother of the ruler of the Eruli, VI. xv. 29, VII. xxxiv. 44; killed in battle, VII. xxxiv. 45

Apadnas, fortress near Amida; strengthened by Justinian, B. II. iv. 20

Apadnas, monastery in Isauria, B. V. ix. 33

Apamea, city of Syria, II. xi. 2, 4, B. V. ix. 27; wood of the Cross preserved there, II. xi. 14; it gives forth a miraculous light in the church, II. xi. 17, 18; visited by Chosroes, II. xi. 14 ff.; entered by Chosroes and robbed of all its treasure, II. xi. 24 ff.; a citizen of, accuses a Persian, II. xi. 36

Apennines, mountains of Italy; Totila and Narses encamp among them, VIII. xxix. 3, 4

Aphelius, monastery of, B. V. ix. 18

Aphrodisias, city on the Chersonese; fortified by Justinian, B. IV. x. 20

Aphrodite, son of Arethas sacrificed to, II. xxviii. 13

Apion, an Egyptian, manager of finances in the Roman army, I. viii. 5

Apis, fortress in Epirus, B. IV. iv. 3

Apollinarius, a native of Italy; comes to Justinian to seek support for Ilderic, IV. v. 7, 8; his good services to the Romans, IV. v. 9; sent to the islands of Ebusa, Majorica, and Minorica, with an army, IV. v. 7

Apollodorus of Damascus, master-builder under Trajan, B. IV. vi. 13

Apostles, Church of the, in Byzantium, B. I. iv. 9–18; reveal their bodies to Justinian, B. I. iv. 19–24; Church of the Apostle John in Ephesus, S.H. iii. 3; Church of the Apostles Peter and Paul at Byzantium, built by Justinian, B. I. iv. 1

Appian Way, built by Appius, V. xiv. 6; description of the road, V. xiv. 6–11; travelled by refugees from Rome, V. xxv. 4; Gothic camp near it, VI. iii. 3, iv. 3, 17

Appiara, fortress in Moesia, B. IV. xi. 20

Appius, builder of the Appian Way, V. xiv. 6–9

Apri, city in Thrace, VIII. xxvii. 8

Apsarus, city near Lazica, VIII. ii. 11; its ancient greatness, VIII. ii. 14; originally named Apsyrtus, VIII. ii. 12; distance from Rhizaeum, VIII. ii. 11; from Petra, VIII. ii. 21

Apsilia, its mountains, VIII. ix. 15; betrayed to the Persians, VIII. x. 2–4

Apsilii, a Christian people subject to the Lazi, VIII. ii. 32, 33, iii. 12, ix. 7, 30, x. 1; their mountainous country, VIII. ix. 20; revolt from the Colchians, VIII. x. 6; won back to allegiance by John, VIII. x. 7; a woman of, VIII. x. 5

Apsyrtus, brother of Medea; his tomb, VIII. ii. 14; ancient name of Apsarus, VIII. ii. 12

Apulia, gained by Totila, VII. vi. 5; its town Canusium, VII. xviii. 18; Mt. Garganon in, VII. xxii. 24; mentioned, VII. xviii. 29

Apulians, a people of southern Italy, V. xv. 21; voluntarily submit to Belisarius, V. xv. 3

Aqueducts, in Rome, VI. iii. 3–7, ix. 1, 2; cut by the Goths, V. xix. 13; stopped up by Belisarius, V. xix. 18; water of one used to turn the mills, V. xix. 8; used by the Goths to shelter a camp, VI. iii. 3–7; Goths attempt to effect an entrance by an aqueduct, VI. ix. 1 ff.; of Byzantium, B. I. xi. 10–14; of Carthage, IV. i. 2; of Naples, V. viii. 45, ix. 11; built or repaired by Justinian at various cities, B.

II. iii. 25, II. v. 11, II. x. 22, II. x. 7, III. iii. 8, III. vii. 1, IV. ix. 16, IV. xi. 13, V. ii. 3, V. iii. 1, V. iii. 19, V. ix. 36, VI. ii. 11; existing aqueducts mentioned, B. II. iii. 21, II. x. 18, I. xi. 11

Aquenisium, district of southern Europe, B. IV. iv. 3

Aquileia, city in northern Italy, III. iii. 9, V. i. 22; its size and importance, III. iv. 30; besieged and captured by Attila, III. iv. 30 ff.

Aquilinus, bodyguard of Belisarius, VI. v. 18. 19

Arabia, its location, I. xix. 20; S.H. xvii. 17; its mountain, Sina, B. V. viii. 1-9

Arabian Gulf, called "Red Sea" by Procopius, I. xix. 2; its description, I. xix. 2 ff., B. V. viii. 2

Aratius, an Armenian commander in the Persian army; in company with Narses defeats Sittas and Belisarius, I. xii. 21, 22; brother of Isaac and Narses, [illegible] 11, VII. xiii. 20; deserts to the Romans, I. xii. 22, xv. 31, VI. xiii. 17; sent to Italy, I. xii. 22, VI. xiii. 17; commander of Armenians, VI. xxvii. 16; holds Auximus in check, VI. xvi. 18; sides with Narses against Belisarius, VI. xviii. 6; stationed at Firmum, VI. xx. 3; sent away from Ravenna, VI. xxix. 29; commander against the Sclaveni, VII. xl. 34; commander of troops sent to the Lombards, VII. xxxiv. 40, VIII. xxv. 11; sent to the Outrigurs with money, VIII. xix. 3, 4; in Illyricum, VIII. xxvii. 13

Arbatias, fortress in Cabetzus, B. IV. iv. 3

Arbitrators, public, S.H. xiv. 4, 13

Arborychi, barbarians in Gaul, formerly subject to the Romans, V. xii. 9; become Roman soldiers, V. xii. 13; absorbed by the Germans, V. xii. 13–15; receive land from Roman soldiers, V. xii. 17

Arcadianae, Baths at Byzantium, B. I. xi. 1

Arcadius, Roman Emperor, elder son of Theodosius; receives the Eastern Empire, III. i. 2; brother of Honorius and Placidia, III. iii. 4; his alliance with the Visigoths, III. ii. 7; when about to die, makes provision for the safety of his heir, I. ii. 1 ff.; succeeded by his son Theodosius, III. ii. 33; the House of, in Byzantium, B. I. ii. 17

Archabis, town near Lazica, VIII. ii. 11

Archaeopolis, first city in Lazica, II. xxix. 18, VIII. xiii. 3; guarded by three thousand Romans, VIII. xiii. 8; objective of Mermeroes, VIII. xiii. 3, 22, 24, 30; passed by him, VIII. xiii. 25-27; attacked by him, VIII. xiv. 3 ff.; attempt to betray it, VIII. xiv. 23–27; held by the Romans and Lazi, VIII. xiv. 45; again attacked by Mermeroes, VIII. xvii. 17; its situation, walls and water supply, VIII. xiv. 1-3; distance from Mocheresis, VIII. xiv. 46

Archangel Michael, *see* St. Michael

Archdeacon of Rome, Pelagius, S.H. xxvii. 17

Archelaus, a patrician; manager of expenditures of the African expedition, III. xi. 17; advises against disembarking on the African coast, III. xv. 2–17; ordered by Belisarius not to take the fleet into Carthage, III. xvii. 16; commands the fleet to anchor off Carthage, III. xx. 11

Architects, mentioned, *see* Master-builders

Architectural terms, *see* Introduction, p. xvi.

ἀνάστασις (*anastasis*), a structure of stones, B. I. x. 13; work of building, B. II. i. 9

ἀντιτείχισμα (*antiteichisma*), protective flanking wall along a *peribolos*, B. V. iv. 6; a dam before another wall, B. II. iii. 16

'Αντίφορος (*Antiphoros*), B. II. vii. 6 and note

ἀρίς (*aris*), dam with gates, called also *phraktes* and *antiteichisma*, B. II. iii. 18, 21

ἀρχιτέκτων (*architekton*), "master-builder," used of Apollodorus of

INDEX

Architectural terms (*cont.*)
Damascus, B. IV. vi. 13. *See* Introduction, p. xv.
ἄσβεστος (*asbestos*), *see titanos*
ἄσφαλτος (*asphaltos*), asphalt, used for bonding masonry, B. I. i. 53
αὐλή (*aulê*), court outside a church, B. I. iv. 7, viii. 10, V. vi. 24; aisle of a church, B. I. i. 58. *See also peristylos*
ἀψίς (*apsis*), arch, B. I. i. 39, 43, 68, 71, iv. 15, x. 14; arch of a bridge, B. IV. viii. 17, V. v. 11; arch carried on columns at propylaea of a church, B. V. vi. 24
διατείχισμα (*diateichisma*), connecting wall or cross-wall, B. II. vii. 15, IV. iii. 21, 25, x. 5, xi. 12, 17
ἐκμαγεῖον (*ekmageion*), model or plan of a structure, B. II. iii. 10
ἐκτύπωμα (*ektypoma*), model or plan of a structure, B. I. i. 22, II. iii. 8
ἔμβολος (*embolos*), roofed colonnade in a city-wall, B. III. v. 11
ἐπάλξεις (*epalxeis*), battlements, B. II. i. 15–17, viii. 16, IV. ii. 4, x. 13
ἐπιτείχισμα (*epiteichisma*), wall built for the purpose of attacking a city, B. II. v. 4; mostly metaphorical, of cities or forts, "threat," "check," B. II. i. 4, 11, vii. 14, viii. 11, V. iv. 9, VI. ii. 8, vi. 17
ἡμίκυκλος (*hemikyklos*), semi-circle, used to describe an apse, B. I. i. 35, 36; an exedra, B. V. vi. 25
ἡμικύλινδρος (*hemikylindros*), semi-cylinder, used to describe an apse, B. I. i. 32
θόλος (*tholos*), dome or vault; dome, σφαιροειδὴς θόλος, B. I. i. 45; B. I. viii. 13, x. 9; vault, B. I. i. 56, x. 14, V. vi. 7; στοὰ ἐν θολωτῷ τείχει, B. IV. xi. 16; θόλος ἐν στοᾶς τρόπῳ, B. IV. x. 13
ἰνδάλματα (*indalmata*), plans of a building, B. I. i. 24
κτίσις (*ktisis*), a building, B. IV. viii. 3; masonry, B. I. i. 78
λόφος (*lophos*), pier, called also *pessos*, B. I. i. 37, 38, 51, 52
λῶρος (*loros*, Lat. *lorus*), arch, B. I. i. 68, 75
μέταυλος (θύρα) (*metaulos* [*thyra*]), door leading from a court into a building, I. xxvi. 9, III. xii. 4; leading from a court into a church, B. I. iv. 7, V. vi. 24

Architectural terms (*cont.*)
μηχανικός (*mechanikos*), "master-builder" (*see* Introduction, p. xiv.), B. I. i. 71, 76, II. iii. 11; λόγιος ἐπὶ σοφίᾳ τῇ καλουμένῃ μηχανικῇ, II. xiii. 26 (*cf.* B. I. i. 24); τοὺς τὰ μηχανικὰ εὐδοκιμοῦντας, B. II. iii. 7
μηχανοποιός (*mechanopoios*), master-builder (*see* Introduction, p. xiv.), B. I. i. 24, 68, II. iii. 2, 14, viii. 25
μῶλος (*molos*), "mole," at the junction of a wall with the sea, called also *probolos*, B. IV. x. 7
νάρθηξ (*narthex*), narthex of a church; term explained, B. I. iv. 7, V. vi. 23
οἰκοδομή (*oikodomê*), work or act of building, B. I. i. 23
οἰκοδόμημα (*oikodomema*; selected examples), structure, B. I. i. 35, V. vi. 6; a structure *or* a building operation, B. II. vii. 5, IV. i. 10
οἰκοδομία (*oikodomia*; selected examples), a building *or* a structure, VI. ix. 4, B. II. viii. 14, x. 22, III. i. 3, ii. 12, vii. 9, 25, IV. i. 1, 2, vi. 37, ix. 7, V. i. 2, vi. 7, 9; a structure as part of a building (*see also* the following sense), B. I. i. 32, 41, IV. viii. 21, V. v. 10; masonry (sometimes difficult to distinguish from the preceding and the following senses), VI. ix. 5, 6, xxvii. 19, VIII. xi. 34, B. I. iv. 16, II. i. 10, iii. 27, v. 5, vi. 11, vii. 10, xi. 8, III. iv. 3, vii. 6, IV. vi. 18, vii. 6, ix. 14, V. v. 13, VI. iv. 3; plan or method of construction, B. II. ix. 19, IV. vi. 2; work or act of constructing, B. II. i. 6, 7, ii. 10, vi. 4, x. 20, III. iv. 12
περίβολος (*peribolos*), circuit-wall, *passim* in B.; distinguished from other types of walls, B. II. i. 20, vii. 5, viii. 20, x. 17, 18
περίστυλος (*peristylos*), "colonnaded" (adj.), applied to market-place, B. I. x. 5; court, B. I. xi. 12, II. x. 20; aisle of a church, B. I. i. 58; stoa, B. I. iv. 26

INDEX

Architectural terms (*cont.*)

πεσσός (*pessos*), pier, B. I. i. 37, 69, 71. *See also lophos*

πλευραί (*pleurai*) arms of a cruciform church, B. I. iv. 13, 16

πρόβολος (*probolos*), structure built at the ends of a wall where it joined the sea, B. IV. x. 15, called also *molos*, B. IV. x. 7; built to protect a city-wall against flood, B. II. viii. 18; starling added to the pier of a bridge to reduce the disturbance of the current, called also *promachos*, B. V. iv. 3; metaphorical, of places or forts, B. II. viii. 11, IV. i. 33, vi. 7

πρόθυρον (*prothyron*) porch or vestibule before the door of a church, B. I. iv. 7

πρόμαχος (*promachos*), *see probolos*

προμαχών, προμαχεών (*promachon, promacheon*), rampart or parapet on a wall, B. IV. ii. 5, vi. 24, x. 14

προπύλαια (*propylaia*) propylaea, I. xxiv. 9, B. I. iv. 7, x. 3, V. vi. 24

πρόστωον (*prostoön*) portico before a house or palace, III. xii. 5, IV. xxviii. 8

πτερόν (*pteron*), structure added to a city-wall; name explained, B. II. viii. 14

προτείχισμα (*proteichisma*), outworks, *passim* in B.; distinguished from *peribolos*, B. II. i. 21, iii. 16, vii. 5, viii. 20

στοά (*stoa*), covered colonnade along a street, I. xxiv. 9, VI. iv. 9, B. I. x. 3; about a market-place, B. VI. v. 10; about a court before or around a church, B. I. iv. 26, vi. 13, viii. 12; porch of a building, B. I. x. 9; narthex of a church, B. I. iv. 7, V. vi. 23; aisle of a church, B. I. i. 55–58, V. vi. 22; covered portico in a city-wall, B. II. i. 16, IV. x. 13, xi. 16; in the Hippodrome at Byzantium, I. xxiv. 49; undefined uses (probably mostly covered colonnades along streets), V. xxii. 21, B. I. xi. 21, II. viii. 25, ix. 7, x. 22, III. iv. 18, IV. i. 23, V. ii. 5; a device composed of poles used to protect soldiers attacking a wall, VI. xix. 6, 14

Architectural terms (*cont.*)

(*cf.* Polyb., I. xlviii. 2; Caes., *Bell. Civ.*, II. ii. 3); the "Royal Portico" at Constantinople, called *basileios stoa*, S.H. xiv. 13, and *basileos stoa*, containing four colonnades (*stoai*), about a peristyle court (*peristylos aulê*), B. I. xi. 12–14. *See* Introduction, p. xvi.

σύνθεσις (λίθων) (*synthesis* [*lithon*]), joints of masonry, *or* the process of joining stones, B. I. viii. 18, II. i. 9, IV. viii. 9

συνθήκη (λίθων) (*syntheke* [*lithon*]), joints of masonry, B. II. viii. 17; masonry, B. V. v. 11; courses of stones, B. I. ii. 1; binding of bricks, V. xxiii. 15; or of stones, VIII. xi. 34

τέλμα (*telma*), the space between stones which was filled with mortar or lead, B. I. i. 53, II. i. 9

τέμενος (*temenos*), *see* note on B. I. iii. 17

τίτανος (*titanos*), lime, called also *asbestos* in Procopius's time, II. xxx. 18, VI. xxvii. 21, VII. xxiv. 4, B. I. i. 53, II. i. 9, III. ii. 12

τρίγων (*trigon*), pendentive, B. I. i. 43

φράκτης (*phraktes*), dam with gates, called also *aris* and *antiteichisma*, B. II. iii. 18

Arcunes, fortress in Cabetzus, B. IV. iv. 3

Ardaburius, son of Aspar; Roman general, sent against the usurper John, III. iii. 8; destroyed by Leon, III. vi. 27

Ardeia, fortress in Cabetzus, B. IV. iv. 3

Arelatum, city in Gaul, VII. xxxiii. 5

Areobindus, Roman general; son-in-law of Olyvrius, I. viii. 1, S.H. v. 31; flees with his army before Cabades, I. viii. 10, 11; summoned to Byzantium, I. ix. 1

Areobindus, a Senator; sent as general to Lybia, IV. xxiv. 1; his inexperience in warfare, *ib.*, IV. xxv. 25; xxvi. 16; husband of Preiecta, VII. xxxi. 3; accompanied by his wife and his sister, IV. xxiv. 3; shares the rule of

Libya with Sergius, IV. xxiv. 4, 5; sends John against Antalas and Stotzas, IV. xxiv. 6; writes to Sergius to unite with John, IV. xxiv. 7; made sole commander of Libya, IV. xxiv. 16; sends Gontharis against the Moors, IV. xxv. 4, 5; arranges with Coutzinas to turn traitor against the other Moors, IV. xxv. 15; informs Gontharis of his dealings with Coutzinas, IV. xxv. 16; persuaded by Gontharis to postpone the engagement, IV. xxv. 17, 18; his death planned and finally accomplished by Gontharis, IV. xxv. 22–xxvi. 33, VII. xxxi. 3; treasure left by him in the Palace, IV. xxviii. 35; sister of, IV. xxiv. 3; placed in a fortress for protection, IV. xxvi. 18; removed from the fortress by Gontharis, IV. xxvii. 20

Areobindus, servant of Theodora, who becomes enamoured of him, S.H. xvi. 11

Areon, fort built by Justinian in Armenia, B. III. iv. 10

Ares, worshipped by the inhabitants of Thule, VI. xv. 25; House of; portion of the imperial residence in Byzantium, I. xxiv. 9, B. I. x. 3

Arethas, son of Gabalas; made king of the Saracens of Arabia by Justinian and pitted against Alamundaras, I. xvii. 47–48; VIII. xi. 10, S.H. ii. 23, 28; with the Roman army, I. xviii. 7; at the battle on the Euphrates, I. xviii. 26, 35; quarrels with Alamundaras, II. i. 3–7; joins Belisarius in Mesopotamia, II. xvi. 5; sent by Belisarius to plunder Assyria, II. xix. 11, 15 ff.; returns another way, II. xix. 26 ff.; wages war against Alamundaras, II. xxviii. 12–14; son of, sacrificed to Aphrodite, II. xxviii. 13

Arethusa, harbour of Syracuse, III. xiv. 11

Argamo, fortress in Moesia, B. IV. xi. 20

Arganocili, fortress in Aquenisium, B. IV. iv. 3

Argek, a guardsman; his effective fighting against the Persians at Edessa, II. xxvi. 26, 27

Argentares, fortress in Aquenisium, B. IV. iv. 3

Argicianum, fortress in Macedonia, B. IV. iv. 3

Argo, the ship said to have been built by Jason, VIII. ii. 30

Argos, Diomedes repulsed thence, V. xv. 8

Argus, fortress in Epirus, B. IV. iv. 3

Argyas, fortress in Epirus, B. IV. iv. 3

Argyronium, place on the Bosporus, B. I. ix. 12

Aria, fortress in Dardania, B. IV. iv. 3

Ariadne, daughter of Leon, wife of Zeno, and mother of Leon the younger, III. vii. 2; flees to Isauria with Zeno, III. vii. 18

Arians, schismatics; comprise the Goths, III. ii. 5, VII. xviii. 21, VIII. iv. 11; also the Vandals, III. viii. 4, xxi. 20; the Franks, V. v. 9; and the Gepaedes, VII. xxxiv. 24; some among the Roman soldiers, IV. i. 4, xiv. 12, 21; Gelimer a steadfast adherent, IV. ix. 14; also Amalaric, V. xiii. 10; the wealth of their holdings, S.H. xi. 16–18; persecuted by Justinian, S.H. xviii. 10; debarred from the office of Emperor, III. vi. 3; not trusted by the Roman soldiers in Gaul, V. xii. 17; Arian priests expelled from Rome, VII. ix. 21; Arian priests of the Vandals, III. xxi. 23, 25

Ariminum, city of northern Italy, VII. xi. 32; occupied by John, VI. x. 5 ff.; besieged by Vittigis, VI. xi. 3, xii. 1 ff., VI. xvi. 3; abandoned by the Goths, VI. x. 6; Ildiger and Martinus sent thither, VI. xi. 4, 21; its relief advocated by Narses, VI. xvi. 5 ff.; messenger sent thence to Belisarius, VI. xvi. 14; saved for the Romans, VI. xvi. 21–xvii. 22; entered by Narses, VI. xix. 10; Sabinianus and Thurimuth flee to, VII. xi. 30; captured by the Goths, VII. xxxvii. 23; commanded by Usdrilas, VIII. xxviii. 2; distance from Ravenna,

VI. x. 5; from Ancon, VI. xi. 4; from Urbinus, VI. xix. 1; three women cannibals in its vicinity, VI. xx. 27 ff.; passed by Narses, VIII. xxviii. 11, xxix. 3; its bridge, VIII. xxviii. 5, 6

Arimuth, Roman commander in Illyricum, VIII. xxvii. 13

Arina, fortress in Moesia, B. IV. xi. 20

Aristotle, studied the current at Chalcis, VIII. vi. 20

Armenia, location of, VIII. ii. 5, 20, B. III. i. 13; its limit Amida, I. xvii. 24; Lesser, extends to Amida, B. III. i. 17, iv. 15; Greater, seat of the King of Armenia, B. III. i. 8; adjoins the land of the Tzani, VIII. i. 9; source of the Sarus River, B. V. v. 8; a part of, known as Sophanenê, B. III. ii. 2, iii. 1; another part as Chorzanê, B. III. iii. 9; divided by the Euphrates, B. III. v. 1; garrisoned by Justinian, B. III. i. 16, 17; buildings of Justinian in, B. III. i. 1, iv. 1 ff., vi. 1, vii. 24; two heirs contend for its throne, B. III. i. 8 ff.; protected by Justinian, B. III. i. 2, 3; its city Melitenê, B. I. vii. 3, III. iv. 20; cities Sebasteia and Nicopolis, B. III. iv. 11; ruled by Parthian Kings, B. III. i. 6; attacked by the Huns, S.H. ii. 29; visited by Bessas, VIII. xiii. 11; Bessas appointed General of, VIII. ix. 4; King of, appointed by the Emperor, B. III. i. 8, 14, 26; Count of, B. III. i. 15; General of, III. xi. 5, VIII. viii. 22, B. III. v. 12; Dukes of, B. III. ii. 1; Satraps of, B. III. i. 17, 24; enabled to defy Persia, B. III. v. 12; wages war against Persia, I. v. 10 ff.; claims the site of Artemis' temple, VIII. v. 24; tribes of, B. III. iii. 8; Armenians serving in the Roman army, VII. vi. 10, xxvi. 24, xxvii. 3. 10, B. III. i. 27; in the Palace Guard, S.H. xxiv. 16; render signal service at Auximus, VI. xxvii. 16; Armenians sent with Areobindus to Libya, IV. xxiv. 2; follow Artabanes in entering the service of Gontharis, IV. xxvii. 9; support Artabanes in his plot against Gontharis, IV. xxviii. 8, 34, 36; the Armenian language, VII. xxvi. 24; Armenian history, I. v. 9, 40, B. III. i. 6; the following Armenians are mentioned: Anzalas, VIII. xxxi. 13; Arsaces, VII. xxxii. 1; Artabanes, VII. xxxii. 11; Artabazes, VII. iii. 10; Chanaranges, VII. xxxii. 11; Gilacius, VII. xxvi. 24; Isaac, VII. xiii. 20; John (Gouzes), son of Thomas, VIII. viii. 15, xi. 57; Narses, VI. xxvi. 3; Varazes, VII. xxvii. 3

Arrian, the historian; cited, VIII. xiv. 48

Arsa, fortress in Dardania, B. IV. iv. 3

Arsaces, Parthian King of Armenia, progenitor of the Arsacidae, II. iii. 32, B. III. i. 6

Arsaces, King of Armenia, descendant of Arsaces I, wages a truceless war with Persia, I. v. 10 ff.; slandered to Pacurius, I. v. 16 ff.; victim of stratagem of Magi, betrays himself to Pacurius, I. v. 19 ff.; confined in the Prison of Oblivion, I. v. 29 ff.; kills himself, I. v. 39 ff.

Arsaces, King of Armenia; descendant of Arsaces I; has two sons, Tigranes and Arsaces, B. III. i. 8, 9; his abdication, II. iii. 35; and death, B. III. i. 10

Arsaces, brother of Tigranes; joint-king of Armenia, B. III. i. 8 ff.; bestows the kingdom of Armenia upon the Romans, II. iii. 35; B. III. i. 12, 13, v. 2

Arsaces, commander in Sura; killed while valiantly defending the city, II. v. 11

Arsaces, of the Arsacidae, VII. xxxii. 1, 3; had made overtures to Chosroes, VII. xxxii. 2; mildly punished by Justinian, VII. xxxii. 3; plots against Justinian, VII. xxxii. 4–51; instigates Artabanes, VII. xxxii. 5–11; enlists Chanaranges, VII. xxxii.

11, 31; seeks in vain to enlist Germanus through his son Justinus, VII. xxxii. 21, 28; confers with Artabanes VII. xxxii. 22; his escape feared by Marcellus, VII. xxxii. 24

Arsacidae, descendants of Arsaces I, King of Armenia, II. iii. 32, 35, IV. xxiv. 2, xxvii. 16; of Parthian origin, B. III. i. 6

Arsaza, fortress in southern Europe, B. IV. iv. 3

Arsena, fortress in southern Europe, B. IV. iv. 3

Arsenius, favourite of the Empress, S.H. xxvii. 6; a Samaritan, S.H. xxvii. 7; spared by Justinian, but excluded from the Palace, S.H. xxvii. 10; accompanies Paulus, S.H. xxvii. 11; pretends conversion, S.H. xxvii. 12; investigated by Justinian, S.H. xvii. 16; impaled by Liberius, S.H. xxvii. 19

Arsinus River, tributary to the Euphrates, I. xvii. 21

Artabanes, son of John, of the Arsacidae; slays Sittas, II. iii. 25; a relative of Arsaces, VII. xxxii. 1; sent to Libya in command of Armenians, IV. xxiv. 2; known to Chosroes by reason of his brave deeds, IV. xxvii. 17; brother of John, IV. xxiv. 15; uncle of Gregorius, IV. xxvii. 10; joins Areobindus, IV. xxv. 4; supports him against Gontharis, IV. xxvi. 7, 13, 19; enters the service of Gontharis, IV. xxvii. 9; his plot to kill the tyrant, IV. xxvii. 10; urged on by Gregorius, IV. xxvii. 11–19; sent against Antalas, IV. xxvii. 23, 25; joins battle, but allows the enemy to escape, IV. xxvii. 27–29; threatened by Ulitheus, IV. xxvii. 30; his excuses, IV. xxvii. 31, 32; after deliberation returns to Carthage, IV. xxvii. 33, 35; entertained by Gontharis at a banquet, IV. xxviii. 3; arranges to carry out his plot against Gontharis, IV. xxviii. 6–9; Artasires makes a request of him, IV. xxviii. 12, 13; succeeds in destroying Gontharis, IV. xxviii. 15–30, VII. xxxi. 2; assisted by Peter, cuts down the bodyguards, IV. xxviii. 33; directs Athanasius to look after the treasure of Areobindus, IV. xxviii. 35; sends John and others to Byzantium, IV. xxviii. 40; wins great fame, IV. xxviii. 42; rewarded with money by Preiecta, IV. xxviii. 43; made General of Libya, *ib.*, VII. xxxi. 4; summoned to Byzantium, IV. xxviii. 44; wishes to marry Preiecta, VII. xxxi. 4; secures his recall, VII. xxxi. 4, 7; admired by the Byzantines, VII. xxxi. 8, 9; honoured by the Emperor, VII. xxxi. 9, 10; not permitted to marry Preiecta, VII. xxxi. 11; had left a former wife, VII. xxxi. 11–13; whom he is forced to take back, VII. xxxi. 14; outraged thereby, VII. xxxi. 15; sends his wife away again, VII. xxxi. 16; incited by Arsaces to plot against Justinian, VII. xxxii. 5–51; consulted by Chanaranges, VII. xxxii. 31; Marcellus shews concern for him, VII. xxxii. 40; imprisoned by Justinian and examined, VII. xxxii. 42, 44; mildly punished, VII. xxxii. 51; sent by Justinian to relieve Liberius, VII. xxxix. 8, xl. 14; driven back by storm, VII. xl. 15–17; distinguishes himself in a skirmish, VIII. viii. 25–27; Commander-in-chief in Sicily, VIII. xxiv. 1; receives appeals from Croton, VIII. xxv. 24

Artabanes, a Persarmenian; deserted to the Romans, VIII, viii. 21–24

Artabazes, an Armenian officer in the Roman army; leads an advance party into Verona, VII. iii. 10 ff.; escapes with difficulty, VII. iii. 21; reproaches the commanders, VII. iii. 22; delivers a speech, VII. iv. 2–8; fights in single combat with Valaris, VII. iv. 22 ff.; sustains a severe wound, VII. iv. 25 ff.; his death, VII. iv. 29

INDEX

Artace, suburb of Cyzicus, I. xxv. 31

Artaleson, town in Armenia, fortified by Justinian, B. III. iii. 13, 14

Artasires, a Persian; bodyguard of Belisarius, VI. ii. 10; sent to Rome, VII. xi. 37; makes a sally, VII. xiii. 2–4

Artasires, bodyguard of Artabanes; shares knowledge of his plot against Gontharis, IV. xxvii. 10, 18; renders good service in the execution of the plot, IV. xxviii. 7–32; his ingenious protection for his arm, IV. xxviii. 10, 11, 31

Artemis, among the Taurians, temple of, in Celesene, I. xvii. 11, VIII. v. 23; sanctuary of, founded by Orestes in Pontus, I. xvii. 15; another in Cappadocia, I. xvii. 18; a monument to, VIII. xxii. 27; Artemis Bolosia, VIII. xxii. 29

Artemisium, fortress built by Justinian near the Rhecius, B. IV. iii. 30

Arufus, commander of Eruli; escapes with John, VII. xxvi. 23; flees to Dryus, VII. xxvi. 28

Aruth, of the Eruli; son-in-law of Mauricius, VIII. xxvi. 13; in the army of Narses, *ib.*

Arzamon, town in Mesopotamia; distance from Constantina, I. viii. 10

Arzanenê, district of Persia on the Nymphius River, I. viii. 21, II. xv. 7, B. III. ii. 3; invaded by Celer, I. viii. 21

Arzes, bodyguard of Belisarius; his remarkable wound, VI. ii. 16–18; treatment of his wound, VI. ii. 25–29; of the household of Belisarius, VI. ii. 25

Arzum, fortress in Thrace, B. IV. xi. 20

Asbadus, bodyguard of Justinian; defeated by the Sclaveni, VII. xxxviii. 4–6, 9

Asbadus, a Geped in the army of Narses, VIII. xxvi. 13; pursues and wounds Totila, VIII. xxxii. 22–24; wounded by Scipuar, VIII. xxxii. 24, 25

Asbestus, the contemporary term for lime, VI. xxvii. 21, B. I. i. 53

Ascalon, city in Palestine, S.H. xxix. 17, 21; its Senate, *ib.* 17

Ascan, a Massagete chief, at the battle of Daras, I. xiii. 21, xiv. 44; his exploits at the battle on the Euphrates and his death, I. xviii. 38

Asclepiades, a native of Palestine and friend of Theodorus, IV. xviii. 3; reveals the plot of Maximinus to Theodorus and Germanus, IV. xviii. 4

Asclepiodotus, of Naples, an orator; with Pastor opposes the plan to surrender the city, V. viii. 22 ff.; they address the Neapolitans, V. viii. 29–40; bring forward the Jews, V. viii. 41; his effrontery after the capture of the city, V. x. 39, 43–45; bitterly accused by Stephanus, V. x. 40–42; killed by the mob, V. x. 46

Asculum, city in Picenum; besieged by Totila, VII. xi. 39; surrenders to him, VII. xii. 12

A Secretis, title of confidential secretary to the Emperor, II. vii. 15, S.H. xiv. 4

Asgarzus, fortress in Haemimontum, B. IV. xi. 20

Asgizus, fortress in Haemimontum, B. IV. xi. 20

Asia, one of the continents, VIII. ii. 32, iii. 7, 11, vi. 12–15; its boundary with Europe discussed, VIII. vi. 1–15, ii. 28; to the right as one sails into the Mediterranean, III. i. 5; distance from Europe at different points, III. i. 7, 8; distance along the Asiatic side of the Euxine, III. i. 11; approaches Europe at Byzantium, B. I. v. 6, 8, IV. viii. 2; opposite the Chersonese, B. IV. x. 2; bounded (*sic*) by the Nile, B. VI. i. 7; adjoins Libya, V. xii. 1; entered from the Hellespont by the Huns, II. iv. 9; invaded by the barbarians, S.H. xxiii. 6; buildings of Justinian in, B. V. i. 1, 3

Asiaticus, father of Severianus, IV. xxiii. 6

Asilba, fortress in Moesia, B. IV. xi. 20

Asinarian Gate, in the circuit-wall of Rome, V. xiv. 14; betrayed by

four Isaurians, VII. xx. 4–15; opened to the Gothic army, VII. xx. 14, 15
Asinarius, Gothic commander in Dalmatia, V. vii. 1, xvi. 8; gathers an army among the Suevi, V. xvi. 12, 14; joins Uligisalus and proceeds to Salones, V. xvi. 15, 16
Asise, town in Tuscany; besieged by Totila, VII. xii. 12; surrendered to him, VII. xii. 18
Aspar, Roman general; father of Ardaburius, III. iii. 8; of the Arian faith, III. vi. 3; his great power in Byzantium, III. iv. 8; sent against the usurper John, III. iii. 8; defeated by the Vandals in Libya, III. iii. 35; returns home, III. iii. 36; makes Leon Emperor of the East, III. v. 7; his friendship sought by Basiliscus, III. vi. 2; quarrels with Leon, III. vi. 3; urges Basiliscus to spare the Vandals, III. vi. 4, 16; destroyed by Leon, III. vi. 27; the Emperor Marcian had been his adviser, III. iv. 7
Aspebedes, uncle of Chosroes, I. xi. 5, xxiii. 6; negotiates a treaty with Celer, I. ix. 24; shares command of invading army, I. xxi. 4; put to death by Chosroes, I. xxiii. 6
Aspetiani, an Armenian tribe; inclined toward alliance with the Romans, II. iii. 12–18
Asphalt, produced at Babylon, B. I. i. 53
Assessments, Prorated, a new tax, S.H. xxiii. 9, 17–21
Assessor, Councillor or Quaestor (*cf.* I. xi. 11), S.H. vi. 13, xiii. 12, xviii. 10
Assyria, Jews exiled in, B. II. xi. 2; plundered by Arethas, II. xix. 15 ff.; open to Roman attack, S.H. ii. 25; the Assyrians, V. xxiv. 36
Asterius, Dancing Master of the Greens, S.H. ix. 5
Asthianenê, section of Armenia, B. III. iii. 7
Astica, region in Thrace; plundered by the Sclaveni, VII. xl. 43
Astrologers, treatment of, S.H. xi. 37; mentioned, III. iii. 11
Atachas, fortress in Mesopotamia, B. II. iv. 14
Atalaric, grandson of Theoderic, son of Amalasuntha; King of the Goths, III. xiv. 5, VII. xxxix. 15, VIII. xxi. 11; succeeded his grandfather Theoderic, III. xiv. 6, V. ii. 1; reared by his mother Amalasuntha, V. ii. 1; who attempts to educate him, V. ii. 6 ff.; corrupted by the Goths, V. ii. 19 ff.; receives the envoy Alexander, V. vi. 26; divides Gaul with his cousin Amalaric, V. xiii. 4, 6; returns the treasures of Carcasiana to him, V. xiii. 6; attacked by a wasting disease, V. iii. 10, iv. 5; his death, V. iv. 4, 19; foreshadowed by the crumbling of a mosaic in Naples, V. xxiv. 24; his benefactions to the Romans, VII. xxi. 12; his Quaestor Fidelius, V. xiv. 5
Athanasius, brother of Alexander. V. vi. 26; father-in-law of Leontius, VII. xxxii. 34, VIII. xxiv. 11; sent with Areobindus to Libya, IV. xxiv. 2; summoned by Areobindus, IV. xxvi. 6; pretends pleasure at Gontharis' invitation, IV. xxvi. 21, 22; with Areobindus entertained by Gontharis, IV. xxvi. 31; spared by assassins of Areobindus, IV. xxvi. 33; entertained by Gontharis at a second banquet, IV. xxviii. 3; directed by Artabanes to look after the treasure of Areobindus, IV. xxviii. 35; envoy of Justinian, V. vi. 25, vii. 24; returned by the Goths, VI. xxii. 23; made Praetorian Prefect by the Emperor, VI. xxii. 24; returns to Italy, VI. xxix. 30
Athena, her statue stolen from Troy, V. xv. 9; different views as to the existence of the statue in the time of Procopius, V. xv. 11–14; a copy of it in the temple of Fortune in Rome, V. xv. 11; Greek statues of, V. xv. 13
Athenae, village near Lazica, II. xxix. 22, xxx. 14, VIII. ii. 10, 11

INDEX

Athenaea, ancient ruler of a region near the Black Sea, VIII. ii. 10

Athenodorus, an Isaurian, bodyguard of Belisarius, V. xxix. 20, 21

Athens, chief city of Greece; home of Xenophon, B. I. i. 13; and of Phidias, VIII. xxi. 12, B. I. xi. 7; its distance from Megara the measure of one day's journey, III. i. 17; not far from Euboea, B. IV. iii. 16; work of Justinian in, B. IV. ii. 24; suffers neglect under him, S.H. xxvi. 33

Athyras, city near Rhegium; improved by Justinian, B. IV. viii. 18, 19

Atreus, father of Agamemnon, VIII. xxii. 27

Attachas, place in Armenia; distance from Martyropolis, I. xxi. 9

Attalus, declared Emperor of the Romans by Alaric, III. ii. 28; of noble family, *ib.*; his lack of discretion, III. ii. 29; marches with Alaric against Ravenna, *ib.*; sends commanders alone to Libya against the advice of Alaric, III. ii. 30, 32; failure of his attempt upon Libya, *ib.*; quarrels with Alaric, and is reduced from the kingship, III. ii. 36

Attila, leader of the Huns, V. i. 3; overruns Europe, III. iv. 29, B. IV. v. 6; besieges and captures Aquileia, III. iv. 30 ff.; defeated by Aetius, III. iv. 24

Auduin, a Lombard; Regent for Valdarus, VII. xxxv. 17; assumes the royal power, VII. xxxv. 18; demands surrender of Ildiges, VII. xxxv. 20; married the sister of Amalafridas, VIII. xxv. 12; sends envoy to ask a truce, VIII. xviii. 7; reports his victory to Justinian, VIII. xxv. 15; sends allies to Narses, VIII. xxvi. 12; robs Ildigisal of the throne, VIII. xxvii. 1; demands Ildigisal, VIII. xxvii. 4, 22; refuses to surrender Ustrigothus, VIII. xxvii. 26, 27

Augarus, toparch of Edessa, II. xii. 8; friend of Augustus, II. xii. 8, 9; his visit to Rome, II. xii. 9 ff.; with difficulty persuades Augustus to allow him to return, II. xii. 11 ff.; receives from Augustus the promise of a hippodrome for Edessa, II. xii. 18; his enigmatic reply to the enquiries of the citizens, II. xii. 19; stricken with gout, seeks relief from physicians, II. xii. 20, 21; invites Christ to come to Edessa, II. xii. 24; cured upon receiving the reply of Christ, II. xii. 28; son of, an unrighteous ruler, delivers over Edessa to Persia, II. xii. 28

Augila, two cities in Libya, B. VI. ii. 14; distance from Boreium, B. VI. ii. 15; their inhabitants Christianized by Justinian, B. VI. ii. 15–19

Augustaeum, market-place before the Senate-House in Byzantium, B. I. ii. 1 ff., x. 5

Augustas, fortress in Thrace, B. IV. xi. 20

Augustae, city on the Danube, restored by Justinian, B. IV. vi. 29, 30

Augustulus, name given to Augustus, Emperor of the West, V. i. 2; dethroned by Odoacer, V. i. 7, VI. vi. 16

Augustus, first Emperor of the Romans; allowed the Thuringians to settle in Gaul, V. xii. 10; builder of a great bridge over the Narnus, V. xvii. 11; his reputed affection for Augarus, II. xii. 8–19; promises a hippodrome to Edessa, II. xii. 18

Augustus, Emperor of the West, III. vii. 15, V. i. 2

Augustus, priest in Byzantium, II. xxx. 53, 54

Augustus (Sebastos), title of Justinian, S.H. xxvii. 23

Aulon, city on the Ionian Gulf, V. iv. 21

Aulon, fortress in Macedonia, B. IV. iv. 3

Aumetra, fortress in Byzacium; walled by Justinian, B. VI. vi. 18

Aurasius, mountain in Numidia, B. VI. vii. 2–5; distance from Carthage, III. viii. 5, IV. xiii.

22; its great size, fruitful plateaus, and defences, IV. xiii. 23–25; source of the Abigas River there, IV. xiii. 20, xix. 11; adjoins First Mauretania, IV. xx. 30; taken by the Moors from the Vandals, III. viii. 5, IV. xiii. 26; its west side also held by the Moors, IV. xiii. 27; Moors of, ruled by Iaudas, IV. xii. 29, xiii. 1; Solomon marches thither, IV. xiii. 18; Iaudas establishes himself there, IV. xiii. 21; ascended by Solomon, IV. xiii. 30 ff.; the Romans eluded by the Moors on the mountain, IV. xiii. 35, 36; Solomon prepares more carefully for a second attempt, IV. xiii. 40; in which he succeeds in dislodging the Moors from there, IV. xix. 5–xx. 20; fortified and held by the Romans, IV. xx. 22; capture of Iaudas' treasure there, IV. xx. 23–29; fugitive Vandals return thither, IV. xiv. 19; made secure by Justinian, B. VI. vii. 8

Aurelian Gate, in Rome, called also the Gate of Peter, V. xix. 4, xxviii. 15; near the Tomb of Hadrian, V. xxii. 12

Auriliana, fortress in Aquenisium, B. IV. iv. 3

Authiparu, fortress in Haemimontum, B. IV. xi. 20

Auximus, city in Picenum; its strong position, VI. x. 3, xxiii. 6, 7; metropolis of Picenum, VI. xi. 2; considered by Vittigis the key to Ravenna, VI. xxiv. 7, 10, xxvi. 13; strongly garrisoned by the Goths, VI. xi. 2, xviii. 19 ff., xx. 2, xxiii. 8, xxvi. 13; well provisioned, VI. xx. 2; its garrison feared by the Romans, VI. xvi. 3, 8, 17; held in check by Aratius, VI. xvi. 18–20; besieged by Belisarius, VI. xxiii. 1, 5–xxiv. 17, xxvi. 2–xxvii. 24, 27; surrenders to him, VI. xxvii. 28–34; besieged by the Goths, VII. xi. 19; fighting around it, VII. xi. 19–31; its spring and cistern, VI. xxvii. 2; distance from its port, Ancon, VI. xiii. 7; from Firmum, VI. xvi. 1; from Ravenna and the Ionian Gulf, VI. xxiii. 6; Goths retreat thither, VIII. xxiii. 40

Auxomis, capital city of the Homeritae, I. xix. 17; distance from Adulis, I. xix. 22; from Elephantina and the Roman boundary, I. xix. 27

Auxomitae, name applied to some of the Ethiopians, I. xix. 17, B. V. viii. 2

Axiopa, fortress in Moesia, B. IV. xi. 20

Azarethes, Persian general, invades Roman territory, I. xvii. 1, xviii. 1; retires before Belisarius, I. xviii. 9 ff.; exhorts the Persian army, I. xviii. 27 ff.; arrays them for battle, I. xviii. 30; dishonoured by Cabades, I. xviii. 51 ff.; at the siege of Edessa, II. xxvii. 41

Azeta, fortress in Dardania, B. IV. iv. 3

B, *see also* names indexed under V

Babas, commander in the Roman army; sent to Lazica, VIII. ix. 5; commander of Archaeopolis, VIII. xiii. 8; addresses his men, VIII. xiv. 14–21; leads a sally, VIII. xiv. 22 ff.

Babas, fortress in Macedonia, B. IV. iv. 3

Babosis, place in Numidia, IV. xix. 16

Babylon, its Queen Semiramis, B. I. i. 53

Bacchus and Sergius, shrine of, in Byzantium, B. I. iv. 3

Bacchus, brother of Solomon and father of Cyrus and Sergius, IV. xxi. 1, 19, S.H. v. 28; father of Solomon the younger, IV. xxi. 19, xxii. 17

Bacusta, fortress in Epirus, B. IV. iv. 3

Bacustê, fortress in Epirus, *ib.*

Badê, city in Numidia; walled by Justinian, B. VI. vii. 8

Badziania, fortress in Cabetzus, B. IV. iv. 3

Baeca, fortress in Haemimontum, B. IV. xi. 20

Bagais, a deserted city near the Abigas River, IV. xix. 7

INDEX

Bagradas River, in Libya, IV. xv. 13
Baiberdon, fort built by Justinian in Armenia, B. III. iv. 10
Balan, term applied by barbarians to a white-faced horse, V. xviii. 6, 7
Balas, leader of the Massagetae, III. xi. 12
Balausum, fortress in Scassetana, B. IV. iv. 3
Balbae, fortress in Cabetzus, B. IV. iv. 3
Baleae, city of Northern Greece; fortified by Justinian, B. IV. ii. 16
Ballesiana, fortress in Dardania, B. IV. iv. 3
Ballista, description of, V. xxi. 14–18
Banasymeon, fortress in Mesopotamia, B. II. iv. 14
Bandalarius, *see* Visandus Vandalarius
Bandifer, "standard-bearer," IV. x. 4
Bandum, Latin term for "standard," IV. ii. 1
Banes, fortress in Cabetzus, B. IV. iv. 3
Baptist, John the, Church of, at Byzantium, B. I. viii. 15, 16
Barachtestes, fortress in southern Europe, B. IV. iv. 3
Baradotus, priest of Constantina, his godliness, II. xiii. 13; persuades Cabades to spare Constantina, II. xiii. 14, 15
Baras, fortress in Mesopotamia, B. II. iv. 22–24
Barbalissus, fortress in Euphratesia, B. II. ix. 10; distance from Obbane, II. xii. 4
Barbarian Plain, a region near Sergiopolis, II. v. 29
Barbaricini, term applied to Moors on Sardinia, IV. xiii. 44, B. VI. vii. 13
Barbaries, fortress in Cabetzus, B. IV. iv. 3
Barbation, a Thracian; guard of Belisarius, VII. xi. 37; makes a sally from Rome, VII. xiii. 2–4; sent forward with troops, VII. xxviii. 5; returns with news of defeat, VII. xxviii. 17
Barbatus, commander of Roman cavalry, III. xi. 7, IV. xv. 50; on the Roman right wing at the battle of Tricamarum, IV. iii. 4; his death, IV. xv. 59
Barchon, fortress built by Justinian in Tzanica, B. III. vi. 20
Baresmanas, Persian general, at the battle of Daras, I. xiii. 16, xiv. 32, 45; standard bearer of, attacked and killed by Sunicas, I. xiv. 47–50
Barlaus, Gate of, in the wall of Edessa, II. xxvii. 44
Barsymes, surname of Peter (*q.v.*), favourite of Theodora
Bartholomew, Apostle, Church of, in Daras, built by Justinian, B. II. ii. 1, iii. 26
Bascum, fortress in Thrace, B. IV. xi. 20
Basibunum, fortress in Haemimontum, B. IV. xi. 20
Basileon, fortress in Mesopotamia, strengthened by Justinian, B. II. iv. 18
Basilica Amyntou, fortress in Macedonia, B. IV. iv. 3
Basilides, appointed Quaestor in place of Tribunianus, I. xxiv. 18
Basiliscus, brother of Berine; commander of an expedition against the Vandals, III. vi. 2; his aspirations to the throne, *ib.*, urged by Aspar to spare the Vandals, III. vi. 4; landing in Africa, makes a complete failure of the expedition, III. vi. 10–24, x. 2; returning to Byzantium, becomes a suppliant, III. vi. 26; saved by Berine, *ib.*; usurps the throne in Byzantium, III. vii. 18; his misrule, III. vii. 19; sends an army under Harmatus to meet Zeno, III. vii. 20; becomes a suppliant, III. vii. 22; exiled to Cappadocia and dies, III. vii. 24, 25
Basiliscus, son of Harmatus, III. vii. 21; made Caesar and then removed by Zeno, III. vii. 23
Basilius, father of John of Edessa, II. xxi. 27, S.H. xii. 6
Basilius, a Patrician; escapes from Rome, VII. xx. 18
Bassaces, an Armenian; son-in-law of John, accompanies him on a mission to Bouzes, II. iii. 29; escapes with his companions from an ambush, II. iii. 30; leads an embassy to the Persian King, II. iii. 31; comes with Armenians to Byzantium, II. xxi. 34

INDEX

Bassicius, trusted friend of the Armenian king Arsaces, I. v. 17; flayed by Pacurius, I. v. 28

Bassidina, fortress in Moesia, B. IV. xi. 20

Bassus, Praetorian Prefect; his honesty, S.H. xxi. 6, 7

Basternas, fortress in Moesia, B. IV. xi. 20

Batnê (Batnae), fortress one day's journey distant from Edessa, II. xii. 31; secured by Justinian, B. II. vii. 18

Bazinus, fortress in Macedonia, B. IV. iv. 3

Bebius, *see* Vesuvius

Becis, fortress in Moesia, B. IV. xi. 20

Beculi, fortress in Haemimontum, B. IV. xi. 20

Bederiana, *see* Vederiana

Begadeus, Monastery of, in Mesopotamia, B. V. ix. 32

Beirut, centre of silk industry, S.H. xxv. 14

Belabitenê, province of Armenia, B. III. i. 26

Belaïdipara, fortress in Thrace, B. IV. xi. 20

Belapaton, city in Persia, VIII. x. 9

Belas, fortress in Dardania, B. IV. iv. 3

Belastyras, fortress in Haemimontum B. IV. xi. 20

Beledina, fortress in Moesia, B. IV. xi. 20

Belisarius, greatest General of the age of Justinian; husband of Antonina, I. xxv. 11, S.H. i. 12; a native of Germany, III. xi. 21; in company with Sittas, invades Persarmenia, I. xii. 20, 21; defeated by Narses and Aratius, I. xii. 22; appointed Commander of troops in Daras, with Procopius as Adviser, I. xii. 24; at the command of Justinian, undertakes to build a fort in Mindouos, I. xiii. 2, 3; prevented by the Persians, I. xiii. 4 ff.; appointed General of the East, I. xiii. 9; in company with Hermogenes, prepares to meet the Persians at Daras, I. xiii. 12 ff.; at the Battle of Daras, I. xiii. 19 ff.; sends letters to Mirranes, I. xiv. 1 ff., 7; addresses his soldiers, I. xiv. 20 ff.; arrays the army on the second day of battle, I. xiv. 28; wins a brilliant victory, I. xiv. 47 ff.; recalls the Romans from pursuit, I. xiv. 53; accused by Peter and John, S.H. iv. 4; hastens to meet the invasion of Azarethes, I. xviii. 4; follows the retiring Persian army, I. xviii. 9 ff.; ridiculed by his army, I. xviii. 12, 24; attempts to dissuade the Romans from battle, I. xviii. 16 ff.; arrays them for battle, I. xviii. 25, 26; fights valiantly after most of the Roman army had been routed, I. xviii. 41 ff.; returns to Byzantium in order to go against the Vandals, I. xxi. 2; his share in quelling the Nika Insurrection, I. xxiv. 40 ff.; appointed General of the East and despatched to Libya, I. xxvi. 1; victorious in Italy, II. i. 1; brings Vittigis to Byzantium, II. iv. 13; shares the command of the East with Bouzes, II. vi. 1; summoned from Italy to Byzantium, II. xiv. 8; sent against Chosroes, II. xiv. 8, 13, S.H. ii. 1; gathers an army in Mesopotamia, II. xvi. 1 ff.; invades Persia, II. xviii. 1 ff.; defeats Nabedes at Nisibis, II. xviii. 24, 25, S.H. ii. 28; feared by Chosroes, S.H. ii. 37; sends Arethas into Assyria, II. xix. 15; hears accusation of Photius, S.H. ii. 6–11; distrusted by him, S.H. ii. 12; meets Antonina, S.H. iii. 1; his deep love for her, *ib.*; subdued by her magic charms, S.H. iii. 2; attacks Sisauranon, II. xix. 4 ff.; captures it, II. xix. 24; VII. iii. 11; S.H. ii. 18; holds consultation with commanders, II. xix. 35 ff.; recalled to Byzantium, II. xix. 49; S.H. iii. 4; returns to Roman territory, II. xix. 45; journeys swiftly to East to confront Chosroes, II. xx. 20; gathers a force at Europum, II. xx. 24 ff.; receives Abandanes, envoy of Chosroes, II. xxi. 2 ff.; forces Chosroes to retire, II. xxi.

21; gives John of Edessa as a hostage, II. xxi. 27, S.H. xii. 6, 7; fails in third invasion of Persia, S.H. iii. 30, 31; replaced by Martinus and deprived of his bodyguard, S.H. iv. 13; summoned to Byzantium, II. xxi. 34, III. ix. 25; his great fame, II. xxi. 28, 29; ordered to be in readiness to lead the African expedition, III. x. 21; made Commander-in-Chief with unlimited powers, III. xi. 18, 20; adopts Theodosius, S.H. i. 15, 16; surprises Theodosius with Antonina, S.H. i. 18; protected by Theodosius, S.H. iii. 14; orders death of Theodosius, S.H. i. 22; laments his loss, S.H. i. 38–40; consoled by Constantinus, S.H. i. 24; deceived by Antonina, S.H. i. 26; sets sail for Africa, III. xii. 2, B. VI. v. 6; punishes two Massagetes for murder, III. xii. 9; addresses the army at Abydus, III. xii. 21; provides for the safe navigation of the fleet, III. xiii. 1–4; disembarks the army at Methone, III. xiii. 9 ff.; provides a supply of bread, III. xiii. 20; his wife preserves the drinking water, III. xiii. 23, 24; sends Procopius to Syracuse as intelligence officer, III. xiv. 3 ff.; his anxiety regarding the Vandals and the attitude of his own soldiers, III. xiv. 1, 2; leaves Sicily for Africa, III. xiv. 15; holds a consultation on disembarkation, III. xv. 1 ff.; disembarks the army and fortifies a camp, III. xv. 31–33; orders the fleet not to put in at Carthage, III. xvii. 16; orders that five men remain on each ship, III. xv. 36; punishes certain soldiers for stealing and addresses the army, III. xvi. 1–8; advances to Decimum, where he wins a victory over the Vandals, III. xvi. 9–xix. 33, xxi. 16, xxii. 14; captures with ease the unwalled cities of Libya, III. v. 9; restrains his army before Carthage, III. xx. 2; obeyed by the greater part of the fleet, III. xx. 15; enters Carthage, III. xx. 17; exhorts his soldiers to moderation, III. xx. 18–20; sits upon the throne of Gelimer, III. xx. 21; hears and answers complaints of Carthaginian citizens, III. xx. 22, 23; lunches in Gelimer's Palace, III. xxi. 1, 5; enjoys great renown because of the peaceful entry into Carthage, III. xxi. 8; his treaties with the Moors, III, xxv. 2–9, IV. viii. 11 ff., xi. 9; considers the fortification of Carthage, III. xxi. 11; presses on the work of repairing them, III. xxiii. 19, 20; spares the messengers of Tzazon, III. xxiv. 6; and the envoys of Gelimer, III. xxiv. 17; prevents desertions to the Vandals, IV. i. 7–11; addresses the army, IV. i. 12–25; defeats the Moors in the battle of Tricamarum, IV. ii. 1–iii. 18; attacks the Vandal camp, IV. iii. 10; [illegible] the Roman army, IV. iv. 6–8; sends John to pursue Gelimer, IV. iv. 9; himself follows, IV. iv. 13; mourns death of John the Armenian, IV. iv. 24; spares Uliaris, IV. iv. 25; continues pursuit of Gelimer, IV. iv. 26; leaves Pharas to besiege him, IV. iv. 28; sends suppliant Vandals to Carthage, IV. iv. 32; captures Boniface with the treasures of Gelimer, IV. iv. 33–41; returns to Carthage, IV. v. 1; sends out detachments to recover lost areas, IV. v. 1–10; makes an unsuccessful expedition to Sicily, IV. v. 11; writes a letter to the Goths, IV. v. 12–17; their reply, IV. v. 18-24; reports to Justinian, IV. v. 25; receives the report of Pharas regarding Gelimer, IV. vii. 10; sends Cyprian with instructions, IV. vii. 11; receives Gelimer at Aclas, IV. vii. 13, 14; reports his capture, IV. vii. 17, S.H. iv. 32; the victim of unjust slander, IV. viii. 1, 2, S.H. xviii. 9; given choice of returning to Byzantium or remaining in Carthage, chooses the latter, IV. viii. 4, 5; learns of charges against him, IV. viii. 8; hears report of Moorish uprising, IV. viii. 22; leaves Solomon in charge of Libya, IV. viii. 23; summoned from Africa, S.H. xviii. 9; in Byzantium, receives signal honours, IV. ix. 1 ff.; brings Vandals with him, IV. ix. 1, xiv. 17; pays honour to Justinian in the hippodrome, IV. ix. 12; later celebrates a "triumph" in the old manner, IV. ix. 15; becomes Consul, *ib.*; distributes much wealth of the Vandals to the people, IV. ix. 16; subjugates Sicily, IV. xiv. 1; winters in Syracuse, IV. xiv. 4, 41; his return to Africa besought by Solomon, IV. xiv. 41, 42; arrives opportunely at Carthage, IV. xv. 9, 10; pursues and overtakes fugitives, IV. xv. 11, 12; encamps and prepares for battle, IV. xv. 13–15; addresses his army, IV. xv. 16–29; defeats Stotzas, IV. xv. 40 ff.; plunders enemy camp, IV. xv. 46, 47; returns to Carthage, IV. xv. 47; sails for Sicily, IV. xv. 48, 49; Solomon lends suspected soldiers to him, IV. xix. 3; credited with destruction of Vandal power, IV. xi. 44, V. v. 1; sent by sea against the Goths, V. v. 2; Commander-in-Chief of the expedition, V. v. 4; sent first to Sicily, V. v. 6, 7, xiii. 14, S.H. i. 21; takes its cities except Panormus, by surrender, V. v. 12; captures Panormus, V. v. 12–16; enjoys great fame, V. v. 17 ff.; lays down consulship in Syracuse, V. v. 18, 19; commissioned to make settlement with Theodatus, V. vi. 25–27, S.H. iv. 43; obliged to hasten into Italy, V. vii. 26, viii. 1; receives the deserter Ebrimous, V. viii. 3; invites surrender of Naples, V. viii. 5 ff.; lays siege to it, V. viii. 42; unsuccessful in storming its wall, V. viii. 43; cuts its aqueduct, V. viii. 45, ix. 12; despairs of success in the siege, V. ix. 8, 10; learns of a possible entry by the aqueduct, V. ix. 10 ff.; makes necessary preparations, V. ix. 18–21; makes final appeal to the Neapolitans, V. ix. 22 ff.; realizes his plan of using the aqueduct, V. x. 1 ff.; captures Naples, V. x. 21 ff.; addresses the army, V. x. 29–34; protects Gothic prisoners, V. x. 37; addressed by Asclepiodotus, X. x. 39 ff.; forgives Neapolitans, V. x. 48; prepares to march on Rome, V. xiv. 1, 4; garrisons Cumae, V. xiv. 2; invited into Rome by citizens, V. xiv. 5; enters the city, V. xiv. 14; sends Leuderis and the keys of Rome to Justinian, V. xiv. 15; repairs defences of the city, *ib.*; prepares for a siege in spite of citizens, V. xiv. 16, 17; places ballistae and "wild asses" on the wall, V. xxi. 14, 18; guards the gates with "wolves," V. xxi. 19; smallness of his force in Rome, V. xxii. 17, xxiv. 2; receives submission of part of Samnium, Calabria and Apulia, V. xv. 1–3; controls all southern Italy, V. xv. 15; sends troops to occupy strongholds north of Rome, V. xvi. 1 ff.; Vittigis eager to catch him in Rome, V. xvi. 20, 21, xvii. 8; recalls troops from Tuscany, V. xvii. 1, 2; fortifies the Mulvian Bridge, V. xvii. 14; comes thither with troops, V. xviii. 2; unexpectedly engages the Goths, V. xviii. 3 ff.; his excellent horse, V. xviii. 6; shut out of Rome by his own men, V. xviii. 20; drives Goths from the moat, V. xviii. 26, 27; enters the city, V. xviii. 28; disposes the guards, V. xviii. 34; hears false report of disaster, V. xviii. 35–37; forestalls further rumours, V. xviii. 38, 39; ridiculed by the Romans, V. xviii. 42; finally partakes of food, V. xviii. 43; arranges guard of each gate, V. xix. 14–18; his name given to Samnite child, V. xx. 1–4; omen of victory for him, V. xx. 4; stops up the aqueducts, V. xix. 18, VI. ix. 6; operates mills on the Tiber, V. xix. 19 ff.; reproached by the citizens, V. xx. 6, 7; receives envoys from Vittigis, V. xx. 8; his reply to them, V. xx. 15–18; appoints Fidelius Pretorian Prefect, V. xx. 20; report of Gothic envoys concerning him, V. xxi. 1; from the wall, shoots two Goths, V. xxii. 2–5; checks Gothic advance, V. xxii. 7–9; assigns Constantinus to the Aurelian Gate, V. xxii. 15; prevented from repairing "Broken Wall," V. xxiii. 5; summoned to Vivarium, V. xxiii. 13; where he conducts a successful defence, V. xxiii. 14–23; praised by the Romans, V. xxiii. 27; writes the Emperor for reinforcements, V. xxiv. 1 ff.; receives an encouraging reply, V. xxiv. 21; sends non-combatants to Naples, V. xxv. 2; uses Roman [illegible] the wall, V. xxv. 11, 12; exiles Silverius and Senators from Rome, V. xxv. 13, 14; his precautions against corruption of the guards, V. xxv. 15, 16; against surprise at night, V. xxv. 17; unable to defend Portus, V. xxvi. 18; receives reinforcements, V. xxvii. 2; outwits the Goths, V. xxvii. 13–14; who try his methods in vain, V. xxvii. 18–23; applauded by the Romans, V. xxvii. 25; explains his confidence, V. xxvii. 26–29; compelled by Romans to risk a pitched battle, V. xxviii. 2, 3; addresses the army, V. xxviii. 5–14; leads out forces and disposes them for battle, V. xxviii. 15–19; commands in person at the great battle, V. xxix. 16 ff.; grieves for Chorsomantis, VI. i. 34; provides safe-conduct of Euthalius, VI. ii. 1–24; appealed to by citizens, VI. iii. 12 ff.; his reply, VI. iii. 23–32; sends Procopius to Naples, VI. iv. 1; garrisons stronghold near Rome, VI. iv. 4 ff.; receives John's troops into Rome, VI. v. 5 ff.; opens Flaminian Gate, VI. v. 8; outgenerals the Goths, VI. v. 9 ff.; receives Gothic envoys, VI. vi. 3 ff.; arranges an armistice, VI. vi. 36, vii. 10; goes to Ostia, VI. vii. 3, 4; receives Gothic envoys, VI. vii. 21 ff.; sends out cavalry, VI. vii. 25 ff.; appealed to from Milan, VI. vii. 35, 38; quarrels with Constantinus, VI. viii. 1 ff.; puts him to death, VI. viii. 17, 18, S.H. i. 28; in bad odour, S.H. i. 30; investigates the aqueduct, VI. ix. 9–11; learns of Vittigis' stratagem, VI. ix. 20; punishes his accomplice, VI. ix. 22; sends message to John, VI. x. 1, 7; attacks departing Goths, VI. x. 14 ff.; again sends message to John, VI. xi. 4–7; sends assistance to Milan, VI. xii. 26; moves against Vittigis, VI. xiii. 1; takes two cities by surrender, [illegible] 2, 3; garrisons them, VI. xiii. 4; receives reinforcements, VI. xiii. 16–18; joins forces with Narses, VI. xvi. 1; they confer, VI. xvi. 2 ff.; arranges relief of Ariminum, VI. xvi. 14–17 ff.; advances through the mountains, VI. xvii. 12 ff.; arrives at Ariminum, VI. xviii. 2; suspects John, VI. xviii. 3; his plan blocked by Narses, VI. xviii. 4–11; protests in a speech, VI. xviii. 12–22; displays a letter from Justinian, VI. xviii. 27, 28; accused by Narses, VI. xviii. 29; besieges Urbinus, VI. xix. 1 ff.; abandoned by Narses, VI. xix. 8, 9; takes Urbinus by surrender, VI. xix. 17; stations Aratius at Firmum, VI. xx. 3; marches against Urviventus, VI. xx. 3, 4; besieges the city, VI. xx. 5 ff.; sends troops against Uraïas, VI. xxi. 1, 16; receives word from Martinus, VI. xxi. 13; orders John and Justinus to Milan, VI. xxi. 16; quarrels with John, nephew of Vitalian, S.H. v. 7; avoided by him, S.H. v.

13; writes to Narses, VI. xxi. 17–22; moves into Picenum, VI. xxii. 1; reports fall of Milan to the Emperor, VI. xxii. 2, 3; made sole Commander, VI. xxii. 4; fails to restrain the Eruli, VI. xxii. 5; Justinian wishes to send him against the Persians, VI. xxii. 21; holds Gothic envoys, VI. xxii. 23; plans capture of Auximus and Fisula, VI. xxiii. 1 ff.; lays siege to the former, VI. xxiii. 5–xxiv. 17, xxvi. 2–xxvii. 4, 27; takes it by surrender, VI. xxvii. 28–34; hears of arrival of Franks, VI. xxv. 15; writes to Theudibert, VI. xxv. 19–23; narrowly escapes a serious wound, VI. xxvii. 13, 14; lays siege to Ravenna, VI. xxviii. 1 ff.; sends envoys to Vittigis, VI. xxviii. 8 ff.; sends Vitalius into Venetia, VI. xxviii. 24; sends Thomas to the Cottian Alps, VI. xxviii. 29 ff.; repudiates terms of Emperor's envoys, VI. xxix. 4, 5; addresses the officers, VI. xxix. 7–14; secures written statement from them, VI. xxix. 16; offered kingship by the Goths, VI. xxix. 18; unwilling to accept, VI. xxix. 19, 20; but uses the opportunity to take Ravenna, VI. xxix. 20 ff.; calls a second council, VI. xxix. 22; writes to Vittigis, VI. xxix. 24; receives Gothic envoys, VI. xxix. 26–28; dismisses unfriendly commanders, VI. xxix. 29; enters Ravenna with army, VI. xxix. 30 ff.; guards Vittigis not in disgrace, VI. xxix. 35, S.H. iv. 32, 43; protects the Goths, VI. xxix. 38; takes over several strongholds, VI. xxix. 39–41; receives envoys from Ildibadus, VI. xxix. 41; slandered to the Emperor, VI. xxx. 1; summoned to Byzantium, VI. xxx. 2, 3; Gothic offer repeated, VI. xxx. 24–27; his refusal, VI. xxx. 28; proceeds to Byzantium, VI. xxx. 30; VII. i. 1, 25, 31, S.H. i. 35, 42; denied a triumph by the Emperor, VII. i. 3; his popularity with the people, VII. i. 4, 5; his prominent position in Byzantium, VII. i. 17–22; Justinian forced to send him against Totila, VII. ix. 23, x. 1; relieves Dryus, VII. x. 6, 7, 12; removes to Pola, VII. x. 13; receives feigned letter of Bonus, VII. x. 15; and spies of Totila, VII. x. 17; answers letter, VII. x. 18; reaches Ravenna, VII. xi. 1; delivers a speech, VII. xi. 1–9; sends a force into Aemilia, VII. xi. 11; to Auximus, VII. xi. 19; seizes Pisaurus, VII. xi. 33, 34; sends a force to Rome, VII. xi. 37; his forces not a match for the Goths, VII. xi. 38; sends John to Byzantium with a letter, VII. xii. 1–10; hostile to Herodian, VII. xii. 16; regrets decision to operate from Ravenna, VII. xiii. 13, 14; proceeds to Epidamnus, VII. xiii. 19; writes to Justinian, *ib.*; receives reinforcements, VII. xiii. 21; sends a force to Portus, VII. xv. 1; reinforced by John and Isaac, VII. xviii. 1; disapproves John's plan, VII. xviii. 1, 2; concerned for Rome, VII. xviii. 3; sends John to Calabria and sails for Rome, VII. xviii. 5; leaves Dryus, VII. xviii. 8; arrives at Portus, VII. xviii. 11; awaits John in vain, VII. xviii. 25, 29; attempts to provision Rome, VII. xix. 1 ff.; leaves Antonina with Isaac in Portus, VII. xix. 7; which he guards with a special force, VII. xix. 25; instructs Bessas to divert barbarians, VII. xix. 12; fires a tower, VII. xix. 18, 19; and captures a bridge, VII. xix. 21; report of his success reaches Portus, VII. xix. 23; hears of Isaac's rashness, VII. xix. 29; abandons the attack, VII. xix. 30; falls sick, VII. xix. 32, 33; Justinian refers Totila to him, VII. xxi. 25; dissuades Totila from destroying Rome, VII. xxii. 7–17; held in Portus, VII. xxii. 18; permits Martinianus to feign desertion VII. xxiii. 1;

INDEX

receives captives from Spolitium, VII. xxiii. 7; makes visit of inspection to Rome, VII. xxiii. 8–11; routs a Gothic ambush, VII. xxiii. 10, 11; reoccupies Rome, VII. xxiv. 1, 2; repairs its defences, VII. xxiv. 3–6; provisions the city, VII. xxiv. 7; successfully defends it against Totila, VII. xxiv. 8–26; replaces gates and sends keys of the city to Justinian, VII. xxiv. 34; suspicious of John, VII. xxv. 22–24; urges Justinian to send reinforcements, VII. xxvii. 1; receives a letter from him, VII. xxvii. 12; sails to Sicily, VII. xxvii. 16; thence for Tarentum, VII. xxviii. 1; puts in at Croton, VII. xxviii. 3; encamps, sending a larger force forward, VII. xxviii. 4, 5; hastily returns to Messana, VII. xxviii. 18; joined by Valerian, VII. xxx. 2; summons John and sails for Rusciane, VII. xxx. 9; decides to go to [illegible] 10, respected and feared by the Goths, VII. xxv. 14; summoned to Byzantium, VII. xxx. 25; his inglorious return, VII. xxxv. 1; abandons Perusia to its fate, VII. xxxv. 2; awaited at Byzantium, VII. xxxii. 19, 38, 42; feared by conspirators, VII. xxxii. 38; who desire his death, VII. xxxii. 39; takes up residence in Byzantium, VII. xxxv. 3; his wealth and fame, *ib.*; owned property in a suburb, VII. xxxv. 4; his wealth coveted by Theodora, S.H. v. 20; his money confiscated, S.H. iv. 17; garrisons Rome, VII. xxxvi. 1; returns to Byzantium, VII. xxxvi. 4; appoints commanders in Rhegium, VII. xxxvii. 20; assisted by Sinnion, VIII. xix. 7; honoured by the Emperor, VIII. xxi. 1; regarded as First Citizen of the Empire, VIII. xxi. 2, 3; brought Amalafridas to Byzantium, VIII. xxv. 12; treated with indignity, S.H. iv. 20, 21; ridiculed, S.H. v. 27; his utter disgrace, S.H. iv. 16; his friends kept from him, S.H. iv. 15; reconciled with Antonina, S.H. iii. 12; recalled to favour after despair, S.H. iv. 22–31; seeks reappointment, S.H. iv. 38; made commander of the Royal Grooms and sent to Italy, S.H. iv. 39; exacts money from Ita ians, S.H. v. 4, 5; expected to lead an insurrection, S.H. iv. 40; fails in Italian expedition, S.H. iv. 42, 43; abandons Italy, S.H. v. 17; his inconstant character, S.H. v. 24–26; his good fortune foretold by a sign, VII. xxxv. 3–8; his qualities as a man and as a commander, VII. i. 6–16; disgraceful acts of, S.H. i. 10 ff.; his wife Antonina, VII. xix. 7, 30, xxviii. 4, xxx. 2, 3, 25; his treatment by Theodora, S.H. xvii. 1; his daughter courted by Sergius, S.H. v. 33; her marriage, S.H. v. 18–21; swayed by Antonina, S.H. v. 14, 27; his great wealth, S.H. iv. [illegible]; accused of self-interest, S.H. ii. 21; his navigation officer Demetrius, VII. vi. 20; his bodyguards, II. xix. 15, etc.; his "household," VI. xxviii. 8, VII. i. 20, 21, xxxvi. 16, S.H. i. 15; his followers, S.H. ii. 4, iii. 8; in mosaic at Byzantium, B. I. x. 16; the "teaching of Belisarius," VI. xxi. 30

Bella, fortress in Dardania, B. IV. iv. 3

Bemastes, fortress in Cabetzus, B. IV. iv. 3

Beneventus (Beneventum), town in Samnium, called in ancient times Maleventus, V. xv. 4; its strong winds, V. xv. 7; founded by Diomed, V. xv. 8; relics of the Caledonian boar preserved in, *ib.*; meeting of Diomed and Aeneas at, V. xv. 9; its defences destroyed by the Goths, VII. xxv. 11

Bepara, fortress in Thrace, B. IV. xi. 20

Bercadium, fortress in southern Europe, B. IV. iv. 3

Bereïarus, fortress in Thrace, B. IV. xi. 20

Bergisum, fortress in Thrace, B. IV. xi. 20

Bergomum, city near Milan; occupied by Mundilas, VI. xii. 40
Berine, wife of Emperor Leon, and sister of Basiliscus, III. vi. 2; gains clemency for Basiliscus, III. vi. 26
Beriniana, fortress in Dardania, B. IV. iv. 3
Beripara, fortress in Thrace, B. IV. xi. 20
Beripara, fortress in Moesia, B. IV. xi. 20
Bermezium, fortress in Dardania, B. IV. iv. 3
Bernicê, city in Libya; fortified by Justinian, B. VI. ii. 5
Beroea, a town of Syria between Hieropolis and Antioch, II. vii. 2; distance from Chalcis, II. xii. 1; Chosroes demands money from the inhabitants, II. vii. 5; the citizens retire to the acropolis, II. vii. 7; the lower city entered by Chosroes and a large part of it fired, II. vii. 10, 11; acropolis valiantly defended against Chosroes, II. vii. 12; miserable plight of the besieged, II. vii. 13; citizens capitulate to Chosroes, II. vii. 35
Beroea, city in Thrace; restored by Justinian, B. IV. xi. 19
Beros, *see* Verus
Bersabus, a Persian notable, VIII. xv. 8; captured by Valerian, VIII. xv. 9; imprisoned in Byzantium, VIII. xv. 10; returned to Isdigousnas, VIII. xv. 11
Berzana, fortress in Dardania, B. IV. iv. 3
Besaiana, fortress in Dardania, B. IV. iv. 3
Besi, a barbarian tribe, VI. xxvi. 3
Besiana, fortress in Dardania, B. IV. iv. 3
Bessas, of Thrace; Roman general, I. viii. 3, V. v. 3; by birth a Goth, V. xvi. 2; his ability, V. xvi. 2, 3, VI. i. 3; commander in Martyropolis, I. xxi. 5; at the capture of Naples, V. x. 2, 5, 10–12, 20; sent against Narnia, V. xvi. 2; which he takes by surrender, V. xvi. 3; recalled to Rome, V. xvii. 1, 2; returning slowly, meets the Goths in battle, V. xvii. 4, 5; arrives in Rome, V. xvii. 6; commanding at the Praenestine Gate, sends false report, V. xviii. 35, xix. 15; summons Belisarius to the Vivarium, V. xxiii. 13; makes a sally against the Goths, V. xxvii. 18; saves Belisarius from Constantinus, VI. viii. 15; sent away from Ravenna, VI. xxix. 29; with others, left in charge of Italy, VI. xxx. 2, confers with other commanders, VII. iii. 2, 3; joins in relief expedition to Florentia, VII. v. 4; holds Spolitium, VII. vi. 8; then Rome, VII. xi. 37; disapproves a sally, VII. xiii. 2; refuses to support an advance from Portus, VII. xv. 2–6; appealed to by citizens, VII. xvii. 2–8; replies to them, VII. xvii. 8; hoards and sells grain, VII. xvii. 10, 16, xix. 14, xx. 1; instructed by Belisarius to attack, VII. xix. 12; his failure to obey, VII. xix. 13; neglects discipline, VII. xx. 1, 2; questions Gothic captives, VII. xx. 10, 11; disregards their warning, VII. xx. 12; escapes from Rome by flight, VII. xx. 18, 20; his accumulated wealth falls to Totila, VII. xx. 26; his guards, VII. xvii. 12; sent to Lazica as General of Armenia, VIII. ix. 4; sent against the Abasgi, VIII. ix. 12; besieges Petra, VIII. xi. 11 ff.; undermines the wall, VIII. xi. 14–18; leads the assault in person, VIII. xi. 39, 40; is wounded, but saved, VIII. xi. 44–50; returns to the assault, VIII. xi. 51; refuses a request of the Persians, VIII. xii. 3–13; sends captives to Justinian and dismantles the wall of Petra, VIII. xii. 28; unwisely leaves Lazica, VIII. xiii. 11–13; regains his reputation lost at Rome, VIII. xii. 30–34, xxxiii. 24
Besuparum, fortress in Thrace, B. IV. xi. 20
Bethlehem, city in Palestine; secured by Justinian, B. V. ix. 12; its Monastery of John, B. V. ix. 13
Betzas, fortress in Cabetzus, B. IV. iv. 3

INDEX

Biculea, fortress in southern Europe, B. IV. iv. 3
Bidzo, fortress in Cabetzus, B. IV. iv. 3
Bigranaê, fortress on the Danube, built by Justinian, B. IV. vi. 28
Billeting of Roman troops and of barbarians, S.H. xxiii. 22, 24
Bimerus, fortress in Cabetzus, B. IV. iv. 3
Bineus, fortress in Cabetzus, B. IV. v. 3
Birginaso, fortress in Moesia, B. IV. xi. 20
Bisdina, fortress in Moesia, B. IV. xi. 20
Bishops, of Rome, V. iii. 5, xiv. 4, xxv. 13, xxvi. 2, VII. xvi. 1, S.H. xxvii. 17; of Alexandria, S.H. xxvii. 3, 22; of Antioch, II. vii. 16; of Apamea, II. xi. 16; of Byzantium, III. xii. 2, S.H. vi. 26; of Cyzicus, I. xxv. 37; of Ephesus, S.H. iii. 4
Bismapha, fortress in Moesia, B. IV. xi. 20
Bithynia, location, VIII. ii. 2; its city Helenopolis, B. V. ii. 1; Nicaea, B. V. iii. 1 ff.; source of grain [illegible]; its dangerous highway repaired by Justinian, B. V. iii. 12–15; its hot spring, B. V. iii. 16; Bithynians offer access to Byzantium, II. xxviii. 23
Bitzimaeas, fortress in Cabetzus, B. IV. iv. 3
Bizana, town in Armenia, B. III. iv. 13, B. III. v. 13–15; distance from Tzumina, B. III. v. 15
Blachernae, quarter in Byzantium; its church, B. I. iii. 3
Black Gulf, off the Thracian Chersonese, II. iv. 8, V. xv. 18
Black Sea, *see* Euxine
Blases, brother of Perozes, chosen king in place of Cabades, deposed, I. v. 2; imprisoned and blinded by Cabades, I. vi. 17
Blebois, fortress near Pauta, B. IV. iv. 3
Blemyes, a people of upper Egypt, I. xix. 28; receive annual payment from the Roman emperor, I. xix. 32, 33; Diocletian purposes to hold them in check by means of the Nobatae, I. xix. 30; their religion, I. xix. 35, 36
Bleschames, commander of the Persian soldiers in Sisauranon, II. xix. 3; sent to Byzantium by Belisarius with Persian captives, II. xix. 24, VII. iii. 11, S.H. ii. 28, B. II. iv. 8
Blezo, fortress in Dardania, B. IV. iv. 3
Blue Faction, one of the dominant popular parties of the Hippodrome; struggles with the Green Faction, I. xxiv. 2–6; colonnade of the Blues in the Hippodrome at Byzantium, I. xxiv. 49; championed by Justinian, II. xi. 32, S.H. vii. 1, 2, 6, 22, ix. 33, x. 16, xxix. 27, 35; their novel styles of clothing, S.H. vii. 8 ff.; non-militant members, S.H. vii. 17; accept supplication of Theodora's mother, S.H. ix. 7; seem very moderate, S.H. x. 19; in the Nika Insurrection, I. xxiv. 7 ff.; riot in Byzantium, S.H. xxix. 33; attack Malthanes, S.H. xxix. 36; also called "Veneti," *q.v.*; in Antioch, S.H. xii. 28; in Tarsus, S.H. xxix. 30, 32; their patron [illegible], S.H. xxix. 35; *cf.* Vol. VI. Appendix I
Boas River, considered by Procopius the upper portion of the Phasis, II. xxix. 14–16; description of, VIII. ii. 6, 9
Bochas, a Massagete, bodyguard of Belisarius, VI. ii. 10; sent to the Plain of Nero, VI. ii. 20; helps to rout the Goths, but is surprised and wounded, VI. ii. 21–23; after inflicting great losses upon the Goths, VI. ii. 36; rescued by Valerian and Martinus, VI. ii. 24; dies of his wound, VI. ii. 32
Bodas, fortress in Moesia, B. IV. xi. 20
Boeotia, in central Greece; damaged by earthquakes, VIII. xxv. 16; its town Scarphea, VIII. xxv. 19; labours of Justinian in, B. IV. ii. 24
Boes, a Persian general, I. xii. 10
Boethius, a Roman senator, son-in-law of Symmachus, V. i. 32; husband of Rusticiana, VII. xx. 27, 29; his death, V. i. 34; his children receive from Amalasuntha his property, V. ii. 5
Bogas, fortress in Macedonia, B. IV. iv.
3

INDEX

Bolbus, fortress in Macedonia, B. IV. iv. 3

Bolosia, epithet of Artemis, VIII. xxii. 29

Bolum, fortress in Persarmenia, near the Persian gold mines, I. xv. 18; betrayed to the Romans by Isaac, I. xv. 32, 33; its return demanded by Chosroes, I. xxii. 3; relinquished by the Romans, I. xxii. 18, VIII. xiii. 19

Boniface, Roman general; his splendid qualities, III. iii. 14, 15; rival of Aetius, III. iii. 15; made General of all Libya, III. iii. 16; slandered by Aetius, III. iii. 17; summoned to Rome by Placidia, III. iii. 18; refuses to come, III. iii. 20; makes an alliance with the Vandals, III. iii. 22, 25; the true cause of his conduct discovered by his friends, III. iii. 27, 28; urged by Placidia to return to Rome, III. iii. 29; unable to persuade the Vandals to withdraw, meets them in battle and is twice defeated, III. iii. 30–35, xxi. 16; returns to Rome, III. iii. 36

Boniface, the Libyan, a native of Byzacium; entrusted by Gelimer with his wealth, IV. iv. 33, 34; falls into the hands of Belisarius, IV. iv. 35–41

Bononia, city in Aemilia; captured by Vitalius, VII. xi. 12

Bononia, fortress on the Danube, B. IV. vi. 24

Bonus, nephew of John; commander in Genua, VII. x. 14, 16, 18

Boraïdes, nephew of Justinian; assists in making Hypatius prisoner, I. xxiv. 53; brother of Germanus, VII. xxxi. 17, xxxii. 18

Borbrega, fortress in Cabetzus, B. IV. iv. 3

Boreium, city in Pentapolis, B. VI. ii. 11; near the Moors, B. VI. ii. 21; distance from Augila, B. VI. ii. 15; fortified by Justinian, B. VI. ii. 12, 13

Boriades, bodyguard of Belisarius; sent to capture Syllectus, III. xvi. 9

Bospara, fortress in Thrace, B. IV. xi. 20

Bosporus, city on the Euxine, I. xii. 7, VIII. v. 26, 27; citizens of, submit to Justinian, I. xii. 8; Justinian accused of seizing it, II. iii. 40; strengthened by him, B. III. vii. 10, 12

Bostra, its poor-house, B. V. ix. 22

Bottes, fortress in Cabetzus, B. IV. iv. 3

Boulla, Plain of, distance from Carthage, III. xxv. 1; near the boundary of Numidia, *ib.*; the Vandals gather there, III. xix. 32, xxv. 1; the only territory left to the Vandals, III. xxv. 16; Gelimer and Tzazon meet there, III. xxv. 22; mutineers gather there, IV. xv. 1

Boulpiansus, fortress in Epirus, B. IV. iv. 3

Bourboöden, fortress in Macedonia, B. IV. iv. 3

Bourgaon, mountain in Numidia; scene of a battle with the Moors, IV. xii. 3 ff.

Bourgousnoes, fortress in Tzanica, B. III. vi. 24; distance from Sisilisson, *ib.*

Bouzes, commander in Lebanon; brother of Coutzes, I. xiii. 5; brother of Venilus, VIII. ix. 5; uncle of Domentiolus, VII. xxxix. 3; sent to support Belisarius at Mindouos, I. xiii. 5; commander in Martyropolis, I. xxi. 5; at the battle of Daras, I. xiii. 19, 25 ff.; sent against the Armenians, II. iii. 28; his offer of friendship distrusted by them, II. iii. 28, 29; slays John treacherously, II. iii. 31; shares command of the East with Belisarius, II. vi. 1; makes suggestions as to the defence of Hieropolis, II. vi. 2 ff.; abandons the city, II. vi. 7, 8; prevents the Edessenes from ransoming captives, II. xiii. 6; favours invasion of Persia, II. xvi. 16; takes refuge in Hierapolis, II. xx. 20; they invite Belisarius to join them, II. xx. 21 ff.; but later come to him at Europum, II. xx. 28; sent to help the Lombards, VII. xxxiv. 40; confided in by Germanus, VII. xxxii. 41; testifies in his favour, VII. xxxii. 45; accused by

INDEX

Peter and John, S.H. iv. 4; summoned to Byzantium and cruelly confined by Theodora, S.H. iv. 6–12, xvii. 1
Braducius, interpreter of Isdigousnas, II. xxviii. 41; by whom, possibly, he was slandered, VIII. xi. 9; slain by Chosroes, VIII. xi. 8
Braeola, fortress in the district of Aquenisium, B. IV. iv. 3
Brarcedum, fortress in southern Europe, B. IV. iv. 3
Bratzista, fortress in southern Europe, B. IV. iv. 3
Bre, fortress in Rhodope; built by Justinian, B. IV. xi. 20
Brebatê, fortress in Epirus, B. IV. iv. 3
Brebeta, fortress in Epirus, B. IV. iv. 3
Bredas, fortress in Haemimontum, B. IV. xi. 20
Bregedaba, fortress in Cabetzus, B. IV. iv. 3
Brigizes, fortress in Macedonia, B. IV. iv. 3
Briparo, fortress in the district of Remisianisia, B. IV. iv. 3
Briparum, fortress in Dardania, B. IV. iv. 3
Britain, counted in the Western Empire, III. i. 18; compared in size with Thule, VI. xv. 4; much larger than Sicily, VI. vi. 28; its position with reference to Brittia, VIII. xx. 4–6; inhabited by barbarians, S.H. xix. 13; revolts from the Romans, III. ii. 31; not recovered, but held by tyrants, III. ii. 38; offered to the Goths by Belisarius, VI. vi. 28
Britons, V. xxiv. 36
Brittia, an island lying off Gaul, VIII. xx. 5; its numerous population, causing annual migrations to the mainland, VIII. xx. 6–10; horses unknown there, VIII. xx. 29; its dividing wall, VIII. xx. 42–46; the destination of departing spirits, VIII. xx. 47 ff.; its people wage war on the Varni, VIII. xx. 1 ff.; a maiden of, VIII. xx. 12, 41; remote from the Varni, VIII. xx. 18; distance from the mouth of the Rhine, VIII. xx. 4
Brittones, one of the three nations of Brittia, VIII. xx. 7
Brittura, fortress in the district of Remisianisia, B. IV. iv. 3
Brochi, place on the Bosporus, B. I. viii. 3
Broken Wall, a portion of the defences of Rome, V. xxiii. 3, 4; not rebuilt by Belisarius, V. xxiii. 5; never attacked by the Goths, V. xxiii. 6, 7; never rebuilt, V. xxiii. 8
Bronze Gate, entrance of the Palace in Byzantium, I. xxiv. 47, B. I. x. 3, 11 ff.
Bruchi, a people of the Caucasus, VIII. iv. 1
Brundisium, city in Calabria, VII. xviii. 11; Goths retire to, VII. xviii. 6; Verus encamps near, VII. xxvii. 6; distance from Cannae, VII. xviii. 18; from Dryus, VII. xviii. 6
Bruttii, a people of southern Italy, V. xv. 22, 23
Bruttium, province of Italy, V. viii. 4; gained by Totila, VII. vi. 5; influence of Tullianus in, VII. xviii. 20; John in, VII. xviii. 25; guarded by Rhecimundus, VII. xviii. 26; Lucanian mountains extend to, VII. xxviii. 7
Bugarama, fortress in Cabetzus, B. IV. iv. 3
Bulibas, fortress in Epirus, B. IV. iv. 3
Bulicas, harbour of the Homeritae, I. xix. 21
Bupus, fortress in Epirus, B. IV. iv. 3
Burcentius, Roman soldier; sent as a messenger by the Goths, VI. xxvi. 3 ff., 14, 15; denounced to Valerian, VI. xxvi. 25; confesses and is killed, VI. xxvi. 26
Burdepto, fortress in Haemimontum, B. IV. xi. 20
Burdopes, fortress in southern Europe, B. IV. iv. 3
Burgarama, fortress in Cabetzus, B. IV. iv. 3
Burgonobore, fortress on the Danube, B. IV. vi. 20
Burgualtu, fortress on the Danube, B. IV. vi. 22
Burgundians, a barbarian people of Gaul, V. xii. 11; attacked by the Franks, V. xii. 23; alliance

formed against, V. xii. 24, 25; driven back by the Franks, V. xii. 26, 28–30; and completely subjugated, V. xiii. 3; sent as allies to the Goths, VI. xii. 38, 39; subjugated by the Franks, VI. xxviii. 17; reported to be in Liguria, VI. xxi. 13; rewarded by the Goths, VI. xxi. 39

Burnus, town in Liburnia, V. xvi. 13, 15

Burtudgiz, fortress in Haemimontum, B. IV. xi. 20

Busta Gallorum, in central Italy; remains of Gothic pyres, VIII. xxix. 5

Buteries, fortress in Cabetzus, B. IV. iv. 3

Buttis, fortress in Scassetana, B. IV. iv. 3

Byrsia, fortress in Cabetzus, B. IV. iv. 3

Byzacium, district in Africa held by Moors, III. xix. 32, VIII. xvii. 21, B. VI. vi. 1; a dry region, III. xv. 34; its town Hermione, III. xiv. 10; its city Caputvada, B. VI. vi. 8; Moors of, defeat the Vandals, III. ix. 3; seek alliance with the Romans, III. xxv. 3; Moors of, revolt, IV. viii. 9, x. 2, xii. 1, 2; Roman forces annihilated there, IV. x. 3 ff.; objective of Solomon's expedition, IV. xi. 14; Moors of, suffer a crushing defeat, IV. xii. 21–25; abandoned by them, IV. xii. 29; except those under Antalas, IV. xii. 30; plundered by the Leuathae, IV. xxi. 17; Moors gather there once more, IV. xxiii. 1; Himerius commander in, IV. xxiii. 3, 14; Moors march thence against Carthage, IV. xxv. 2; defeated by John, IV. xxviii. 46; subsequent battles, IV. xxviii. 47 ff.; works of Justinian in, B. VI. vi. 17; home of Boniface, the Libyan, IV. iv. 33

Byzantines, residents of Byzantium, B. I. i. 21, ii. 1; their identification of the Palladium, V. xv. 14; reverence the Church of the Mother of God, S.H. iii. 23; their admiration of Belisarius, VII. i. 5; mock Alexander, VII. i. 30; make direful forecasts, VII. xxix. 17; well supplied with water, B. I. xi. 14; frequent Pythia, B. V. iii. 17

Byzantium, capital of the Roman Empire, both East and West; called Constantinople (*q.v.*) only rarely, in the *Buildings*; at the limit of the Mediterranean, B. IV. ix. 2; at the "beginning" of the Euxine, VIII. ii. 1; its harbours, B. I. v. 1–13, V. i. 10; the Nika insurrection in, I. xxiv. 1 ff., B. I. i. 20; its suburbs ravaged by Huns, II. iv. 4; visited by the pestilence, II. xxii. 9 ff., S.H. iv. 1; accessible to the Persians by way of the Euxine, II. xxviii. 23; supplies rowers in the Roman fleet, III. xi. 16; supplies forces to Narses, VIII. xxvi. 10; ashes from Vesuvius fell there, VI. iv. 27; visited by earthquakes, VII. xxix. 4, 5, 17; harassed by a whale, VII. xxix. 9; its Palace, VII. i. 3, xxxii. 22, 39, 43, 51, B. I. iv. 2, 8, x. 3, 4, 10 ff.; its long walls, VII. xl. 43; suburbs of, B. IV. ix. 3; its suburb Panteichion, VII. xxxv. 4; fortresses adjacent to, B. IV. viii. 2 ff.; its grain supply, B. V. i. 16; its chief priest Epiphanius, III. xii. 2; distance from Adrianople, VII. xl. 36; from Carthage, III. x. 14; from the mouth of the Danube, III. i. 10; from Topirus, VII. xxxviii. 9; from its long walls, B. IV. ix. 6; buildings erected or repaired by Justinian in, B. I. i.; its Senate House, V. v. 19, B. I. x. 6; home of the master-builder John, B. II. viii. 25

Byzas, eponymous hero of Byzantium, B. I. v. 1

Cabades, youngest son of Perozes, I. iv. 2; father of Chosroes, S.H. ii. 26; grandfather of Cabades, VIII. xxvi. 13; chosen King of Persia, I. iv. 34, B. II. ii. 19; unpopular because of innovations, I. v. 1; cast into the Prison of Oblivion, I. v. 7; escapes therefrom, I. vi. 7, 8, 10; enters Persia

INDEX

with an army of Ephthalitae, I. vi. 10–17; appoints Adergoudounbades "Chanaranges," I. vi. 15, 18; deposes Blases, I. vi. 17; institutes a new office, I. vi. 18, 19; appeals to Anastasius for a loan, I. vii. 1; invades Roman territory, I. vii. 3, S.H. xxiii. 7; grants request of Jacobus, the hermit, I. vii. 9–11; besieges Amida, I. vii. 12–29; and captures it, I. xii. 29, B. III. ii. 8; puts Glones in command of the city, I. vii. 33; his treatment of the captives, I. vii. 34; routs Roman armies, I. viii. 8–19; spares Constantina, II. xiii. 15; desires capture of Edessa and Constantina, II. xiii. 8; abandons Edessa, II. xiii. 9 ff.; retires to meet Hunnic invasion, I. viii. 19; seizes the Caspian Gates, I. x. 12; protests fortification of Daras, I. x. 16; solicitude as to his successor, I. xi. 2 ff.; cured by Stephanus of Edessa, II. xxvi. 31; hates his oldest son Caoses, I. xi. 3, II. ix. 12; requests Justinus to adopt Chosroes, I. xi. 9, 20 ff.; unwilling to save Seoses, I. xi. 36, 37; tries forcibly to convert the Iberians, I. xii. 2 ff.; sends an army against them, I. xii. 10; sends an army into Roman Armenia, I. xv. 1; captures Theodosiopolis, B. III. v. 3; passes Martyropolis, B. III. ii. 4; receives the submission of Martyropolis, B. III. ii. 6, 7; his gold mines at Pharangium, I. xv. 27; deprived of their revenue, I. xv. 28, 29; treats with Rufinus, I. xvi. 1 ff.; punishes Mirranes, I. xvii. 26 ff.; plans a new Roman campaign, I. xvii. 29; advised by Alamundaras, I. xvii. 30 ff.; whose advice he adopts, I. xviii. 1; dishonours Azarethes, I. xviii. 51 ff.; refuses to negotiate with Hermogenes, I. xxi. 1; bought pearl from the Ephthalitae, I. iv. 16; his last illness, I. xxi. 17 ff.; his ability as a ruler, I. vi. 19

Cabades, son of Zames, nephew of Chosroes, VIII. xxvi. 13; plot to set him on the Persian throne in place of Chosroes, I. xxiii. 4; ordered to be killed by Chosroes, I. xxiii. 7; escapes by the help of the Chanaranges, I. xxiii. 9 ff.; in the army of Narses, VIII. xxvi. 13; one claiming his name entertained by Justinian in Byzantium, I. xxiii. 23, 24

Cabaon, a Moorish ruler, prepares to meet the Vandals, III. viii. 15, 16; sends spies to Carthage, III. viii. 17 ff.; receives the report of his spies, III. viii. 24; prepares for the conflict, III. viii. 25, 26, IV. xi. 17; defeats the enemy, III. viii. 28

Cabetzus, district of southern Europe, B. IV. iv. 3

Cabotumba, fortress in Haemimontum, B. IV. xi. 20

Cadiseni, in the Persian army at the battle of Daras, I. xiv. 38, 39

Cadmean victory (proverb), V. vii. 5

Caenopolis, contemporary name of Taenarum, III. xiii. 9

Caesar, title applied by the Persians to the Roman Emperor, II. xi. 35, xxi. 9; a title given to one next below the emperor in station, III. vii. 21, 23; *see* Augustus

Caesarea, city in Palestine; home of Procopius, I. i. 1, S.H. xi. 25; of Evangelus, S.H. xxx. 18

Caesarea, city in Thessaly; restored by Justinian, B. IV. iii. 9, 10

Caesarea, city in Cappadocia, B. V. iv. 7–14

Caesarea, chief city of "Second Mauritania," IV. xx. 31; situated at its eastern extremity, IV. x. 29; distance from Carthage, IV. v. 5; recovered for the Romans by Belisarius, *ib.*, IV. xx. 32

Caesena, fortress in northern Italy, V. i. 15; distance from Ravenna, *ib.*; garrisoned by Vittigis, VI. xi. 3; John sent thither by Narses, VI. xix. 19; attacked unsuccessfully by him, VI. xix. 20, 21; taken over by Belisarius, VI. xxix. 40; captured by Totila, VII. vi. 1

Caïsus, a Homerite; fugitive because of murder, I. xx. 9, 10

INDEX

Calabria, on the left of the Ionian Gulf, VI. v. 2, VII. xl. 15, B. IV. i. 11; in southern Itlay, VI. v. 2; provisions brought thence by the Romans, VI. xxiv. 14; gained by Totila, VII. vi. 5; mentioned, VII. xviii. 2, 7, 8, xxiii. 18, xxvii. 12; its city Tarentum, VII. xxiii. 12

Calabrians, their location, V. xv. 21, 22; voluntarily submit to Belisarius, V. xv. 3; won over by John, VII. xviii. 17; plan revolt from the Goths, VII. xxiii. 17; a Calabrian accuses a Gothic soldier, VII. viii. 12

Calamaa, city in Numidia; strengthened by Justinian, B. VI. vii. 10

Calarnus, fortress in Macedonia, B. IV. iv. 3

Calbentia, fortress in southern Europe, B. IV. iv. 3

Calis, fortress in southern Europe, B. IV. iv. 3

Callatis, fortress in Moesia, B. IV. xi. 20

Calligonus, a eunuch; accompanies Photius, S.H. iii. 2, 5; surrendered to Antonina, S.H. iii. 15; his great influence, S.H. v. 27

Callinicum, city in Mesopotamia; rebuilt by Justinian, II. xi. 28, B. II. vii. 1, 17, ix. 2; on the Euphrates, I. xviii. 13; Roman army conveyed thither by boats after the battle on the Euphrates, I. xviii. 50; taken by Chosroes, II. xxi. 30 ff., S.H. iii. 31

Callinicus, Governor of "Second Cilicia"; slain by Theodora, S.H. xvii. 2, 3

Callinicus, title given to Justinian by victorious troops, II. viii. 29, xxx. 3, IV. xxviii. 36

Callipolis, city in Chersonese; fortified by Justinian, B. IV. x. 22; supplied with store-houses, B. IV. x. 23

Calonymus, of Alexandria, admiral of the Roman fleet, III. xi. 14; ordered by Belisarius not to take the fleet into Carthage, III. xvii. 16; enters the harbour Mandracium with a few ships, and plunders the houses along the sea, III. xx. 16; bound by oath to return his plunder, III. xx. 23; disregards his oath, but later dies of apoplexy in Byzantium, III. xx. 24, 25

Calydonian Boar, its tusks preserved in Beneventum, V. xv. 8

Calypso, the island of, VIII. xxii. 19, 21

Camillus, early Roman General, VIII. xxix. 4

Caminus, fortress in Macedonia, B. IV. iv. 3

Campani, a people of southern Italy, V. xv. 22

Campania, district in Italy, VII. xxii. 20, xxiii. 18, VIII. xxxiv. 22–24; sought by Roman fugitives, V. xvii. 20; by refugees from Rome, V. xxv. 4, 10; by Procopius, VI. iv. 1 ff.; by Antonina, VI. iv. 14; Roman forces unite in, VI. v. 2; Procopius gathers soldiers and provisions in, VI. iv. 19; entered by Totila, VII. vi. 1; held by the Goths, VII. x. 4; Senators rescued from, VII. xxvi. 2–13; Senators summoned thence by Totila, VII. xxxvii. 3; prisoners sent thither by him, VIII. xxii. 2, xxxiv. 5, 6; its cities: Naples, V. viii. 5; and Cumae, V. xiv. 2, VIII. xxxiv. 19; its mountain, Vesuvius, VIII. xxxv. 1

Campses, fortress on the Danube, B. IV. vi. 5

Candaras, fortress near Germenne, B. IV. iv. 3

Candida, fortress in Macedonia, B. IV. iv. 3

Candidati, an imperial corps serving as bodyguards; Asbadus one of them, VII. xxxviii. 5

Candidiana, fortress in Moesia; restored by Justinian, B. IV. vii. 9

Candidus, priest of Sergiopolis, makes agreement with Chosroes, II. v. 31; punished by Chosroes for failing to keep his agreement, II. xx. 2 ff., 15, 16

Candilar, fortress in southern Europe, B. IV. iv. 3

Cannae, town in Apulia; scene of the great battle, VII. xviii. 19; distance from Canusium, *ib.*

Cantabaza, fortress on the Danube, B. IV. vi. 5

INDEX

Canusium, town in Apulia; taken by John, VII. xviii. 18; distance from Beneventum, *ib.*; from Cannae, VII. xviii. 19

Caoses, oldest son of Cabades, I. xi. 3; hated by his father, II. ix. 12; claims the throne of Persia upon the death of Cabades, I. xxi. 20; prevented by Mebodes from becoming king, I. xxi. 22

Capaza, fortress in Epirus, B. IV. iv. 3

Capisturia, fortress in Thrace, B. IV. xi. 20

Capitol, hill in Rome, S.H. viii. 20

Capitolinus, *see* Jupiter

Capomalba, fortress in Dardania, B. IV. iv. 3

Cappadocia, section of Asia embracing a portion of the Taurus, I. x. 1; desired by Chosroes, II. xxviii. 23; visited by Orestes, I. xvii. 16; buildings by Justinian in, B. V. iv. 7–18; Theodoriscus and George natives of, V. xxix. 20; Basiliscus exiled thither, III. vii. 24

Caprae, place in Italy; scene of Totila's death, [illegible]

Capua, town in Campania; garrisoned by Totila, VII. xviii. 24, 29; Roman Senators rescued from, VII. xxvi. 4 ff.; distance from Minturnae, VII. xxvi. 4; terminus of the Appian Way, V. xiv. 6

Caput Bovis, fortress on the Danube, B. IV. vi. 6

Caputvada, city in Byzacium, B. VI. vi. 8; distance from Carthage, III. xiv. 17; Roman army lands there, *ib.*; improved by Justinian, B. VI. vi. 13–16

Caranalis, town in Sardinia; captured by Tzazon, III. xxiv. 1, xxv. 10; IV. xiii. 44; VIII. xxiv. 34

Carasthyra, fortress in Thrace, B. IV. xi. 20

Carberus, fortress in Haemimontum, B. IV. xi. 20

Carcasiana, city in Gaul; battle fought near it, V. xii. 35 ff.; besieged by the Franks, V. xii. 41; siege raised at the approach of Theoderic, V. xii. 44; its treasures conveyed to Ravenna, V. xii. 47; later returned to Amalaric, V. xiii. 6

Carmina, fortress in Epirus, B. IV. iv. 3

Carnii, a people of Central Europe, V. xv. 27

Carrhae, city of Mesopotamia, citizens of, offer money to Chosroes, II. xiii. 7; able to see smoke of the burning "agger" at Edessa, II. xxvii. 15; strengthened by Justinian, B. II. vii. 1, 17

Carso, fortress in Moesia, B. IV. xi. 20

Carthage, first city of Africa, B. VI. v. 2; founded by Dido, IV. x. 25; grows to be metropolis of Libya, IV. x. 26, 27; walls preserved by Gizeric, III. v. 8; the only walled city in Libya, III. xv. 9; defences neglected by the Vandals, III. xxi. 11, 12, B. VI. v. 4, 5; ostensible destination of Belisarius' expedition, V. v. 6; entered by Belisarius, III. xx. 17, 21; defences restored by him, III. xxiii. 19, 20; besieged by Gelimer, IV. i. 3; by Stotzas, IV. xv. 8; its surrender prevented by Belisarius, IV. xv. 9, 10; the harbours, Stagnum, III. xv. 15, xx. 15; and Mandracium, III. xx. 3, 14; IV. xxvi. 10; the shipyard Misouas, IV. xiv. 40; its suburbs, Aclas, IV. vii. 13; and Decimum, III. xvii. 11; its aqueduct, IV. i. 2; its hippodrome, IV. xiv. 31, xviii. 11; its Palace, III. xx. 21, S.H. i. 33, B. VI. v. 9; its priest Reparatus, IV. xxvi. 24, 31; monastery built and fortified there by Solomon, IV. xxvi. 17; an ancient saying among its children, III. xxi. 14–16; its Church of St. Cyprian and annual festival, III. xxi. 17, 18: distance from Aurasius, III. viii. 5, IV. xiii. 22; from the plain of Boulla, III. xxv. 1; from Byzantium, III. x. 14; from Caesarea, IV. v. 5; from Caputvada, III. xiv. 17; from Decimum, III. xvii. 17; from Grasse, III. xvii. 8; from Hippo Regius, IV. iv. 26; from Iouce, III. xv. 8; from Membresa, IV. xv. 12; from Mercurium, III. vi. 10; from Siccaveneria, IV. xxiv. 6; from Stagnum, III. xv. 15, xx. 15; from Tebesta, IV. xxi. 19; from Tricamarum, IV. ii. 4; later called

Justinianê; restored by Justinian, B. VI. v. 8–12; mentioned, VIII. xxiv. 36, S.H. i. 18, v. 34
Caseëra, fortress in Rhodopê; built by Justinian, B. IV. xi. 20
Casibonon, fortress in Haemimontum, B. IV. xi. 20
Casius, epithet of Zeus, VIII. xxii. 25
Casope, town in Cercyra, VIII. xxii. 26
Caspian Gates, a strategically important pass through the Caucasus Mountains, I. x. 1 ff., VIII. iii. 4; fortified by Alexander, I. x. 9; offered to Anastasius by Ambazouces, I. x. 10; seized by Cabades, I. x. 12, xvi. 4, 7, xxii. 5; guarded by the Persians, II. x. 21
Cassandria, ancient Potidaea; captured by Huns, II. iv. 5, B. IV. iii. 21
Cassia, fortress in southern Europe, B. IV. iv. 3
Cassopas, fortress in Macedonia, B. IV. iv. 3
Cassopes, fortress in Macedonia, B. IV. iv. 3
Castella, Latin word for "towers," B. II. v. 9
Castellium, fortress in Dardania, B. IV. iv. 3
Castellium, fortress in southern Europe, B. IV. iv. 3
Castellium, fortress in southern Europe, B. IV. iv. 3
Castellobretara, fortress in Dardania, B. IV. iv. 3
Castellonovo, fortress in Moesia, B. IV. xi. 20
Castellonovo, fortress in the district of Aquenisium, B. IV. iv. 3
Castellum, city in Moesia, B. IV. xi. 20
Castellus, fortress in Epirus, B. IV. iv. 3
Castelona, fortress in Dardania, B. IV. iv. 3
Castimum, fortress in Dardania, B. IV. iv. 3
Castina, fortress in Epirus, B. IV. iv. 3
Castoria, lake in Northern Greece, B. IV. iii. 1
Castra Martis, town near the Danube, fortified by Justinian, B. IV. vi. 33
Castrazarba, fortress in Thrace, B. IV. xi. 20.
Casula, garment befitting one of humble station (Latin), IV. xxv. 26
Casyella, fortress in Dardania, B. IV. iv. 3
Catana, town in Sicily; taken by Belisarius, V. v. 12; without walls, VII. xl. 21
Catassu, fortress in Moesia, B. IV. xi. 20
Catellus, an Italian notable; slain by the Goths, VII. x. 22
Catholicus, title of the bishop of Doubios, II. xxv. 4
Catrasema, fortress in Dardania, B. IV. iv. 3
Catrelates, fortress in Dardania, B. IV. iv. 3
Cattapheterus, fortress in Dardania, B. IV. iv. 3
Cattarecus, fortress in Dardania, B. IV. iv. 3
Cattarus, fortress in Dardania, B. IV. iv. 3
Caucana, place in Sicily, III. xiv. 4, 11, 14; distance from Syracuse, III. xiv. 4
Caucasus Mountains, a range extending eastward from the Euxine, I. xv. 26; VIII. ii. 26, iii. 11, 12, iv. 1; inhabited by Huns, II. xv. 3, 29, xxviii. 22; by Alani, etc., II. xxix. 15; barbarians in, held in check by Lazica, II. xxviii. 22; contain the source of the Phasis, VIII. ii. 27; described, VIII. iii. 1–4; no tradition of Amazons there, VIII. iii. 6, 7; extend to the Euxine, VIII. ix. 15; Opsites takes refuge in, VIII. ix. 29; home of the Sabiri, VIII. xi. 23, 26
Cavallarius, envoy of Eraric to Justinian, VII. ii. 16
Cebrus, fortress on the Danube, B. IV. vi. 28
Cecola, fortress in Dardania, B. IV. iv. 3
Ceimenus, fortress in Epirus, B. IV. iv. 3
Celer, Roman general, I. viii. 2; invades Arzanene, I. viii. 21, II. xv. 7; with Patricius and Hypatius besieges Amida, I. ix. 1; negotiates a treaty with Aspebedes, I. ix. 24

INDEX

Celesene, district in Armenia, I. xvii. 11, 21, VIII. v. 24; contains a sanctuary of Artemis, I. xvii. 11

Celliriana, fortress in Dardania, B. IV. iv. 3

Celtica, Celtic mountains at the head-waters of the Po, V. i. 18; contain the sources of the Danube, VIII. v. 30

Celts, " earlier " name of the Gauls, B. IV. v. 9

Cena, place in Tzanica, B. III. vi. 22

Centauropolis, fort in Thessaly, B. IV. iii. 13; restored by Justinian, B. IV. iii. 14

Centaurs, home of, in Thessaly, B. IV. iii. 11, 12

Centenarium, a sum of money, so called because it " weighs one hundred pounds," I. xxii. 3, 4, II. iii. 7, etc.

Centumcellae, town in Etruria, VII. xiii. 12, xxxvi. 11, 15; abandoned by the Goths, VI. vii. 18; occupied by the Romans, VI. vii. 23; besieged by Totila, VII. xxxvii. 8–18; its surrender demanded by him, VII. xxxix. 25; attacked by Narses' order VIII. xxxiv. 20; distance from Rome, VI. vii. 19

Centuriae, place in Numidia, IV. xiii. 2

Cephallenia, Demetrius a Cephallenian, VII. vi. 20; touched at by Artabanes, VII. xl. 14

Cepi, town on the Euxine, VIII. v. 28

Ceras, the " Golden Horn " at Byzantium, B. I. v. 1

Cerataeum, a quarter of Antioch; II. x. 7

Cercineou, fortress in Thessaly, B. IV. iv. 3

Cercyra, island in the Adriatic Sea; ravaged by the Goths, VIII. xxii. 30; legend as to its inhabitants, VII. xxvii. 19; once called the Land of the Phaeacians, VIII. xxii. 18, 19

Ceremonial, Court, innovations in, made by Justinian and Theodora, S.H. xxx. 21–26, 30, 31; yet Justinian easily approached, S.H. xiii. 1, xv. 11, 12; obeisance required of courtiers by Justinian, S.H. xv. 15, 16, 27, 35, xxx. 22, 23

Ceriparon, fortress in Haemimontum, B. IV. xi. 20

Ceroessa, reputed mother of Byzas, B. I. v. 1

Cervarium, town in Apulia, VII. xviii. 29

Cesiana, fortress in Dardania, B. IV. iv. 3

Cesuna, fortress in Dardania, B. IV. iv. 3

Cethegus, a Patrician of Rome, VII. xiii. 12; *cf.* VII. xxxv. 10

Cethreon, fortress in Epirus, B. IV. iv. 3

Chaereüs, town near Alexandria, B. VI. i. 2 ff.

Chaeronea, city in Greece; destroyed by earthquake, VIII. xxv. 17

Chalaro, fortress in Aquenisium, B. IV. iv. 3

Chalazar, a Massagete; guardsman, in command of Illyrians, VII. xxx. 6; mutilated and killed by Totila, VII. xxx. 20, 21

Chalcedon, city opposite Byzantium, III. i. 8, 9; distance from the [illegible], III. i. 11; at the " beginning " of the Euxine, VIII. ii. 1, v. 31, 33

Chalcis, city of Euboea, B. IV. iii. 18; visited by Aristotle, VIII. vi. 20

Chalcis, city of Syria; saved from Chosroes by money payment, II. xii. 1, 2; fortified by Justinian, B. II. xi. 1, 8, 9; distance from Beroea, II. xii. 1; from Gabboulon, I. xviii. 8

Chalkê, *see* Bronze Gate

Chanaranges, a Persian title, *lit.* " Commander of Frontier Troops," I. v. 4, vi. 12, xxiii. 7 ff.

Chanaranges, Persian general, shares command of invading army, I. xxi. 4; besieges Martyropolis, I. xxi. 14, 15; retires, I. xxi. 27

Chanaranges, a Persarmenian, VII. xxxii. 11; his unstable character, VII. xxxii. 12; involved in a plot against Justinian, VII. xxxii. 11–51; entrapped by Justinus, VII. xxxii. 29–40; consults Artabanes, VII. xxxii. 31

Charadrus, fortress in Macedonia, B. IV. iv. 3

INDEX

Charton, fortress in Tzanica; restored by Justinian, B. III. vi. 18, 19

Charybdis, the story of, located at the Strait of Messina, V. viii. 1, VIII. vi. 23, xxii. 19

Cherduscera, fortress near Pauta, B. IV. iv. 3

Cheroenum, fortress in Haemimontum, B. IV. xi. 20

Cherson, city on the Euxine, I. xii. 7, VIII. v. 27, 28; restored by Justinian, B. III. vii. 10; distance from the mouth of the Ister, VIII. v. 29

Chersonese (Thracian), *mod.* Gallipoli Peninsula, S.H. xviii. 20; its size and extent, V. xv. 18, B. IV. x. 8; assailed by the Huns, II. iv. 8; its former worthless defences, B. IV. x. 5–9; invaded by barbarians, B. IV. x. 9; strongly protected by Justinian, B. IV. x. 10–23 meaning of the name, B. IV. x. 4

Chesdupara, fortress in southern Europe, B. IV. iv. 3

Chilbudius, Roman general, VII. xiii. 26; his services to the empire, VII. xiv. 1–6; impersonated by a barbarian of the same name, VII. xiv. 7 ff.

Chilbudius, one of the Antae; captured in battle, VII. xiv. 8; serves his master well, VII. xiv. 9, 10; ransomed and taken home to the Antae, VII. xiv. 16 ff.; forced to pretend to be the Roman general, VII. xiv. 31; unmasked by Narses, VII. xiv. 35, 36

Chiliarch, title given to commander of a detachment of Vandals, III. v. 18, IV. iii. 8

Chimaerae, fortress in Epirus, B. IV. iv. 3

Chinialon, leader of the Cutrigurs, VIII. xviii. 15; receives a message from Justinian, VIII. xix. 3

Chiton, garment of the Armenian satraps, B. III. i. 22; as worn by the Factionists, S.H. vii. 12

Chorianes, Persian commander, VIII. i. 4; makes camp on the river Hippis, VIII. viii. 1; advances to meet the Romans and Lazi, VIII viii. 17; receives fugitives, VIII viii. 28; killed in battle, VIII. viii. 34, 35

Chorsamantis, a Massagete, bodyguard of Belisarius; alone pursues the Goths to their camp, VI. i. 21–25; wounded in a second encounter, VI. i. 26, 27; goes out alone against the Goths and is killed, VI. i. 28–33

Chorsomanus, a Massagete; bodyguard of Belisarius, V. xvi. 1

Chorzanê, land between the two Armenias, B. III. iii. 9

Chorzianenê, region of Armenia, II. xxiv. 14

Chosroes, King of Persia; third son of Cabades, I. xi. 5; offered to Justinus for adoption, I. xi. 6 ff.; awaits outcome of negotiations, I. xi. 27; retires in anger to Persia, I. xi. 30; declared successor by Cabades, I. xxi. 17 ff.; chosen King, I. xxi. 22; meets Roman ambassadors, I. xxii. 1 ff.; failure of their negotiations, I. xxii. 12 ff.; grants prayer of Rufinus, I. xxii. 15; concludes the "endless peace," I. xxii. 16, 17; unpopular among the Persians, I. xxiii. 1–3; plot to dethrone him, I. xxiii. 5 ff.; slays Zames and other male relatives, I. xxiii. 6; orders slaughter of Zames' son, I. xxiii. 7; hears he has been spared, I. xxiii. 13; his punishment of Adergoudounbades, I. xxiii. 14 ff.; destroys Mebodes, I. xxiii. 25 ff.; vexed at Roman success in Libya, I. xxvi. 2; demands share of spoils, I. xxvi. 3; desires to break Roman treaty, II. i. 1; charges Justinian with violation of the treaty, II. i. 12–14, x. 13, 16; hears with favour ambassadors of Vittigis, II. ii. 12, VI. xxii. 17; receives Armenian embassy, II. iii. 32 ff.; decides to open hostilities, II. iii. 55; makes four invasions, VIII. vii. 2, S.H. xviii. 23, xxiii. 7; admonished by Justinian, II. iv. 17 ff.; detains Anastasius, II. iv. 26; dismisses him, II. v. 27; first invasion of Roman territory, II. v. 1; marches toward Syria,

INDEX

II. v. 4; refrains from attacking Zenobia, II. v. 7; besieges Sura, II. v. 8 ff.; captures it by strategem, II. v. 22 ff., B. II. ix. 1; marries Euphemia, II. v. 28; releases captives for ransom, II. v. 29; hears plea of Megas, II. vi. 18 ff.; exacts money from the Hierapolitans, II. vi. 22–24; offers to depart for ten centenaria, II. vi. 25; demands money from Beroeans, II. vii. 5; enters and fires Beroea, II. vii. 10, 11; besieges the acropolis, II. vii. 11 ff.; reproached by Megas, II. vii. 19; his reply, II. vii. 20 ff.; allows capitulation, II. vii. 35; moves against Antioch, II. viii. 1; demands money from it, II. viii. 4; hears ambassadors, II. viii. 5; insulted by the citizens, II. viii. 6; storms the city wall, II. viii. 8 ff.; captures the city, II. viii. 20, B. II. x. 10; reproached by Zaberganes, II. viii. 30 ff.; addresses ambassadors, II. ix. 1 ff.; hesitates to enter the city, II. viii. 22–24, ix. 7; orders plunder of Antioch, II. ix. 14; burns the city, II. ix. 17, 18; addressed by ambassadors, II. x. 10 ff.; demands money from them, II. x. 19 ff.; accept terms of peace, II. x. 24; visits Seleucia, II. xi. 1; and Daphne, II. xi. 5 ff.; burns sanctuary of Michael, II. xi. 12, 13; proceeds to Apamea, II. xi. 14; enters city and seizes treasures, II. xi. 24 ff.; a spectator in the hippodrome, II. xi. 31 ff.; impales an adulterer, II. xi. 37, 38; exacts money from Chalcis, II. xii. 1, 2; crosses the Euphrates, II. xii. 3 ff.; eager to capture Edessa, II. xii. 6 ff., 29, 31; exacts money, II. xii. 33, 34; receives letter from Justinian, II. xiii. 1, 2; negotiates with Carrhae, II. xiii. 7; accepts money from Constantina, II. xiii. 8; claims Constantina by inheritance, *ib.*, II. xiii. 15; besieges Daras, II. xi. 28, xiii. 16, B. II. ii. 20, 21; abandons siege upon receipt of money, II. xiii. 28; charged by Justinian with breaking the treaty, II. xiii. 29; settles captives of Antioch, II. xiv. 1 ff.; called in by the Lazi, II. xv. 1, 12 ff.; prepares to invade Lazica, II. xv. 31–35; Belisarius sent against him, II. xiv. 8, S.H. ii. 1, iii. 30, iv. 38; invades Lazica, II. xvii. 1 ff.; commands attack on Petra, II. xvii. 4; impales Aniabedes, II. xvii. 11; besieges and captures Petra, II. xvii. 13–27, VIII. xii. 21, B. III. vii. 7; retires from Lazica, II. xix. 48; third invasion of Roman territory, II. xx. 1 ff.; besieges Sergiopolis in vain, II. xx. 11 ff., B. II. ix. 9; punishes Candidus, II. xx. 2 ff., 15, 16; takes much treasure from Sergiopolis, II. xx. 7; sends envoy to Belisarius, II. xxi. 1, 23; retires before Belisarius, II. xxi. 15 ff.; crosses the Euphrates, II. xxi. 21; takes Callinicum, II. xi. 28, xxi. 30–32, S.H. iii. 31; receives the hostage John, II. xxi. 27, S.H. iii. 7; awaits Roman envoys, II. xxiv. 1 ff.; his army visited by pestilence, II. xxiv. 8, 12; retires into Assyria, II. xxiv. 12; fourth invasion, II. xxvi. 1 ff.; makes attempt upon Edessa, II. xxvi. 5 ff., VIII. xiv. 35; comes to terms, II. xxvii. 46; sanctions five-year truce, II. xxviii. 7 ff.; lays plans against Daras and Lazica, II. xxviii. 15 ff.; attempts ruse against Daras, II. xxviii. 31 ff.; plans Euxine fleet, II. xxix. 1; foiled by the Romans, B. III. vii. 8; sends Phabrizus into Lazica, II. xxix. 2 ff.; and relief army to Petra, II. xxix. 13; violates Roman treaty, VI. xxii. 20, 21; receives overtures from Arsaces, VII. xxxii. 2; invited into Lazica, VIII. iv. 5, xvi. 5, 27, 29; which he is eager to acquire, VIII. vii. 1, 13, xii. 17; reviled by the Persians, VIII. vii. 3; oppresses the Lazi, VIII. viii. 10; summons Sceparnas, VIII. ix. 14; father of Anasozadus, VIII. x. 8; whom he banishes, VIII. x. 8–10; falls violently ill, VIII. x. 10; sickly by nature, *ib.*; gathered many physicians, VIII. x. 11; devoted to Tribunus, VIII. x. 11–14; grants him a favour, VIII. x. 14–16; defeats and punishes Anasozadus, VIII. x. 19–22; receives Petrus, VIII. xi. 2, 3; executes Bradueius, VIII. xi. 8; captures and garrisons Petra, VIII. xii. 21; builds aqueduct of three channels, VIII. xii. 22; prepares to break the "endless peace," VIII. xiv. 39; his envoy Isdigousnas, VIII. xv. 1, 11; wishes to ransom Bersabus, VIII. xv. 8, 10; exacts heavy payments from the Romans, VIII. xv. 17, S.H. xi. 12; retires from Lazica, S.H. ii. 25, 26; plots death of Gubazes, VIII. xvi. 2; reported to be in Lazica, VIII. xvi. 8, 11; hated by Gubazes, VIII. xvi. 32; receives report of Isdigousnas, VIII. xvii. 9; attacks Armenians, S.H. ii. 29; criticized by his commanders, S.H. ii. 31; whom he silences, S.H. ii. 32–36; indirectly approached by Theodora, S.H. ii. 34; whom he scorns, S.H. ii. 36; increases pay of spies, S.H. xxx. 13; his character, II. ix. 8–12, S.H. xviii. 28; disregards treaties, B. II. x. 1; uncle of Cabades, VIII. xxvi. 13; acquainted with Artabanes, IV. xxvii. 17

Christ, S.H. xiii. 4, 7; name of, S.H. xxvii. 28; prophecy of, B. V. vii. 6; his suffering, II. xi. 14; his temple in Byzantium, III. vi. 26; his Apostle Peter, V. xix. 4; his grandmother Anna, B. I. iii. 11, 12; his Apostles, B. I. iv. 1; sanctuaries dedicated to, B. I. ii. 18. *See also* Jesus

Christianity, errors of, corrected by Justinian, B. I. i. 9

Christians, the "true followers" of Christ, B. V. vii. 3; converted temples into churches, I. xvii. 18; boast impregnability of Edessa, II. xii. 7; persecuted, S.H. xxvii. 8, 27; among the Homeritae, abused by Jews, I. xx. 1; persecuted by Honoric, III. viii. 3, 4, xxi. 19; by Gundamundus, III. viii. 7; courted by Trasamundus, III. viii. 9, 10; not molested by Ilderic, III. ix. 1; Justinian reproached for not protecting them, III. x. 19; deprived of a church, III. xxi. 19; consoled by a dream, III. xxi. 21; recover Church of St. Cyprian, III. xxi. 25; in Jerusalem, receive Temple treasures, IV. ix. 9; landowners, S.H. xi. 30; backsliders among, S.H. xi. 32, 33; reverence churches and ritual, III. viii. 17, 18, 20, 24, S.H. iii. 24; celebrate finding of Apostles' bodies, B. I. iv. 22; honour feast of Easter, I. xviii. 15, IV. xiv. 7; those not of orthodox faith excluded by, IV. xiv. 14; Christian precepts violated by Basiliscus, III. vii. 22; doctrines of, favoured by the Romans, V. xxv. 23; distraught by Justinian and Theodora, S.H. x. 15, xxvii. 32; the Christian name, S.H. xxvii. 7, 26; harass Justinian, S.H. xxvii. 10; Church of, in Edessa; restored by Justinian, B. II. vii. 6; established on Mt. Garizin, B. V. vii. 7; shrines of, on Mt. Garizin, B. V. vii. 17; converts in Libya, B. VI. ii. 19; Hebrew converts, B. VI. ii. 23; Moorish converts, B. VI. iii. 10; dogmas of, VII. xxxv. 11; S.H. xxvii. 12; heresies of, S.H. xi. 14, 15, 25, xix. 11; *see* heresy; disagree on doctrine, V. iii. 5, 6; VIII. xxv. 13; scriptures of, IV. xxi. 21, xxvi. 28, VII. xxxii. 9; their Feast of Easter, S.H. xxviii. 17; sacraments of, S.H. vi. 27; their rite of adoption, S.H. i. 16; of baptism, III. xii. 2, IV. xxvi. 25, 28; oaths of, S.H. ii. 13, 16; priests of, S.H. iii. 26; the following are mentioned as Christians: Abasgi, VIII. iii. 19, 21; Apsilii, VIII. ii. 33; Arborychi and Germans, V. xii. 15; Eruli, VI. xiv. 33, 34; Franks, VI. xxv. 10; Gadabitani, B. VI. iv. 12; Lazi and Iberians, I. xii. 3, II. xxviii. 26; Lombards, VI. xiv. 9; Neapolitans, V. ix. 27;

Romans, VIII. xii. 8; Samaritans, B. V. vii. 16; Tetraxitae, VIII. iv. 9; Tzani, B. III. vi. 7, vii. 6; neighbours of Lazica, VIII. ii. 17
Chrysanthus, fortress in Haemimontum, B. IV. xi. 20
Chryses, master-builder; his services at Daras, B. II. iii. 2 ff.
Chrysomallo, a dancing-girl, S.H. xvii. 33, 34
Chrysomallo, a second dancing-girl, S.H. xvii. 34
Ciberis, city in the Chersonese; fortified by Justinian, B. IV. x. 20; adorned with buildings, B. IV. x. 21
Cidamê, Moorish city in Africa, B. VI. iii. 9
Cilana, city in Numidia; strengthened by Justinian, B. VI. vii. 10
Cilicae, fortress in Epirus, B. IV. iv. 3
Cilicia, district in Asia Minor, divided into two provinces, S.H. xvii. 2; B. V. v. 1; objective of Chosroes' invasion, II. v. 4, vi. 21; Cilicians as sailors in the African expedition, III. xi. 14; disorders in, S.H. xxix. 29; misgoverned by Malthanes, *ib.*; Cilicians attack Callinicus, S.H. xvii. 2; Theodosius sent thither, S.H. iii. 5; refuge of Ephraemius, II. vii. 17; and of Germanus, II. vii. 18; home of Paulus, VII. xxxvi. 16; of Malthanes, S.H. xxix. 28; its cities Mopsuestia, B. V. v. 4; and Anazarbus, S.H. xviii. 41; buildings of Justinian in, B. V. vi. 1; Cilician screens, to protect attacking soldiers, II. xxvi. 29
Cimmerians, the ancient name of the tribes on the Maeotic Lake, VIII. iv. 8; and of the Huns, VIII. v. 1; discover the possibility of crossing the Maeotic Lake, VIII. v. 7–9; cross it and attack the Goths, VIII. v. 10, 11; Cimmerian Strait, considered by some the boundary between Europe and Asia, VIII. vi. 15; B. VI. i. 7
Cionin, fortress in Epirus, B. IV. iv. 3
Ciphas, fortress in Mesopotamia, B. II. iv. 14
Cipipene, fortress in Aquenisium, B. IV. iv. 3
Circaeum, mountain near Taracina, V. xi. 2; considered to be named from the Homeric Circe, *ib.*; its resemblance to an island, V. xi. 3, 4
Circe, her meeting with Odysseus, V. xi. 2
Circesium, fortress on the Euphrates, II. v. 2, B. II. vi. 2; its excellent defenses, II. v. 3
Cisseron, mountain in Palestine, B. V. ix. 20
Cistidizus, fortress in Moesia, B. IV. xi. 20
Citharizon, fortress in Armenia; four days from Theodosipolis, II. xxiv. 13; B. III. iii. 9; seat of a Duke, B. III. ii. 1; fortified by Justinian, B. III. iii. 7
Cithinas, fortress in Epirus, B. IV. iv. 3
Classes, harbour of Ravenna, VI. xxix. 31
Claudian, Roman commander of Salones; sent with a force against Indulf, VII. xxxv. 27
Cleft, The, defile in Greece; filled by a violent earthquake, VIII. xxv. 23
Clemades, fortress in Aquenisium, B. IV. iv. 3
Clementiana, fortress in Epirus, B. IV. iv. 3
Clementinus, a Patrician of Rome; refuses to follow John, VII. xxvi. 13
Clesbestita, fortress in Cabetzus, B. IV. iv. 3
Clipea, city in Africa, IV. x. 24
Clipea, *see* Shield Mountain
Clisura, fortress in Haemimontum, B. IV. xi. 20
Clisura, Latin term (*clausura*) for a narrow road shut in by mountains, II. xxix. 25, B. III. iii. 2, vii. 5, B. IV. ii. 17
Cloadarius, ruler of the Franks; sanctions treaty with Theodatus, V. xiii. 27
Clusium, city in Tuscany; garrisoned by Vittigis, VI. xi. 1; surrenders to Belisarius, VI. xiii. 2, 3; garrisoned by him, VI. xiii. 4
Cobenciles, fortress in Dardania, B. IV. iv. 3

INDEX

Coccas, a Roman deserter, VIII. xxxi. 12; slain in single combat, VIII. xxxi. 14–16
Coetaeon, reputed earlier name of Cotais (*q.v.*), VIII. xiv. 49
Coinage, Persian, VII. xxxiii. 6; Frankish, VII. xxxiii. 5, 6; barbarian, *ib.*; Roman coinage debased by Justinian, S.H. xxii. 38; xxv. 12; clipping of coins, VII. i. 31; follis, S.H. xxv. 12; stater, S.H. xx. 18, xxiv. 28, xxv. 12, xxix. 25
Colchians, inhabitants of Lazica, or Colchis, VIII. i. 8; identified with the Lazi, VIII. i. 10; at the "end" of the Euxine, VIII. ii. 1; not neighbours of the Trapezuntines, VIII. ii. 15; ancient location of their dwellings, VIII. ii. 31; their king Gubazes, VIII. viii. 1; the Apsilii revolt from them, VIII. x. 6; the Colchian Phasis, VIII. vi. 13, 14, B. VI. i. 7
Colchis, ancient name of Lazica (*q.v.*), I. xi. 28, etc.; at the end of the Euxine, III. i. 11; invaded by the Persians, VIII. i. 3 ff., viii. 39, S.H. xviii. 24; abandoned by Chosroes, S.H. ii. 25, 26; held entirely by the Persians, VIII. xvi. 7
Colobona, fortress in Macedonia, B. IV. iv. 3
Coloneia, founded by Pompey in Armenia, B. III. iv. 6
Colonnade, Royal, at Byzantium, S.H. xiv. 13, B. I. xi. 12, 13
Colophonia, fortress in Epirus, B. IV. iv. 3
Comana, city in Armenia, VIII. v. 24
Comana, city in Pontus, distinguished from Comana "among the Taurians," I. xvii. 12
Comê, fortress in Old Epirus, B. IV. iv. 3
Comê, fortress in Epirus, B. IV. iv. 3
Comet, The, its appearance in the heavens, II. iv. 1, 2; various explanations of the meaning of the phenomenon, II. iv. 3
Comito, sister of Theodora, S.H. ix. 3; commences her career, S.H. ix. 9
Commagene, old name for Euphratesia, I. xvii. 2, 23, II. xx. 17; invaded by the Persians, I. xviii. 2, B. II. viii. 4
Comum, city near Milan; occupied by Mundilas, VI. xii. 40
Conon, commander of Isaurians, VI. v. 1; proceeds to Ostia by sea, VI. v. 3; captures Ancon, VI. xi. 5; nearly loses it by a blunder, VI. xiii. 8 ff.; commander of Naples; besieged by Totila, VII. vi. 2 ff.; sends Demetrius to the Roman fleet, VII. vi. 22; urges Maximinus to relieve Naples, VII. vii. 2; allowed his liberty by Totila, VII. vii. 16; treated kindly by him, VII. viii. 6–9; commander of Rome; appealed to by the citizens, VII. xvii. 2–8; hoards and sells grain, VII. xvii. 10; disregards warning of captives, VII. xx. 12; flees from Rome, VII. xxiii. 1; left in command of Rome by Belisarius, VII. xxvii. 16; killed by his soldiers, VII. xxx. 7
Constantiana, fortress in Moesia, B. IV. xi. 20
Constantianus, an Illyrian, II. xxiv. 4; envoy to Chosroes with Sergius, II. xxiv. 3; appointed general, II. xxviii. 2; sent as envoy to Chosroes with Sergius a second time, II. xxviii. 3 ff.
Constantianus, commander of Royal Grooms; sent to Illyricum, V. vii. 26; his successful campaign in Dalmatia, V. vii. 27–36; controls territory as far as Liburnia, V. xv. 15; prepares to defend Salones, V. xvi. 14, 15; sent to Ravenna, VI. xxx. 2; receives offer of surrender from Totila, VII. ii. 8; which he agrees to accept, VII. ii. 9; confers with other commanders, VII. iii. 2, 3; shares chief command with Alexander, VII. iii. 4; holds Ravenna, VII. vi. 8; appeals to Justinian, VII. ix. 5; receives confidence of Germanus, VII. xxxii. 41; testifies in his favour, VII. xxxii. 45; sent to help the Lombards, VII. xxxiv. 40; commander against the Sclaveni, VII. xl. 34; his standard captured, VII. xl. 42; later recovered, VII. xl. 45
Constantina, city in Mesopotamia, I.

xxii. 3; distance from Arzamon, I. viii. 10; Cabades desirous of capturing the city, II. xiii. 8; spared by Cabades owing to the entreaties of Baradotus, II. xiii. 13 ff.; claimed by Chosroes as an inherited possession, II. xiii. 8, 15; citizens of, their offer of money accepted by Chosroes, II. xiii. 8

Constantina, city in Africa; distance from Gazophyla, IV. xv. 52

Constantine the Great, Emperor; divided the Roman Empire, III. i. 3; enlarged Byzantium and gave it his name, *ib.*; said to have discovered the Palladium in Byzantium, V. xv. 14; his burial-place, B. I. iv. 19; Forum of, in Byzantium, I. xxiv. 9, 24, V. xv. 14, B. I. iv. 27, x. 3; his mother Helen, B. V. ii. 1; honours the city of her birth, B. V. ii. 2; built the fortress Daphnê, B. IV. vii. 7

Constantinople, later name for Byzantium (q.v.), B. I. i. ff., vi. 1, II. i. 1, V. i. 8; first city of Europe, B. IV. ix. 14; its buildings by Justinian, B. IV. viii. 3

Constantinus, of Thrace, Roman general, V. v. 3; sent into Tuscany, V. xvi. 1; takes Spolitium and Perusia and certain other strongholds, V. xvi. 3; defeats a Gothic army and captures the commanders, V. xvi. 6, 7; recalled to Rome, V. xvii. 1–3; leaves garrisons in Perusia and Spolitium, V. xvii. 3; assigned to guard the Flaminian Gate, V. xix. 16; assigned to the Aurelian Gate and the adjoining wall, V. xxii. 15, 16; leaves the gate during an attack, V. xxii. 18; returns, V. xxii. 25; leads the Huns in a signally successful skirmish, VI. i. 4–10; incurs hatred of Antonina, S.H. i. 24; his disagreement with Belisarius, VI. viii. 1 ff.; killed by his order, VI. viii. 17

Constantinus, chosen king by the soldiers in Britain, III. ii. 31; his invasion of Spain and Gaul, *ib.*; defeated and killed in battle, III. ii. 37

Constantinus, Quaestor, S.H. xx. 20; beloved by Justinian, S.H. xx. 21; unscrupulous, S.H. xx. 21–23

Constantius, Emperor, son of Constantine the Great; builder of the original Church of the Apostles, B. I. iv. 19

Constantius, husband of Placidia, partner in the royal power with Honorius; his brief reign and death, III. iii. 4; father of Valentinian, III. iii. 5

Consul, this office held by Romans during Gothic rule, VI. vi. 20; held by Appius, V. xiv. 6; by Belisarius, IV. ix. 15, V. v. 19; by Gothigus, VII. xxxv. 10; by Justinus, VII. xxxii. 15; by Theoderic, VI. vi. 16; office abolished, S.H. xxvi. 15; mentioned, VIII. xxi. 2, S.H. xvii. 7

Copustorus, fortress in Moesia, B. IV. xi. 20

Coracii, city of Northern Greece; fortified by Justinian, B. IV. ii. 16

Cordes, a suburb of Daras, B. II. ii. 2

Corinth, city in Greece, B. IV. ii. 1; near the head of the Crisaean Gulf, V. xv. 17; damaged by earthquakes, S.H. xviii. 42, B. IV. ii. 24

Coronea, city in Greece; destroyed by earthquake, VIII. xxv. 17

Corsica, called Cyrnus in ancient times, IV. v. 3, VIII. xxiv. 39; Cyril sent thither with an army, IV. v. 3; recovered by the Romans, IV. v. 4; attacked and captured by the Goths, VIII. xxiv. 31–33; mentioned, VIII. xxiv. 37

Cosmas, Saint of Syria, B. II. xi. 4; shrine of Cosmas and Damian at Byzantium, B. I. vi. 5–8; Cosmas and Damian bring relief to Justinian from an ailment, B. I. vi. 5; House of, in Pamphylia, B. V. ix. 37

Costume, of Persian dignitaries, I. xvii. 27, 28; of the Moorish rulers, III. xxv. 7; of the Armenian satraps, B. III. i. 18–23;

of the Huns, S.H. vii. 10–14; of the Vandals, IV. vi. 7; of the Sclaveni and the Antae, VII. xiv. 26; of the Factionists at Constantinople, S.H. vii. 10–14; in the theatres, S.H. ix. 20; silk garments, formerly called Medic, now Seric, I. xx. 9, IV. vi. 7; Roman dress worn by the Gauls, V. xii. 19; the "casula" worn by Areobindus, IV. xxvi. 26; armour of Totila, VIII. xxxi. 18; equestrian statue of Justinian in Constantinople, in costume called "Achilles," B. I. ii. 7–12; red boots of the Persian King, B. III. i. 23; and of the Roman Emperor, *ib.*

Cotais, later name for Cotiaion, VIII. xiv. 48; near Uthimereos, VIII. xiv. 51; fortified by Mermeroes, VIII. xvi. 16; Persians retire thither, VIII. xvii. 19

Cotiaion, fortress in Lazica, VIII. xiv. 48

Cottian Alps, between Gaul and Liguria, VI. xxviii. 28; strongholds in, partly taken over by Belisarius, VI. xxviii. 29 ff.; subjugated by Theudibert, VIII. xxiv. 6

Coucarizon, place in Armenia, B. III. iv. 12

Council of Chalcedon, S.H. xxvii. 5

Count of Armenia, appointed by Emperor, B. III. i. 14, 15

Court, *see* Ceremonial

Coutzes, Roman general, brother of Bouzes, sent to support Belisarius at Mindouos, I. xiii. 5; captured by the Persians, I. xiii. 8

Coutzinas, a Moorish ruler, joins in an attack upon a Roman force, IV. x. 6; agrees to turn against the other Moors, IV. xxv. 2, 15, VIII. xvii. 21; his further dealings with Areobindus, IV. xxv. 17, 18; ignorant of Antalas' knowledge of his plot, IV. xxv. 20, 21; separates from Antalas and sides with Gontharis, IV. xxvii. 24; marches with Artabanes against Antalas, IV. xxvii. 25, 27; in alliance with John, IV. xxviii. 50

Coxyline Tzani, *see* Tzani

Crataea, fortress in Macedonia, B. IV. iv. 3

Cratiscara, fort in Dardania; built by Justinian, B. IV. i. 32

Creas, fortress in Moesia, B. IV. xi. 20

Crisaean Gulf, the Gulf of Corinth, V. xv. 17, VIII. xxv. 16; location of, B. IV. ii. 1

Crispa, fortress on the Danube, B. IV. vi. 23

Cross, of Christ, II. xi. 14, 16, 20, 29; a Christian symbol, B. I. iv. 11, 13

Croton, city in southern Italy, V. xv. 23, VII. xxviii. 2, 3, xxx. 12, 14, 23; distance from Messana, VII. xxviii. 18; sends appeal for help, VIII. xxv. 24; relief sent thither by Justinian, VIII. xxvi. 1, 2

Cryniana, fortress in Macedonia, B. IV. iv. 3

Cteanus, surname of Theodorus, III. xi. 7

Ctesiphon, town on the Tigris River, II. xxviii. 4, 5, S.H. ii. 25; distance from Antioch of Chosroes, II. xiv. 1; from Belapaton, VIII. x. 9

Cuas, fortress in Remisianisia, B. IV. iv. 3

Cubinus, fortress in Dardania, B. IV. iv. 3

Cuino, fortress in Dardania, B. IV. iv. 3

Cuintu, fortress in Dardania, B. IV. iv. 3

Cululis, city in Byzacium; fortified by Justinian, B. VI. vi. 18

Cumae, coast city in Campania, V. xiv. 3; garrisoned by Belisarius, V. xiv. 2; one of the only two fortresses in Campania, V. xiv. 2; the abode of the Sibyl, V. xiv. 3; captured by Totila, VII. vi. 3; money deposited there by him, VIII. xxxiv. 19, 21; attacked by Narses' order, VIII. xxxiv. 20; besieged, VIII. xxxiv. 22; taken by the Romans, VIII. xxxv. 38; distance from Naples, V. xiv. 3

Cumarciana, fortress in Macedonia, B. IV. iv. 3

Cumudeba, fortress in Remisianisia, B. IV. iv. 3

Cunae, fortress in Cabetzus, B. IV. iv. 3

INDEX

Cupi, fortress on the Danube; strengthened by Justinian, B. IV. vi. 1, 2

Curicum, town in Mesopotamia, B. V. ix. 34

Currency, debased by Justinian, S.H. xxii. 38, xxv. 12

Curtuxura, fortress in Thrace, B. IV. xi. 20

Cuscabiri, fortress in Rhodopê; built by Justinian, B. IV. xi. 20

Cuscauri, fortress in Moesia, B. IV. xi. 20

Cusculi, fortress in Moesia, B. IV. xi. 20

Cusculis, fortress in Rhodopê; built by Justinian, B. IV. xi. 20

Cusines, fortress in Dardania, B. IV. iv. 3

Customs duties, imposed under Justinian, S.H. xxv. 1–6, 16

Cutilas, a Thracian, bodyguard of Belisarius, VI. ii. 10; his remarkable wound, VI. ii. 14, 15, 18; which causes his death, VI. ii. 30, 31

Cutrigur(s), progenitor of the Cutrigur Huns, [illegible], a Hunnic tribe, origin of the name, VIII. v. 2–4; settle in the country from which the Goths were expelled, VIII. v. 15, 22, 23; continue to ravage Roman territory, VIII. v. 16; become allies of the Gepaedes, VIII. xviii. 14, 15; accused by Justinian, VIII. xviii. 18–20; receive money annually from Byzantium, VIII. xviii. 19; attacked by the Utigurs, VIII. xviii. 21–24, xix. 8; their Roman prisoners escape, VIII. xix. 2; a remnant settled in Thrace, VIII. xix. 7; Cutrigur Huns engage with Ildigisal and Goar, VIII. xxvii. 10, 11; accused by the Utigurs, VIII. xix. 15 ff.

Cutzusura, fortress in Cabetzus, B. IV. iv. 3

Cyanean Rocks, "Dark Blue Rocks," at the upper end of the Bosporus, III. i. 8

Cydnus River, in Cilicia; swollen by snows, B. V. v. 17; floods Tarsus, S.H. xviii. 40, B. V. v. 14–18; controlled by Justinian, B. V. v. 19, 20

Cynoscephale, *see* Dog's Head

Cyntodemus, fortress in Moesia; restored by Justinian, B. IV. vii. 5

Cynton, fortress in Moesia; built by Justinian, B. IV. vii. 6

Cyprian, Saint, especially reverenced at Carthage, III. xxi. 17; his Church and Festival, III. xxi. 18, 23, 25; sends a dream to devout Christians, III. xxi. 21

Cyprian, commander of Roman auxiliaries, III. xi. 6; at the battle of Tricamarum, IV. iii. 4; sent to conduct Gelimer, IV. vii. 11; sent against Fisula, VI. xxiii. 2; with Justinus presses its siege, VI. xxiv. 18; receives its surrender, VI. xxvii. 26; marches with others to the relief of Florentia, VII. v. 4; holds Perusia, VII. vi. 8; its surrender demanded by Totila, VII. xii. 18; slain by Ulifus, VII. xii. 19, 20, xxiii. 6, xxv. 21, VIII. xxxiii. 10, 12

Cypriana, a periodic storm on the African coast, III. xx. 12

Cyprus, island, [illegible]

Cyrene, city in Africa; western limit of Pentapolis, B. VI. i. 11; marking the division between the Eastern and Western Empire, III. i. 16

Cyrenus, monastery of, in Mesopotamia, B. V. ix. 32

Cyridana, fortress in Haemimontum, B. IV. xi. 20

Cyril, Roman commander at the battle of Daras, I. xiii. 21; sent as commander of an army to Sardinia, III. xi. 1, 6; avoids Sardinia and sails to Carthage, III. xxiv. 19; sent to Sardinia and Corsica with an army, IV. v. 2, 3; wins them back for the empire, IV. v. 4; commander of auxiliaries in Numidia, IV. xv. 50; his death, IV. xv. 59

Cyrillus, father of a bride, S.H. xvii. 32

Cyrnus, ancient name of Corsica (*q.v.*), IV. v. 3, VIII. xxiv. 39

Cyrrou, fortress in Macedonia, B. IV. iv. 3

Cyrus, King of Persia, II. ii. 15; releases Jews, B. II. xi. 2; an ideal king, B. I. i. 12, 15

Cyrus, son of Bacchus and brother of

INDEX

Sergius; becomes ruler of Pentapolis in Libya, IV. xxi. 1, 16; brother of Solomon the younger, IV. xxi. 19; marches with Solomon against the Moors, *ib.*
Cyrus, fortress of Syria, B. II. xi. 2–7
Cyzicus, city on the Propontis; Factionists of, S.H. xvii. 41; John the Cappadocian exiled thither, I. xxv. 31

Dabanas, fortress in Mesopotamia, B. II. iv. 14
Dabanus, fortress in Dardania, B. IV. iv. 3
Dabusis, fortress in Numidia; walled by Justinian, B. VI. vii. 8
Dacia, province on the Danube, VIII. v. 30, B. IV. v. 10; limit of the Gothic rule, S.H. xviii. 16; taken by the Gepaedes, VII. xxxiii. 8, xxxiv. 17, 35; parts taken by the Eruli, VII. xxxiii. 13; formerly under Gothic power, VII. xxxiv. 10; Goths driven from, VII. xxxiv. 15; its fortress Pontes, B. IV. vi. 15; Dacians, V. xv. 27
Daciviza, station on the Post Route, S.H. xxx. 8
Dagaris, a Roman spy, captured by the Huns, I. xv. 6; returned to the Romans, I. xxii. 18; his later services to the Romans, I. xxii. 19
Dagisthaeus, Roman commander; leads an army to succour the Lazi, II. xxix. 10, VIII. viii. 1; with Gubazes besieges Petra, II. xxix. 11 ff.; sends an insufficient force to guard the pass into Lazica, II. xxix. 33–34; his incompetent conduct of the siege of Petra, II. xxix. 34 ff.; deceived by Mirranes, II. xxx. 7; abandons Petra, II. xxx. 11; with Phoubelis attacks Mermeroes, II. xxx. 22; with Gubazes attacks and almost annihilates the Persians, II. xxx. 39 ff.; undermines the wall of Petra, VIII. xi. 11, 14, 15; leads the Roman army to battle, VIII. viii. 16; fights against the Persians, VIII. viii. 29; slandered by the Lazi, VIII. ix. 1–3; released from prison and sent to Italy, VIII. xxvi. 13; commands on the left wing, VIII. xxxi. 4; in the assault on Rome, VIII. xxxiii. 21; lost Petra, recovered Rome, VIII. xxxiii. 24
Dalatarba, fortress in Haemimontum, B. IV. xi. 20
Dalatarba, fortress in Rhodope; built by Justinian, B. IV. xi. 20
Dalmatas, fortress in Remisianisia, B. IV. iv. 3
Dalmatia, area east of the Ionian Gulf, VIII. xxvii. 5; adjoining Precalis and Liburnia, V. xv. 25; held by the rebel Marcellianus, III. vi. 7; counted in the western empire, V. xv. 25; its strong winds, V. xv. 5, 6; opposite to Italy, V. xv. 5, 7; Mundus sent thither by Justinian, V. v. 2; conquered by him, V. v. 11; invaded by the Goths, V. vii. 1 ff.; recovered for the empire by Constantinus, V. vii. 27–36; an army sent thither by Vittigis, V. xvi. 8, 9; plundered by the Lombards, VII. xxxiii. 12; visited by a Gothic fleet, VII. xxxv. 24–29; invaded by the Sclaveni, VII. xl. 7; Roman army winters in, VII. xl. 11, 27, 30; Goths offer to resign claim to, VIII. xxiv. 4; mentioned, VI. xxi. 41, xxviii. 2, xxx. 2, VII. xiii. 19
Damascus, city in Syria, B. V. ix. 26; home of Apollodorus, B. IV. vi. 13
Damian, Saint of Syria, B. II. xi. 4; Cosmas and, shrine of, B. I. vi. 5–8; Cosmas and, House of, B. V. ix. 37
Damianus, nephew of Valerian; sent from Rome with troops, VI. vii. 26; detained in Ariminum by John, VI. xi. 22; escorts the Lombards from Italy, VIII. xxxiii. 2
Damianus, Senator of Tarsus, S.H. xxix. 32; patron of the Blues; killed in a raid, S.H. xxix. 33
Dancing Master, official of the Hippodrome, S.H. ix. 5
Danedebae, fortress in Cabetzus, B. IV. iv. 3
Dani, a barbarian nation in Europe, VI. xv. 3, 29
Danube River, called also the Ister (*q.v.*), III. i. 10, VIII. v. 29; fortification of, B. IV. v. 1 ff.

INDEX

Daphnê, suburb of Antioch, II. viii. 25; visited by Chosroes, who sacrifices there, II. xi. 5 ff.; church of the Archangel Michael and other buildings burned by the Persians, II. xi. 6; portent of its uprooted cypresses, II. xiv. 5, 6; law that the cypresses may not be cut down, *ib.*; church at, B. V. ix. 29

Daphnê, fortress in Moesia; built by Constantine, B. IV. vii. 7; destroyed by barbarians; rebuilt by Justinian, B. IV. vii. 8

Daras, town on the Persian border; hastily fortified by Anastasius, I. x. 13; VIII. vii. 9; S.H. xii. 9, B. II. i. 4–10; its importance for the Romans, B. II. i. 13; its formidable defences, II. xiii. 17; well provisioned, VIII. vii. 7; its remarkable spring, VIII. vii. 7, 8; a menace to the Persians, I. xvi. 6; battle of, I. xiii. 12 ff.; the Persians demand that its wall be abolished, I. xvi. 7; its abandonment by the Romans a condition of the "endless peace," I. xxii. 16; revolt of John, I. xxvi. 5–12; besieged by Chosroes, II. xi. 28, xiii. 16 ff.; VIII. vii. 5; citizens of, make a settlement with Chosroes, II. xiii. 28; Chosroes plans its capture by a ruse, II. xxviii. 17; failure of the attempt, II. xxviii. 31 ff.; fortified by Justinian, B. II. i. 11–27, iii. 1, III. v. 10, 11; and its river controlled, B. II. iii. 1–23; water supply of, protected by Justinian, B. II. ii. 1–21; home of Solomon, III. xi. 9; distance from Sisauranon, B. II. iv. 9; from Nisibis and the Persian boundary, I. x. 14; from Ammodios, I. xiii. 15; from Theodosiopolis, B. II. ii. 16; road from, to Rhabdios, B. II. iv. 1; mentioned, B. II. iv. 14

Dardania, section of the Balkan Peninsula; fortresses of, B. IV. iv. 3, viii. 1

Dardanians, a people of southern Europe, B. IV. i. 17

Dardapara, fortress in Dardania, B. IV. iv. 3

Dardapara, fortress in the district of Remisianisia, B. IV. iv. 3

Datius, priest of Milan; asks aid of Belisarius, VI. vii. 35

Datius, brought as king from Thule by the Eruli, VI. xv. 29

Dausaron, fortress in Mesopotamia, B. II. vi. 14

Deacon, Pelagius of Rome, VII. xvi. 5; Psoes of Alexandria, S.H. xxvii. 14

Death, Gate of, in Byzantium, I. xxiv. 52

Debrê, fortress in Haemimontum, B. IV. xi. 20

December, month in the Roman calendar, IV. iii. 28, V. xiv. 14

Decennovium, river near Rome, V. xi. 2

Decimum, suburb of Carthage, III. xvii. 11, 17, xviii. 5, xix. 1, 14, 23, 33, xx. 6, 7, 10, xxi. 23, 24, IV. xxv. 12; the Vandals routed there, III. xviii. 7–11, xix. 31; distance from Carthage, III. xvii. 17; from Pedion Halon, III. xviii. 12

Decius, a Patrician; escapes from Rome, VII. xx. 18

Dedbera, fortress in southern Europe, B. IV. iv. 3

Deixas, fortress in Haemimontum, B. IV. xi. 20

Delphi, shrine in Greece; tripods first made there, III. xxi. 3

Delphix, a term used by the Romans to designate a royal banquet-room, III. xxi. 2, 3; in the Palace of Gelimer, III. xxi. 5

Delphrax, Monastery of, in Mesopotamia, B. V. ix. 32

Demetrias, city of Thessaly; fortified by Justinian, B. IV. iii. 5

Demetrius, of Philippi, envoy of Justinian, V. iii. 5, 13, 29

Demetrius, Roman commander of infantry, V. v. 3; VI. xxiii. 2; sent to Italy, VII. vi. 13, 14; endeavours in vain to relieve Naples, VII. vi. 15–24; escapes capture, VII. vi. 25; sent by Maximinus to Naples, VII. vii. 3; captured by the Goths, VII. vii. 6; forced by Totila to advise Neapolitans to surrender, VII. vii. 8–10

INDEX

Demetrius, a Cephallenian; Governor of Naples, VII. vi. 20; his wanton abuse of Totila, VII. vi. 21; goes secretly to the Roman fleet, VII. vi. 22, 23; captured and mutilated by the Goths, VII. vi. 26
Demon, believed to have "possessed" Justinian, S.H. xii. 14, 26–28, 32, xviii. 1, 36, 37, xxii. 28, xxx. 34; and Theodora, S.H. xii. 14
Demosthenes, his property "inherited" by Justinian, S.H. xii. 5
Demurrer, a legal protest, III. iii. 3. *See also* Limitation, Statute of
Denizus, fortress in Rhodope; built by Justinian, B. IV. xi. 20
Deoniana, fortress in Moesia, B. IV. xi. 20
Deopheron, a notable Italian, VII. xxx. 6; brother of Tullianus, *ib.*; sent as envoy to Totila, VII. xxx. 19
Dertallus, fortress in Thrace, B. IV. xi. 20
Destreba, fortress in Remisianisia, B. IV. iv. 3
Deuphracus, fortress in Epirus, B. IV. iv. 3
Deurias, fortress in Remisianisia, B. IV. iv. 3
Deuteron, a section of Byzantium, at the "second" milestone from the centre of the old city, B. I. iii. 11
Diaremata, boats used for the transshipment of grain in Egypt, B. VI. i. 3
Dido, her emigration from Phoenicia, IV. x. 25
Dieramata, *see* Diaremata
Dinarthison, monastery in Libya; fortified by Justinian, B. VI. ii. 7, 8
Dingium, fortress in Thrace, B. IV. xi. 20
Diniscarta, fortress in Moesia, B. IV. xi. 20
Dinium, fortress in Dardania, B. IV. iv. 3
Diocletian, Roman Emperor; readjusts the boundary in Egypt, I. xix. 29 ff.; builds the fortress of Philae, I. xix. 34, 35; fortresses in Mesopotamia, B. II. viii. 7; ordained food distribution in Alexandria, S.H. xxvi. 41; founded Circesium, B. II. vi. 2, 4
Diocletianopolis, city of Thessaly, B. IV. iii. 1; condemned by Justinian, B. IV. iii. 4
Diogenes, a guardsman of Belisarius; commander of cavalry, II. xxi. 2, 18, 20, VII. xxxvii. 9; his notable exploit on a scouting expedition, III. xxiii. 5–18; sent out against the Goths, V. xxvii. 11, 12, VI. v. 9; sent to investigate the aqueduct, VI. ix. 9; commands the garrison of Rome, VII. xxxvi. 1 ff.; escapes from Rome, VII. xxxvi. 15; commander of the Centumcellae, VII. xxxvii. 9; receives and answers proposals from Totila, VII. xxxvii. 11–17; repudiates his agreement with Totila, VII. xxxix. 25, 26
Diogenes, resident of Byzantium; accused by Theodora, but acquitted, S.H. xvi. 23–28
Diomedes, son of Tydeus; founder of Beneventus; V. xv. 8; received the tusks of the Caledonian boar from his uncle Meleager, *ib.*; meets Aeneas there, V. xv. 9; gives the Palladium to him, V. xv. 9, 10
Dionoia, fortress in Epirus, B. IV. iv. 3
Dionysius, his property "inherited" by Justinian, S.H. xii. 6
Dionysus, fortress in Epirus, B. IV. iv. 3
Dityvistus, companion of the youthful Justinus, S.H. vi. 2
Dodona, in Greece; ravaged by the Goths, VIII. xxii. 31
Dog's Head, eastern point of Cercyra, VII. xxvii. 19
Dolebin, fortress in Epirus, B. IV. iv. 3
Dolomites, an independent people in Persia; in the Persian army, VIII. xiv. 5–7; their fighting equipment, VIII. xiv. 8; accustomed to the mountains, VIII. xiv. 9; assist in the attack on Archaeopolis, VIII. xiv. 12; flee with the Persian army, VIII. xiv. 42

Dolones, the large sails used on ships, III. xvii. 5
Domesticus, title of confidential adviser, III. iv. 7, xi. 5; Domestici, a section of the Palace Guard, S.H. xxiv. 24, xxvi. 28
Domitian, Roman Emperor; resembled by Justinian, S.H. viii. 13–21; his excellent wife, S.H. viii. 15; strange statue of, S.H. viii. 18–21
Domnentiolus, Roman commander; nephew of Bouzes, II. xxiv. 15; defends Messana, VII. xxxix. 3
Domnicus, Senator, acccompanies Germanus to Libya, IV. xvi. 2; at the battle of Scalae Veteres, IV. xvii. 4; summoned to Byzantium, IV. xix. 1; envoy to Vittigis, VI. xxix. 1, 7
Dordas, fortress in Haemimontum, B. IV. xi. 20
Dorostolus, fortress on the Danube; restored by Justinian, B. IV. vii. 10, 11
Dorotheus, Roman commander at the battle of Daras, I. xiii. 21
Dorotheus, General of Armenia; attacks invading Persians, I. xv. 3 ff.; makes a sally, I. xv. 11 ff.; commander of auxiliaries, III. xi. 5; his death, III. xiv. 14
Dorthon, town on the Po, VI. xxiii. 5
Dorticum, fortress on the Danube, B. IV. vi. 20
Dory, land on the Euxine, B. III. vii. 13; its situation and character, B. III. vii. 15–17; protected against the Goths, B. III. vii. 17; fortified by Justinian, B. III. vii. 16, 17
Doubios, district in Persarmenia, II. xxv. 1, 2; its trade with India, II. xxv. 3; distance from Theodosiopolis, II. xxv. 1; Mermeroes stops there with his army, II. xxx. 33; Bishop of, called Catholicus, II. xxv. 4; sent to urge the Romans to make peace, II. xxiv. 6, 7
Dracon, river in Campania, VIII. xxxv. 7; its high banks, VIII. xxxv. 8
Dracon, river in Bithynia, B. V. ii. 6
Drasimarca, fortress in Remisianisia B. IV. iv. 3
Dromon, a swift ship of war, III. xi. 15, 16, xv. 36
Drullus, fortress in Dardania, B. IV. iv. 3
Dryus, city on the east coast of Italy, called also Hydrus, III. i. 9, 12, V. xv. 20, VI. v. 1; besieged by the Goths, VII. ix. 22, x. 8; its garrison parley with the Goths, VII. x. 5; relieved by Valentinus, VII. x. 6, 7, 9; its siege raised by the Goths, VII. xviii. 6; only city of southern Italy held by the Romans, VII. xxii. 22, xxiii. 13; distance from Brundisium, VII. xviii. 6; from Rome, VII. xviii. 4; from Tarentum, VII. xxiii. 12; mentioned, VII. xviii. 5, 8, xxii. 20, xxvi. 28, xxvii. 4, xxx. 2, 9; held by the Romans, VIII. xxiii. 17, xxxiv. 10, 13; commanded by Pacurius, VIII. xxvi. 4
Ducepratum, fortress on the Danube, B. IV. vi. 5
Duiana, fortress in Cabetzus, B. IV. iv. 3
Duke, of Armenia, appointed by Justinian, B. III. i. 28, ii. 1; stationed at Citharizon, B. III. iii. 8; of Tzanica, B. III. vi. 17
Duliares, fortress in southern Europe, B. IV. iv. 3
Durbuliana, fortress in Dardania, B. IV. iv. 3
Duries, fortress in Cabetzus, B. IV. iv. 3
Dusmanes, fortress in southern Europe, B. IV. iv. 3
Dux, Latin title of a military commander, I. xvii. 46, B. II. vi. 9, III. iii. 14. *See also* Duke
Dyrrachin, fortress in Epirus, B. IV. iv. 3
Dyrrachium, contemporary name of Epidamnus (*q.v.*), III. i. 16, xi. 8

Easter, Feast of; preceded by days of fasting, B. I. vii. 7; especially observed by Christians, I. xviii. 15, IV. xiv. 7, S.H. ix. 53, xxviii. 17; by Justinian, S.H. xiii. 29, B. I. vii. 7, 8; Arians resent exclusion from rites, IV. xiv. 15
Earthquakes throughout Greece, VIII. xxv. 16–18, 23; at Byzantium

and elsewhere, VII. xxix. 4, 5, 17; at Antioch, II. xiv. 6, S.H. xviii. 41; at Seleucia in Pieria, *ib.*; at Anazarbus, *ib.*; at Ibora, Amasia, Polybotus, Philomede, Lychnidus, Corinth, S.H. xviii. 42

Ebrimous, son-in-law of Theodatus; deserts to the Romans, V. viii. 3; honoured by the Emperor, *ib.*

Ebusa, island in the western Mediterranean, so-called by the natives, III. i. 18; Apollinaris sent thither with an army, IV. v. 7

Echinaeus, city of Thessaly; visited by a tidal wave, VIII. xxv. 19; fortified by Justinian, B. IV. iii. 5

Edana, fortress in Macedonia, B. IV. iv. 3

Edessa, city on the Persian border; centre of Osroene, I. xvii. 24; story of its Toparch Augarus, II. xii. 8 ff.; believed impregnable, II. xii. 7, 26, 30; letter of Christ inscribed on its wall, II. xii. 26; delivered to the Persians, II. xii. 28; recovered by the citizens, II. xii. 29; pays Chosroes two centenaria, II. xii. 34; citizens of, eager to ransom captives of Antioch, II. xiii. 3 ff.; its capture desired by Chosroes, II. xii. 6, 7, 31, xiii. 8; who abandons his hope, II. xiii. 9 ff.; attacked by him, II. xxvi. 5 ff., VIII. xiv. 35; home of Sergius, II. xxiv. 4; of John, son of Basilius, S.H. xii. 6; of Procopius, prefect of Samaria, B. V. vii. 14; its hippodrome, B. II. vii. 9; built by Augustus, II. xii. 18; a portent in, VIII. xiv. 39–41; flooded, S.H. xviii. 38; restored by Justinian, B. II. vii. 1 ff.

Edetzio, fortress in Dardania, B. IV. iv. 3

Egypt, adjoins Libya, B. VI. i. 5; formerly marked limit of Phoenicia, IV. x. 15; traversed by the Nile, V. xii. 2; VIII. vi. 2, 13, 14, B. VI. i. 6; topography of, I. xix. 3; suffers from pestilence, II. xxii. 6; and from flood, VII. xxix. 6–8, S.H. xviii. 39; densely populated, IV. x. 19; Hebrews migrate thence, IV. x. 13; traversed by Phoenicians, IV. x. 18; John of Cappadocia sent thither, I. xxv. 43, S.H. xvii. 40; Kings of, B. II. i. 3; its "city of Antinous," (Antinopolis) VIII. xxvii. 6; Post Route to, S.H. xxx. 10; its Prefect Zeno, S.H. xii. 1; home of John Laxarion, S.H. xxix. 1; visited by Theodora, S.H. xii. 30; Egyptian sellers of grain, S.H. xxvi. 37; the Egyptian god Osiris, B. VI. i. 12; ancient statues of, V. xv. 13

Eileithuia, ancient name of Artemis Bolosia, VIII. xxii. 29

Eirenaeus, Roman general; sent to Lazica, I. xii. 14; property of, confiscated by Justinian, S.H. xxix. 16

Eirenê, Church of, beside the Church of Sophia, B. I. ii. 13; Church of; on the Golden Horn, B. I. vii. 1, 2

Eirenê, fortress in Epirus, B. IV. iv. 3

Eisdicaea, fortress in Thrace, B. IV. xi. 20

Elaeae, fortress in Europe, B. IV. xi. 20

Elaeus, city at the base of the Chersonese, B. IV. x. 3; near Sestus, B. IV. x. 26; fortified by Justinian, B. IV. x. 27

Elemundus, king of the Gepaedes; his death, VIII. xxvii. 19; father of Ustrigothus, VIII. xxvii. 19, 26

Elephantine, city in Egypt, on the Roman boundary, I. xix. 27; near Philae, I. xix. 34, 35

Elephants, used in warfare by the Persians, VIII. xiii. 4, xiv. 35 ff., xvii. 11, B. II. i. 11

Elpidius, physician of Theoderic, V. i. 38

Emastus, fortress in Dardania, B. IV. iv. 3

Emesa, city in Syria, S.H. xxviii. 1 ff.; home of Severianus, IV. xxiii. 6; of Priscus, S.H. xxviii. 1; Church of, S.H. xxviii. 2–6

Emporium, port of the city of Perga, B. V. ix. 38

Endielon, place near Amida, I. vii. 5

Endyneia, fortress in Epirus, B. IV. iv. 3

Ennes, commander of the Isaurians in the Roman army, V. v. 3; brother of Tarmutus, V. xxviii. 23; at the capture of Naples, V. x. 1, 3, 13; saves his brother, V. xxix. 42; sent to Milan with Isaurians, VI. xii. 27, 40

Ephesus, city in Asia Minor; refuge of Theodosius, S.H. i. 23, ii. 14, 17, iii. 2, 9; its Church of John rebuilt by Justinian, S.H. iii. 3, B. V. i. 4–6; bishop of V. iii. 5, S.H. iii. 4

Ephraemius, bishop of Antioch; accused of treason by Julian, II. vii. 16; retires to Cilicia, II. vii. 17

Ephthalite Huns, called White Huns, their manners and customs, I. iii. 1, 2; wage war with Perozes, I. iii. 1 ff.; entrap the Persian army, I. iii. 8 ff.; in a second war with Perozes completely destroy his army, I. iv. 1 ff.; force the Persians to pay tribute, I. iv. 35; receive Cabades after his escape from the Prison of Oblivion, I. vi. 10; Cabades owes their king money, I. vii. 1, 2; punished for impiety towards Jacobus, the hermit, I. vii. 8; eight hundred Ephthalitae killed by the Persians, I. viii. 13

Epidamnus, town near Dardania, B. IV. i. 17; on the sea adjoining Epirus, V. ii. 24, xv. 24; Amalasuntha sends a ship thither, V. ii. 26, 28, iii. 14; reached by Lombard invasions, VII. xxxiii. 12; by the Sclaveni, VII. xxix. 1; used as a naval port, VII. xiii. 19, 21, xviii. 1; recruiting station for Constantianus, V. vii. 27, 28; called also Dyrrachium, III. i. 16, xi. 8; home of John, III. xi. 8

Epidaurus, harbour on the eastern side of the Ionian Gulf, V. vii. 28, 32

Epidunta, fortress in Epirus, B. IV. iv. 3

Epileum, fortress in Epirus, B. IV. iv. 3

Epiphanius, bishop of Byzantium; blesses the fleet, III. xii. 2

Epirus, on the right of the Ionian Gulf B. IV. i. 11, viii. 1; adjoining Precalis, V. xv. 24; Maximinus delays there, VII. vi. 11; strengthened by Justinian, B. IV. i. 35, viii. 1; fortresses in, B. IV. iv. 3; its city Lychnidon, S.H. xviii. 42; mentioned, B. IV. ii. 1

Episcopia, fortress near Rhegium; built by Justinian, B. IV. viii. 19 ff.

Episterba, fortress in Epirus, B. IV. iv. 3

Epizephyrian Locrians, among the Bruttii, V. xv. 23

Eraria, fortress in southern Europe, B. IV. iv. 3

Eraric, one of the Rogi; serving in the Gothic army, VII. ii. 1; declared king of the Goths by the Rogi, VII. ii. 4; hated by the Goths, VII. ii. 10; who plot his destruction, VII. ii. 12, 13; sends envoys to Justinian, VII. ii. 15–17; slain by the Goths, VII. ii. 6, 18, iii. 1

Erculente, fortress in Moesia, B. IV. xi. 20

[illegible], [illegible] B. IV. xi. 20

Eridanus, a name sometimes given to the Po River, (*q.v.*), V. i. 18, VII. iii. 22; Placentia situated on, VII. xiii. 9

Eruli, a barbarian tribe, usually allied with the Romans; history of their wanderings etc., VI. xiv. 1–34; their worthless character, IV. iv. 30; VI. xiv. 35, 36, 41; some emigrate to Thule, VI. xv. 1 ff.; revolt from the Romans, VI. xiv. 37; kill their king and summon one from Thule, VI. xiv. 38, 42, xv. 27, 30; their king a figurehead, VI. xiv. 39, 40; decide to ask Justinian to nominate a king, VI. xv. 30 ff.; welcome Suartuas as king, VI. xv. 33, VIII. xxv. 11; abandon him, VI. xv. 34, 35; submit to Gepaedes, VI. xv. 36; fight without protective armour except a shield, II. xxv. 27, 28; in the Roman army, II. xxi. 4, VI. xiii. 18, xix. 20, VII. xxvii. 3, xxxiii. 13; at the battle of Daras, I. xiii. 19, xiv. 33, 39; under Mundus, I. xxiv. 41; in the army of Valerian, II. xxiv. 12;

of Martinus, II. xxiv. 14; follow Peter into Persia, II. xxiv. 18; in the battle of Anglon, II. xxv. 20 ff.; in African expedition, III. xi. 11; dissuade Stotzas from attacking Germanus, IV. xvii. 14, 15; supporters of Narses, VI. xviii. 6, VIII. xxvi. 17; refuse to remain with Belisarius, VI. xxii. 5; meet army of Uraïas, VI. xxii. 6; reach Venetia, then Byzantium VI. xxii. 7, 8; follow Narses into Thrace, VII. xiii. 21, 22; defeat the Sclaveni, VII. xiii. 25; receive parts of Dacia from the Emperor VII. xxxiii. 13, xxxiv. 37; overrun Illyricum and Thrace, VII. xxxiii. 13, 14; receive payments from the Emperor, VII. xxxiii. 14; arrayed against Gepaedes, VII. xxxiv. 42; in the army of Narses, VIII. xxvi. 13, xxx. 18, xxxi. 5; kill Usdrilas, VIII. xxviii. 10; in the assault on Rome, VIII. xxxiii. 19; side with Gepaedes, VII. xxxiv. 43; their leader Aordus defeated by the Romans, VII. xxxiv. 44, 45; feared by Roman commanders, VII. xxxiv. 46; commanded by Arufus, VII. xxvi. 23; by Verus, VII. xxvii. 8; by Vitalius, VII. i. 34, 35; of the Arian faith, IV. xiv. 12; the following individuals are named: Philemuth, VII. xxxix. 10; Uligagus, VIII. ix. 5

Esdilasas, a Moorish ruler; joins in an attack upon a Roman force, IV. x. 6 ff.; surrenders himself to the Romans, IV. xii. 26; brought to Carthage IV. xii. 29

Esimiphaeus, established as king of the Homeritae, I. xx. 1; desposed by insurgents, I. xx. 3; makes idle promise to Justinian, I. xx. 9 ff.

Etaeries, fortress in Cabetzus, B. IV. iv. 3.

Ethiopians, a people of Africa, B. V. viii. 2; location of their country, I. xix. 17; the ships used there, I. xix. 23; iron not produced there nor imported from elsewhere, I. xix. 24, 25; sought as allies by Justinian, I. xix. 1, xx. 9 ff., II. iii. 40; unable to buy silk from the Indians, I. xx. 12

Euageës, brother of Hoamer; imprisoned by Gelimer, III. ix. 9, 14; killed in prison by Ammatas, III. xvii. 12

Euboea, island near Marathon, B. IV. iii. 16; description of, B. IV. iii. 17 ff.; its strait Euripus, VIII. vi. 20; its town Geraestus, VIII. xxii. 27

Eudaemon, a consular, uncle of John Laxarion, S.H. xxix. 4; Treasurer of the Emperor's funds, *ib.*; approaches Justinian, S.H. xxix. 5; seeks recall of Liberius, S.H. xxix. 10; dies intestate, S.H. xxix. 12

Eudocia, daughter of Eudoxia; taken captive by Gelimer, III. v. 3; married to Honoric, III. v. 6

Eudoxia, daughter of Theodosius and wife of Valentinian, III. iv. 15, 20; mother of Eudocia and Placidia, III. v. 3; forced to be the mistress of Maximus, III. iv. 36; invites Gizeric to avenge her, III. iv. 37–39; taken captive by Gizeric, III. v. 3; sent to Byzantium, III. v. 6

Eugenius, Martyr, aqueduct of, at Trapezus, B. III. vii. 1

Eugenius, slave of Antonina, S.H. i. 27

Eulogius, Roman envoy to Godas, III. x. 32, 33; returns with his reply, III. x. 34

Eulysia, a country on the Euxine, VIII. iv. 7

Eunomians, a religious sect, S.H. i. 15

Eunuchs, Narses, I. xxv. 24; Euphratas, VIII. iii. 19; serving in the Palace, S.H. vi. 26, xv. 26, 34, xxix. 13

Euphemia, Empress; prevents marriage of Justinian, S.H. ix. 47; her innocuous career and death, S.H. ix. 48, 49; *see* Lupicina

Euphemia, daughter of John the Cappadocian, I. xxv. 13

Euphemia, captive of Sura; married by Chosroes, II. v. 28

Euphratas, a eunuch of the Abasgi, VIII. iii. 19; director of palace eunuchs; dies, S.H. xxix. 13

Euphrates River, its source in Armenia, I. xvii. 4; disappears in a strange marsh, I. xvii. 6 ff.; its

INDEX

course from Celesene to its junction with the Tigris, I. xvii. 21, 22; receives the Aborrhas, II. v. 2, B. II. vi. 1; protects one side of Circesium, *ib.*, B. II. vi. 1, 4; important battle on its banks, I. xviii. 30 ff.; crossed by Chosroes, S.H. iii. 31; nature of the land to the right of it, B. II. viii. 2; flows by the following cities: Zenobia, B. II. viii. 16; Sura, B. II. ix. 1; Melitenê, B. III. iv. 15; Pentacomia, B. II. ix. 10; boundary of Lesser Armenia, B. III. i. 17

Euphratesia, later name of Commagene I. xvii. 2, 23, II. xx. 17, 20, B. II. viii. 4; chosen by Azarethes as the starting point for an invasion of Roman territory, I. xvii. 2; fortified by Justinian, B. II. ix. 10; its Church of St. Sergius, B. II. ix. 3

Euripus, strait between Euboea and mainland, VIII. vi. 20; puzzled Aristotle, *ib.*; bridged by a timber, B. IV. iii. 19

Euroea, city in Illyricum; shifted and fortified by Justinian, B. IV. i. 39–42

Europe, continent opposite Asia, III. i. 7, xxii. 15; distance from Africa and Asia at different points, III. i. 7, 8; distance along the European side of the Euxine, III. i. 10; extent of Western Empire in, III. i. 14; in effect an island, B. IV. i. 12; to the left of Gibraltar, V. xii. 1; separated from Asia by the Phasis, VIII. ii. 32, vi. 14; or by the Tanais, VIII. vi. 15; borders the Mediterranean, B. IV. ix. 1; its boundaries, VIII. ii. 28, 29, vi. 1–5; as delimited by Herodotus, VIII. vi. 12–14; approaches Asia at Byzantium, B. I. v. 6; description of, V. xii. 3 ff.; plundered by the Visigoths, III. ii. 7, 13; invaded by the Huns, II. iv. 4 ff.; ravaged by the Sclaveni, VII. xl. 33; overrun by barbarians, S.H. xxiii. 6, 8; unrest among its peoples, VIII. xviii. 1; losses by war in, S.H. xviii. 22; contains no Amazons, VIII. iii. 11; defended by Danube fortresses, B. IV. i. 33; buildings of Justinian in, B. III. vii. 25, IV. i. 3, 10, 13, 14, V. i. 1; fortresses of, B. IV. iv. 1, vii. 21; Byzantium, its "acropolis," B. IV. viii. 2, ix. 14

Europe, a region comprising a part of Thrace, B. IV. xi. 20; fortresses in, B. IV. xi. 20; well watered, B. IV. ix. 14

Europê, fortress in Epirus, B. IV. iv. 3

Europus, town in Euphratesia, B. II. ix. 10; headquarters of Belisarius, II. xx. 24, 27, 28

Eurymenê, fortress in Thessaly; rebuilt by Justinian, B. IV. iii. 14

Eusebius, Roman ambassador to the Persian king Perozes, I. iii. 8; warns Perozes of the stratagem of the Ephthalitae, I. iii. 13

Eusebius, Bishop of Cyzicus, I. xxv. 37, 38

Eustratius, sent to Libya to assess taxes, IV. viii. 25

Euthalius, paymaster of Roman troops in Italy, VI. ii. 1; secures safe conduct from Belisarius, VI. ii. 2 ff., 24

Eutropius, place near Byzantium named from, B. I. xi. 22

Eutyches, heresy of, III. vii. 22

Eutychiana, fortress in Dardania, B. IV. iv. 3

Euxine Sea, the modern Black Sea; entrance to, from Byzantium, S.H. xxv. 2; B. I. viii. 2, ix. 7, 11; formed by the Mediterranean, B. IV. ix. 1; distance around it, III. i. 10, 11; joins the Aegean at Byzantium, B. I. v. 3, 5; bordered on north by barbarian tribes, VIII. vii. 12, S.H. xxv. 4; touched by the Caucasus, VIII. ix. 15; does not "end" at Byzantium, VIII. vi. 25; receives the waters of the Phasis, II. xxix. 16, III. i. 11, VIII. vi. 8; and of the Ister, VIII. v. 30; also the outflow from the Maeotic Lake, VIII. vi. 4; description of, VIII. i. 7–v. 33, B. VI. i. 8; forms part of boundary between Europe and Asia, VIII. vi. 3, 5; has Anchialus on its shore, B. III. vii. 18,

19; buildings of Justinian about it, B. III. vii. 1, 19; fortresses on, B. III. vii. 24, B. IV. xi. 20; home of dolphins, VII. xxix. 11; desired as an outlet by Chosroes, II. xxviii. 23
Evangelus, wealthy Senator of Caesarea, S.H. xxx. 18; rebuked by Justinian, S.H. xxx. 19
Evaris, builder of a church near Antioch, II. xi. 7
Excubitor, Latin word for "guard," IV. xii. 17
Exentaprista, fortress in Moesia, B. IV. xi. 20

Factions, popular parties of the Hippodrome; their unruly conduct, S.H. vii. 1–42; *see* Blue Faction *and* Green Faction, *also* Vol. VI. App. 1
Fanus, fortress in Italy, on the Adriatic, VII. xi. 32; dismantled by Vittigis, *ib.*, VII. xxv. 7, 8
Fata, (Latin) "Fates"; Temple of, in Rome, V. xxv. 19, 20
Faustinus, a Samaritan turned Christian; Senator; accused of maltreating Christians, S.H. xxvii. 26, 27
Faventia, city in Aemilia; distance from Ravenna, VII. iii. 22
Fidelius, native of Milan, V. xiv. 5; previously Quaestor to Atalaric, *ib.*; envoy of the Romans to Belisarius, *ib.*; Praetorian Prefect sent to Milan in company with troops, VI. xii. 27, 28; taunts the Gothic envoys, V. xx. 19, 20; killed by the Goths, VI. xii. 34, 35
Firmum, city in Italy; on the Adriatic VI. xvi. 1; Aratius stationed there to hold Auximus in check, VI. xx. 3; besieged by Totila VII. xi. 39; surrenders to him, VII. xii. 12; distance from Auximus, VI. xvi. 1
Fisula, town in Etruria; Belisarius plans its capture, VI. xxiii. 1; besieged by Cyprian and Justinus, VI. xxiii. 2, xxiv. 18, xxv. 19; surrenders to the Romans, VI. xxvii. 27
Flaminian Gate, in Rome; the Goths pass out through it, V. xiv. 14; threatened by a Gothic camp, V. xix. 2; next to the Pincian, V. xix. 16, xxiii. 3; held by Constantianus, V. xix. 16; closed by Belisarius, *ib.* VI. v. 6; not attacked by the Goths, V. xxiii. 2; guarded by Ursicinus, V. xxiii. 3; opened by Belisarius, VI. v. 8, 12
Flaminian Way, road leading northward from Rome, VIII. xxviii. 13; passed Narnia, Spolitium and Perusia, VI. xi. 9; left by Narses, VIII. xxviii. 13
Florentia, city in Etruria; besieged by the Goths, VII. v. 1; relieved by a Roman army, VII. v. 4, 5; held by Justinus, VII. vi. 8; distance from Mucellis, VII. v. 5
Florentiana, fortress in Aquenisium, B. IV. iv. 3
Florentianae, city in Numidia; walled by Justinian, B. VI. vii. 8
Florentius, a Thracian; distinguishes himself at the battle of Satala, I. xv. 15, 16
Foederati, auxiliary troops of the Roman armies, III. xi. 2, 3, 5, xix. 13, 14; IV. iii. 4, vii. 11, xv. 50, V. v. 2, VII. xxxi. 10, xxxiii. 13, VIII. v. 13
Foedus, (Latin) "treaty," III. xi. 4
Forocornelius, ancient town in northern Italy, VI. xix. 22
Fortune, Temple of, in Rome, V. xv. 11
Forty Martyrs, Monastery of, near Theodosiopolis, B. III. iv. 14
Forty Saints, The, B. I. vii. 3 ff.
Forty-five Saints, Monastery of, B. III. iv. 13
Forum of Peace, in Rome, VIII. xxi. 11
Fosala, fortress in Numidia; strengthened by Justinian, B. VI. vii. 10
Fossatum, fortress in Moesia, B. IV. xi. 20
Franks, collective name of Germanic tribes, III. iii. 1, V. xi. 29, xii. 8; account of the growth of their kingdom up to the time of Procopius, V. xii. 8–xiii. 13; their ruler Theudibert, VI. xii. 38; persuaded by Justinian to ally themselves with him, V. v. 8–10; their war with the Goths, V. xi. 17, 18, 28; occupy the Visi-

INDEX

gothic portion of Gaul, V. xiii. 11, 12; invited to form alliance with Theodatus, receiving the Gothic portion of Gaul, V. xiii. 14; Vittigis advises forming of such an alliance with them, V. xiii. 19–24; make the treaty with some reserve, V. xiii. 26–28; send Burgundians as allies, VI. xii. 38; have the Suevi subject to them, V. xv. 26; the nations north of Langovilla subject to them, V. xv. 29; their reported alliance with the Goths, VI. xviii. 21; distrusted by the Goths, VI. xxii. 10; regardless of treaties, VI. xxv. 2; decide to enter the war. VI. xxv. 1; their fighting equipment, VI. xxv. 3, 4, 12; their atrocities at Ticinum, VI. xxv. 9; attack and rout a Gothic and a Roman force, VI. xxv. 11–14; suffer from lack of food, VI. xxv. 16–18; their previous alliance with the Romans, VI. xxv. 21; retire from Italy, VI. xxv. 24, xxvi. 12; feared by Belisarius, [illegible]; send envoys to Vittigis without success, VI. xxviii. 7–23; seek the Emperor's approval of their occupation of Gaul, VII. xxxiii. 4; conduct themselves as equals of the Romans, VII. xxxiii. 5; issue gold coinage, VII. xxxiii. 5, 6; acquire most of Venetia, VII. xxxiii. 7; received lands from Justinian, VII. xxxiv. 37; Milan a bulwark against them, VI. xxi. 6; adherents of Christianity, but retaining much of their pagan religion, VI. xxv. 10; their leader repudiates Totila's proposal of marriage with his daughter, VII. xxxvii. 1, 2; separated from the Varni by the Rhine, VIII. xx. 2; receive immigrants from Brittia, VIII. xx. 8–10; their ruler Theudibert, VIII. xx. 11; Hermegisclus allied with them by marriage, VIII. xx. 15; the Varni urged to favour them, VIII. xx. 17; close to the Varni, VIII. xx. 18; said to be holding a large part of Italy, VIII. xxiv. 4; usurp parts of Italy, VIII. xxiv. 6–8; make alliance with the Goths, VIII. xxiv. 9, 10; bribed by Justinian, VIII. xxiv. 13; hostile to the Goths, VIII. xxiv. 21, 22; refuse free passage to Narses, VIII. xxvi. 18–20; friendly to the Goths, VIII. xxvi. 19; prevent the surrender of Verona, VIII. xxxiii. 5; their alliance desired by Teïas, VIII. xxxiii. 7, xxxiv. 9, 17; desire Italy for themselves, VIII. xxxiv. 18; despaired of by Teïas, VIII. xxxiv. 21; mentioned, VIII. xx. 30, 49

Fricê, city in Numidia; walled by Justinian, B. VI. vii. 9

Frissones, one of the nations of Brittia, VIII. xx. 7

Frontier troops, called "Limitanei," S.H. xxiv. 12–14

Fuscias, sent by Gelimer as envoy to Spain, III. xxiv. 7 ff.

Gabalas, a Saracen; father of Arethas, I. xvii. 47

Gabboulon, fortress in Euphratesia, B. II. ix. 10; distance from Chalcis, I. xviii. 8

Gabraeum, fortress in Epirus, B. IV. iv. 3

Gadabitani, barbarians of Africa; converted to Christianity, B. VI. iv. 12

Gadira (Gades), town in Libya near the Pillars of Heracles, III. i. 4, 5; width of the strait, III. i. 7; distance from Tripolis, III. i. 14; and from the Ionian Sea, III. i. 15; marked limit of Mauritania, IV. x. 29; Vandals cross there, III. iii. 26; improved by Justinian, B. VI. vii. 14–16; *see* Pillars of Heracles

Gaeana, fortress in Numidia; walled by Justinian, B. VI. vii. 8

Galatia, region of Asia Minor, adjoining Cappadocia and Bithynia, II. xxviii. 23, S.H. xxiv. 25; lands in, given to Gelimer, IV. ix. 13; its river Siberis, B. V. iv. 1

Garces, fortress in southern Europe, B. IV. iv. 3

Garganon, mountain in Apulia, VII. xxii. 24

Garizin, mountain in Palestine, B. V.

vii. 1; fortified and provided with sanctuaries by Justinian, B. V. vii. 16, 17

Gaul, region extending from the Pyrenees to Liguria, V. xii. 4; its great expanse, V. xii. 5, 6; its rivers, lakes, and population, V. xii. 7–11; invaded by Constantinus, III. ii. 31; separated from Liguria and Italy by the Alps, V. xii. 4, 20, VI. vii. 37, VI. xxv. 5, xxviii. 28; formerly subject to the Romans, V. xii. 9; occupied by the Goths, V. xi. 16, 28; the Franks become established there, V. xi. 29, xii. 1 ff., VII. xxxiii. 4; partly occupied by the Visigoths, III. ii. 13, 37, V. xii. 12, 20; guarded by Roman soldiers, V. xii. 16; divided between the Franks and the Goths, V. xii. 32, 45; really under the sway of Theoderic, V. xii. 47; divided between the Goths and the Visigoths, V. xiii. 4, 5; the Visigothic portion taken over by the Franks, V. xiii. 12; Visigoths retire thence to Spain, V. xiii. 13; portion of, offered to Franks as the price of alliance, V. xiii. 14, VI. xxviii. 19, VII. xxxiii. 2; held by the Goths under Marcias, V. xiii. 15, xvi. 7; threatened by the Franks, V. xiii. 16; given to them by Vittigis, V. xiii. 26, 27; largely held by Germans, S.H. xviii. 17; limit of the Gothic rule, S.H. xviii. 16; fronts Brittia, VIII. xx. 5; gold mined in, VII. xxxiii. 5

Gauls, defeated by Camillus, VIII. xxix. 4, 5; later name of the Celts, B. IV. v. 9

Gaulus, island between the Adriatic and Tyrrhenian Seas, III. xiv. 16

Gauti, nation in Thule, VI. xv. 26

Gaza, limit of Arabia in olden times, I. xix. 20

Gazophyla, place in Numidia, IV. xv. 52; distance from Constantina, *ib.*; Roman commanders take sanctuary there, IV. xv. 59

Geilaris, son of Genzon and father of Gelimer, III. ix. 6

Gelimer, king of the Vandals, V. v. 1, vi. 2, xxix. 8, VII. i. 3, xxxv. 4, VIII. xix. 7, S.H. iv. 32, B. VI. v. 6, vi. 8; son of Geilaris, III. ix. 6; brother of Tzazon, III. xi. 23, xxiv. 1; and of Ammatas, III. xvii. 11; uncle of Gibamundus, III. xviii. 1; his character, III. ix. 7; his wealth, S.H. iv. 34; encroaches upon the authority of Illderic, III. ix. 8; secures the royal power, *ib.*; holds Lilybaeum, IV. v. 13; imprisons Illderic, Hoamer, and Euagees, III. ix. 9; defies Justinian, shewing cruelty to imprisoned princes, III. ix. 14; replies to Justinian, III. ix. 20–23; who prepares an expedition against him, III. x. 1 ff.; sends envoys to Spain, III. xxiv. 7; his slave Godas becomes tyrant of Sardinia, III. x. 25–27; sends an expedition thither, III. xi. 22, 23; ignorant of Roman plans, III. xiv. 10; entrusts wealth to Boniface, IV. iv. 34; imprisons Roman merchants, III. xx. 5, 6; expected by Belisarius to attack, III. xvii. 4; writes to his brother, III. xvii. 11; follows the Roman army, III. xvii. 14; plans his attack, III. xviii. 1; comes upon the Romans with cavalry, III. xix. 18; anticipates them in seizing a hill, III. xix. 20–22; blunders and loses opportunity, III. xix. 25–29; routed by Belisarius, III. xix. 30, 31, xxi. 16; flees to the Plain of Boulla, III. xix. 32; Belisarius sits upon his throne, III. xx. 21; his palace and provisions used by the Romans, III. xxi. 1-6; his reason for abandoning Carthage, III. xxi. 12; encourages Libyan farmers to kill Roman soldiers, III. xxiii. 1–4; eluded by Roman scouts, III. xxiii. 6–16; receives letter from Tzazon, III. xxiv. 2–4; collects the Vandals in the Plain of Boulla, III. xxv. 1; writes Tzazon, III. xxv. 10–18; leads the Vandals against Carthage, IV. i. 1; cuts the aqueduct and attempts siege, IV. i. 2, 3; arms and addresses his army, IV. ii. 8–

INDEX

22; at the battle of Tricamarum, IV. iii. 9; flees from the camp, IV. iii. 20; pursued by John the Armenian, IV. iv. 9, 14; and by Belisarius, IV. iv. 13, 26; escapes and takes refuge on Mt. Papua, IV. iv. 26; Moors there friendly to him, IV. iv. 27; Pharas sent to guard him, IV. iv. 28, 31; suffers great misery, IV. vi. 4; receives a letter from Pharas, IV. vi. 15–26; replies thereto, IV. vi. 27–30; the meaning of his strange request, IV. vi. 31–33; finally compelled to surrender, IV. vii. 1–6; again writes Pharas, IV. vii. 6–9; Cyprian comes to Papua to take him prisoner, IV. vii. 11; surrenders himself, IV. vii. 12; meets Belisarius at Aclas, IV. vii. 14; his unexpected laughter, IV. vii. 14–16; marvels at restored Carthage, III. xxiii. 20, 21; his capture reported by Belisarius, IV. vii. 17; reaches Byzantium with Belisarius, IV. ix. 1, II. xxi. 28; a captive in Belisarius' triumph, IV. ix. 10; before Justinian in the Hippodrome, IV. ix. 11, 12; given lands in Galatia, IV. ix. 13, 14; nephew of, IV. vii. 4

Gembero, fortress in Aquenisium, B. IV. iv. 3

Gemellomontes, fortress in Moesia, B. IV. xi. 20

Gemenus, fortress in Epirus. B. IV. iv. 3

Geminianus, Rock of, on Mt. Aurasius, IV. xx. 23

General of Armenia, B. III. i. 16. v. 12

Genoa, seaport of Italy, VI. xii. 29; commanded by Bonus, VII. x. 14

Gentianum, fortress in Macedonia, B. IV. iv. 3

Genysius, fortress in Epirus, B. IV. iv. 3

Genzana, fortress in Dardania, B. IV. iv. 3

Genzon, son of Gizeric, receives Libyan slaves, III. v. 11; tries to save John, III. vi. 24; father of Gundamundus and Trasamundus, III. viii. 6, 8; and of Geilaris, III. ix. 6; his death, III. viii. 1

George, Martyr, sanctuary of, B. III. iv. 13

George, confidant of Belisarius, persuades the inhabitants of Sisauranon to capitulate, II. xix. 22, 23; saves the city of Daras, II. xxviii. 33 ff.

George, a Cappadocian; guard of Martinus, conspicuous for valour, V. xxix. 20, 21

Gepaedes, a Gothic people, III. ii. 2; ruled by Thorisin, VIII. xviii. 3; and by Elemundus, VIII. xxvii. 19; their location, III. ii. 6; at war with the Goths, V. iii. 15, xi. 5; relations with the Eruli, VI. xiv. 25–27; who submit to them, VI. xv. 36; take possession of Dacia, VII. xxxiii. 8, xxxiv. 17, 35; oppress the population, VII. xxxiii. 8; in pay of Roman Emperors, VII. xxxiii. 9; allied with the Romans, VII. xxxiv. 10, 31; receive gifts from the Emperor, VII. xxxiv. 10; Lombards settle near them, VII. xxxiii. 11; to whom they become hostile, VII. xxxiv. 1, 2, xxxv. 19; [illegible] 3, 28; seek alliance with Justinian, VII. xxxiv. 4–39; who rejects their proposal, VII. xxxiv. 40; a Roman army sent against them, VII. xxxiv. 41; have most of the Eruli as allies, VII. xxxiv. 43; make settlement with Lombards, VII. xxxiv. 45; feared by Roman commanders, VII. xxxiv. 46; some of them follow Ildiges, VII. xxxv. 21; a Lombard flees to them, VII. xxxv. 12 ff.; make a treaty with the Lombards, VIII. xviii. 1; but resort to war again, VIII. xviii. 2 ff.; negotiate with Auduin, VIII. xviii. 8 ff.; seek alliance with Huns, VIII. xviii. 13 ff.; send the Cutrigurs into Roman territory, VIII. xviii. 16, 17; ferry the Sclaveni over the Ister, VIII. xxv. 5, 10; Justinian seeks an understanding with them, VIII. xxv. 6; prepare to fight Lombards, VIII. xxv. 7; send envoys to Byzantium, VIII. xxv. 8; Justinian sends troops against them, VIII. xxv. 10; defeated by the Lombards, VIII. xxv.

14; in the army of Narses, VIII. xxvi. 13; receive Goar and Ildigisal, VIII. xxvii. 22-25; Ustrigothus a refugee from, VIII. xxvii. 19-20; make peace with Justinian and the Lombards, VIII. xxvii. 21; refuse to surrender Illdigisal, VIII. xxvii. 22-25; the following individuals are named: Asbadus, VIII. xxvi. 13, xxxii. 22; Philegagus, VIII. viii. 15

Geraestus, town in Euboea, VIII. xxii. 27

Gergesites, ancient people of Phoenicia, IV. x. 17; emigrate to Egypt and then to Libya, IV. x. 18, 19

Germae, town in Dardania, rebuilt by Justinian, B. IV. i. 31

Germani Fossatum, site of fort built by Justinian, B. III. iv. 11

Germania, home of Belisarius, III. xi. 21

Germans, a numerous group of many tribes, VIII. xx. 3; their territory, S.H. xviii. 17; called "Franks," III. iii. 1; according to one account, killed Gontharis, III. iii. 33; receive from the Goths a portion of Gaul, VII. xxxiii. 2; *see* Franks

Germanus, nephew of Justinian, II. vi. 9; VII. xii. 11, xxxvii. 24, xxxix. 9; brother of Boraïdes, VII. xxxi. 17; father of Justinus, VII. xxxii. 14; and of Justinian, VII. xxxii. 17, xxxix. 17, xl. 10, VIII. xxv. 11; husband of Passara, VII. xxxix. 14; and of Matasuntha, *ib.*; wins displeasure of Theodora, S.H. v. 8; arranges marriage of his daughter, S.H. v. 9, 10; father-in-law of John, VII. xii. 11, xxxix. 10, xl. 10, VIII. xxvi. 11; commander at the battle of Daras, I. xiii. 21; sent to meet the invasion of Chosroes, II. vi. 9; establishes himself in Antioch and inspects the fortifications, II. vi. 10; retires into Cilicia, II. vii. 18; sent to Libya, IV. xvi. 1; makes a count of loyal soldiers, IV. xvi. 3; wins over mutineers, IV. xvi. 4-6; prepares to meet Stotzas in battle, IV. xvi. 7; arrays his army, IV. xvi. 10; addresses his troops, IV. xvi. 11-24; follows the mutineers into Numidia, IV. xvii. 2; prepares for battle at Scalae Veteres, IV. xvii. 3-6; receives offer of desertion from Moors, IV. xvii. 9; whom he distrusts, IV. xvii. 10; Stotzas prepares to attack his division, IV. xvii. 13; rallies the Romans, IV. xvii. 18; routs the mutineers, IV. xvii. 19-20; his horse killed under him, IV. xvii. 23; arranges countersign, IV. xvii. 22; captures and plunders enemy camp, IV. xvii. 24-29; tries to restore order, IV. xvii. 30; defeats Stotzas in second battle, IV. xvii. 34; learns of a plot, IV. xviii. 4; invites Maximinus to join his bodyguards, IV. xviii. 5-6; frustrates plot, IV. xviii. 8-15; impales Maximinus, IV. xviii. 17, 18; summoned to Byzantium, IV. xix. 1; false report of his coming to Carthage, IV. xxiii. 23, 25; vexed by interference of Justinian in settling brother's estate, VII. xxxi. 18; attempt to involve him in plot against Justinian, VII. xxxii. 10, 13-31, 44; confers with Marcellus, VII. xxxii. 22, 24-27; through his son entraps Chananranges, VII. xxxii. 27-38; plot to name him Emperor, VII. xxxii. 38; reveals plot to Bouzes and Constantianus, VII. xxxii. 41; successfully defended by Marcellus, VII. xxxii. 44; and by Constantianus and Bouzes, VII. xxxii. 45; experiences the Emperor's anger, VII. xxxii. 47; saved by Marcellus, VII. xxxii. 48; appointed commander against the Goths, VII. xxxvii. 24; replaced by Liberius, VII. xxxvii. 26; reappointed, VII. xxxix. 9; makes ambitious preparations, VII. xxxix. 11 ff.; parleys with Roman deserters, VII. xxxix. 22; awaited by Diogenes, VII. xxxix. 26, 28; detained by an invasion of Sclaveni, VII. xl. 1-4; by whom he is feared, VII. xl. 4-6; had defeated the Antae, VII. xl. 6; prepares to leave for Italy, VII. xl. 8; dies of disease, VII. xl. 9, 27, VIII. xxi. 1; character and attainments, VII. xxxvii. 24; his sons as commanders, VIII. xxv. 1

Germas, fortress near Germenne, B. IV. iv. 3

Germatza, fortress in Dardania, B. IV. iv. 3.

Germenne, city in southern Europe, B. IV. iv. 3

Geronticê, fortress in Thessaly, B. IV. iv. 3.

Gesilafossatum, fortress in Haemimontum, B. IV. xi. 20

Getic, a name sometimes applied to the Gothic peoples, III. ii. 2, V. xxiv. 30; the "Getic peril," V. xxiv. 29, 30

Getrinas, fortress in Haemimontum, B. IV. xi. 20

Getristaus, fortress in Haemimontum, B. IV. xi. 20

Gezon, Roman infantryman, paymaster of his company, IV. xx. 12; scales the fortress of Toumar, IV. xx. 13–16

Gibal, Gothic commander; sent against Ancon, VIII. xxiii. 1; in command of ships, VIII. xxiii. 12

Gibamundus, nephew of Gelimer, III. xviii. 1; sent to attack the Roman army on the left, *ib.*; his force destroyed at Pedion Halon, III. xviii. 12, 19, xix. 18, 19, xxv. 15

Gibimer, Gothic commander, stationed at Clusium, VI. xi. 1

Gilacius, an Armenian, general in the Roman army, VII. xxvi. 24, 26; captured and put to death by the Goths, VII. xxvi. 25–27

Girgis, city in Africa, B. VI. iv. 14

Giselicus, illegitimate son of Alaric, chosen King of the Visigoths, V. xii. 43; his death, V. xii. 46

Gizeric, King of the Vandals, III. iii. 23, VII. i. 4, B. VI. v. 2; son of Godigisclus and brother of Gontharis, III. iii. 23; father of Honoric, Genzon, and Theodorus, III. v. 6, 11, vi. 24; becomes joint ruler of the Vandals, III. iii. 23; according to one account destroyed his brother, III. iii. 33; his great ability, III. iii. 24; invited to share Libya, III. iii. 25; leads the Vandals into Libya, III. iii. 33; besieges Hippo Regius, III. iii. 32, 34; discovers Marcian among Roman captives, III. iv. 3–8; spares his life and exacts oath, III. iv. 9–10; secures possession of Libya, III. xxi. 16, xxii. 4; makes compact with Valentinian, III. iv. 12–14, xvi. 13; receives back his son, III. iv. 14; receives Vandal ambassadors, III. xxii. 7; refuses their petition, III. xxii. 9–11; makes attempt on Taenarum, III. xxii. 16; massacres Zacynthians, III. xxii. 17–18; invited to punish Maximus, III. iv. 38, 39; despoils Rome, III. v. 1 ff., IV. ix. 5, 8; captures Eudoxia and her daughters, III. v. 3; removes the walls of Libyan cities, III. v. 8, xv. 9; thereby winning ridicule in later times, III. v. 9; destroyed tax records of Libya, IV. viii. 25; enslaves and empoverishes Libyans, III. v. 11, 12; exempts confiscated land from taxation, III. v. 14; with the Moors invades Roman provinces, III. v. 22–25; Aspar urges Basiliscus to spare him, III. vi. 4; favours Olyvrius as Emperor, III. vi. 6; fears Leon, III. vi. 11; persuades Basiliscus to delay, III. vi. 12–16; destroys Roman fleet, III. vi. 17–21; receives Majorinus in disguise, III. vii. 6, 7, 9–10; prepares to meet the army of Majorinus, III. vii. 12; forms a compact with Zenon, III. vii. 26, ix. 23; his death and his will, III. vii. 29–30, ix. 10, xvi. 13; the "law of Gizeric," III. ix. 12

Gladiators, of an earlier period, VI. i. 5

Glones, a Persian, in command of the garrison in Amida, I. vii. 33; destroyed by a strategem, I. ix. 5–17; son of, I. ix. 4, 18

Glutton, epithet of the general John, II. xix. 15, etc.

Glycerius, Emperor of the West; dies after a very short reign, III. vii. 15

Goar, a Gothic captive from Dalmatia;

exiled to Egypt, VIII. xxvii. 5, 6; flies from Byzantium with Ildigisal, VIII. xxvii. 7 ff.; surprises Roman officers, VIII. xxvii. 17; reaches the Gepaedes, VIII. xxvii. 18

Godas, a Goth, slave of Gelimer; sets up a tyranny in Sardinia, III. x. 25–27, xi. 22, xxv. 11; invites Justinian to support him, III. x. 28–31; receives the envoy Eulogius, III. x. 33; sends him back with a letter, III. x. 34; the Vandals send an expedition against him, III. xi. 23, xiv. 9; killed by Tzazon, III. xxiv. 1, 3, IV. ii. 27

Godidisclus, a Goth; officer in the Roman army, I. viii. 3

Godigisclus, chief of the Vandals, III. xxii. 3, 5; allowed by Honorius to settle in Spain, III. iii. 2; succeeded by his sons Gontharis and Gizeric, III. iii. 23

Golden Gate, in the land-wall of Byzantium, B. I. iii. 9, ix. 16

Golden Horn, harbour of Byzantium; beautified by Justinian, B. I. v. 1, vii. 2, viii. 1

Gombes, fortress on the Danube, B. IV. vi. 22

Gomphi, city of Thessaly; fortified by Justinian, B. IV. iii. 5

Gontharis, son of Godigisclus and brother of Gizeric; becomes ruler of the Vandals with his brother, III. iii. 23; his mild character, III. iii. 24; invited by Boniface to share Libya, III. iii. 25; his death, III. iii. 32, 33

Gontharis, Roman commander; occupies Albani, VI. iv. 8

Gontharis, bodyguard of Solomon; sent forward against the Moors, IV. xix. 6, VII. xxxi. 3; camps near the Abigas River, IV. xix. 7; defeated by the Moors and besieged in his camp, IV. xix. 8; receives support from Solomon, IV. xix. 9; attempts to set up a tyranny, IV. xxv. 1 ff.; summoned to Carthage and sent against the Moors, IV. xxv. 4, 5; makes an agreement with Antalas to betray the Romans, IV. xxv. 6, 10; recalls Roman skirmishers, IV. xxv. 14; hears of the treasonable plan of Coutzinas, IV. xxv. 16; persuades Areobindus to postpone the engagement, IV. xxv. 17, 18; reveals the plot to Antalas, IV. xxv. 19; plans to kill Areobindus, IV. xxv. 22; persuades him to join battle with the Moors, IV. xxv. 23 ff.; openly sets about establishing his tyranny, IV. xxv. 28 ff.; summons Athanasius, IV. xxvi. 21; and Areobindus, IV. xxvi. 23; his reception of Areobindus, IV. xxvi. 27–32; has him assassinated, IV. xxvi. 32, 33; offends Antalas by sending him the head of Areobindus, IV. xxvii. 1, 2; receives the mutineers under John, IV. xxvii. 7, 8; removes the wife and sister of Areobindus from the fortress, IV. xxvii. 20; compels Prejecta to write a false report in a letter to Justinian for his own advantage, IV. xxvii. 20–22; sends Artabanes against Antalas, IV. xxvii. 23; Coutzinas sides with him, IV. xxvii. 24; Artabanes determines to kill him, IV. xxvii. 34; prepares a larger army against Antalas, IV. xxvii. 36; destroys many in the city, IV. xxvii. 37, 38; entertains Artabanes and others at a banquet, IV. xxviii. 1 ff.; his murder planned by Artabanes, IV. xxviii. 6 ff.; his death, IV. xxviii. 27–30, VII. xxxi. 2, xxxii. 6

Gorgo, city of the Ephthalitae, against the Persian frontier, I. iii. 2, iv. 10

Gorzoubitae, people on the Euxine, B. III. vii. 11

Gospels, Christian writings; used to witness oaths, IV. xxi. 21, S.H. v. 28

Gothaeus, sent to Spain as envoy by Gelimer, III. xxiv. 7 ff.

Gothigus, patrician and ex-consul; urges Justinian to defend Italy, VII. xxxv. 10

Goths, used regularly to designate the Ostrogoths; called also " Getic," V. xxiv. 30; their fortunes previous to the war with Justinian,

V. i. 1 ff., xv. 28; general description of the Gothic peoples, III. ii. 2 ff.; their migrations, III. ii. 6 ff., VIII. v. 12–14; their common religion and language, III. ii. 5; bounded by the Danube, B. IV. i. 5; inhabit Dory, B. III. vii. 13, 17; followed Arian heresy, VIII. iv. 11; their original home, VIII. v. 5; defeated by the Cimmerians, VIII. v. 11; extent of their sway, S.H. xviii. 16; held Dacia, VII. xxxiv. 10; which was taken away from them, by Justinian, VII. xxxiii. 8, xxxiv. 15; march under Belisarius against Chrosoes, II. xiv. 10, xviii. 24, xxi. 4; enter Pannonia, then settle for a time in Thrace, III. ii. 39; subdue the Western Empire, III. ii. 40; ruled by Theoderic, S.H. xxiv. 9; led into Italy by him, V. xvi. 2, VI. xiv. 24; make no new laws in Italy, VI. vi. 17; tolerant in religious matters, VI. vi. 18; respect churches, VI. vi. 19; allowed Romans to fill offices, ib.; prevented by Amalasuntha from injuring the Romans, V. ii. 5; their leaders hostile to her, V. iii. 11; oppose her efforts to educate Atalaric, V. ii. 8 ff.; grieve at her death, V. iv. 28; defeated in Dalmatia, V. v. 11; enter Dalmatia again, V. vii. 1 ff.; again defeated, V. vii. 27–36; garrison Naples strongly, V. viii. 5; but lose it, V. x. 26; dissatisfied with Theodatus, declare Vittigis King, V. xi. 1, 5; furnish a market in Sicily, III. xiv. 5; refuse to give up Lilybaeum, IV. v. 11; receive letter of remonstrance from Belisarius, IV. v. 12–17; their reply, IV. v. 18–24; form alliance with Franks, V. xii. 24, 25; their crafty hesitation, V. xii. 26, 27; reproached by their allies, V. xii. 31; secure a portion of Gaul, V. xii. 32; mingle with the Visigoths, V. xii. 49; divide Gaul with the Visigoths, V. xiii. 4, 5, 7, 8; remit tribute imposed by Theoderic, V. xiii. 6; their war with the Franks, V. xi. 17, 18, 28; yield Gaul to them, V. xiii. 12; in Italy, attacked by Belisarius, IV. xiv. 1; withdraw from Rome, V. xi. 26, xiv. 12–14; defeat the Romans at the Mulvian Bridge, V. xviii. 3 ff.; establish seven camps about Rome and begin the siege, V. xix. 2–5, 11, xxiv. 26; cut the aqueducts, V. xix. 13; assault the wall, V. xxi.–xxiii; capture Portus, V. xxvi. 14; outwitted in three attacks, V. xxvii. 6–14; again defeated when they try Belisarius' tactics, V. xxvii. 15–23; inferiority of their soldiers to the Romans, V. xxvii. 27; a troublesome Goth killed at the Salarian Gate, V. xxiii. 9–11; defeat the Romans in a pitched battle, V. xxix. 16 ff.; but suffer great losses in the Plain of Nero, VI. ii. 19 ff.; respect the Church of Paul, VI. iv. 10; suffer famine and pestilence, VI. iv. 16, 17; retire from the camp near the Appian Way, VI. iv. 18; decide to abandon the siege, VI. vi. 1, 2; send envoys to Rome, VI. vi. 3; arrange an armistice with Belisarius, VI. vi. 36, vii. 13; abandon Portus, VI. vii. 16, 22; and Centumcellae, VI. vii. 18; and Albani, VI. vii. 20; attempt to enter Rome by stealth, VI. ix. 1 ff.; assault the Pincian Gate, VI. ix. 12 ff.; abandon Ariminum, VI. x. 6; raise the siege of Rome, VI. x. 8, 12, 13; defeated at the Mulvian Bridge, VI. x. 15 ff.; besiege Ariminum, VI. xii. 1 ff.; defeated at Ticinum, VI. xii. 31, 33; besiege Milan, VI. xii. 39, 40; raise the siege of Ariminum, VI. xvii. 21, 22; control Aemilia, VI. xviii. 25; surrender Urbinus, VI. xix. 17; take Milan by surrender, VI. xxi. 38 ff.; become masters of Liguria, VI. xxi. 42; seek alliance with Lombards, VI. xxii. 9–12; decide to stir up Chosroes, VI. xxii. 17; besieged in Auximus, VI. xxiii. 9–xxiv. 17, xxvi. 2–xxvii. 24, 27; surrender to Belisarius, VI. xxvii. 28–34; surrender Fisula, VI. xxvii. 25, 26;

disappointed in the Franks, VI. xxv. 6 ff.; many in the Cottian Alps surrender to Belisarius, VI. xxviii. 28–35; accept terms offered by Justinian, VI. xxix. 3; distrust the Romans, VI. xxix. 6; dissatisfied with Vittigis, wish to make Belisarius king, VI. xxix. 17 ff.; arrange to receive Belisarius into Ravenna, VI. xxix. 24 ff.; attempt a new national government, VI. xxx. 3 ff.; their power reorganized by Ildibadus, VII. i. 25 ff.; take Placentia by surrender, VII. xvi. 3; capture Rome, VII. xx. 14 ff.; and Rusciane, VII. xxx. 21; give Franks a portion of Gaul, VII. xxxiii. 2; whom they cannot restrain, VII. xxxiii. 7; dreaded by the Gepaedes, VII. xxxiv. 10; capture Perusia, VII. xxxv. 2; Gothic captives of Belisarius, VII. i. 12; in the retinue of Belisarius, VII. i. 6; besiege Rome, VII. xxxvi. 1 ff.; capture Portus, VII. xxxvi. 3; besiege Centumcellae, VII. xxxvii. 10–18; invade Sicily, VII. xxxvii. 18; capture Ariminum, VII. xxxvii. 23; fear Germanus as Commander, VII. xxxvii. 24; defeat a Roman force, VII. xxxvii. 28; attack Rhegium, VII. xxxix. 1, 2; plunder all Sicily, VII. xxxix. 4; terrified by reports of Germanus' preparations, VII. xxxix. 21; capture Rome, VIII. xii. 32, 33; offer to relinquish Sicily and Dalmatia, VIII. xxiv. 4; hold small part of Venetia, VIII. xxiv. 8; make alliance with Franks, VIII. xxiv. 9, 10; reported hostile to them, VIII. xxiv. 21, 22; on friendly terms with them, VIII. xxvi. 19; despair of holding Italy, VIII. xxxiv. 3; command the sea, VIII. xxxv. 12, 13; in Italy, S.H. v. 6; the Gothic War, VII. xxxiii. 1, VIII. xxi. 1, 4, xxxv. 38, S.H. v. 16; mentioned, S.H. xvi. 1, xxi. 26; Gothic language, V. x. 10, VII. xxvi. 24; King of, in mosaic at Byzantium, B. I. x. 17

Gouboulgoudou, a Massagete, guard of Valerian; renders signal service at Ancon, VI. xiii. 14, 15

Gourasson, fortress in Macedonia, B. IV. iv. 3

Gourgenes, King of Iberia, revolts from the Persians, I. xii. 4 ff., II. xv. 6, xxviii. 20; retires before the Persian army into Lazica, I. xii. 11, 12

Gousanastades, "Chanaranges"; counsels the execution of Cabades, I. v. 4; put to death by Cabades, I. vi. 18

Graecus, fortress in Remisianisia, B. IV. iv. 3

Grain, importation of, to Byzantium, S.H. xxii. 14–19, xxvi. 22, B. V. i. 7–16; for use of the Eastern cities, S.H. xxii. 14; for use of Alexandria, S.H. xxvi. 37, 40–44; dole to Roman beggars, S.H. xxvi. 29; store-houses at Alexandria protected from rioters, B. VI. i. 4; store-houses built on Tenedus, B. V. i. 7–16

Grandetum, fortress in southern Europe, B. IV. iv. 3

Grapso, fortress in Moesia, B. IV. xi. 20

Grasse, a place in Libya, III. xvii. 8, 14, 17; its pleasant park, III. xvii. 9, 10; distance from Carthage, III. xvii. 8

Gratiana, fortress in Moesia, B. IV. xi. 20

Gratiana, city at the extremity of Illyricum, V. iii. 15, 17

Greece, its works of art brought to Rome, VIII. xxi. 14; visited by earthquakes, VIII. xxv. 16 ff.; fleet sent thither by Totila, VIII. xxii. 17; overrun by barbarians, S.H. xviii. 20; oppressed by Justinian, S.H. xxvi. 33; cut off from Euboea, B. IV. iii. 17; plundered by the Huns, II. iv. 11; by Gizeric, III. v. 23; diligently fortified by Justinian, B. IV. ii. 1, 12, 15, 23 ff.; buildings by Justinian in, B. IV. viii. 1

Greeks, of an earlier age; led by Agamemnon, VIII. xxii. 27, 28; traitors at Thermopylae, B. IV. ii. 8; descendants of the ancient Hellenes, S.H. xi. 31; some become Christians, S.H. xi. 32; mistreated by Alexander, S.H. xxvi. 30–34; term of contempt, IV. xxvii. 38, V. xviii. 40, xxix. 11, VII. ix. 12, xxi. 4, 12, 13, S.H. xxiv. 7; "Greeklings," VIII. xxiii. 25; Greek language, VIII. xiv. 48, S.H. xx. 17; ancient Greek faith, *see* Paganism

Green Faction, one of the parties of the Circus; their struggles with the Blue Faction, I. xxiv. 2–6; in the Nika insurrection, I xxiv. 7 ff.; their excesses, S.H. vii. 4, 26; their outlandish costumes, S.H. vii. 8 ff.; their keeper of animals, S.H. ix. 2, 5; reject supplication of Theodora's mother, S.H. ix. 7; singled out for punishment, S.H. xi. 36, xviii. 34; mentioned, S.H. xvi. 18, 23, xvii. 41, xix. 11; favoured by Chosroes at Apamea, II. xi. 32

Gregorius, nephew of Artabanes; with him plans the murder of Gontharis, IV. xxviii. 7–9; urges Artabanes to carry out the plot, [illegible] in the banquet-hall, IV. xxviii. 14; restrains Artasires, IV. xxviii. 16

Gregory, Saint; Monastery of, in Jerusalem, B.V. ix. 2

Gribo, fortress in Aquenisium, B. IV. iv. 3

Grinciapana, fortress in Remisianisia, B. IV. iv. 3

Gripas, Gothic commander, in Dalmatia, V. vii. 1; defeated by Constantianus, V. vii. 27–36; retires to Ravenna, V. vii. 36

Groffes, fortress in southern Europe, B. IV. iv. 3

Gubazes, King of Lazica, VIII. viii. 1; "silentiarius" *in absentia*, II. xxix. 31; surrenders his people to Chosroes, II. xvii. 2 ff.; plotted against by Phabrizus, II. xxix. 2 ff.; begs Justinian for help, II. xxix. 9; with Dagisthaeus besieges Petra, II. xxix. 11 ff.; defends one pass against the Persians, II. xxix. 28 ff.; asks Justinian to send money to the Alani and the Sabeiri, II. xxix. 30; Chosroes plans to put him out of the way, II. xxviii. 30, xxix. 2 ff.; rewarded with money by Justinian, II. xxx. 28; with Dagisthaeus attacks and almost annihilates the Persians, II. xxx. 39 ff.; addresses the Lazic troops, VIII. viii. 6–13; leads the Lazi to the attack, VIII. viii. 14 ff.; fights against the Persians, VIII. viii. 29; hostile to Terdetes, VIII. x. 2; wins back the rebellious Apsilii, VIII. x. 7; friendly to the Romans, VIII. xvi. 2; hides in the mountains, VIII. xvi. 6, 20, 21; false report of his defeat, VIII. xvi. 7; flees before the Persians, VIII. xvi. 19; receives a letter from Mermeroes, VIII. xvi. 23; but is obdurate, VIII. xvi. 32; hostile to Chosroes, *ib.*; with the Roman army, VIII. xvii. 13; his mother a Roman woman, VIII. ix. 9; nephew of Opsites, VIII. ix. 7; the sister of, VIII. xvii. 14

Gudilas, a Thracian; Roman commander, VII. xxx. 6; a guardsman, sent as envoy to Totila, VII. xxx. 19

Gundamundus, son of Genzon, becomes King of the Vandals, III. viii. 6; his reign and death, III. viii. 7; brother of Trasamundus, III. viii. 8

Gundulf, Gothic commander; sent against Ancon, VIII. xxiii. 1; former guardsman of Belisarius, *ib.*; in command of ships, VIII. xxiii. 12; escapes from battle, VIII. xxiii. 38; *see* Indulf

Gurbicum, fortress in southern Europe, B. IV. iv. 3

Guzes, surname of John the Armenian, *q.v.*

Gynaecomites, fortress in Epirus, B. IV. iv. 3

Hadrian, Tomb of, in Rome, V. xxii. 12; its excellent construction and decoration, V. xxii. 13, 14; attacked by the Goths, V. xxii. 19 ff.; statues thereof hurled upon attackers, V. xxii. 22; used as a fortress by Totila, VIII. xxxiii. 14; by Paulus, VII. xxxvi. 17–23

INDEX

Hadrumetum (Adramytus), city in Libya, III. xvii. 8, IV. xxvii. 26, 31, 33; taken by the Moors, IV. xxiii. 11–15; recovered by Paulus, a priest, IV. xxiii. 18–25, 29; guarded for the Emperor, IV. xxvii. 6; dismantled by the Vandals, B. VI. vi. 1–5; restored by Justinian, B. VI. vi. 6; called Justinianê in his honour, B. VI. vi. 7

Haemimontum, region of Thrace, fortresses built by Justinian in, B. IV. xi. 18, 20

Halicaniburgu, fortress on the Danube, B. IV. vi. 18

Halicarnassus, home of Herodotus, VIII. vi. 12

Halmyris, fortress in Scythia; restored by Justinian, B. IV. vii. 20

Hamaxobii, Scythian tribe, B. IV. i. 5

Hannibal, Carthaginian General; his memorable defeat of the Romans, VII. xviii. 19; his camp used by Totila, VII. xxii. 24

Harmata, fortress on the Danube, B. IV. vi. 18

Harmatus, Roman General; marches against Zenon, III. vii. 20; surrenders to him, III. vii. 21; killed by Zenon, III. vii. 23

Hebdomum, suburb of Byzantium, B. I. iv. 28, viii. 15, ix. 16

Hebrews, their migration from Egypt to Palestine, IV. x. 13; History of the, IV. x. 17; Hebrew scripture quoted by Gelimer, IV. ix. 11; laws of the, S.H. xxviii. 16; their King Solomon, B. VI. ii. 22; treasures of Solomon taken from Rome by Alaric, V. xii. 42; a certain Hebrew makes a prophecy, V. ix. 3–6; oppressed by Justinian, S.H. xxviii. 17; of Iotabe; formerly autonomous, become subject to the Romans, I. xix. 4; *see also* Jews

Hebrus River, crossed by the Sclaveni, VII. xxxviii. 1

Hecebolus, magistrate of Pentapolis, dismisses Theorora, S.H. ix. 27, xii. 30

Hedones, fortress in Epirus, B. IV. iv. 3

Hedonia, fortress in Epirus, B. IV. iv. 3

Helega, fortress in Epirus, B. IV. iv. 3

Helen, mother of Constantine, B. V. ii. 1; born in Bithynia, B. V. ii. 2; Palace of, in Byzantium, I. xxiv. 30

Helenopolis, station on the Post Route, S.H. xxx. 8

Hellas, VIII. ii. 15

Hellenic Faith, *see* Paganism

Hellespont, strait between Sestus and Abydus, III. i. 7; beside the Thracian Chersonese, V. xv. 18; approached from Rhaedestus, B. IV. ix. 17; narrowness of its strait, B. V. i. 8; Customs House established on, S.H. xxv. 2 ff.; winds at the, B. V. i. 12; bridged by Xerxes, B. V. iii. 8

Hellestheaeus, King of the Ethiopians, his expeditions against the Homeritae, I. xx. 1 ff.; his vain promises to Justinian, I. xx. 9 ff.

Hemerium, town in Euphratesia, B. II. ix. 10

Hephaestus, Magistrate of Alexandria; oppresses the people, S.H. xxvi. 35–44

Heraclea, city on the Aegean; ancient Perinthus, III. xii. 6, B. IV. ix. 14; restored by Justinian, B. IV. ix. 15, 16; distance from Rhaedestus, B. IV. ix. 17

Heraclea, city on the Euxine, VIII. ii. 2

Heraclea, city of northern Greece; fortified by Justinian, B. IV. ii. 17, 21, 22

Heracles, wrestled with Antaeus in Clipea, IV. x. 24; Pillars of, Gibraltar, III. i. 5, 9, etc.

Heracleius, Roman general; defeats the Vandals in Tripolis, III. vi. 9; returns to Byzantium, III. vi. 25

Heraeum, *see* Hieron.

Hercula, fortress in southern Europe, B. IV. iv. 3

Heresy, variation from Christian doctrine, S.H. xi. 14, 16, xviii. 34, xix. 11, xxvii. 5; of Eutyches, III. vii. 22

Hermegisclus, ruler of the Varni, VIII. xx. 11; marries the sister of Theudibert, *ib.*; foretells his own

death, VIII. xx. 13 ff.; his death, VIII. xx. 21
Hermenefridus, ruler of the Thuringians and father of Amalafridas, VIII. xxv. 11; betrothed to Amalaberga, V. xii. 22; killed by the Franks, V. xiii. 1; wife of, escapes to Theodatus, V. xiii. 2
Hermes, called "Mercury" by the Romans, III. vi. 10; town of Hermes or Mercurium, on the coast of Libya, III. vi. 10, xvii. 15, xx. 10
Hermione, town in Byzacium; distance from the coast, III. xiv. 10, xvii. 4, 11
Hermogenes, Roman general, sent to assist Belisarius, I. xiii. 10; in company with Belisarius prepares to meet the Persians at Daras, I. xiii. 12 ff.; at the battle of Daras, I. xiii. 19 ff.; forbids Andreas to engage in single combat, I. xiii. 35; interchange of letters with Perozes, I. xiv. 1 ff.; address to the troops, I. xiv. 20 ff.; arrays the army on the second day of the battle of Daras, I. xiv. 44; recalls Romans from pursuit of the Persians, I. xiv. 53; returns to Byzantium, I. xvi. 10; sent as ambassador by the Emperor, I. xviii. 16; negotiates unsuccessfully with Chosroes, I. xxi. 1; accompanies the army of Sittas as ambassador, I. xxi. 10, 23; ambassador to Chosroes with Rufinus, I. xxii. 16
Hermogenes, father of Saturninus, S.H. xvii. 32
Herodian, Roman commander of infantry, V. v. 3, VI. xvi. 21; left in command of garrison in Naples, V. xiv. 1; accompanies Belisarius to Byzantium, VII. i. 1; commander of Thracians, VII. vi. 10; sent to Naples, VII. vii. 3; escapes capture, VII. vii. 7; commander of Spolitium, VII. xii. 12; parleys with the Goths, VII. xii. 13; surrenders the town, VII. xii. 15, xxiii. 3; his fear of Belisarius, VII. xii. 16; praised by Totila, VII. xxi. 15, 16; driven to treason by Belisarius, S.H. v. 5, 6; commander of Goths in Cumae, VIII. xxxiv. 19
Herodotus, cited as authority, VIII. vi. 12–15
Hestia, *i.e.* Vesta; identified with the Persian fire divinity, II. xxiv. 2
Hierapolis, city on the Euphrates, I. xiii. 11, xvii. 22; distance from Beroea and Antioch, II. vii. 2; Bouzes and the Roman army stationed there, II. vi. 2; suggested plan for its defence, II. vi. 3 ff.; deserted by Bouzes, II. vi. 7, 8; saved from Chosroes by payment of money, II. vi. 22–24; Justus and Bouzes take refuge there, II. xx. 20; strengthened by Justinian, B. II. ix. 12–17
Hieron, or Heraeum, suburb of Byzantium, III. i. 8, VIII. vi. 17, 19, 25, 28, S.H. xv. 36, xxv. 2, B. I. iii. 10, ix. 13, xi. 22; site of a Palace, B. I. xi. 16
Hilara, her property "inherited" by Justinian, S.H. xii. 5
Himerius, a Thracian, commander in Byzacium, captured by Moors, IV. xxiii. 3–5; guarded by them, IV. xxiii. 10; puts Hadrumetum into their hands, IV. xxiii. 10–15; escapes to Carthage, IV. xxiii. 17; Commander of Rhegium, VII. xxxvii. 20; surrenders to the Goths, VII. xxxix. 5
Hippis River, in Lazica, VIII. i. 6, viii. 1, 2
Hippo Regius, a strong city of Numidia, III. iii. 31, IV. iv. 32; besieged by the Vandals, III. iii. 32, 34; distance from Carthage, IV. iv. 26; Boniface the Libyan captured there, IV. iv. 34, 36, 39
Hoamer, nephew of Ilderic; acts as his general, III. ix. 2; imprisoned by Gelimer, III. ix. 9; blinded by Gelimer, III. ix. 14, 17; his death, III. xvii. 12
Holodoris, fortress in southern Europe B. IV. iv. 3
Holoverum, a trade-name for purple dye, S.H. xxv. 21
Homer, Homeric bowmen compared with contemporaries, I. i. 9–11; his testimony as to Circe's location, V. xi. 2, 4; as to the island

of Calypso, VIII. xxii. 21; quoted, B. I. i. 15

Homeritae, a Saracen tribe, B. V. viii. 2; sought as allies by Justinian, I. xix. 1, xx. 9 ff.; location of their country, I. xix. 15; domestic conflicts and intervention of Hellestheaeus, I. xx. 1 ff.

Homonoia, fortress in Epirus, B. IV. iv. 3

Honoriatae, neighbours of the Bithynians, VIII. ii. 2

Honoric, son of Gizeric; given as a hostage to Valentinian, III. iv. 13; returned, III. iv. 14; marries Eudocia, III. v. 6; receives Libyan slaves, III. v. 11; succeeds to the throne of the Vandals, III. viii. 1, xxi. 19; makes war on the Moors, III. viii. 1, 2; persecutes the Christians, III. viii. 3, 4; his death, III. viii. 5; father of Ilderic, III. ix. 1; in his reign the church of St. Cyprian taken by the Arians, III. xxi. 19

Honorius, Emperor of the West, uncle of Theodosius II; unable to assist him, I. ii. 4; son of Theodosius, III. i. 2, ii. 1; brother of Arcadius and of Placidia, III. iii. 4; his realm overrun by barbarians, III. ii. 1; retires to Ravenna, III. ii. 8, 9; accused of bringing in the Visigoths, III. ii. 10; his stupid remark upon learning of the fall of Rome, III. ii. 25, 26; dethroned by Attalus, III. ii. 28; prepares for flight, III. ii. 32; his good fortune in extreme peril, III. ii. 34–37; allows the Vandals to settle in Spain, III. iii. 2; refuses them ownership of the land, III. iii. 3; shares royal power with Constantius, III. iii. 4; his death, *ib.*

Hormisdas, House of, in Byzantium, B. I. iv. 1, 2, x. 4

Horonon, fortress in Tzanica, B. III. vi. 16, 18

Huns, a nomadic people; of ugly countenance, I. iii. 4; their homeland north of the Euxine Sea, I. x. 6, xii. 7, II. xv. 3, xxviii. 22, VIII. iii. 5, iv. 7, v. 27; bordering on the Danube, B. IV. i. 5; make invasions through the Caucasus, VIII. iii. 3; their war with Cabades, I. viii. 19, ix. 24, x. 15, II. xvi. 3, B. II. i. 5, 6; Justinian attempts to win their support, II. i. 14, iii. 47, x. 16, S.H. xi. 12; capture a Roman spy, I. xv. 6; invade Pallenê, B. IV. iii. 22; control Bosporus, B. III. vii. 12; menace Rhodopê, B. IV. xi. 11; feared by the Persians at Martyropolis, I. xxi. 27; invade Roman territory, I. xxi. 28; often defeated by Dagaris, I. xxii. 19; receive annual payments from the Romans, II. x. 23, S.H. viii. 5, 6, xi. 5; held back by the Lazi, II. xv. 3; in the army of Chosroes, II. xxvi. 5; assist the Romans in the defence of Edessa, II. xxvi. 25, 26; invade Europe, II. iv. 4 ff.; cross the Hellespont into Asia, II. iv. 9; plunder Illyricum and Greece, II. iv. 10–12; fighting in the Roman army, V. iii. 15, v. 4, xxvii. 2, 27, VII. vi. 10; led by Constantinus in a successful skirmish, VI. i. 4–10; encamp at the Church of Paul, VI. iv. 11; harass the Goths, VI. iv. 16; return to Rome, VI. iv. 18; invade Illyricum, VII. xi. 15; frequent invasions of, VII. xiv. 2, S.H. xviii. 20, xxi. 26; Justinian opposes the Antae to them, VII. xiv. 33; Hunnic soldiers asked for by Belisarius, VII. xii. 10; give shelter to Opsites, VIII. ix. 29; in the Persian army, VIII. xvii. 10, 11; their alliance sought by the Gepaedes, VIII. xviii. 13 ff.; ferried over the Ister by the Gepaedes, VIII. xviii. 17; receive a message from Justinian, VIII. xix. 3; come as refugees to Roman territory, VIII. xix. 6; in the army of Narses, VIII. xxvi. 13, xxx. 18, xxxi. 3; invade Thrace, VIII. xxi. 22, xxii. 1; sent against the Armenians, S.H. ii. 29; their losses, S.H. xviii. 25, 26; plunder Europe, S.H. xxiii. 6, 8; once called Cimmerians, VIII. v. 1; women found fighting in their armies, VIII. iii. 10;

INDEX

Hunnic mode of hair-dressing, S.H. vii. 10; and of clothing, S.H. vii. 14; altogether illiterate, VIII. xix. 8; the Hunnic character, VII. xiv. 28; Odolgan a Hun, VII. xxiii. 6; *see* Massagetae, Sabeiri, Cutrigurs

Hydrus, contemporary name of Dryus, *q.v.* V. xv. 20

Hygea, fortress in Macedonia, B. IV. iv. 3

Hylasianae, fortress in Haemimontum, B. IV. xi. 20

Hymauparubri, fortress in Thrace, B. IV. xi. 20

Hypatê, city of Northern Greece; fortified by Justinian, B. IV. ii. 16

Hypatius, Roman general; nephew of Anastasius, I. viii. 2; brother of Pompeius and uncle of John, VII. xxxi. 14; his army routed by Cabades, I. viii. 10–18; his escape, I. viii. 19; sent as envoy to the Persians, I. xi. 24; slandered by Rufinus, I. xi. 38; his punishment, I. xi. 39; excluded from the Palace by Justinian, I. xxiv. 19–21; declared Emperor by the populace, I. xxiv. 22 ff.; his wife Mary, I. xxiv. 23; takes the Emperor's seat in the Hippodrome, I. xxiv. 42; brought before Justinian, I. xxiv. 53; meets his death bravely, I. xxiv. 55, 56

Hypatius, priest of Ephesus; envoy of Justinian, V. iii. 5, 13, 29

Hypatius, a notable citizen, slain by Factionists, S.H. ix. 35

Ia, Saint; shrine of, near the Golden Gate, B. I. ix. 16

Iatron, fortress in Moesia; restored by Justinian, B. IV. vii. 6

Iaudas, ruler of Moors on Mt. Aurasius, IV. xii. 29, xxv. 2; an able warrior, IV. xiii. 13; plunders Numidia, IV. xiii. 1; engages with Althias, IV. xiii. 10–16; Solomon marches against him, IV. xiii. 18; accused before Solomon, IV. xiii. 19; slays Mephanius, *ib.*; establishes himself on Mt. Aurasius, IV. xiii. 21; with the mutineers of Stotzas, IV. xvii. 8; Solomon marches against him, IV. xix. 5; remains on Mt. Aurasius, IV. xix. 19, 21; escapes wounded, IV. xx. 21; expelled from Mt. Aurasius, B. VI. vii. 7; subjugated by John, VIII. xvii. 21; had deposited treasures, IV. xx. 24

Iberia, region at the eastern end of the Euxine, VIII. ii. 20, xvi. 14; near Lazica, VIII. ii. 24, xiii. 12, 15, 21; adjoins the Caucasus, VIII. ii. 26; road from, into Lazica, VIII. xiii. 5; its passes seized by Mermeroes, VIII. xiii. 3

Iberians, a Christian people; side with the Romans, I. xii. 2 ff., II. xv. 6; rule over the Meschi, VIII. ii. 24; come to Byzantium, I. xii. 14; given choice of remaining or returning to their homes, I. xxii. 16; dissatisfied with Persian rule, II. xxviii. 20, 21; Monastery of the, in Jerusalem, B. V. ix. 6; Phazas an Iberian, VII. vi. 10, xxviii. 5; and Peranius, V. v. 3

Ibida, city in Scythia; restored by Justinian, B. IV. vii. 19

Ibora, city in Asia; destroyed by earthquake, S.H. xviii. 42

Idriphthon, fortress in Mesopotamia, B. II. iv. 14

Ilderic, son of Honoric, becomes king of the Vandals, III. ix. 1; an unwarlike ruler, *ib.*; uncle of Hoamer, III. ix. 2; suspected plot of the Goths against him, III. ix. 4; on terms of special friendship with Justinian, III. ix. 5; makes large gifts to Apollinarius, IV. v. 8; allows Gelimer to encroach upon his authority, III. ix. 8; dethroned and imprisoned, III. ix. 8, 9, 14, 17; killed in prison by Ammatas, III. xvii. 11, 12; his sons and other offspring receive rewards from Justinian and Theodora, IV. ix. 13

Ildibadus, Gothic commander of Verona; sends envoys to Belisarius, VI. xxix. 41; suggested for the kingship of the Goths, VI. xxx. 14; summoned from Verona, xxx. 16; declared king, VI. xxx. 17; addresses the Goths, VI. xxx. 18 ff.; sends envoys to Belisarius, promising to obey him as king, VI. xxx. 25, 26; receives the report of his envoys, VI. xxx. 29; his children taken to Byzantium by Belisarius, VII. i. 1; reorganizes the Gothic power, VII. i. 25–27, iv. 12; defeats Vitalius, VII. i. 34, 35; increasing his fame thereby, VII. i. 36; becomes hostile to Uraïas, VII. i. 37 ff.; slays him, VII. i. 41; reproached by the Goths, VII. i. 42; offends Velas, VII. i. 43 ff.; slain by him, VII. i. 47–49, ii. 4, 8, 10; hopes of the Goths in him, VII. ii. 5; they sorrow for his loss, VII. ii. 11; nephew of Theudis, VI. xxx. 15; uncle of Totila, VII. ii. 7

Ildibert, ruler of the Franks; sanctions treaty with Theodatus, V. xiii. 27

Ildiger, son-in-law of Antonina, IV. viii. 24; in the army of Martinus, II. xxiv. 13; sent to Libya with an army, IV. viii. 24; made joint-commander of Carthage, IV. xv. 49; at the battle of Scalae Veteres, IV. xvii. 6, 19; comes to Rome, VI. vii. 15; with Valerian seizes Constantinus, VI. viii. 16; on guard at the Pincian Gate, VI. ix. 13; meets a Gothic attack, VI. ix. 14; sent to Ariminum, VI. xi. 4, 8, 21; assists at the capture of Petra, VI. xi. 10–19; leaves Ariminum, VI. xi. 22; sent in command of a fleet to Ariminum, VI. xvi. 22; takes possession of the Gothic camp, VI. xviii. 1; slighted by John, VI. xviii. 2, 3; sent to guard the Po, VI. xxviii. 24; accompanies Belisarius to Byzantium, VII. i. 1

Ildiges, a Lombard prince; son of Risiulfus; flees to the Sclaveni, VII. xxxv. 16; and thence to the Gepedes, VII. xxxv. 19; his surrender demanded by Audouin, VII. xxxv. 20; returns to the Sclaveni, VII. xxxv. 21; starts to join Totila, VII. xxxv. 22; defeats a Roman force and recrosses the Danube, *ib.*; *see also* Ildigisal

Ildigisal, a Lombard, goes as a fugitive to Byzantium, VIII. xxvii. 1; kindly received by Justinian, VIII. xxvii. 2; demanded by Auduin, VIII. xxvii. 4; flies from Byzantium with Goar, VIII. xxvii. 5 ff.; surprises Roman officers, VIII. xxvii. 17; reaches the Gepaedes, VIII. xxvii. 18; his surrender demanded by Justinian and Auduin, VIII. xxvii. 22; slain by Thorisin, VIII. xxvii. 28, 29; *see also* Ildiges

Ilium, capture of, V. xv. 8, 9; entered by Diomedes and Odysseus as spies, V. xv. 9

Illus, a rebel, B. III. i. 25, 26

Illyricum, adjoins Greece, B. IV. ii. 17; and Thrace, III. xi. 21; borders upon Moesia, B. IV. vii. 3; invaded by the Huns, II. iv. 5, 10, VII. xi. 15; plundered by Gizeric, III. v. 23; by the Sclaveni, VII. xxix. 1–3, xxxviii. 3, 7, 19, VIII. xxv. 1 ff.; by the Lombards, VII. xxxiii. 12; by the Eruli, VII. xxxiii. 13; at the mercy of barbarians, VII. xxix. 3, xxxiii. 1, xxxiv. 46, S.H. xviii. 20; Mundus General of, V. v. 2; Constantianus sent to, V. vii. 26; Justinus General of, VI. xiii. 17; Eruli settled in, VI. xv. 1.; its Prefect Archelaus, III. xi. 17; Illyrians in the Roman army, VII. x. 2, xi. 11, xxx. 6; abandon Vitalius, VII. xi. 13, 14, 16; commanded by Nazares, VII. xi. 18; the region canvassed for recruits by Belisarius, VII. xii. 4; threatened by Totila, VII. xxi. 19; Belisarius reported to be in, VII. xxxii. 19; searched for fugitives, VIII. xxvii. 9, 12; soldiers recruited there by Germanus, VII. xxxix. 9, 17; John General of, VII. xxxix. 10; mountains of, crossed by the Sclaveni, VII. xl. 7; said to be the limit of the Caucasus, VIII. iii. 3; traversed by the Ister, VIII. v. 30, xviii. 17; soldiers recruited in, VIII. xxvi. 10; Generals of, S.H. xxi. 26; fortified by Justinian, B. IV. v. 1, vi. 18, 36, 37, vii. 1; fortresses of, B. IV. vi. 34; buildings by Justinian in, B. IV. viii. 1;

Archbishop of, B. IV. i. 25; its cities: Sardice, VII. xl. 1; Ulpania, VIII. xxv. 13; Gratiana, V. iii. 15; home of Peter, V. iii. 30; Justinus an Illyrian, S.H. vi. 2
Illyrin, fortress in Epirus, B. IV. iv. 3
Illyrisum, pass into Sophanene, B. III. iii. 4
Immortals, a detachment of the Persian army, I. xiv. 31; at the battle of Daras, I. xiv. 44 ff.
Indaro, a dancing-girl, S.H. xvii. 34
India, washed by the "Red Sea," I. xix. 3; source (sic) of the Nile, B. VI. i. 6; tale of its boats built without iron, I. xix. 23, 24; iron neither produced nor imported, I. xix. 24, 25; its export of silk, I. xx. 9, 12; silkworms introduced from, VIII. xvii. 1. ff.; its trade with Doubios, II. xxv. 3
Indulf, bodyguard of Belisarius; deserts to Totila, VII. xxxv. 23; sent to Dalmatia with an army and fleet, VII. xxxv. 24; raids Mouicurum, VII. xxxv. 25, 26; and Laureate, VII. xxxv. 26–29; retires to northern Italy, VIII. xxxv. 37; called also Gundulf, *q.v.*, VIII. xxiii. 2
Innocentius, Roman commander of cavalry, V. v. 3, xvii. 17; Commander of Portus, VII. xv. 1, 7; receives reinforcements, VII. xv. 1
Inscriptions mentioned or quoted, II. xii. 26, S.H. viii. 14; Greek, VIII. xxi. 13, xxii. 23–29; Phoenician, IV. x. 22
Ionian Gulf, the modern Adriatic Sea; described, V. xv. 16 ff.; B. IV. i. 11; its size and width, III. i. 12; its distance from the Pillars of Heracles, III. i. 15; its tides, V. i. 19; mentioned, II. iv. 4; V. i. 13, VIII. xxxiv. 10, 23; S.H. xviii. 20
Ionians, as sailors in the African expedition, III. xi. 14
Iotabe, an island in the "Red Sea," I. xix. 3
Iouce, place on the African coast; distance from Carthage, III. xv. 8
Iourphouthes, Moorish ruler; joins in an attack upon a Roman force, IV. x. 6 ff.
Iphigeneia, daughter of Agamemnon, VIII. xxii. 27; flees from the sanctuary of Artemis, I. xvii. 11 ff.; priestess in Tauris, VIII. v. 23; temple dedicated to her by Orestes, I. xvii. 18
Iris River, in Pontus, I. xvii. 14
Isaac, an Armenian, brother of Aratius and Narses, VII. xiii. 20; betrays Bolum to the Romans and comes to Byzantium, I. xv. 32, 33; commander in Armenia, II. xxiv. 14; rescues Narses from the battle of Anglon, II. xxv. 24; sent to Belisarius, VII. xiii. 20; joins forces with him, VII. xviii. 1; placed in command of Portus, VII. xix. 7; disobeys instructions, VII. xix. 24, 32; crosses the river and attacks a Gothic camp, VII. xix. 24–28; captured by the Goths, VII. xix. 29, 30; executed by Totila, VII. xix. 34
Isauria, district of Asia Minor; its town Apadnas, B. V. ix. 33
Isaurians, wage war against Anastasius, S.H. vi. 4; serving in the Roman army, I. xviii. 5; commanded by Longinus and Stephanacius, I. xviii. 7; at the battle on the Euphrates, I. xviii. 38; their inexperience in war, I. xviii. 39; in the Italian army of Belisarius, V. v. 2; commanded by Ennes, V. v. 3, x. 1; render signal service at the capture of Naples, V. ix. 11 ff., 17–21, x. 1; a force of, reaches Naples, VI. v. 1; arrives in the harbour of Rome, VI. vii. 1; they fortify a camp, VI. vii. 2; guard ships at Ostia, VI. vii. 9; remain in Ostia, VI. vii. 12, 16; occupy Portus, VI. vii. 16, 22; occupy Ancon, VI. xi. 5; with John at Ariminum, VI. xii. 6, 9; sent to Milan under Ennes, VI. xii. 26, 27; sent against Fisula, VI. xxiii. 2; sent to destroy the cistern at Auximus, VI. xxvii. 5 ff.; in Conon's garrison at Naples, VII. vi. 2; form the garrison of Tibur, VII. x. 19–21; four Isaurians negotiate with Totila, VII. xx. 4–10, 12, 13; open the Asinarian Gate to the

Goths, VII. xx. 14, 15, xxi. 15, 16; betray Rome to Totila, VII. xxxvi. 7–14; the following individuals are named: Athenodorus, V. xxix. 20, Longinus, B. III. vi. 23, Mindes, VII. xxxvi. 26; Isaurian javelins, V. xxix. 42
Iscus, town near the Danube; fortified by Justinian, B. IV. vi. 33
Isdigerdes, Persian King, guardian of Theodosius, I. ii. 7 ff.
Isdigousnas, important Persian official, II. xxviii. 16; employed by Chosroes, II. xxviii. 17; attempts a strategem against Daras, II. xxviii. 31 ff.; continues to Byzantium as envoy, II. xxviii. 38 ff.; his unbearable arrogance, VIII. xi. 4–7; makes trivial protest to Justinian, VIII. xi. 10, xv. 1 ff.; secures the return of Bersabus, VIII. xv. 11; departs from Byzantium highly honoured, VIII. xv. 19, 20; reports to Chosroes, VIII. xvii. 9
Isgipera, fortress in Thrace, B. IV. xi. 20
Isidorus of Miletus, master-builder; one of the builders of the Church of Sophia, B. I. i. 24, 50, 70, II. iii. 7
Isidorus of Miletus, nephew of the preceding, master-builder; his services at Zenobia, B. II. viii. 25
Isidorus, the House of, in Byzantium, B. I. ii. 17
Isis, worshipped by the Blemyes and Nobatae, I. xix. 35
Ister River, called also the Danube, III. i. 10, ii. 6; Roman boundary, B. IV. i. 4, 14; boundary of Pannonia, V. xv. 27; Antae settled near its banks, V. xxvii. 2, VII. xiv. 30; borders the settlements of the Sclaveni, VI. xxvi. 19, VII. xiv. 30; its course described, VIII. v. 30, B. IV. i. 12, v. 9, 10; distance from Cherson, VIII. v. 29; bridged by Trajan, B. IV. vi. 11 ff.; destroys Trajan's bridge, B. IV. vi. 14; guarded by the Romans, VIII. xviii. 17; crossed by the Sclaveni, VII. xiii. 24, xxix. 1, xxxviii. 1, 8, xl. 1, 2, 31, VIII. xxv. 5, 10; by the Antae, VII. xl. 5; by the Goths, III. ii. 39, VIII. v. 12; by the Cutrigurs, VIII. v. 16, xviii. 17; by the Lombards, VII. xxxiii. 11; guarded by Chilbudius, VII. xiv. 2, 3; recrossed by Ildiges, VII. xxxv. 22; fortified by Justinian, B. IV. i. 33, 34, v. 1 ff., vii. 1, viii. 1, xi. 20; its line of forts, B. IV. vi. 1, 34, vii. 10, 15; mentioned, VII. xiv. 32, xxxiv. 10, 13, xxxix. 19, VIII. xx. 2, xxv. 6, B. IV. vi. 10; *see* Danube
Isthmus of Corinth, V. xv. 17, B. IV. ii. 1.
Istria, adjoining Liburnia and Venetia, V. xv. 25; Roman fugitives rally in VII. xxxix. 24
Itaberies, fortress in Cabetzus, B. IV. iv. 3
Itadeba, fortress in Cabetzus, B. IV. iv. 3
Italians, often coupled with "Goths," V. i. 1, etc.; their love for Theoderic, V. i. 29; grieve at the death of Amalasuntha, V. iv. 28; oppressed by Alexander, VII. i. 32, 33; said to repent "betraying" the Goths, VII. iv. 16; suffer grievously, VII. vi. 7, ix. 2–4, xviii. 20; their condition improved, VII. xviii. 22, 23; at Rusciane, spared by Totila, VII. xxx. 24; urge Justinian to defend Italy, VII. xxxv. 9; Deopheron an Italian, VII. xxx. 19; in the army of Narses, VIII. xxvi. 20
Italy, description of the land and people, V. xv. 16, 21–25; skirted by the Ister, VIII. v. 30; separated from Sicily by a narrow strait, VIII. vi. 21; from Gaul by the Alps, VI. xxv. 5; its cities and people destroyed by the Visigoths, III. ii. 11, 12; invaded by Gizeric, III. v. 1 ff., 22, 23; by the Goths, VIII. v. 14, B. III. vii. 13; won by Justinian, II. i. 1, B. II. x. 1, claimed by the barbarians, V. i. 4, VI. vi. 15, 17; neglected by the Romans, VI. vi. 21; offered by Amalasuntha to Justinian, V. iii. 28, iv. 18; and by Theodatus, V. vi. 21; desired by the Franks, VI. xxv. 1, xxviii. 7, 15; invaded by Theudibert, VI. xxv. 2–23;

left by him, VI. xxvi. 1; Belisarius Commander in, VII. i. 16, etc.; its revenues taken by Totila, VII. xii. 6, xiii. 1; lost to the Romans, VII. xxxiii. 1; said to be held largely by the Franks, VIII. xxiv. 4; whose departure is demanded, VIII. xxiv. 11; desired by them, VIII. xxxiv. 18; relinquished by the Goths, VIII. xxxv. 36; Belisarius sent thither, S.H. iv. 39; abandoned by him, S.H. v. 17; exploited by Justinian, S.H. v. 4, vi. 25; devastated, S.H. xviii. 13, 14; oppressed by Alexander S.H. xxiv. 9; mentioned, S.H. i. 34, etc.; cities of, in mosaic at Byzantium, B. I. x. 16

Ithaca, home of Odysseus, VIII. xxii. 23

Itzes, fortress in Moesia, B. IV. xi. 20

Jacobus, a holy man among the Syrians, I. vii. 5 ff.

Janus, one of the older Roman gods, V. xxv. 19; Temple of, in Rome, V. xxv. 18, 19; his double-faced statue, V. xxv. 20, 21

Jason, his adventures with Medea, II. xvii. 2, VIII. ii. 31; stole the Golden Fleece, VIII. ii. 15; shared in slaying Apsyrtus, VIII. ii. 12

Jebusites, ancient people of Phoenicia, IV. x. 17; emigrate to Egypt and thence to Libya, IV. x. 18, 19

Jericho, city in Palestine, B. V. ix. 4, 5

Jerusalem, scene of Christ's suffering, II. xi. 14; captured by Titus, IV. ix. 5, V. xii. 42; receives back the treasures of the Temple, IV. ix. 9; its treasures coveted by Chosroes, II. xx. 18; refuge of Photius, S.H. iii. 28; Theodotus sent thither, S.H. ix. 42; its Church of the Mother of God, B. V. vi. 1, 26; monasteries in, B. V. ix. 1, 6, 9; desert of, B. V. ix. 7

Jesus, his life and work in Palestine, II. xii. 22, 23; his visit to Samaria, B. V. vii. 3; invited by Augarus to come to Edessa, II. xii. 24; his reply, II. xii. 25; *see also* Christ

Jews, treasures of, brought to Byzantium by Belisarius, IV. ix. 5; a Jew warns against keeping Temple treasures, IV. ix. 6–8; returned to Jerusalem by Justinian, IV. ix. 9; oppress Christians, I. xx. 1; supporting the Gothic party at Naples, V. viii. 41; stubbornly resist the Romans, V. x. 24–26; near Boreium in Libya, B. VI. ii. 22; built Cyrus, B. II. xi. 2; *see also* Hebrews

Joannina, daughter of Belisarius; betrothed to Anastasius, S.H. iv. 37; whom she ardently loves, S.H. v. 22

John the Apostle, Church of, at Ephesus, B. V. i. 5, S.H. iii. 3; Monastery of, in Mesopotamia, B. V. ix. 31

John the Baptist, shrine of, in Byzantium, B. I. viii. 15, 16

John, Abbot, Monastery of, in Bethlehem, B. V. ix. 13

John the Armenian, financial manager of Belisarius, III. xvii. 1, 2; commanded to precede the Roman army, III. xvii. 2, xviii. 3; engages with Ammatas at Decimum and defeats his force, III. xviii. 5, 6; pursues the fugitives to Carthage, III. xviii. 10, xix. 30; rejoins Belisarius, III. xix. 33; entrusted with the command of a skirmishing force, IV. ii. 1; in the centre at the battle of Tricamarum, IV. iii. 5; begins the fighting, IV. iii. 10, 12, 13; pursues Gelimer, IV. iv. 9, 14; killed accidentally by Uliaris, IV. iv. 18, 19; his character, IV. iv. 20; cared for and buried by his soldiers, IV. iv. 22; mourned by Belisarius, IV. iv. 24

John, father of Artabanes, of the Arsacidae, II. iii. 25; treacherously slain by Bouzes, II. iii. 29–31

John, brother of Artabanes; sent to Africa, IV. xxiv. 2; killed in battle, IV. xxiv. 15

John, commander of auxiliaries, III. xi. 6; at the battle of Tricamarum, IV. iii. 4; sent with an army to Caesarea, IV. v. 5

John, a general under Basiliscus; his excellent fighting against the Vandals, III. vi. 22–24

INDEX

John, son of Basilius, a notable of Edessa; given as a hostage to Chosroes, II. xxi. 27, 33, S.H. xii. 6; retained by Chosroes, S.H. xii. 7; his death, S.H. xii. 10; his property "inherited" by Justinian, S.H. xii. 6

John, Archbishop of Byzantium, S.H. vi. 26

John of Byzantium, master-builder; his services at Zenobia, B. II. viii. 25

John the Cappadocian, Praetorian Prefect, I. xxiv. 11; his character and ability, I. xxiv. 12–15, xxv. 8–10; highly esteemed by Justinian, I. xxv. 5, 25, 33; dismissed from office, I. xxiv. 17; restored to office, I. xxv. 1; hated by Theodora, I. xxv. 4–7; advises against Vandalic War, III. x. 7–17; supplies the army with bad bread, III. xiii. 12 ff., S.H. xxiii. 14; hostile to Belisarius, I. xxv. 12; entrapped by Antonia, I. xxv. 13 ff., S.H. ii. 16; exiled as a priest to Cyzicus, I. xxv. 31; hopes to become Emperor, I. xxv. 8, 19, 44, II. xxx. 50; his easy lot in Cyzicus, I. xxv. 34, 35; accused of the murder of Eusebius, I. xxv. 39, S.H. xvii. 42, 44; his treatment at the trial, I. xxv. 40; his punishment, I. xxv. 42, 43, S.H. i. 14. ii. 15, xvii. 38, 40; robbed and plundered by Justinian, S.H. xxi. 5, xxii. 1; imprisoned in Egypt, I. xxv. 43; returns to Byzantium, II. xxx. 49, 50; the grotesque fulfilment of his dreams, II. xxx. 54; his daughter Euphemia, I. xxv. 13

John of Epidamnus, Commander-in-Chief of infantry, III. xi. 8, IV. xvi. 2

John the Glutton, a guardsman; sent with Arethas into Assyria, II. xix. 15 ff.; commands detachment in invading army, II. xxiv. 15; sent to the Po, VI. xxiii. 3–5; accompanies Narses, VII. xiii. 23; commander against Sclaveni, VII. xl. 34; in the army of Narses, VIII. xxvi. 13; commands on the left wing, VIII. xxxi. 4; accuses Belisarius, S.H. iv. 4

John Guzes, an Armenian, son of Thomas Guzes, in the Roman army, II. xxx. 4, VIII. viii. 15; commander in Lazica, VIII. viii. 15, ix. 13; called John Guzes, VIII. viii. 15; orders his men to fight on foot, VIII. viii. 30; kills one of the Alani, VIII. viii. 38; attacks and circumvents the Abasgi, VIII. ix. 20 ff.; wins over the Apsilii, VIII. x. 7; gains entrance into Petra, VIII. xi. 57, 58; killed by a stone, VIII. xi. 64

John, the Hunchback; Roman general, S.H. vi. 5; warned by a dream to spare Justinus, S.H. vi. 6–9

John Laxarion, replaces Liberius as prefect in Egypt, S.H. xxix. 1; his uncle Eudaemon, S.H. xxix. 4; addressed by Justinian, S.H. xxix. 6; seeks to remove Liberius, S.H. xxix. 7; attacks him, S.H. xxix. 9; killed in a brawl, *ib.*

John, son of Lucas; Roman officer, captured by Alamundaras, I. xvii. 43, 44

John, commander in Mesopotamia; arrests Vittigis' interpreter, II. xiv. 12; attacked by the Persians, II. xviii. 16

John, son of Nicetas; Roman commander at the battle of Daras, I. xiii. 21; urges retirement, II. xix. 36 ff.; commands detachment of invading army, II. xxiv. 15

John of Palestine, Master of the Treasuries; removed from office, S.H. xxii. 33, 34; succeeded by Peter, S.H. xxii. 36

John, brother of Pappus; at the battle of Scalae Veteres, IV. xvii. 6, 16; made General of Libya, IV. xxviii. 45; his varying fortunes in fighting the Moors, IV. xxviii. 46–51; successful as General of Libya, VIII. xvii. 20, 21; sends expedition to Sardinia, VIII. xxiv. 33

John, son of Pompeius; marries Preiecta, VII. xxxi. 14

John, son of Rufinus; ambassador to

Chosroes, II. vii. 15, ix. 1, x. 10, 18 ff.

John, son of Sisiniolus, sent as commander to Libya, IV. xix. 1; especially hostile to Sergius, IV. xxii. 3, 4, S.H. v. 31; marches against the Moors, IV. xxiii. 2; fails to meet Himerius, IV. xxiii. 3–5; quarrels with Sergius, IV. xxiii. 32; sent against Antalas and Stotzas, IV. xxiv. 6; meets the enemy at a great disadvantage, IV. xxiv. 8; his enmity against Stotzas, IV. xxiv. 9; gives him a mortal wound, IV. xxiv. 11; his army routed by the Moors, IV. xxiv. 12; his death, IV. xxiv. 13, 14; mourned by Justinian, IV. xxiv. 16

John, son (illegitimate) of Theodora, S.H. xvii. 17; learns his parentage, S.H. xvii. 18; returns to Byzantium, S.H. xvii. 19, 20; disposed of by Theodora, S.H. xvii. 21–23

John Tzibus, Governor of Lazica; his origin and character, II. xv. 9; persuades Justinian to build Petra, II. xv. 10; monopolizes the retail trade, II. xv. 11, xxix. 21; valiantly defends Petra, II. xvii. 5 ff.; killed by a missile, II. xvii. 16

John, nephew of Vitalian, Roman commander of Thracians, VI. v. 1; his excellent qualities, VI. x. 10; uncle of Bonus, VII. x. 14; reaches Campania, VI. v. 2; approaches Rome, VI. v. 5; reaches Ostia, VI. vii. 1; forms a barricade of waggons, VI. vii. 2; sent out from Rome by Belisarius, VI. vii. 25 ff.; instructed by Belisarius to begin operations, VI. x. 1; defeats and kills Ulitheus, VI. x. 2; passes by Auximus and Urbinus, VI. x. 3–5; enters Ariminum VI. x. 5, 7, 11; wins great fame, VI. x. 9; receives proposal of marriage with Matasuntha, VI. x. 11; directed by Belisarius to leave Ariminum, VI. xi. 4; refuses, VI. xi. 22; prevents the approach of a tower to the wall of Ariminum, VI. xii. 6 ff.; addresses his soldiers, VI. xii. 14 ff.; attacks and inflicts severe losses on the Goths, VI. xii. 23–25; leads his command into Picenum, VI. vii. 25; his conduct discussed by a council of war, VI. xvi. 4 ff.; his friendship with Narses, VI. xvi. 5; writes to Belisarius, VI. xvi. 14–16; his sufferings in the siege of Ariminum, VI. xviii. 2; replies to Belisarius, VI. xviii. 3; becomes suspicious towards him, *ib.*, sides with Narses, VI. xviii. 6, S.H. v. 7; accompanies Belisarius to Urbinus, VI. xix. 1; had previously failed to capture Urbinus, VI. xix. 8; sent by Narses against Caesena, VI. xix. 19; makes an unsuccessful attack upon it, VI. xix. 20, 21; occupies Forum Cornelii and recovers all Aemilia, VI. xix. 22, xxi. 14; refuses to obey Belisarius, VI. xxi. 16, 25; sent by Narses to Milan, VI. xxi. 19, 23; later sent to bring boats, VI. xxi. 24; sent to the Po, VI. xxiii. 3–5; feared by Vittigis, VI. xxiv. 12; his force routed by the [illegible] 11, 19; returns with Martinus, VI. xxvi. 1; comes to the relief of Thomas, VI. xxviii. 33–35; Gothic soldiers desert to him, VI. xxviii. 35; sent away from Ravenna, VI. xxix. 29; with others left in charge of Italy, VI. xxx. 2; confers with colleagues, VII. iii. 2, 3; leads an army to the relief of Florentia, VII. v. 4; chosen by lot to lead advance party, VII. v. 8, 9; suffers repulse, VII. v. 10–12; false report of his death, VII. v. 14, 17; holds Rome, VII. vi. 8; prevents Romans from answering Totila's letter, VII. ix. 20; sent to Byzantium for reinforcements, VII. xii. 1; marries Germanus' daughter, VII. xii. 11, xxxix. 10, xl. 10, VIII. xxvi. 11, S.H. v. 9, 10; his life threatened by Theodora, S.H. v. 12; sent to Belisarius from Byzantium, VII. xiii. 20; defers return, S.H. v. 13; joins forces with Belisarius, VII. xviii. 1; urges a land march on Rome, VII. xviii. 1, 2; sent to Rome, VII.

INDEX

xviii. 5; awaited in vain by Belisarius, VII. xviii. 11, 29; surprises the Goths at Brundisium, VII. xviii. 11–16; wins Calabria, VII. xviii. 17; takes Canusium, VII. xviii. 18; admonished and assisted by Tullianus, VII. xviii. 20–22; his route to Rome blocked at Capua, VII. xviii. 24, 25; disperses a Gothic force in Rhegium, VII. xviii. 27, 28; sends Antae to Tullianus, VII. xxii. 3; Totila marches against him, VII. xxii. 6, 18; retreats to Dryus, VII. xxii. 20; Antae return to him, VII. xxii. 21; intercepts foraging parties, VII. xxii. 23; fortifies Tarentum, VII. xxiii. 12–17; distrusts Belisarius, VII. xxv. 22–24; fails to capture Acherontis, VII. xxvi. 1; rescues Roman Senators, VII. xxvi. 1–13; sends them to Sicily, VII. xxvi. 14; Totila proceeds against him, VII. xxvi. 15; encamps in Lucania, VII. xxvi. 16; surprised and routed by Totila, VII. xxvi. 17–23; flees to Dryus, VII. xxvi. 28; at Dryus, VII. xxvii. 4; marches to Tarentum, VII. xxvii. 11; receives detachment sent by Valerian, VII. xxvii. 15; had garrisoned fortress near Rusciane, VII. xxviii. 8; summoned by Belisarius to Dryus, VII. xxx. 9; disembarks and marches to Picenum, VII. xxx. 15, 17, 18; sent with force to assist Lombards, VII. xxxiv. 41; had returned from Italy, *ib.*; accompanies Germanus as general, VII. xxxix. 10; appointed to succeed him, VII. xl. 10, 27; winters in Salones, VII. xl. 30, VIII. xxi. 4; ordered to await Narses, VIII. xxi. 5, 6; not qualified to be commander-in-chief, VIII. xxi. 8; awaits Narses, VIII. xxii. 1; receives a letter from Valerian, VIII. xxiii. 4–6; sails for relief of Ancon, VIII. xxiii. 7, 8; exhorts his fleet, VIII. xxiii. 14–22; returns to Salones, VIII. xxiii. 42; joins Narses, VIII. xxvi. 11; gives him advice, VIII. xxvi. 24, 25; holds the right wing, VIII. xxxi. 2; in the assault on Rome, VIII. xxxiii. 18; his standard, VIII. xxxiii. 21; sent into Tuscany, VIII. xxxiv. 22; summoned to Campania, VIII. xxxiv. 24; advises acceptance of Gothic terms, VIII. xxxv. 34, 35

John, a Roman soldier; chosen Emperor, III. iii. 5; his virtues as a ruler, III. iii. 6, 7; reduced from power, III. iii. 8; captured and killed, III. iii. 9

John, bodyguard of Belisarius, sent to the Pillars of Heracles with an army, IV. v. 6

John the mutineer, succeeds Stotzas as general of the mutineers, IV. xxv. 3; leads the mutineers to join Gontharis, IV. xxvii. 7; marches with Artabanes against Antalas, IV. xxvii. 25; does not take part in the battle, IV. xxvii. 27; entertained by Pasiphilus at a banquet, IV. xxviii. 5; taken from sanctuary, and sent to Byzantium, IV. xxviii. 39, 40

John, Roman infantryman; becomes tyrant at Daras, I. xxvi. 5–12; his death, I. xxvi. 12

Jordan River, in Palestine, B. V. ix. 3, 19

Joseph, an imperial scribe; sent as envoy to Stotzas, IV. xv. 7; killed by him, IV. xv. 8

Joshua, son of Nun, brings the Hebrews into Palestine, IV. x. 13; subjugates the country, IV. x. 14; mentioned in a Phoenician inscription, IV. x. 22

Jucundianae, near Byzantium; site of a Palace, B. I. xi. 16

Judaeus, fortress on the Danube, B. IV. vi. 21

Julian, Saint, church of, at Antioch, II. x. 8

Julian, brother of Summas; envoy to the Ethiopians and Homeritae, I. xx. 9, II. i. 10; private secretary of Justinian, ambassador to Chosroes, II. vii. 15; forbids giving money to Chosroes, II. vii. 16

Julian, son of Savarus; a rebel leader, S.H. xi. 27

INDEX

Julian, Harbour of; at Byzantium, B. I. iv. 28

Julioballae, fortress in Aquenisium, B. IV. iv. 3

Juliopolis, city in Galatia; protected from its river by Justinian, B. V. iv. 1, 5, 6

July, called "Quintilis" as being the fifth month from March, V. xxiv. 31; mentioned in Sibyl's prophecy, V. xxiv. 28, 30, 31

Junilus, appointed Quaestor, S.H. xx. 17; ignorant of the law, *ib.*; his death, S.H. xx. 20

Jupiter Capitolinus, Temple of, in Rome, plundered by Gizeric, III. v. 4

Justina, daughter of Germanus, married to John, S.H. v. 8–10

Justinian, nephew of Justinus, for whom he acts as Regent, I. xi. 10, S.H. vi. 19, B. I. iii. 3; uncle of Germanus, IV. xvi. 1, VII. xxxvii. 24, xxxix. 9; brother of Vigilantia, and of Boraïdes, VII. xxxi. 17; and of Preiecta, VII. xxxi. 2; IV. xxiv. 3; origin and early career, S.H. vi. 1–3, 19–28; favours adoption of Chosroes by Justinus, I. xi. 10; serving as general, I. xi. 16, xii. 21; declared Co-Emperor with Justinus, S.H. ix. 52, 53; prevented from marrying Theodora, S.H. ix. 47; overshadows Justinus, S.H. ix. 50; changes a law to facilitate marriage, S.H. ix. 51; succeeds Justinus as Emperor, I. xiii. 1, III. vii. 27, V. ii. 2, S.H. ix. 54, B. VI. iv. 6; his ruthless administration, S.H. vi. 22–28; yet possessed of many excellent qualities, B. I. i. 6–16; orders building of a fort in Mindouos, I. xiii. 2; appoints Belisarius General of the East, I. xiii. 9; makes Arethas commander of many tribes, I. xvii. 47; pits Arethas against Alamundaras, I. xvii. 47, 48; orders demolition of Philae, I. xix. 36; courts Ethiopians and Homeritae, I. xix. 1, xx. 9 ff.; receives the Palm Groves as a present, I. xix. 10 ff., B. V. viii. 2; recalls Belisarius and sends Sittas to the East, I. xxi. 2, 3; receives information from a Persian spy, I. xxi. 13; concludes the "endless peace," I. xxii. 16; receives a pretender, I. xxiii. 24; his conduct during the Nika Insurrection, I. xxiv. 10 ff.; his affection for John the Cappadocian, I. xxv. 5, 25, 33; denounced before Chosroes, II. iii. 37 ff.; refuses to sanction treaty, II. xiii. 29; summons Belisarius from Italy and sends him against Chosroes, II. xiv. 8; commands Belisarius to invade Persia, II. xvi. 5; sends him again against Chosroes, II. xx. 20; summons Belisarius for Italian expedition, II. xxi. 34; assists victims of pestilence, II. xxiii. 5 ff.; attacked by the pestilence, II. xxiii. 20, S.H. iv. 1; orders invasion of Persia, II. xxiv. 10; appoints Marcellus and Constantianus generals, II. xxviii. 2; sanctions the five-year peace, II. xxviii. 11; receives Isdigousnas with especial honour, II. xxviii. 38 ff.; sends succour to the Lazi, II. xxix. 10; neglects to send money to Gubazes, II. xxix. 30–32; finally sends funds, II. xxx. 28; sends John Tzibus to Lazica, II. xv. 9; founds Petra in Lazica, II. xv. 10, xxix. 20; makes a money present to Chosroes, I. xxvi. 4; considers the question of Strata, II. i. 7 ff.; accused of tampering with Alamundaras, II. i. 12–14, iii. 47, x. 16; advises Chosroes against war, II. iv. 17 ff.; sends Germanus to Syria, II. vi. 9; sends embassy to Chosroes, II. vii. 15; writes to Chosroes, II. xiii. 1; on terms of especial friendship with Ilderic, III. ix. 5; sends warning to Gelimer, III. ix. 10–13; again warns Gelimer, III. ix. 15–19; receives appeal of Libyans, IV. v. 8; prepares for war upon Gelimer, III. ix. 24, 25; summons Belisarius from the East, III. ix. 25; makes preparations, III. x. 1 ff.; discouraged by John the

INDEX

Cappadocian, III. x. 7 ff.; encouraged by a priest, III. x. 18–20; continues preparations, III. x. 21; besought by Godas for help, III. x. 28–31; sends an envoy, III. x. 32; and later an army, III. xi. 1; dispatches Valerianus and Martinus, III. xi. 24; sends the expedition, III. xii. 1 ff.; secures market from Amalasuntha, III. xiv. 5; their mutual friendship, III. xiv. 6; writes to the Vandals, III. xvi. 12–14; his letter not delivered, III. xvi. 15; invited by Goths to arbitrate, IV. v. 24; receives Belisarius's report on Goths, IV. v. 25; hears slanders against Belisarius, IV. viii. 2; sends Solomon to test him, IV. viii. 4; returns Jewish treasures, IV. ix. 9; receives homage of Gelimer and of Belisarius, IV. ix. 12; distributes rewards, IV. ix. 13; sends Belisarius against the Goths, IV. xiv. 1; sends Germanus to Libya, IV. xvi. 1; entrusts Solomon again with command of Libya, IV. xix. 1; receives letter from Antalas, IV. xxii. 6–10; refuses to recall Sergius, IV. xxii. 11; sends Areobindus to Libya, IV. xxiv. 1; transfers Sergius to Italy, IV. xxiv. 16; appoints Artabanes General of Libya, IV. xxviii. 43; summons him to Byzantium, IV. xxviii. 44; appealed to by Amalasuntha, V. ii. 23; makes friendly reply, V. ii. 24; Theodatus plans to hand over Tuscany to him, V. iii. 4; Amalasuntha wishes to give him Italy, V. iii. 12; sends Alexander to Amalasuntha, V. iii. 14; but ostensibly to make complaints, V. iii. 15–17; his letter to Amalasuntha, V. iii. 16–18; her reply, V. iii. 19–27; sends Peter as envoy, V. iii. 30; receives envoys from Amalasuntha, V. iv. 11; also from Theodatus, V. iv. 15, 16; his secret instructions to Peter, V. iv. 17; champions Amalasuntha, V. iv. 22; hears report of Italian envoys, V. iv. 23 ff.; inaugurates the Gothic War, V. v. 1 ff.; sends Belisarius with a fleet to Sicily, V. v. 2, 6, 7; recovers all Sicily, V. v. 17; gains alliance of Franks, V. v. 8–10, xiii. 28; Theodatus proposes a settlement, V. vi. 2–13; receives a letter from him, V. vi. 14–21; his reply, V. vi. 22–25; addresses a letter to the Gothic nobles, V. vii. 22–24; sends Constantianus to Illyricum and Belisarius to Italy, V. vii. 26; honours the deserter Ebrimous, V. viii. 3; receives the keys of Rome, V. xiv. 15; sends relief to Belisarius, V. xxiv. 18; writes encouragingly to him, V. xxiv. 21; wins friendship of the Eruli, VI. xiv. 33; appoints a king of the Eruli, VI. xv. 30 ff.; attempts to restore Suartuas, VI. xv. 36; sends instructions to the army in Italy regarding Narses, VI. xviii. 27, 28; recalls Narses and makes Belisarius sole Commander, VI. xxii. 4; decides to attack Chosroes, VI. xxii. 21; Belisarius's loyalty to him, VI. xxix. 20, xxx. 28; returns the envoys of Vittigis, VI. xxii. 22; sends envoys of peace, VI. xxix. 1; summons Belisarius from Italy, VI. xxx. 2; treats him coldly, VII. i. 2, 3; not loved by the Italians, VII. i. 33; receives envoys from Eraric, VII. ii. 15–18; provoked at the commanders, VII. iii. 1; appoints Maximinus Praetorian Prefect, VII. vi. 9; sends an army to Italy, VII. vi. 10; sends Demetrius to Italy, VII. vi. 13; forgives Illyrian soldiers, VII. xi. 16; appealed to by Belisarius, VII. xii. 1–10; sends troops to him, VII. xiii. 20; sends Narses to the Eruli, VII. xiii. 21; offers Turris to the Antae, VII. xiv. 32–34; summons Vigilius, VII. xvi. 1; intimate with Pelagius, VII. xvi. 5; receives envoys from Totila, VII. xxi. 18–25; sends troops to Belisarius, VII. xxvii. 1–3; writes him a letter, VII. xxvii. 12; sends troops to Sicily, VII. xxx. 1; pardons soldiers for killing Conon, VII. xxx. 8; summons Belisarius from Italy, VII. xxx. 25; recalls Artabanes from Libya, VII. xxxi. 7; honours him, VII. xxxi. 9, 10; incurs his hostility, VII. xxxi. 15; and that of Germanus, VII. xxxi. 18; alters the will of Boraïdes, *ib.*; had punished Arsaces mildly, VII. xxxii. 3; imprisons conspirators, VII. xxxii. 42; assembles the Senate, VII. xxxii. 43; angry with Germanus, VII. xxxii. 47; persuaded by Marcellus, VII. xxxii. 48–50; punishes conspirators mildly, VII. xxxii. 51; approves the cession of Gaul to the Franks, VII. xxxiii. 3, 4; had taken Dacia from the Goths, VII. xxxiii. 8; witholds payments from the Gepaedes, VII. xxxiii. 9; gives towns to the Lombards, VII. xxxiii. 10; makes payments to the Eruli, VII. xxxiii. 14; his alliance solicited by both Lombards and Gepaedes, VII. xxxiv. 3-39; favours the former, VII. xxxiv. 40; had given lands to Franks, Eruli and Lombards, VII. xxxiv. 37; sends support to Lombards, VII. xxxiv. 40; urged to defend Italy, VII. xxxv. 9, 10; absorbed in Christian dogmas, VII. xxxv. 11; student of the Scriptures, VII. xxxii. 9; appoints Germanus General of Thrace, VII. xl. 6; makes Suartuas ruler of the Eruli, VIII. xxv. 11; requested by Chosroes to send Tribunus, VIII. x. 14; plans to send Belisarius against the Goths, VII. xxxvi. 4; appoints Liberius Commander, VII. xxxvi. 6; sends provisions to Italy, VII. xxxvii. 5; refuses to receive Totila's envoy, VII. xxxvii. 6, 7; despised by Totila, VII. xxxvii. 13; appoints Germanus Commander, VII. xxxvii. 24; substitutes Liberius, VII. xxxvii. 26, xxxix. 6; and then reverses his decision, VII. xxxvii. 27; sends Germanus against Sclaveni, VII. xl. 3, 34; his services to the Abasgi, VIII. iii. 19, 21; receives an envoy from Tetraxitae, VIII. iv. 12, 13; sends Bessas to Lazica, VIII. ix. 4, 12; sends Petrus to Chosroes, VIII. xi. 2; receives Isdigousnas, VIII. xi. 7; sends money to Sabiri, VIII. xi. 25; appoints Bessas General, VIII. xii. 32; adversely criticized, VIII. xii. 33; garrisons Scanda and Sarapanis, VIII. xiii. 17; negotiates with Isdigouspas, VIII. xv. 1 ff.; surrenders Bersabus to him, VIII. xv. 11; shews him undue honour, VIII. xv. 19, 20; domesticates the silkworm, VIII. xvii. 1 ff.; appoints John General of Libya, VIII. xvii. 20; sends embassy to Utigurs, VIII. xviii. 18–21; sends message to Chinialon, VIII. xix. 3; supplicated by Cutrigurs, VIII. xix. 7; receives envoys from Sandil, VIII. xix. 9 ff.; from the Franks, VIII. xx. 10; his reasons for appointing Narses Commander-in-Chief, VIII. xxi. 6, 9; receives many embassies from Totila, VIII. xxiv. 4; invites Theudibald to an alliance, VIII. xxiv. 11; bribes the Franks, VIII. xxiv. 13; receives Frankish envoy, VIII. xxiv. 30; sends troops against the Sclaveni, VIII. xxv. 1; makes alliance with Lombards, VIII. xxv. 7; with the Gepaedes, VIII. xxv. 6–8; sends troops to the Lombards, VIII. xxv. 10; receives a message from Auduin, VIII. xxv. 15; sends relief to Croton, VIII. xxvi. 1; receives offers of surrender from Tarentum and Acherontia, VIII. xxvi. 4; provides lavishly for the Gothic War, VIII. xxvi. 7; persuades Auduin to send allies, VIII. xxvi. 12; receives Ildigisal, VIII. xxvii. 2; refuses to surrender him, VIII. xxvii. 4, 5; makes peace with the Gepaedes, VIII. xxvii. 21; demands surrender of Ildigisal, VIII. xxvii. 22; acquits Solomon, S.H. v. 36, 37; slays Amantius S.H. vi. 26; and Vitalian, S.H. vi. 27, 28; envies wealth of

INDEX

Belisarius, S.H. iv. 33, 34; seriously ill, S.H. ix. 35; orders investigation of killing of Hypatius, S.H. ix. 36, 37; recovers, orders the death of Theodotus, S.H. ix. 39; confiscates property of Callinicus, S.H. xvii. 4; feigns ignorance, S.H. xvii. 45; disasters during his reign, S.H. xviii. 20, 45; seen in a dream, S.H. xix. 1–3; controls trade, S.H. xx. 1–4; establishes monopolies, S.H. xx. 5, xxv. 13, xxvi. 19; institutes two new offices, S.H. xx. 7; bids officials compete, S.H. xx. 13; favours Constantinus, S.H. xx. 21; plunders the wealthy, S.H. xxi. 5, 15; appoints base men, S.H. xxi. 9–14; sells offices, S.H. xxi. 16–19; plunders subjects, S.H. xxi. 20–22; forbids attacks on barbarians, S.H. xxi. 26; ruined John the Cappadocian, S.H. xxii. 1; exploits the grain trade, S.H. xxii. 14; bewitched by Theodora, S.H. xxii. 28; sells positions in Palace Guard, S.H. xxiv. 18; which he also squeezes, S.H. xxiv. 26, 32; oppresses merchants, S.H. xxv. 1 ff.; debases currency, S.H. xxv. 11, 12; controlled silk trade, S.H. xxv. 16, 23, 26; ruined the orators, S.H. xxvi. 1–4; also doctors and teachers, S.H. xxvi. 5, 7; abolishes local treasuries, S.H. xxvi. 6; closes public spectacles, S.H. xxvi. 7–9; stops gratuities, S.H. xxvi. 15; robs the whole population, S.H. xxvi. 16, 17; raises price of bread, S.H. xxvi. 20–22, 25; controls import of grain, S.H. xxvi. 22; neglects aqueduct, S.H. xxvi. 23–25; applauds Alexander Snips, S.H. xxvi. 30, 34, 44; spares Arsenius, S.H. xxvii. 10; begins investigation, S.H. xxvii. 16; executes Rhodon, S.H. xxvii. 18; petitioned by Paulus, S.H. xxvii. 22; attacks Faustinus, S.H. xxvii. 28, 29; by whom he is bribed, S.H. xxvii. 30; his lack of regard for the laws, S.H. xxvii. 33; overrides Hebraic law, S.H. xxviii. 16–19; his treatment of Liberius, S.H. xxix. 1 ff.; contradicts himself, S.H. xxix. 3; writes to Liberius, S.H. xxix. 6; also to John, *ib.*; punishes Liberius, S.H. xxix. 11; seizes inheritances, S.H. xii. 3–11, xxix. 12–16, 24; writes new inheritance law, S.H. xxix. 19; his treatment of Malthanes, S.H. xxix. 26–38; neglects the public post, S.H. xxx. 8–11; and state spies, S.H. xxx. 14; abolished army camels, S.H. xxx. 15, 16; pre-empts Porphyrion, S.H. xxx. 19; makes innovations in court ceremonial, S.H. xxx. 21 ff.; required the presence of great numbers at the Palace, S.H. xxx. 30; rebuilt the Church of Sophia in Byzantium, B. I. i. 20 ff.; equestrian statue of, B. I. ii. 5–8; rebuilt the Hospice of Samson, B. I. ii. 16; fortifies Daras, B. II. iii. 1; and protects it from flood damage, B. II. iii. 1–23; protects the water-supply of Daras, B. II. ii. 1–21; authorizes the building of churches in all parts of the Empire, B. I. viii. 5; garrisons Armenia, B. III. i. 16; makes Syria secure, B. II. xi. 10, 12, III. i. 1; restores Cyrus, B. II. xi. 4–7; construction in Euphratesia, B. II. ix. 20; bitterly hated by Chosroes, B. II. x. 1; repairs cities captured by him, *ib.*; strengthens and adorns Antioch, B. II. x. 2–25; strengthens Hemerium, B. II. ix. 10, 11; protects treasures of Sergiopolis, B. II. ix. 6–9; and fortresses of Euphratesia, B. II. ix. 10 ff.; rebuilds Sura and Callinicum, B. II. ix. 2; secures fortresses on right of the Euphrates, B. II. viii. 1 ff.; checks the Saracens, B. II. vi. 15, 16; restores Annoucas, B. II. vi. 12; strengthens Circesium, B. II. vi. 3–11; repairs Constantina, B. II. v. 2–11; and supplies it with water, B. II. v. 11; fortifies Basileon, B. II. iv. 18; captures and dismantles Sisauranon, B.

INDEX

II. iv. 8; fortifies Rhabdios, B. II. iv. 12, 13; pressed by the barbarians of Europe, B. IV. i. 6; protects the sanatorium of Anchialus, B. III. vii. 23, 24; great extent of his building enterprises, B. IV. i. 1, 2; fortifies Dory, B. III. vii. 16, 17; restores Sebastopolis, B. III. vii. 9; work among the Tzani, B. III. vii. 1 ff.; concerned for the Tzani, B. III. vi. 8; subdues them, B. III. vi. 6; labours in Armenia, B. III. vi. 1; strengthens Theodosiopolis, B. III. v. 9–12; completes wall of Melitenê, B. III. iv. 20; checks Persian inroads, B. III. iii. 13, 14; strengthens Martyropolis, B. III. ii. 11–14; appoints Dukes of Armenia, B. III. i. 28; restored Centauropolis and Eurymenê, B. IV. iii. 14; restored Larissa and Caesarea, B. IV. iii. 9, 10; fortifies the Isthmus of Corinth, B. IV. ii. 27, 28; restores fortresses of northern Greece, B. IV. ii. 22; fortifies Thermopylae, B. IV. ii. 2–15; secures Photicê and Phoenicê, B. IV. i. 38; secures Pallenê, B. IV. iii. 23–26; restores St. Cyril, B. IV. vii. 16; rebuilt Daphnê in Moesia, B. IV. vii. 8; built Securisca in Thrace, B. IV. vii. 4; restores Augustes, B. IV. vi. 30; strengthens Pontes, B. IV. vi. 18; restores Singidunum, B. IV. v. 15; his buildings in Illyricum, B. IV. v. 1; on the Danube, B. IV. v. 7 ff.; protects Anastasiopolis, B. IV. xi. 12, 13; and Toperus, B. IV. xi. 14–17; strengthens Aenus, B. IV. xi. 4, 5; restores Rhaedestus, B. IV. ix. 19, x. 1; protects the Chersonese, B. IV. x. 1 ff.; restores Heraclea, B. IV. ix. 15, 16; repairs the long walls of Byzantium, B. IV. ix. 9–13; builds Episcopia, B. IV. viii. 20 ff.; builds a bridge at Rhegium, B. IV. viii. 17; converts Jews, B. VI. ii. 23; fortifies Teuchira, B. VI. ii. 4; buildings in Taphosiris, B. VI. i. 13; protects grain-warehouses at Alexandria, B. VI. i. 4; builds a Church on Mt. Sina, B. V. viii. 5, 6; his treatment of the Samaritans, B. V. vii. 16; buildings of, in Cilicia, B. V. vi. 1; built Church of the Mother of God in Jerusalem, B. V. vi. 1 ff.; builds hostels in Jerusalem, B. V. vi. 25; replaces the bridge over the Sarus, B. V. v. 13; controls flooding of the Cydnus, B. V. v. 19, 20; restores Septum, B. VI. vii. 15, 16; walls Traiani Forum, B. VI. vii. 12; expels the Moors from Mt. Aurasius, B. VI. vii. 7; walls cities near Mt. Aurasius, B. VI. vii. 7, 8; and secures the rest of Numidia, B. VI. vii. 9–11; fortifies Caputvada, B. VI. vi. 13–16; recovers Libya and restores Hadrumetum, B. VI. vi. 6; fortifies Vaga in Africa, B. VI. v. 13; restores Carthage, B, VI. v. 8–12; restores Leptimagna, B. VI. iv. 1–5; converts the Moors, B. VI. iii. 10; restores a bridge near Mopsuestia, B. V. v. 7; improves a road near Theopolis, B. V. v. 2, 3; restores Mocesus, B. V. iv. 15–18; improves the defences of Caesarea, B. V. iv. 7–14; bridges the Sagaris, B. V. iii. 10, 11; builds a bridge at Nicaea, B. V. iii. 6; controls flooding of the Dracon, B. V. ii. 6 ff.; improves Helenopolis, B. V. ii. 3–5; builds granary on Tenedos, B. V. i. 13–16; rebuilds the Church of John at Ephesus, B. V. i. 6; his buildings in Europe, B. IV. iv. 1 ff., viii. 1, V. i. 1; buildings in Byzantium, B. II. i. 1; his buildings in Mesopotamia, B. II. vii. 1, 6 ff.; restores Zenobia, B. II. viii. 11–15; works in Armenia, B. II. iv. 1 ff.; protects Sophanenê, B. III. iii. 6; strengthens fortresses on the Danube, B. IV. vi. 2, 35, 37, vii. 1 ff.; protects the Chersonese, B. IV. x. 10 ff.; fortified the whole Empire, B. VI. vii. 17; disregarding adverse advice, defeated the Vandals, B. VI. v. 6; repairs damage in Libya, B. VI.

v. 7; buildings, in Bithynia, B. V. iii. 1-20; in Asia B. V. iii. 1 ff.; plot against his life, VII. xxxi. 1–xxxii. 51; intolerant of unorthodox, IV. xiv. 14; indulgent to his generals, VIII. xiii. 14; his bodyguard Asbadus, VII. xxxviii. 5; his incredible baseness, S.H. i. 4, 10; a constant innovator, S.H. vi. 19–21, vii. 39, viii. 24, xi. 1, 2; his passion for building over the sea, S.H. viii. 7, 8, xxvi. 23; squanders money on barbarians, S.H. xi. 5 ff., xix. 4–10, 13–17; his rapacity, S.H. viii. 9–11, xxvii. 25, xix. 11, 12, 17; his personal appearance, S.H. viii. 12–21; his base character, S.H. viii. 22–ix. 1; his base wife Theodora, I. xxv. 4, S.H. ix. 1; whom he loves, S.H. ix. 30; close partner of Theodora, S.H. x. 13, 14, xiii. 19, xv. 19, 20; pretends to disagree with her, S.H. x. 17, 18, 23; his treatment of officials, S.H. x. 20–22; greedy and murderous, S.H. xi. 3, 4; foments strife, S.H. xi. 12, 13; persecutes and robs schismatics, S.H. xi. 15; a systematic robber, S.H. xi. 40, 41, xiii. 20–22, xiv. 5, 6; probably of demonic nature, S.H. xii. 14, 27, xviii. 1–4, 36, 37, xxx. 34; strange tales about him, S.H. xii. 18–23; by easygoing methods encourages decay of the state, S.H. xv. 17, 18; received reports from the girl Macedonia, S.H. xii. 29; approachable, S.H. xiii. 1, xv. 11, 12; but ruthless, S.H. xiii. 2, 3, 8–10, 16–20, xxvii. 1, 2; mistreats the Christians, S.H. xiii. 4–7, xxvii. 32; vain and fickle, S.H. xiii. 10, 11; open to flattery, S.H. xiii. 12; inscrutable, S.H. xiii. 13; exacting from subordinates, S.H. xiii. 23–27; ate and slept little, S.H. xiii. 28–33, xv. 11; a thorough barbarian, S.H. xiv. 2–4; controlled the law-courts, S.H. xiv. 5; easily deceived, S.H. xiv. 11; persuaded to sell justice, S.H. xiv. 17; his secretary Priscus, S.H. xvi. 7; whose fate he ignores, S.H. xvi. 10; murderous, S.H. xviii. 27; his inopportune activities, S.H. xviii. 29, 30; favours one of the Factions, II. xi. 32, S.H. vii. 1, xviii. 33, 34, xxix. 27; an easy victim, S.H. xxii. 29; fickle, S.H. xxii. 31, 32; displeased with John, S.H. xxii. 35; refused to remit taxes, S.H. xxiii. 6, 21, 23; oppressed the army, S.H. xxiv. 1–11; neglects frontier guards, S.H. xxiv. 13; insincere, S.H. xxix. 1, 12; clever and resourceful, B. IV. ii. 11; cured of a severe malady by the Forty Saints, B. I. vii. 6 ff.; his severe self-discipline, B. I. vii. 7–11; fails to capture the whale, VII. xxix. 10; his 'household,' VII. xiv. 1; in mosaic at the Bronze Gate, B. I. x. 16–19; the "Vandals of Justinian," IV. xiv. 17; his birthplace Taurisium, B. IV. i. 15, 17, 18; which he fortified and adorned, B. IV. i. 19–27; years of reign noted, I. xvi. 10, xxii. 17, II. iii. 56, V. 1, xxviii. 11, xxx. 48, III. xii. 1, IV. xiv. 6, xix. 1, xxi. 1, xxviii. 41, V. v. 1, xiv. 14, VIII. xv. 12, xxxiii. 26

Justinian, son of Germanus, brother of Justinus, VII. xxxii. 17, xxxix. 17; appointed to succeed his father, VII. xl. 10, 27; sent in command of troops to the Lombards, VIII. xxv. 11

Justiniana Prima, city built by Justinian in Dardania, B. IV. i. 19

Justiniana Secunda, fortress built by Justinian in Dardania, B. IV. i. 29

Justinianê, later name of Hadrumetum, B. VI. vi. 7; of Tzumina, B. III. v. 15; and of Carthage, B. VI. v. 8

Justinianopolis, city in Epirus, B. IV. i. 36, iv. 3

Justinianopolis, fortress in Moesia, B. IV. xi. 20

Justinianopolis, town in Thessaly, B. IV. iii. 4

Justinopolis, city in Dardania; built by Justinian, B. IV. i. 30

INDEX

Justinus, Emperor; uncle of Justinian, I. xi. 10, III. vii. 27, B. I. iii. 3; his first journey to Byzantium, S.H. vi. 2; an officer in the Roman army, I. viii. 3; escapes death punishment, S.H. vi. 5–9; becomes powerful, S.H. vi. 10; succeeds Anastasius, I. xi. 1, S.H. vi. 11; entirely uneducated, signs decrees with a stencil, S.H. vi. 11–16; his stupidity, S.H. viii. 2, 3; declines to adopt Chosroes, I. xi. 6 ff.; reduces Hypatius from authority, I. xi. 39; captures Peter of Arzanene, II. xv. 7; supports the Iberians, I. xii. 5 ff.; shares throne with Justinian, I. xii. 21, S.H. vi. 19, xi. 5, xii. 29; appoints Procopius Adviser to Belisarius, I. xii. 24; activities of Justinian under, B. I. iv. 29; Ilderic accused of betraying Vandals to him, III. ix. 8; his drab wife Lupicina, S.H. vi. 17; his futile reign, III. ix. 5, S.H. vi. 18; yet left well filled treasuries, S.H. xix. 4; overshadowed by Justinian, S.H. ix. 50; his death, I. xiii. 1, S.H. ix. 54; mentioned, S.H. xix. 1, 8, xxiv. 18

Justinus, General of Illyricum; arrives in Italy, VI. xiii. 17; sides with Narses against Belisarius, VI. xviii. 6; accompanies John's troops, VI. xix. 21; in Aemilia, VI. xxi. 14; refuses to obey Belisarius, VI. xxi. 16; sent by Narses to Milan, VI. xxi. 19, 23; sent against Fisula, VI. xxiii. 2; with Cyprian presses its siege, VI. xxiv. 18; receives the surrender of Fisula, VI. xxvii. 26; besieged in Florentia, VII. v. 1; sends for relief, VII. v. 2; relieved by a Roman army, VII. v. 4, 6; holds Florentia, VII. vi. 8; left in command of Ravenna, VII. xiii. 19; joins Narses, VIII. xxviii. 1; commands Ravenna, VIII. xxviii. 4

Justinus, elder son of Germanus, a consular, VII. xxxii. 14, 15, xxxix. 17; brother of Justinian, VII. xxxii. 17; declines to enter plot, VII. xxxii. 14–21, 28; reports to his father, VII. xxxii. 22; entraps Chanaranges, VII. xxxii. 27–38; accused of conspiracy, VII. xxxii. 44; successfully defended, *ib.*; commander against the Sclaveni, VII. xl. 34; sent to support Lombards, VIII. xxv. 11

Justus, nephew of Justinian; assists in making Hypatius prisoner, I. xxiv. 53; takes refuge in Hierapolis, II. xx. 20; invites Belisarius, II. xx. 21; but comes to Europus, II. xx. 28; commander in invading army, II. xxiv. 15; invades Persia without support, II. xxiv. 20; invades country about Taraunon, II. xxv. 35; his death, II. xxviii. 1

Labellus, fortress in Epirus, B. IV. iv. 3

Laberium, fortress in Dardania, B. IV. iv. 3

Labutza, fortress in Dardania, B. IV. iv. 3

Laccoburgo, fortress on the Danube, B. IV. vi. 20

Lages, fortress in Macedonia, B. IV. iv. 3

Lamfouaomba, city in Numidia; strengthened by Justinian, B. VI. vii. 10

Lamponiana, fortress in Remisianisia, B. IV. iv. 3

Languvilla, home of the Albani, north of Liguria, V. xv. 29

Laodicea, city in Asia Minor, B. V. ix. 30

Lapidarias, fortress in Illyricum; built by Justinian, B. IV. vi. 36

Lapithae, mythical enemies of the Centaurs, B. IV. iii. 12

Laribus, city in Libya, IV. xxii. 14, xxviii. 48; attacked by the Moors, IV. xxii. 18–20

Laribuzuduon, city in Numidia; strengthened by Justinian, B. VI. vii. 10

Larissa, city in Thessaly, B. IV. iii. 7; restored by Justinian, B. IV. iii. 9, 10

Lasbarus, fortress in Dardania, B. IV. iv. 3

Latin language, spoken by Chilbudius,

INDEX

VII. xiv. 36; Latin literature, V. iii. 1
Latin Way, running southward from Rome, V. xiv. 6, VI. iii. 3, v. 2
Laureate, a stronghold in Dalmatia, raided by a Gothic force, VII. xxxv. 26-29
Laurus, a Carthaginian; impaled by Belisarius, IV. i. 8
Lautzones, fortress in southern Europe, B. IV. iv. 3
Lavula, pass between Lucania and Bruttium, VII. xxviii. 7
Lawrence, Saint; shrine of, in Byzantium, B. I. vi. 2
Laws, confusion of, caused by Justinian, S.H. vii. 7, 31, ix. 51, xi. 1, 2, xiii. 20, 21, xiv. 9, 10, xxvii. 33, xxviii. 16, xxix. 15; *see* Legislation.
Laxarion, surname of John, S.H. xxix. 1, 2
Lazarus, Roman commander, defeated by Ildiges, VII. xxxv. 22
Lazi, a people located on the Pontus, wrongly distinguished from the "Colchians," VIII. i. 8, 10, ii. 10, 16, vi. 18; their Bishops, VIII. ii. 17; rule over Scymnia and Suania, VIII. ii. 23; their dwellings in Europe, VIII. ii. 29; rule over the Abasgi, VIII. iii. 12; invite Chosroes into their country, VIII. iv. 5; surrender Petra to the Persians, B. III. vii. 7; wish to fight independently of the Romans, VIII. viii. 3-5; harangued by Gubazes, VIII. viii. 6-13; engage with the Persians, VIII. viii. 14 ff.; pursue the defeated Persians, VIII. viii. 36; capture the Persian camp, VIII. viii. 38; slander Dagisthaeus, VIII. ix. 1; rule over the Apsilii, VIII. x. 1; powerless to defend Apsilia, VIII. x. 4; win back the Apsilii, VIII. x. 7; have only Petra south of the Phasis, VIII. xiii. 2; destroy frontier forts, VIII. xiii. 20; and Rhodopolis, VIII. xiii. 22; build and later destroy a fortress, VIII. xiv. 47; guard Uthimereos, VIII. xiv. 51; embrace the Persian cause, VIII. xvi. 3, S.H. xviii. 24; excluded from their own land by the Persians, VIII. xvi. 14, 15; suffer hardships in the mountains, VIII. xvi. 21, 30; their kings, Opsites, VIII. ix. 7; Gubazes, VIII. xvi. 2, 6; the following individuals are mentioned, Terdetes, VIII. x. 2; Theophobius, VIII. xvi. 4; one of the Lazi given a commission by Mermeroes, VIII. xiv. 23-27; kings of, married Roman women, VIII. ix. 8; Monastery of the, B. V. ix. 7
Lazica, later name of "Colchis" (*q.v.*), I. xi. 28; its cities, II. xxix. 18; an unproductive country, I. xii. 17, II. xxviii. 27; imported salt and other necessities, II. xv. 5, xxviii. 27; contains many fortresses, II. xxx. 27; difficult to traverse, II. xxix. 24, 25, S.H. ii. 26; situation, inhabitants, etc., VIII. i. 5 ff., ii. 3, 6, 8, 22, vi. 29, xi. 26; called Coetoeon, VIII. xiv. 49; borders on Iberia, VIII. xiii. 12; claimed by the Persians, I. xi. 28; its forts occupied by them, I. xii. 19; Chosroes refuses to give them up, I. xxii. 3; finally restored, I. xxii. 18; invaded by Chosroes, I. xxiii. 12, II. xv. 1, xvii. 1 ff.; in limited subjection to the Romans, II. xv. 2-4; placed under a Roman magistrate, II. iii. 39; restive under Roman misrule, II. xv. 6 ff.; appeals to Chosroes, II. xv. 1, 12 ff.; demanded back from Chosroes, II. xxviii. 6; Chosroes plans to colonize it, II. xxviii. 17; restive under Persian rule, II. xxviii. 25; bulwark against the barbarians of the Caucasus, II. xxviii. 22; its importance to Persia, II. xxviii. 18 ff.; scene of the story of Jason and Medea, II. xvii. 2, VIII. ii. 30; in ancient times allied with Persia, II. xv. 15; becomes ally of Romans, II. xv. 16; its people Christian, II. xxviii. 26; invaded by the Persians, VIII. i. 5; placed in

charge of Bessas, VIII. ix. 4; invaded by Nabedes, VIII. ix. 6; passes from Iberia seized by Mermeroes, VIII. xiii. 3; road into, from Iberia, VIII. xiii. 5; practically handed over to the Persians by Bessas, VIII. xiii. 13; scarcity of fodder in, VIII. xiv. 44; mostly held by the Persians, VIII. xiv. 45, 53; contested by Romans and Persians, VIII. xv. 2, 11; held by the Persians, VIII. xv. 11, 14; oppressed by the Roman soldiers, VIII. xvi. 1 ff.; captured by the Persians, S.H. xxx. 14; securely held by them, VIII. xvi. 13, 14, xvii. 9; its chief city Archaeopolis, VIII. xiii. 3; its cities, Rhodopolis, VIII. xiii. 21; Petra, II. xv. 10, etc.; its frontier forts Scanda and Sarapanis, VIII. xiii. 15; its fortress Losorion, B. III. vii. 5; its fertile section, Mocheresis, VIII. xiv. 46; boundaries of, VIII. ii. 21; its "clisurae," B. III. vii. 5; its Church restored by Justinian, B. III. vii. 6; its city Petra improved by Justinian, B. III. vii. 7; mentioned, S.H. ii. 29, 31, B. III. vii. 8

Lead, used in the construction of the Church of St. Sophia, B. I. i. 53

Lebanon, mountain in Phoenicia, I. xiii. 5, II. viii. 2, xvi. 17, xix. 33, S.H. xii. 6, B. II. xi. 10, V. i. 2

Lechaeum, at the head of the Crisaean Gulf, V. xv. 17

Lederata, earlier name of Literata, B. IV. vi. 3

Legion, unit of the Roman army, B. I. vii. 3, III. iv. 16

Legislation, on marriage of Senators, S.H. ix. 51; touching the Samaritans, S.H. xi. 24; sodomy, S.H. xi. 34; bribery, S.H. xxi. 16; price of silk, S.H. xxv. 16; statute of limitations, S.H. xxviii. 7–9; legacies, S.H. xxviii. 9, xxix. 19; touching the Hebrews, S.H. xxviii. 16; inheritance, S.H xxviii. 6–15, xxix. 17–25; *see* Laws.

Leon, Emperor of the East, III. v. 7; sends an expedition against the Vandals, III. vi. 1 ff.; quarrels with Aspar, III. vi. 3; appoints Anthemius Emperor of the West, III. vi. 5; wins over the tyrant Marcellianus and sends him against the Vandals in Sardinia, III. vi. 8; dreaded by Gizeric, III. vi. 11; his expedition destroyed by the Vandals, III. vi. 17 ff.; destroys Aspar and Ardaburius, III. vi. 27; his death, III. vii. 2; husband of Berine, III. vi. 2; father of Ariadne, III. vii. 2; mentioned, S.H. vi. 2

Leon, the younger son of Zeno and Ariadne, III. vii. 2; becomes Emperor while an infant, *ib.*; dies soon afterward, III. vii. 3

Leon, a Cilician; Referendarius, S.H. xvii. 32; introduced bribery S.H. xiv. 16, 17; father-in-law of Malthanes, S.H. xxix. 28; perverts justice, S.H. xiv. 18–22; cursed by the Blues, S.H. xxix. 33; bribes Justinian, S.H. xxix. 35; bribes Factionists, S.H. xxix. 36

Leonianus, Roman commander in Illyricum, VIII. xxvii. 13; slain, VIII. xxvii. 17

Leontarium, city of northern Greece; fortified by Justinian, B. IV. ii. 16

Leontius, son-in-law of Athanasius, assists in detecting a plot, VII. xxxii. 34–37, VIII. xxiv. 11; reports to Marcellus, VII. xxxii. 40; exonerates Germanus, VII. xxxii. 44; sent as envoy to Theudibald, VIII. xxiv. 11; addresses him, VIII. xxiv. 12–24; dismissed by him, VIII. xxiv. 30

Leontius, son of Zaunas, sent as commander to Libya, IV. xix. 1; fights valorously at the capture of Toumar, IV. xx. 19; brother of Rufinus, *ib.*

Leontius, a rebel, B. III. i. 25, 26

Leontius, Saint, B. V. ix. 26

Leptimagna, city in Africa, III. xvii. 8, B. VI. iv. 1; buried in sand, restored by Justinian, B. VI. iv. 1–5; buildings of Justinian in, B. VI. iv. 11; threatened by the Leuathae, IV. xxi. 2, 13, 15; captured by the Moors, B. VI.

iv. 6; vision of flame seen in, B. VI. iv. 7–10
Lesbos, island in the Aegean; passed by the fugitive Vandals, IV. xiv. 18
Leuathae, a Moorish tribe, B. VI. iv. 6; present demands to Sergius, IV. xxi. 2; their representatives received by him and killed, IV. xxi. 4–10, S.H. v. 28; come in arms against Leptimagna, IV. xxi. 12; routed by the Romans, IV. xxi. 14; march against the Romans a second time, IV. xxi. 16; scorn the overtures of Solomon, IV. xxi. 20–22; capture him, IV. xxii. 13; release him, IV. xxii. 16, S.H. v. 34; besiege Laribus, IV. xxii. 18; depart to their homes, IV. xxii. 20; join the Moors of Byzacium against the Romans, IV. xxviii. 47
Leudardus, Frankish envoy to Justinian, VIII. xxiv. 30
Leuderis, a Goth; left in command of the garrison in Rome, V. xi. 26; his reputation for discretion, *ib.*; remains in Rome after the withdrawal of the garrison, V. xiv. 13; sent to the Emperor, V. xiv. 15, xxiv. 1
Libelarius of Thrace, Roman general; invades Mesopotamia, I. xii. 23; dismissed from office, I. xii. 24
Liberius, Roman senator; envoy of Theodatus, V. iv. 15, 21; makes a true report to Justinian, V. iv. 23, 24; chosen to lead an expedition to Italy, VII. xxxvi. 6, xxxvii. 26; but detained in Byzantium, VII. xxxvii. 27; an incompetent commander, VII. xxxix. 7; sent with a fleet to Sicily, VII. xxxix. 6; reaches Syracuse, VII. xl. 12; withdraws to Panormus, VII. xl. 18; recalled to Byzantium, VII. xxxix. 8, VIII. xxiv. 1; praefectus augustalis, at Alexandria, S.H. xxvii. 17; impales Arsenius, S.H. xxvii. 19; removed from office, S.H. xxix. 1; supported by Pelagius, S.H. xxix. 2, 3; addressed by Justinian, S.H. xxix. 6; asked by John to retire, S.H. xxix. 7; refuses, S.H. xxix. 8; attacked in force, S.H. xxix. 9; recalled to Byzantium, S.H. xxix. 10
Liburnia, adjoining Dalmatia and Istria, V. xv. 25; subdued by Constantianus, V. vii. 36; invaded by Goths, V. xvi. 12
Libya, continent to the right of Gibraltar, V. xii. 1, etc.; its natural features, V. xii. 2; considered part of Asia, III. i. 5; its geographical location, VIII. vi. 3; adjoins Egypt, B. VI. i. 5; west of the Nile, B. VI. i. 9; its various divisions, B. VI. i. 10; its desert, B. VI. ii. 1; extends to Gibraltar, B. VI. vii. 14; best crops of, produced on Mt. Aurasius, B. VI. vii. 5; its aborigines, IV. x. 23; the Phoenicians emigrate thither, IV. x. 19; Phoenician tongue used there, IV. x. 20; subjugated by the Romans, IV. x. 28; Visigoths fail to subdue, III. ii. 30, 32, 36; lost by Valentinian, III. iii. 12; occupied by the Vandals, III. iii. 26, xxii. 4, VIII. v. 10, etc.; who remove the walls of the cities, III. v. 8, xv. 9; won by Justinian, B. II. x. 1; recovered for the Romans by Belisarius, III. xvi. 9 ff. S.H. i. 16 ff.; prospers under the rule of Solomon, IV. xix. 3, xx. 33; who restores the city-walls, IV. xix. 3, xx. 29; overrun by the Moors, IV. xxiii. 26–31, xxviii. 49; Huns escape from the army there, V. iii. 15; Ildiger comes thence, VI. vii. 15; Artabanes General of, VII. xxxi. 4; a successor appointed, VII. xxxi. 7; saved by Germanus, VII. xxxix. 11, 12; situation in, favourable to the Romans, VIII. xvii. 20, 21; desolation in, VIII. xvii. 22; John General of, VIII. xxiv. 33; buildings of Justinian in, B. V. i. 3; damage to, repaired by Justinian, B. VI. v. 7; exploited by him, S.H. vi. 25; home of Junilus, S.H. xx. 17; mentioned, S.H. v. 28 etc.; cities of; in mosaic at Byzantium, B. I. x. 16

INDEX

Libyans, enslaved and impoverished by Gizeric, III. v. 11–13, 15–17; cannot trust the Vandals, III. xvi. 3; suffer at their hands, III. xx. 19; oppressed by the Moors, IV. viii. 20, xxiii. 27; reoccupy Hadrumetum, B. VI. vi. 3, 4; enjoy peace at last, IV. xxviii. 52; Hannibal a Libyan, VII. xviii. 19, xxii. 24

Lignius, fortress in Cabetzus, B. IV. iv. 3

Liguria, region of Italy on the boundary of Gaul, V. xii. 4, VII. xl. 27; separated from Gaul by the Cottian Alps, V. xii. 20, VI. xxviii. 28; its chief city Milan, VI. vii. 37, 38, V. xiv. 5; bounded by the Po, V. xv. 28; occupied by the Romans, VI. xii. 36; by Uraïas, VI. xviii. 19, 22, xxiv. 20, xxviii. 35; Franks reported present in, VI. xviii. 21; also Burgundians, VI. xxi. 13; falls under power of the Goths, VI. xxi. 42, xxviii. 3; Eruli proceed thither, VI. xxii. 5; entered by the Franks, VI. xxv. 5, 7; gained by Ildibadus, VII. i. 27; the army of Marjorinus halts there, III. vii. 4, 11; partly subject to Theudibert, VIII. xxiv. 6

Ligurians, in Milan, slain by the Goths, VI. xxi. 29, 39; in the army of Uraïas, VI. xxviii. 31; sent as envoys to Chosroes by Vittigis, II. ii. 1, VI. xxii. 18, 19

Lilybaeum, a promontory of Sicily; presented to Amalafrida, III. viii. 13; Belisarius attempts unsuccessfully to take it, IV. v. 11; he asserts his claim, IV. v. 12 ff.; the claim denied by the Goths, IV. v. 19 ff.; subject of complaint by Justinian, V. iii. 15 ff., iv. 19

Lime, called "asbestus" in Procopius' time, VI. xxvii. 21, B. I. i. 53

Limitanei, Latin term for frontier troops, S.H. xxiv. 12–14

Limitation, Statute of, III. iii. 3, S.H. xxviii. 7. *See* Demurrer

Limnaae, fortress in Macedonia, B. IV. iv. 3

Limnederium, fortress in Macedonia B. IV. iv. 3

Limo, fortress in Moesia, B. IV. xi. 20

Liste, fortress in Dardania, B. IV. iv. 3

Listria, fortress in Epirus, B. IV. iv. 3

Literata, fortress on the Danube; strengthened by Justinian, B. IV. vi. 3, 4

Locrians, *See* Epizephyrian Locrians

Logothete, treasury official, VII. i. 28, xxi. 14, S.H. xviii. 15, xxiv. 1, 5, 6, 7, 9, 10

Lombards, a Christian people; subjugated by the Eruli, VI. xiv. 9; attacked wantonly by Rudolphus, VI. xiv. 12 ff.; rout his army and kill him, VI. xiv. 21, 22; defeat the Eruli, VI. xv. 1; their alliance sought by the Goths, VI. xxii. 11, 12; receive certain towns from Justinian, VII. xxxiii. 10; cross the Danube, VII. xxxiii. 11; plunder Dalmatia and Illyricum, VII. xxxiii. 12; become hostile to the Gepaedes, VII. xxxiv. 1, 2, xxxv. 19; seek alliance with Justinian, VII. xxxiv. 3–39; who favours their cause, VII. xxxiv. 40; outnumbered by the Gepaedes, VII. xxxiv. 3, 28; receive lands from Justinian, VII. xxxiv. 37; Justinian sends them Roman troops, VII. xxxiv. 40, 44; make hasty settlement with the Gepaedes, VII. xxxiv. 45, xxxv. 20; their ruler promises Germanus support, VII. xxxix. 20; make treaty with the Gepaedes, VIII. xviii. 1; but finally resort to war again, VIII. xviii. 2 ff.; expect Romans as allies, VIII. xviii. 13; Cutrigurs invoked against them, VIII. xviii. 14; prepare for war with the Gepaedes, VIII. xxv. 7; in alliance with Justinian, *ib.*; demand help against the Gepaedes, VIII. xxv. 10; receive only small Roman detachment, VIII. xxv. 13; advance on the Gepaedes, VIII. xxv. 14; sent to assist Narses, VIII. xxv. 15, xxvi. 19, xxx. 18, xxxi. 5; their unruly conduct, VIII. xxxiii. 2; sent home by him, VIII. xxxiii. 2, 3; follow Ildigisal to Byzantium, VIII. xxvii. 1, 3; flee with Ildigisal and

INDEX

Goar, VIII. xxvii. 8 ff.; receive a fugitive, Ustrigothus, VIII. xxvii. 19, 20; make peace with Gepaedes, VIII. xxvii. 21, 25; unwilling to betray Ustrigothus, VIII. xxvii. 28; their kings, Auduin, VII. xxxiv. 4, etc.; Vaces, VII. xxxv. 13; and Valdarus, VII. xxxv. 17; a Lombard fugitive, VII. xxxv. 12 ff.

Longiana, fortress in Remisianisia, B. IV. iv. 3

Longini Fossatum, Roman camp in Tzanica, B. III. vi. 23

Longiniana, fortress on the Danube, B. IV. vi. 23

Longinus, commander of Isaurians, I. xviii. 7; distinguished for valour, VI. x. 19, 20

Longinus, sent to Emesa, S.H. xxviii. 10; unmasks Priscus, S.H. xxviii. 14, 15

Longinus, Roman general, revolt of, B. III. vi. 23

Lori, name for arches, B. I. i. 68, 75

Losorion, fortress built by Justinian in Lazica, B. III. vii. 5

Lossonus, fortress in Thessaly, B. IV. iv. 3

Lournes, fortress in Mesopotamia, B. II. iv. 14

Lucani, a people of southern Italy, V. xv. 22; Totila marches against them, VII. xxii. 6, 18

Lucania, in southern Italy, V. viii. 4; gained by Totila, VII. vi. 5; Tullianus influential in, VII. xviii. 20; mountains of, VII. xxviii. 7; mentioned, VII. xviii. 25, xxii. 1 ff., xxiii. 18, xxvi. 16

Lucas, father of John, I. xvii. 44

Lucernariaburgu, fortress in Illyricum; constructed by Justinian, B. IV. vi. 36, vii. 4

Lucunanta, fortress in Scassetana, B. IV. iv. 3

Luke, the Apostle; his body revealed to Justinian, B. I. iv. 18, 21

Lupicina, barbarian wife of Justinus; becomes Empress, S.H. vi. 17; *See* Euphemia

Lupophantana, fortress in Remisianisia, B. IV. iv. 3

Lutzolo, fortress in Remisianisia, B. IV. iv. 3

Lycaones, in the army of Belisarius, I. xviii. 40

Lychnidus, city in Epirus; destroyed by earthquake, S.H. xviii. 42

Lydicae, fortress in Europe, B. IV. xi. 20

Lysina, island off the coast of Dalmatia, V. vii. 32

Lysiormum, fort restored by Justinian in Armenia, B. III. iv. 10

Lysippus, Greek sculptor, VIII. xxi. 12, 13, B. I. xi. 7

Lytararizon, fort in Armenia restored by Justinian, B. III. iv. 10

Maccuniana, fortress in Dardania, B. IV. iv. 3

Macedon, Macedonia, home of Alexander, B. III. i. 5; buildings of Justinian in, B. IV. iii. 15, 26, IV. iv. 3, viii. 1; its city Philippi, V. iii. 5

Macedonia, slave of Belisarius, S.H. i. 21; cruelly slain by Antonina, S.H. i. 26, 27, ii. 12

Macedonia, dancer in Antioch, S.H. xii. 28; her great influence, S.H. xii. 29; reassures Theodora, S.H. xii. 30

Macedonians, founders of Seleucia and Ctesiphon, II. xxviii. 4; Parthians revolt against, B. III. i. 5; Alexander, *ib.*, B. VI. ii. 16

Maddeni, tribe of Saracens subject to the Homeritae, I. xix. 14, xx. 9

Maeotic Lake, the modern sea of Azov; description and surrounding peoples, VIII. iv. 7-v. 11, 23, vii. 12; receives the waters of the Tanais, VIII. vi. 4, 15; called "Mother of the Euxine", VIII. vi. 16; borders the land of the Cutrigur Huns, VIII. xviii. 14; also that of the Utigurs, VIII. xviii. 18; home of the Vandals, III. iii. 1; at the eastern extremity of the "Mediterranean", III. i. 4; limit of the Euxine, III. i. 10, B. III. vii. 8, 10; first crossing of the Cimmerians, VIII. v. 7–9

Magdalathon, fortress in Mesopotamia, B. II. vi. 14

Magi, advise Perozes to deceive the Ephthalitae, I. iii. 18 ff.; entrap

INDEX

Arsaces, I. v. 19 ff.; advice to Cabades at the siege of Amida, I. vii. 19; announce to Chosroes that he will capture Sura, II. v. 9; answer Cabades' enquiry with regard to Edessa, II. xiii. 9, 10; guardians of the fire-sanctuary, II. xxiv. 2
Magimias, fortress in Scassetana, B. IV. iv. 3
Magister, title of Commander of Palace Troops (*Magister Officiorum*), I. viii. 2, S.H. xvi. 5, xvii. 32, xxii. 12, xxiv. 22, xxv. 3
Magna Graecia, in southern Italy, V. xv. 23
Magnus, Roman commander of cavalry, V. v. 3; at the capture of Naples, V. x. 1, 3, 7, 8, 13; sent to Tibur with Sinthues, VI. iv. 7; repairs the defences, VI. iv. 15; sent to guard the Po, VI. xxviii. 1; besieged in Auximus, VII. xi. 19, 26
Majorica, island in the western Mediterranean, III. i. 18; Apollinarius sent thither with an army, IV. v. 7
Majorinus, Emperor of the West; makes an expedition against the Vandals, III. vii. 4–13; disguised as an envoy and received by Gizeric, III. vii. 8–10; his death, III. vii. 14
Malea, southern promontory of the Peloponnesus, III. xiii. 5
Maleventus, ancient name of Beneventus, city in Samnium, V. xv. 4
Malthanes, son-in-law of Leon, S.H. xxix. 28; misgoverns Cilicia, S.H. xxix. 29; reviled in public, S.H. xxix. 30; punishes offenders, S.H. xxix. 31; cursed by the Blues, S.H. xxix. 33; investigation ordered, S.H. xxix. 34; well received by Justinian, S.H. xxix. 35; attacked by Blues, S.H. xxix. 36; the incident ignored, S.H. xxix. 38
Mamaea, mother of Alexander Severus, B. III. i. 5
Mamas, priest of Daras; assists in the overthrow of John, I. xxvi. 8
Mambri, fortress in Mesopotamia; restored by Justinian, B. II. viii. 7
Mamilianus, of Caesarea, S.H. xxix. 17; his death, S.H. xxix. 22
Mammes, city in Byzacium; Solomon encamps there, IV. xi. 15; battle fought there, IV. xi. 47–54; fortified by Justinian, B. VI. vi. 18
Mammianus, eminent citizen of Emesa, S.H. xxviii. 3, 6
Mandracium, the harbour of Carthage, III. xx. 14, 15, IV. viii. 7, xxvi. 10, B. VI. v. 11; opened to the Roman fleet, III. xx. 3; entered by Calonymus with a few ships, III. xx. 16
Maniana, fortress in Dardania, B. IV. iv. 3
Manichaeans, a religious group, S.H. xi. 26; admired by Peter Barsymes, S.H. xxii. 25
Manroballe, fortress in Moesia, B. IV. xi. 20
Mantua, city in northern Italy; distance from Verona, VII. iii. 5
Marathon, near Euboea, B. IV. iii. 16
Marcelliana, fortress in Dardania, B. IV. iv. 3
Marcellianus, rules as rebel over Dalmatia, III. vi. 7; won over by Leon and sent to Sardinia against the Vandals, III. vi. 8; destroyed by treachery, III. vi. 25
Marcellus, nephew of Justinian; appointed general, II. xxviii. 2
Marcellus, Roman commander at the battle of Daras, I. xiii. 21; Commander of Palace Guards, sent by Theodora to assassinate John the Cappadocian, I. xxv. 24 ff.; wounded in the encounter, I. xxv. 29; consulted by Germanus, VII. xxxii. 22; his austere character, VII. xxxii. 23; advises cautious action, VII. xxxii. 24–27; wishes to secure direct evidence, VII. xxxii. 26, 27; provides the services of Leontius, VII. xxxii. 33, 34; his death plotted, VII. xxxii. 39; hearing Leontius' report, still defers action, VII. xxxii. 40; reports to Justinian, VII. xxxii. 42; exonerates Germanus, VII. xxxii. 44; saves Germanus from the Emperor's wrath, VII. xxxii.

INDEX

48–50; gains a high reputation, VII. xxxii. 50

Marcellus, commander of auxiliaries, III. xi. 6; on left wing at battle of Tricamarum, IV. iii. 4; Commander-in-Chief of Roman forces in Numidia, IV. xv. 50, 51; leads his army against Stotzas, IV. xv. 52; his death, IV. xv. 59

Marcentius, commander in Byzacium; persuaded to join Antalas, IV. xxvii. 5, 6, 31; serves in Italy, VI. v. 1

Marcerota, fortress in Moesia, B. IV. xi. 20

Marcerota, fortress in Haemimontum, B. IV. xi. 20

March, first month in the early Roman calendar, V. xxiv. 31

Marcian, confidential adviser of Aspar, III. iv. 7; taken prisoner by Gizeric, III. iv. 2; his career foreshadowed by a sign, III. iv. 4–8; spared by Gizeric, III. iv. 9, 10; becomes Emperor of the East, III. iv. 10, 39; his successful reign, III. iv. 11; his death, III. v. 7

Marcian, commander of infantry, III. xi. 7

Marcian, a man of note in Venetia; assists the Romans to capture Verona, VII. iii. 6 ff.

Marciana, fortress in Epirus, B. IV. iv. 3

Marcianopolis, fortress in Moesia, B. IV. xi. 20

Marcianum, fortress in Haemimontum, B. IV. xi. 20

Marcias, commands a Gothic garrison in Gaul, V. xiii. 15; summoned thence by Vittigis, V. xiii. 29, xix. 12; his absence prevents Vittigis from leaving Ravenna, V. xvi. 7; commands a Gothic camp in the Plain of Nero, V. xix. 12, xxix. 2

Marcipetra, fortress in Dardania, B. IV. iv. 3

Mareburgu, fortress on the Danube, B. IV. vi. 18

Margdis, fortress in Mesopotamia, B. II. iv. 14

Maria, lake near Alexandria, B. VI. i. 2

Maritime Market, in Carthage, B. VI. v. 10

Marmarata, fortress in Epirus, B. IV. iv. 3

Maron, the Wall of, B. V. ix. 28

Martinianus, a Byzantine; flees from Rome, VII. xxiii. 1; goes over as a pretended deserter to Totila, VII. xxiii. 1, 2; captures the amphitheatre at Spolitium from the Goths, VII. xxiii. 4–7

Martinus, given as hostage to the Persians, I. xxi. 27; commander of auxiliaries, III. xi. 6, 29; sent in advance to Africa, III. xi. 24; joins fleet at Methone, III. xiii. 9; at the battle of Tricamarum, IV. iii. 4; escapes with Solomon from mutiny in Carthage, IV. xiv. 37–40; sent back to Numidia, IV. xiv. 40; summoned to Byzantium, IV. xix. 2; sent to Italy, V. xxiv. 18–20; arrives in Rome, V. xxvii. 1; sent out against Goths, V. xxvii. 22, 23; sent to Plain of Nero, VI. ii. 8; fights there with varying fortune, VI. ii. 19 ff.; with Valerian rescues Bochas, VI. ii. 24; sent to Taracina, VI. iv. 6, 14; recalled to Rome, VI. v. 4; sent with Ildiger to Ariminum, VI. xi. 4, 8–21; they capture Petra, VI. xi. 10–19; leave Ariminum, VI. xi. 22; sent to Ariminum with land army, VI. xvi. 23, xvii. 20; sent to succour Milan, VI. xxi. 1; delays, VI. xxi. 2 ff.; writes to Belisarius, VI. xxi. 13–15; John and Justinus sent to assist him, VI. xxi. 16, 19, 22, 23; marches toward Rome, VI. xxi. 42; sent to the Po, VI. xxiii. 3–5; defeated by the Franks, VI. xxv. 14, 19; returns with John, VI. xxvi. 1; comes to relief of Thomas, VI. xxviii. 33; accompanies Belisarius to Byzantium, VII. i. 1; sent to the East, II. xiv. 9; defends Daras against Chosroes, II. xiii. 16 ff.; ordered into Persia with Valerianus, II. xxiv. 10; General of the East, encamps at Citharizon, II. xxiv. 13; S.H. iv. 13; follows Peter invading Persia, II. xxiv. 19; commands

INDEX

the centre at the battle of Anglon, II. xxv. 17; with Peter and Peranius defends Edessa, II. xxvi. 25 ff.; deceived by Persian commanders, II. xxvi. 44 ff., xxvii. 5, 6; arranges settlement with Chosroes, II. xxvii. 45, 46; serving in Lazica, VIII. xvii. 12; his bodyguards Theodoriscus and George, V. xxix. 20

Martis, fortress in Epirus, B. IV. iv. 3

Martius, fortress in Epirus, B. IV. iv. 3

Martyropolis, town on Persian border, B. II. iv. 3, III. ii. 3; near the river Nymphius, I. viii. 22; distance from Amida, I. xxi. 6, B. III. ii. 4; near Phison, II. xxiv. 15, B. III. iii. 1; exposed to barbarians, B. III. ii. 3, 4; captured by Cabades, B. III. ii. 5, 6; relinquished by Anastasius, B. III. ii. 9; besieged by Persians, I. xxi. 5, 6; Sittas and Hermogenes fear for safety of, I. xxi. 23; siege of, abandoned by Persians, I. xxi. 27; weakness of its wall, B. III. ii. 10; strengthened by Justinian, B. III. ii. 11–14; seat of a Duke, B. III. ii. 1

Mary, Mother of God, B. I. iii. 1–3; her mother Anna, B. I. iii. 11; her Church at Pegê, B. I. iii. 6; at Hieron, B. I. iii. 10; in Blachernae, B. I. vi. 3; shrine of, on the Bosporus, B. I. viii. 20; *see also* St. Mary *and* Virgin

Mary, wife of Hypatius; tries to restrain her husband, I. xxiv. 23, 24

Mascas, fortress in Dardania, B. IV. iv. 3

Massagetae, called "Huns" in Procopius' time, III. xi. 9, S.H. vii. 10; their love of wine, III. xii. 8; observe certain rules of priority in battle, III. xviii. 14; their austere manner of life, VII. xiv. 28; reported to be preparing to join the Persians, I. xxi. 13; in the army of Aetius, III. iv. 24; in the African expedition, III. xi. 11, xii. 8–10, xvii. 3, xviii. 3, 13, 17, xix. 18, 33, IV. xiii. 2; their doubtful allegiance, IV. i. 5, 6, 9–11, ii. 3, iii. 7, 16; with the mutineers under John, IV. xxvii. 8; their savage conduct at the capture of Naples, V. x. 29; Chalazar a Massagete, VII. xxx. 6; *see* Huns

Massilia, colony of Phocaea in Gaul, VII. xxxiii. 4; subjugated by the Franks, *ib.*

Massonas, Moorish ruler; accuses Iaudas, IV. xiii. 19

Master of the Treasuries, *Praefectus Aerarii*, S.H. xxii. 33, xxv. 19, 26

Master-builders (see *Introduction*, p. xiv); the following are mentioned: Anthemius of Tralles, B. I. i. 24, 50, 70, B. II. iii. 7; Apollodorus of Damascus, B. IV. vi. 13; Evaris, II. xi. 7; Isidorus of Miletus, B. I. i. 24, 70, B. II. iii. 7; Isidorus the Younger, nephew of the preceding, B. II. viii. 25; John of Byzantium, B. II. viii. 25; Theodorus, II. xiii. 26

Mastigas, Moorish ruler, IV. xx. 31

Mastinas, ruler of Moors in Mauretania, IV. xiii. 19

Matasuntha, daughter of Amalasuntha; wedded by Vittigis, V. xi. 27; opens negotiations with John, VI. x. 11; suspected of burning grain stores in Ravenna, VI. xxviii. 26; marries Germanus, VII. xxxix. 14

Mauricius, son of Mundus; Roman general, slain in battle, V. vii. 2, 3, 12; father of Theudimundus, VII. i. 36; father-in-law of Aruth, VIII. xxvi. 13

Mauritania, occupied by the Moors, IV. x. 29; Moors of, seek alliance with the Romans, III. xxv. 3; ruled by Mastinas, IV. xiii. 19; fugitive Vandals return thither, IV. xiv. 19; Iaudas retires thither, IV. xx. 21; "First Mauritania" called Zabe, subjugated by Solomon, IV. xx. 30; "Second Mauritania," IV. xx. 31; Stotzas comes thence to join Antalas, IV. xxii. 5; adjoins Numidia, III. xxv. 21; city of Caesarea there, IV. v. 5

Maxentiolus, bodyguard of Constantinus, VI. viii. 3, 13

INDEX

Maxentius, bodyguard of Belisarius, V. xviii. 14
Maxentius, fortress in Moesia; improved by Justinian, B. IV. vii. 6
Maximianopolis, city of Rhodopê; fortified by Justinian, B. IV. xi. 10
Maximinus, envoy from Justinian to Vittigis, VI. xxix. 1, 7; appointed Pretorian Prefect, VII. vi. 9; sails to Epirus, VII. vi. 11; a timid warrior, VII. vi. 12, vii. 1; puts in at Sicily, VII. vii. 1; urged by Roman commanders to come to their relief, VII. vii. 2; sends his force to Naples, VII. vii. 3
Maximinus, bodyguard of Theodorus the Cappadocian; tries to set up a tyranny, IV. xviii. 1–3; upon invitation of Germanus, becomes a bodyguard of his, IV. xviii. 6, 7; examined by Germanus and impaled, IV. xviii. 17, 18
Maximus, the Elder; his tyranny, III. iv. 16; festival celebrating his defeat, *ib.*
Maximus, Roman Senator, III. iv. 16; his wife outraged by Valentinian, III. iv. 17–22; plans to murder Valentinian, III. iv. 24; slanders and destroys Aetius, III. iv. 25–27; kills Valentinian and usurps the throne, III. iv. 36, V. xxv. 15; stoned to death, III. v. 2
Maximus, Roman senator; exiled by Belisarius, V. xxv. 14, 15; takes sanctuary, VII. xx. 19; slain by the Goths, VIII. xxxiv. 6
Mebodes, a Persian official, sent as envoy to the Romans, I. xi. 25; slanders Seoses, I. xi. 31; persuades Cabades to leave a written declaration concerning Chosroes, I. xxi. 17–19; opposes the claim of Caoses, I. xxi. 20; secures the election of Chosroes as King, I. xxi. 22; his tragic death, I. xxiii. 25 ff.
Medara, city in Numidia; strengthened by Justinian, B. VI. vii. 10
Medea, the tale of, II. xvii. 2; her slaying of Apsyrtus, VIII. ii. 12; assisted Jason to steal the Fleece, VIII. ii. 15; her flight with Jason, VIII. ii. 31; "Medea's Oil", used by Persians at Petra VIII. xi. 36, 61
Medeca, fortress in Cabetzus, B. IV. iv. 3
Medela, city in Numidia; strengthened by Justinian, B. VI. vii. 10
Medeos, city in Numidia, IV. iv. 27
Medes, name used by Procopius as equivalent to "Persians", *q.v.*, I. i. 17, etc.; capture the Jews. B. II. xi. 2; encamp on the Hippis River, VIII. viii. 1; ravages of, S.H. xi. 11; invasions of, S.H. xxiii. 6; Medic garments, *i.e.* of silk, I. xx. 9, IV. vi. 7
Mediana, fortress in southern Europe, B. IV. iv. 3
Medic garments, called in Procopius' time "seric", as coming from the Chinese (Seres), I. xx. 9; worn by the Vandals, IV. vi. 7
Medisinissas, Moorish ruler; joins in attack on a Roman force, IV. x. 6 ff.; slays Rufinus, IV. x. 11
Megara, city in Greece; one day's journey distant from Athens, III. i. 17
Megas, bishop of Beroea, sent to Chosroes, II. vi. 17; begs him to spare the Roman cities, II. vi. 18 ff.; goes to Antioch, II. vii. 1; fails to persuade the citizens of Antioch to pay money to Chosroes, II. vii. 14; his conference with Chosroes at Beroea, II. vii. 19 ff.
Melanchlaenae, old name for the Goths, III. ii. 2, VIII. v. 6
Melas, Gulf of; near the Hellespont, B. IV. x. 3; *see* Black Gulf
Meleager, slayer of the Caledonian boar, V. xv. 8
Meleum, city in Numidia; walled by Justinian, B. VI. vii. 8
Meligedius, Roman deserter; commander of Perusia, VIII. xxxiii. 10; surrenders the city to Narses, VIII. xxxiii. 11, 12
Melichiza, fortress in Macedonia, B. IV. iv. 3
Melita, island between the Adriatic and the Tyrrhenian Seas, III. xiv. 16, VII. xl. 17

INDEX

Melitenê, city in Armenia, on the Euphrates, B. I. vii. 3, III. iv. 16; chief city of Armenia Minor, I. xvii. 22; its importance increased, B. III. iv. 18; walled by Anastasius and by Justinian, B. III. iv. 19, 20

Membresa, city in Libya, IV. xv. 12; distance from Carthage, *ib.*

Menaeus, Martyr; shrine of, at Hebdomum, B. I. ix. 16

Menas, Martyr; shrine of, at Hebdomum, B. I. ix. 16

Menephesse, place in Byzacium, IV. xxiii. 3

Mephanias, a Moor; father of Massonas and father-in-law of Iaudas, IV. xiii. 19; treacherously slain by Iaudas, *ib.*

Mercurium, town near Carthage, III. vi. 10, xvii. 15, xx. 10

Mercurius, Latin name of Hermes, III. vi. 10

Meridio, fortress in Aquenisium, B. IV. iv. 3

Meriopontede, fortress in Aquenisium, B. IV. iv. 3

Mermeroes, Persian general; invades Roman Armenia, I. xv. 1 ff.; driven back by Dorotheus and Sittas, I. xv. 8; invades Roman territory a second time, I. xv. 9; defeated at Satala, I. xv. 12 ff.; shares command of an invading army, I. xxi. 4; leads an army to the relief of Petra, II. xxix. 13, xxx. 1 ff.; forces the pass into Iberia, II. xxx. 8–10; reaches Petra, II. xxx. 15; taunts the Romans, II. xxx. 17; leaving garrison in Petra, starts back, II. xxx. 20; attacked by Phoubelis and Gubazes, II. xxx. 22; departs from Lazica with the greater part of his army, II. xxx. 32, 33; sends most of the Sabiri away, VIII. xiii. 7; marches towards Petra, VIII. xiii. 1; turns against Archaeopolis, VIII. xiii. 2, 3, 20; marches against the Roman army, VIII. xiii. 23; passes Archaeopolis, VIII. xiii. 25–27; eluded by the Roman army, VIII. xiii. 29; marches on Archaeopolis, VIII. xiii. 30; attacks, VIII. xiv. 3 ff.; sends Dolomites against the upper town, VIII. xiv. 5, 10; has a fire started in the city, VIII. xiv. 25–27; withdraws to Mocheresis, VIII. xiv. 45; restores Cotaïs, VIII. xiv. 50; controls most of Lazica, VIII. xiv. 53; gains Uthimereos by treason, VIII. xvi. 4 ff.; garrisons three fortresses in Lazica, VIII. xvi. 16, 17; lures deserters from the Lazi, VIII. xvi. 22; writes to Gubazes, VIII. xvi. 23–31; reinforced by Huns, VIII. xvii. 10; moves against strongholds of Lazica, VIII. xvii. 11; attacks a fortress, VIII. xvii. 14; then Archaeopolis, VIII. xvii. 17

Meschi, a people subject to the Iberians, VIII. ii. 24; character of their country, VIII. ii. 25

Mesopotamia, bounded by the Tigris and the Euphrates, I. xvii. 23; its hot climate, II. xix. 31; partly comprised in Armenia, B. III. ii. 1 ff.; regular route of Persian invasions, I. xvii. 25; avoided by a Persian army, I. xvii. 2; invaded by the Persians, I. xxi. 4 ff.; secured against the Persians, B. II. iv. 21, viii. 1; its fortress Circesium, B. II. vi. 1; churches in, B. V. ix. 31 ff.; mentioned, B. II. vii. 1

Messana, city of Sicily, V. viii. 1; distance from Croton, VII. xxviii. 18; opposite Rhegium, *ib.*; attacked by Totila, VII. xxxix. 2, 3

Metallus, fortress in Moesia, B. IV. xi. 20

Metanastae, Scythian tribe, B. IV. i. 5

Methone, on the coast of the Peloponnesus, III. xiii. 9; Roman fleet stops there, III. xiii. 9–21

Metizus, fortress in Macedonia, B. IV. iv. 3

Metropolis, city of Thessaly; fortified by Justinian, B. IV. iii. 5

Michael, the Archangel, *see* St. Michael

Milan, chief city of Liguria, VI. vii. 37, 38; second only to Rome among the cities of the West, *ib.*, VI. xxi. 6; distance from Rome and the Alps, VI. vii. 38; from the Po, VI. xxi. 2; bulwark against the Franks, VI. xxi. 6; receives assistance from Belisarius against the Goths, VI. xii. 26 ff.; occupied by the Romans, VI. xii. 36; besieged by Uraïas, VI. xii. 39, 40, xviii. 19, 22, 24, xxi. 1 ff.; Paulus seeks relief for the city, VI. xxi. 3–11; John and Justinus sent thither, VI. xxi. 16, 19, 22, 23; surrenders to the Goths, VI. xxi. 38, xxii. 2; razed to the ground, VI. xxi. 39; held by Uraïas, VI. xxiii. 4, xxvi. 9; its priest Datius, VI. vii. 35

Miletes, fortress in Dardania, B. IV. iv. 3

Miletus, home of Isidorus, B. I. i. 24, II. viii. 25

Milk Mountain, in Campania, VIII. xxxv. 15

Millareca, fortress in southern Europe, B. IV. iv. 3

Mindes, an Isaurian; in the Roman army, VII. xxxvi. 26

Mindouos, place near Persian boundary which Justinian attempts to fortify, I. xiii. 2, xvi. 7

Minorica, island in the western Mediterranean, III. i. 18; Apollinarius sent thither with an army, IV. v. 7

Minturnae, town in Latium, VII. xxvi. 4, 8; distance from Capua, VII. xxvi. 4

Mirranes, a Persian term (*lit.* "Mithra-son", denoting properly, not an office, but a patrician family); *see* Perozes; also commander in Petra, deceives Dagistheus, II. xxx. 7; besieges Daras, B. II. ii. 19

Misuas, shipyard of Carthage, IV. xiv. 40

Mocatiana, fortress on the Danube, B. IV. vi. 25

Mocesus, fortress in Cappadocia; restored by Justinian, B. V. iv 15–18

Mochadium, promontory on the Bosporus, B. I. ix. 13

Mocheresis, important city of Lazica, II. xxix. 18; also a section of Lazica, VIII. i. 5, xvi. 14; distance from Archaeopolis, VIII. xiv. 46; populous and productive, *ib.*; key to Suania and Scymnia, VIII. xiv. 54; Mermeroes retires thither, VIII. xiv. 45; left by him, VIII. xvii. 11; Persians retire thither, VIII. xvii. 19

Mocius, Martyr; Church of, in Byzantium, B. I. iv. 27

Moesia, called Mysia, B. IV. vii. 3, 15; fortresses in, B. IV. xi. 20

Molatzes, commander of troops in Lebanon, brings succour to Antioch, II. viii. 2; flees precipitately with the soldiers, II. viii. 17–19

Monopolies, established by Justinian, S.H. xx. 5, xxv. 13, xxvi. 19; in Alexandria, S.H. xxvi. 36

Montani, schismatics, S.H. xi. 14; their self-immolation, S.H. xi. 23

Monteferetra, town in Italy; garrisoned by Vittigis, VI. xi. 3

Monteregine, fortress in Moesia, B. IV. xi. 20

Moors, a black race of Africa, II. ii. 8, iii. 46, IV. xiii. 29, B. VI. iii. 9, 10; origin and migrations, IV. x. 13 ff., B. VI. vi. 17; near Boreium, B. VI. ii. 21; have Hadrumentum at their mercy, B. VI. vi. 4, 5; driven away from Carthage, IV. x. 27, 28; gain much of Libya, IV. x. 29, B. VI. ii. 2; take Mt. Aurasius, IV. xiii. 26, 27, B. VI. vii. 6; their ruler Ortaïas, IV. xiii. 28; and Iaudas, IV. xii. 29, xiii. 1; and Mastinas, IV. xiii. 19; inhabit Mt. Papua, IV. iv. 27, vi. 19, 20; not merged with the Vandals, III. v. 21, B. VI. iv. 6; their alliance secured by Gizeric, III. v. 22; make war on Vandals, III. viii. 1, 2; make Mt. Aurasius independent, III. viii. 5; their wars with Gundamundus, III. viii. 7; inflict a great defeat on Vandals, III. viii. 15–28; defeat Vandals in Byzacium, III. ix. 3; most of them seek alliance with the Romans, III. xxv. 2–4, IV. viii. 11 ff.; their doubtful fidelity, III. xxv. 9; stationed in rear in battle, IV. iii. 8; threaten Roman power in Tripolis, IV. v. 10;

repulse Pharas from Mt. Papua, IV. vi. 1–3; rise in Byzacium and Numidia, IV. viii. 20–23, x. 1, 2; caught in ambush, IV. x. 5; in turn annihilate the Roman force, IV. x. 6 ff.; receive warning letter from Solomon, IV. xi. 1–8; their reply, IV. xi. 9–13; Solomon marches against them, IV. xi. 14; prepare for battle, IV. xi. 17, 18, 37–46; defeated by the Romans, IV. xi. 47–54; again rise against the Romans, IV. xii. 1; seize Mt. Burgaon, IV. xii. 3–9; suffer a crushing defeat, IV. xii. 17 ff.; realize meaning of prophecy, IV. xii. 28; emigrate to Numidia, IV. xii. 29; those under Antalas remain in Byzacium, IV. xii. 30; rise under Iaudas, IV. xiii. 1 ff.; checked by Althias, IV. xiii. 8, 9; in the army of Solomon, IV. xiii. 20; elude Solomon, IV. xiii. 35, 36; Solomon prepares another expedition against them, IV. xiii. 40; with the mutineers of Stotzas, IV. xvii. 8; their uncertain allegiance IV. xvii. 9–12; join in pursuit of mutineers, IV. xvii. 31; Solomon marches against them, IV. xix. 5; defeat Gontharis, IV. xix. 8; flood the Roman camp, IV. xix. 14; retire to Mt. Aurasius, IV. xix. 16; defeated by Solomon, retire, IV. xix. 17, 18; abandon Zerboule, IV. xix. 23–32; overwhelmingly defeated, IV. xx. 1 ff.; defeat Solomon, IV. xxi. 25–28; gather under Antalas, IV. xxii. 5; tricked by Solomon the younger, IV. xxii. 12–17; attack Laribus, IV. xxii. 18–20; again gathered by Antalas, IV. xxiii. 1; capture Himerius and Hadrumetum, IV. xxiii. 10–15; lose Hadrumetum, IV. xxiii. 25; pillage all Libya, IV. xxiii. 26–32; defeat Romans at Siccaveneria, IV. xxiv. 8–12; march against Carthage, IV. xxv. 1, 2; in the army of Artabanes, IV. xxvii. 25; defeated by John, IV. xxviii. 46, VIII. xvii. 21; with the Leuathae defeat John, IV. xxviii. 47, 48; routed in third battle, IV. xxviii. 50, 51; in alliance with John, IV. xxviii. 50; in Sardinia, objective of an expedition, IV. xiii. 41, 45, B. VI. vii. 13; had been sent thither by the Vandals, IV. xiii. 43; overrun the island, IV. xiii. 42, 44; called Barbaricini, IV. xiii. 44; allies in the Roman army in Italy, V. v. 4; make night attacks on Goths, V. xxv. 9; sent out at night by Belisarius, V. xxv. 17; in the battle in the Plain of Nero, V. xxix. 22; in the retinue of Belisarius, VII. i. 6; deserters in Gothic army, VII. xviii. 26, 28; a Moor distinguishes himself at the siege of Auximus, VI. xxiii. 36–39; practice polygamy, IV. xi. 13; untrustworthy by nature, IV. xiii. 37, xvii. 10; even among themselves, IV. xxv. 16; suspicious towards all, IV. xxvi. 2; hardy as a people, IV. vi. 5, 10–13; reckless in character, IV. viii. 10; their female oracles, IV. viii. 13; their method of cooking bread, IV. vii. 3; include women in armies, IV. xi. 18, 19; undesirable allies, IV. xiii. 40; unpracticed in storming walls, IV. xxii. 20; guard captives carelessly, IV. xxiii. 17; receive symbols of kingship from Roman Emperors, III. xxv. 5–7; an old Moor, guardian of treasure, slain by a Roman soldier, IV. xx. 24, 27; a Moorish woman, IV. vii. 3; their chief Cutzinas, VIII. xvii. 21; power destroyed by Justinian, VI. xxii. 16, B. VI. iv. 10, vii. 7, 9; called "pacati," B. VI. iii. 11; mentioned, S.H. xviii. 7

Mopsuestia, city of Cilicia, II. x. 2; on the Pyramus River, B. V. v. 4

Moras, Gothic commander in Urbinus, VI. xi. 2, xix. 10; at Acherontia, where he negotiates surrender, VIII. xxvi. 4

Mosaics, in the Bronze Gate of the Palace in Byzantium, B. I. x. 15–20; portrait of Theoderic at Naples, V. xxiv. 22–27; technique of preparation, B. I. x. 15

INDEX

Moses, leader of the Hebrews, IV. x. 13; received the laws on Mt. Sinai, B. V. viii. 8

Mother of God, Church of the, in Antioch, B. II. x. 24; in Theodosiopolis, B. III. iv. 12; in Jerusalem, B. V. vi. 1 ff.; on Mt. Sinai, B. V. viii. 5, 6; in Jericho, B. V. ix. 5; in Porphyreon, B. V. ix. 23; in Libya, B. VI. ii. 20; in Leptimagna, built by Justinian, B. VI. iv. 4; in Carthage; restored by Justinian, B. VI. v. 9; at Septum, B. VI. vii. 16

Motreses, fortress in Aquenisium, B. IV. iv. 3

Mouicurum, town near Salones; raided by Goths, VII. xxxv. 25

Mucellis, town in northern Italy; distance from Florentia, VII. v. 5

Mulato, fortress in Dardania, B. V. iv. 3

Mulvian Bridge, over the Tiber, VII. xxiv. 32; guarded by the Goths, V. xix. 3

Mundepa, fortress in Rhodopê; built by Justinian, B. IV. xi. 20

Mundilas, bodyguard of Belisarius, distinguished for his valour, VI. x. 19; sent out against the Goths, V. xxvii. 11, 12; accompanies Procopius to Naples, VI. iv. 3; returns to Rome, VI. iv. 4; kills a brave Goth, VI. v. 15; sent to Milan with troops, VI. xii. 27, 36; grieves at death of Fidelius, VI. xii. 35; occupies cities near Milan, VI. xii. 40; sends for relief, VI. xxi. 27–29; addresses the soldiers, VI. xxi. 29–37; kept under guard by the Goths, VI. xxi. 39

Mundus, Roman general; assists in quelling the Nika insurrection, I. xxiv. 40 ff.; father of Mauricius, V. vii. 1–8; VII. i. 36; VIII. xxvi. 13; General of Illyricum; sent against Salones, V. v. 2; secures Salones, V. v. 11; slain in battle, V. vii. 4, 5, 12; prophecy concerning him, V. vii. 6–8

Murciara, fortress in Epirus, B. IV. iv. 3

Murideba, fortress in Moesia, B. IV. xi. 20

Museum, fortress in Macedonia, B. IV. iv. 3

Mutzianicastellum, fortress in southern Europe, B. IV. iv. 3

Mutzipara, fortress in Aquenisium, B. IV. iv. 3

Myrmex, channel into the harbour of Rhegium, B. IV. viii. 16

Myron, the Greek sculptor, VIII. xxi. 14

Myropoles, fortress of Northern Greece; restored by Justinian, B. IV. ii. 21

Mysia, name used by Procopius for "Moesia," B. IV. vii. 3, 15, xi. 20

Nabedes, Persian commander in Nisibis, II. xviii. 9; makes a sally against Romans, II. xviii. 19 ff., S.H. ii. 28; General of Persarmenia, favours peace, II. xxiv. 6; takes up position in Anglon, II. xxv. 6; defeats Roman armies, II. xxv. 20 ff.; invades Lazica, VIII. ix. 6; carried off Theodora, VIII. ix. 7

Naïsopolis, Naïssus, town in Dardania, VII. xl. 1; rebuilt by Justinian, B. IV. i. 31

Naphtha, called "Medea's oil," VIII. xi. 36

Naples, city in Campania, on the sea, V. viii. 5; one of the only two fortresses in Campania, V. xiv. 2; distance from Cumae, V. xiv. 3; from Vesuvius, VI. iv. 22; its mosaic of Theoderic, V. xxiv. 22 ff.; its inhabitants Romans and Christians, V. ix. 27; commanded by Uliaris, V. iii. 15; strongly garrisoned by the Goths, V. viii. 5; Belisarius attempts to bring about its surrender, V. viii. 6 ff.; strength of its position, V. viii. 44; besieged by Belisarius, V. viii. 43 ff.; its aqueduct cut by him, V. viii. 45; and investigated by an Isaurian, V. ix. 11 ff.; the city captured thereby, V. x. 1–26; slaughter by the soldiers, V. x. 28, 29; garrisoned by Belisarius, V. xiv. 1; women etc. sent thither by Belisarius, V. xxv. 2; Procopius sent thither, VI. iv. 1; Antonina retires thither, VI. iv. 6; Isaurian soldiers arrive there, VI. v. 1; offered to Belisarius by the Goths, VI. vi. 30; Goths sent thither by Belisarius, VI. xiii. 4; besieged by Totila, VII. vi. 2 ff.; its relief attempted by Demetrius, VII. vi. 15 ff.; governed by another Demetrius, VII. vi. 20; second attempt to relieve it, VII. vii. 3 ff.; inhabitants addressed by Totila, VII. vii. 11–16; surrendered to him, VII. vii. 20, xiii. 6; its defences partially demolished, VII. viii. 10; fortress near Naples, VII. xxvi. 13; *see* Neapolitans

Narnia, strong city of Tuscany; Bessas sent against it, V. xvi. 2; named from the Narnus River, V. xvii. 9; surrenders to Bessas, V. xvi. 3; battle fought there, V. xvii. 4, 5; garrisoned by Bessas, V. xvii. 6; avoided by Vittigis, V. xvii. 8, VI. xi. 9; taken by Narses, VIII. xxxiii. 9; distance from Rome, V. xvii. 6

Narnus River, flows by Narnia, V. xvii. 9; its great bridge, V. xvii. 10, 11

Narses, a Persarmenian, imperial steward; receives deserters, I. xv. 31; a eunuch, I. xxv. 24; sent on a mission by Theodora, *ib.*; overhears a conversation, I. xxv. 26; sent to Italy, VI. xiii. 16; joins forces with Belisarius, VI. xvi. 1; they hold a council, VI. xvi. 2 ff.; his friendship with John, VI. xvi. 5; defends him in a speech, VI. xvi. 6–13; accompanies Belisarius to Ariminum, VI. xvi. 24; considered by John responsible for the relief of Ariminum, VI. xviii. 3; persuaded to separate from Belisarius, VI. xviii. 4–9; blocks plans of Belisarius, VI. xviii. 10, 11; replies to Belisarius' speech of protest, VI. xviii. 23–26; supported by Justinian, VI. xviii. 28; his perverse interpretation, VI. xviii. 29; accompanies Belisarius to Urbinus, VI. xix. 1; encamps apart, VI. xix. 2; retires with part of the army, VI. xix. 8, 9; proceeds to Ariminum, VI. xix. 10; vexed at Belisarius' success at Urbinus, VI. xix. 18; sends John against Caesena, VI. xix. 19; receives a letter from Belisarius, VI. xxi. 17–22; John awaits his command, VI. xxi. 25; sends John and Justinus to Milan, VI. xxi. 23; recalled by Justinian, VI. xxii. 4, 5; sent to the Eruli, VII. xiii. 21; unmasks the pretender Chilbudius, VII. xiii. 26–xiv. 36; Commander of Italian expedition, awaited by John at Salones, VIII. xxi. 6, xxii. 1; marches against Totila, VIII. xxi. 19, 20; loses provision ships, VIII. xxii. 32; receives Lombards as allies, VIII. xxv. 15; sets out from Salones, VIII. xxvi. 5; his active preparations, VIII. xxvi. 8–10; refused free passage by the Franks, VIII. xxvi. 18, 19; considers his route of march, VIII. xxvi. 20; receives advice from John, VIII. xxvi. 24, 25; joined by Valerian and Justinus, VIII. xxviii. 1; prepares to leave Ravenna, VIII. xxviii. 4; passes Ariminum, VIII. xxviii. 5 ff.; leaves the Flaminian Way, VIII. xxviii. 13; reaches the Apennines, VIII. xxix. 4; sends a message to Totila, VIII. xxix. 6; receives his reply, VIII. xxix. 9; occupies a point of vantage, VIII. xxix. 13 ff.; makes Paulus a guardsman, VIII. xxix. 28; exhorts his army, VIII. xxx. 1–7; holds the right wing, VIII. xxxi. 2; disposes his forces, VIII. xxxi. 5; bends the line, VIII. xxxi. 6; exhorts his army, VIII. xxxi. 9; refuses Totila's request for a conference, VIII. xxxi. 21; not caught unprepared, VIII. xxxii. 3; arrays his army, VIII. xxxii. 5; informed of Totila's death, VIII. xxxii. 32; sends Lombards home, VIII. xxxiii. 1, 2; sends Valerian to guard Po, VIII. xxxiii. 8; receives surrender of Perusia, VIII. xxxiii. 11, 12; advances on Rome, VIII. xxxiii. 13; attacks the wall of Rome, VIII. xxxiii. 18; sends Dagisthaeus to an undefended spot, VIII. xxxiii. 21; attacks Hadrian's tomb, VIII.

xxxiii. 25; sends forces against Cumae and Centumcellae, VIII. xxxiv. 20; sends a force into Tuscany, VIII. xxxiv. 22; concentrates forces in Campania, VIII. xxxiv. 24; builds towers, VIII. xxxv. 14; receives overtures from the Goths, VIII. xxxv. 33, 34; accepts them, VIII. xxxv. 36; a generous commander, VIII. xxvi. 14, 15; popular with officers and soldiers, VIII. xxvi. 16, 17; his bodyguard Anzalas, VIII. xxxi. 13; the standards of, VIII. xxxiii. 21

Narses, a Persarmenian; brother of Isaac and of Aratius, II. xxiv. 14, VI. xvi. 21, etc.; Persian general, successfully fights Belisarius, I. xii. 21, 22; deserts to Romans, I. xv. 31, VI. xiii. 17; dismantles sanctuaries, I. xix. 37; commander in Italy, VI. xiii. 17, xxvi. 3, xxvii. 16; sides with Narses the eunuch against Belisarius, VI. xviii. 6; sent away from Ravenna, VI. xxix. 29; encamps near Theodosiopolis, II. xxiv. 12; leads attack at Anglon, II. xxv. 20; dies bravely, II. xxv. 24

Naupactus, city in Greece; destroyed by earthquake, VIII. xxv. 17

Nazares, an Illyrian commander; distinguished for bravery, VII. xi. 18; fights the Sclaveni, VII. xl. 34

Neaïoduno, fortress in Moesia, B. IV. xi. 20

Neapolis, fortress in Macedonia, B. IV. iv. 3

Neapolis, city in Palestine, B. V. vii. 1

Neapolitans, residents of Naples in Campania, send Stephanus to Belisarius, V. viii. 7; appeal to Theodatus for help, V. ix. 1; Belisarius makes final appeal to them, V. ix. 22 ff.; their obduracy, V. ix. 30; protected by Belisarius, V. x. 29, 34–36; kill Asclepiodotus, V. x. 46; impale body of Pastor, V. x. 47; forgiven by Belisarius, V. x. 48; approve Totila's proposal, VII. vii. 17; *see also* Naples

Neocaesarea, fortress in Euphratesia, B. II. ix. 10, 18–20

Nepa, fortress in Italy; captured by the Romans, VIII. xxxiv. 16

Nepos, Emperor of the West; dies after a reign of a few days, III. vii. 15

Nero, Roman Emperor, S.H. i. 9; Plain of, near Rome; a Gothic camp established there, V. xix. 3, 12, xxviii. 17; troops sent thither by Belisarius, V. xxviii. 15 ff.; operations there on the day of the great battle, V. xxix. 22 ff.; Marcias ordered by Vittigis to remain there, V. xxix. 2; Constantinus wins a signal success in, VI. i. 4–10; skirmish in, VI. i. 21; Martinus and Valerian sent to, VI. ii. 8; Goths victorious in, VI. ii. 19 ff.; but with heavy losses, VI. ii. 36; its "stadium," VI. i. 5

Nicaea, city in Bithynia, improved by Justinian, B. V. iii. 1–6

Nicê, fortress in Haemimontum, B. IV. xi. 20

Nicetas, father of the general John, I. xiii. 21, II. xix. 36, xxiv. 15

Nicholas, Saint, shrine of, in Byzantium, B. I. vi. 4

Nicocles, according to Procopius father of Themistocles, B. I. i. 7

Nicomedia, city in Bithynia, B. V. iii. 7

Nicopolis, town of Acarnania, plundered by the Goths, VIII. xxii. 31

Nicopolis, city in Armenia, restored by Justinian, B. III. iv. 11, 13

Nicopolis, town in Illyricum, restored by Justinian, B. IV. i. 37

Nicopolis, fortress in Moesia, B. IV. xi. 20

Nika Insurrection, a popular uprising, I. xxiv. 1 ff., S.H. xii. 12, xix. 12, B. I. i. 20

Nile River, boundary between Europe and Africa, VIII. vi. 13, 14; course of, B. VI. i. 6–10; its source unknown, V. xii. 2; its annual flooding, VII. xxix. 6–8, 17, 19; its prolonged flood, S.H. xviii. 39; the Nobatae dwell along its banks, I. xix. 28, 29; its island, Philae, I. xix. 34; made by Justinian accessible from Alexan-

dria, B. VI. i. 1–4; mentioned, VIII. vi. 2
Nisconis, fortress in Moesia, B. IV. xi. 20
Nisibis, city on the Persian frontier, distance from the Tigris, I. x. 14; from Daras, I. x. 14; from Sisauranon, II. xix. 2, S.H. ii. 24, 28; bulwark of the Persian Empire, II. xviii. 7; its capture by the Persians, I. xvii. 25; its territory invaded by Libelarius, I. xii. 23; by Belisarius, II. xviii. 1 ff.; negotiations with Chosroes there, I. xxii. 10
Nobatae, a people of upper Egypt, I. xix. 28; settled along the Nile by Diocletian, I. xix. 29 ff.; receive annual payment from the Roman Emperor, I. xix. 32, 33; their religion, I. xix. 35
Nogeto, fortress in southern Europe, B. IV. iv. 3
Nono, fortress in Moesia, B. IV. xi. 20
Norici, a people of central Europe, V. xv. 27
Novae, fortress on the Danube, strengthened by Justinian, B. IV. vi. 1–3, 5
Novaria, city near Milan, occupied by Mundilas, VI. xii. 40
Novas, fortress in Moesia, B. IV. xi. 20
Novejustiniana, fortress in Moesia, B. IV. xi. 20
Novus, fortress on the Danube, B. IV. vi. 24
Nuceria, city in Campania, VIII. xxxv. 7
Numa, early Roman king, V. xxiv. 31
Numidia, section of Africa, adjoining Mauritania, III. xxv. 21; its boundary near the Plain of Boulla, III. xxv. 1; Mt. Papua on its borders, IV. iv. 27; includes Mt. Aurasius, III. viii. 5, B. VI. vii. 2–5; and the city of Hippo Regius, III. iii. 31, IV. iv. 26; and Tigisis, IV. x. 21; Moors of, seek alliance with the Romans, III. xxv. 3; plundered by the Moors, IV. viii. 9, x. 2; by Iaudas, IV. xiii. 1, 18; retreat of mutineers, IV. xv. 44, 50, xvii. 1; left by the Romans, IV. xx. 30; Gontharis commander there, IV. xxv. 1; Moors of, march against Carthage, IV. xxv. 2; fortresses of, strengthened by Justinian, B. VI. vii. 1–11; mentioned, VIII. xvii. 21
Nun ("Naues"), father of Joshua ("Jesus"), IV. x. 13, 22
Nymphium, fortress in Macedonia, B. IV. iv. 3
Nymphius River, in Armenia, B. III. ii. 2; near Martyropolis, I. viii. 22, xxi. 6; forms boundary between Roman and Persian territory, I. xxi. 6; boundary of Arzanene, I. viii. 21, II. xv. 7

Oasis, city in upper Egypt, former home of the Nobatae, I. xix. 30
Obbane, town on the Euphrates, distance from Barbalissum, II. xii. 4
Obeisance, required of courtiers by Justinian, S.H. xv. 15, 16, 27, 35, xxx. 22, 23
Ocean, conceived by Procopius as encircling the earth, III. i. 4
Ocenitae, a section of the Tzani, B. III. vi. 18, 21
Ochus, king of the Eruli, VI. xiv. 38
Octava, place in Armenia; distance from Satala, I. xv. 9
Octavus, fortress on the Danube, near Singidunum, B. IV. v. 16
Odoacer, bodyguard of the Emperor, V. i. 6; usurps the throne, V. i. 7, 8, xii. 20, VI. vi. 21; distributes land in Tuscany, V. i. 28; concedes all Gaul to the Visigoths, V. xii. 20; Zeno unable to cope with him, VI. vi. 15, 16; Theoderic persuaded to attack him, V. i. 10, VI. vi. 23; defeated by Theoderic, V. i. 14, xii. 21; besieged in Ravenna, V. i. 15, 24; his agreement with Theoderic, V. i. 24; killed by Theoderic, V. i. 25
Odolgan, a Hun, Commander of Perusia, sends aid to Martinianus VII. xxiii. 6
Odonachus, commander in the Roman army; sent to Lazica, VIII. ix. 5; in command of Archaeopolis. VIII. xiii. 8; addresses his men, VIII. xiv. 14–21; leads a sally, VIII. xiv. 22 ff.

INDEX

Odonathus, husband of Zenobia, King of the Saracens, II. v. 5, B. II. viii. 8; his services to the Romans, II. v. 6
Odriuzo, fortress in Aquenisium, B. IV. iv. 3
Odysseus, with Diomedes stole the Palladium from Troy, V. xv. 9; his meeting with Circe, V. xi. 2; his wanderings, VIII. xxii. 21, 23
Odyssus, fortress in Moesia, B. IV. xi. 20
Oenochalacon, place in Armenia, II. iii. 15
Oilas, bodyguard of Belisarius, V. xxvii. 13
Olbus, fortress in Epirus, B. IV. iv. 3
Old Epirus, fortresses of, B. IV. iv. 3
Olives, Mt. of, at Jerusalem, B. V. ix. 8
Olyvrius, Roman Senator, husband of Placidia, III. v. 6, vi. 6; becomes Emperor of the West, killed after a short reign, III. vii. 1; father-in-law of Areobindus, I. viii. 1
Olyvrius, a Roman patrician, takes sanctuary, VII. xx. 19
Onalus, fortress in Epirus, B. IV. iv. 3
Onopnictes, torrent at Antioch, B. II. x. 16
Onus, fortress on the Danube, built by Justinian, B. IV. vi. 28
Opilio, Roman senator, envoy of Theodatus, V. iv. 15, 21; makes a false report to Justinian, V. iv. 25
Opsites, ruler of the Abasgi, VIII. ix. 11; escapes to Caucasus, VIII. ix. 29
Opsites, king of Lazica, uncle of Gubazes, VIII. ix. 7; his consort Theodora carried off by Nabedes, *ib.*
Optaris, a Goth, hostile to Theodatus, V. xi. 7, 8; pursues and kills him, V. xi. 6, 9
Optas, fortress in Macedonia, B. IV. iv. 3
Optio (Latin), a kind of adjutant in the Roman army, III. xvii. 1, IV. xx. 12
Optium, fortress in Macedonia, B. IV. iv. 3
Orestes, son of Agamemnon, the story of his flight from Tauris, I. xvii. 11 ff., VIII. v. 24
Orestes, father of Augustus, for whom he acts as Regent, V. i. 2; his death, V. i. 5
Orestes, Roman ex-consul, takes sanctuary, VII. xx. 19; unable to flee with John, VII. xxvi. 13
Origenes, Senator, counsels moderation, I. xxiv. 26 ff.
Orocassias, mountain at Antioch, II. vi. 10, B. II. x. 9, 16
Orontes River, at Antioch, II. vi. 10, viii. 3, 35, B. II. x. 6, 7
Ortaias, Moorish ruler beyond Mt. Aurasius, IV. xiii. 19, 28; accuses Iaudas to Solomon, IV. xiii. 19; with the mutineers of Stotzas, IV. xvii. 8; his report of the country beyond his own, IV. xiii. 29
Osdas, Gothic commander; burned to death, VII. xix. 20
Osiris, god of the Egyptians, B. VI. i. 12; worshipped by the Blemyes and Nobatae, I. xix. 35
Osroenê, section of Armenia, B. III. iv. 5; including Edessa, I. xvii. 24; its strongly fortified cities, I. xvii. 34; fortresses in, B. II. viii. 1
Osroes, ancient king of Edessa, I. xvii. 24
Ostia, city at the mouth of the Tiber, neglected in Procopius' time, V. xxvi. 8; no good road thence to Rome, V. xxvi. 13, VI. vii. 6; the only port on the Tiber left to Rome, V. xxvi. 16, VI. iv. 2; distance from Anthium, V. xxvi. 17; Paulus and Conon sent thither, VI. v. 3; reached by John, VI. vii. 1; Rome provisioned by way of Ostia, VI. vii. 1 ff.
Othoni, islets near Cercyra, VIII. xxii. 20
Ozormê, fortress in Thrace, B. IV. xi. 20

Pacue, fortress in Epirus, B. IV. iv. 3
Pacurius, King of Persia, I. v. 10; entraps Arsaces, I. v. 16 ff.; imprisons him, I. v. 29; flays Bassicius, I. v. 28; grants a favour, I. v. 30 ff.

Pacurius, son of Peranius, commander of Dryus, VIII. xxvi. 4; sent to Italy, VII. xxvii. 2; negotiates with Ragnaris, VIII. xxxiv. 9; tricked by him, VIII. xxxiv. 9–12; defeats him in battle, VIII. xxxiv. 13–15

Padisara, fortress in Moesia, B. IV. xi. 20

Paganism, the ancient "Hellenic" or "Greek" faith, II. xiii. 7; in Egypt, I. xix. 35–37; among the Homeritae, I. xx. 1; in Byzantium I. xxv. 10, S.H. xix. 11; among the Gadibitani, B. VI. iv. 12; in Libya, B. VI. ii. 15; efforts to suppress paganism in the Roman Empire, I. xix. 35–37, S.H. xi. 21-23, 31–33; "Polytheism," S.H. xi. 26, B. VI. ii. 15

Painting, mural, by encaustic method, B. I. x. 15

Palace, imperial residence in Rome, S.H. xxvi. 27; said to be named from Pallas, III. xxi. 4; despoiled by Gizeric, III. v. 3, 4, IV. ix. 5; in Byzantium, VII. xi. 9; S.H. iii. 15. 19, iv. 24, etc., B. I. iv. 2, 8, etc.; its underground chamber, S.H. iv. 7; Palace Guard, called Scholarii, VIII. xxvii. 2, S.H. vi. 3, etc.; Palace officials, S.H. xxii. 12; the eunuchs in, VII. xl. 35, VIII. iii. 19, S.H. iv. 13, etc.; Arsenius excluded from, S.H. xxvii. 10, 12; at Hieron, B. I. xi. 16, 17; in Carthage, S.H. i. 33; restored by Justinian, B. VI. v. 9; in Ravenna, VI. xxix. 37, S.H. i. 33

Palatiolum, fortress near the Danube, restored by Justinian, B. IV. vi. 34, 35

Palestine, bounded by the "Red Sea," I. xix. 2; settled by the Hebrews, IV. x. 13; Moors emigrated thence, IV. x. 27; Hebrews exiled from, B. II. xi. 2; Saracens dwelling in, I. xix. 10; objective of Chosroes' invasion, II. xx. 18; visited by the pestilence, II. xxii. 6; disturbed by sedition, S.H. xi. 24, xxvii. 9; by persecution, S.H. xxvii. 27; protected from the Saracens, B. V. viii. 9; home of Arsenius, S.H. xxvii. 6; of John, S.H. xxii. 34; of Tribunus, VIII. x. 11; crown lands in, S.H. xxvii. 31; "Third Palestine" a section of Arabia, B. V. viii. 1

Palladius, Commander of Croton, VIII. xxv. 24

Pallas, an "eponymous hero;" to explain "Palatium," III. xxi. 4

Pallenê, peninsula, in the northern Aegaean, fortified by Justinian, B. IV. iii. 20, 25

Palm Groves, in Arabia, held by Saracens, I. xix. 8, 9, II. iii. 41; presented to Justinian, I. xix. 10 ff., B. V. viii. 2

Palmatis, fortress in Moesia; enlarged by Justinian, B. IV. vii. 12

Palmyra, city in Phoenice Libanensis, II. i. 6, B. V. i. 2; restored by Justinian, B. II. xi. 10–12

Palyrus, fortress in Epirus, B. IV. iv. 3

Pamilinus, fortress in Dardania, B. IV. iv. 3

Pamphylia, district in Asia Minor, B. V. ix. 37, 38; its city Perga, B. V. ix. 38

Pancratian Gate, in the wall of Rome, across the Tiber, V. xxviii. 19; false report of its capture, V. xviii. 35; threatened by the Goths, V. xxiii. 1; guarded by Paulus, V. xxiii. 2

Pancratius, saint from whom the Pancratian Gate was named, V. xviii. 35

Pannonia, region on the Danube, entered by the Goths, III. ii. 39; bestowed upon the Lombards, VII. xxxiii. 10; Pannonians, V. xv. 27

Panormus, city in Sicily, VII. xl. 18; Goths in, defy Belisarius, V. v. 12; taken by him, V. v. 12–16; garrisoned by him, V. viii. 1

Pantaleia, town in Dardania; rebuilt by Justinian, B. IV. i. 31

Panteichion, suburb of Byzantium, VII. xxxv. 4

Panteleëmon, Saint, shrine of, on the Bosporus, B. I. ix. 11; Monastery of, in the Jordan desert, B. V. ix. 3

Paphlagonians, a people of Asia Minor, VIII. ii. 2; term of contempt, S.H. xvi. 7

INDEX

Pappus, brother of John, IV. xvii. 6, xxviii. 45; commander of cavalry, III. xi. 7; on the right wing at the battle of Tricamarum, IV. iii. 4

Papua, mountain in Numidia, IV. iv. 27; Gelimer takes refuge there, IV. iv. 26, 28; its ascent attempted by Pharas, IV. vi. 1; closely besieged, IV. iv. 28, vi. 3; Cyprian sent thither to receive Gelimer, IV. vii. 11

Paratonium, fortress in Libya, built by Justinian, B. VI. ii. 2

Paraturon, city in Numidia, strengthened by Justinian, B. VI. vii. 10

Paretium, fortress in Epirus, B. IV. iv. 3

Parian marble, used in Hadrian's Tomb, V. xxii. 13; in a colonnade at Byzantium, B. I. iii. 3

Parmus, fortress in Epirus, B. IV. iv. 3

Parnusta, fortress in Cabetzus, B. IV. iv. 3

Parthians, kinship with the first Arsaces, II. iii. 32; Parthian Kings, B. III. i. 6; rise against Macedon, B. III. i. 5

Parthion, fortress in Macedonia, B. IV. iv. 3

Pascas, fortress in Macedonia, B. IV. iv. 3

Pasiphilus, mutineer; supporter of Gontharis, IV. xxvii. 21, 22, 36, 38; entertains John at a banquet, IV. xxviii. 3; his death, IV. xxviii. 39

Passara, wife of Germanus; her death, VII. xxxix. 14

Pastor, of Naples, an orator, opposes surrender of the city, V. viii. 22 ff.; addresses the Neapolitans, V. viii. 29–40; brings forward the Jews, V. viii. 41; his death, V. x. 38; impaled by the mob, V. x. 47

Patapa, fortress in Epirus, B. IV. iv. 3

Patrae, city of Greece; destroyed by earthquake, VIII. xxv. 17

Patrician, title of honour, III. ii. 15, etc.; how conferred, V. vi. 3; Patricians hunted down by the Goths, VIII. xxxiv. 6; certain Patricians consult Sibylline prophecies, V. xxiv. 28 ff.; the title refused Gelimer because of Arianism, IV. ix. 14

Patriciolus, officer in the Roman army, I. viii. 3

Patricius, a Phrygian, Roman general, I. viii. 2; routed by Cabades, I. viii. 10–18; his escape, I. viii. 19; entraps two hundred Persians, I. ix. 5–18

Patrimonium, property administered directly by the Emperor, V. iv. 1, vi. 26, S.H. xxii. 12

Paucaris, an Isaurian, bodyguard of Belisarius, V. ix. 17; prepares the aqueduct of Naples for troops, V. ix. 19–21

Paul, the Apostle; Church of, at Rome, VI. iv. 9; respected by the Goths, VI. iv. 10; its site fortified, VI. iv. 11; Church of, in Byzantium, B. I. iv. 1; Gate of, in the wall of Rome, VI. iv. 3, VII. xxxvi. 7, 10

Paulimandra, fortress in Moesia, B. IV. xi. 20

Paulus, priest of Hadrumetum; rescues the city from the Moors, IV. xxiii. 18–25; comes to Byzantium, IV. xxiii. 29

Paulus, Patriarch of Alexandria, S.H. xxvii. 3, 4; accompanied by Arsenius, S.H. xxvii. 11, 19; accuses Psoes, S.H. xxvii. 14; investigated by Justinian, S.H. xxvii. 16; unfrocked, S.H. xxvii. 18; petitions Justinian, S.H. xxvii. 21; opposed by Vigilius, S.H. xxvii. 24

Paulus, commander of infantry, V. v. 3; on guard at the Pancratian Gate, V. xxiii. 2; sent to Milan with Thracians, VI. xii. 27, 40

Paulus, commander of Isaurians, VI. v. 1; proceeds to Ostia by sea, VI. v. 3; remains in Ostia, VI. vii. 12, 16; occupies Portus, VI. vii. 16, 22

Paulus, messenger of Mundilas, VI. xxi. 3; swims the Po and delivers his message, VI. xxi. 4–9; returns to Milan, VI. xxi. 11

Paulus, a Cilician; commander in the Roman army, VII. xxxvi. 16; seizes and holds the Tomb of Hadrian, VII. xxxvi. 17–25; surrenders and is sent to Byzantium by Totila, VII. xxxvi. 26–28

INDEX

Paulus, a Roman soldier distinguished for valour, VIII. xxix. 22, 26, 27; made a bodyguard of Narses, VIII. xxix. 28

Paulus, interpreter of Chosroes, II. vi. 22; a Roman reared in Antioch, II. vi. 23; presents the Persian demands at Hierapolis, II. vi. 22; at Beroea, II. vii. 5; at Antioch, II. viii. 4; where he exhorts the citizens to prudence, II. viii. 7; at Chalcis, II. xii. 1; at Edessa, II. xii. 33, xxvi. 14, xxvii. 24, 45

Pauta, city of southern Europe, B. IV. iv. 3

Peace, Forum of, in Rome, VIII. xxi. 11; Temple of, VIII. xxi. 12

Pearl, story of the, I. iv. 17–31

Pedion Halon, in Libya; scene of destruction of forces of Gibamundus, III. xviii. 12

Pegasius, physician, friend of Solomon the younger, IV. xxii. 14, 15; ransoms him and is killed by him, S.H. v. 33–35, 38

Pegê, suburb of Byzantium; its shrine, B. I. iii. 6

Pelagius, a priest of Rome; intimate with Justinian, VII. xvi. 5; relieves suffering in Rome, VII. xvi. 6; envoy to Totila, VII. xvi. 7–xvii. 1; pleads for the Romans, VII. xx. 23–25; intercedes for Senators, VII. xxi. 17; envoy to Justinian, VII. xxi. 18; sent to Alexandria, S.H. xxvii. 17; acts as substitute for Vigilius, S.H. xxvii. 17, 24; intercedes for Liberius, S.H. xxix. 2

Pelargus, Street of; in Byzantium, B. I. ix. 15

Pelecum, fortress in Macedonia, B. IV. iv. 3

Peleum, fortress in Epirus, B. IV. iv. 3

Pelion, mountain in Thessaly, B. IV. iii. 6, 7

Peloponnesus, the southern peninsula of Greece, its resemblance to Spain, V. xii. 3; escapes plunder by the Huns, II. iv. 11; a rendezvous for Roman forces, III. xi. 24; touched at by Vandals, IV. xiv. 18; plundered by Gizeric, III. v. 23, xxii. 16; oppressed by Alexander, S.H. xxvi. 32; refuge of Roman ships, VII. xl. 16; its cities unwalled, B. IV. ii. 27, 28; protected by a wall at the Isthmus, *ib.*; and at Thermopylae, S.H. xxvi. 31

Pelusium, city in Egypt; source of the pestilence, II. xxii. 6

Penates, gods of ancient Rome, V. xxv. 19

Peneus, river in Thessaly, B. IV. iii. 6, 7

Pentacomia, town in Euphratesia, B. II. ix. 10

Pentapolis, section of Libya, B. VI. i. 11; distance from Alexandria, B. VI. ii. 3; from Tripolis, B. VI. iii. 12; its cities: Boreium, B. VI. ii. 11; Teuchira, B. VI. ii. 4; governed by Hecebolus, S.H. ix. 27; by Cyrus, IV. xxi. 1; fortresses in, built by Justinian, B. VI. ii. 7, 8

Pentebagae, city in Numidia; walled by Justinian, B. VI. vii. 8

Pentecost, festival of the Christians, B. V. vii. 5

[illegible] 3

Peplabius, fortress in Cabetzus, B. IV. iv. 3

Peranius, son of Gourgenes, King of Iberia, I. xii. 11, V. v. 3; father of Pacurius, VII. xxvii. 2, VIII. xxvi. 4; uncle of Phazas, VII. vi. 10; had deserted to the Romans, V. v. 3; commander in invading army, II. xxiv. 15; invades country about Taraunon, II. xxv. 35; defends Edessa, II. xxvi. 25 ff.; surrender of, demanded by Chosroes, II. xxvi. 38; at the siege of Rome, summons Belisarius, V. xxiii. 13; leads a sally, VI. i. 11; sent against Urviventus, VI. xix. 1; persuades Belisarius to march against it, VI. xx. 4; his death, II. xxviii. 1

Perbyla, fortress in Thessaly, B. IV. iv. 3

Percus, fortress in Epirus, B. IV. iv. 3

Perga, city in Pamphylia, B. V. ix. 38

Perinthus, ancient name of Heraclea, III. xii. 6, B. IV. ix. 14

Peripatetic philosophers, S.H. viii. 23

Perozes, Persian King; wages war against the Ephthalitae, I. iii. 1, 8; entrapped by the Ephthalitae, I. iii. 10 ff.; escapes with his army, I. iii. 22; his second expedition, I. iv. 1 ff.; destroyed with his army, I. iv. 14 ff.; his famous pearl, I. iv. 14

Perozes, Persian general, I. xiii. 16; exchanges letters with Belisarius and Hermogenes, I. xiv. 1 ff.; addresses his troops, I. xiv. 13 ff.; defeated by Belisarius, I. xiv. 28 ff.; punished by Cabades, I. xvii. 26 ff.; *see also* Mirranes

Perozes, father of murderers of Symeon, II. iii. 3

Persarmenia, region adjoining Iberia, VIII. ii. 20, 26, viii. 22, B. III. iii. 3, vi. 15; includes a portion of the Taurus range, I. x. 1; its river Arsinus, I. xvii. 21; its fortresses, I. xv. 18, II. xxv. 35, VIII. viii. 22; its General Nabedes, II. xxiv. 6; its trade with India, II. xxv. 3; devastated by Sittas and Belisarius, I. xii. 20; Persarmenians in the Persian army, I. xv. 1; the following individuals are named: Artabanes, VIII. viii. 21; Chanaranges, VII. xxxii. 11; Varazes, VIII. xiii. 10

Persia, adjoining Iberia, V. v. 3; boundary of, B. II. i. 3, etc.; territory of, B. II. ii. 21, etc.; frontier of, closed, B. II. iv. 21, V. 1; its province Arxanenê, B. III. ii. 3; Dolomites live in, VIII. xiv. 6, 7; Post Route to, S.H. xxx. 10

Persians, called also Medes, I. i. 17, etc.; refuse kingship to any mutilated man, I. xi. 4, VIII. x. 22; their kings called "King of Kings," I. xiv. 18, xvii. 33; Cyrus, II. ii. 15, B. I. i. 12, 15, II. xi. 2; Xerxes, B. V. iii. 8; Cabades, I. iv. 2, etc.; Chosroes, I. xxi. 22, etc.; their king wears red shoes, B. III. i. 23; coin silver, but not gold, VII. xxxiii. 6; wear hair long, S.H. vii. 9; tenacious of custom, I. v. 33; worship the rising sun, I. iii. 20; their fire-worship, II. xxiv. 2; do not bury the dead, I. xi. 35, xii. 4; their set character, II. xxviii. 25; their trade in Indian silk, I. xx. 9, VIII. xvii. 1 S.H. xxv. 16; arrogance of their officials, I. xi. 33; their magistracies hereditary, I. vi. 13; have gold mines, I. xv. 18, 27; check losses of armies, I. xviii. 52 ff.; infantry inefficient, I. xiv. 25; bowmen inferior to Romans, I. xviii. 32, 33; their long shields, V. xxii. 20; use elephants in battle, VIII. xiii. 4, xiv. 35 ff., B. II. i. 11; skill in bridging rivers, II. xxi. 22; maintain spies at public expense, I. xxi. 11; subjected by Alexander, B. III. i. 5; make alliance with Tigranes, B. III. i. 11; feared by Arsaces, B. III. i. 12; fought constantly by the Romans, III. xix. 7; defeated by Ephthalitae, I. iv. 13; to whom they pay tribute, I. iv. 35; make peace with Theodosius, I. ii. 12–15, B. II. i. 5; unable to halt fortification of Daras, I. x. 15, B. II. i. 11; capture Amida, I. vii. 29; return Amida, I. ix. 4; wage war with the Huns, I. ix. 24; seize forts in Lazica, I. xii. 19; prevent fortification of Mindouos, I. xiii. 7, 8; defeated at Daras, I. xiv. 47 ff.; in Persarmenia, I. xv. 8; and in Armenia, I. xv. 16; disregard Mesopotamia, I. xvii. 25; victorious on the Euphrates, I. xviii. 37; invade Mesopotamia, I. xxi. 4; besiege Martyropolis in vain, I. xxi. 5 ff.; make peace with the Romans, I. xxii. 17, 18; capture Sura, II. v. 25, B. II. ix. 1; and Beroea, II. vii. 12 ff.; and Antioch, II. viii. 20 ff.; and Petra, II. xvii. 27; besiege Edessa in vain, II. xxvi. 5 ff., xxvii. 46; save Petra from the Romans, II. xxix. 41 ff.; suffer severe defeat in Lazica, II. xxx. 39 ff.; at Nisibis, S.H. ii. 28; make peace with the Romans, III. i. 1, ix. 25, 26; fight against Vandals, IV. xiv. 18; in the Roman army, VII. iii. 11, VIII. xxvi. 13; five-year truce with the Romans, VIII. i. 3; invade Lazica,

VIII. i. 3, viii. 39; have Alani as allies, VIII. iii. 4; maintain army in Lazica, VIII. iv. 5, 6; which they wish to acquire, VIII. vii. 1, 12, 13; threaten rebellion against Chosroes, VIII. vii. 4, S.H. ii. 31; led into Apsilia, VIII. x. 2, 3; extend sway, VIII. x. 4, B. III. vii. 7; hold Petra, VIII. x. 4, B. III. vii. 7; repair its wall, VIII. xi. 15, 16; have Hunnic allies, VIII. xi. 24, S.H. xi. 12; lose Petra but hold acropolis, VIII. xi. 62, 63; exhorted by Bessas, VIII. xii. 1 ff.; burned alive, VIII. xii. 14, 15; improve difficult road into Lazica, VIII. xiii. 5; take Scanda and Sarapanis, VIII. xiii. 19; rebuild Scanda, VIII. xiii. 20; have Dolomites as mercenaries, VIII. xiv. 6, 7; attack Archaeopolis, VIII. xiv. 11; control most of Lazica, VIII. xiv. 45; receive payments from the Romans, VIII. xv. 3, 6; make treaty with the Romans, VIII. xv. 12; whom they practically hold tributary, VIII. xv. 16–18; aim at Byzantium through Lazica, VIII. xv. 15; which they hold securely, VIII. xvi. 6, 7; gain Uthimereos, VIII. xvi. 13; and Scymnia and Suania, VIII. xvi. 14; Persian standards captured, VIII. xiv. 43; receive Rhabdios in exchange, B. II. iv. 3; their fortress Sisauranon, B. II. iv. 8; receive tribute from Rhabdios, B. II. iv. 11; held in check by Zenobia, B. II. viii. 10, 11; contest possession of Armenia, B. III. i. 13; defied by the Armenians, B. III. v. 12; the Persian War, VI. xxx. 2, VII. xxx. 25

Perusia, first city of Tuscany, V. xvi. 4, VII. xxxv. 2; submits to Constantinus, V. xvi. 3; battle fought near it, V. xvi. 6; garrisoned by Constantinus, V. xvii. 3; avoided by Vittigis, V. xvii. 7, VI. xi. 9; held by Cyprian, VII. vi. 8; its surrender demanded by Totila, VII. xii. 18; support obtained thence by Martinianus, VII. xxiii. 5–7; besieged by the Goths, VII. xxv. 1, 2; Totila summoned thither, VII. xxv. 19, 20; he moves against it, VII. xxv. 24; abandoned by Belisarius and captured by the Goths, VII. xxxv. 2, S.H. v. 17; betrayed to the Romans, VIII. xxxiii. 10–12

Pestilence, S.H. iv. 1, vi. 22, xviii. 44; devastates the whole world, II. xxii. 1 ff.; in Byzantium, II. xxii. 9 ff.; in Persia, II. xxiv. 8, 12; in the siege of Rome, VI. iii. 1, iv. 17, 18

Peter the Apostle, buried near Rome, where one of the city-gates bore his name, V. xix. 4; his promise to guard "Broken Wall," V. xxiii. 5; reverenced by the Romans above all others, V. xxiii. 5; his Church, V. xxii. 21, VI. ix. 17, VII. xx. 22, xxxvi. 17, S.H. xxvi. 29; Church of, in Byzantium, B. I. iv. 1

Peter the Illyrian, a Patrician; envoy of Justinian to Italy, V. iii. 30, iv. 17; his ability, V. iii. 30; delays at Aulon, V. iv. 20, 21; sent on with letter to Amalasuntha, V. iv. 22; arrives in Italy, V. iv. 25; denounces Theodatus V. iv. 30; whom he seeks to terrify, V. vi. 1; and who tries to prove his innocence, V. iv. 31; and suggests an agreement, V. vi. 2–6; recalled and given further instructions, V. vi. 7–13; reports to Justinian, V. vi. 14; sent again to Italy, V. vi. 25, 26, vii. 24, S.H. xvi. 2 ff.; reproaches Theodatus, V. vii. 13; who replies in a speech, V. vii. 14–16; replies thereto, V. vii. 17–21; destroys Amalasuntha, S.H. xvi. 5, xxiv. 23; delivers letter from Justinian, V. vii. 22; dismissed by the Goths, VI. xxii. 23; made Magister by the Emperor, VI. xxii. 24, S.H. xvi. 5; plunders the Scholarii, S.H. xxiv. 22; a very clever thief, S.H. xxiv. 23; sent as ambassador to Chosroes, VIII. xi. 2

Peter of Thrace, bodyguard of Solomon; at the banquet of Gontharis, IV. xxviii. 3; approves

INDEX

Artabanes' plot, IV. xxviii. 24, 28; with Artabanes cuts down remaining guards, IV. xxviii. 33

Peter the General, captured as a boy by Justinus, II. xv. 7; becomes general; sent to Lazica, I. xii. 9; summoned to Byzantium, I. xii. 14; bodyguard of the commander Justinian, I. xviii. 6; at the battle on the Euphrates, I. xviii. 42; favours invasion of Persia, II. xvi. 16; accuses Belisarius, S.H. iv. 4; accused by the Massagetae, IV. i. 6; attacked before Nisibis, II. xviii. 16 ff.; commander in army of invasion, II. xxiv. 13; precipitately enters Persia, II. xxiv. 18; commands right wing at the battle of Anglon, II. xxv. 17; assists in defence of Edessa, II. xxvi. 25 ff.; his surrender demanded by Chosroes, II. xxvi. 38; his base character and misrule in Lazica, II. xv. 6–8

Peter Barsymes, a Syrian, clever and unscrupulous, S.H. xxii. 3–5; appointed to succeed Theodotus, S.H. xxii. 6; his management, S.H. xxii. 17; favoured by Theodora, S.H. xxii. 22; whom he bewitched, S.H. xxii. 24, 32; student of sorcery, S.H. xxii. 25; removed from office, S.H. xxii. 33; appointed to a new one, *ib.*; succeeds John, S.H. xxii. 36; depreciates currency, S.H. xxii. 37, 38; oppresses farmers, S.H. xxiii. 14; controls the silk trade, S.H. xxv. 20–22

Petra, strong city of Lazica, built by Justinian, II. xv. 10, xvii. 3, xxix. 20, VIII. ii. 32; on the Asiatic side of the Phasis, VIII. ii. 29; its impregnable defences, II. xvii. 18 ff., VIII. xi. 12; attacked by the Persians, II. xvii. 4 ff.; besieged by Chosroes, II. xvii. 13 ff., VIII. iv. 5, 6; captured by him, II. xvii. 26, S.H. ii. 26; strongly garrisoned and provisioned by him, II. xix. 48, VIII. xii. 17–19, 21; besieged by Romans and Lazi, II. xxix. 11 ff.; valour of the Persian defenders, II. xxix. 35; the siege abandoned, II. xxx. 11; Persian garrison receives supplies, VIII. viii. 39; neglected by Dagisthaeus, VIII. ix. 2; keeps Romans and Lazi engaged, VIII. x. 4; besieged by Romans, VIII. xi. 11 ff., xiv. 4; captured by the Romans, VIII. xi. 62, xiii. 11, 12; its wall razed, VIII. xii. 28, B. III. vii. 7; Mermeroes learns of its loss, VIII. xiii. 1, 2; improved by Justinian, B. III. vii. 7; only stronghold in Lazica south of the Phasis, VIII. xiii. 2; lost by Dagisthaeus, recovered by Bessas, VIII. xxxiii. 24; distance from Apsarus, VIII. ii. 21; its water-supply, VIII. xii. 20–22; monopoly established in, II. xv. 11, xxix. 21

Petra Pertusa, fortress on the Flaminian Way, its naturally strong position, VI. xi. 10–14; allowed by Vittigis to retain its original garrison, VI. xi. 2; captured by the Romans, VI. xi. 10 ff.; captured by Totila, VII. vi. 1; held by the Goths, VIII. xxviii. 13; captured by the Romans, VIII. xxxiv. 16, 24

Petrae, ancient capital of the Arabs, I. xix. 20

Petres, fortress in Aquenisium, B. IV. iv. 3

Petrios, place in Armenia, B. III. iv. 12

Petrizen, fortress in Dardania, B. IV. iv. 3

Petroniana, fortress in Epirus, B. IV. iv. 3

Pezium, fortress in Epirus, B. IV. iv. 3

Phabrizus, high Persian official, II. xxviii. 16; employed by Chosroes, II. xxviii. 17; attempts to destroy Gubazes, II. xxix. 2 ff.; left as Commander in Lazica, II. xxx. 32; his forces almost annihilated, II. xxx. 42 ff.; defeats Anasozadus, VIII. x. 19

Phaeacia, Phaeacians, the island of Cercyra and its inhabitants, VIII. xxii. 18–23

Phanaguris, town on the Euxine, VIII. v. 28

Phanitheus, Erulian commander, VI.

xiii. 18; slain at Caesena, VI. xix. 20, xxii. 8
Pharangium, fortress in Persarmenia, occupied by the Romans, I. xv. 18; near Persian gold mines, I. xv. 27, 29; near source of the Boas River, II. xxix. 14; given over to the Romans, I. xv. 29, II. iii. 1; its return demanded by Chosroes, I. xxii. 3; given up by the Romans, I. xxii. 18, VIII. xiii. 19
Pharanores, fortress in southern Europe, B. IV. iv. 3
Pharas, Erulian chief, reports to Belisarius, IV. vii. 10; his good qualities, IV. iv. 29, 31; an uneducated man, IV. vi. 15; at the battle of Daras, I. xiii. 19, 25 ff., xiv. 32, 33, 39; in the African expedition, III. xi. 11; takes over siege of Gelimer, IV. iv. 28, 31, vi. 1, 3; his correspondence with Gelimer, IV. vi. 15–30, vii. 6–9; humours his prisoner, IV. vi. 31–34
Pharesmanes, of Colchis; officer in Roman army, I. viii. 3; father of Zaunas, IV. xix. 1, xx. 19
Pharsalus, city in Thessaly; fortified by Justinian, B. IV. iii. 5
Pharsanses, a man of note among the Lazi, II. xxix. 4; his friendship sought by Phabrizus, II. xxix. 5; saves Gubazes, II. xxix. 7
Phasciae, fortress in Macedonia, B. IV. iv. 3
Phasis River, in Lazica, VIII. i. 10, ii. 15, 31, v. 33, xiii. 3, 9, 23, 26, xvi. 6, 18, xvii. 12; its source in the Taurus, II. xxix. 16; its course through Lazica, II. xxix. 16, VIII. ii. 27, 32; considered a boundary between Europe and Asia, VIII. ii. 28, vi. 7, 8, 13, 14, 15, B. VI. i. 7; Petra only town south of, in Lazica, VIII. xiii. 2; its size and strong current, II. xxx. 25, 26; strongly defended by the Lazi, II. xxx. 27; forded by them, II. xxx. 37; crossed by Roman army, VIII. xiii. 28; distance from Chalcedon, III. i. 11
Phazas, an Iberian, nephew of Peranius, commander of Armenians, VII. vi. 10; sent to Naples, VII. vii. 3; escapes capture, VII. vii. 7; sent forward by Belisarius, VII. xxviii. 5; dies fighting bravely, VII. xxviii. 15
Pheidias, Athenian sculptor, VIII. xxi. 12, 13, B. I. xi. 7
Pheison, town in Armenia, II. xxiv. 15, B. III. iii. 1; distance from Martyropolis, B. III. iii. 1; strengthened by Justinian, B. III. iii. 6
Phialê, section of Alexandria, B. VI. i. 3
Phichas, fortress in Mesopotamia, B. II. vi. 14
Philae, fortress on an island in the Nile, I. xix. 34–36; its temples dismantled by Justinian, I. xix. 36, 37
Philegagus, Roman commander of horse, VIII. viii. 15; orders his men to fight on foot, VIII. viii. 30
Philemouth, an Erulian chief; encamps near Martinus, II. xxiv. 14; with Beros follows Peter into Persia, II. xxiv. 18; succeeds Phanitheus as Commander of the Eruli, VI. xxii. 8, VII. xiii. 22, xxxiv. 42, VIII. xxvi. 13; accompanies Germanus, VII. xxxix. 10; in the assault on Rome, VIII. xxxiii. 19; sent into Tuscany, VIII. xxxiv. 22; summoned to Campania, VIII. xxxiv. 24
Philippi, city in Macedonia, home of Demetrius, V. iii. 5
Philippopolis, city in Thrace, VIII. xxi. 21; restored by Justinian, B. IV. xi. 19
Philomede, city in Pisidia, S.H. xviii. 42
Phocaea, its colony Massilia, VII. xxxiii. 4
Phocas, Saint, B. V. ix. 24
Phocas, made Pretorian Prefect, I. xxiv. 18, S.H. xxi. 6, 7
Phocas, bodyguard of Belisarius, sent to Portus, VII. xv. 1; with Valentinus plans a sally, VII. xv. 2; not supported by Bessas, VII. xv. 3, 4; meets his death in a second sally, VII. xv. 5–8
Phoenicê, town in Illyricum, restored by Justinian, B. IV. i. 37, 38

INDEX

Phoenicia, its earlier extent, IV. x. 15; ruled by one king in ancient times, IV. x. 16; home of various peoples, IV. x. 17; Dido's emigration from, IV. x. 25; Phoenician tongue spoken in Libya, IV. x. 20; Phoenician inscriptions, IV. x. 22; centre of the silk industry, S.H. xxv. 14; home of Rhodon, S.H. xxvii. 3; Moors said to be a Phoenician race, B. VI. iii. 9; buildings of Justinian in, B. V. ix. 23 ff.; its city Palmyra, B. II. xi. 10, V. i. 2; guarded by a Roman force, II. xvi. 17

Phollis, a small coin, S.H. xxv. 12

Photice, town in Illyricum, B. IV. i. 37, iv. 3

Photius, stepson of Belisarius, V. v. 5, S.H. i. 31; his jealous nature, S.H. i. 32; accompanies Belisarius to Italy, V. v. 5; at the capture of Naples, V. x. 5, 8, 9, 20; driven from Italy by Antonina, S.H. i. 34; accompanies Belisarius, S.H. ii. 1; Antonina desires his removal, S.H. ii. 3, 4; accuses his mother, S.H. ii. 5; his assistance entreated by Belisarius, S.H. ii. 6–11, iv. 41; promises help, S.H. ii. 12; yet distrusts Belisarius, *ib.*; goes to Ephesus, S.H. ii. 14, iii. 2, 9; sends Theodosius to Cilicia, S.H. iii. 5; returns to Byzantium, *ib.*; cruelly punished by Theodora, S.H. iii. 12, xvii. 1; refuses to give information, S.H. iii. 13, 14; confined by Theodora, S.H. iii. 22; makes two escapes, S.H. iii. 22–24; flees to Jerusalem, S.H. iii. 28; becomes a monk, S.H. iii. 29; had received promise of Belisarius, S.H. v. 25; his groom Valentinus, V. xviii. 18; his intimates, S.H. iii. 8

Phoubelis, a notable among the Lazi; attacks Mermeroes, II. xxx. 22

Phracellan, fortress in Thessaly, B. IV. iv. 3

Phredas, friend of Areobindus; sent to Gontharis, IV. xxvi. 8, 9

Phrerraria, fortress in Remisianisia, B. IV. iv. 3

Phrygia, adjoins Bithynia, B. V. iii. 12; home of the Montani, S.H. xi. 23; source of grain, S.H. xxii. 17; its city Polybotus, S.H. xviii. 42

Phthia, ancient name of a district in Thessaly, B. IV. iii. 7

Physicians, S.H. xxvi. 5–7; Elpidius, physician of Theoderic, V. i. 38; Tribunus of Palestine, physician of Chosroes, II. xxviii. 8 ff., VIII. x. 11–16; Stephanus of Edessa, II. xxvi. 31; Pegasius of Laribus in Libya, IV. xxii. 14; Theoctistus VI. ii. 26 ff.

Picenum, district of central Italy, John sent thither, VI. vii. 28; raided by him, VI. x. 1 ff., xvii. 1; its metropolis Auximus, VI. xi. 2, xxiii. 6; its strongholds, Auximus, Petra and Urbinus, VI. xi. 2; Caesena and Monteferetra, VI. xi. 3; its town Alba, VI. vii. 25; story of an infant abandoned there, VI. xvii. 2 ff.; refuge for famine-sufferers, VI. xx. 18; ravaged by famine, VI. xx. 21, xxiv. 15; invaded by Totila, VII. xi. 39; Totila sends a force into, VII. xxx. 18; mentioned, VI. xviii. 9, xxii. 1, VII. xxx. 15, 17; its inhabitants, Piceni, V. xv. 21

Pillars of Heracles, the Strait of Gibraltar, III. i. 5, 9, 15, 18, vii. 11, IV. x. 20, B. VI. vii. 14

Pinci, fortress on the Danube, strengthened by Justinian, B. IV. vi. 1, 2

Pincian Gate, in the wall of Rome, next to the Flaminian Gate, V. xix. 16, xxiii. 3; held by Belisarius, V. xix. 14; often mentioned in describing the great siege, V. xxviii. 15, etc.

Pinna, a sea-creature which produces "wool," B. III. i. 20

Pinzus, fortress in Thrace, B. IV. xi. 20

Pisaurus, fortress on the Adriatic, VII. xi. 32; dismantled by Vittigis, VII. xi. 32, xxv. 7, 8; seized by Belisarius, VII. xi. 33, 34

Piscinae, fortress in Epirus, B. IV. iv. 3

Pisidia, region in Asia, home of Principius, V. xxviii. 23; Pisidians called "Wolf-Skulls," VII. xxvii.

20; its city Philomede, S.H. xviii. 42
Pissas, Gothic commander, sent into Tuscany, V. xvi. 5; defeated and captured, V. xvi. 6, 7
Pistes, fortress in southern Europe, B. IV. iv. 3
Pitius, *see* Pityus
Pityaxes, Persian general at the battle of Daras, I. xiii. 16, xiv. 32, 38
Pityus, fortress in Lazica, II. xxix. 18; distance from Sebastopolis, VIII. iv. 4; dismantled by the Romans, VIII. iv. 6, B. III. vii. 8
Pitzas, a Goth, surrenders part of Samnium to Belisarius, V. xv. 1, 2
Placentia, first city of Aemilia, on the Po, VII. xiii. 9; besieged by the Goths, VII. xiii. 8–11; inhabitants hard pressed, VII. xvi. 2, 3; surrender to the Goths, VII. xvi. 3
Placidia, sister of Arcadius and wife of Constantius, III. iii. 4; mother of Valentinian, whom she corrupts, III. iii. 10; appoints Boniface General of Libya, III. iii. 16; hears Aetius' slander of Boniface, III. iii. 17, 18; summons him to Rome, III. iii. 18; sends men to Boniface at Carthage, III. iii. 27; learns the truth and tries to bring him back, III. iii. 28, 29; finally receives him back, III. iii. 36; her death, III. iv. 15
Placidia, daughter of Eudoxia, wife of Olyvrius, taken captive by Gizeric, III. v. 3, vi. 6; sent to Byzantium, III. v. 6
Placidiana, fortress in Macedonia, B. IV. iv. 3
Placillianae, Palace in Byzantium, I. xxiv. 30
Plague, *see* Pestilence
Plataea, city in Greece, work of Justinian in, B. IV. ii. 24
Platanon, called a suburb of Theopolis (*i.e.* Antioch), B. V. v. 1
Plato, Saint, his shrine in Byzantium, B. I. iv. 27
Platonic teachings, espoused by Theodatus, V. iii. 1, vi. 10
Pleurum, fortress in Macedonia, B. IV. iv. 3
Plotinopolis, city in Thrace, restored by Justinian, B. IV. xi. 19
Plumia, adornment of the costume of the Armenian satraps, B. III. i. 22
Po River, in Italy, called also Eridanus, V. i. 18; boundary of Liguria, V. xv. 28; and of Aemilia, V. xv. 30; distance from Milan, VI. xxi. 2; spanned by a bridge at Ticinum, VI. xxv. 8; proposed as a boundary between Gothic and Roman territory, VI. xxix. 2, VII. ii. 15; remarkable falling of its water, VI. xxviii. 3–5; crossed by Mundilas, VI. xii. 30, 31; Paulus swims across it, VI. xxi. 4; Martinus and Uliaris delay on its banks, VI. xxi. 2, 13; guarded by Roman troops, VI. xxiii. 3–5, xxviii. 33; crossed by Uraïas, VI. xxiv. 21; by the Franks, VI. xxv. 7–11, xxviii. 19; guarded by Magnus and Vitalius, VI. xxviii. 1, 2; and by Belisarius and Ildiger, VI. xxviii. 24; by Valerian, VIII. xxxiii. [illegible]; mentioned, VI. xxix. 35, xxx. 3, VIII. xxvi. 22, xxxiii. 6, xxxiv. 8, xxxv. 37; *see also* Eridanus
Pola, city in Illyricum, VII. x. 13
Polybotus, city in Phrygia, S.H. xviii. 42
Polytheism, *see* Paganism
Pompeius, father of John and brother of Hypatius, VII. xxxi. 14; nephew of Anastasius, sent from the Palace by Justinian, I. xxiv. 19–21; brought before him as a prisoner, I. xxiv. 53; his death, I. xxiv. 56; his children, I. xxiv. 58
Pompey, Roman General, B. III. iv. 6
Pontes, fortress on the Danube, B. IV. vi. 8 ff.; improved by Justinian, B. IV. vi. 18
Ponteserium, fortress on the Danube, B. IV. vi. 23
Pontici, a people on the Euxine, II. xxix. 19, VIII. ii. 2; visited by Bessas, VIII. xiii. 11
Pontus, region of Asia, visited by Orestes, I. xvii. 14; its city Amasia, S.H. xviii. 42
Pontus, *see* Euxine

INDEX

Pontzas, fortress in Aquenisium, B. IV. iv. 3
Poor-House, near Apamea, B. V. ix. 27; in Bostra, B. V. ix. 22; of St. Conon, B. V. ix. 35; in Curicum, B. V. ix. 34; in Pamphylia, B V. ix. 38
Porphyreon, town in Phoenicia, B. V. ix. 23; purchased by Evangelus, S.H. xxx. 19
Porphyrius, a whale which harassed Byzantium, VII. xxix. 9 ff.
Portus, harbour of Rome, V. xxvi. 3; its situation, V. xxvi. 4–7; distance from Rome, V. xxvi. 4; approached by a good road, V. xxvi. 9, VI. vii. 6, VII. xix. 11, 18; captured and garrisoned by the Goths, V. xxvi. 14, 15, xxvii. 1, VI. vii. 11; strength of its defences, V. xxvi. 7, 19; abandoned by the Goths and occupied by Paulus, VI. vii. 16, 22; receives reinforcements, VII. xv. 1; sally from, VII. xv. 7, 8; Roman ships interrupted at, VII. xv. 11–13; cut off from Rome by Totila VII. xviii. 10; protected by a special force, VII. xix. 6; held by Isaac, VII. xix. 7; report of Belisarius' success reaches it, VII. xix. 23; its loss feared by Belisarius, VII. xix. 30; who returns thither, VII. xix. 32; checkmated by a garrison at Algedon, VII. xxii. 18; guarded by the Romans, VII. xxiv. 2; refuge of Roman fugitives, VII. xxvi. 12; occupied by the Goths, VII. xxxvi. 3; sought by Gothic refugees, VIII. xxxiii. 23; surrendered to the Romans, VIII. xxxiv. 16
Poseidon, fortress in Epirus, B. IV. iv. 3
Post, Imperial, II. xx. 20, III. xvi. 12, B. V. iii. 3; its uses and efficiency, S.H. xxx. 1–7; neglected by Justinian, S.H. xxx. 8–11
Potamucastellum, fortress in Thrace, B. IV. xi. 20
Potes, fortress in the district of Aquenisium, B. IV. iv. 3
Potidaea, ancient town in Pallenê, known later as Cassandria, B. IV. iii. 21; captured by the Huns, II. iv. 5
Praenestine Gate, in the wall of Rome; commanded by Bessas, V. xviii. 35, xix. 15; threatened by a Gothic camp, V. xix. 2; near the Vivarium, V. xxii. 10
Praetor, III. x. 3
Praetor of the Demes, S.H. xx. 9, 10; *cf.* S.H. vii. 19, xi. 37, xvi. 19, 20, xviii. 33, xx. 7, 13, xxviii. 10
Praetorians, soldiers of the Imperial Guard, S.H. xxii. 5; *see* Prefect, Praetorian
Praxiteles, Greek sculptor, B. I. xi. 7
Precalis, district east of the Ionian Gulf, V. xv. 25
Prefect, Praetorian, called "Prefect of the Court," I. xxiv. 11, 18, III. x. 3, 7, xi. 17, xiii. 12, VI. xii. 27, xxi. 40, VII. vi. 9, S.H. xxi. 1; of the army, a disbursing officer, III. xi. 17, xv. 13, xvii. 16, IV. xvi. 2; of the city, S.H. ix. 37; of the Demes, S.H. xx. 1
Preïdis, fortress in Moesia, B. IV. xi. 20
Preiecta, daughter of Vigilantia and wife of Areobindus; accompanies him to Libya, IV. xxiv. 3, VII. xxxi. 3; niece of Justinian, VII. xxxi. 2; placed in a fortress for safety, IV. xxvi. 18; compelled to make false report, IV. xxvii. 20; presents a great sum to Artabanes, IV. xxviii. 43; betrothed to him, VII. xxxi. 2; to whom she owes a debt of gratitude, VII. xxxi. 3; sent to the Emperor by Artabanes, VII. xxxi. 4; Artabanes unable to marry her, VII. xxxi. 11; married to John, son of Pompeius, VII. xxxi. 14
Presidio, fortress in Moesia, B. IV. xi. 20
Presidius, a Roman of Ravenna, VI. viii. 2; escapes to Spolitium, *ib.*; robbed of two daggers by Constantinus, VI. viii. 3, S.H. i. 28; appeals to Belisarius, VI. viii. 4 ff.
Pretzouries, fortress in Remisianisia, B. IV. iv. 3
Priapus, worshipped by the Blemyes and Nobatae, I. xix. 35
Primiana, fortress in Remisianisia, B. IV. iv. 3

INDEX

Primoniana, fortress in Dardania, B. IV. iv. 3

Principius, a Pisidian, bodyguard of Belisarius, V. xxviii. 23–29; fights valiantly, V. xxix. 39, 40; killed in battle, V. xxix. 41

Priniana, fortress in Macedonia, B. IV. iv. 3

Priscupera, fortress in Dardania, B. IV. iv. 3

Priscus, Saint; shrine of, in Byzantium, B. I. vi. 4

Priscus, Secretary of Justinian, S.H. xvi. 7; opposed by Theodora, S.H. xvi. 8; becomes a priest, S.H. xvi. 9; forgotten by Justinian, S.H. xvi. 10

Priscus of Emesa; a clever forger, S.H. xxviii. 1; his operations, S.H. xxviii. 4 ff.; unmasked by Longinus, S.H. xxviii. 14, 15

Prison of Oblivion, in Persia; reason for the name, I. v. 8; its rule abated for Arsaces, I. v. 9–29; Cabades confined therein, I. v. 7

Privata, personal funds of the Emperor, [illegible]

Proba, a notable woman of Rome; said to have betrayed the city, III. ii. 27

Probinu, fortress in Haemimontum, B. IV. xi. 20

Probus, nephew of Anastasius; sent to Bosporus, I. xii. 6, 9

Proclus, Quaestor, S.H. vi. 13; counsels Justinus, I. xi. 11 ff.; saves Theodatus, S.H. ix. 41

Proconsularis (provincia), area adjoining Carthage, B. VI. v. 12

Procopius of Caesarea, author of the *History of the Wars*, I. i. 1; eyewitness of the events described, I. i. 3; religious views, V. iii. 6–9; chosen Legal Adviser to Belisarius, I. i. 3, xii. 24; in Byzantium at the time of the pestilence, II. xxii. 9; had seen Cappadocia and Armenia, I. xvii. 17; his frankness in writing, I. i. 5; sails with Belisarius for Africa, III. xii. 3; his reassuring dream, III. xii. 3–5; sent to Syracuse, III. xiv. 3, 4, 7–13; praised by Belisarius, III. xiv. 15; congratulates Belisarius upon a good omen, III. xv. 35; escapes from Carthage with Solomon, IV. xiv. 39; goes to Belisarius in Syracuse, IV. xiv. 41; writer of the *Gothic War*, V. vii. 37, etc.; sent to Naples, VI. iv. 1; gathers soldiers and provisions in Campania, VI. iv. 19; assisted by Antonina, VI. iv. 20; witnesses the infant reared by a goat, VI. xvii. 10; makes a useful suggestion to Belisarius, VI. xxiii. 23–28

Procopius of Edessa, Prefect of Samaria, B. V. vii. 14

Procurers, banished from Byzantium, B. I. ix. 6

Prometheus, the alleged scene of his punishment, VIII. i. 12, vi. 15

Pronathidum, fortress in Epirus, B. IV. iv. 3

Proöchthi, place on the Bosporus, B. I. viii. 3

Propontis, modern Sea of Marmara, B. I. xi. 1

Prorated assessments, a new tax, S.H. xxiii. 9, 17–21

[illegible] 1–10

Protectores, section of the Palace Guard, S.H. xxiv. 24

Protiana, fortress in Dardania, B. IV. iv. 3

Psoes, deacon in Alexandria, S.H. xxvii. 14; dies under torture, S.H. xxvii. 15

Ptocheiou, fortress in Epirus, B. IV. iv. 3

Ptocheium, fortress in Dardania, B. IV. iv. 3

Ptolemaïs, city in Libya; restored by Justinian, B. VI. ii. 9–11

Ptolemaïs, town in Phoenicia, B. V. ix. 25

Pudentius of Tripolis; recovers the region for the Romans, III. x. 22–24, xi. 22, IV. xxi. 3; supported by Belisarius, IV. v. 10; advises Sergius, IV. xxi. 3; fights against the Leuathae, IV. xxi. 13, 14; his death, IV. xxi. 15

Pulchra Theodora, fortress in Moesia, B. IV. xi. 20

Pumpkin, nickname of Theodotus, S.H. ix. 37

Pupsalus, fortress in Epirus, B. IV. iv. 3

INDEX

Pusinum, fortress in Thrace, B. IV. xi. 20
Putedis, fortress on the Danube, B. IV. vi. 28
Pylades, companion of Orestes, I. xvii. 11 ff.
Pyramids, compared with the buildings of Justinian, B. II. i. 3
Pyramus, river near Mopsuestia, B. V. v. 4
Pyrenees Mountains, on the northern boundary of Spain, V. xii. 3
Pyrgo-castellum, a fortress formed by a single tower, B. II. v. 8
Pythia, place in Bithynia, B. V. iii. 16

Quadratus, messenger to Belisarius, S.H. iv. 24, 26
Quaesitor, public prosecutor, S.H. xx. 9, 11
Quaestor, Councillor of the Emperor, S.H. vi. 13, ix. 41, xiv. 3, xx. 15; office held by Fidelius, V. xiv. 5; mentioned, VII. xl. 23
Quartermaster, paymaster of the army, S.H. xxiii. 12, xxiv. 13
Quartiana, fortress in Aquenisium, B. IV. iv. 3
Questris, fortress in Moesia; restored by Justinian, B. IV. vii. 12
Quimedaba, fort in Dardania; built by Justinian, B. IV. i. 32
Quintilis, early name of July, as being the "fifth" month from March, V. xxiv. 31

Raculê, fortress in Haemimontum, B. IV. xi. 20
Radigis, son of Hermegisclus, VIII. xx. 12; advised by his father to marry his stepmother, VIII. xx. 20; brought to terms by his rejected fiancée, VIII. xx. 22 ff.
Ragnaris, Gothic commander of Tarentum; negotiates for its surrender, VIII. xxvi. 4; refuses to surrender, VIII. xxxiv. 9; tricks Pacurius, VIII. xxxiv. 10–12; defeated in battle, VIII. xxxiv. 14, 15
Ram, siege-engine for battering walls, V. xxi. 5–12, xxii. 1, 11, II. xvii. 9, 10; a lighter type made by the Sabiri, VIII. xi. 29 ff., xiv. 5
Ratiaria, city on the Danube; improved by Justinian, B. IV. vi. 24
Ravenna, city in northern Italy, refuge of Honorius, III. ii. 9, 25; its situation, V. i. 16 ff.; attacked by Alaric and Attalus, III. ii. 29; limit of Picene territory, V. xv. 21; besieged by the Goths, V. i. 14, 24; surrendered to Theoderic, V. i. 24; treasures deposited in, V. xii. 47; occupied by Vittigis, V. xi. 26; Roman senators killed there, V. xxvi. 1; held by Vittigis, VI. xvi.–xxix.; besieged by Belisarius, VI. xxviii. 1 ff.; its stores of grain burned, VI. xxviii. 25, 26; entered by Belisarius and his army, VI. xxix. 30 ff.; left by Belisarius, VII. i. 25; administered by Alexander, VII. i. 32; held by Constantianus, VII. vi. 8; headquarters of Belisarius, VII. xi. 1 ff.; found unsuitable, VII. xiii. 13, 14; left in charge of Justinus, VII. xiii. 19, VIII. xxviii. 4; protected by Auximus, VI. xxiv. 7, xxvi. 13; centre of Roman strength in Italy, VII. xxxix. 23, xl. 30, VIII. xxiii. 4, 17, 42, xxvi. 20, 25, xxviii. 1, 2; Romans defeated near, VII. xxxvii. 28; overtaxed by Belisarius, S.H. v. 4; distance from Ariminum, VI. x. 5; from Auximus, VI. xxiii. 6; from Caesena, V. i. 15; from Faventia, VII. iii. 22; from Milan, VI. vii. 37, 38; from the Tuscan Sea, V. xv. 19; its harbour Classes, VI. xxix. 31; its Palace, VI. xxix. 37, S.H. i. 33; priest of, V. i. 24
Red Sea, description of (confused by Procopius with the Arabian Gulf), I. xix. 2 ff., II. iii. 41; near Mt. Sina, B. V. viii. 1, 2
Referendarius, a palace official, II. xxiii. 6, S.H. xiv. 11, xvii. 32, xxix. 28
Regata, place near Rome, V. xi. 1; Goths gather at, V. xi. 1, 5
Remisianisia, district in southern Europe, B. IV. iv. 3
Reparatus, priest of Carthage; messenger of Gontharis, IV. xxvi. 23, 24; persuades Areobindus, IV.

xxvi. 24–27; dismissed by Gontharis, IV. xxvi. 31
Reparatus, brother of Vigilius; escapes execution, V. xxvi. 2; Praetorian Prefect; his death, VI. xxi. 40
Repentance, a convent on the Bosporus, S.H. xvii. 5, B. I. ix. 9
Requisition, a burden imposed upon landholders, S.H. xxii. 19, xxiii. 9–14
Residina, fortress in Moesia, B. IV. xi. 20
Rex, title of barbarian kings, V. i. 26, VI. xiv. 38; "Reges," title of an infantry detachment, V. xxiii. 3
Rhabdios, Roman town surrounded by Persian territory, B. II. iv. 1–7; distance from Sisauranon, B. II. iv. 9; neglected by the Romans, B. II. iv. 10; fortified by Justinian, B. II. iv. 12, 13
Rhabestum, fortress in Dardania, B. IV. iv. 3
Rhaedestus, city near the Hellespont, fortified by Justinian; distance from Heracleum, B. IV. ix. 17, 18
Rhasios, fortress in Mesopotamia, B. II. iv. 14
Rhechius, river near Thessalonicê, B. IV. iii. 27, 30
Rhecimer, slays his father-in-law Anthemius, Emperor of the West, III. vii. 1
Rhecimundus, Gothic notable; in command of Bruttium, VII. xviii. 26; attacked and routed by John, VII. xviii. 27, 28
Rhecinarius, envoy to Chosroes, II. xxvii. 24, 25
Rhecithangus, of Thrace; commander in Lebanon, II. xvi. 17 ff.; eager to return thither, II. xix. 33, 34; commander in Lazica, II. xxx. 29; in Illyricum, VIII. xxvii. 13
Rhegium, city in southern Italy, V. viii. 1, VII. xviii. 27, xxiii. 12; opposite Messana, VII. xxviii. 18; Belisarius departs thence with his army, V. viii. 4; attacked by the Goths, VII. xxxvii. 19–22, xxxix. 1; surrendered to them, VII. xxxix. 5
Rhegium, town on the Egnatian Road, B. IV. viii. 5, 7; its harbour, B. IV. viii. 10 ff.; near Athyras, B. IV. viii. 18
Rheon River, in Lazica, VIII. xiii. 3, xiv. 47
Rhepordenes, fortress in Remisianisia, B. IV. iv. 3
Rhesium, suburb of Byzantium, B. I. iv. 28
Rhiginocastellum, fortress near Germenne, B. IV. iv. 3
Rhine River, in Gaul, V. xii. 7, VIII. xx. 32, 33; distance from Brittia, VIII. xx. 4; separates the Varni from the Franks, VIII. xx. 2, 3, 18; reached by the Vandals, III. iii. 1
Rhipaean Mountains, contain the source of the Tanais, VIII. vi. 5, 6
Rhipalthas, fortress in Mesopotamia, B. II. iv. 14
Rhizaeum, city near Lazica, II. xxix. 22, xxx. 14, VIII. ii. 3, 10; distance from Apsarus, VIII. ii. 11; fortified by Justinian, B. III. vii. 3
Rhodon, praefectus augustalis; at Alexandria, [illegible]; tortures Psoes, S.H. xxvii. 15; investigated by Justinian, S.H. xxvii. 16; executed, S.H. xxvii. 18
Rhodopê, region of Thrace; fortified by Justinian, B. IV. xi. 6–17; fortresses in, B. IV. xi. 20
Rhodopolis, important city of Lazica, II. xxix. 18, VIII. xiii. 21; destroyed by the Lazi, VIII. xiii. 22
Rhone River, in Gaul, V. xii. 7; boundary of Visigothic power, V. xii. 12, xiii. 5; limit of Roman power, V. xii. 20; separates Goths from Franks, V. xii. 45
Rhotun, fortress in Dardania, B. IV. iv. 3
Ricilas, bodyguard of Belisarius, sent to Auximus, VII. xi. 19; his rash encounter with the Goths, VII. xi. 22–24; his death, VII. xi. 25
Ripesia, section of Dacia, on the Danube, B. IV. v. 10
Risiulfus, a Lombard, nephew of Vaces and heir to the throne, VII. xxxv. 13; banished by him, VII. xxxv. 14; flees to the Varni, VII.

xxxv. 15; his two children, VII. xxxv. 15, 16
Rock of Blood, pass between Lucania and Bruttium, VII. xxviii. 7
Rodolphus, leader of the Eruli, VI. xiv. 11; forced by his people to march against the Lombards, VI. xiv. 12 ff.
Rogi, a barbarian people, allies of the Goths, VI. xiv. 24, VII. ii. 1–3; elevate Eraric to the Gothic throne, VII. ii. 4
Rolligeras, fortress near Germenne, B. IV. iv. 3
Romaniana, fortress in Dardania, B. IV. iv. 3
Romans, in ancient times, captured Jerusalem, V. xii. 42; ancient Roman dress preserved in Gaul, V. xii. 18, 19; subjects of the Eastern Empire, both in the East and in the West, mentioned frequently throughout; lack of discipline in Roman armies, I. xiv. 14; their bowmen superior to those of the Persians, I. xviii. 34; lived in luxury under Theoderic, V. xx. 11; poverty of Roman soldiers, IV. iv. 3; marry Vandal women, IV. xiv. 8; desire Vandal estates, IV. xiv. 10; raise a mutiny, IV. xiv. 7 ff.; make peace with the Persians, III. ix. 26; accustomed to enter subject cities in disorder, III. xxi. 9; require especial oaths from bodyguards, IV. xviii. 6; Roman deserters in the Gothic army, VII. xxiii. 3, xxvi. 10, xxxix. 22, VIII. xxvi. 6, xxxii. 20, xxxiii. 10; purchase silk from the Persians, VIII. xvii. 1, S.H. xxv. 16; maintain spies at public expense, I. xxi. 11, S.H. xxx. 1, 12 ff.; specifically, the residents of Rome, celebrate a festival commemorating the overthrow of Maximus, III. iv. 16; honour Christian teachings, V. xxv. 23; suffer hardships during the siege of Rome, V. xx. 5, etc.; send non-combatants to Naples, V. xxv. 2, 10; again suffer during siege by Totila, VII. xiii. 4, etc.; especially devoted to their city, VIII. xxii. 5; Roman Emperor, alone privileged to coin gold, VII. xxxiii. 5, 6; wears red shoes, B. III. i. 23; Romans, Field of the, on the Persian border, B. II. iv. 5, 6
Romanus, Abbot, Monastery of, B. V. ix. 11
Rome, Capital and first city of the West, VI. vii. 38, S.H. xxvi. 12; terminus of the Appian Way, V. xiv. 6; its territory adjoins Campania, V. xv. 22; abandoned by Honorius, III. ii. 8, 9; sacked by the Visigoths, III. ii. 13; attacked by Alaric, III. ii. 14–23; suffers under his siege, III. ii. 27; delivered to him, according to report, by Proba, III. ii. 27; sacked by Alaric, III. ii. 24, V. xii. 41; despoiled by Gizeric, III. v. 1 ff., IV. ix. 5; visited by envoys from Justinian, V. iii. 5, 16; garrisoned by Vittigis, V. xi. 25, 26; abandoned by the Goths, V. xi. 26, xiv. 12, 13; entered by Belisarius, V. xiv. 14; keys of, sent to Justinian, V. xiv. 15; defences improved by Belisarius, *ib.*; ill situated for a siege, V. xiv. 16, xxiv. 13; its territories secured by Belisarius, V. xvi. 1; its wall embracing the Tiber, V. xix. 6–10; provisioned for siege, V. xvii. 14; its siege begun by the Goths, V. xxiv. 26; not entirely shut in by them, V. xxv. 6; visited by famine and pestilence, VI. iii. 1; abandoned by the Goths, VI. x. 12 ff.; garrisoned by Belisarius, VI. xiii. 1; avoided by Totila, VII. vi. 1; held by John, VII. vi. 8; garrison of Naples, moves thither VII. viii. 6–9; placarded by Totila, VII. ix. 21; Belisarius sends a small force thither, VII. xi. 37; besieged by Totila, VII. xiii. 1 ff.; Vigilius seeks to revictual the city, VII. xv. 9 ff.; sufferings of the population during siege, VII. xiii. 4 ff., xvi. 4, 7, xvii. 1, 9–25, xx. 3; concern of Belisarius for, VII. xviii. 3; its approaches guarded by Totila, VII. xviii. 8; captured by him, VII. xx. 16 ff.; its walls partly razed, VII. xxii. 7,

xxiv. 3; saved from destruction by a letter from Belisarius, VII. xxii. 8–17; left without inhabitants, VII. xxii. 19; visited by Belisarius, VII. xxiii. 8; reoccupied and held by him, VII. xxiv. 2–26; its walls hastily rebuilt, VII. xxiv. 3, 4; its keys sent to Justinian, VII. xxiv. 34; its garrison kills Conon, VII. xxx. 7; at the mercy of the Goths, VII. xxxv. 2; assailed by Totila, VII. xxxvi. 1 ff.; captured through treachery, VII. xxxvi. 7–14; previously betrayed by Isaurians, VII. xxxvi. 7; commanded by Diogenes and Paulus, VII. xxxvi. 16; its population invited by Totila to return, VII. xxxvi. 29; its defences previously destroyed in part by him, VII. xxxvii. 2, VIII. xxii. 3; damage repaired by Totila, VII. xxxvii. 3; commanded by Bessas, VIII. xii. 31; captured by the Goths, VIII. xii. 32; Procopius there, VIII. xxi. 10; adorned by works of art from Greece, VIII. xxi. 14; prophecy concerning, VIII. xxi. 16; defended by the Goths, VIII. xxxiii. 13 ff.; its wall too long for them to defend, VIII. xxxiii. 17; lost by Bessas, won by Dagisthaeus, VIII. xxxiii. 24; captured the fifth time during the reign of Justinian, VIII. xxxiii. 27; held by the Romans, VIII. xxxiv. 6; its Palace, VI. viii. 10, ix. 5, S.H. xxvi. 27; its bishop Silverius, V. xi. 26, xiv. 4, xxv. 13; Vigilius, V. xxv. 13, xxvi. 2, VII. xv. 9, xxxv. 9; its priest Pelagius, VII. xvi. 5; who becomes its Chief Deacon, S.H. xxvii. 17; a priest of, V. xvi. 20; its Church of Peter the Apostle, VI. ix. 17; its aqueducts, VI. iii. 3–7, ix. 1, 2; cut by the Goths, V. xix. 13; their number and size, *ib.*; stopped up by Belisarius, V. xix. 18; water of one used to turn mills, V. xix. 8; its fourteen gates, V. xix. 1; the Asinarian, V. xiv. 14; the Aurelian, V. xix. 4; the Flaminian, V. xix. 2; the Pancratian, V. xviii. 35; of Paul, VI. iv. 3; of Peter, V. xix. 4; the Pincian, V. xix. 14; the Praenestine, V. xix. 2; the Salarian, V. xviii. 39; the Transtiburtine, V. xix. 4, its sewers, V. xix. 29; its "stadium" in the Plain of Nero, VI. i. 5; its ancient storage chambers, VI. i. 11; its harbour Portus, V. xxv. 4, xxvi. 3, 7, 9; Ostia, VI. iv. 2; distance from Algedon, VII. xxii. 18; from Centumcellae, VI. vii. 19; from Dryus, VII. xviii. 4; from Narnia, V. xvii. 6; from Portus and the sea, V. xxvi. 4; from Tibur, VI. iv. 7; road between Rome and Portus, VII. xix. 11, 18; its harbour, VII. vi. 18

Rome, name of a cock of the Emperor Honorius, III. ii. 26

Romyliana, fortress in Aquenisium, B. IV. iv. 3

Roumisiana, fort in Dardania, built by Justinian, B. IV. i. 32

Rubusta, fortress in Moesia, B. IV. xi. [illegible]

Ruderic, Gothic commander, VII. v. 1; defeated by Isaac, VII. xix. 25, 26; dies of wounds, VII. xix. 34

Rufinianae, suburb of Byzantium, I. xxv. 21, 23

Rufinus, envoy to the Persians, I. xi. 24; slanders Hypatius, I. xi. 38; ambassador to Hierapolis, I. xiii. 11; treats with Cabades, I. xvi. 1 ff.; reports to the Emperor, I. xvi. 10; meets Chosroes on the Tigris, I. xxii. 1; sent to Byzantium, I. xxii. 7; false report of his death, I. xxii. 9; negotiates with Chosroes, I. xxii. 13, 14; slandered to the Emperor, I. xxii. 15; sent again as envoy to Chosroes, I. xxii. 16; brother of Timostratus, I. xvii. 44; father of John, the ambassador, II. vii. 15

Rufinus, of Thrace, of the House of Belisarius and his standard-bearer, IV. x. 3, 4; commander of cavalry, III. xi. 7; makes successful attack upon the Moors, IV. x. 5; his force in turn annihilated by the Moors, IV. x. 6 ff.;

captured and killed, IV. x. 10, 11, xi. 22
Rufinus, commander in Libya, IV. xix. 1; fights valiantly, IV. xx. 19
Rusciane, harbour of Thurii, VII. xxviii. 8; strong fortress near it, *ib.*; which is besieged by Totila, VII. xxix. 21; makes terms with the Goths, VII. xxx. 5; Belisarius attempts to relieve it, VII. xxx. 9–14; surrenders to Totila, VII. xxx. 19–21
Rusticiana, daughter of Symmachus and wife of Boethius; reduced to beggary, VII. xx. 27, 28; hated by the Goths, VII. xx. 29; protected by Totila, VII. xx. 30
Rusticus, a priest of Rome; sent with Peter to Justinian, V. vi. 13, 14

Sabbatiani, schismatics, S.H. xi. 14
Sabbatius, father of Justinian, S.H. xii. 18
Sabeiri Huns, their location, II. xxix. 15; in the Persian army, I. xv. 1, VIII. xiv. 11, xvi. 8, xvii. 10; in the Roman army, VIII. xi. 22–26; form alliance with Gubazes, II. xxix. 29; receive money from Justinian, II. xxx. 28, VIII. xi. 25, 26; display skill in building rams, VIII. xi. 27–32; allied with Persians, VIII. xiii. 6; distrusted by Mermeroes, VIII. xiii. 7; directed to build rams, VIII. xiv. 4, 5; their leader slain, VIII. xvii. 18
Sabines, a people of Italy, V. xvii. 12
Sabinianus, bodyguard of Belisarius, sent to Auximus, VII. xi. 19; decides to leave Auximus, VII. xi. 26, 27; attacked by Totila, but escapes, VII. xi. 29–31; sent to Pisaurus, VII. xi. 34
Sabiniribes, fortress in southern Europe, B. IV. iv. 3
Sabrathan, city in Africa, walled by Justinian, B. VI. iv. 13
Saccice, mother of Alamundaras, I. xvii. 1
Saccus, city in northern Greece, fortified by Justinian, B. IV. ii. 16
Sacissus, fortress in Thrace, B. IV. xi. 20
Sacred Island, at the mouth of the Tiber, V. xxvi. 5
Sagaris, *see* Sangarius
Saginae, a people near Lazica, VIII. ii. 16, iv. 3, 5, 7
St. Agathonicus, Church of, in Byzantium, B. I. iv. 30
St. Anna, mother of Mary, her shrine in Deuteron, B. I. iii. 11
St. Anthimus, shrine of, in Byzantium, B. I. vi. 9
St. Bacchus, Church of St. Sergius and, B. I. iv. 3
St. Conon, Poor-House of, B. V. ix. 35
St. Cyril, principal fortress in Scythia, restored by Justinian, B. IV. vii. 16
St. Donatus', two fortresses in Epirus, B. IV. iv. 3
St. Elissaeus, Monastery of the Spring of, B. V. ix. 9
St. Gregory, Monastery of, in Jerusalem, B. V. ix. 2
St. John, Monastery of, B. V. ix. 19
St. John, Church of, in Laodicea, B. V. ix. 30
St. John, Monastery of, in Mesopotamia, B. V. ix. 31
St. Julian, fortress in Haemimontum, B. IV. xi. 20
St. Lawrence, shrine of, in Byzantium, B. I. vi. 2
St. Leontius, House of, in Damascus, B. V. ix. 26
St. Mary, Monastery of, at Jerusalem, B. V. ix. 8; *see also* Mary *and* Virgin
St. Michael (Archangel), churches of, in Byzantium, B. I. iii. 14, S.H. xvi. 18; at Anaplus, B. I. viii. 2; opposite Anaplus, B. I. viii. 19; at Mochadium, B. I. ix. 14; at Antioch, B. II. x. 25; at Daphne, suburb of Antioch, II. xi. 6, 13; at Tretum, near Antioch, II. xi. 7, 12; at Pythia, B. V. iii. 20; Poor-House of, at Emporium in Pamphylia, B. V. ix. 38
St. Nicholas, shrine of, in Byzantium, B. I. vi. 4
St. Pancratius, from whom a gate at Rome was named, V. xviii. 35
St. Panteleëmon, Monastery of, B. V. ix. 3
St. Phocas, Monastery of, B. V. ix. 24

INDEX

St. Plato, his shrine in Byzantium, B. I. iv. 27
St. Prima, local Saint of Carthage, shrine of, restored by Justinian, B. VI. v. 9
St. Romanus, Poor-House of, B. V. ix. 27
St. Sabianus, fortress in Epirus, B. IV. iv. 3
St. Sabinus', fortress in Epirus, B. IV. iv. 3
St. Samuel, Monastery of, B. V. ix. 15
St. Sergius, from whom Sergiopolis was named, II. v. 29; Church of, in Euphratesia, B. II. ix. 3; Monastery of, B. V. ix. 20; House of, B. V. ix. 25; Church of Sts. Sergius and Bacchus, B. I. iv. 3
St. Stephen's, fortress in Epirus, B. IV. iv. 3
St. Thalelaeus, Monastery of, in Jerusalem, B. V. ix. 1
St. Theodore, fortress in Haemimontum, B. IV. xi. 20
St. Theodotê, sanctuary of, at Hebdomum, B. I. iv. 28
St. Trajan, fortress in Thrace, B. IV. xi. 20
Salarian Gate, in the wall of Rome, III. ii. 17, 22, V. xviii. 19, etc.; held by Belisarius, V. xix. 14; attacked by the Goths, V. xxii. 1–9; successfully defended, V. xxiii. 24, 25
Salebries, fortress in Cabetzus, B. IV. iv. 3
Sallust, Roman historian; the house of, burned by Alaric, III. ii. 24
Salones, city in Dalmatia, V. v. 2, VII. x. 3, 12; taken by Mundus, V. v. 11; battle near, V. vii. 2 ff.; its inhabitants mistrusted by the Goths, V. vii. 10, 31; weakness of its defences, V. vii. 31; occupied by the Goths, V. vii. 27; abandoned by them, V. vii. 32; occupied by Constantianus, V. xvi. 14, 15; Vittigis sends an army against it, V. xvi. 9, 10; strengthened by Constantianus, V. xvi. 14, 15; invested by the Goths, V. xvi. 16; commanded by Claudian, VII. xxxv. 27; Roman army winters in, VII. xl. 11, 30; John winters in, VIII. xxi. 4, 5, xxii. 1, xxiii. 4; left by him, VIII. xxiii. 8; John returns to, VIII. xxiii. 42; left by Narses, VIII. xxvi. 5; near Mouicurum, VII. xxxv. 25
Saltopyrgus, fortress on the Danube; restored by Justinian, B. IV. vii. 10, 11
Samaritans, formerly held Mt. Garizin, B. V. vii. 2; expelled therefrom, B. V. vii. 7; prophecy concerning, B. V. vii. 3; attack Christians, B. V. vii. 5; burn Christian sanctuaries, B. V. vii. 17; shew disrespect to Christian ritual, B. V. vii. 5; christianized by Justinian, B. V. vii. 16; rise in revolt, B. V. vii. 9, 11–14; forcibly suppressed by Justinian, S.H. xi. 24, 29; punished by him, S.H. xviii. 34; the following individuals are mentioned: Arsenius, S.H. xxvii. 7; Faustinus, S.H. xxvii. 26, 27
Samnites, a people of central Italy, V. xv. 21; gruesome play of Samnite children, V. xx. 1–4
Samnium, [illegible] v. 2; a portion of, surrendered to Belisarius, V. xv. 1, 15; the remainder held by the Goths, V. xv. 2; entered by Totila, VII. vi. 1
Samosata, city on the Euphrates, I. xvii. 22; on the boundary of Euphratesia, I. xvii. 23
Samson, Hospice of, in Byzantium, B. I. ii. 14–16
Sandil, leader of the Utigurs, VIII. xviii. 23; remonstrates to Justinian, VIII. xix. 8 ff.
Sangarius River, in Bithynia, VII. xxix. 12; bridged by Justinian, B. V. iii. 8–11
Sani, VIII. i. 8; *see* Tzani
Saphchae, pass into Sophanenê, B. III. iii. 4
Saracens, nomads of the region of Arabia; experts at plundering, but not at storming cities, II. xix. 12, B. II. ix. 3, 4; in Persia, ruled by Alamundaras, I. xvii. 45; some in alliance with the Romans, I. xvii. 46; their king, Odonathus, II. v. 5, B. II. viii. 8; in Arabia, ruled by Arethas, I. xvii. 47, S.H. ii. 28; receive

annual payments from the Romans, II. x. 23; settled in the Palm Groves, I. xix. 7, 8; and in Palestine, I. xix. 10; cannibals in Arabia, I. xix. 15; never mentioned in treaties, II. i. 5; observe holiday at the vernal equinox, II. xvi. 18; dispute possession of Strata, II. i. 6; in the army of Chosroes, II. xxvii. 30; of Azarethes, I. xvii. 1, xviii. 30; with the army of Belisarius, I. xviii. 7, 26, 35, 36, II. xvi. 5; wage war among themselves, II. xxviii. 12–14; accused by Isdigousnas, VIII. xi. 10; subject of dispute between Romans and Persians, VIII. xv. 2; ravages of, S.H. xi. 11, xviii. 22, xxiii. 6, 8, xxiv. 12, B. II. vi. 15, xi. 10–12; called Homeritae, B. V. viii. 2; Palestine guarded against them, B. V. viii. 9

Sarapanis, city in Lazica, II. xxix. 18; held in turn by Lazi, Romans and Persians, VIII. xiii. 15–19; occupied by Mermeroes, VIII. xvi. 17

Sarapis, commander of Roman infantry, III. xi. 7, IV. xv. 50; his death, IV. xv. 59

Sardanapalus, King of Assyria, S.H. i. 9

Sardicê, town in Dardania, VII. xl. 1, 4; rebuilt by Justinian, B. IV. i. 31, iv. 3

Sardinia, island previously called Sardo, VIII. xxiv. 37, 38, B. VI. vii. 12; compared in size with Sicily, IV. xiii. 42; half way between Rome and Carthage, *ib.*; recovered by the Romans, III. vi. 8, 11; occupied by the tyrant Godas, III. x. 26, 27; Gelimer sends an expedition to recover it, III. xi. 22, 23; subdued by Tzazon, III. xxiv. 1, 3, IV. ii. 25; avoided by Cyril, III. xxiv. 19; Tzazon summoned thence, III. xxv. 10, 17, 24, 25; recovered by Cyril, IV. v. 2, 4; Moors in, fought by Solomon, IV. xiii. 41–45; attacked and captured by the Goths, VIII. xxiv. 31–33; unsuccessful attempt to recapture, VIII. xxiv. 33–36

Sardo, island later called Sardinia, VIII. xxiv. 37, 38, B. VI. vii. 12

Sardonic, term derived from Sardo (Sardinia), VIII. xxiv. 38

Sarmates, fortress in southern Europe, B. IV. iv. 3

Sarmathê, Monastery of, in Mesopotamia, B. V. ix. 32

Sarmathon, fortress in Haemimontum, B. IV. xi. 20

Sarus, river in Cappadocia, I. xvii. 17; near Adana, B. V. v. 8, 9

Satala, town in Armenia; its location, I. xv. 9, 10; battle of, I. xv. 12 ff.; fortified by Justinian, B. III. iv. 2–5

Satraps, governors in Armenia, B. III. i. 17, 24–26

Saturninus, son of Hermogenes, S.H. xvii. 32; his marriage, S.H. xvii. 32, 36; complains and is punished, S.H. xvii. 36, 37

Sauras, fortress in Mesopotamia, B. II. iv. 14

Sauromatae Hamaxobii, Scythian tribe, VIII. v. 6, B. IV. i. 5; old name of the Goths, III. ii. 2

Savarus, father of Julian, S.H. xi. 27

Scalae Veteres, place in Numidia, IV. xvii. 3

Scanda, city of Lazica, II. xxix. 18; frontier fortress, held by the Lazi, Romans and Persians in turn, VIII. xiii. 15–18; destroyed and rebuilt, VIII. xiii. 20

Scaplizo, fortress near Germenne, B. IV. iv. 3

Scardon, city in Dalmatia, V. vii. 32, xvi. 13; touched at by John, VIII. xxiii. 8

Scares, fortress in Cabetzus, B. IV. iv. 3

Scariotasalucra, fortress in Thrace, B. IV. xi. 20

Scaripara, fortress in Aquenisium, B. IV. iv. 3

Scarphea, town in Boeotia; visited by tidal wave, VIII. xxv. 19

Scassetana, district of southern Europe, B. IV. iv. 3

Scatrina, fortress in Moesia, B. IV. xi. 20

Scedeba, fortress in Moesia, B. IV. xi. 20

Sceminites, fortress in Epirus, B. IV. iv. 3

INDEX

Scemnas, fortress in Thrace, B. IV. xi. 20

Scentudies, fortress in Cabetzus, B. IV. iv. 3

Sceparnas, ruler of the Abasgi, VIII. ix. 11; summoned by Chosroes, VIII. ix. 13, 14

Schamalinichon, fortress in Tzanica, B. III. vi. 26; site of church built by Justinian, B. III. vi. 12

Scholarii, Palace Guards, S.H. xxiv. 15, 21, xxvi. 28 (cf. VIII. xxvii. 2)

Scholasticus, a eunuch; commander against the Sclaveni, VII. xl. 35

School, section of the Imperial Guard, VIII. xxvii. 2

Scidreus, fortress in Thessaly, B. IV. iv. 3

Scilê, fortress in Numidia; strengthened by Justinian, B. VI. vii. 11

Scinzeries, fortress near Germenne, B. IV. iv. 3

Scipuar, a Gothic commander; sent against Ancon, VIII. xxiii. 1, 12; accompanies Totila in flight, VIII. xxxii. 22; wounds Asbadus, [illegible] self, VIII. xxxii. 25

Sciri, a Gothic people, V. i. 3

Scirtus, river in Mesopotamia, S.H. xviii. 38; damages Edessa, B. II. vii. 2–5

Scitaces, fortress in Thrace, B. IV. xi. 20

Sclaveni, a barbarian nation, VI. xv. 2, xxvi. 18, B. IV. i. 5; in the Roman army, V. xxvii. 2; settled near the Ister, VI. xxvi. 19; neighbours of the Antae, VII. xl. 5; formerly called Spori, VII. xiv. 29; held extensive territory, VII. xiv. 30; their frequent invasions, VII. xiv. 2; defeat Chilbudius, VII. xiv. 4, 5; make war on the Antae, VII. xiv. 7; cross the Danube, VII. xiii. 24; defeated by the Eruli, VII. xiii. 25; invade Illyricum, VII. xxix. 1–3; Ildiges flees to them, VII. xxxv. 16; many of them follow him, VII. xxxv. 19; Ildiges returns to them, VII. xxxv. 21, 22; their democratic government, VII. xiv. 22; religious beliefs, etc., VII. xiv. 23–28; one of them renders a service to Belisarius, VI. xxvi. 20 ff.; invade Roman territory, VII. xxxviii. 1–23; commit atrocities, VII. xxxviii. 6, 20–22; ambush travellers, B. IV. vii. 13, 17, 18; inexperienced in storming cities, VII. xxxviii. 7; capture Topirus, VII. xxxviii. 9–18, B. IV. xi. 14; invade Roman territory, VII. xl. 1 ff.; fear Germanus, VII. xl. 4, 5, 7; turn aside to Dalmatia, VII. xl. 7; continue inroad, VII. xl. 31–33; defeat a Roman army, VII. xl. 36–41; find great booty, VII. xl. 42, 43; finally depart, VII. xl. 44, 45; invade Illyricum, VIII. xxv. 1 ff.; ferried over the Ister by the Gepaedes, VIII. xxv. 10; overrun Europe, S.H. xi. 11, xviii. 20, xxiii. 6; their losses, S.H. xviii. 25, 26

Scopentzana, fortress in Dardania, B. IV. iv. 3

Scriptures, of the Christians, Areobindus seeks to protect himself by them, IV. xxvi. 27; *see also* [illegible]

Scrithiphini, nation on Thule; their manner of life, customs, etc., VI. xv. 16–25

Scuanes, fortress in Cabetzus, B. IV. iv. 3

Sculcoburgo, fortress in Aquenisium, B. IV. iv. 3

Scumbro, fortress in Remisianisia, B. IV. iv. 3

Scupium, fortress in Dardania, B. IV. iv. 3

Scydreon, city in Epirus, B. IV. iv. 3

Scylaeum, mountain in Italy, VII. xxvii. 17, VIII. xxvi. 3

Scylla, the story of, located at the Strait of Messina, V. viii. 1, VII. xxvii. 17; the "Strait of Scylla" (Strait of Messina), VII. xviii. 26

Scymnia, region near Lazica, VIII. ii. 23; shut off by Mermeroes, VIII. xiv. 53; gained by the Persians, VIII. xvi. 14

Scythia, region fronting the Danube, B. IV. i. 5; defences of, B. IV. vii. 16 ff.; Scythian wilderness, S.H. xviii. 21

Scythians, a barbarian people, III. xix. 7; in the army of Attila, III. iv.

24; formerly included many nations, VIII. v. 6, 24; their location, VIII. v. 23
Scythias, fortress in Moesia, B. IV. xi. 20
Scythopolis, town in Palestine, S.H. xxvii. 8
Sebasteia, city in Armenia; restored by Justinian, B. III. iv. 11
Sebastopolis, fortress in Lazica, II. xxix. 18, VIII. iv. 4; dismantled by the Romans, B. III. vii. 8; restored and greatly improved by Justinian, B. III. vii. 9; distance from Pityus, VIII. iv. 4
Secretary, Confidential; called *A Secretis*, S.H. xiv. 4
Securisca, fortress in Thrace; built by Justinian, B. IV. vii. 4
Seleucia, city on the Tigris, founded by the Macedonians, II. xxviii. 4
Seleucia, (in Pieria), distance from Antioch, II. xi. 1; visited by Chosroes, who bathes in the sea and sacrifices there, *ib.*; destroyed by earthquake, S.H. xviii. 41
Selymbria, city of Thrace, its defences restored by Justinian, B. IV. ix. 12
Semiramis, Queen in Babylon, S.H. i. 9, B. I. i. 53
Senate, in Rome, III. iv. 16, etc.; in Byzantium, B. I. x. 7, etc.; a mere shadow, S.H. xiv. 8; depicted in mosaic at Byzantium, B. I. x. 18
Senate-House, in Byzantium, B. I. ii. 1, x. 6–9
Senators, removed from Rome by Totila, VII. xxii. 19; rescued by John, VII. xxvi. 1, 2, 14; brought back to Rome by Totila, VII. xxxvi. 29, xxxvii. 3; their sufferings, VIII. xxxiv. 2 ff.; sent into Campania, VIII. xxxiv. 5
Senecius, bodyguard of Sittas, given as a hostage to the Persians, I. xxi. 27
Senogallia, town in Italy near Ancon, VIII. xxiii. 9
Seoses, close friend of Cabades, rescues him from the Prison of Oblivion, I. vi. 4, 10; receives the office of "Adrastadaran Salanes," I. vi. 18, 19; envoy to the Romans, I. xi. 25; brought to trial, I. xi. 31 ff.; condemned to death, I. xi. 37
Septecasaê, fortress in Aquenisium, B. IV. iv. 3
Septum, fortress at the Pillars of Heracles, III. i. 6; John sent thither with an army, IV. v. 6; improved by Justinian, B. VI. vii. 14–16
Seretus, fortress in Dardania, B. IV. iv. 3
Sergiopolis, city in Mesopotamia, II. v. 29, B. II. ix. 3–9; citizens of, give much treasure to Chosroes, II. xx. 7; saved from capture by Ambrus, II. xx. 10; besieged in vain by Chosroes, II. xx. 11 ff.
Sergius and Bacchus, Saints, church of, in Byzantium, B. I. iv. 3
Sergius of Edessa, Orator, II. xxiv. 4; envoy to Chosroes, II. xxiv. 3, xxviii. 3 ff.
Sergius, son of Bacchus, brother of Cyrus, becomes ruler of Tripolis, IV. xxi. 1; brother of Solomon, the younger, IV. xxi. 19, S.H. v. 33; threatened by an army of Leuathae, IV. xxi. 2; receives their representatives, IV. xxi. 3 ff.; meets them in battle, IV. xxi. 13, 14; retires into the city, IV. xxi. 15; receives help from Solomon, IV. xxi. 16, 19; succeeds Solomon in command. IV. xxii. 1; his misrule, IV. xxii. 2. S.H. v. 28; his recall demanded by Antalas, IV. xxii. 9, 10; Justinian refuses to recall him, IV. xxii. 11; neglects Hadrumetum, IV. xxiii. 20, 21; quarrels with John, son of Sisiniolus, IV. xxii. 3, xxiii. 32; shares rule of Libya with Areobindus, IV. xxiv. 4, 5; departs to Numidia, IV. xxiv. 6; causes defection of troops, S.H. v. 30; hated by John, S.H. v. 31; effeminate, S.H. v. 32; suitor of Belisarius' daughter, S.H. v. 33; disregards Areobindus' instructions, IV. xxiv. 7, 8; recalled and sent to Italy, IV. xxiv. 16, xxv. 1, VII. xxvii. 2
Seric, *see* Medic garments, IV. vi. 7

Serinda, a land above India, VIII. xvii. 2, 7

Sestus, city on the Hellespont, II. iv. 9, III. i. 8, S.H. xxv. 2, B. V. i. 8; opposite Abydus, B. IV. x. 24; protected by Justinian, B. IV. x. 25; near Elaeus, B. IV. x. 26

Setlotes, fortress in Aquenisium, B. IV. iv. 3

Severianus, son of Asiaticus, a Phoenician, his daring encounter with the Moors, IV. xxiii. 6–9; escapes to Carthage, IV. xxiii. 17

Severus, Palace of, in Leptimagna, B. VI. iv. 5

Sewers, S.H. xxii. 14, B. II. x. 22

Shield Mountain (Clipea), ancient fortress on Mt. Aurasium, IV. xiii. 33

Shoal's Head, *see* Caputvada, III. xiv. 17

Shoes, as worn by the Factionists in Byzantium, S.H. vii. 14

Siberis, river in Galatia, B. V. iv. 1

Sibyl, her prophecy concerning Mundus, V. vii. 6–8; prophecies of, consulted by patricians, V. xxiv. 28; difficulty of understanding them, V. xxiv. 34–37; her cave shewn at Cumae, V. xiv. 3

Siccaveneria, city in Numidia, distance from Carthage, IV. xxiv. 6; strengthened by Justinian, B. VI. vii. 10

Sicilians, marked for vengeance by Totila, VII. xvi. 14–21, 31

Sicily, island, compared in size with Sardinia, IV. xiii. 42; smaller than Britain, VI. vi. 28; its mountain Aetna, VIII. xxxv. 2; important source of supplies for all Italy, VI. xxiv. 14, VII. vi. 15, xiii. 7, xvi. 20, VIII. xxxv. 13; separated from Italy by a strait, VIII. vi. 21; invaded by Gizeric, III. v. 22, 23; Vandals receive concessions in, III. viii. 13, IV. v. 21; reached by Roman fleet, III. xiii. 22; expedition sent thither by Belisarius, IV. v. 11; claimed by the Goths, IV. v. 19; subjugated by Belisarius, IV. xiv. 1, S.H. i. 21; mutiny in, IV. xv. 48, 49; refuge of Libyans, IV. xxiii. 28; Belisarius sent thither with a fleet, V. v. 6, xiii. 14; taken by him, V. v. 12 ff.; with an insignificant force, VII. xvi. 18, 19; garrisoned by him, V. xxiv. 2; Theodatus proposes to withdraw from, V. vi. 2; grain brought thence by Belisarius, V. xiv. 17; refuge of Roman fugitives, V. xxv. 10; offered to Belisarius by the Goths, VI. vi. 27; Goths sent thither by Belisarius, VI. xiii. 4; Totila prepares to invade it, VII. xxxvii. 4, 8; invaded by the Goths, VII. xxxvii. 18, xxxix. 2 ff.; plundered throughout, VII. xxxix. 4, xl. 19; Liberius sent thither with a fleet, VII. xxxix. 6; Artabanes sent thither, VII. xxxix. 8, VIII. xxv. 24; evacuated by Totila, VII. xl. 24, 26–29; conquest of, by Artabanes, VIII. xxiv. 1 ff.; Goths offer to renounce claim thereto, VIII. xxiv. 4; mentioned, VI. xviii. 9, etc.

Siclae, fortress in Macedonia, B. IV. iv. 3

Sicyon, home of Lysippus, B. I. xi. 7

Sidon, city at the extremity of Phoenicia, IV. x. 15

Sigeum, promontory, at the Hellespont, III. xiii. 5

Silentiarius, Privy Councillor in the Palace at Byzantium, II. xxi. 2, xxix. 31, S.H. xxvi. 28, B. IV. viii. 24

Siletheus, Monastery of, B. V. ix. 10

Silk, traffic in, controlled by the Persians, I. xx. 9, 12; culture of silk-worms introduced by Justinian, VIII. xvii. 1–7; market of, controlled by him, S.H. xxv. 14–26; Beirut the centre of the industry, S.H. xxv. 14; impossible for the Ethiopians to buy silk from the Indians, I. xx. 12; used in dress of Armenian satraps, B. III. i. 22; in "Medic garments," I. xx. 9

Silvanus, father of Rufinus, I. xi. 24, xvi. 4

Silverius, Bishop of Rome, V. xi. 26; influences the citizens to yield to Belisarius, V. xiv. 4; dismissed by Belisarius, V. xxv. 13; victim

of Antonina and Theodora, S.H. i. 14, 27
Simmas, Massagete chief, in the Roman army, I. xiii. 21, xiv. 44
Sina, mountain in Arabia, B. V. viii. 1–9; its Monastery and Church, B. V. viii. 4–6
Sinas, fortress in Mesopotamia, B. II. iv. 14
Singidunum, city on the Danube, III. ii. 6, V. xv. 27, VI. xv. 30; destroyed by the barbarians, B. IV. v. 12, 13; restored by Justinian, B. IV. v. 15; towns near it given to the Eruli, VII. xxxiii. 13
Sinnion, leader of the Massagetae, III. xi. 12; and of the Cutrigurs, VIII. xix. 7
Sinope, city on the Euxine, VIII. ii. 2
Sinthues, bodyguard of Belisarius; sent to Tibur with Magnus, VI. iv. 7; repairs the defences, VI. iv. 15; wounded in battle, *ib.*
Siphilas, bodyguard of Constantianus; at the taking of Salones, V. vii. 34
Siphrios, fortress near Amida, I. viii. 10, B. II. iv. 14
Sirmium, town in Pannonia, III. ii. 6, V. iii. 15, xi. 5, xv. 27, S.H. xviii. 16, 18; taken by the Gepaedes, VII. xxxiii. 8; held by them, VII. xxxiv. 17, 35, S.H. xviii. 18
Sisauranon, fortress in Mesopotamia, II. xix. 2, S.H. ii. 24; attacked by Belisarius, II. xix. 4; capitulates to him, II. xix. 23, 24, VII. iii. 11, S.H. ii. 18, 28, B. II. iv. 8; distance from Daras and from Rhabdios, B. II. iv. 9
Siscii, a people of central Europe, V. xv. 26
Sisifridus, a Goth; commander of the Roman garrison of Asise, VII. xii. 12; killed in a sally, VII. xii. 17
Sisigis, commander of a Gothic stronghold; submits to Belisarius, VI. xxviii. 30, 32; besieged by Uraïas, VI. xxviii. 33
Sisilisson, fortress in Tzanica, B. III. vi. 22; distance from Bourgousnoes, B. III. vi. 24
Sisiniolus, father of John, IV. xix. 1, xxii. 3, etc.
Sitifis, metropolis of First Mauretania, IV. xx. 30; walled by Justinian, B. VI. vii. 9
Sittas or Tzittas, Roman general, with Belisarius in invading army, I. xii. 20, 21; defeated by Narses and Aratius, I. xii. 22; attacks Persian army of invasion, I. xv. 3 ff.; occupies hills about Satala, I. xv. 10; attacks unexpectedly, I. xv. 12; first defeats and then conciliates the Tzani, I. xv. 24, B. III. vi. 6; proceeds to the East, I. xxi. 3; awaits Persians at Attachas, I. xxi. 9; negotiates at Martyropolis, I. xxi. 23 ff.; sent against the Armenians, II. iii. 8 ff.; his death, II. iii. 25, IV. xxvii. 17; his valour and achievements, II. iii. 26
Smornes, fortress on the Danube, B. IV. vi. 5
Snail, Gate of the, in the Palace at Byzantium, I. xxiv. 43
Snips, nickname of Alexander, VII. i. 30, S.H. xxvi. 29
Sodomy, punishable by law, S.H. xi. 34, xvi. 19, 23, xix. 11, xx. 9
Soinian Gate, in the wall of Edessa, II. xxvii. 41
Solbanu, fortress in Thrace, B. IV. xi. 20
Solomon, King of the Hebrews, IV. ix. 7, B. VI. ii. 22; his treasures taken from Rome by Alaric, V. xii. 42
Solomon, commander of auxiliaries, III. xi. 5; a eunuch, III. xi. 6; native of the country about Daras, III. xi. 9; uncle of Cyrus, IV. xxi. 1; and of Sergius, VII. xxvii. 2; sent to report Belisarius' victory, III. xxiv. 19; returns to Libya, IV. viii. 4; left in charge of Libya, IV. viii. 23; receives reinforcements, IV. viii. 24; disturbed by reports, IV. x. 1 ff.; writes to Moorish leaders, IV. xi. 1–8; their reply, IV. xi. 9–13; moves against the Moors, IV. xi. 14; addresses his troops, IV. xi. 23–36; wins a decisive victory, IV. xi. 15 ff.; informed of second uprising, marches back, IV. xii. 2; wins a brilliant victory, IV. xii. 3 ff.; moves against Iaudas, IV.

xiii. 18; instigated against him, IV. xiii. 19; encamps on the Abigas River, IV. xiii. 20; ascends Mt. Aurasius, IV. xiii. 30–33; eluded by the Moors, IV. xiii. 35, 36; returns to Carthage, IV. xiii. 39; prepares second expedition, IV. xiii. 40; also against Sardinia, IV. xiii. 41, 45; winters in Carthage, IV. xiv. 4; opposed by the soldiers, IV. xiv. 10; plan to assassinate him, IV. xiv. 22; his guards implicated, IV. xiv. 23; failure of the conspiracy, IV. xiv. 24–27; tries to win back loyalty of his men, IV. xiv. 30; insulted openly, IV. xiv. 31; sends Theodorus to the mutineers, IV. xiv. 32; his enmity towards Theodorus, IV. xiv. 33; his acquaintances killed by the mutineers, IV. xiv. 36; flees to sanctuary in the Palace, IV. xiv. 37; returns to house of Theodorus, IV. xiv. 38; escapes by boat, IV. xiv. 40; departs for Syracuse, IV. xiv. 41; begs Belisarius to come to Carthage, IV. xiv. 42; returns with him, IV. xv. 9; again in command of Libya, IV. xix. 1; his prosperous rule, IV. xix. 3, 4, xx. 33; again marches against Iaudas, IV. xix. 5; sends Gontharis ahead, IV. xix. 6; learns of defeat of Gontharis, IV. xix. 9; advances to Babosis, IV. xix. 16; defeats the Moors, IV. xix. 17; returns to Zerboule, IV. xix. 20; which he captures, IV. xix. 25–31; cares for water-supply during siege of Toumar, IV. xx. 3; addresses the army, IV. xx. 4–9; seeks a vulnerable point, IV. xx. 10, 11; fortifies Mt. Aurasius, IV. xx. 22; fortifies Libyan cities, IV. xix. 3, xx. 29; subjugates First Mauretania, IV. xx. 30; appealed to by Sergius, IV. xxi. 16; incurs enmity of Antalas, IV. xxi. 17, xxii. 7, 8; marches against the Moors, IV. xxi. 19; scorned by the Leuathae, IV. xx. 20–22; refuses to distribute booty, IV. xxi. 23, 24; defeated by the Moors and slain, IV. xxi. 25–28, S.H. v. 30; Justinian's regard for him, IV. xxii. 11; built and fortified a monastery in Carthage, IV. xxvi. 17; standards of, recovered from the Moors, IV. xxviii. 46

Solomon the younger, brother of Cyrus and Sergius, S.H. v. 29; marches against the Moors, IV. xxi. 19; his capture and release, IV. xxii. 12–17; murders Pegasius S.H. v. 33–35; cleared by Justinian, S.H. v. 36, 37; his death, S.H. v. 38

Solomon, an Armenian, according to one report, slew Sittas, II. iii. 27

Sophanenê, part of Armenia, I. xxi. 6, B. III. ii. 2, iii. 1, 3; Theodorus Satrap of, B. III. ii. 6; relinquished by Anastasius, B. III. ii. 9; protected by Justinian, B. III. iii. 6

Sophia, Church of, in Byzantium, destroyed by fire, I. xxiv. 9; description of the restored building, B. I. i. 27 ff.; its treasures, II. xxx. 53; used as a sanctuary, S.H. iii. 24, xvii. 9; desecrated by Factionists, S.H. ix. 35; appropriateness of its name, III. vi. 26, B. I. i. 21; mentioned, B. I. ii. 13

Sorcery, I. xxv. 8, III. iii. 11, S.H. i. 26, ii. 2, iii. 2

Spain, first country of Europe, beginning from Gibraltar, V. xii. 3, VIII. xx. 5, B. IV. ix. 1; its size compared with that of Gaul, V. xii. 5; which adjoins, V. xv. 29; settled by the Vandals, III. iii. 2, 22; invaded by Constantinus, III. ii. 31; settled by the Visigoths, III. iii. 26, xxiv. 7, IV. iv. 34, V. xii. 12, xiii. 13, VIII. v. 10; really under sway of Theoderic, V. xii. 47; formerly subject to the Romans, V. xii. 9; Theudis establishes an independent power in, V. xii. 50–54; Spanish woman becomes his wife, V. xii. 50

Spartan marble, B. I. x. 20

Spathizus, fortress in Moesia, B. IV. xi. 20

Speloncа, fortress in Remisianisia, B. IV. iv. 3

INDEX

Speretium, fortress in Epirus, B. IV. iv. 3

Spibyrus, fortress in Moesia, B. IV. xi. 20

Spies, maintained by the State, I. xxi. 11, S.H. xxx. 1, 12 ff.

Spinus, a Roman, counsellor of Totila, VII. xl. 20; captured in Catana, VII. xl. 21; secures his release, VII. xl. 24, 25; persuades Totila to leave Sicily, VII. xl. 26–29

Spolitium, city in Italy, submits to Constantinus, V. xvi. 3; garrisoned by him, V. xvi. 4, xvii. 3; avoided by Vittigis, V. xvii. 7, VI. xi. 9; refuge of Presidius, VI. viii. 2; held by Bessas, VII. vi. 8; besieged by Totila, VII. xii. 12; surrendered to him, VII. xii. 15, 16, xxi. 15, S.H. v. 6; its walls razed by the Goths, VII. xxiii. 3; Roman prisoners sent there, VII. xxiii. 2; its amphitheatre used as a garrison, VII. xxiii. 3; captured by Martinianus, VII. xxiii. 4–7; ordered to be rebuilt by Narses, VIII. xxxiii. 9; home of Spinus, VII. xl. 20

Spori, ancient name of the Antae and the Sclaveni, VII. xiv. 29

Stadium, place in Byzantium, B. I. xi. 27

Stagirus, home of Aristotle, VIII. vi. 20

Stagnum, a harbour near Carthage, affords anchorage for Roman fleet, III. xv. 15, xx. 15, 16

Stamazo, fortress in Cabetzus, B. IV. iv. 3

Stater, a gold coin, S.H. xx. 18, xxiv. 28, xxv. 12, xxix. 25

Staurin, mountain at Antioch, B. II. x. 16

Stendas, fortress in Aquenisium, B. IV. iv. 3

Stenecorta, fortress in Cabetzus, B. IV. iv. 3

Stenes, fortress in Remisianisia, B. IV. iv. 3

Stenes, fortress near Sardica, B. IV. iv. 3

Stephanacius, commander of Isaurians, I. xviii. 7

Stephaniacum, fortress in Epirus, B. IV. iv. 3

Stephanus, a physician of note, intercedes with Chosroes for Edessa, II. xxvi. 31 ff.

Stephanus, a Neapolitan, remonstrates with Belisarius, V. viii. 7–11; urged by Belisarius to win over the Neapolitans, V. viii. 19; his attempts to do so, V. viii. 20, 21; assisted by Antiochus, V. viii. 21; opposed by Pastor and Asclepiodotus, V. viii. 22–24; goes again to Belisarius, V. viii. 25; summoned once more by Belisarius, V. ix. 23; returns to the city, V. ix. 29; bitterly accuses Asclepiodotus, V. x. 40–43

Stephanus, ambassador of Totila, VII. xxxvii. 6

Stiliburgu, fortress on the Danube, B. IV. vi. 18

Stoa, Royal, in Byzantium, S.H. xiv. 13, B. I. xi. 12, 13

Stotzas, bodyguard of Martinus, destined not to return to Byzantium, III. xi. 30; chosen tyrant by mutineers, IV. xv. 1; marches on Carthage, IV. xv. 2; solicits Vandals, IV. xv. 3, 4; demands surrender of Carthage, IV. xv. 5; kills an envoy and besieges Carthage, IV. xv. 8; addresses his troops, IV. xv. 30–39; defeated by Belisarius, IV. xv. 40 ff.; his troops gather in Numidia, IV. xv. 50; Romans march against him, IV. xv. 52; enters Roman army alone, IV. xv. 53–57; received with favour, IV. xv. 58; kills Roman commanders in a sanctuary, IV. xv. 59; eager to fight battle with Germanus, IV. xvi. 8; hopes for defection from Carthage, IV. xvi. 9, 10; his hopes falsified, IV. xvii. 1; defeated by Germanus, IV. xvii. 3 ff., VII. xxxix. 12; escapes with a few men, IV. xvii. 24; hopes to renew battle, IV. xvii. 32; escapes with difficulty, IV. xvii. 33; suffers another defeat, IV. xvii. 34; withdraws to Mauritania, IV. xvii. 35; end of his mutiny, *ib.*, IV. xix. 3; joins Antalas, IV. xxii. 5, xxiii. 1; receives Roman captives, IV. xxiii. 10, 17; joins Moors in plundering Libya, IV. xxiii. 26–31;

INDEX

Areobindus sends force against him, IV. xxiv. 6; his enmity against John, IV. xxiv. 9; mortally wounded by him in battle, IV. xxiv. 11; carried out of the battle, IV. xxiv. 12; his death, IV. xxiv. 14; succeeded by John as tyrant, IV. xxv. 3

Strabo, historian; his account of the Amazons, VIII. iii. 6

Stramentias, fortress in Cabetzus, B. IV. iv. 3

Stranbasta, fortress in southern Europe, B. IV. iv. 3

Strata, a region claimed by the Saracens, II. i. 6; meaning of the name, II. i. 7; unproductive, II. i. 11

Strategius, guardian of the royal treasures, envoy of Justinian, II. i. 9; his advice concerning Strata, II. i. 11

Streden, fortress in Epirus, B. IV. iv. 3

Stronges, fortress in Remisianisia, B. IV. iv. 3

Strongylum, fortress near Byzantium B. IV. viii. 4

Struas, fortress in Dardania, B. IV. iv.3

Suabastas, fortress near Pauta, B. IV. iv. 3

Suania, region near Lazica, VIII. ii. 23; shut off by Mermeroes, VIII. xiv. 53; gained by the Persians, VIII. xvi. 14

Suartuas, an Erulian, appointed King of the Eruli by Justinian, VI. xv. 32, VIII. xxv. 11; attempts to destroy Eruli, sent to Thule, VI. xv. 34; flees to Byzantium, VI. xv. 35; Justinian attempts to restore him, VI. xv. 36; sent to the Lombards, VIII. xxv. 11

Subaras, fortress in Remisianisia, B. IV. iv. 3

Sudanel, fortress in Rhodopê, built by Justinian, B. IV. xi. 20

Suegogmense, fortress near Germenne, B. IV. iv. 3

Suevi, a barbarian people of Gaul, V. xii. 11; in two divisions, V. xv. 26; Asinarius gathers an army among them, V. xvi. 9, 12

Summus, father of Julian, commander in Palestine, II. i. 9, 10; his advice concerning Strata, II. i. 11

Sunicas, Massagete chief, in the Roman army, I. xiii. 20, xiv. 39, 40, 44; charges the standard-bearer of Baresmanas, I. xiv. 47; kills Baresmanas, I. xiv. 50

Sunitae, allies in the Persian army, I. xv. 1

Suntas, bodyguard of Belisarius, VI. vii. 27

Supernumerary, an enlistment in the Roman army beyond the required number, S.H. xxiv. 19, 20

Sura, fortress near Zenobia, captured by Chosroes, II. v. 10 ff., B. II. ix. 1; strengthened by Justinian, B. II. ix. 1, 2; on the Euphrates, I. xviii. 14, II. v. 8; distance from Sergiopolis, II. v. 29; Bishop of, begs Chosroes to spare the city, II. v. 13 ff.; a woman of, made captive, II. ix. 9, 10

Suras, fortress in Haemimontum, B. IV. xi. 20

Suricum, fortress in Dardania, B. IV. iv. 3

Susanna, Monastery of, B. II. ix. 17

Susiana, fortress on the Danube, B. IV. vi. 18

Susurmena, village near Trapezus, VIII. ii. 3

Sybotae, islands near Cercyra, VIII. xxii. 30

Sycae, suburb of Byzantium, II. xxiii. 9, B. I. v. 9

Syceae, place in Galatia, B. V. iv. 1

Sycibida, fortress near the Danube; restored by Justinian, B. IV. vi. 34, 35

Sycidaba, fortress in Moesia, B. IV. vii. 10

Syllectus, city in Libya, III. xvi. 9; captured by Romans, III. xvi. 11; entered by the Roman army, III. xvii. 6

Symeon, sanctuary of, at Amida, I. ix. 18

Symeon, manager of Persian gold mine, I. xv. 27; goes over to the Romans, I. xv. 28, 29; presented with Armenian villages, II. iii. 1; murdered by sons of Perozes, II. iii. 2; uncle of Amazaspes, II. iii. 3

Symmachus, Roman Senator, accompanies Germanus to Libya, IV.

xvi. 2; summoned to Byzantium, IV. xix. 1
Symmachus, Senator and consular, father-in-law of Boethius, V. i. 32; father of Rusticiana, VII. xx. 27, 29; his death, V. i. 34; his children receive his property from Amalasuntha, V. ii. 5
Symphygium, fortress in Epirus, B. IV. iv. 3
Syracuse, city in Sicily, III. xiv. 13, S.H. i. 21; its harbour Arethusa, III. xiv. 11; Procopius sent thither, III. xiv. 3, 7; Belisarius winters there, IV. xiv. 4, 41; surrenders to Belisarius, V. v. 12; entered by him on last day of consulship, V. v. 18, 19; garrisoned by him, V. viii. 1; visited by Maximinus, VII. vii. 1; besieged by the Goths, VII. xl. 12; distance from Caucana, III. xiv. 4
Syria, open to invasion by the Persians, I. xvii. 34 ff., II. xvi. 17, xix. 34; attacked by Chosroes II. v. 4, vi. 21; made secure by Justinian, B. II. xi. 10; its fortress Cyrus, B. II. xi. 2; home of Antiochus of Naples, V. viii. 21; of Peter Barsymes, S.H. xxii. 3; of Addaeus, S.H. xxv. 7; Syriac tongue, II. ii. 3
Syrtes, Great, a succession of shoals off the coast of north Africa, B. VI. iii. 1 ff.; explanation of the name, B. VI. iii. 5, 6; crescent gulf formed by, B. VI. iv. 15, v. 1; alternation of tides over, B. VI. iv. 15–23
Syrtes, Lesser, B. VI. iv. 14

Tabellio, Latin word for "Recorder," S.H. xxviii. 6
Tacapê, city in Africa, B. VI. iv. 14
Taenarum, promontory of the Peloponnesus, later called Caenopolis, III. xiii. 8; Gizeric repulsed thence, III. xxii. 16
Taginae, town in Italy, VIII. xxix. 3
Tamonbari, fortress in Thrace, B. IV. xi. 20
Tamugadê, city in Numidia, dismantled by the Moors, IV. xiii. 26, xix. 20; walled by Justinian, B. VI. vii. 8
Tanais River, empties into the Maeotic Lake, VIII. iv. 7, v. 23, vi. 4; also its outlet, VIII. iv. 10; rises in the Rhipaean Mountains, VIII. vi. 5; said to divide Europe from Asia, VIII. vi. 2, 6, 7, 13, 15, B. VI. i. 7; crossed by the Utigurs, VIII. xviii. 22
Tanaitis, name of a wind rising near the Maeotic Lake, VIII. iv. 10
Tanata, fortress on the Danube, B. IV. vi. 5
Taphosiris, city in Libya, B. VI. i. 12
Taracina, city near Rome, V. xi. 2; at the limit of Campania, V. xv. 22; Euthalius stops in, VI. ii. 1; Belisarius sends men thither, VI. ii. 3; occupied by Martinus and Trajan, VI. iv. 6, 14; left by them, VI. v. 4
Taraunon, district in Persarmenia, invaded by Justus and Peranius, II. xxv. 35
Tarbesium, stronghold in Venetia, surrenders to Belisarius, VI. xxix. 40; Vitalius defeated near it, VII. i. 35; commanded by Totila, VII. ii. 7; who proposes to surrender it, VII. ii. 8, 9
Tarentum, city in Calabria; fortified by John, VII. xxiii. 12–17; its location, VII. xxiii. 14, xxviii. 2; captured by Totila, VII. xxxvii. 23; Goths escape thither, VIII. xxvi. 3; commanded by Ragnaris, VIII. xxvi. 4, xxxiv. 9; threatened by Pacurius, VIII. xxxiv. 14, 15; its harbour, VII. xxiii. 14; distance from Dryus, VII. xxiii. 12; mentioned, VII. xxvii. 11, 17 xxviii. 1
Tarmutus, an Isaurian, brother of Ennes, V. xxviii. 23–29; fights valiantly, V. xxix. 39, 40; his remarkable escape, V. xxix. 42, 43; his death, V. xxix. 44
Tarporum, fortress near Pauta, B. IV. iv. 3
Tarsus, city in Cilicia, flooded by the Cydnus, S.H. xviii. 40, xxix. 30, 31, B. V. v. 17, 18; protected by Justinian from the Cydnus, B. V. v. 19, 20
Tartarus, pit of Hades, S.H. iv. 7
Tatianus, Quartermaster at Antioch, II. x. 2

Tatianus, Senator, his property "inherited" by Justinian, S.H. xii. 5

Tattimuth, sent in command of an army to Tripolis, III. x. 23; receives help from Belisarius, IV. v. 10

Taulantii, a people of Illyricum, III. ii. 9, V. i. 13

Taurians, a people on the Euxine, I. xvii. 11 ff., 21, B. III. vii. 10, IV. i. 5; their land, Taurica, VIII. v. 23

Taurisium, town in Dardania, birthplace of Justinian, B. IV. i. 17; fortified and renamed by Justinian, B. IV. i. 18; adorned by him, B. IV. i. 19–27

Taurocephali, Market of, in Thrace, B. IV. xi. 20

Taurocomum, fortress in Haemimontum, B. IV. xi. 20

Tauroscythians, a people on the Euxine, B. III. vii. 10

Taurus Mountains, size and extent, I. x. 1, 2, xv. 20, xvii. 17, B. V. v. 15, 16

Taxation, S.H. xxiii. 1–24, xii. 12, 13; assessment of taxes, S.H. xviii. 10; rigorous collection of taxes of Justinian, S.H. xviii. 10, xxi. 1, xxiii. 1–6; new taxes imposed by him, S.H. xxi. 2, xxii. 19, xxiii. 9–21; "pub ic" and "imperial" taxes, III. x. 3; customs duties, S.H. xxv. 1–6, 16; taxes conveyed by Imperial Post, S.H. xxx. 2; taxation in Armenia, II. iii. 7; Anastasius remits the taxes of Amida after its sack by the Persians, I. vii. 35, S.H. xxiii. 7; taxes levied in Libya by the Vandals, III. v. 11–15; who destroy the Roman records of taxation there, IV. viii. 25; two Roman officials sent to Libya to assess new taxes, *ib.*; taxes to be paid by the Goths for Sicily and Dalmatia after they had withdrawn, VIII. xxiv. 4

Tebesta, city in Libya, distance from Carthage, IV. xxi. 19

Teësimonte, fortress in Haemimontum, B. IV. xi. 20

Teïas, Gothic commander, blocks roads against Narses, VIII. xxvi. 21, 22, 24; summoned by Totila, VIII. xxix. 1; chosen King of the Goths, VIII. xxxiii. 6, xxxiv. 9, 17; seeks alliance with the Franks, VIII. xxxiii. 7, xxxiv. 9; slays Roman children, VIII. xxxiv. 8; prepares to fight Narses, VIII. xxxiv. 21; reaches Campania, VIII. xxxiv. 23; fights heroically and dies, VIII. xxxv. 20–29

Teleptê, city in Byzacium, fortified by Justinian, B. VI. vi. 18

Tenedos, island near the Hellespont, its granary built by Justinian, B. V. i. 7–16

Terdetes, a notable of the Lazi, betrays Apsilia to the Persians, VIII. x. 2, 3

Terebinthius, Christian Bishop, attacked by Samaritans, B. V. vii. 5

Terentius, Roman commander of infantry, III. xi. 7, IV. xv. 50

Terias, fortress in Dardania, B. IV. iv. 3

Tetrapyrgia, fortress in Dardania, built by Justinian, B. IV. i. 18

Tetraxitae, a Gothic tribe near the Maeotic Lake, VIII. iv. 9, v. 5; Christians, VIII. iv. 9; their history, VIII. v. 1 ff.; send embassy to Justinian, VIII. iv. 12, 13; attacked and taken across the Maeotic Lake by the Utigurs, VIII. v. 18–21; in alliance with the Utigurs, VIII. xviii. 22

Teuchira, city in Africa, B. VI. ii. 4

Tezulê, fortress in Dardania, B. IV. iv. 3

Thalelaeus, Saint, Monastery of, in Jerusalem, B. V. ix. 1

Thannourios, name of two fortresses in Mesopotamia, B. II. vi. 14, 15

Tharsandala, fortress in Rhodope, built by Justinian, B. IV. xi. 20

Theatre, in Byzantium, frequented by the Factions, S.H. vii. 13; by the youthful Theodora, S.H. ix. 20; closing of theatres, S.H. xxvi. 8

Thebes, city in Egypt, VII. xxix. 6

Thebes, city of Boeotia, fortified by Justinian, B. IV. iii. 5

INDEX

Thecla, Martyr, shrine of, in Byzantium, B. I. iv. 28
Themeres, fortress in Mesopotamia, B. II. vi. 14
Themiscyra, town on the Thermodon River, VIII. ii. 2; traditional seat of the Amazons, VIII. iii. 5
Themistocles, the Athenian, his boast, B. I. i. 7
Theoctistus, commander in Lebanon, brings succour to Antioch, II. viii. 2; flees precipitately, II. viii. 17–19; objects to plan of Belisarius, II. xvi. 17 ff.; eager to return to Lebanon, II. xix. 33, 34; commander in invading army, II. xxiv. 13
Theoctistus, a skilful physician, VI. ii. 26 ff.
Theodatus, King of the Goths, IV. xiv. 1; son of Amalafrida and nephew of Theoderic, V. iii. 1, VI. xxx. 5, VII. viii. 21; brother of Amalaberga, V. xiii. 2; father of Theodegisclus, V. xi. 10; father-in-law of Ebrimous, V. viii. 3; father of Theodenanthe, *ib.*; his unstable character, V. vii. 11; accustomed to consult oracles, V. ix. 3; opposed by Amalasuntha, V. iii. 2, 3; plans to deliver Tuscany to Justinian, V. iii. 4, 29; meets envoys of Justinian secretly, V. iii. 9; accused by the Tuscans, V. iv. 1; compelled by Amalasuntha to make restitution, V. iv. 2; her attempts to gain his support, V. iv. 9 ff.; his accession, V. iv. 10, 19; imprisons Amalasuntha, V. iv. 13–15; sends envoys and a letter to Justinian, V. iv. 15, 16; receives the envoy Peter, V. iv. 17; opposed by Justinian, V. iv. 22; defended by Opilio, V. iv. 25; persuaded to kill Amalasuntha, V. iv. 26, 27, S.H. xvi. 5; denounced by Peter, V. iv. 30; his excuses, V. iv. 31; suggests agreement with Justinian, V. vi. 1–5; recalls Peter and consults him further, V. vi. 6–13; his letter to Justinian, V. vi. 14–21; reply of Justinian, V. vi. 22–25; receives envoys from him, V. vi. 26; refuses to put his agreement into effect, V. vii. 11, 12; makes speech regarding envoys, V. vii. 13–16; receives a letter addressed to Gothic nobles, V. vii. 22; guards the envoys Peter and Athanasius, V. vii. 25; proposes alliance with the Franks, V. xiii. 14, 24; appealed to by the Neapolitans, V. ix. 1; terrified by a sign, V. ix. 2–7; defeated by Belisarius, S.H. iv. 43; dethroned by the Goths, V. xi. 1, VI. xxx. 5; flees towards Ravenna, V. xi. 6; justly hated by Optaris, V. xi. 7, 8; killed on the road, V. xi. 9, xiii. 15, xxix. 6
Theodegisclus, son of Theodatus, imprisoned by Vittigis, V. xi. 10
Theodenanthe, daughter of Theodatus, wife of Ebrimous, V. viii. 3
Theoderic, King of the Goths, I. viii. 3, VII. i. 4, 32, xxxix. 15, 21, VIII. v. 14, S.H. xxiv. 9, xxvi. 27, 28, B. III. vii. 13; brother of Amalafrida, III. viii. 11, 13, V. iii. 1, VIII. xxv. 11; father of Amalasuntha, V. ii. 23, xxiv. 25, VII. xxxix. 14, S.H. xxiv. 23; of Theodichusa, V. xii. 22; grandfather of Atalaric, III. xiv. 6, V. ii. 1, xxiv. 24, VIII. xxi. 11; of Amalaric, V. xii. 43, 46; of Matasuntha, V. xi. 27, xxix. 8; uncle of Theodatus, V. iii. 1, VI. xxx. 5; the family of, V. iv. 6; Patrician and consular, V. i. 9, VI. vi. 16; makes alliance with the Vandals, III. viii. 11–13, IV. v. 21; conciliates the Rogi, VII. ii. 2; begged to send garrison to Sicily, VII. xvi. 17; becomes hostile to the Vandals, III. ix. 3; refrains from attacking them, III. ix. 5; leads Gothic rebellion, V. i. 9; persuaded to attack Odoacer, V. i. 10, VI. vi. 16, 23; leads the Goths into Italy, V. i. 12; not followed by all Goths, V. xvi. 2; besieges Ravenna, V. i. 24; agrees with Odoacer, then kills him, V. i. 24, 25; makes war on the Gepaedes, V. xi. 5; forms alliance with the Thuringians and the Visigoths, V. xii. 21, 22; feared by the Franks, V. xii. 23;

forms alliance with them, V. xii. 24; gains Burgundian territory by craft, V. xii. 26–28, 31, 32; disregarded by the Franks, V. xii. 33; sends army to Alaric, V. xii. 34; reproached by the Visigoths, V. xii. 37; drives the Franks from Carcasiana, V. xii. 44; recovers eastern Gaul, V. xii. 45; makes Amalaric King of the Visigoths, V. xii. 46; sends army to Spain, V. xii. 50; tolerates tyranny of Theudis, V. xii. 51–54; virtually ruler of Gaul, Spain and Italy, V. xii. 47–49; imposed tribute on the Visigoths, V. xii. 47, 48, xiii. 6; removed treasures of Carsasiana, V. xiii. 6; kills Symmachus and Boethius, V. i. 34; terrified by fish's head, V. i. 35 ff.; his death, III. xiv. 6, V. i. 39, xiii. 1; succeeded by Atalaric, V. ii. 1; made no new laws in Italy, VI. vi. 17; mosaic picture of, in Naples, V. xxiv. 22; kept the Romans in luxury, [illegible]; forbade education of Gothic children, V. ii. 14; ignorant of letters, V. ii. 16; character as a sovereign, V. i. 26 ff., xi. 26; beloved by subjects, V. i. 29–31; benefits of his reign, VII. ix. 10, xxi. 12, 23; his wealth carried to Byzantium, VII. i. 3; statues of, destroyed, VII. xx. 29

Theodichusa, daughter of Theoderic, betrothed to Alaric the younger, V. xii. 22; mother of Amalaric, V. xii. 43

Theodora, Empress, her birth and early career, S.H. vi. 1, xii. 28; parentage and childhood, S.H. ix. 3, 9; her lewd practices, S.H. ix. 10–25; avoided by the respectable, S.H. ix. 25, 26; engaged by Hecebolus, S.H. ix. 27; returns to Byzantium, S.H. ix. 27, 28, xii. 30; beloved by Justinian, S.H. ix. 30; becomes wealthy, S.H. ix. 31; married by Justinian, S.H. ix. 51; becomes Empress without opposition, S.H. ix. 54, x. 1, 9; greatly beloved by Justinian, I. xxv. 4; her hatred of John the Cappadocian, *ib.*, S.H. xvii. 38–44; counsels firmness in dealing with the Nika Insurrection, I. xxiv. 33 ff.; encourages Antonina to entrap John the Cappadocian, I. xxv. 22; succeeds in punishing him, I. xxv. 30, S.H. xxii. 1; mutilates two youths, S.H. xvii. 44; pleased with Peter Barsymes, S.H. xxii. 5, 26, 32, 33; opposes Justinian, S.H. xxii. 22; bewitched by Peter Barsymes, S.H. xxii. 24; student of sorcery, S.H. xxii. 27; bewitched Justinian, S.H. xxii. 28, 32; distributes rewards to Gelimer and others, IV. ix. 13; compels Artabanes to take back his wife, VII. xxxi. 14; personal appearance, S.H. x. 11; close partner of Justinian, S.H. x. 13, 14, xi. 40, 41, xv. 19, 20, B. I. ii. 17, ix. 5; with whom she pretends to disagree, S.H. x. 17, 18, 23; probably of demonic nature, S.H. xii. 14; her strange dream, S.H. xii. 31, 32; persistently base, S.H. xv. 1–4; independent, S.H. xv. 2; meticulous in care of her person, S. H. xv. 6–9; influential in government, S.H. xv. 10, xvii. 27; difficult of access, S.H. xv. 13–16; and one cause of State's decay, S.H. xv. 17, 18; supervises reforms, S.H. xv. 21; robs citizens and perverts justice, S.H. xv. 22, 23; ridicules a Patrician, S.H. xv. 24–35; her suburban residence, S.H. xv. 36–38; her treatment of enemies, S.H. xv. 39; fears Amalasuntha, S.H. xvi. 1; and destroys her, S.H. xvi. 2 ff.; opposes Priscus, S.H. xvi. 8; and sends him off, S.H. xvi. 9; writes to Zaberganes, S.H. ii. 32–36; summons Belisarius to Byzantium, S.H. iii. 4; her ruthlessness, S.H. iii. 6 ff., xv. 4, xvi. 14–17; surprises Antonina, S.H. iii. 15–18; confines Photius, S.H. iii. 21, 22; summons Belisarius and Bouzes to Byzantium, S.H. iv. 5, 6; confiscates money of Belisarius, S.H. iv. 17; friendly to Antonina, S.H. iv. 18, 19; sends message to Belisarius, S.H. iv. 24–28;

whose wealth she envies, S.H. iv. 33, 34, v. 20; her grandson Anastasius, S.H. iv. 37; hostile to Germanus, S.H. v. 8; frustrates a marriage planned by him, S.H. v. 11, 12; threatens to kill John, S.H. v. 12; forces marriage of Belisarius' daughter to her grandson, S.H. v. 18–21; distrusts Antonina, S.H. v. 20; persecutes Areobindus, S.H. xvi. 11; her tireless vigilance, S.H. xvi. 12, 13; punishes Vasianus, S.H. xvi. 18–21; respected nothing, S.H. xvi. 22, xvii. 10; attacks Diogenes, S.H. xvi. 23–28; causes execution of Callinicus, S.H. xvii. 3; tries to check social crime, S.H. xvii. 5; makes matches for two women, S.H. xvii. 7–15; her son John, born before marriage, S.H. xvii. 16, 17; whom she disposes of, S.H. xvii. 21–23; protects adulteresses, S.H. xvii. 24; arbitrarily arranges marriages, S.H. xvii. 28–37; punishes a fastidious youth, S.H. xvii. 37; penalized silk merchants, S.H. xxv. 19; her favourite Arsenius, S.H. xxvii. 6; annoyed by him, S.H. xxvii. 13; urges investigation, S.H. xxvii. 16; has Arsenius impaled, S.H. xxvii. 19; innovations of, in court ceremonial, S.H. xxx. 21–26; her death, II. xxx. 49, VII. xxx. 4, S.H. v. 23, 27; depicted in mosaic at the Bronze Gate, B. I. x. 17; statue of, in Byzantium, B. I. xi. 8

Theodora, consort of Opsites, carried off by Nabedes, VIII. ix. 7; a Roman by birth, VIII. ix. 8

Theodora, fortress on the Danube, B. IV. vi. 15; abandoned by Justinian, B. IV. vi. 18

Theodore, Saint, sanctuary of, in Rhesium, B. I. iv. 28

Theodorianae, baths in Carthage, built by Justinian, B. VI. v. 10

Theodorias, name applied to Vaga, in Africa, B. VI. v. 14

Theodoriscus, a Cappadocian, bodyguard of Martinus, V. xxix. 20, 21

Theodoropolis, city in Moesia, built by Justinian, B. IV. vii. 5

Theodoropolis, fortress on the Danube, B. IV. vi. 18

Theodoropolis, fortress in Rhodopê, built by Justinian, B. IV. xi. 20

Theodoropolis, fortress in Haemimontum, B. IV. xi. 20

Theodorus, youngest son of Gizeric, his death, III. v. 11

Theodorus Cteanus, commander of infantry, III. xi. 7

Theodorus, commander of guards, ascends Mt. Bourgaon, IV. xii. 17; killed by the mutineers, IV. XIV. 35; an excellent soldier, *ib.*

Theodorus, Silentiarius, B. IV. viii. 24

Theodorus, friend of Diogenes, S.H. xvi. 25; tortured, S.H. xvi. 26, 27

Theodorus the Cappadocian, sent to Libya with an army, IV. viii. 24; sent by Solomon to quiet the mutineers, IV. xiv. 32; his enmity against Solomon, IV. xiv. 33; elected general by the mutineers, IV. xiv. 34; allows Solomon and Martinus to escape, IV. xiv. 38; bidden by Solomon to care for Carthage, IV. xiv. 41; refuses to surrender Carthage to Stotzas, IV. xv. 6; made joint ruler of Carthage with Ildiger, IV. xv. 49; at the battle of Scalae Veteres, IV. xvii. 6, 19; learns of the plot of Maximinus, IV. xviii. 4

Theodorus of Daras, builder, II. xiii. 26

Theodorus, Referendarius at Byzantium, II. xxiii. 6

Theodorus, Satrap of Sophanene, B. III. ii. 6; confirmed in office by Cabades, B. III. ii. 7; his action condoned by Anastasius, B. III. ii. 9

Theodorus, Orator in Rome, sent as envoy to Justinian, VII. xxi. 18

Theodosiopolis, city on the Persian frontier, I. x. 18, xv. 2, II. xxiv. 12, B. II. v. 1; near the sources of the Euphrates and Tigris, I. xvii. 4; in Armenia, B. III. i. 1, iii. 9, iv. 14, v. 2; near Bolum, I. xv. 32; distance from Doubios, II. xxv. 1; from Citharizon, II. xxiv. 13; captured by Cabades, B. III. v. 3; strengthened by Anas-

tasius, I. x. 19, B. III. v. 4, 5; its defences improved by Justinian, B. II. v. 1, III. v. 6–12; its Church of the Mother of God, B. III. iv. 12
Theodosiopolis, city near the Aborrhas River, II. xix. 29; distance from Daras, B. II. ii. 16; its surrounding fortresses, B. II. vi. 13
Theodosius I, Roman Emperor, father of Arcadius and Honorius, III. i. 2; overthrows the tyranny of Maximus, III. iv. 16
Theodosius II, son of Arcadius, youthful Roman Emperor, I. ii. 1 ff., B. III. i. 11; his accession, III. ii. 33; Honorius considers taking refuge with him, III. ii. 32; rears Valentinian, III. iii. 5; makes him Emperor of the West, III. iii. 8; sends an army against the tyrant John, *ib.*; makes treaty with the Persians, I. ii. 12, 15, B. II. i. 5; receives the kingdom of Arsaces, II. iii. 35, B. III. i. 12, v. 2; founds Theodosiopolis, B. III. v. 3, 4, 5; his death, III. iv. 39; succeeded by Marcian, III. iv. 2, 10; father of Eudoxia, III. iv. 15
Theodosius, head of the household of Belisarius, VI. xxviii. 8; sent as envoy to Vittigis, *ib.*
Theodosius, Senator, cruelly punished by Theodora, S.H. iii. 9–11
Theodosius, of the household of Belisarius, S.H. i. 15; formally adopted by Belisarius, S.H. i. 16; beloved by Antonina, *ib.*; surprised by Belisarius, S.H. i. 19, 20; sentenced to death by him, S.H. i. 22; escapes to Ephesus, S.H. i. 23; recalled by Belisarius, S.H. i. 26; unable to return to Italy, S.H. i. 31, 34; justly hated by Photius, S.H. i. 32; returns after Photius' departure, S.H. i. 34; in Byzantium, becomes afraid, S.H. i. 36; retires to Ephesus as a monk, S.H. i. 37; refuses to return, S.H. i. 40, 41; awaiting Belisarius' absence, S.H. i. 42; returns to Antonina, S.H. ii. 3, 5; denounced by Belisarius, S.H. ii. 11; returns to Ephesus, S.H. ii. 14, 17; takes sanctuary, S.H. iii. 3; sent to Cilicia, S.H. iii. 5; his money confiscated, *ib.*; sought by Theodora, S.H. iii. 12; summoned to Byzantium, S.H. iii. 15; restored to Antonina, S.H. iii. 17; dies, S.H. iii. 20
Theodotus, Monastery of, in Mesopotamia, B. V. ix. 32
Theodotus, Prefect of Byzantium, S.H. ix. 37; accused by Justinian, S.H. ix. 39; saved by Proclus, S.H. ix. 41; retires to Jerusalem, S.H. ix. 42, 43; replaced John the Cappadocian, S.H. xxii. 2; gives way to Peter, S.H. xxii. 6
Theophobius, of the Lazi, betrays Uthimereos, VIII. xvi. 4–13
Theopolis, name of Antioch, *q.v.* B. II. x. 2, V. v. 1, ix. 29
Therma, fortress in Macedonia, B. IV. iv. 3
Therma, fortress in Epirus, B. IV. iv. 3
Therma, fortress in Moesia, B. IV. xi. 20
Thermodon River, reputed home of the Amazons, VIII. ii. 2, iii. 5, 7
Thermopylae, Pass of, attacked by the Huns, II. iv. 10; fortified by Justinian, B. IV. ii. 2–15, 23; its garrison, VIII. xxvi. 1, S.H. xxvi. 31; vulnerable, B. IV. ii. 20, 25, 28
Thesaurus, fortress in Epirus, B. IV. iv. 3
Thescus, fortress in Thrace, built by Justinian, B. IV. x. 28
Thessalonicê, city in northern Greece, B. IV. iii. 27; home of Peter, V. iii. 30; its capture planned by the Sclaveni, VII. xl. 3; avoided by them, VII. xl. 7; threatened by Huns, VIII. xxi. 22; visited by Antonina, S.H. i. 11
Thessaly, in northern Greece, adjoining Boeotia, VIII. xxv. 19; plundered by the Huns, II. iv. 10; fortresses of, B. IV. iv. 3; buildings of Justinian in, B. IV. iii. 1 ff.; Thessalian cape, or *chlamys*, III. xxv. 7
Thesteum, fortress in Macedonia, B. IV. iv. 3
Theudibald, succeeds his father Theudibert as King of the Franks, VIII. xxiv. 11; addressed by

Leontius, VIII. xxiv. 12–24; replies to him, VIII. xxiv. 25–29; invited by Teïas to an alliance, VIII. xxxiv. 17
Theudibert, King of the Franks, gives his sister in marriage to Amalaric, V. xiii. 4; appealed to by her, V. xiii. 10; defeats Amalaric in battle, V. xiii. 11; takes over Visigothic portion of Gaul, V. xiii. 12; sanctions treaty with Theodatus, V. xiii. 27; sends allies to Vittigis, VI. xii. 38, 39; leads an army into Italy, VI. xxv. 2–24, VIII. xxiv. 11, 15; receives a letter from Belisarius, VI. xxv. 19–23; retires from Italy, VI. xxv. 24, xxvi. 1, 12; his actions defended by Theudibald, VIII. xxiv. 26; marries his sister to Hermegisclus, VIII. xx. 11; his death, VIII. xxiv. 6; succeeded by Theudibald, VIII. xxiv. 11; the sister of, VIII. xx. 41
Theudimund, son of Mauricius, escapes from peril, VII. i. 36
Theudis, King of the Visigoths, IV. iv. 34, V. xii. 50–54, xiii. 13; receives envoys from Gelimer, III. xxiv. 7–16; uncle of Ildibadus, VI. xxx. 15
Thilasamon, village near Amida, I. ix. 14
Thiolla, fortress in Mesopotamia, B. II. vi. 14
Thocyodis, fortress in Haemimontum, B. IV. xi. 20
Thomas, bishop of Apamea; displays the wood of the cross, II. xi. 16 ff.; goes before Chosroes, II. xi. 20 ff.; saves the wood of the cross, II. xi. 29, 30
Thomas, Roman commander, sent by Belisarius to take over strongholds, VI. xxviii. 29 ff.; besieged by Uraïas, VI. xxviii. 33
Thomas, ambassador to Chosroes, I. xxii. 1
Thomas Guzes, commander in Lazica, II. xxx. 5; father of John Guzes, VIII. viii. 15, 38, ix. 13, x. 7, xi. 57, 64
Thorisin, ruler (by usurpation) of the Gepaedes, VII. xxxiv. 4, VIII. xviii. 3, xxvii. 19; negotiates with Auduin, VIII. xviii. 8 ff.; refuses to surrender Ildigisal, VIII. xxvii. 22–25
Thrace, at the eastern limit of the Mediterranean, B. IV. ix. 1; on the Euxine, B. III. vii. 18; in form, an isthmus, B. IV. ix. 2, 3; protected by the Chersonese, B. IV. x. 2; dominated by Byzantium, B. IV. viii. 2; adjoins "Germania," III. xi. 21; contains royal horse-pastures, III. xii. 6; starting point of Alaric's invasion, III. ii. 7; the Goths settle in, III. ii. 39, V. xvi. 2, VIII. v. 13; at the mercy of barbarians, VII. xxxiii. 1; named as the limit of the Caucasus, VIII. iii. 3; traversed by the Ister, VIII. v. 30; its towns, B. III. vii. 18 ff., IV. vii. 1 ff.; Adrianople, VII. xl. 36; Apri, VIII. xxvii. 8; Topirus, VII. xxxviii. 9; Tzurullum, VII. xxxviii. 5; source of grain, S.H. xxii. 17; invaded and ravaged by the Sclaveni, VII. xxxviii. 3, 7, 19; Artabanes appointed General of, VII. xxxix. 8; Germanus General of, VII. xl. 6; Cutrigurs given homes in, VIII. xix. 5, 7, xxvii. 10; Narses passes through, VIII. xxi. 21; Lombards settle in, VIII. xxvii. 3; invaded by barbarians, B. IV. x. 9; crossed by Ildigisal and Goar, VIII. xxvii. 11; held by barbarians, S.H. xviii. 20; generals of, S.H. xxi. 26; a force of Thracians reaches Dryus, VI. v. 1; sent to Milan under Paulus, VI. xii. 26, 27; Thracians in Roman armies, II. xix. 32, xxi. 4, VI. xi. 5, VII. vi. 10, x. 1, 2, x i. 4, xxxix. 9, 17, 18, VIII. xxvi. 10; home of several Roman commanders, I. xiii. 5, III. xi. 10; of Babas, VIII. ix. 5; of Barbation, VII. xi. 37; of Constantine and Bessas, V. v. 3; of Cutilas, VI. ii. 10; of Gudilas, VII. xxx. 6; of Himerius, IV. xxiii. 3; of Peter, IV. xxviii. 3; of Theodosius, S.H. i. 15; of Ulimuth, VI. xiii. 14; buildings by Justinian in, B. IV. viii. 2 ff., xi. 18, 20; Narses leads the Eruli thither, VII. xiii.

INDEX

22; invaded by the Antae, VII. xiv. 11; overrun by the Eruli, VII. xxxiii. 13; Chilbudius General of, VII. xiv. 2; mentioned, VII. xxxii. 38, VIII. xviii. 17, xxvii. 9

Thrasarichu, fortress in Haemimontum, B. IV. xi. 20

Thrasou, fortress in Rhodopê, built by Justinian, B. IV. xi. 20

Thule, an "island" situated in the extreme north, VIII. xx. 6, xxv. 11; its position with reference. to Brittia, VIII. xx. 4; description, inhabitants, long nights, etc., VI. xv. 4 ff.; Eruli settled there, VI. xv. 29; a king summoned thence by the Eruli, VI. xiv. 42, xv. 27, 30; return of the messengers, VI. xv. 33

Thurii, city in southern Itlay, V. xv. 23, VII. xxiii. 12; between Croton and Tarentum, VII. xxviii. 3; its harbour Rusciane, VII. xxviii. 8

Thurimuth, bodyguard of Belisarius, sent into Aemilia, VII. xi. 11; with Vitalius defeats Goths, VII. xi. 17; returns to Ravenna, VII. xi. 18; sent to Auximus, VII. xi. 19; defeats Goths, VII. xi. 25; decides to leave Auximus, VII. xi. 26, 27; attacked by Totila, but escapes, VII. xi. 29–31; sent to Pisaurus, VII. xi. 34; commander of Rhegium, VII. xxxvii. 20; distinguishes himself in its defence, VII. xxxix. 1; surrenders to the Goths, VII. xxxix. 5

Thuringians, barbarians of Gaul, V. xii. 10, 11; form close alliance with Theoderic, V. xii. 21, 22; their ruler Hermenefridus, V. xii. 22, VIII. xxv. 11; subjugated by the Franks, V. xiii. 1, VI. xxviii. 17

Thyrsus, Martyr, shrine of, in Byzantium, B. I. iv. 28

Tiber River, flowing through Rome, an obstacle to Vittigis, V. xvii. 13–15; defended by Belisarius, V. xvii. 18, xviii. 2 ff.; crossed by Vittigis, V. xviii. 1 ff., xxiv. 3; crossed by the Goths to storm the wall, V. xxii. 18, 25; used by Belisarius to turn mills, V. xix. 19 ff.; Rome provisioned by way of it, VI. vii. 8 ff.; description of its mouths, V. xxvi. 5–8; navigable, V. xxvi. 6, 10–12; its tortuous course, V. xxvi. 11; flowed near the Aurelian Gate, V. xxii. 16, VI. ix. 16; sewers of Rome discharge into, V. xix. 29; bridge over, distance from Rome, V. xvii. 13; fortified by Belisarius, V. xvii. 14; abandoned by the garrison, V. xvii. 19; bridged within the city, V. xix. 6–10, VII. xvii. 22; guarded by a bridge built by Totila, VII. xviii. 9, 10, xix. 16; most of bridges destroyed by the Goths, VII. xxiv. 31, xxv. 22; mentioned, VII. vi. 1, x. 23, etc.

Tiberias, town in Palestine, B. V. ix. 21

Tibur, town near Rome, occupied by Sinthues and Magnus, VI. iv. 7; taken by Totila, VII. x. 19, 21, xi. 1; its inhabitants slain, VII. x. 19–22; held by the Goths as a check on Rome, VII. x. 23; its defences destroyed, VII. [illegible]; occupied by Totila, VII. xxiv. 31; strengthened by him, VII. xxiv. 32

Ticinum, strongly fortified city in northern Italy, VI. xii. 32; battle fought near, VI. xii. 31, 33; Uraïas proceeds thither, VI. xxiv. 20, 21, xxx. 4; a bridge there over the Po, VI. xxv. 8; held by the Goths, VII. i. 27, iii. 3, iv. 12, VIII. xxxiii. 6, xxxv. 37; money deposited there by Totila, VIII. xxxiii. 7, xxxiv. 19

Tigas, fortress in Moesia, restored by Justinian, B. IV. vii. 6

Tigisis, city in Numidia, IV. x. 21, 22, its great spring, IV. xiii. 5; strengthened by Justinian, B. VI. vii. 10

Tigra, fortress in Moesia, B. IV. xi. 20

Tigranes, son of Arsaces, joint-King of Armenia, B. III. i. 8 ff., makes alliance with Persia, B. III. i. 11, 13

Tigris River, its source in Armenia, I. xvii. 4; its course into Assyria, I. xvii. 5, 6; distance from Nisibis, I. xi. 27; its junction with the Euphrates, I. xvii. 22; flows between Seleucia and Ctesiphon,

II. xxviii. 5; limit of Parthian rule, B. III. i. 5; crossed by Arethas, S.H. ii. 23, 25, 28
Tilicion, fortress in Moesia, built by Justinian, B. IV. vii. 14
Tillito, fortress in Moesia, B. IV. xi. 20
Timaciolum, fortress in the district of Aquenisium, B. IV. iv. 3
Timathochiom, fortress in the district of Aquenisium, B. IV. iv. 3
Timena, fortress on the Danube, B. IV. vi. 18
Timiana, fortress in southern Europe, B. IV. iv. 3
Timostratus, brother of Rufinus, captured by Alamundaras, I. xvii. 43, 44
Timothy, the Apostle, his body revealed to Justinian, B. I. iv. 18, 21
Tithyra, fortress in Epirus, B. IV. iv. 3
Titiana, fortress in Epirus, B. IV. iv. 3
Titus, son of Vespasian, Roman Emperor, IV. ix. 2; his capture of Jerusalem, IV. ix. 5
Tiuncona, fortress in southern Europe, B. IV. iv. 3
Tomes, fortress in Remisianisia, B. IV. iv. 3
Tomis, fortress in Moesia, B. IV. xi. 20
Toparum, fortress in Rhodopê, built by Justinian, B. IV. xi. 20
Topera, fortress in Remisianisia, B. IV. iv. 3
Topirus, coast city of Thrace, captured by the Sclaveni, VII. xxxviii. 9–18, B. IV. xi. 14; strengthened by Justinian, B. IV. xi. 14–17; distance from Byzantium, VII. xxxviii. 9
Totila, ruler of the Goths, V. xxiv. 32; nephew of Ildibadus, VII. ii. 7; offers to surrender Tarbesium, VII. ii. 8, 9; invited to become King of the Goths, VII. ii. 11; his conditions, VII. ii. 12; assumes the power, VII. ii. 18, iii. 1; in Ticinum, VII. iii. 3; moves against the Romans, VII. iv. 1; addresses his army, VII. iv. 10–18; crosses the Po and defeats the Romans, VII. iv. 19 ff.; sends a force against Florentia, VII. v. 1; treats Roman captives kindly, VII. v. 19; captures Caesena, Petra and Beneventum, VII. vi. 1; besieges Naples, VII. vi. 2 ff.; captures a fortress, VII. xxvi. 13; captures Cumae, VII. vi. 3; treats Senators' wives chivalrously, VII. vi. 4; gains much of lower Italy, VII. vi. 5; feared by Roman soldiers, VII. vi. 19; insulted by Demetrius, VII. vi. 21; intercepts a relieving fleet, VII. vi. 24; humiliates Demetrius, VII. vii. 8, 9; addresses the Neapolitans, VII. vii. 11–16; receives the surrender of Naples, VII. vii. 18–20; his humane treatment of the Neapolitans, VII. viii. 1–5; and kindness to the Roman garrison, VII. viii. 8, 9; partially dismantles defences of Naples, VII. viii. 10; imprisons a guard, VII. viii. 25; appeases Gothic notables, VII. viii. 14–24; executes the guard, VII. viii. 25; writes to the Roman Senate, VII. ix. 19; has Rome placarded, VII. ix. 20, 21; sends force against Dryus and moves on Rome, VII. ix. 22; receives report from Dryus, VII. x. 9; sends out spies, VII. x. 14–18; takes Tibur, VII. x. 19–21; sends force to Bononia, VII. xi. 16; eluded by the Romans, VII. xi. 20; ambushes the Romans, VII. xi. 28–30; threatens Pisaurus, VII. xi. 35, 36; attacks several towns, VII. xi. 38, 39; besieges Tuscan towns, VII. xii. 12; takes Firmum and Asculum by surrender, VII. xii. 12; also Spolitium, VII. xii. 15, S.H. v. 6; and Asise, VII. xii. 18; demands surrender of Perusia, *ib.*; has Cyprian murdered, VII. xii. 19, 20; besieges Rome, VII. xiii. 1 ff.; urges farmers to cultivate the land, VII. xiii. 1; takes the revenue, *ib.*; sends a force into Aemilia, VII. xiii. 8–11; ambushes a Roman force, VII. xv. 7, 8; mutilates a Roman Bishop, VII. xv. 14, 15; treats with Pelagius, VII. xvi. 7–xvii. 1; hears of Belisarius' arrival, VII. xviii. 6; guards approaches to Rome, VII. xviii. 8; builds bridge over the Tiber, VII. xviii. 9, 10, xix. 16;

INDEX

receives a depleted force, VII. xviii. 16; sends a force to Capua, VII. xviii. 24; appoints Rhecimundus to Bruttium, VII. xviii. 26; executes Isaac, VII. xix. 34; negotiates with four Isaurians, VII. xx. 4–13; captures Rome, VII. xx. 14 ff.; allows Romans to flee, VII. xx. 20, 21; prays in the Church of Peter, VII. xx. 22; appealed to by Pelagius, VII. xx. 23–25; stops slaughter, VII. xx. 25; secures accumulated wealth of Bessas, VII. xx. 26; protects Roman women, VII. xx. 30, 31; addresses the Goths, VII. xxi. 1–11; and the Roman Senate, VII. xxi. 12–16; persuaded to spare Senators, VII. xxi. 17; sends envoys and letter to Justinian, VII. xxi. 18–24; referred by Justinian to Belisarius, VII. xxi. 25; who eludes him, S.H. v. 2; sends Senators to Campania, VII. xxvi. 2; sends a force against Tullianus, VII. xxii. 4; decides to dismantle Rome, VII. xxii. 6; does so in part, VII. xxii. 7, xxiv. 3, 9; dissuaded by Belisarius, VII. xxii. 8–17; garrisons Algedon and marches against John, VII. xxii. 18; disposes of his prisoners, VII. xxii. 19; persuades Roman farmers to return, VII. xxii. 20; master of southern Italy except Dryus, VII. xxii. 22; encamps on Mt. Garganon, VII. xxii. 24; receives Martinianus kindly, VII. xxiii. 1, 2; captures Acherontis and goes to Ravenna, VII. xxiii. 18; attacks Belisarius in Rome, VII. xxiv. 8–26; reproached by Gothic notables, VII. xxiv. 27; worshipped by them while successful, VII. xxiv. 29; retires to Tibur, VII. xxiv. 31; had sent a force against Perusia, VII. xxv. 1; called to its assistance, VII. xxv. 2; addresses the Goths, VII. xxv. 3–24; moves against Perusia, VII. xxv. 24; sends a force into Campania, VII. xxvi. 3; receives report of defeat, VII. xxvi. 9; marches against John, VII. xxvi. 15; surprises and routs him, VII. xxvi. 17–23; surprises a force under Verus, VII. xxvii. 6–9; kept away by Roman fleet, VII. xxvii. 10; sends troops to Rusciane, VII. xxviii. 9; who return to him defeated, VII. xxviii. 11; surprises the Roman force, VII. xxviii. 13–15; besieges fortress near Rusciane, VII. xxix. 21; drives off Roman fleet, VII. xxx. 13, 14; Romans attempt diversion, VII. xxx. 16, 18; sends force into Picenum, VII. xxx. 18; takes Rusciane by surrender, VII. xxx. 19–21; treats captives with moderation, VII. xxx. 21, 22; Ildiges plans to join him, VII. xxxv. 22; receives Indulf as a deserter, VII. xxxv. 23; sends him to Dalmatia, VII. xxxv. 24; Indulf returns to him, VII. xxxv. 29; marches on Rome, VII. xxxvi. 1; captures Rome by treachery, VII. xxxvi. 7–14; attacks Tomb of Hadrian, VII. xxxvi. 18–20; receives its surrender, VII. xxxvi. 24–28; wishes Rome to be inhabited, VII. xxxvi. 29; his proposal of marriage rejected by Franks, VII. xxxvii. 1, 2; repairs and provisions Rome, VII. xxxvii. 3; prepares to invade Sicily, VII. xxxvii. 4; captures provision ships, VII. xxxvii. 5; sends ambassador to Justinian, VII. xxxvii. 6; besieges Centumcellae, VII. xxxvii. 8; negotiates with Diogenes, VII. xxxvii. 11–17; attacks Rhegium, VII. xxxvii. 19–22; captures Tarentum, VII. xxxvii. 23; attacks Messana, VII. xxxix. 2; demands surrender of Centumcellae, VII. xxxix. 25; retires with great booty, VII. xl. 19; chooses Spinus as counsellor, VII. xl. 20; seeks to rescue him, VII. xl. 22; leaves Sicily, VII. xl. 24, 26–29; suspected of intrigue, VII. xl. 32, 33; Narses marches against him, VIII. xxi. 19; prepares for Narses, VIII. xxii. 1 ff.; sends fleet to Greece, VIII. xxii. 17; sends army into Picenum, VIII. xxiii. 1; his power weakened,

viii. xxiii. 42; sends vain embassies to Justinian, viii. xxiv. 4; gives lands to Theudibert, viii. xxiv. 27; sends expedition to Corsica and Sardinia, viii. xxiv. 31–33; Roman deserters to, viii. xxvi. 6, xxxii. 20; blocks roads, viii. xxvi. 21, 23, 24; awaits Teïas near Rome, viii. xxix. 1; moves against the Romans, viii. xxix. 2; receives message from Narses, viii. xxix. 6; his reply, viii. xxix. 8; suspected by Narses, viii. xxix. 9; appears before the Roman camp, viii. xxix. 10; tries to gain a vantage point, viii. xxix. 16 ff.; exhorts his army, viii. xxx. 7–20; arranges his forces, viii. xxxi. 8; displays his prowess, viii. xxxi. 17–20; proposes conference, viii. xxxi. 21; withdraws to camp, viii. xxxii. 1; changes armour, viii. xxxii. 2; gives a foolish order, viii. xxxii. 7; his flight and death, viii. xxxii. 22–30; his death verified by the Romans, viii. xxxii. 31, 32; another version of his end, viii. xxxii. 33–36; deposited money in Ticinum, viii. xxxiii. 7; instigated murder of Cyprian, viii. xxxiii. 10; burned much of Rome, viii. xxxiii. 14; sent Senators to Campania, viii. xxxiv. 5; held Roman children as hostages, viii. xxxiv. 7, 8; deposited money in Ticinum and Cumae, viii. xxxiv. 19

Toumar, place on the summit of Mt. Aurasius, iv. xix. 22; besieged by the Romans, iv. xx. 1 ff.; scaled and captured, iv. xx. 1–20

Trachea, a strongly defended pass in Abasgia, viii. ix. 19, 21, 22

Traiani Forum, city on Sardinia, walled by Justinian, B. vi. vii. 12, 13

Trajan, Roman Emperor, iv. ix. 2, viii. ii. 16, B. iii. iv. 17, iv. vi. 6; founded Turris, vii. xiv. 32; his conquest of Dacia, B. iv. vi. 11 ff.

Trajan, bodyguard of Belisarius, sent into Assyria, ii. xix. 15 ff.; returns by a different route, ii. xix. 28 ff.; makes a successful attack on the Goths, v. xxvii. 4 ff.; sent to Taracina, vi. iv. 6; which he occupies with Martinus, vi. iv. 14; summoned back to Rome, vi. v. 4; sent against the Goths, vi. v. 9, 10; in the battle at the Pincian Gate, vi. v. 21; his strange wound, vi. v. 24–27

Trajanopolis, city in Rhodopê, fortified by Justinian, B. iv. xi. 10

Tralles, home of Anthemius, B. i. i. 24

Trana, fortress in Epirus, B. iv. iv. 3

Transtiburtine Gate, in the wall of Rome, threatened by a Gothic camp, v. xix. 4

Trapezus, city on the Euxine, ii. xxix. 22, xxx. 14, viii. ii. 2; location, viii. i. 8; extent of its territory, viii. ii. 3; its boundaries, viii. iv. 5; not near Colchis, viii. ii. 15; adjoins Rhizaeum, viii. ii. 3, B. iii. vii. 3; its unusual honey, viii. ii. 4; refuge of Roman garrisons, viii. iv. 6; supplied with water, B. iii. vii. 1

Trasamundus, brother of Gundamundus, becomes King of the Vandals, iii. viii. 8; tries to win over the Christians, iii. viii. 9, 10; asks the hand of Amalafrida, iii. viii. 11; becomes a friend of Anastasius, iii. viii. 14; his death, iii. viii. 29

Trasiana, fortress in Aquenisium, B. iv. iv. 3

Trasmariscas, fortress in Moesia, B. iv. vii. 7, 9

Tredetetilious, fortress in Aquenisium, B. iv. iv. 3

Tretum, place near Antioch, its Church of Michael, ii. xi. 7

Tria Fata, statues in Rome, v. xxv. 19

Tribunianus, a Pamphylian, flatters Justinian, i. xxiv. 11, S.H. xiii. 12; becomes Quaestor, i. xxiv. 11, S.H. xx. 16; his dexterity in manipulating laws, i. xxiv. 16; dismissed from office, i. xxiv. 17; restored to office, i. xxv. 1, 2; his death, i. xxv. 2; his property seized by Justinian, S.H. xx. 17

Tribunus, a physician, beloved by Chosroes, ii. xxviii. 8 ff., viii. x.

11–14; receives a favour from him, VIII. x. 15, 16
Tricamarum, place in Libya, distance from Carthage, IV. ii. 4; Vandals defeated there, IV. iii. 1 ff., iv. 35, v. 2, 9
Tricca, city of Thessaly, fortified by Justinian, B. IV. iii. 5
Tricesa, fortress on the Danube, B. IV. vi. 28
Tripolis, district in Africa, III. i. 14, B. VI. iii. 9, v. 1; Vandals defeated there, III. vi. 9, 11; won for the Emperor, B. VI. iv. 10; Moors dwelling there, III. viii. 15; lost again by the Vandals, III. x. 22–24; Gelimer despairs of recover ing it, III. xi. 22; Belisarius sends army thither, IV. v. 10; rule of, falls to Sergius, IV. xxi. 1; Leuathae come thence with army, IV. xxviii. 47; ashes from Vesuvius fell in, VI. iv. 27; distance from Gadira, III. i. 14; from Pentapolis, B. VI. iii. 12
Tripyrgia, quarter of Edessa, II. xxvii. 41
Trisciana, fortress in Cabetzus, B. IV. iv. 3
Triumph, description of the manner of celebration, IV. ix. 1–14; triumphal procession of Belisarius, IV. ix. 15, 16; who on another occasion is denied a triumph, VII. i. 3
Trosmes, fortress in Moesia, B. IV. xi. 20
Troy, capture of, III. xxi. 4, VIII. xxii. 31; a man of Troy, V. xv. 10
Tryphon, Martyr, shrine of, on the Bosporus, B. I. ix. 15
Tryphon, sent to Libya as tax-assessor, IV. viii. 25
Tucca, fortress near Carthage, built by Justinian, B. VI. v. 15
Tudera, town in Italy, garrisoned by Vittigis, VI. xi. 1; surrenders to Belisarius, VI. xiii. 2, 3; garrisoned by him, VI. xiii. 4
Tugurias, fortress in Cabetzus, B. IV. iv. 3
Tulcoburgo, fortress in Remisianisia, B. IV. iv. 3
Tuleus, fortress in Thrace, B. IV. xi. 20
Tullianus, son of Venantius, advises John, VII. xviii. 20–22; influential in Bruttium and Lucania, VII. xviii. 20; brother of Deopheron, VII. xxx. 6; rouses the rustics, VII. xxii. 2; defeats a Gothic force, VII. xxii. 4–6; makes off in flight, VII. xxii. 21
Turicla, fortress in Cabetzus, B. IV. iv. 3
Turribas, fortress in Aquenisium, B. IV. iv. 3
Turris, town above the Danube, founded by Trajan, VII. xiv. 32
Turules, fortress in Moesia, B. IV. xi. 20
Turus, fortress in Cabetzus, B. IV. iv. 3
Tuscan Sea, south of Gaul, V. xii. 6, 7; distance from Ravenna, V. xv. 19; separated from the Adriatic by Gaulus and Melita, III. xiv. 16; severity of its storms, IV. iv. 37
Tuscans, inhabitants of Tuscany, accuse Theodatus, V. iv. 1; welcome Constantinus into their cities, V. xvi. 4; gifted with prophecy, VIII. xxi. 16, 17
Tuscany, area between Aemilia and Rome, V. xv. 30, largely owned by Theodatus, V. iii. 2, 29; who plans to surrender it, V. iii. 3, iv. 17; invaded by Constantinus, V. xvi. 1 ff.; by Totila, VII. xii. 12; by Teïas, VIII. xxxiii. 9; by John and Philemouth, VIII. xxxiv. 22; crossed by Totila, VII. vi. 1, VIII. xxix. 3; famine in, VI. xx. 19; refuge of Romans, VI. xxv. 14; shut off from Rome, VII. x. 23; its cities: Centumcellae, VI. vii. 18, 19; Clusium, VI. xi. 1; Genoa, VI. xii. 29; Narnia, V. xvi. 2; Perusia, V. xvi. 3, VII. xxxv. 2; Spolitium, V. xvi. 3; its fortress Nepa, VIII. xxxiv. 16; its Lake Vulsina, V. iv. 14
Tusudeaas, fortress in Cabetzus, B. IV. iv. 3
Tuttiana, fortress in Dardania, B. IV. iv. 3
Tydeus, father of Diomedes, V. xv. 8
Tynnichus, an artist, VIII. xxii. 29
Tyrcanus, fortress in Epirus, B. IV. iv. 3
Tyre, city in Phoenicia, its silk indus-

try, S.H. xxv. 14; home of Hecebolus, S.H. ix. 27
Tzani, called Sani in early times, I. xv. 21; their location, II. xxix. 14, VIII. i. 8, 9; character of the people and country, B. III. vi. 2 ff.; divided into tribes, B. III. vi. 18; averse to agriculture, B. III. vi. 21; their boundaries, B. III. vi. 15; subdued by the Romans, I. xv. 19 ff., II. iii. 39, B. III. vi. 6; serve in Roman armies, II. xxix. 10, 41, VIII. xiii. 10; defend a Roman camp, II. xxx. 13; return to their homes, II. xxx. 14; become Christians, I. xv. 25, B. III. vi. 7; Justinian fears their relapse, B. III. vi. 8; rendered accessible by Justinian, B. III. vi. 13; his buildings among them, B. III. vi. 1 ff., vii. 1; Coxyline Tzani, B. III. vi. 26
Tzanica, land of the Tzani, B. III. vi. 5, 9; its mountains, VIII. ii. 5, 6; its point of entrance for Romans, B. III. vi. 17; fortresses of, B. III. vi. 14, vii. 24
Tzanzacon, fortress in Tzanica, B. III. vi. 26
Tzasclis, fortress in Moesia, B. IV. xi. 20
Tzazon, brother of Gelimer, sent to Sardinia, III. xi. 23; overthrows and kills Godas, III. xxiv. 1; writes to Gelimer, III. xxiv. 2–4; receives a letter from him, III. xxv. 10–18; departs for Libya, III. xxv. 19–21; meets Gelimer at the Plain of Boulla, III. xxv. 24; addresses his troops separately, IV. ii. 23–32; commands in the centre at the battle of Tricamarum, IV. iii. 1, 8, 10, 12; his death, IV. iii. 14; his head taken to Sardinia, IV. v. 2, 4
Tzertzenutzas, fortress in Remisianisia, B. IV. iv. 3
Tzibile, fortress in Apsilia, VIII. x. 1, 7; guarding approach to Abasgia, VIII. xvii. 16
Tzibus, *see* John Tzibus
Tzimes, fortress in Cabetzus, B. IV. iv. 3
Tzitaetus, fortress in Haemimontum, B. IV. xi. 20
Tzittas, *see* Sittas
Tzonpolegon, fortress in Haemimontum, B. IV. xi. 20
Tzumina, place in Armenia, site of a city built by Justinian, B. III. v. 15; distance from Bizana, *ib.*
Tzur, a pass over the Caucasus, VIII. iii. 4
Tzurullum, town in Thrace, VII. xxxviii. 5
Tzutrato, fortress in Aquenisium, B. IV. iv. 3
Tzyeidon, fortress in Haemimontum, B. IV. xi. 20

Ucum, fortress in Haemimontum, B. IV. xi. 20
Uliaris, bodyguard of Belisarius, III. xix. 23; his stupid action at Decimum, III. xix. 24; kills John the Armenian accidentally, IV. iv. 15 ff.; takes refuge in a sanctuary, IV. iv. 21; spared by Belisarius, IV. iv. 25
Uliaris, Gothic commander, VII. v. 1; in command of Naples, V. iii. 15
Ulias, a Goth, given as a hostage, VI. vii. 13
Ulibula, fortress in Epirus, B. IV. iv. 3
Ulifus, bodyguard of Cyprian, whom he kills; commander of Perusia, VII. xii. 19, 20, VIII. xxxiii. 10; his death, VIII. xxxiii. 11, 12
Uligagus, of the Eruli, commander in the Roman army, VIII. ix. 5; sent to Lazica, VIII. ix. 5, 13, xiii. 9; attacks the Abasgi, VIII. ix. 20 ff.
Uligisalus, Gothic commander, sent to Dalmatia, V. xvi. 8; enters Liburnia alone, V. xvi. 12; defeated, retires to Burnus, V. xvi. 13; proceeds with Asinarius to Salones, V. xvi. 16; stationed in Tudera, VI. xi. 1
Ulimuth, of Thrace, bodyguard of Belisarius, renders signal service at Ancon, VI. xiii. 14, 15
Ulitheus, uncle of Vittigis, defeated and killed by John, VI. x. 2
Ulitheus, bodyguard of Gontharis, IV. xxv. 8; bears messages to Antalas, IV. xxv. 8–11, 19; assassinates Areobindus, IV. xxvi. 32, 33, xxvii. 20; marches against Antalas, IV. xxvii. 25 ff.; killed

by Artasires at banquet, IV. xxviii. 19 ff.
Ulmiton, fortress in Scythia, restored by Justinian, B. IV. vii. 17, 18
Ulpiana, city in Dardania, VIII. xxv. 13; rebuilt and renamed by Justinian, B. IV. i. 28, 29
Unigastus, bodyguard of Belisarius, whom he saves, VI. xxvii. 14
Unilas, Gothic commander; sent into Tuscany, V. xvi. 5; defeated and captured, V. xvi. 6, 7
Unnon, fortress near the Danube; strengthened by Justinian, B. IV. vi. 33, 34
Unnum, city of northern Greece; fortified by Justinian, B. IV. ii. 16
Uraïas, nephew of Vittigis, VI. xxx. 4, 12; sent into Liguria, VI. xii. 37; besieges Milan, VI. xviii. 19, xxi. 1; makes terms with the Eruli, VI. xxii. 6; held in check by John and others, VI. xxiii. 4; sent to Ticinum, VI. xxiv. 20–22; summoned by Vittigis, VI. xxvi. 9; leads relief expedition to Ravenna, VI. xxviii. 31; turns aside to the Alps, VI. xxviii. 33; unable to continue, VI. xxviii. 35; invited to assume kingship of the Goths, VI. xxx. 4 ff.; declines the offer, VI. xxx. 11 ff.; becomes hostile to Ildibadus, VII. i. 37 ff.; slain by him, VII. i. 41, 49
Urbinus, city in Picenum, VI. x. 5; its situation, VI. xix. 3, 4; distance from Ariminum, VI. xix. 1; passed by John, VI. x. 5, 7; garrisoned by Vittigis, VI. xi. 2; besieged by Belisarius, VI. xix. 1 ff.; failure of its water-supply, VI. xix. 12, 13; captured in midwinter, VI. xix. 17, xx. 1
Urbriana, fortress in southern Europe, B. IV. iv. 3
Urdaus, fortress in Thrace, B. IV. xi. 20
Ursicinus, Roman commander of cavalry, V. v. 3, xxiii. 3
Urvisalia, town in Picenum, destroyed by Alaric, VI. xvi. 24; its goat-nursed infant, VI. xvii. 1 ff.
Urviventus, town near Rome, garrisoned by Vittigis, VI. xi. 1, xviii. 19; its situation, VI. xx. 7–10; Peranius sent against it, VI. xix. 1; Belisarius marches against it, VI. xx. 3, 4; besieged by him, VI. xx. 5 ff.
Usdrilas, Gothic commander of Ariminum, VIII. xxviii. 2; writes insolently to Valerian, VIII. xxviii. 2–4; leads a scouting party, VIII. xxviii. 8, 9; killed in a skirmish, VIII. xxviii. 10, 11, xxix. 3
Usiana, fortress in Dardania, B. IV. iv. 3
Ustrigothus, son of Elemundus, VIII. xxvii. 19; dethroned by Gepaedes and flees, VIII. xxvii. 19, 20; his surrender demanded by Thorisin, VIII. xxvii. 26; slain by Auduin, VIII. xxvii. 28, 29
Uthimereos, fortress in Lazica, VIII. xiv. 51; shut off by Mermeroes, VIII. xiv. 53; betrayed by him, VIII. xvi. 4 ff.; garrisoned by him, VIII. xvi. 16
Utigur, progenitor of the Utigur Huns, VIII. v. 2
Utigur Huns, tribe near the Maeotic Lake, VIII. iv. 8; origin of the name, VIII. v. 2–4; feared by the Tetraxitae, VIII. iv. 13; return home, VIII. v. 17; taking with them the Tetraxitae, VIII. v. 18–22; receive an embassy from Justinian, VIII. xviii. 18–21; attack the Cutrigurs, VIII. xviii. 24, xix. 4, 6; their king Sandil, VIII. xix. 8; *see* Cimmerians
Utos, fortress near the Danube, built by Justinian, B. IV. vi. 35

V, *see also* names indexed under B
Vaces, ruler of the Lombards, VI. xxii. 11, VII. xxxv. 13; friend of the Emperor, VI. xxii. 12; uncle of Risiulfus, VII. xxxv. 13; father of Valdarus, VII. xxxv. 17; banishes Risiulfus, VII. xxxv. 14; bribes the Varni to kill him, VII. xxxv. 16; dies of disease, VII. xxxv. 17
Vacimus, Gothic commander, sent against Ancon, VI. xiii. 5, 8
Vacis, a Goth; harangues the Romans, V. xviii. 39–41.
Vaga, city near Carthage, walled by

Justinian, B. VI. v. 12, 13; renamed Theodorias, B. VI. v. 14
Valaris, a Goth, challenges the Roman army, VII. iv. 21; fights with Artabazes, VII. iv. 23; slain by him, VII. iv. 24, 28
Valdarus, son of Vaces, becomes King of the Lombards, VII. xxxv. 17
Valentinian, son of Constantius, reared by Theodosius, III. iii. 5; becomes Emperor of the West, III. iii. 8; captures and kills John, III. iii. 9; vicious from early training, III. iii. 10, 11; loses Libya to the empire, III. iii. 12; receives tribute from Gizeric, III. iv. 13; returns his hostage, III. iv. 14; slays Aetius, III. iv. 27; outrages the wife of Maximus, iii. iv. 16 ff.; slain by him, III. iv. 15, 36, V. xxv. 15; father of Eudocia and Placidia, III. v. 3, vi. 6; husband of Eudoxia, III. iv. 15; his family receive awards, IV. ix. 13
Valentiniana, fortress in Moesia, B. IV. xi. 20
Valentinus, Bishop, mutilated by Totila, VII. xv. 13–15
Valentinus, Roman commander; sent to relieve Dryus, VII. x. 6, 7; his men defeated, VII. x. 10, 11; returns to Salones, VII. x. 12; sent to Portus, VII. xv. 1; with Phocas makes a sally, VII. xv. 2; not supported by Bessas, VII. xv. 3, 4; meets his death in a second sally, VII. xv. 5–8
Valentinus, groom of Photius, fights valiantly, V. xviii. 18
Valerian, commander of auxiliaries, III. xi. 6; sent in advance to Africa, III. xi. 24, 29; meets fleet at Methone, III. xiii. 9; at the battle of Tricamarum, IV. iii. 4; Martinus sent to him in Numidia, IV. xiv. 40; summoned to Byzantium, IV. xix. 2; sent to Italy, V. xxiv. 19; winters in Aetolia, V. xxiv. 20; ordered to hasten to Rome, V. xxiv. 18; arrives in Rome, V. xxvii. 1; sent out against the Goths, V. xxvii. 22; sent to the Plain of Nero, VI. ii. 8; fights there with varying fortune, VI. ii. 19 ff.; with Martinus rescues Bochas, VI. ii. 24; establishes a camp, VI. iv. 11; returns to the city, VI. iv. 12; with Ildiger seizes Constantinus, VI. viii. 16; assists Belisarius at Auximus, VI. xxvi. 17 ff.; accompanies Belisarius to Byzantium, VII. i. 1; appointed General of Armenia, II. xiv. 8, VII. xxvii. 3, S.H. ii. 30; receives Persian envoys, II. xxiv. 6–8; reports to Justinian, II. xxiv. 9; ordered to invade Persia with Martinus, II. xxiv. 10; encamps near Theodosiopolis, II. xxiv. 12; follows Peter invading Persia, II. xxiv. 19; commands left wing at the battle of Anglon, II. xxv. 17; serving as general in Armenia, VIII. viii. 22; captures the Persian Bersabus, VIII. xv. 9; sent to Italy, VII. xxvii. 3; hesitates, VII. xxvii. 13, 14; sends a small detachment, VII. xxvii. 15; ordered by Justinian to proceed, VII. xxx. 1; crosses to Dryus, VII. xxx. 2; accompanies Belisarius to Rusciane, VII. xxx. 9; expected to proceed by land to Picenum, VII. xxx. 15, 18; instead sails to Ancon, VII. xxx. 17; writes to John, VIII. xxiii. 4–6; comes to Scardon, VIII. xxiii. 8; exhorts his fleet, VIII. xxiii. 14–22; returns to Ravenna, VIII. xxiii. 42; joins Narses, VIII. xxviii. 1; receives letter from Usdrilas, VIII. xxviii. 2; commands on the right wing, VIII. xxxi. 4; escorts Lombards from Italy, VIII. xxxiii. 2; encamps near Verona, VIII. xxxiii. 3; receives proposals of surrender, VIII. xxxiii. 4; retires, VIII. xxxiii. 5; sent to guard Po, VIII. xxxiii. 8; captures Petra Pertusa, VIII. xxxiv. 24; summoned to Campania, *ib.*; uncle of Damian, VI. vii. 26; his bodyguard Gouboulgoudou, VI. xiii. 14
Valeriana, fortress on the Danube, walled by Justinian, B. IV. vi. 31
Vandals, a Gothic people, III. ii. 2; their original home, III. i. 1, iii. 1 ff., VIII. v. 5; a portion of them

INDEX

lost to memory, III. xxii. 3, 13; settle in Spain, III. iii. 2; their alliance sought by Boniface, III. iii. 22, 25; migrate to Africa, III. iii. 26, VIII. v. 10; gain Africa, B. VI. v. 2; dismantle Hadrumetum, B. VI. vi. 2, 5; hold Libya, B. VI. vii. 6; do not control beyond Mt. Aurasius, B. VI. vii. 9; neglect Septum, B. VI. vii. 14; defeated by the Romans, II. ii. 8, iii. 46, V. iii. 22, v. 1, xxix. 8, VI. xxii. 16, VII. i. 3, B. VI. iv. 6, etc.; suffer heavy casualties, S.H. xviii. 6, 9; defeat Boniface in battle, III. iii. 31; besiege Hippo Regius, III. iii. 32, 34; defeat second Roman army, III. iii. 35; gain possession of Libya, III. xxii. 4; send Moors to Sardinia, IV. xiii. 43; take a church, III. xxi. 19; invade Italy and sack Rome, III. v. 1 ff.; their numbers with the Alani, III. v. 18–20; absorb all peoples except Moors, III. v. 21; Leon sends expedition against [illegible], III. vi. 1 ff.; expelled from Sardinia, III. vi. 8; defeated in Tripolis, III. vi. 9; lose Mt. Aurasius, IV. xiii. 26; make "endless peace" with Zeno, III. vii. 26; make war on the Moors, III. viii. 1, 2; defeated by them, III. viii. 15–28, B. VI. iv. 6; become hostile to the Goths, III. ix. 3; defeated often by the Moors, IV. x. 29; their king Gelimer, VIII. xix. 7; Justinian prepares an expedition against them, III. x. 1 ff.; lose Tripolis, III. x. 22–24; and Sardinia, III. x. 25–27; receive letter from Justinian, III. xvi. 12–14; recover Sardinia, III. xxiv. 1; defeated at Decimum, III. xviii. 1 ff.; greatly feared by Roman army, III. xix. 27; collected by Gelimer, III. xxv. 1 ff.; accumulated great wealth in Africa, IV. iii. 26; not trusted by Libyans, III. xvi. 3; their effeminacy as a nation, IV. vi. 5–10; their women incite mutiny, IV. xiv. 8, 9; likewise their Arian priests, IV. xiv. 13; Vandals' estates, established by Gizeric, III. v. 12; Vandals of Justinian, IV. xiv. 17; in the retinue of Belisarius, VII. i. 6; captives of Belisarius, VII. i. 12; King of, in mosaic at Byzantium, B. I. x. 17

Vararanes, Persian King, invades Roman territory, I. ii. 11 ff.; concludes peace with the Romans, I. ii. 15

Varazes, an Armenian, commander in the Roman army; sent to Italy, VII. xxvii. 3; unexpectedly rescues Verus, VII. xxvii. 10; lands and marches to Tarentum, VII. xxvii. 11; with the Roman army in Lazica, VIII. xiii. 10

Variana, city on the Danube, restored by Justinian, B. IV. vi. 31

Varizes, title of a Persian general (*lit.* "Victorious"), properly a family name, I. xii. 10; *cf.* Varazes

Varni, a barbarian nation, VI. xv. 2; Risiulfus flees to them, VII. xxxv. 15; involved in war with Brittia, VIII. [illegible]; ruled by Hermegisclus, VIII. xx. 11; advised to favour Franks, VIII. xx. 15, 16; engage with the islanders, VIII. xx. 33; do not ride on horses, VIII. xx. 31; their king Radigis, VIII. xx. 20

Varrames, son of Adergoudounbades, shares a secret, I. xxiii. 10; reveals the truth to Chosroes, I. xxiii. 13; made Chanaranges, I. xxiii. 22

Vasianus, punished by Theodora, S.H. xvi. 18–21

Vazaine, district in Persia, VIII. x. 9; distance from Ctesiphon, *ib.*

Vederiana, in Illyricum, home of Justinus, S.H. vi. 2; rebuilt by Justinian, B. IV. i. 17, 28

Velas, a Goth, offended by Ildibadus, VII. i. 43 ff.; slays him, VII. i. 47, 48

Vellurus, village in Rhodopê, fortified by Justinian, B. IV. xi. 7, 8

Venantius, father of Tullianus, VII. xviii. 20

Veneti, a people north of Italy, V. xv. 25

Veneti, name of one of the circus-factions, I. xxiv. 2-6; supported by Justinian, II. xi. 32, S.H. vii. 1, etc.; the "Blue Faction," II. xi. 32; *cf. also* Volume VI, Appendix I

Venetia, home of the Veneti, held by the Goths, V. xi. 16; Vitalius sent thither, VI. xxviii. 24; gained by Ildibadus, VII. i. 27; partly gained by the Franks, VII. xxxiii. 7; largely subject to Theudibert, VIII. xxiv. 6, xxxiii. 5, S.H. xviii. 17; little of, left to the Goths, VIII. xxiv. 8; reached by Narses, VIII. xxvi. 18; Teïas summoned thence, VIII. xxix. 1; its towns: Tarbesium, VI. xxix. 40; Verona, VII. iii. 3; mentioned, VI. xxi. 41, xxii. 7, VII. i. 34, xxxv. 22

Venilus, brother of Bouzes, commander in the Roman army, VIII. ix. 5; sent to Lazica, VIII. ix. 5, xiii. 9

Veredarii, imperial messengers, III. xvi. 12

Veredi, government post-horses, II. xx. 20

Vergentinus, Roman Senator, makes escape, V. xxvi. 2; proceeds to Dalmatia, VI. xxi. 41

Verina, Empress; *see* Berine

Verona, city in upper Italy, commanded by Ildibadus, VI. xxix. 41, xxx. 16, VII. iii. 3; attacked by a Roman army, VII. iii. 4 ff.; entered by Artabazes, VII. iii. 13; recovered by the Goths, VII. iii. 16, iv. 18; its garrison depleted by Totila, VII. iv. 1; held by the Goths, VIII. xxvi. 20–22; threatened by Valerian, VIII. xxxiii. 3, 4; distance from Mantua, VII. iii. 5

Verus, commander of Eruli, encamps near Martinus, II. xxiv. 14; with Philemouth follows Peter into Persia, II. xxiv. 18; sent to Italy, VII. xxvii. 3; arrives at Dryus, VII. xxvii. 4; his uncontrolled nature, VII. xxvii. 5, 6; almost captured by Totila, VII. xxvii. 9; rescued by Varazes, VII. xxvii. 10; defeated and slain in battle, VII. xxxvii. 28, xxxix. 24

Verus, fortress in Haemimontum, B. IV. xi. 20

Vespasian, Roman Emperor, father of Titus, IV. ix. 5; and of Domitian, S.H. viii. 13

Vesta, *see* Hestia

Vesuvius, volcanic mountain in Campania, description of, VI. iv. 22–24; distance from Naples, VI. iv. 22; its heavy ash-showers, VI. iv. 25–27; periodicity of its eruptions, VI. iv. 28; its fertility, VI. iv. 29; its salubrious atmosphere, VI. iv. 30; its eruptions described, VIII. xxxv. 1–6; its springs, VIII. xxxv. 7; threatens an eruption, VI. iv. 21

Vevon, place in Bruttium, VII. xviii. 27

Via, fortress in Haemimontum, B. IV. xi. 20

Vicanovo, fortress in Aquenisium, B. IV. iv. 3

Victoriana, fortress in Dardania, B IV. iv. 3

Victorias, fortress in Dardania, B. IV. iv. 3

Vidamas, fortress in Mesopotamia, B. II. vi. 14

Vidigis, fortress in Moesia, B. IV. xi. 20

Vigilantia, mother of Prejecta, and sister of Justinian, IV. xxiv. 3

Vigilius, brother of Reparatus, V. xxvi. 2; appointed bishop of Rome, V. xxv. 13; sends supplies to Rome, VII. xv. 9 ff.; goes to Byzantium, VII. xvi. 1; urges Justinian to defend Italy, VII. xxxv. 9; his agent Pelagius, S.H. xxvii. 17; opposes reappointment of Paulus, S. H. xxvii. 24

Viminacium, city on the Danube, restored by Justinian, B. IV. v. 17, vi. 1

Vimisdeon, fortress in Mesopotamia, B. II. vi. 14

Vindimiola, fortress in Aquenisium, B. IV. iv. 3

Virgin, Church of the, in Abasgia, VIII. iii. 21; in Blachernae, B. I. iii. 3, vi. 3, S.H. iii. 23; at Pegê, B. I. iii. 6; at Hieron, B. I. iii. 10; on the Asiatic shore, B. I. viii. 20; at Antioch, B. II. x. 24; at Theodosiopolis, B. III. iv. 12; at Jerusalem, B. V. vi. 1; on Mt. Garizin, B. V. vii. 7; on Mt. Sina, B. V. viii. 5; at Jericho, B. V. ix. 5;

INDEX

on the Mount of Olives, B. V. ix. 8; at Porphyreon, B. V. ix. 23; at Augila, B. VI. ii. 20; in Leptimagna, B. VI. iv. 4; in Carthage, B. VI. v. 9; at Septum, B. VI. vii. 16; afforded protection by her sanctuaries, B. I. iii. 9, VI. ii. 20; *see also* Mary *and* St. Mary

Virthon, fortress near Amida, strengthened by Justinian, B. II. iv. 20

Visandus, Erulian commander, VI. xiii. 18; left in Venetia, VI. xxii. 8; killed in battle, VII. i. 36

Visandus Vandalarius, a Goth, distinguished for bravery, V. xviii. 29; his unexpected recovery, V. xviii. 30–33; stationed at Auximus, VI. xi. 2

Visigoths, a Gothic people, III. ii. 2; their original home, VIII. v. 5; occupy all Spain and part of Gaul, V. xii. 12; their ruler Alaric the younger, V. xii. 22; form close alliance with Theoderic, V. xii. 21, 22; attacked by the Franks, V. xii. [illegible]; encamp against them, V. xii. 35; compel Alaric to fight, V. xii. 36–38; defeated in battle, V. xii. 40; wreak destruction in Italy, III. ii. 11, 12; choose Giselicus as King, V. xii. 43; then Amalaric, V. xii. 46; mingle with the Ostrogoths, V. xii. 49; separate from them, V. xiii. 7, 8; defeated by the Franks, V. xiii. 11; withdraw to Spain, III. iii. 26, IV. iv. 34, V. xiii. 13, VIII. v. 5; their alliance with Arcadius, III. ii. 7; invited to form alliance with the Vandals, III. xxiv. 7; their king Theudis, VI. xxx. 15

Vitalian, son of Patriciolus, becomes tyrant, I. viii. 3; uncle of John, VI. v. 1, etc.; hostile to Anastasius, I. xiii. 10; his adviser Hermogenes, *ib.*; slain by Justinian, S.H. vi. 27, 28

Vitalius, General of Illyricum, VII. x. 2; meets the Eruli in Venetia, VI. xxii. 7; guards the Po near Ravenna, VI. xxviii. 2; sent into Venetia, VI. xxviii. 24; defeated by Ildibadus, VII. i. 34, 35; escapes, VII. i. 36; confers with other commanders, VII. iii. 2, 3; returns through Thrace with Belisarius, VII. x. 2 ff.; persuades him to proceed to Ravenna, VII. xiii. 14; repulses an attack of the Goths, VII. xi. 16, 17; sent into Aemilia, VII. xi. 11; captures Bononia, VII. xi. 12

Vittigis, King of the Ostrogoths, V. xi. 5, VIII. xxvii. 5, 6; his good birth and military achievements, V. xi. 5; uncle of Uraïas, VI. xii. 37, xxx. 4, 12; nephew of Ulitheus, VI. x. 2; husband of Matasuntha, V. xi. 27, VI. x. 11, xxviii. 26, VII. i. 2; pursues Theodatus, V. xi. 6; imprisons son of Theodatus, V. xi. 10; advises withdrawal to Ravenna, V. xi. 11 ff.; withdraws, leaving garrison in Rome, V. xi. 26; unable to recall Goths from Gaul, V. xiii. 16; addresses the Goths, V. xiii. 17–25; forms alliance with the Franks, V. xiii. 26–28; summons Marcias from Gaul, V. xiii. 29; sends army into Tuscany, V. xvi. 5; eager to leave Ravenna, V. xvi. 7, 11; sends army to Dalmatia, V. xvi. 8, 9; finally moves against Rome, V. xvi. 19; his feverish haste, V. xvi. 20, 21, xvii. 8; passes by Perusia, etc., V. xvii. 7, 8; advances through Sabine territory, V. xvii. 12; halts at the Tiber, V. xvii. 13; sends Vacis to the Salarian Gate, V. xviii. 39; commands one Gothic camp, V. xix. 12; his name given in play to a Samnite child, V. xx. 1–4; sends envoy to Belisarius, V. xx. 7; hears their report, V. xxi. 1; prepares to storm the wall, V. xxi. 2, 3; constructs engines of war, V. xxi. 4–12; makes a general assault, V. xxii. 1 ff.; leads attack on the Vivarium, V. xxii. 10 ff.; where he presses the Romans hard, V. xxiii. 13; breaks down outer wall, V. xxiii. 17, 19; his force cut to pieces, V. xxiii. 20–22; kills Roman senators, V. xxvi. 1; seizes Portus, V. xxvi. 3, 14;

tries to use Roman tactics, V. xxvii. 15–23; exhorts his army, V. xxix. 1–15; commands in person at the great battle, V. xxix. 16 ff.; abandons Portus, VI. vii. 16, 22; investigates aqueduct, VI. ix. 1 ff.; tries a new stratagem, VI. ix. 16 ff.; abandons Rome, VI. x. 8, 12, 13; marches to Ariminum, VI. xi. 1–3; which he besieges, VI. xii. 1 ff.; sends army into Liguria, VI. xii. 37; receives Frankish allies, VI. xii. 38; Belisarius marches against him, VI. xiii. 1; sends army against Ancon, VI. xiii. 5; garrisons Auximus, VI. xxiii. 8; learns of Belisarius' approach, VI. xvii. 17, 18; holds Ravenna, VI. xviii. 19, xxiii. 1, xxiv. 24; seeks alliance of Lombards, VI. xxii. 9–12; persuaded to stir up Chosroes, II. ii. 1, 4 ff., VI. xxii. 13 ff.; fate of his envoys, II. xiv. 11, 12, VI. xxii. 22; receives appeals from Auximus, VI. xxiv. 1–16, xxvi. 2, 5–15; and from Fisula, VI. xxiv. 19; sends Uraïas to Ticinum, VI. xxiv. 20; besieged in Ravenna, VI. xxviii. 1 ff.; receives envoys from the Franks and from Belisarius, VI. xxviii. 7–22; favours the latter, VI. xxviii. 23; despairs of success, VI. xxviii. 27; capitulates, VI. xxix. 2, 3, VII. ii. 15; Goths dissatisfied with him, VI. xxix. 17; offers kingship to Belisarius, VI. xxix. 21; invited to make good his promise, VI. xxix. 24; places himself in the hands of the Romans, VI. xxx. 21; guarded by Belisarius, VI. xxix. 35, S.H. iv. 32, 43; brought to Byzantium by Belisarius, II. iv. 13, xxi. 28, VII. i. 1, 2, VIII. xxv. 12; where he remains, II. xiv. 10; had dismantled Pisaurus and Fanus, VII. xi. 32, xxv. 7; his death, VII. xxxix. 14; his wealth, S.H. iv. 34

Vivarium, an enclosure in the walls of Rome, V. xxii. 10; built for the keeping of wild animals, V. xxiii. 16; a very vulnerable point in the wall, V. xxiii. 13, 15; attacked by Vittigis, V. xxii. 10, 11, xxiii. 13–23; successfully defended by Belisarius, V. xxiii. 14–23

Vledas, Gothic commander, VII. v. 1

Vulsina, lake in Tuscany, Amalasuntha imprisoned there, V. iv. 14

White Syrians, old name for the inhabitants of Armenia Minor, I. xvii. 21

Wild Ass, a ballistic weapon, "like a sling," V. xxi. 18, 19

Wolf, contrivance for guarding gate, V. xxi. 19–22

Wolf-Helmet, mountain in Pisidia, VII. xxvii. 20

Wolf-Skulls, name applied to certain of the Pisidians, VII. xxvii. 20

Xenophon, the historian, B. I. i. 13

Xeropotamus, fortress in Epirus, B. IV. iv. 3

Xerxes, King of Persia, bridged the Hellespont, B. V. iii. 8

Zabe, called "First Mauritania", subjugated by Solomon, IV. xx. 30

Zaberganes, a Persian; misrepresents Mebodes to Chosroes, I. xxiii. 25, 26; reproaches Chosroes, II. viii. 30 ff.; receives envoys of Edessa, II. xxvi. 16–19; receives a letter from Theodora, S.H. ii. 32; his embassy to Byzantium, S.H. ii. 33

Zachariah, the Prophet, appears to Photius, S.H. iii. 27

Zacharias, Abbot, Monastery of, B. V. ix. 16

Zacynthus, island west of Greece, III. xiii. 21; victim of Gizeric's atrocity, III. xxii. 15, 17, 18

Zaïdus, commander of Roman infantry, III. xi. 7

Zaldapa, fortress in Moesia, B. IV. xi. 20

Zamarthas, fortress in Mesopotamia, B. II. vi. 14

Zames, son of Cabades, disqualified for kingship, I. xi. 4, II. ix. 12, VIII. xxvi. 13; plot to put him in power, I. xxiii. 4, 5; slain by Chosroes, I. xxiii. 6

Zanes, fortress in the district of Aquenisium, B. IV. iv. 3; on the Danube, B. IV. vi. 6, 8

INDEX

Zarter, a Massagete, bodyguard of Belisarius, V. xvi. 1

Zaunas, son of Paresmanes, and father of Leontius and Rufinus, IV. xix. 1, xx. 19

Zdebren, fortress in Haemimontum, B. IV. xi. 20

Zeapouries, fortress near Pauta, B. IV. iv. 3

Zebinus, Monastery of, in Mesopotamia, B. V. ix. 32

Zechi, a barbarian tribe, their location, II. xxix. 15, VIII. iv. 1, 2

Zemarcu, fortress in Haemimontum, B. IV. xi. 20

Zeno, Roman Emperor, I. iii. 8, B. III. i. 25, 26, V. vii. 5; husband of Ariadne and father of Leon, III. vii. 2; shares rule with infant son, III. vii. 3; flees into Isauria, III. vii. 18; marches against Basiliscus, III. vii. 20; receives surrender of opponents, III. vii. 21; captures and banishes Basiliscus, III. vii. 22, 24; again becomes Emperor, III. vii. 23; kills Harmatus, *ib.*; forms [illegible] with [illegible], III. vii. 26; persuades Theoderic to attack Odoacer, V. i. 10, VI. vi. 16, 23; punishes Samaritans, B. V. vii. 7; allows Palace Guards to degenerate, S.H. xxiv. 17

Zeno, Roman commander of cavalry, VI. v. 2; given as hostage, VI. vii. 13

Zeno, grandson of Anthemius, sent to Egypt, S.H. xii. 1; his property seized, S.H. xii. 2; his death, S.H. xii. 3

Zenobia, wife of Odonathus, Queen of the Saracens, B. II. viii. 8; founder of the city Zenobia, II. v. 5

Zenobia, city on the Euphrates, II. v. 4, B. II. viii. 16; its unique situation, B. II. viii. 12–15; founded by Zenobia, II. v. 5, B. II. viii. 9; spared by Chosroes, II. v. 7; restored by Justinian, B. II. viii. 11–25; near to Sura, B. II. ix. 1

Zerboule, fortress on Mt. Aurasius, IV. xix. 19, 20; besieged by the Romans, IV. xix. 23–27; abandoned by the Moors, IV. xix. 28–32

Zernes, fortress on the Danube, B. IV. vi. 5

Zetnucortu, town near the Danube, fortified by Justinian, B. IV. vi. 33

Zeugma, fortress in Euphratesia, B. II. ix. 18–20

Zeus Casius, VIII. xxii. 25

Zeuxippus, Bath of, in [illegible], [illegible], destroyed by fire, I. xxiv. 9

Zicideba, fortress in Moesia, B. IV. xi. 20

Zimarchus, companion of the youthful Justinus, S.H. vi. 2

Zincyro, fortress in Thrace, B. IV. xi. 20

Zisnudeba, fortress in Moesia, B. IV. xi. 20

Zoê, Martyr, shrine of in Byzantium, B. I. iii. 13

Zositersum, fortress in Thrace, B. IV. xi. 20

Zysbaes, fortress in Dardania, B. IV. iv. 3

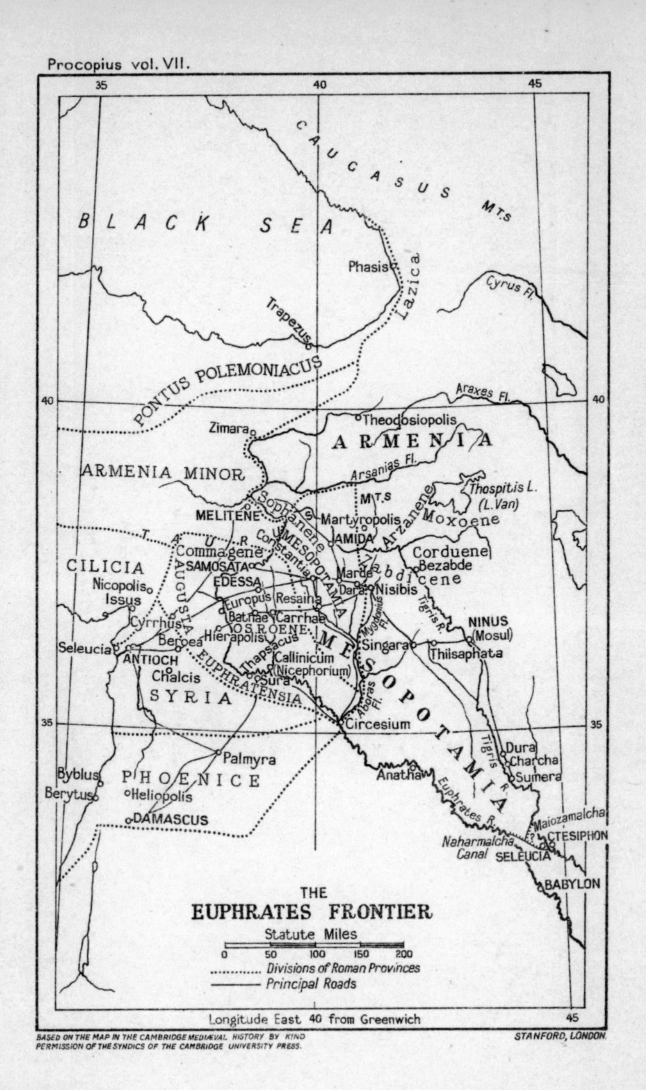
CAUCASUS MTS
BLACK SEA
Phasis
Lazica
Cyrus Fl.
Trapezus
PONTUS POLEMONIACUS
Araxes Fl.
Theodosiopolis
Zimara
ARMENIA
ARMENIA MINOR
Arsanias Fl.
MTS
Thospitis L.
(L. Van)
MELITENE
Sophanene
Martyropolis
Arzanene
Moxoene
TAURUS
AMIDA
Commagene
Constantia
MESOPOTAMIA
Corduene
Bezabde
CILICIA
SAMOSATA
Zabdicene
AUGUSTA
EDESSA
Mardes
Dara
Nisibis
Nicopolis
Issus
Europus
Resaina
Tigris R.
Batnae
Carrhae
NINUS
(Mosul)
Cyrrhus
OSROENE
Mygdonius Fl.
Seleucia
Beroea
Hierapolis
Singara
Thilsaphata
ANTIOCH
Thapsacus
Callinicum
(Nicephorium)
Chalcis
Sura
EUPHRATENSIA
SYRIA
Aboras Fl.
Circesium
Palmyra
Dura
Charcha
Tigris R.
Sumera
Byblus
PHOENICE
Anatha
Berytus
Heliopolis
Euphrates R.
DAMASCUS
Maiozamalcha
CTESIPHON
Naharmalcha Canal
SELEUCIA
BABYLON
35
40
45
THE EUPHRATES FRONTIER
Statute Miles
0 50 100 150 200
Divisions of Roman Provinces
Principal Roads
Longitude East 40 from Greenwich
BASED ON THE MAP IN THE CAMBRIDGE MEDIÆVAL HISTORY BY KIND PERMISSION OF THE SYNDICS OF THE CAMBRIDGE UNIVERSITY PRESS.
STANFORD, LONDON.

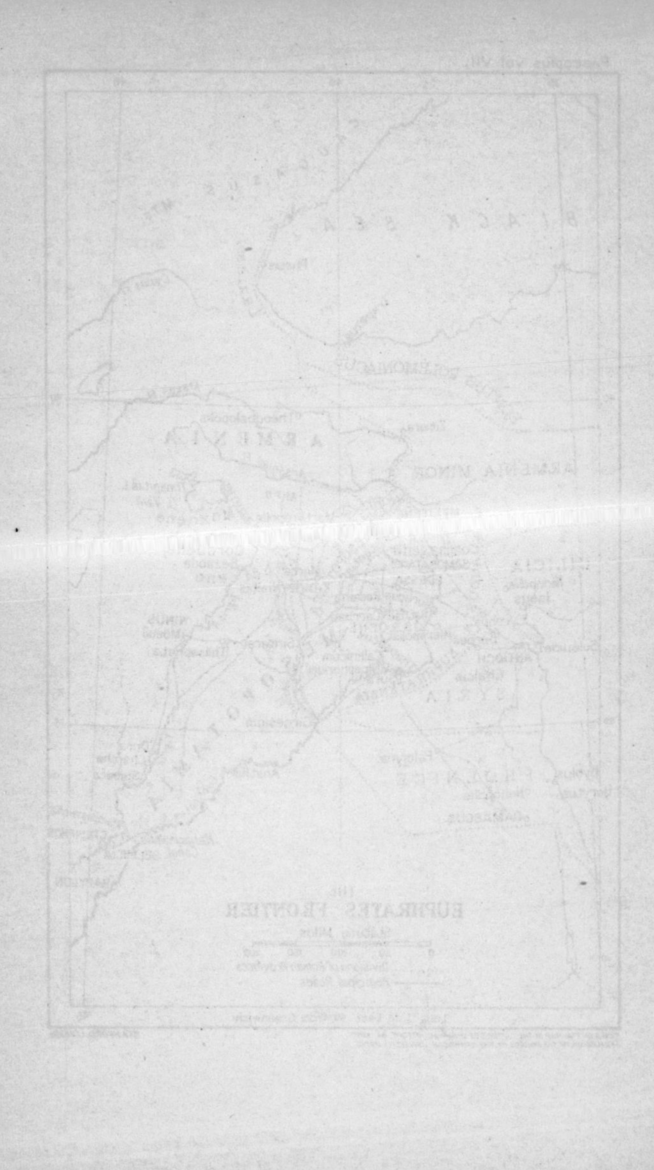

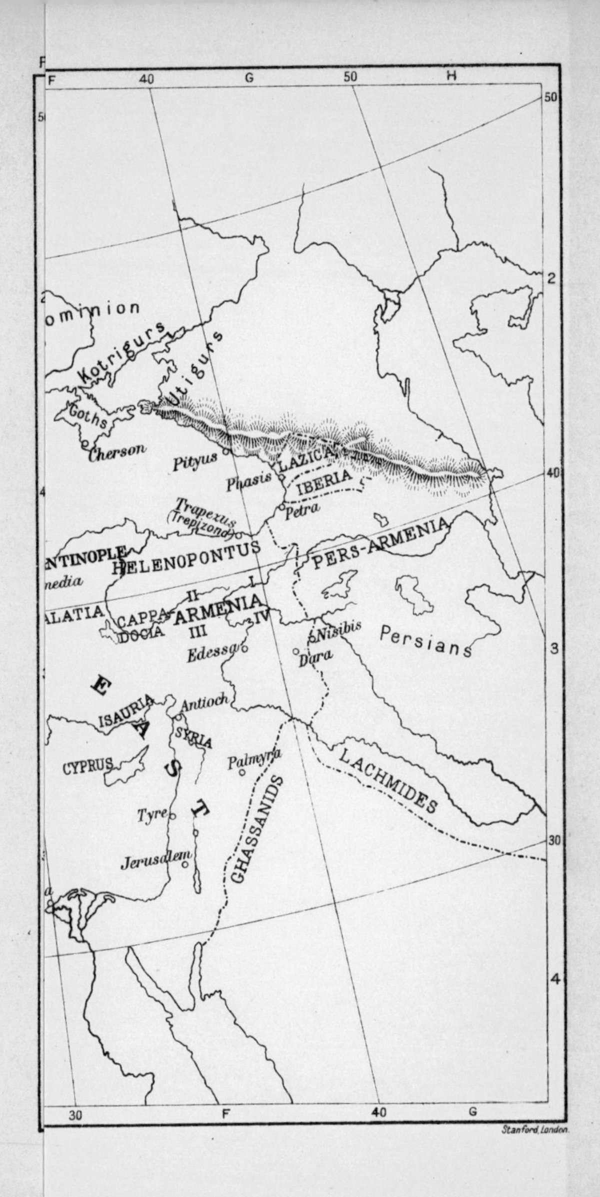

F
40
G
50
H
50
2
ominion
Kotrigurs
Utigurs
Goths
Cherson
Pityus
Phasis
LAZICA
IBERIA
Trapezus
(Trepizond)
Petra
NTINOPLE
HELENOPONTUS
PERS-ARMENIA
nedia
I
II
ALATIA
CAPPA-
DOCIA
ARMENIA
III
IV
Nisibis
Persians
Edessa
Dara
40
3
E
ISAURIA
Antioch
SYRIA
A
CYPRUS
S
Palmyra
LACHMIDES
Tyre
T
GHASSANIDS
Jerusalem
30
4
30
F
40
G
Stanford, London.

Printed in Great Britain by
Richard Clay and Company, Ltd.,
Bungay, Suffolk.

THE LOEB CLASSICAL LIBRARY

VOLUMES ALREADY PUBLISHED

Latin Authors

AMMIANUS MARCELLINUS. Translated by J. C. Rolfe. 3 Vols.
APULEIUS: THE GOLDEN ASS (METAMORPHOSES). W. Adlington (1566). Revised by S. Gaselee. (*6th Imp.*)
AULUS GELLIUS. J. C. Rolfe. 3 Vols.
AUSONIUS. H. G. Evelyn White. 2 Vols.
BEDE. J. E. King. 2 Vols.
BOETHIUS: TRACTS AND DE CONSOLATIONE PHILOSOPHIAE. Rev. H. F. Stewart and E. K. Rand. (*3rd Imp.*)
CAESAR: CIVIL WARS. A. G. Peskett. (*4th Imp.*)
CAESAR: GALLIC WAR. H. J. Edwards. (*8th Imp.*)
CATO AND VARRO: DE RE RUSTICA. H. B. Ash and W. D. Hooper. (*2nd Imp.*)
CATULLUS. F. W. Cornish; TIBULLUS. J. B. Postgate; AND PERVIGILIUM VENERIS. J. W. Mackail. (*11th Imp.*)
CELSUS: DE MEDICINA. W. G. Spencer. 3 Vols. (Vol. I. *2nd Imp. revised.*)
CICERO: BRUTUS, AND ORATOR. G. L. Hendrickson and H. M. Hubbell.
CICERO: DE FINIBUS. H. Rackham. (*3rd Imp. revised.*)
CICERO: DE NATURA DEORUM AND ACADEMICA. H. Rackham.
CICERO: DE OFFICIIS. Walter Miller. (*4th Imp.*)
CICERO: DE REPUBLICA AND DE LEGIBUS. Clinton W. Keyes.
CICERO: DE SENECTUTE, DE AMICITIA, DE DIVINATIONE. W. A. Falconer. (*4th Imp.*)
CICERO: IN CATILINAM, PRO FLACCO, PRO MURENA, PRO SULLA. Louis E. Lord.
CICERO: LETTERS TO ATTICUS. E. O. Winstedt. 3 Vols. (Vol. I. *5th Imp.*, Vol. II. *3rd Imp.* and Vol. III. *2nd Imp.*)
CICERO: LETTERS TO HIS FRIENDS. W. Glynn Williams. 3 Vols.
CICERO: PHILIPPICS. W. C. A. Ker. (*2nd Imp.*)
CICERO: PRO ARCHIA, POST REDITUM, DE DOMO, DE HARUSPICUM RESPONSIS, PRO PLANCIO. N. H. Watts. (*2nd Imp.*)

CICERO: PRO CAECINA, PRO LEGE MANILIA, PRO CLUENTIO, PRO RABIRIO. H. Grose Hodge.

CICERO: PRO MILONE, IN PISONEM, PRO SCAURO, PRO FONTEIO, PRO RABIRIO POSTUMO, PRO MARCELLO, PRO LIGARIO, PRO REGE DEIOTARO. N. H. Watts.

CICERO: PRO QUINCTIO, PRO ROSCIO AMERINO, PRO ROSCIO COMOEDO, CONTRA RULLUM. J. H. Freese.

CICERO: TUSCULAN DISPUTATIONS. J. E. King.

CICERO: VERRINE ORATIONS. L. H. G. Greenwood. 2 Vols.

CLAUDIAN. M. Platnauer. 2 Vols.

FLORUS. E. S. Forster, and CORNELIUS NEPOS; J. C. Rolfe.

FRONTINUS: STRATAGEMS AND AQUEDUCTS. C. E. Bennett and M. B. McElwain.

FRONTO: CORRESPONDENCE. C. R. Haines. 2 Vols.

HORACE: ODES AND EPODES. C. E. Bennett. (11*th Imp. revised.*)

HORACE: SATIRES, EPISTLES, ARS POETICA. H. R. Fairclough. (5*th Imp. revised.*)

JEROME: SELECTED LETTERS. F. A. Wright.

JUVENAL AND PERSIUS. G. G. Ramsay. (6*th Imp.*)

LIVY. B. O. Foster, Evan T. Sage, A. C. Schlesinger and F. G. Moore. 13 Vols. Vols. I.–VI., IX.–XII. (Vol. I. 3*rd Imp.*, Vols. II., III. and IX. 2*nd Imp. revised.*)

LUCAN. J. D. Duff.

LUCRETIUS. W. H. D. Rouse. (4*th Imp. revised.*)

MARTIAL. W. C. A. Ker. 2 Vols. (3*rd Imp. revised.*)

MINOR LATIN POETS: from PUBLILIUS SYRUS to RUTILIUS NAMATIANUS, including GRATTIUS, CALPURNIUS SICULUS, NEMESIANUS, AVIANUS, and others with "Aetna" and the "Phoenix." J. Wight Duff and Arnold M. Duff. (2*nd Imp.*)

OVID: THE ART OF LOVE AND OTHER POEMS. J. H. Mozley. (2*nd Imp.*)

OVID: FASTI. Sir James G. Frazer.

OVID: HEROIDES AND AMORES. Grant Showerman. (3*rd Imp.*)

OVID: METAMORPHOSES. F. J. Miller. 2 Vols. (Vol. I. 7*th Imp.*, Vol. II. 6*th Imp.*)

OVID: TRISTIA AND EX PONTO. A. L. Wheeler. (2*nd Imp.*)

PERSIUS. Cf. JUVENAL.

PETRONIUS. M. Heseltine; SENECA: APOCOLOCYNTOSIS. W. H. D. Rouse. (7*th Imp. revised.*)

PLAUTUS. Paul Nixon. 5 Vols. (Vol. I. 4*th Imp.*, Vols. II. and III. 3*rd Imp.*)

PLINY: LETTERS. Melmoth's Translation revised by W. M. L. Hutchinson. 2 Vols. (Vol. I. *5th Imp.*, Vol. II. *4th Imp.*)
PLINY: NATURAL HISTORY. H. Rackham and W. H. S. Jones. 10 Vols. Vols. I.–III.
PROPERTIUS. H. E. Butler. (*5th Imp.*)
QUINTILIAN. H. E. Butler. 4 Vols. (Vols. I., II. and IV. *2nd Imp.*)
REMAINS OF OLD LATIN. E. H. Warmington. 4 Vols. Vol. I. (ENNIUS AND CAECILIUS.) Vol. II. (LIVIUS, NAEVIUS, PACUVIUS, ACCIUS.) Vol. III. (LUCILIUS AND LAWS OF XII TABLES.) Vol. IV. (INSCRIPTIONS.)
ST. AUGUSTINE, CONFESSIONS OF. W. Watts (1631). 2 Vols. (Vol. I. *4th Imp.*, Vol. II. *3rd Imp.*)
ST. AUGUSTINE, SELECT LETTERS. J. H. Baxter.
SALLUST. J. Rolfe. (*2nd Imp. revised.*)
SCRIPTORES HISTORIAE AUGUSTAE. D. Magie. 3 Vols. (Vol. I. *2nd Imp. revised.*)
SENECA: APOCOLOCYNTOSIS. Cf. PETRONIUS.
SENECA: EPISTULAE MORALES. R. M. Gummere. 3 Vols. (Vol. I. *3rd Imp.*, Vol. II. *2nd Imp. revised.*)
SENECA: MORAL ESSAYS. J. W. Basore. 3 Vols. (Vol. II. *2nd Imp. revised.*)
SENECA: TRAGEDIES. F. J. Miller. 2 Vols. (Vol. I. *3rd Imp.*, Vol. II. *2nd Imp. revised.*)
SIDONIUS: POEMS AND LETTERS. W. B. Anderson. 2 Vols. Vol. I.
SILIUS ITALICUS. J. D. Duff. 2 Vols. (Vol. II. *2nd Imp.*)
STATIUS. J. H. Mozley. 2 Vols.
SUETONIUS. J. C. Rolfe. 2 Vols. (*5th Imp. revised.*)
TACITUS: DIALOGUS. Sir Wm. Peterson and AGRICOLA AND GERMANIA. Maurice Hutton. (*5th Imp.*)
TACITUS: HISTORIES AND ANNALS. C. H. Moore and J. Jackson. 4 Vols. (Vol. I. *2nd Imp.*)
TERENCE. John Sargeaunt. 2 Vols. (Vol. I. *6th Imp.*, II. *5th Imp.*)
TERTULLIAN: APOLOGIA AND DE SPECTACULIS. T. R. Glover. MINUCIUS FELIX. G. H. Rendall.
VALERIUS FLACCUS. J. H. Mozley. (*2nd Imp. revised.*)
VARRO: DE LINGUA LATINA. R. G. Kent. 2 Vols.
VELLEIUS PATERCULUS AND RES GESTAE DIVI AUGUSTI. F. W. Shipley.
VIRGIL. H. R. Fairclough. 2 Vols. (Vol. I. *14th Imp.*, Vol. II. *11th Imp. revised.*)
VITRUVIUS: DE ARCHITECTURA. F. Granger. 2 Vols.

Greek Authors

ACHILLES TATIUS. S. Gaselee.

AENEAS TACTICUS: ASCLEPIODOTUS AND ONASANDER. The Illinois Greek Club.

AESCHINES. C. D. Adams.

AESCHYLUS. H. Weir Smyth. 2 Vols. (Vol. I. *4th Imp.*, Vol. II. *3rd Imp.*)

APOLLODORUS. Sir James G. Frazer. 2 Vols. (Vol. I. *2nd Imp.*)

APOLLONIUS RHODIUS. R. C. Seaton. (*4th Imp.*)

THE APOSTOLIC FATHERS. Kirsopp Lake. 2 Vols. (Vol. I. *5th Imp.*, Vol. II. *4th Imp.*)

APPIAN'S ROMAN HISTORY. Horace White. 4 Vols. (Vol. I. *3rd Imp.*, Vols. II., III. and IV. *2nd Imp.*)

ARATUS. Cf. CALLIMACHUS.

ARISTOPHANES. Benjamin Bickley Rogers. 3 Vols. Verse trans. (Vols. I. and II. *4th Imp.*, Vol. III. *3rd Imp.*)

ARISTOTLE: ART OF RHETORIC. J. H. Freese. (*2nd Imp.*)

ARISTOTLE: ATHENIAN CONSTITUTION, EUDEMIAN ETHICS, VICES AND VIRTUES. H. Rackham. (*2nd Imp.*)

ARISTOTLE: METAPHYSICS. H. Tredennick. 2 Vols. (*2nd Imp.*)

ARISTOTLE: MINOR WORKS. W. S. Hett. On Colours, On Things Heard, On Physiognomies, On Plants, On Marvellous Things Heard, Mechanical Problems, On Indivisible Lines, On Position and Names of Winds.

ARISTOTLE: NICOMACHEAN ETHICS. H. Rackham. (*3rd Imp. revised.*)

ARISTOTLE: OECONOMICA AND MAGNA MORALIA. G. C. Armstrong; with Metaphysics, Vol. II. (*2nd Imp.*)

ARISTOTLE: ON THE HEAVENS. W. K. C. Guthrie.

ARISTOTLE: ON THE SOUL, PARVA NATURALIA, ON BREATH. W. S. Hett. (*2nd Imp. revised.*)

ARISTOTLE: ORGANON. H. P. Cooke and H. Tredennick. 2 Vols. Vol. I.

ARISTOTLE: PARTS OF ANIMALS. A. L. Peck; MOTION AND PROGRESSION OF ANIMALS. E. S. Forster.

ARISTOTLE: PHYSICS. Rev. P. Wicksteed and F. M. Cornford. 2 Vols. (Vol. II. *2nd Imp.*)

ARISTOTLE: POETICS AND LONGINUS. W. Hamilton Fyfe; DEMETRIUS ON STYLE. W. Rhys Roberts. (*3rd Imp. revised.*)

ARISTOTLE: POLITICS. H. Rackham.

ARISTOTLE: PROBLEMS. W. S. Hett. 2 Vols.

ARISTOTLE: RHETORICA AD ALEXANDRUM (with PROBLEMS, Vol. II.). H. Rackham.

ARRIAN: HISTORY OF ALEXANDER AND INDICA. Rev. E. Iliffe Robson. 2 Vols.
ATHENAEUS: DEIPNOSOPHISTAE. C. B. Gulick. 7 Vols.
CALLIMACHUS AND LYCOPHRON. A. W. Mair; ARATUS. G. R. Mair.
CLEMENT OF ALEXANDRIA. Rev. G. W. Butterworth. (*2nd Imp.*)
COLLUTHUS. Cf. OPPIAN.
DAPHNIS AND CHLOE. Thornley's Translation revised by J. M. Edmonds; AND PARTHENIUS. S. Gaselee. (*3rd Imp.*)
DEMOSTHENES: DE CORONA AND DE FALSA LEGATIONE. C. A. Vince and J. H. Vince. (*2nd Imp. revised.*)
DEMOSTHENES: MEIDIAS, ANDROTION, ARISTOCRATES, TIMOCRATES AND ARISTOGEITON: I. AND II. Translated by J. H. Vince.
DEMOSTHENES: OLYNTHIACS, PHILIPPICS AND MINOR ORATIONS: I.–XVII. AND XX. J. H. Vince.
DEMOSTHENES: PRIVATE ORATIONS. A. T. Murray. 4 Vols. Vols. I., II and III.
DIO CASSIUS: ROMAN HISTORY. E. Cary. 9 Vols. (Vols. I and II. *2nd Imp.*)
DIO CHRYSOSTOM. J. W. Cohoon and F. W. Crosby. 5 Vols. Vols. I.–III.
DIODORUS SICULUS. C. H. Oldfather. In 12 Volumes. Vols. I.–III.
DIOGENES LAERTIUS. R. D. Hicks. 2 Vols. (Vol. I. *3rd Imp.*)
DIONYSIUS OF HALICARNASSUS: ROMAN ANTIQUITIES. Spelman's translation revised by E. Cary. 7 Vols. Vols. I–III.
EPICTETUS. W. A. Oldfather. 2 Vols.
EURIPIDES. A. S. Way. 4 Vols. (Vol. II. *6th Imp.*, Vols. I and IV. *5th Imp.*, Vol. III. *3rd Imp.*) Verse trans.
EUSEBIUS: ECCLESIASTICAL HISTORY. Kirsopp Lake and J. E. L. Oulton. 2 Vols. (Vol. II. *2nd Imp.*)
GALEN: ON THE NATURAL FACULTIES. A. J. Brock. (*2nd Imp.*)
THE GREEK ANTHOLOGY. W. R. Paton. 5 Vols. (Vols. I. and II. *4th Imp.*, Vols. III. and IV. *2nd Imp.*)
GREEK ELEGY AND IAMBUS WITH THE ANACREONTEA. J. M. Edmonds. 2 Vols.
THE GREEK BUCOLIC POETS (THEOCRITUS, BION, MOSCHUS). J. M. Edmonds. (*6th Imp. revised.*)
GREEK MATHEMATICAL WORKS. Ivor Thomas. 2 Vols. Vol. I. (Thales to Euclid.)

HERODES. Cf. THEOPHRASTUS: CHARACTERS.
HERODOTUS. A. D. Godley. 4 Vols. (Vols. I.–III. *3rd Imp.*, Vol. IV. *2nd Imp.*)
HESIOD AND THE HOMERIC HYMNS. H. G. Evelyn White. (*5th Imp. revised and enlarged.*)
HIPPOCRATES AND THE FRAGMENTS OF HERACLEITUS. W. H. S. Jones and E. T. Withington. 4 Vols. (Vol. I. *2nd Imp.*)
HOMER: ILIAD. A. T. Murray. 2 Vols. (*4th Imp.*)
HOMER: ODYSSEY. A. T. Murray. 2 Vols. (*5th Imp.*)
ISAEUS. E. W. Forster.
ISOCRATES. George Norlin. 3 Vols. Vols. I. and II.
JOSEPHUS. H. St. J. Thackeray and Ralph Marcus. 9 Vols. Vols. I.–VI. (Vol. V. *2nd Imp.*)
JULIAN. Wilmer Cave Wright. 3 Vols. (Vols. I. and II. *2nd Imp.*)
LUCIAN. A. M. Harmon. 8 Vols. Vols. I.–V. (Vols. I. and II. *3rd Imp.*)
LYCOPHRON. Cf. CALLIMACHUS.
LYRA GRAECA. J. M. Edmonds. 3 Vols. (Vol. I. *3rd Imp.*, Vol. II. *2nd Ed. revised and enlarged*, Vol. III. *2nd Imp. revised*).
LYSIAS. W. R. M. Lamb.
MARCUS AURELIUS. C. R. Haines. (*3rd Imp. revised.*)
MENANDER. F. G. Allinson. (*2nd Imp. revised.*)
MINOR ATTIC ORATORS (ANTIPHON, ANDOCIDES, DEMADES, DEINARCHUS, HYPEREIDES). K. J. Maidment. 2 Vols. Vol. I.
NONNOS. W. H. D. Rouse. 3 Vols.
OPPIAN, COLLUTHUS, TRYPHIODORUS. A. W. Mair.
PAPYRI (SELECTIONS). A. S. Hunt and C. C. Edgar. 4 Vols. Vols. I. and II.
PARTHENIUS. Cf. DAPHNIS AND CHLOE.
PAUSANIAS: DESCRIPTION OF GREECE. W. H. S. Jones. 5 Vols. and Companion Vol. (Vols. I. and III. *2nd Imp.*)
PHILO. 10 Vols. Vols. I.–V.; F. H. Colson and Rev. G. H. Whitaker. Vols. VI.–VIII. (Vol. IV. *2nd Imp.*); F. H. Colson.
PHILOSTRATUS: THE LIFE OF APOLLONIUS OF TYANA. F. C. Conybeare. 2 Vols. (Vol. I. *3rd Imp.*, Vol. II. *2nd Imp.*)
PHILOSTRATUS: IMAGINES; CALLISTRATUS: DESCRIPTIONS. A. Fairbanks.
PHILOSTRATUS AND EUNAPIUS: LIVES OF THE SOPHISTS. Wilmer Cave Wright.
PINDAR. Sir J. E. Sandys. (*6th Imp. revised.*)